MODERN UKRAINIAN

Modern Ukrainian

by

Assya Humesky
University of Michigan

3rd Edition

КІУС
CIUS

CANADIAN INSTITUTE OF UKRAINIAN STUDIES
2001
EDMONTON - TORONTO

Canadian Cataloguing in Publication Data

Humesky, Assya, 1925–
Modern Ukrainian

Second Edition, includes index

ISBN 978-1-895571-29-5

1. Ukrainian language — Textbooks for second language learners — English speakers.* 2. Ukrainian language — Grammar. I. Title.

PG3823.H84 1999 491.7'982421 C99-931380-0

(The Canadian Library in Ukrainian Studies)

Cover design: Yuriy Diakunchak

This book is dedicated
to the memory of my father
Serhij Pylypenko

ACKNOWLEDGEMENTS

This project was in part supported by the Harvard Ukrainian Research Institute and the University of Michigan. The following persons have read the manuscript, some more than once, and offered their valuable suggestions: Vera Pereshluha, Prof. Dmytro Kyslytsia, Prof. Bohdan Struminskyj, Dr. Susan Wobst, Tatiana Kardinalowska, Wayles Browne, Martha Kuchar and Natalia Duzhyk. To all these people I want to express my heartfelt gratitude. My special thanks go to Prof. Horace G. Lunt for his expert advice and criticism.

Recording of tapes was done at the University of Michigan Language Laboratory with the assistance of James Bixler, Laboratory Associate Director. The voices on the tapes are those of Rev. Olexander Bykovec, Mrs. Zena Ijewlew, Prof. Dmytro Kyslytsia (on most recordings), Julian Kytasty (he plays the bandura and sings), Luba Litus and myself. I thank all the people who helped with the recording.

I am also grateful to Prof. Omeljan Pritsak, Director of the Harvard Ukrainian Research Institute for his support of the project and to Prof. George Luckyj, Associate Director of the Canadian Institute of Ukrainian Studies who made the publication of the book possible.

I thank Prof. Benjamin Stolz, Chairman of the Slavic Department of the University of Michigan, for suggesting the idea of writing this book and for encouraging me in this task.

Finally I want to thank my husband Eugene for his patience and moral support.

The publication of this book was subsidized by a grant from the Ministry of Culture and Recreation of the Province of Ontario.

TABLE OF CONTENTS

ABBREVIATIONS AND NOTATIONS

A	accusative case	N	nominative case
adj.	adjective	p.	person
adv.	adverb	P	perfective aspect
conj.	conjunction	pfv.	perfective aspect
D	dative case	pl.	plural
dim.	diminutive	sg.	singular
E.Ukr.	East Ukrainian	U	uni-directional verb
f.; fem.	feminine gender;	V	vocative
	female	W.Ukr.	West Ukrainian
G	genitive case	Ø	zero ending
I	instrumental case;	=	same as; explanation
	imperfective aspect	+	government; sequence
imfv.	imperfective aspect	/	or; either-or
indecl.	indeclinable	()	or (variant); explanation;
interj.	interjection		pfv. aspect (in cumulative
inf.	infinitive		vocabularies)
L	locative case	{	aspectual pair (lesson
lit.	literally		vocabularies)
M	multi-directional verb	;	divides sg. from pl. (Ukr. vo-
m.; masc.	masculine gender		cabularies); divides different
n.; ntr	neuter gender		meanings (English vocabularies)

Italics indicate transcription (actual sounds).
Bold faced Ukrainian letters and syllables indicate spelling.
See also special notations in the vocabularies at the end of the book.

СПИСОК ДІЯЛОГІВ

PREFACE

This book is a first year Ukrainian grammar which presents the fundamental morphology and vocabulary and includes limited notations on syntax and intonation. It consists of twenty lessons arranged in such a way that they can be covered within an academic year. The approximate time alloted per lesson is one week, however some lessons may take longer. Additional time is also necessary for review exercises which appear at regular intervals.

1. **Dialogues**. These serve as a pattern for conversation, and are **NOT** intended for memorization.

2. **Lesson vocabulary**. It contains all the new words and idioms in the given lesson.

3. **Explanatory notes**. They are provided for general information and point out cultural connotation and usage, stylistic coloring, regional variants, etc.

4. **Grammar notes**. They are divided by topic and consist of rules, explanation, examples, and a list of corresponding exercises respectively.

5. **Exercises.** There are specific exercises for each grammar point (as marked in the grammar notes) and exercises of a general nature (e.g. reading, translation). Questions to the dialogues and reading passages are provided. Review exercises appear after every four lessons.

6. **Appendices**. These contain structural and phonetic information presented in a systematic and organized fashion for easy reference.

7. **Vocabulary**. It includes all the lexical items and idioms presented in the vocabulary lists and explanatory notes and grammar notes in both English-Ukrainian and Ukrainian-English order.

SUGGESTIONS FOR USE OF BOOK

1. **The dialogue** should be introduced through group reading and/or by example of the teacher. It is also recommended that the dialogue be repeated throughout the lesson both to illustrate the grammar and vocabulary and as a pattern for sentence formation. The dialogue should serve as a basis for conversation and questions have been provided at the end of the lesson for this purpose.

2. **The vocabulary** must be learned thoroughly. Exercises and dialogue serve as an aid to vocabulary memorization. The vocabulary may be introduced either by the teacher or by having the student listen to it on tape.

3. **Explanatory notes** are to be read by the student outside of class. Should a grammar point arise it would then be discussed during class time.

4. It is strongly recommended that **grammar notes** be assigned as homework to be prepared for classroom discussions. The amount of grammar to be covered during each class is left to the teacher's discretion. The presentation of each grammar point should be immediately followed by exercises.

5. Certain exercises are better suited for classroom use, (e.g. structural drills, questions directed to the individual student, drills involving choice), others are intended for homework (e.g. translation, vocabulary). The purpose of the readings is multifold. They may be used a) for reading (group and individual), b) for dictation, c) for grammar and vocabulary review, d) for conversation, e) as a guide for composition, f) for listening comprehension.

SUGGESTED ORDER OF PRESENTATION

The teacher should not follow the order in which the items are presented in the text, for the dialogues, vocabulary, grammar and exercises are all interrelated. It is advisable to first acquaint the student with the vocabulary before proceeding to the other parts of the lesson. The grammar should be presented immediately **preceding** a corresponding dialogue (Do **NOT** do all the dialogues at once!).

The following is a sample presentation of a new lesson:

Day 1. Towards end of classtime read the vocabulary for the new lesson. Assign the grammar to be discussed the following day, and quickly go over the corresponding dialogue(s).

Day 2. Begin the class with exercises to review the material previously covered (This may be in the form of dictation, structure drills, question and answer, oral/aural comprehension).

Review the new dialogue(s).

Discuss the grammar which was assigned for homework asking leading questions and referring back to the dialogue for illustration.

Practice the new grammar by means of appropriately selected exercises.

Assign the next day's grammar and corresponding dialogue(s).

The above is only a suggested schedule and the teacher should vary it to avoid monotony.

USE OF TAPES *

1. **Pronunciation practice**. Sound patterns and pronunciation and sound discrimination exercises which appear in the introductory chapter on the Ukrainian Sound System have all been recorded and should be used at the beginning of the course and later for review.

2. **Vocabulary**. Tapes for each lesson begin with vocabulary. It is recorded at slow speed with pauses for repetition.

3. **Dialogues**. There are 57 dialogues and narrative passages in the book. They are recorded twice, the first time with pauses for repetition and the second time at normal speed.

4. **Listening comprehension.** Review passages which appear in the text as reading and translation exercises are recorded for listening comprehension. First listen to the recording done at normal speed and try to answer the questions to these passages which are provided in the text. Next, listen to the recording with pauses for pronunciation practice.

5. **Songs and poems**. The text mentions a few poems and songs. The words have been provided in the Explanatory notes and recorded with pauses for repetition (some with music).

---

* Tapes are available from the U. of Michigan, Language Research Center, c/o Vickie Earle, Rm. 2018, Modern Languages Building, Ann Arbor, Mich. 48109, tel. (734) 764-0424. ($92.00US + $4.50 S&H for 12 cassettes) Supplementary teaching aids and readers (student workbooks with tapes) are available from the Foreign Language Publications, Ohio State U., 33 West 11th Ave., Suite 311N, Columbus, OH 43210-2013 tel. (614) 292-3838 fax (614) 688-3355.

INTRODUCTION

Ukrainian is a Slavic language belonging to the East Slavic group, together with Belarusian and Russian. They are closely related to the West Slavic (Polish, Czech, Slovak, and the Upper and Lower Sorbian languages of eastern Germany) and the South Slavic (Slovene, Serbo-Croatian, Macedonian, and Bulgarian) languages. The Slavic languages as a whole are related to the Baltic languages (Lithuanian and Latvian) and, less closely, to the other members which make-up the Indo-European language family: Indic (Sanskrit and many modern Indian languages), Iranian (including modern Persian), Greek, Albanian, Italic (including Latin and the modern Romance languages), Germanic (including English), and Celtic. Ukrainian and English are thus related, but both have undergone farreaching changes from the hypothetical common prototype, and the relationship is not readily apparent except in a few words (e.g. *brat* — brother, *sestra* — sister).

Ukrainian is the mother tongue of over fifty million Ukrainians, most of whom live in Ukraine. Ukrainians also live in Poland, Romania, Russia, Belarus, the Baltic Republics, the Central Asia Republics, Slovakia and in what formerly was Yugoslavia, as well as in the United States, Canada, Australia, South America, and other countries.

Ukrainian is of course not uniform over the large area where it is spoken: local varieties of speech differ from one another in pronunciation, morphology, syntax and especially in vocabulary.

Linguists distinguish three groups of dialects: the northern, the southwestern (including Galicia, Transcarpathia and Bukovina) and the southeastern. *Kyjiv* (Kyiv), the major political center, is situated in the zone transitional from the northern to the southeastern dialect areas.

The development of a modern literary Ukrainian language began in the last years of the 18th century and proceeded rapidly in the early 19th century. The poet Taras Shevchenko (1814–1861), a gifted and many-sided artist and writer, wrote powerfully and persuasively in Ukrainian, welding together elements from different dialects and from older works into a new and effective means of expression. He was joined and followed by many, and a new literary language began to flourish. But the Ukrainian lands were divided between Austria and Russia, and Ukrainian remained at best a subordinate language in public life. Indeed it was forbidden to print works in Ukrainian in the Russian Empire from 1863 to 1905. Under such conditions it was hard for a unified standard language to develop, and writers tended to use large admixtures of their native local dialects in their works.

In 1917 Ukrainians proclaimed their independence from the Russian Empire and Ukrainian became the official language of the Ukrainian People's Republic. The same decree was passed in the Western Ukrainian lands which won their independence from Austria in 1918. Soon afterwards, West Ukraine fell under Polish rule, while the Eastern lands became incorporated into the Soviet Union. During the two decades (1918–1938) strong efforts were made to standardize Ukrainian in Galicia, which was part of Poland, and in the Soviet Ukraine. Inevitably there was considerable difference in the detailed selection of possible linguistic elements. Both the local dialects and the two languages, Polish and Russian, played a role. Since 1945 all the Ukrainian lands have been absorbed into the Ukrainian S.S.R., today's independent Ukraine, and standard literary Ukrainian is taught in public schools.

The western type of standard Ukrainian which flourished in Poland until 1939 has been important in the American Ukrainian communities, for the largest body of Ukrainian immigrants to the U.S. and Canada came from Galicia, Bukovina and Transcarpathia, that is from Austro-Hungary before 1918 and from Poland, Romania and Czechoslovakia between 1918 and 1938. The majority of post-1945 immigrants also came from western Ukraine, including many leading scholars who were active in Ukrainian cultural life here. The chief differences from the contemporary usage in Ukraine lie in the spelling conventions, some small grammatical points, word stress, and above all in the choice of vocabulary. In this book we follow with some modifications the standard established by the Ukrainian Academy of Science in 1929 in accordance with the decisions of the All-Ukrainian linguistic conference held in Kharkiv in 1927, and adhered to by all the leading Ukrainian scientific institutions outside Ukraine.

THE UKRAINIAN SOUND SYSTEM

There are six vowels and 22 basic consonants in Ukrainian. They are represented below in a transcription form.*

THE VOWELS

a	—	pronounced approximately as in English f*a*ther, st*a*rt	
e	—	about like *e* in met, b*e*t	
y	—	about like *i* in b*i*t, t*i*n	
i	—	about like *ee* in b*ee*t, m*ee*t	
o	—	about like *o* in abort, sh*o*rt	greater lip rounding
u	—	about like *oo* in b*oo*t, s*oo*n	

(Exercise 1)

Note 1. All Ukrainian vowels are plain, i.e. there are no diphthongs. Pay particular attention to the Ukrainian *o*: it is one short sound, not like its English counterpart.

Note 2. Stressed and unstressed vowels have about the same sound quality.**

THE CONSONANTS

One of the main features which distinguishes Ukrainian consonants from English consonants is the existence of two sets, hard and soft (or, in linguistic terminology, non-palatalized and palatalized).

We shall first learn the 22 hard consonants.

THE HARD CONSONANTS

p	—	approximately as in s*p*ot
b	—	approximately as in English
f	—	"
v	—	"
m	—	"

---

* This trascription will be used throughout the book whenever necessary for elucidating a point in grammar or spelling. We shall use a transliteration system in spelling Ukrainian names elsewhere, e.g. in translating dialogues, exercise model sentences, etc. The student will find this transliteration system provided at the end of the book in Appendix 2.

** In this text stress will be indicated on all words, mono-and polysyllabic, except those which never receive stress.

t	—	pronounced with the tip of the tongue against the front teeth (not against the upper gum as in English) and without aspiration
d	—	pronounced with the tip of the tongue against the front teeth
n	—	” ” ” ”
s	—	approximately as in *s*o
z	—	approximately as in *z*one
c	—	approximately like the *ts* in be*ts*, pronounced as one unit
ʒ	—	approximately like *ds* in be*ds*, pronounced as one unit
ǯ	—	approximately as in *j*ob, ju*dge*
č	—	approximately as in mu*ch*
š	—	approximately as in hu*sh*
ž	—	approximately as in a*z*ure, mea*s*ure
l	—	approximately as in tab*l*e, ha*ll*
r	—	trilled with the tip of the tongue, as in Spanish or Italian
k	—	pronounced without aspiration, as in s*k*ate
g	—	approximately as in *g*um
h	—	NOT like English *h* which is voicelless (like *p, t, k, s*), but fully voiced (like *b, d, g, z*); very approximately as in per*h*aps
x	—	does not occur in English (it is like the German sound in Ba*ch*). Produced by placing the tongue in position for *k* and lowering it slightly so that a stream of air passes between the back of the tongue and the roof of the mouth. It is a sound that can be prolonged, like *s, f,* and *v*.

Note 1. Ukrainian consonants are never pronounced with aspiration which is typical of the initial English *p, t, k*.

Note 2. The Ukrainian sounds *d, t, n, l* are pronounced with the tip of the tongue touching the upper (or, in some speakers, the lower) teeth and are called "dental." By contrast, the English *d, t, n, l* are produced with the tongue touching the upper gum.

Note 3. With a few exceptions only hard consonants occur before the vowels *e* and *y*. (See Note 5 to Conditioned Soft Consonants.)

Note 4. Most Ukrainian consonants, both hard and soft, can appear in a lengthened form (in writing they are doubled). This can occur only between vowels or at the beginning of a word. In transcription, we use the superscript ¯ over the doubled consonant.

(Exercise 2)

THE SOFT CONSONANTS

All the hard consonants in Ukrainian have their soft counterparts. The soft or palatalized consonants have the articulatory features of the hard or non-palatalized consonants plus an additional feature in which the tongue arches toward the middle of the roof of the mouth. The acoustic effect is one of higher pitch.

In transcription, we use a single quotation mark ' to indicate palatalization.

There are two kinds of soft consonants: independent and conditioned.

INDEPENDENT SOFT CONSONANTS

The independent soft consonants may occur

1) in word final position
2) before the vowels *a, o, u, i*
3) before certain consonants*

t'	—	very approximately as in s*te*w (British pronunciation)
d'	—	very approximately as in *d*ew (British pronunciation)
n'	—	very approximately as in *n*ews (British pronunciation)
s'	—	very approximately as in *s*uit (British pronunciation)
z'	—	very approximately as in pre*s*ume (British pronunciation)
l'	—	very approximarely as in mi*ll*ion (British pronunciation)
r'	—	palatalized trilled *r*. Only before vowel.
c'	—	very approximately as in "the ha*ts y*ou bought"
ʒ'	—	very approximately as in "the be*ds y*ou bought"
j	—	pronounced approximately as in *yes* or *boyish***

(Exercise 3)

CONDITIONED SOFT CONSONANTS

The conditioned soft consonants occur only when followed by *i*.

p'	—	very approximately as i *spew*
b'	—	very approximately as in im*b*ue
f'	—	very approximately as in *f*ew
v'	—	very approximataly as in *v*iew
m'	—	very approximately as in *m*use
č'	—	very approximately as in *ch*eap
š'	—	very approximately as in *sh*eet
ž'	—	very approximately as in plea*s*ure
ǯ'	—	very approximately as in *j*uice
k'	—	very approximately as in *c*ue
g'	—	very approximately as in ar*g*ue
h'	—	soft *h*. No English equivalent.
x'	—	soft *x*. No English equivalent.

Note 1: Strictly speaking, the conditioned soft consonants are only semi-soft, since their palatalization is slight.

---

* For example, the consonant *k* (*bát'ko, nýz'ko, nén'ka*), the consonant *s* (*nedbál'stvo*)

** The consonant *j* is considered "soft" because morphologically it functions as a soft consonant.

Note 2: The consonants *č, š, ž* when doubled or lengthened are palatalized when followed by *i* as well as *a* and *u* (*oblýč’͡č’a* ‘face’, *r’ič’͡č’u* ‘thing’).

Note 3: In a few words a palatalized *v* appears before *a* (*s’v’áto* ‘holiday’, *c’v’áx* ‘nail’).

Note 4: Conditioned soft consonants may appear before vowels *e* in foreign borrowings, especially the consonants *b’, p’, v’, m’, f’, k’, h’*.

Note 5: All consonants are normally hard before the vowels *e* and *y*. In a few words soft *n’ l’* and *t’* occur before *e*, e.g. *sýn’e* ‘blue’ *l’l’é* ‘pours’, *trét’e* ‘third” (orthographic є).

(Exercise 4)

GLIDES

Ukrainian has two glide consonants. We have encountered one of them, the ‘soft’ *j*. The other is *w*. It occurs only at the end of a word or before a consonant.

(Exercise 5)

SUMMARY OF THE SOUND SYSTEM

We have learned the basic rules about the Ukrainian Sound System. More features will be discussed later. Let us now sum up the important points.

VOWELS

1. There are 6 vowels in Ukrainian:

a, e, y, i, o, u

2. There is little qualitative distinction between stressed and unstressed vowels.

CONSONANTS

1. There are 22 basic consonants: *p, b, f, v, m, t, d, n, s, z, c, ʒ, ǯ, č, š, ž, l, r, k, g, h, x*
2. There are two glides, *j* and *w*. The glide *w* occurs only at the end of a word or before a consonant.
3. All the basic consonants have their soft counterparts.
4. Soft consonants can be independent or conditioned.
5. All consonants are *soft* before *i* (some are only semi-soft).
6. Consonants are *hard* before the vowels *e* and *y* (except that *n’e, l’e* and *t’e* are found in certain words). see note 5 above.
7. Most consonants can be short or lengthened (doubled).

STRESS AND SYLLABIFICATION

Ukrainian words normally have only one stress. The stressed syllable is pronounced with a greater force than the rest of the syllables.

The position of the stress differs in different words. It may also shift within the same word as the word form changes:

knýžka (book)	—	*knyžký* (books)
hovorýty (to speak)	—	*hovóryt'* (speaks)

The number of syllables per word is determined by the number of vowels it contains:

ho-vo-r'ít' po-vó-l'i	—	Speak slowly!

If there is a consonantal cluster within the word, one consonant is assigned to the preceding syllable and the rest to the following:

švýd-ko	—	fast
po-an-hl'íj-s'ko-mu	—	in English

Ukrainians think about spelling their words in terms of the pronunciation of the syllables, so that the question "How do you spell it?" comes out in Ukrainian as "How do you say it by syllables?" or even "How do you write it?" (there is no verb "to spell" in Ukrainian):

ják cé pýšec͡'c'a?	—	How do you spell (lit. "write") it?
hon-ča-rén-ko	—	Hončarenko

Note: In Ukrainian, some monosyllabic words are never stressed while others may or may no be stressed depending on the context. For example, the preposition до is never stressed while the interrogative pronoun щó "what" is stressed as opposed to the conjunction, що. For this reason, we provide stress marks over monosyllabic words wherever needed.

THE ALPHABET

Here are the letters of the Ukrainian alphabet.* The names of the letters are written in transcription.

á	А а	zé	З з	ó	О о	čé	Ч ч
bé	Б б	ý	И и	pé	П п	šá	Ш ш
vé	В в	í	І і	ér	Р р	ščá	Щ щ
hé	Г г	jí	Ї ї	és	С с	jú	Ю ю
gé	Ґ ґ	jót	Й й	té	Т т	já	Я я
dé	Д д	ká	К к	ú	У у	mjakýj znák	Ь ь
é	Е е	él	Л л	éf	Ф ф		
jé	Є є	ém	М м	xá	Х х		
žé	Ж ж	én	Н н	cé	Ц ц		

Note. *Mjakýj znák* the name of the last letter means "soft sign". Note in particular the letters *в, н, р, с, у* and х. They look like familiar Roman letters, but in Ukrainian they represent quite different sounds.

---

* It is an adaptation of the old Slavonic alphabet called Cyrillic. (See Appendix 1)

EVERYDAY AND CLASSROOM EXPRESSIONS

Here are some everyday and classroom expressions. Practice reading and saying them until you know them well.

I. Greetings

1.	Дóбрий дéнь! dóbryj dén'	Good day! Hello!
2.	Добрúдень! dobrýden'	Hello! Good day!
3.	Дóброго рáнку! dóbroho ránku	Good morning!
4.	Дóбрий вéчір! dóbryj véč'ir	Good evening!
5.	Дóброго здорóв'я! dóbroho zdoróv'ja	Greetings!

II. Farewell wishes

1.	До побáчення. do pobáčen'n'a	Good-bye.
2.	Добрáніч. dobrán'ič	Good night.
3.	На добрáніч. na dobránič	Good night.
4.	На всé дóбре. na wsé dóbre	Good-bye! (All the best!)

III. An inquiry about health

1.	Я́к здорóв'я? ják zdoróv'ja	How is your health?
2.	Дóбре, дя́кую. dóbre, d'akuju	Fine, thanks.
3.	Я́к вú себé почувáєте? ják vý sebé počuvájete	How do you feel?
4.	Дя́кую, дóбре. А вú? d'ákuju, dóbre; a vý	Fine, thanks. And you?
5.	Дýже дóбре, дя́кую. dúže dóbre, d'ákuju	Very well, thank you.
6.	Дя́кую, непогáно. d'ákuju, nepoháno	Not bad, thanks.
7.	Непогáно. nepoháno	Not bad.

IV. Requests, expressions of thanks

1.	Прóшу, ... próšu	Please, ...
2.	Будь лáска, ... bud' láska	Please, ...
3.	Дя́кую. d'ákuju	Thanks.
4.	Щúро дя́кую. ščýro d'akuju	My sincere thanks.
5.	Дя́кую дýже. d'ákuju dúže	Thanks (thank you) very much.
6.	Я́ вáм дýже дя́кую. dúže d'ákuju	I thank you very much.
7.	Спасúбі. spasýbi	Thank you.
8.	Прóшу. próšu	You are welcome
9.	Прóшу дýже. próšu dúže	You are very welcome

V. Introductions

1.	Прóшу, знайóмтеся. próšu znajómtes'ja	Please, meet each other.
2.	(Я́) Гончарéнко. (já) hončarénko	(I'm) Hončarenko.
3.	Васи́ль Гончарéнко. vasýl' hončarénko	Vasyl' Hončarenko
4.	Приє́мно. pryjémno	Pleased to meet you.
5.	Ду́же приє́мно. dúže pryjémno	I'm very pleased to meet you.
6.	Дóбрий дéнь. dóbryj dén'	Hello!

VI. Classroom expressions

(A)

1.	Ви́бачте я не розумíю. výbačte, já ne rozum'íju	Excuse me, I don't understand
2.	Щó ви́ сказáли? ščó vý skazály	What did you say?
3.	Прóшу, повторíть. próšu, powtor'ít'	Please, repeat.
4.	Прóшу, повторíть щé раз. próšu, powtor'ít' ščé raz	Please, repeat once more.
5.	Не тáк шви́дко. ne ták švýdko	Not so fast.
6.	Прóшу, не говорíть так шви́дко. próšu, ne hovor'ít' ták švýdko	Please, don't speak so fast.
7.	Прóшу, говорíть повíльно. próšu hovor'ít' povíl'no	Please, speak slowly.
8.	Ду́же дя́кую, тепéр я́ розумíю. dúže d'jákuju, tepér já rozum'íju	Thank you very much, now I understand.

(B)

1.	Цé непрáвильно. cé neprávyl'no	This is incorrect.
2.	Скажíть щé раз, будь лáска. skaž'ít' ščé raz, bud' láska	Say it once more, please.
3.	Тепéр крáще. tepér krášče	Now it's better
4.	Ви́ розумíєте? vý rozum'íjete	Do you understand?
5.	Відповідáйте гóлосно. v'ídpovidájte hólosno	Answer loudly!
6.	Голоснíше, будь лáска! holos'n'íše, bud' láska	Louder, please!
7.	Прóшу, повторíть усí рáзом. prósu powtor'ít' us'í rázom	Please repeat all together.

(C)

1.	Скажíть це по-украї́нському. skaž'ít' cé poukrajín's'komu	Say it in Ukrainian.
2.	Тáк, цé прáвильно. ták, cé právyl'no	Yes, this is correct.
3.	А як цé по-англíйському? a ják cé poanhl'íjs'komu	And how is this in English?
4.	Нí, цé непрáвильно. n'i, cé neprávyl'no	No, it's wrong.
5.	Тепéр дóбре. tepér dóbre	Now it's good.
6.	Прóшу, дáлі. prósu dál'i	Please go on! (or: Next, please!)
7.	Прóшу, всí рáзом! prósu ws'í rázom	All together, please!

VOCABULARY TO EVERYDAY AND CLASSROOM EXPRESSIONS

а	and
будь ла́ска	please
ва́м	you
Васи́ль	Vasyl'
ве́чір	evening
ви́	you
Ви́бачте!	Excuse me!
Відповіда́йте!	Answer!
всі́ = усі́	
Говорі́ть!	Speak!
голосні́ше	louder
го́лосно	loud
Гончаре́нко	Hončarenko
да́лі	further; next!
де́нь	day
до	to; till
До поба́чення!	Good-bye!
Добра́ніч!	Good night!
до́бре	good, well
На все́ до́бре!	All the best!
Добри́день!	Good day! Hello!
до́брий	good, kind
До́брий де́нь!	Good day!
До́брий ве́чір!	Good evening!
До́брого ра́нку!	Good morning!
ду́же	very
Дя́кую!	Thanks!
Дя́кую ду́же!	Thanks very much
здоро́в'я	health
знайо́мтеся	be acquainted
зна́к	sign
кра́ще	better
м'яки́й	soft
м'яки́й зна́к	soft sign
На все́ до́бре!	All the best!
На добра́ніч!	Good night!
не	not
непога́но	not bad
непра́вильно	incorrect; wrong
ні́	no

по-англі́йському	(in) English
поба́чення	meeting; date; appointment
по-украї́нському	(in) Ukrainian
пові́льно	slowly
Повторі́ть!	Repeat!
пра́вильно	correct; right
прие́мно (ду́же п.)	please! (very p.)
Про́шу!	Please! You are welcome.
Про́шу ду́же!	You are very welcome.
ра́з	once
ра́зом	together
ра́нок	morning
Розумі́єте?	Do you understand?
розумі́ю	I understand
Скажі́ть!	Say (it)!
сказа́ли	said (you, they, we s.)
спаси́бі	thanks
та́к	yes
тепе́р	now
усі́	all; everyone
це́	this
шви́дко	fast; quickly
ще́	more
ще́ раз	once more; again
щи́ро	sincerely
що́	what
я́	I
я́к	how
Я́к ви́ себе́ почува́єте?	How do you feel?

NOTES ON THE CONVENTIONAL GREETINGS AND OTHER FORMS OF POLITENESS

Ukrainian has no general greeting corresponding to English 'hello', neither does it have an equivalent to the English phrase 'How are you?'. The most ordinary opening remark on meeting someone is "good day", for which "good evening" is substituted from late afternoon on.

There are two ways of saying 'good day' in Ukrainian: **Добри́день** and **До́брий де́нь**. The first is less formal than the second.

'Good morning' **До́брого ра́нку** is an elliptical phrase with the words 'I bid you' being understood, i.e 'I bid you good morning' **Я́ Ва́м бажа́ю до́брого ра́нку**. This greeting tends to have a stronger meaning as an expression of good will than does 'good day'.

When parting Ukrainians usually say **До поба́чення** which literally means 'Until seeing/meeting'. The noun **поба́чення** is also used in the sense of date, appointment and prison visit. Another formula used at parting is **На все́ до́бре.** Literally translated into English it means 'All the best', but in practical usage it is an equivalent to 'Goodbye'. The expression **Добра́ніч** 'Good night' is used only before actually going to bed.

A typical request would begin with **Про́шу** for the West Ukrainian speaker and with **Будь ла́ска** for the easterner.

To express gratitude a Ukrainian may say **Дя́кую** or **Спаси́бі**, or if he wishes to be extra polite or feels especialy thankful he would say **Ду́же дя́кую** or **щиро дя́кую** 'thank you very much'). The response to that is either **Про́шу** 'You are welcome' or **Про́шу ду́же** 'You are very welcome'. There are other forms of politeness which we will discuss later.

When being introduced, Ukrainians, especially easterners, may respond with the same formulas which are used for greeting, i.e. 'good day', 'good evening', etc. A more formal response is 'Pleased' or 'Very pleased' with the verb **познайо́митися** 'to get acquainted' being understood, or with the complete phrase:

Прие́мно (познайо́митися). pryjémno poznajómytys'a	Pleased (to meet you).
Ду́же прие́мно (познайо́митися). dúže pryjémno poznajómytys'a	Very pleased (to meet you).
Мені́ ду́же прие́мно з ва́ми познайо́митися. meni dúže pryjémno zvámy poznajómytys'a	I am very pleased to meet you.

THE CORRESPONDENCE BETWEEN THE SOUND SYSTEM AND THE WRITING SYSTEM

1. Consonants

The Ukrainian alphabet provides only 21 consonant-letters to represent the 45 consonant-sounds defined above, i.e. both the hard and the soft varieties. To tell whether a consonant is hard or soft one has to look at the letter which follows it (see p. xxvii, "Sound sequence and spelling").

п-	*p, p'*	т-	*t, t'*	ц-	*c, c'*	к-	*k, k'*
б-	*b, b'*	д-	*d, d'*	ч-	*č, č'*	ґ-	*g, g'*
ф-	*f, f'*	с-	*s, s'*	ш-	*š, š'*	х-	*x, x'*
в-	*v, v'*	з-	*z, z'*	ж-	*ž, ž'*	г-	*h, h'*
	w	н-	*n, n'*			й-	*j*
		л-	*l, l'*				
		р-	*r, r'*				

The consonant-sounds *ʒ* and *ǯ* with their soft counterparts *ʒ'* and *ǯ'* do not have separate letter symbols but are represented instead by combinations of the letters **д + з** or **д + ж**:

з	з'	дз
ǯ	ǯ'	дж

On the other hand, there is a sequence of consonant-sounds which is represented by one letter **щ**:

šč'	š'č'	щ

Note: The letter ґ is used to indicate the pronunciation *g* in Soviet dictionaries, textbooks, and linguistic works; in ordinary spelling the letter ґ is written г, and one must know which words are to be pronounced with *g (g')* and which with *h (h')*. The letter ґ is found in older printed works and it is regularly used in most publications issued outside Ukraine. Today it is being re-introduced but not consistently.

2. Vowels

There are ten vowel letters in Ukrainian representing the six vowel-sounds:

a-	а, я	*o-*	о
e-	е, є	*u-*	у, ю
y-	и	*ji-*	ї
i-	і		

The letters **я, є, ю** may represent a jotized vowel, i.e. the glide *j* plus vowel (see p. xxviii); for ї this is always true.

3. Sound sequence * and spelling rules

(a) Consonants

The consonant sound *w* is spelled with **в**. It occurs only at the end of a word or before a consonant.

повторíть	*powtor'ít'*
всí	*ws'í*
Львíв	*l'v'íw* (Lviv)
писáв	*pysáw* (he wrote)

The consonant-sound *j* may be represented in different ways: it is spelled with the letter **й** if it occurs at the end of a word, before a consonant, or before the vowel **o**.

---

* See also Appendix 3.

For example:

до́брий	*dóbryj*
відповіда́йте	*v'idpov'idájte*
його́	*johó* (his)

It is always represented by the vowel-letter ї if it is followed by the sound *i:*

по-украї́нському	*poukrajín's'komu*

It is represented by the vowel-letters **я, є, ї, ю** in initial position or after at vowel:

я́к	*ják*
почува́єте	*počuvájete*
розумі́ю	*rozumíju*

It is represented by the vowel-letters **у, є, ї, ю** preceded by an apostrophe after a labial, i.e. *b, p, v, m, f*.

For example:

м'яки́й	*mjakýj*
п'ю́	*pjú* (I drink)
б'є́	*bjé* (he hits)
в'ї́зд	*vjízd* (entry)
ве́рф'ю	*vérf'ju* (with the shipyard)

(b) Vowels

The vowel **и** never occurs in initial position or after any soft consonant (including j).

The Euphony Rule

In many common words the vowels **у** and і change into **в** and **й** respectively. This occurs after a vowel:

ви́ всі́	*vý ws'í* (you all)
не йди́	*ne jdý* (don't go)
ви + учити = **ви́вчити**	*výwčyty* (to learn)
при + іти = прийти́	*pryjtý* (to come)

This rule has many exceptions, (a) foreign words such as **університе́т** 'university', **іде́я** 'idea', (b) words with the initial stressed **у** or **і**, cf. **і́нший** 'other', **у́спіх** 'success', (c) a number of specific words, including **по-украї́нському** (d) words separated by a pause in speech (including a slight pause between the first name and a patronymic, as **Дмитро́ Іва́нович**) preserve their initial vowels.

(c) Indication of softness of consonants

As has been mentioned above (p. xxviii) softening (palatalization) is indicated by the letter which follows the given consonant, and hardness is likewise recognized by the spelling. Thus:

Softness:

Softness of a consonant may be indicated by a "soft sign":

де́нь	*dén'*
непра́вильно	*neprávyl'no*
сьогóдні	s'ohódn'i (today)

Softness of a consonant may also be indicated by the presence of the vowel-letters **я, є, ю** immediately following it:

дя́кую	*d'ákuju*
малю́нок	*mal'únok* (picture)
тре́тє	*trét'e* (third)

All consonants are soft to a greater or lesser degree when followed by the vowel i:

пово́лі	*powól'i*
всí	*ws'í*
скажíть	*skaž'ít'*
ве́чір	*véč'ir*

Note: There are many instances when the "soft sign" and the letters **я, є, ю** may not be written. The notable exceptions are: (1) no "soft sign" after labials and palatals (**б, п, в, ф, м, ж, ч, ш, щ, д, ж**) and after р (2) no letters **я, є, ю** after palatals **ж, ч, ш, щ** unless there is consonant lengthening ("doubling").

4. Sound sequence not reflected by spelling. Assimiliation*

On the whole, the Ukrainian consonant-letters in conventional spelling reflect the pronunciation faithfully. The exceptions are in groups of consonants. There is a tendency for some feature of the last consonant in a group to be adopted by a preceding consonant. This is called *assimilation* for the first consonant *assimilates* (i.e. becomes similar) to the following one.

The most important assimilation is of the element of softness: if the second consonant is soft, the preceding one will also ordinarily be pronounced as soft; however, this assimilation is not indicated in spelling:

поба́чення	*pobáčen'n'a*
голоснíше	*holos'n'íše*
по-украї́нському	*poukrajín's'komu*
(but збíжжя	*zb'íž'ž'a*)

* For further remarks on assimilation see Appendix 3.

UKRAINIAN HANDWRITING

Here is the Ukrainian alphabet in italics and in script. Note that Ukrainian italics are designed on the model of the script.

А а	Аа	*З з*	Зз	*О о*	Оо	*Ч ч*	Чч
Б б	Бб	*И и*	Ии	*П п*	Пп	*Ш ш*	Шш
В в	Вв	*І і*	Іі	*Р р*	Рр	*Щ щ*	Щщ
Г г	Гг	*Ї ї*	Її	*С с*	Сс	*Ю ю*	Юю
Ґ ґ	Ґґ	*Й й*	Йй	*Т т*	Тт	*Я я*	Яя
Д д	Дд	*К к*	Кк	*У у*	Уу	*Ь ь*	Ьь
Е е	Ее	*Л л*	Лл	*Ф ф*	Фф		
Є є	Єє	*М м*	Мм	*Х х*	Хх		
Ж ж	Жж	*Н н*	Нн	*Ц ц*	Цц		

Four letters have alternative shapes in common use: з has З beside з, т is written Т as well as т, р is written р and р and д is written д as well as д. Further, it is possible to add a cross-piece above the т and under ш: т, т̄, ш, ш̱. This is a great help in reading normally careless handwriting, e.g. мити, пиши

Note that ш is not like English w; the rigth-hand stroke must come down to the line.

It is very important to make the initial little hooks on л, м, я e.g. **ра́зом, дя́кую, пово́лі, будь ла́ска, земля**: разом, дякую поволі, будь ласка, земля

The tails on ц ц and щ щ must be small, not long like у у: **ця́, ву́лиця, кра́ще** ця, вулиця, краще

The soft-sign ь does not rise above the mid-line; в does, e.g. **говорі́ть пра́вильно** говоріть правильно

Do not confuse л, г and ч: **дала́, да́ча, ага́, голова́, чолові́к** дала, дача, ага, голова, чоловік

The capital **У, Ч** and **Ф** do not go below the line: У, Ч, Ф

Note the particular letters which look like Roman script but have different sound value: В, в, д И, и, п, р, С, с, у, х

Note: In the West Ukrainian regions there was a tradition for writing certain letters in a somewhat different manner than is the current modern usage, e.g. к k є Є я ЄЛ. The student is advised to follow the script given above.

(Exercise 4).

Exercise 1.

Practice the following syllables and words (preferably in the language laboratory, repeating after the speaker).

a	*ma*	*ba*	*va*	*máma* Mom	*bába* grandma	*páva* peacock
e	*me*	*be*	*ve*	*mené* me	*sebé* oneself	*véna* vein
y	*my*	*by*	*vy*	*mámy*	*báby*	*pávy*
i	*mi*	*bi*	*vi*	*mámi*	*bábi*	*pávi*
o	*mo*	*bo*	*vo*	*mámo*	*bábo*	*pávo*
u	*mu*	*bu*	*vu*	*mámu*	*bábu*	*pávu*

Exercise 2.

Practice the following words with hard consonants.

p	*pó* along	*mápa* map	*popá* priest's	*popý* priests		
	páva peacock	*paný* lords	*pána* lord's	*máp* maps		
b	*banán* banana	*váb* attract!				
v	*vám* you					
f	*fá* the note F	*týf* typhus				
m	*móva* language	*mené* me	*sám* self			
t	*tám* there	*tút* here!	*tabú* tabu	*týn* fence	*máty* mother	
	tó that	*táto* Dad	*tebé* you	*mát* check-mate		
d	*dám* I'll give	*móda* fashion	*dáta* date	*dým* smoke	*dé* where	*méd* honey
n	*dnó* bottom	*ná* here	*nápad* assault	*núdno* boring	*pán* lord	
s	*samá* herself	*syný* sons	*sóm* catfish	*súd* trial	*sadýty* to plant	

	stán	*sný*	*sebé*	*bás*		
	waist	dreams	self	basso		
z	*znýzu*	*váza*	*dózy*	*póza*	*zúb*	
	from below	vase	doses	beyond	tooth	
	zúby	*zébu*	*zóna*	*báz*		
	teeth	zebu	zone	bases		
c	*клácaty*	*cáp*	*cé*	*cytáta*		
	to chatter (teeth)	goat	this	quote		
	cúpko	*cabé*	*bác*			
	fast	gee-up	bang			
ʒ	*ʒvóny*	*ʒbán*	*ʒús*	*ʒúm*	*gúʒ*	
	bells	jug	shoo	buzz	knot	
ǯ	*ǯút*	*ǯáz*	*saǯú*	*ǯygún*	*v'idpóv'iǯ*	
	jute	jazz	I plant	libertine	answer (rare)	
č	*čás*	*čytáty*	*čésno*	*čomú*	*báč*	
	time	to read	honestly	why	see	
š	*náša*	*šúm*	*čéše*	*šýna*	*šósta*	*váš*
	our	noise	combs	tire	sixth	your
ž	*žába*	*móže*	*žýto*	*mážu*	*bóže*	*máž*
	toad	can	rye	I spread	God!	spread!
l	*láma*	*luná*	*lémko*	*lób*	*volý*	*vál*
	llama	echo	Lemko	forehead	oxen	billow
r	*ráz*	*rýba*	*róža*	*dérevo*	*rudá*	*sýr*
	once	fish	rose	tree	ore	cheese
k	*káva*	*komú*	*kýt*	*kumá*	*rakéta*	*mák*
	coffee	whom	whale	god-mother	rocket	poppy
g	*gánok*	*gáva*	*gráty*	*gúʒ*	*ʒýg*	
	porch	crow	bars	knot	pegtops	
h	*hárno*	*háslo*	*nóhy*	*bóhu*		
	nicely	slogan	legs	to God		
	horá	*hrybý*	*bóh*			
	mountain	mushrooms	God			
x	*xáta*	*múxy*	*xóču*	*suxé*	*múxu*	*púx*
	house	flies	I want	dry	fly	down

Exercise 3.

Practice the following words with independent soft consonants.

t'	*mýt'*	*klápot'*	*páporot'*	*trét'a*	*t'óxkaty*	*let'účka*
	instant	piece	fern	third	to warble	leaflet
d'	*vyhód'*	*búd'*	*porád'*	*syd'át'*	*d'jum*	*d'ohót'*
	come out!	be!	advise!	they sit	inch	tar
n'	*stán'*	*bán'*	*klún'*	*sýn'a*	*sýn'oho*	*sýn' u*
	stand!	bath houses	barns	blue	blue	blue
s'	*ós'*	*rýs'*	*vynós'*	*s'ád'*	*s'óme*	*s'udý*
	here	lynx	carry out!	sit down!	seventh	this way
z'	*zláz'*	*máz'*	*kolód'az'*	*vz'áty*	*hr'az'úka*	
	climb down	salve	well	to take	mud	
l'	*brýl'*	*koról'*	*nól'*	*pol'á*	*l'úba*	*l'ón*
	straw hat	king	zero	fields	darling	flax
r'	*búr'a*	*búr'u*	*čotyr'óx*			
	storm	storm	four			
c'	*mic'*	*zájec'*	*prác'*	*c'ohó*	*c'ác'ka*	*prác'u*
	might	hare	jobs	this	toy	job
ʒ'	*géʒ'*	*ʒ'ób*	*ʒ'úbaty*			
	horse fly	beak	to peck			
j	*já*	*jijí*	*jomú*	*d áj*		
	I	her	him	give!		

Exercise 4.

Practice the following words with conditioned soft consonants.

p'	*p'ít*	*p'iná*	*sop'íty*
	sweat	foam	to snort
b'	*b'ís*	*rob'ít'*	*sob'í*
	devil	do!	oneself

f'	*sof'íja*	*f'íkus*	*vérf'i*		
	Sophia	ficus	docks		
v'	*v'ík*	*v'idpov'idájte*	*sov'í*	*s'v'atýj*	*c'v'áx*
	age	answer!	owl	saint	nail
m'	*m'ína*	*zam'ítka*	*solóm'i*		
	mine	note	straw		
č'	*óč'i*	*č'ítko*	*peč'ínka*	*p'íč'͡č'u*	*oblýč'͡č'a*
	eyes	clearly	liver	oven	face
š'	*hróš'i*	*lyš'ít'*	*š'íst'*	*p'id͡dáš'͡š'a*	*p'id͡dáš'͡š'u*
	money	leave!	six	loft	loft
ž'	*sáž'i*	*ž'ínka*	*skaž'ím*	*podrúž'͡ž'a*	*podrúž'͡ž'u*
	soot	woman	let us say	married couple	married couple (Dative case)
ǯ	*dr'iž'ǯi*				
	yeast				
k'	*k'ít*	*sók'il*	*dok'íja*		
	tom cat	falcon	Dokia (name)		
g'	*g'íps*	*g'imnázija*			
	plaster	high school			
h'	*h'il'͡l'á*	*h'ídno*	*h'íst'*		
	branches	properly	guest		
x'	*x'ibá*	*sux'í*	*rax'ítu*		
	really	dry	rickets		

Exercise 5.

Practice the glide consonants *j* and *w*.

j	*mar'íja*	*júška*	*jósyp*	*míj*	*mýlyj*	*sýn'ij*
	Maria	broth	Joseph	my	dear	blue
w	*stáw*	*máwpa*	*wpáw*	*žówtyj*	*lév'iw*	
	pond	monkey	fell down	yellow	lions	

Exercise 6.

Practice the following contrastive pairs with hard and soft consonants.

Hard/Independent Soft

t / t'

pút	*pút'*
fetters	road
stáw	*st'áw*
became	cut down
tó	*t'óx*
that	warble
tú	*t'ú*
that	interjection

d / d'

búd	*búd'*
booths	be
dáta	*d'áka*
date	gratitude
dówho	*d'óhot'*
long	tar
dúže	*d'úžyna*
very	dozen

l/l'

lúk	*l'úk*
bow	hatch
lák	*l'ák*
lacquer	fright
lóno	*l'ónu*
bosom	flax
malá	*mal'á*
small	tiny tot
s'íl	*s'íl'*
villages	salt

z / z'

láz	*láz'*
passage	crawl
zabráw	*z'ábra*
took	gills

s / s'

ós	*ós'*
wasps	here
rosá	*poros'á*
dew	piglet
sómom	*s'ómym*
cat fish	seventh
sudý	*s'udý*
courts	this way

r / r'

cár	------
tsar	
rádu	*r'ádu*
council	row
tróxy	*tr'óx*
some	three
truná	*tr'umó*
casket	pier-glass

c / c'

kóc	*kýc'*
blanket	kitty
sýna	*sýn'a*
son	blue
cáp	*c'áp*
goat	splash!
cýt'	*c'íp*
hush!	flail

n / n'

stán	*stán'*
state	stand
p'ísnú	*p'ís'n'u*
meatless	song
(u) nóhu	*(u) n'óho*
(in) step	(by) him

Hard / Conditioned Soft

pýk	*p'ík*	*pokažý*	*pokaž'ít'*
mugs	spade (card)	show!	show!
býk	*b'ík*	*skýs*	*k'ís*
bull	side	became sour	braids
výn	*v'ín*	*šýška*	*š'ístka*
wines	he	cone	six
mýr	*m'ír*	*svyščý*	*xruš'č'í*
peace	measures	whistle	May bugs
syčý	*syč'í*		
hiss!	barn owls		

Exercise 7.

Practice writing the "Everyday and classroom expressions" (pp. xxi), then refer to these pages for checking.

I. *Добрий день!*
Добридень!
Доброго ранку!
Добрий вечір!
Доброго здоров'я!

II. *До побачення.*
Добраніч.
На добраніч!
На все добре.

III. *Як здоров'я?*
Добре, дякую.
Як ви себе почуваєте?
Дякую, добре. А ви?
Дуже добре, дякую.
Дякую, непогано.
Непогано.

IV. Прошу, ...
Будь ласка, ...
Дякую. Дякую дуже.
Дякую дуже.
Я вам дуже дякую.
Щиро дякую.
Спасибі.
Дуже дякую.
Прошу.
Прошу дуже.

V. Прошу, знайомтеся.
(Я) Гончаренко.
Василь Гончаренко.
Приємно.
Дуже приємно.
Добрий день.

VI. (A) Вибачте, я не розумію.
Що ви сказали?
Прошу, повторіть.
Прошу, повторіть ще раз.
Не так швидко.
Прошу, не говоріть так швидко.
Прошу, повторіть повільно.
Дуже дякую, тепер я розумію.

(B) Це неправильно.
Скажіть ще раз, будь ласка.
Тепер краще.
Ви розумієте?
Відповідайте голосно.
Голосніше, будь ласка.
Прошу, повторіть усі разом.

(C) *Скажіть це по-українському.*

Так, це правильно.

А як це по-англійському?

Ні, це неправильно.

Тепер добре.

Прошу, далі.

Прошу, всі разом.

ПЕРША ЛЕКЦІЯ

1.	До́брий день!	Good day!
2.	Я́ ва́ш профе́сор.	I am your professor.
3.	Моє́ пр́ізвище Гончаре́нко, моє́ ім'я́ Васи́ль, а по ба́тькові Миха́йлович.	My name is Hončarenko, my first name is Vasyl', and my patronymic is Myxájlovyč.
4.	Я́к ва́ше ім'я́?	What is your name?
5.	Моє́ ім'я́ Марко́.	My name is Marko.
6.	А ва́ше?	And yours?
7.	Моє́ ім'я́ О́ля.	My name is Olja.
8.	А я́к ва́с по ба́тькові?	And what's your patronymic?
9.	Миха́йлівна. О́льга Миха́йлівна.	Myxájlivna. Ol'ha Myxájlivna.
10.	Його́ ім'я́ Марко́, а ї́ї ім'я́ О́льга.	His name is Marko and her name is Ol'ha.

11.	Ві́н студе́нт. Вона́ студе́нтка.	He is a student. She is a student.
12.	Вони́ студе́нти.	They are students.
13.	Хто́ ти́? — Я́ студе́нт.	Who are you? — I am a student.
14.	Хто ти́? — Я́ студе́нтка.	Who are you? — I am a student (f).
15.	Чи ви́ всі́ студе́нти?	Are you all students?
16.	Та́к, ми́ всі́ студе́нти.	Yes, we are all students.
17.	Чи я́ студе́нт?	Am I a student?
18.	Ні́, ви́ не студе́нт, ви́ профе́сор.	No, you are not a student, you are a professor.
19.	Це́ сті́л, а це́ стіле́ць.	This is a table, (and) this is a chair.
20.	Це́ мі́й стіле́ць, а то́ ва́ш.	This is my chair, and that is yours.

21.	Це́ кни́жка, а це́ зо́шит	This is a book, this is a notebook.
22.	Це́ моя́ кни́жка, а то́ ва́ша.	This is my book, and that is yours.
23.	Це́ ру́чка і оліве́ць.	This is a pen and a pencil.
24.	Ру́чка його́, а оліве́ць ї́ї.	The pen is his and the pencil is hers.
25.	О́сь до́шка, а о́н вікно́.	Here is a blackboard, and there a window.
26.	Це́ на́ша до́шка і на́ше вікно́.	It's our blackboard and our window.
27.	О́н две́рі. Це́ на́ші две́рі.	There is a door. It's our door.
28.	Це́ кімна́та. Це́ на́ша кімна́та.	This is a room. It's our room.
29.	Чиє́ це́ мі́сце?	Whose place is this?
30.	Це́ ї́хнє мі́сце, а ва́ше о́н та́м.	It's their place, (and) yours is over there.

31.	Чи́й це́ словни́к?	Whose dictionary is this?
32.	Це́ ї́хній словни́к, а ва́ш о́сь ту́т.	It's their dictionary, (and) yours is here.
33.	Чия́ це́ кни́жка?	Whose book is this?
34.	Це́ ї́хня кни́жка, а о́сь ва́ша.	It's their book, and here is yours.
35.	Де́ зо́шит? — О́сь він.	Where is the notebook? — Here it is.
36.	Де́ ру́чка? — О́сь вона́.	Where is the pen? — Here it is.
37.	Де́ ва́ше мі́сце? — О́сь воно́.	Where is your seat? — Here it is. (It's here).
38.	Де́ студе́нти? — О́сь вони́.	Where are the students? — Here they are.
39.	Ця́ кни́жка моя́, а та́ твоя́.	This book is mine, and that one is yours.
40.	Це́й словни́к мі́й, а то́й тві́й.	This dictionary is mine, and that is yours.

41.	Це́ мі́сце моє́, а те́ твоє́.	This seat is mine, and that is yours.
42.	Чи та́м є́ мі́сце? — Та́к, є́.	Is there any room here? Yes, there is.
43.	Чи та́м є́ студе́нти? — Та́к, є́.	Are there any students there? Yes, there are.
44.	Що́ це́? — Це́ украї́нське сло́во.	What's this? It's a Ukrainian word.
45.	Що́ це́? — Це́ украї́нський словни́к.	What's this? It's the Ukrainian dictionary.
46.	Чи це́ украї́нська мо́ва?	Is this the Ukrainian language?
47.	Та́к, це́ на́ша пе́рша ле́кція.	Yes, this is our first lesson.
48.	Чи то́й студе́нт — украї́нець?	Is that student a Ukrainian?
49.	Та́к, ві́н украї́нець.	Yes, he is Ukrainian.
50.	Чи та́ студе́нтка — украї́нка?	Is that student a Ukrainian?
51.	Та́к, вона́ украї́нка.	Yes, she is Ukrainian.
52.	Дя́кую, це́ все́.	Thank you. That's all.

СЛОВНИК / VOCABULARY

ва́ш (m), ва́ша (f), ва́ше (n)	your (s)
вікно́ (n)	window
ві́н (m), вона́ (f), воно́ (n), вони́ (pl)	he, she, it, they
ве́сь (m), вся́ (f), все́ (n), всі́ (pl) (уве́сь, уся́, усе́, усі́)	all
впра́ва (f), впра́ви (pl)	exercise
две́рі (pl)	door
де́	where
до́шка (f)	(black) board
є́	is, are
зо́шит (m)	notebook

і	and
ім'я́ (n)	name; given name
її́	her (s)
ї́хній, ї́хня, ї́хнє	their (s)
його́	his, its
кімна́та (f)	room
кни́жка (f)	book
ле́кція (f)*	lecture, lesson
ми́	we
мі́й, моя́, моє́	my, mine
мі́сце (n)	place, seat; room (space)
мо́ва (f)	language
на́ш, на́ша, на́ше	our (s)
olіве́ць (m)	pencil
о́н, о́н та́м	there, over there
о́сь, о́сь ту́т	here, over here
пе́рший	first
прі́звище (n)	last name
профе́сор (m)	professor
по ба́тькові	patronymic
Я́к ва́с по ба́тькові?	What's your patronymic?
ру́чка (f)	pen
словни́к (m)	dictionary, vocabulary
сло́во (n)	word
сті́л (m)	table, desk
стіле́ць (m)	chair
студе́нт (m)	student (m)
студе́нтка (f)	student (f)
студе́нти (pl.)	students (males or mixed groups)
та́м	there
тві́й, твоя́, твоє́	your (s)
ти́	you
то́	that
то́й, та́, те́	that one
ту́т	here
украї́нець (m)	Ukrainian (m)
украї́нка (f)	Ukrainian (f)
украї́нськ -ий, -а, -е	Ukrainian
усе́ = все́	all, everything
хто́	who
це́й, ця́, це́	this (one)
чи́	interrogative particle
чи́й, чия́, чиє́	whose

* This word is considered oldfashioned in Ukraine when used in the sense of 'lesson', as in 'private lesson'. The word уро́к is given instead.

NAMES

Васи́ль Миха́йлович Гончаре́нко,
Марко́*, О́ля, О́льга Миха́йлівна

IDIOMS

Я́к ва́ше ім'я?	What's your first name?
Я́к ва́с по ба́тькові?	What's your patronymic?
Я́к ва́ше прі́звище?	What's your last name?

SUPPLEMENT

на́зва	name (other than a person's)
зва́ти (Як ва́с зва́ти)	to call, to name (What do they call you?)

EXPLANATORY NOTES

1. **Студе́нти** refers to college undergraduates. Graduate students are called **аспіра́нти** (**аспіра́нт** m., **аспіра́нтка** f.), while grade and high school students are called **у́чні** (**у́чень** m., **учени́ця** f.) or **школярі́** (**школя́р** m., **школя́рка** f.).

2. **Прі́звище** means 'last' or 'family' name, while **ім'я** stands for 'first name' (occasionally it may refer to the last name). The expression **по ба́тькові** is called patronymic.** It is a form derived from the father's first name, i.e. 'son of' or 'daughter of'.

Я́к ва́ше ім'я?	What is your name?
Моє́ ім'я Васи́ль.	My name is Vasyl.
Я́к ва́с по ба́тькові?	What is your patronymic?
Миха́йлович.	Myxájlovyč.
Я́к ва́ше прі́звище?	What is your last name?
Гончаре́нко.	Hončarenko.

3. The nouns **украї́нець, украї́нка** are used to designate people, and the adjective **украї́нський** is used as a modifier of other nouns. The adverb **по-українському** is used to modify verbs. None of these words are capitalized in Ukrainian and the initial sound *u* is not subject to the *u* — *w* alternation rule*** (see The Sound System, p. xxvii), for example:

* This name admits both stresses **Ма́рко** and **Марко́** the first being the prescribed norm and the second a colloquial variant. Henceforth all variant stresses will be given in parantheses.

** Further discussion of this form will be found in Lesson 2.

*** The name of the country itself — **Україна** — does admit such alteration in poetry — **Вкраїна** (e.g. на Вкраїні, Т. Шевченко).

Вона́ украї́нка.	She is a Ukrainian.
Це́ украї́нське ім'я́.	This is a Ukrainian name.
Говорі́ть по-украї́нському!	Speak Ukrainian!

The adverb **по-украї́нському** has another form **по-украї́нськи**. Some grammars make a distinction between the two forms assigning the meaning 'in the Ukrainian language' to the first and 'in the Ukrainian way' to the second. However, in actual speech this distinction is often ignored and the form **по-украї́нськи** is used throughout. In this textbook we shall use the form **по-украї́нському** following the example of the most recent textbooks published in Ukraine and abroad.

When the adjective **украї́нський** accompanies a noun which designates a person it refers to the national origin of that person, so that the sentence

Це́ на́ш украї́нський профе́сор.

means 'He is our professor, who is Ukrainian' (i.e. he is of Ukrainian nationality or he comes from Ukraine) and not 'He is our professor of the Ukrainian language' (the latter would be Це́ на́ш профе́сор украї́нської мо́ви).

4. The particle **чи** is normally used in questions in the absence of any other interrogatory words such as 'who', 'where', 'why', etc.

Чи всі́ ту́т?	Is everybody here?
Чи це́ пра́вильно?	Is this correct?
Чи це́ твоє́ ім'я́?	Is that your name?

As an interrogative particle **чи** is not translatable into English.

5. По ба́тькові derives from 'ба́тько,' 'father' and 'по' 'after,' 'according to.' The phrase Як вас по-ба́тькові is eliptic, the verb 'зва́ти' to call being understood (e.g. 'Як вас звати по-батькові' 'What do they call you after your father?').

NOTES ON GRAMMAR

I. ABSENCE OF THE ARTICLE

Ukrainian has no definite or indefinite articles corresponding to the English *the* and *a*. Definiteness can be expressed by other means, however, for example by word order:

О́н та́м до́шка.	There is a board there.
До́шка о́н та́м.	The board is over there.

i.e. under neutral or non-emphatic intonation the subject or object is usually indefinite in the final position and definite in the initial position.

II. GENDER OF NOUNS

Nouns in Ukrainian have a grammatical gender, either masculine, feminine, or neuter.* Gender implies that every noun which is masculine will be referred to as **він**, 'he', every feminine noun as **вона́**, 'she', and every neuter noun as **воно́**, 'it', regardless of whether it is animate or inanimate. There are also some nouns which have no gender and are used only in the plural. They are referred to as **вони́**, 'they'. An example from this lesson is **две́рі**, 'door'. Thus:

Masculine

Де́ стіле́ць? О́сь **він**.	Where is the chair? Here it is.
Де́ студе́нт? О́сь **він**.	Where is the student? Here he is.

Feminine

Де́ студе́нтка? О́сь **вона́**.	Where is the student? Here she is.
Де́ кни́жка? О́сь **вона́**.	Where is the book? Here it is.

Neuter

Де́ на́ше мі́сце? О́сь **воно́**.	Where is our place? Here it is.
Де́ на́ше дівча́? О́сь **воно́**.	Where is our girl? Here she is.

Most masculine nouns end in a stem-final consonant, most feminine nouns have a vowel ending **-а** or **-я** following the stem, while neuters usually end in **-о, (нн) -я, (тт) -я** or less frequently in **-е** and **-я**.

Masculine	*Feminine*	*Neuter*
зо́шит	до́шк -а	вікн-о́
стіле́ць	О́л-я	мі́сц-е
		поба́ченн-я
		ім'я́

III. NOMINATIVE CASE

The nominative case is the dictionary form used in definitions, statements of location, presence, existence:

Марко́ студе́нт.	Marko is a student.
Це́ кни́жка.	This is a book.
Ва́ша кімна́та та́м.	Your room is over there.

---

* There are some nouns designating human beings which can be applied to either men or women, without changing their gender or form, cf.:

Він на́ш професор.	He is our professor.
Вона́ наш професор.	She is our professor.

IV. PERSONAL PRONOUNS

There are five personal pronouns in the singular and three in the plural. They are referred to as 'persons' — 1st, 2nd and 3rd. They are as follows:

	Singular			*Plural*	
1st	я́	I	1st	ми́	we
2nd	ти́	you	2nd	ви́	you
3rd	він	he	3rd	вони́	they
3rd	вона́	she			
3rd	воно́	it			

The 2nd person singular **ти́** 'you' is called familiar form and used in addressing a close friend or relative, or a child. Its plural form **ви́** is used in reference to several persons. **Ви́** is also used in addressing one person with whom the speaker is not on familiar terms. In some rural areas, вони́ is used in reference to an absent parent or grandparent.

Ukrainians do not capitalize the pronoun **я́ 'I'; Ви́**, on the other hand, is normally capitalized in correspondence with a person with whom one maintains a formal relationship, or with a stranger (often it is a sign of respect for one's age, or position, or both).

(Exercises 1 and 2)

V. POSSESSIVE PRONOUNS

The possessive pronouns for 1st and 2nd person (singular and plural) and for 3rd person plural have the same number, gender and case as the word which they modify (such correspondence is called agreement):

Вона́ на́ш профе́сор.	She is our professor.*
Це́ ва́ші две́рі.	This is your door.
О́сь моє́ вікно́.	Here is my window.
Де́ ї́хня кімна́та?	Where is their room?
Тві́й зо́шит о́н та́м.	Your notebook is over there.

However, the 3rd person singular possessive pronouns **його́** 'his' or 'its' and **її́** 'hers' or 'its' never change:

Це́ її́ кімна́та, її́ сті́л, її́ две́рі.	This is her room, her table, her door.
Це́ його́ вікно́, його́ кни́жка, його́ сті́л.	This is his window, his book, his table.

* If the noun is masculine the modifier is also masculine, if it is feminine the modifier is f. for women and m. for men, e.g.

Вона́ до́бра голова́.	She is a good head(person) (chairperson).
Він до́брий голова́.	He is a good headman (chairman).

Possessives can be used predicatively or as modifiers:

Це мій олівéць.	This is / my pencil (modifier).
Цéй олівéць мій.	This pencil / is mine (predicate).

Below is the table of possessive pronouns.

	Masculine	*Feminine*	*Neuter*
My (mine)	мíй	моя́	моє́
your (s)	твíй	твоя́	твоє́
our (s)	нáш	нáша	нáше
your (s)	вáш*	вáша	вáше
their (s)	ї́хній	ї́хня	ї́хнє

The forms for the 3rd person singular are:

his	йогó
her (s)	ї́ї
its	йогó

VI. INTERROGATIVE POSSESSIVE

The interrogative pronoun **чи́й, чия́, чиє́** ('whose') is also possessive and agrees in gender, number and case with the noun to which it refers:

Masculine
Чи́й цé олівéць? **Мíй.** — Whose pencil is this? Mine.

Feminine
Чия́ цé кімнáта? **Моя́.** — Whose room is this? Mine.

Neuter
Чиє́ цé ім'я́? **Моє́.** — Whose name is this? Mine.

Plural
Чиї́ цé двéрі? **Нáші.** — Whose door is this? Ours.

(Exercises 3, 4, 5)

---

* **Вáш**; corresponds to **Ви́**, **твíй** corresponds to **ти́**.

VII. DEMONSTRATIVE PRONOUNS

There are two basic types of demonstrative pronouns:

це́й 'this' and **то́й** 'that':

	Masculine	*Feminine*	*Neuter*
This	це́й	ця́	це́
That	то́й	та́	те́

Like the possessives, the demonstrative pronouns agree in gender, number and case with the noun they modify:

Це́й студе́нт, ця́ студе́нтка, це́ ім'я́.
То́й студе́нт, та́ студе́нтка, те́ ім'я́.

In coloquial Ukrainian demonstrative pronouns are often accompanied by the adverbs **о́сь** 'here' and **о́н** 'there' for additional emphasis:

О́сь це́й студе́нт — украї́нець.	This student over here is a Ukrainian.
О́н та́ студе́нтка — украї́нка.	That student over there is a Ukrainian.

The demonstrative **це́й** 'this' has a much wider usage than its counterpart **то́й** 'that', the latter being reserved for definite contrast with something closer at hand. Ukrainians will often use **це́** where English would use 'that':

Це́ вікно́, а це́ две́рі.	This is a window and that is a door.
Що́ це́ та́м?	What is that over there?

The form **це́** has a special function. It is used in questions or statements asking for or giving a definition or an identification of something not yet defined:

Що́ це́? Це́ сті́л.	What is this? It's a table.
Хто́ це́? Це́ студе́нти.	Who are they? They are students.
Це́ до́бре.	That's fine. (It is good.)

Note that in English **це́** may be rendered as 'it', 'that', 'this', 'these', 'those'.

The form **то́** has a similar though a more restricted use referring to something distant:

То́ моє́ мі́сце!	That is may place over there!
То́ студе́нти.	Those are students over there.

(Exercises 6, 7)

VIII. ADJECTIVES

Adjectives are qualifying or attributive words which are used mostly as modifiers of nouns with which they agree in gender, number and case:

Це́ украї́нська кни́жка.	This is a Ukrainian book.
Це́ украї́нське ім'я́.	This is a Ukrainian name.
Це́ украї́нський словни́к.	This is a Ukrainian dictionary.
Це́ украї́нські студе́нти.	These are Ukrainian students.

Adjectives may also be used as the predicate in descriptive sentences:

Він до́брий.	He is kind.
Це́ мі́сце до́бре.	This place is good.

IX. PRESENT TENSE OF THE VERB 'TO BE'

The present tense of the verb 'to be' in modern Ukrainian has only one form є which can be used with any subject singular or plural:

Ту́т є́ украї́нські студе́нти?	Are there any Ukrainian students here?
Чи та́м є́ словни́к?	Is there a dictionary there?
Та́к, є́.	Yes, there is.

The form є is used to indicate possession, existence or availability, as in the above examples otherwise it is omitted:*

Я́ профе́сор.	I am a professor.
Де́ две́рі?	Where is the door?
О́сь студе́нти.	Here are the students.
Вона́ до́бра.	She is kind.

Compare:

Availability, existence	*Identification, description, location*
Чи ту́т є́ словни́к? Та́к, є́. Is there a dictionary here? Yes, there is.	Чи це́ словни́к? Та́к, словни́к. Is this a dictionary? Yes, it is (a dictionary).
Чи ту́т є́ до́брий словни́к? Та́к, є́. Is there a good dictionary here? Yes, there is.	Чи це́й словни́к до́брий? Та́к, до́брий. Is this a good dictionary? Yes, it is.

* In scientific style є may be used when giving a definition, for example, Порівняння не є́ до́казом, 'A comparison is not a proof', or Що́ є́ пра́вда? 'What is truth?'

Та́м є украї́нський професор.
There is (They have) a Ukrainian professor over there.

Ця́ украї́нка — профе́сор.
This Ukrainian woman is a professor.

Note the use of dash in place of the copula when the predicate and the subject are nouns.

(Exercises 13, 14)

X. CONJUNCTIONS а AND і

Both conjunctions а and і may be translated into English as 'and', but they differ in meaning. The conjunction і is used to connect items viewed as similar or identical, or else simply enumerated, such as the items on a list. The conjunction а, on the other hand, contains a sense of contrast: it connects items which in some way are distinct from each other.

Compare:

і	а
(and, also, likewise, too)	(and, but, as for, while)
Ві́н профе́сор, і вона́ профе́сор. He is a professor and she is a professor also.	Ві́н профе́сор, а вона́ студе́нтка. He is a professor and/but she is a student.
О́сь сті́л і стіле́ць. Here is a table and a chair.	О́сь сті́л, а о́н та́м стіле́ць. Here is a table and there is a chair.
І ти́ ту́т? And you too (also) are here?	А ти́ хто́? But who are you?

(Exercise 15)

XI. WORD ORDER AND INTONATION

1. Word order

Ukrainian does not require a change in word order when a statement is changed into a question, cf.:

Ві́н студе́нт.	He is a student.
Ві́н студе́нт?	Is he a student?

In a Ukrainian sentence words sometimes may be shifted around with no sudstantial change in meaning, only in stylistic shading, such as a shift of emphasis. For example:

О́сь на́ш до́брий профе́сор.	Here is our good professor.
О́сь до́брий на́ш профе́сор.	Here is our good professor.
Ві́н ду́же до́бре говори́ть по-англі́йському.	He speaks English very well.
Ві́н говори́ть по-англі́йському ду́же до́бре.	He speaks English very well.

It does not mean, however, that Ukrainian has a 'free' word order. There are basic norms and patterns for the position of words within a sentence. Word order which adheres to these norms is considered normal or neutral, and any deviation from the norms results in an inverted or emphatic word order. Here are the basic rules for Ukrainian word order.

2. Logical center

Every sentence in Ukrainian has a "key" word or words which may be called the logical center or focus (some linguists use the term 'rheme'). These are words which contain the main point made by the sentence, and therefore receive a heavier stress (indicated here by bold print). For example:

Хтó він?	Who is he?
Він **українець.**	He is a Ukrainian.
Дé твій зошит?	Where is your notebook?
Мíй зошит **óн тáм.**	My notebook is over there.
Óн тáм **україньський словни́к.**	There is a Ukrainian dictionary over there.

The logical center in questions containing an interrogatory word ('who', 'where', etc.) is normally at the beginning of the sentence, while in answers or in statements the logical center is normally at the end of the sentence (cf. the above examples). No such rule can be formulated for questions lacking an interrogatory word or with the interrogative **чи**. cf .:

(Чи) Він **говори́ть** по-україньському?	Does he speak Ukrainian?
Тáк, говори́ть.	Yes, he does.
(Чи) Він говори́ть **по-україньському?**	Is he speaking Ukrainian?
Тáк, по-україньському.	Yes, he is.

3. Position of the adverb

In Ukrainian the normal position of **-o/-e** adverbs is before the verb:*

Чи ви́ себé дóбре почувáєте?	Do you feel well?
Вонá непогáно говорить по-україньському.	She speaks Ukrainian quite well.

Adverbs of the -ському- type are normally placed after the verb:

Говорíть по-україньському!	Speak Ukrainian!
Я́ розумíю по-англíйському.	I understand English.

---

* The position of the adverb may be reversed for special emphasis, as in commands: Відповідáйте гóлосно! Говорíть повóлі! or statements such as Вонá говори́ть повóлі.

4. Position of the negative particle не.

The place of the negative particle не is before the word it negates, e.g.

Він не говóрить по-українському.	He doesn't speak Ukrainian.
Він говóрить не по-українському, а по-англíйському.	He doesn't speak Ukrainian, he speaks English. (i.e. "it's not Ukrainian he speaks but English.")

5. Intonation

Intonation contours

Basically we distinguish between two kinds of intonation pattern or contour in a sentence: a falling contour and a rising contour. This means that the level or pitch at the beginning of the sentence is either higher than at the end (= falling contour), or it is lower (= rising contour). For example:

Він українець? ↗ Is he Ukrainian?	— rising (Question without a question word)
Він українець. ↘ He is Ukrainian.	— falling (Statement or Reply)
↗ ↘ Хтó українець?↗↘ Who is Ukrainian?	— falling (Question with a question word)

Intonation levels

In addition to the basic rising or falling contour each sentence normally has intonation fluctuation within it. This fluctuation is perceived in terms of relative pitch as in musical scale.*

A typical fluctuation in a statement is between levels 1 and 2:

2	Твоє́ мíсце ↘	Your place ↘
1	óн тáм.	is over there.

Intonation in questions usually fluctuates between levels 1 and 4 with the logical center rising to level 4:

4	студéнтка?	a student?
3	↗	↗
2	ти́ ↗	you ↗
1	Чи ↗	Are ↗

* Individual words may have intonation fluctuation within them too, but normally the pitch does up or down on the stressed syllable only.

4	Дé ↗			Where is ↘			
3	↘				↘		
2		професор ↘				Professor ↘	
1			Гончаренко?				Hončarenko?

When a question contains no interrogatory word the student must be careful to raise the pitch to level 4 at the logical center since a mere increase in loudness will result in an emphatic statement rather than a question.* cf .:

Question						*Emphatic statement*			
4		↗ дóбре			3	Він ↘			
3	Він	↘			2		ДÓБРЕ ↘		
2			говори́ть ↘		1			говори́ть ↘	
1				по-украї́нському?					по-українському
	Does he speak Ukrainian well?					He speaks Ukrainian very well.			

ВПРАВИ

I. Answer the questions replacing nouns by personal pronouns.

Model: Дé Гончарéнко? Óсь **він**.
Дé кни́жка? Óсь **воні́**.

(зóшит, стілéць, дóшка, олівéць, двéрі, стíл, студéнти, словни́к, рýчка, Маркó, вікнó, Óля)

II. Answer the questions replacing nouns by pronouns.

Model: Хтó профéсор Гончарéнко? **Він** украї́нець.

1. Хтó Маркó? . . . . . студéнт.
2. Чи вáша студéнтка тýт? Тáк, ... тýт.
3. Дé вáше мíсце? . . . . . óсь тýт.
4. Чи цéй украї́нський словни́к дóбрий? Тáк,. . . . . . дóбрий.
5. Чи студéнти сказали “добри́день”? Тáк, ... сказáли добри́день.
6. Хтó Васи́ль Михáйлович? . . . . . профéсор.
7. Чи Óля профéсор? Ні́, ... не профéсор, ... студéнтка.
8. Дé моя́ рýчка? . . . . . . óн тáм.
9. Дé твій зóшит? . . . . . óсь тýт.
10. Дé вáше мíсце? . . . . . óн тáм.

* Speech intonation differs with individuals: women, for example, are known for greater intonation fluctuation, especially women from the Poltava region and from certain areas of the Carpathian mountains.

III. Answer the questions using various possessive pronouns.

Model: Чи́й це́ студе́нт? Це́ **ва́ш** студе́нт.
Чия́ це́ студе́нтка? Це́ **на́ша** студе́нтка.

(сті́л, мі́сце, кни́жка, оліве́ць, пр́ізвище, кімна́та, стіле́ць, ім'я́, зо́шит, ру́чка)

IV. Finish the questions providing corresponding pronouns.

Model: Це́ **моя́** кни́жка. А це́ **чия́**?

1. Це́ ва́ше мі́сце. А це́ . . . . . ?
2. О́сь його́ сті́л. А це́ . . . . . ?
3. Ця́ ру́чка моя́. А ця́ . . . . . ?
4. О́н її́ оліве́ць. А то́ . . . . . ?
5. Це́ моє́ ім'я́. А це́ . . . . . ?
6. О́сь ту́т ї́хнє прі́звище. А о́сь ту́т . . . . . ?
7. Це́ на́ша до́шка. А це́ . . . . . ?
8. Мі́й оліве́ць о́сь ту́т. А це́ . . . . . ?
9. Ва́ш словни́к та́м. А це́ . . . . . ?
10. Це́й зо́шит її́. А це́й . . . . . ?

V. Answer in the negative.

Model: Чи це́ **тві́й** стіле́ць? Ні́, це́ **не мі́й** стіле́ць.

(ва́ш словни́к, на́ша студе́нтка, її́ сті́л, твоя́ кни́жка, ї́хнє мі́сце, ва́ше ім'я́, твоє́ прі́звище, ва́ша ру́чка, його́ мі́сце, ва́ш профе́сор, мі́й оліве́ць, на́ша кімна́та)

VI. Supply the corresponding forms of the demonstrative and possessive pronouns **це́й, мі́й, то́й, ва́ш.**

Model: Це́й сті́л **мі́й**, а **то́й ва́ш.**
Ця́ кімна́та **моя́**, а **та́ ва́ша**.

(зо́шит, кни́жка, оліве́ць, мі́сце, ру́чка, стіле́ць)

VII. Supply the corresponding forms of the demonstrative pronouns.

Model: Це́ сло́во до́бре, і те́ сло́во до́бре.

1. . . . . . мі́сце до́бре, і . . . . . мі́сце до́бре.
2. . . . . . словни́к до́брий, і . . . . . словни́к до́брий.
3. . . . . . ім'я́ украї́нське, і . . . . . ім'я́ украї́нське.
4. . . . . . студе́нтка украї́нка, і . . . . . студе́нтка украї́нка.
5. . . . . . сло́во украї́нське, і . . . . . сло́во украї́нське.
6. . . . . . студе́нт на́ш, і . . . . . студе́нт на́ш.
7. . . . . . до́шка на́ша, і . . . . . до́шка на́ша.
8. . . . . . профе́сор до́брий, і . . . . . профе́сор до́брий.

VIII. Reconstruct questions to the following answers.

Model: Він óн тáм. (Дé він?)

1. Тáк, він студéнт.
2. Ні, цé не моя́ ру́чка.
3. Її вікнó óн тáм.
4. Тáк, цé мíй стіл.
5. Тáк, вонá профéсор.
6. Цé нáша студéнтка Óля.
7. Ні, вони́ не студéнти.
8. Ні, цé недóбре.
9. Цé словни́к.
10. Він профéсор.

IX. Reconstruct questions to the following answers.

1. Тáк, словни́к.
2. Ні, не моя́.
3. Тáк, ту́т.
4. Тáк, мíй.
5. Ні, непрáвильно.
6. Тáк, розумíю.
7. Ні, погáно.
8. Тáк, вáше.
9. Ні, óн тáм.
10. Ні, не тáм.

X. Answer the following questions.

1. Чи цéй студéнт украї́нець?
2. Чи вонá студéнтка?
3. Дé вáша кімнáта?
4. Чи цé прáвильно?
5. Чи всí ту́т?
6. Дé твоє́ мíсце?
7. Чи цé пéрша лéкція?
8. Я́к вáше прíзвище?
9. Я́к її ім'я́?
10. Чи ви́ розумíєте по-украї́нському?
11. Вáше мíсце ту́т?
12. Чи вонá профéсор?
13. Чи ви́ Маркó?
14. Хтó Васи́ль Михáйлович?

XI. Follow the instructions formulated below.

1. Скажі́ть, хто́ ви́.
2. Скажі́ть, де́ ва́ш зо́шит.
3. Скажі́ть, чи вона́ студе́нтка.
4. Скажі́ть, я́к моє́ пр́ізвище.
5. Скажі́ть, чи я́ студе́нт.
6. Скажі́ть, де́ всі́ студе́нти.
7. Скажі́ть, чи ви́ студе́нтка?
8. Скажі́ть, чи це́ ва́ша кни́жка.
9. Скажі́ть, я́к ї́ї ім'я́.
10. Скажі́ть, чи ви́ профе́сор.

XII. Complete the following sentences.

1. Це́ . . . . . мо́ва.
2. Відповіда́йте . . . . . !
3. Я́ не ду́же до́бре . . . .
4. Про́шу, ... голосні́ше!
5. Васи́ль Миха́йлович — на́ш . . . . .
6. Його́ ім'я́ Васи́ль, а я́к його́ . . . . . ?
7. Я́к ви́ себе́ . . . . . ?
8. Дя́кую, ... , а ви́?
9. Про́шу, не . . . . . всі́ ра́зом.
10. Про́шу говорі́ть по- . . . . . !

XIII. Supply the verb 'to be' in the present tense (є) wherever necessary.

1. Хто́ ві́н . . . . . ? Ві́н . . . . . студе́нт.
2. Що́ це́ . . . . . там? Там . . . . . мі́й зо́шит.
3. Чи ту́т . . . . . до́шка? Та́к, ...
4. Ми́ . . . . . студе́нти. А ви́ хто́ . . . . . ?
5. Ту́т . . . . . мі́сце. Це́ мі́сце не́ . . . . . на́ше.
6. Де́ . . . . . . словни́к? О́сь . . . . . ві́н.
7. Що́ та́м . . . . . . ? Та́м . . . . . ле́кція.
8. Я́ . . . . . ту́т. А де́ . . . . . ти́?
9. Ти́ не . . . . . . украї́нець! Я́ . . . . . украї́нець.
10. Це́ . . . . . до́бре.

XIV. Translate into Ukrainian.

1.What is this? 2. Are you there? 3. Is there a dictionary there? 4. The students are here. 5. This is correct. 6. This IS NOT sorrect! 7. Are there any students there? 8. That's good. 9. Here is a chair. 10. This is not your pen. 11. There is room (place) here. 12. Who is he? 13. He is Ukrainian. 14. No, he IS NOT Ukrainian! 15. The door is over there. 16. Is there a blackboard here? 17. His name is not Vasyl, his name is Marko.

XV. Supply the conjunctions **а** and **і** where necessary.

1. Я́ студе́нтка, ... ти́ хто́?
2. Він студе́нт, ... ти́ студе́нт.
3. Це́ словни́к, ... це́ що́?
4. Марко́ . . . . . О́ля — студе́нти.
5. Це́ моє́, ... це́ моє́. Це́ все́ моє́.
6. О́сь кни́жка, ... де́ зо́шит?
7. О́ля ту́т, ... де́ Марко́?
8. Це́ украї́нський словни́к, ... це́?
9. Це́ твоє́ мі́сце, ... де́ моє́?
10. Це́й сті́л ва́ш, ... де́ мі́й?
11. Його́ пр́ізвище Гончаре́нко, ... я́к твоє́ пр́ізвище?
12. Її́ ім'я́ О́ля, ... я́к твоє́ ім'я́?
13. Кни́жка ту́т, ... зо́шит ту́т.
14. Вона́ профе́сор, ... хто́ він?
15. Це́ до́бре, ... це́?

XVI. Read and translate.

Це́ украї́нський студе́нт. Його́ ім'я́ Марко́. О́сь його́ кімна́та. Це́ його́ сті́л, стіле́ць, о́сь зо́шит і словни́к. О́сь украї́нська кни́жка. Він ду́же до́брий студе́нт. Він на́ш пе́рший студе́нт.

О́н та́ студе́нтка — украї́нка. Її́ ім'я́ О́ля. Вона́ на́ша студе́нтка. Її́ мі́сце о́н та́м. О́н її́ ру́чка і олíве́ць, а о́н її́ зо́шит і кни́жка. Це́ украї́нська мо́ва.

Це́ на́ші студе́нти. Вони́ всі ту́т. Це́ на́ша кімна́та, о́сь на́ша до́шка. Це́ на́ш профе́сор. Він украї́нець. Його́ ім'я́ Васи́ль Миха́йлович Гончаре́нко.

XVII. Intonation practice.

(a) Read the following sentences as statements, then change the intonation to interrogative.

1. Це́ ва́ша кімна́та.
2. О́ля украї́нка.
3. Гончаре́нко — це́ украї́нське пр́ізвище.
4. Ви́ до́бре розумі́єте по-украї́нському.
5. Це́ украї́нський словни́к.
6. Це́ тві́й зо́шит.

(b) Read the following sentences as emphatic statements, then as questions.

1. Це́ моє́ мі́сце.
2. Він до́брий студе́нт.
3. Це́ украї́нська мо́ва.

4. Ва́ш сті́л о́н та́м.
5. Я́ до́бре розумі́ю.
6. Марко́ студе́нт.

(c) Read the questions, then make them into emphatic statements.

1. Васи́ль Миха́йлович украї́нець?
2. Ви́ все́ розумі́єте?
3. Студе́нти всі́ ту́т?
4. Це́ словни́к?
5. Це́ пе́рша ле́кція?
6. Ця́ кімна́та моя́?

(d) Read the questions with appropriate intonation.

1. Що́ це́?
2. Хто́ та́м?
3. Чи це́ ти́?
4. Де́ мі́й зо́шит?
5. Це́ ва́ше прі́звище?
6. Чи вона́ украї́нка?
7. Чи́й це́ оліве́ць?
8. Ви́ до́бре розумі́єте?
9. Я́к ва́ше ім'я́?

XVIII. Pronunciation practice.

(1) Listen to the initial consonants of the following words and mark them as either hard ('H') or soft ('S') on the sheet below. Then check the key list below.

	1	2	3	4	5	6	7	8	9	10	11	12	13	14	15
H															
S															

(2) Listen to the final stem-consonant (in some cases followed by a vowel) of the following words. Then mark them as soft or hard on the sheet below.

	16	17	18	19	20	21	22	23	24	25	26	27	28	29	30
H															
S															

(3) Now you will hear a set of pairs of words whose initial consonants differ one being soft and the other hard. Mark them accordingly on the sheet below.

	1	2	3	4	5	6	7	8	9	10	11	12	13	14	15
	1, 2	1, 2	1, 2	1, 2	1, 2	1, 2	1, 2	1, 2	1, 2	1, 2	1, 2	1, 2	1, 2	1, 2	1, 2
H															
S															

(4) Watch for the final stem-consonant in the following pairs. Mark them as hard or soft.

	1	2	3	4	5	6	7	8	9	10	11	12
	1, 2	1, 2	1, 2	1, 2	1, 2	1, 2	1, 2	1, 2	1, 2	1, 2	1, 2	1, 2
H												
S												

(5) Now you will hear single words and see pairs of words on your sheet. Mark the correct one on your sheet.

1. (a) рáсу (b) ря́су
2. (a) везý (b) вíзу
3. (a) ки́т (b) кíт
4. (a) сéла (b) си́ла
5. (a) вели́кий (b) вели́кій
6. (a) руки́ (b) роки́
7. (a) взя́ти (b) в'язáти
8. (a) змія (b) зми́є
9. (a) бур'я́н (b) бурáн
10. (a) пливé (b) пливи́

ANSWER KEYS

Key (1):

1. Маркó (H)
2. він (S)
3. вонá (H)
4. дéнь (H)
5. ні (S)
6. цéй (H)
7. кімнáта (S)
8. ми́ (H)
9. мíй (S)
10. чи́й (H)
11. ви́бачте (H)
12. відповідáйте (S)
13. дýже (H)
14. дáлі (H)
15. чия́ (H)

Key (2):

16. украї́нець (S)
17. зóшит (H)
18. говорíть (S)
19. óсь (S)
20. всé (H)
21. всí (S)
22. олівéць (S)
23. тýт (H)
24. повторíть (S)
25. стíл (H)
26. Васи́ль (S)
27. ця́ (S)
28. мíсце (H)
29. вéчір (H)
30. ї́хнє (S)

Key (3):

1. **ви́є — віє** (H - S)
2. **мі́й — ми́й** (S - H)
3. **са́н — Ся́н** (H - S)
4. **ту́к — тю́к** (H - S)
5. **ле́в — лле́** (H - S)
6. **ню́х — ну́** (S - H)
7. **лі́к — ли́к** (S - H)
8. **пи́ти — піти́** (H - S)
9. **рябий — раби́** (S - H)
10. **бурда́ — бюро́** (H - S)
11. **ти́сну — ті́сно** (H - S)
12. **сі́ль — си́л** (S - H)
13. **си́ч — Сі́ч** (H - S)
14 **мі́ль — ми́ль** (S - H)
15. **жи́то — жі́нка** (H - S)

Key (4):

1. **са́д — ся́дь** (H - S)
2. **гула́ — гуля́** (H - S)
3. **ми́ти — ми́ті** (H - S)
4. **вози́ — в нозі́** (H - S)
5. **пора́д — пора́дь** (H - S)
6. **па́ри — в па́рі** (H - S)
7. **по́вінь — по́вен** (S - H)
8. **мала́ — маля́** (H - S)
9. **ра́ді — ра́ди** (S - H)
10. **си́ня — си́на** (S - H)
11. **ра́ни — ра́ні** (H - S)
12. **ба́зи — ба́зі** (H - S)

Key (5):

1(a), 2(a), 3(b), 4(b), 5(b), 6(a), 7(b), 8(a), 9(a), 10(b).

ДРУГА ЛЕКЦІЯ

1 Новий телевізор
A new television set

Dialogue Participants
Оксáна - О, Михáйло - М, Андрíй - А
Oksana - O, Myxajlo - M, Andrij - A

1. А- Оксáно, дé Михáйло?	A- Oksana, where is Myxajlo?
2. О- Я́ не знáю. А́, óсь він.	O- I don't know. Oh, here he is.
3. М- Добри́день, Андрíйку! Щó новóго?	M- Hello, Andrijko! What's new?
4. А- Нічóго, а óсь я́ бáчу, щó ви́ мáєте нови́й телевізор.	A- Nothing, but I see that you have a new television set.
5. М- Тáк. Хóчеш рáзом диви́тися сьогóдні ввéчері?	M- Yes. Would you like to watch (it) together tonight?
6. А- Звичáйно. Ти́ знáєш, щó телебáчення — цé моя́ любóв.	A- I sure would. You know that I love television.

2 Оля читає
Olja is reading

Dialogue Participants
О́ля - О, Микóла - М, Вíктор - В
Olja - O, Mykola - M, Viktor - V

1. М- Вíкторе, щó О́ля рóбить?	M- Viktor, what is Olja doing?
2. В- Вонá рóбить домáшнє завдáння абó ди́виться прогрáму, абó тé й дрýге. О́лю, щó ти рóбиш?	V- She is doing her homework or watching a TV program, or both. Olja, what are you doing?
3. О- Я́ читáю. А щó?	O- I'm reading. Why?
4. В- Тýт Микóла питáє, щó ти́ рóбиш.	V- Mykola here is asking what you are doing.
5. О- А́, добри́день, Микóло!	O- Oh, hello, Mykola!
6. М- Добри́день, О́лю! Щó ти́ читáєш?	M- Hello, Olja! What are you reading?
7. О- О́сь, бáчиш?	O- Here, see?
8. М- (читáє): "У-кра-ї-на". Цé щó, істóрія?	M- (reads) "U-kra-ji-na". What's that, history?
9. О- Ні. Цé про тé, як украї́нці живýть тепéр.	O- No. It's about the way Ukrainians live today.
10. М- Цікáво.	M- That's interesting.

3 Важко читати
It's hard to read

Dialogue Paticipants:
Тетя́на Миха́йлівна - Т, Лі́да - Л
Tetjana Myxajlivna - T, Lida - L

1. Л- Тетя́но Миха́йлівно! Ви́бачте, але́ я́ не мо́жу о́сь ту́т прочита́ти: чи це́ "пита́ння" чи "писа́ння"?
2. Т- "Пита́ння". А ти́ я́к надрукува́ла?
3. Л- "Писа́ння" Зно́ву помили́лася.
4. Т- Ви́бач, Лі́до! Я́ зна́ю, я́ та́к пога́но пишу́, шо ва́жко чита́ти.
5. Л- Це́ нічо́го, я́ за́раз ви́правлю поми́лку. О́сь вже́. А тепе́р ще́ одне́: о́сь ту́т яка́ літера —"т" чи "п"?
6. Т- Ту́т "т", пита́ння: "Відповіда́йте на пита́ння".
7. Л- Дя́кую за відповідь на моє́ пита́ння. І ви́бачте, що я́ Ва́с усе́ турбу́ю.
8. Т- Ні, ні. Ти́ мене́ зо́всім не турбу́єш.

1. L- Tetjana Myxajlivna, excuse me, but I cannnot read it here. Is it *pytannja* or *pysannja*?
2. T- *Pytannja*. And what did you type?
3. L- *Pysannja*. Made another error.
4. T- I'm sorry, Lida. I know, I write so badly that it's hard to read.
5. L- That's all right. I will correct that error right away. Here, it's done. And one more thing, this letter here, is it *t* or *p*?
6. T- It's *p*, *pytannja*: "Answer the questions (pytannja)."
7. L- Thank you for answering my question. And forgive me for asking you all the time.
8. T- No, no. It's no trouble at all.

4 Журнал Україна
The magazine Ukraina

Dialogue Participants
проф. Васи́ль Гончаре́нко - Г, па́ні Марі́я - М, па́н Петро́ - П
Prof. Vasyl' Hončarenko - H, pani Maria - M, pan Petro - P

1. М- Добри́день, па́не профе́соре!
2. Г- До́брого здоро́в'я, па́ні Марі́є! Чи ви́ ма́єте журна́л "Украї́на"?
3. М- Боюсь, що ні. Пе́тре, чи ми́ ма́ємо журна́л "Украї́на"?
4. П- Ні, не ма́ємо. А хто́ це́ пита́є? А́, це́ ви́, па́не Васи́лю! Добри́день!
5. Г- Добри́день, па́не Пе́тре! Що́ ново́го?
6. П- Нічо́го ново́го. О́сь дивлю́ся програ́му: зно́в стари́й фі́льм, вже́ дру́гий ра́з його́ ба́чу.
7. М- А я́ кажу́, що́ кра́ще чита́ти, ніж диви́тися телеба́чення. Ви́ так не ду́маєте, па́не профе́соре?
8. Г- Та́к, але́ ціка́вий фі́льм я́ те́ж люблю́ диви́тися.
9. П- Ага́, ба́чиш!

1. M- Hello, professor!
2. H- Good day to you, pani Maria! Do you have the magazine "Ukraina"?
3. M- I'm afraid not. Petro, do we have the magazine "Ukraina"?
4. P- No, we don't. And who is asking? Oh, it's you, pan Vasyl'! Hello!
5. H- Hello, pan Petro! What's new?
6. P- Nothing. I'm watching a program: an old film again, I'm seeing it for the second time already.
7. M- And I say that reading is better than watching TV. Don't you think so, Professor?
8. H- Yes, but I also like to watch an interesting film.
9. P- Aha, see!

СЛОВНИК

або́	or, either
або́ ... або́	either ... or
ага́!	aha!
але́	but
ба́чити, ба́чать*	to see
боя́тися, боя́ться (+G)**	to be afraid
ва́жко	hard; difficult; heavy
вас	you
ввече́рі*** (увече́рі)	in the evening
сього́дні ввече́рі	tonight
вже́ (уже́)	already
ви́правити, ви́правлять	to correct
відповіда́ти, відповіда́ють	to answer
ві́дповідь (f)	answer
(говори́ти, говорю́, гово́рять)****	to speak, to talk
диви́тися, дивлю́ся, ди́вляться (на + A)*****	to look; to watch
дома́шній, -я, -є	home (adj.)
дома́шнє завда́ння	home work
дру́гий	second
ду́мати, ду́мають	to think
дя́кувати, дя́кують	to thank

* Verb notation will be as follows: lessons 2–5 — inf., 3rd pl., and 1st sg. where there is a stress shift and / or consonant mutation; lessons 6–15 — inf., 3rd pl. (written out); lessons 16–20 — inf. showing the stem and 3rd pl. (ending only or written out if the stress shifts to the preceding syllable).

** Case notation (see grammar notes to this lesson) will be as follows: N-nominative, A-accusative, G-genitive, D-dative, I-instrumental, L-locative.

*** This adverb has another spelling form, ввечо́рі.

**** Verbs in brackets have appeared in the Sound System.

***** The verb дивитися, like all reflexives, may not take a direct object, but the common usage in Ukraine is to say "дивитися телебачення" 'to watch TV'.

жи́ти, живу́ть	to live
журна́л	magazine
за (+ A)	for
завда́ння (n)	assignment
звича́йно	usually; certainly; of course
здоро́в'я (n)	health
до́брого здоро́в'я	Good day!
зна́ти, зна́ють	to know
зно́в (зно́ву)	again
істо́рія (f)	history; story
його́ (A case)	it; him
каза́ти, кажу́, ка́жуть	to say; to tell
лі́тера (f)	letter
люби́ти, люблю́, лю́блять	to love
любо́в (f)	love
ма́ти, ма́ють	to have
на	on, at, for
надрукува́ти, надруку́ють	to type
ні́ж	than
нічо́го (нішо́)	nothing
нови́й, -а́, -е́	new
Що́ ново́го?	What's new?
Нічо́го ново́го.	Nothing new.
оди́н, одна́, одне́	one; a
о́х!	oh!
па́н (m)	Mr., Sir, gentleman
па́ні (f. indecl.)	Mrs., Madam, lady
писа́ти, пишу́, пи́шуть	to write
пита́ння (n) sg./pl.	question (s)
пита́ти, пита́ють	to ask
пога́но	badly
поми́лка (f)	error, mistake
помили́тися, поми́ляться	to make a mistake
усе́	all the time, always
про (+ A)	about
програ́ма (f)	program
прочита́ти, прочита́ють	to read (through)
роби́ти, роблю́, ро́блять	to do; to work
(розумі́ти, розумі́ють)	to understand
стари́й, -а́, -е́	old
сього́дні	today
те́ж	also
телеба́чення	television
телеві́зор	television set
турбува́ти, турбу́ють	to trouble, to disturb
уве́чері = вве́чері	
уже́ = вже́	
Украї́на	Ukraine
украї́нці	Ukrainians

фільм	film
хотіти, хо́чуть I	to want
ціка́вий, -а, -е (adj.)	interesting
ціка́во (adv.)	interesting
чи	or, whether, if
чи ... чи	whether ... or
чита́ння	reading
чита́ти, чита́ють	to read
що	that (conj.)
яки́й, яка́, яке́	what (kind of), which

SUPPLEMENT

бу́ква (f)	letter
№. но́мер (m), число́ (n), ч.	number, no
старе́нький	old (affectionate)
телевізі́йний	television (adj.)

IDIOMS

А що́?	Why (do you ask)?
те́ й дру́ге	both (this and that)
відповіда́ти на	to answer a/the
пита́ння	question
це́ нічо́го	that's all right
Вже́	Ready/Done
Ще́ одне́	One more thing

NAMES

Андрі́й	Andrew
Андрі́йко	dim. of Андрі́й
Марі́я	Mary
Окса́на	Oksana
Тетя́на Миха́йлівна	
Ві́ктор	Victor
Лі́да (Лі́дія)	Lida (Lydia)
Миха́йло	Michael
Петро́	Peter
Мико́ла	Mykola (Nicholas)

EXPLANATORY NOTES

1. **До́брого здоро́в'я** is another way to greet a person, literally wishing him good health.

2. Істо́рія can refer to history or story, tale (of an incident). A literary story is called оповіда́ння.

3. Forms of address change with time and from region to region. Thus the formal titles **па́н** and **па́ні** were common throughout the Ukraine before 1917. Today they are used among the emigré Ukrainians, while in Ukraine they are used more and more since the declaration of independence. The use of the first name and the second person singular **ти́** has always been the custom among close friends and relatives. A more distant relationship requires the use of the first name and the second person plural **ви** (Eastern Ukrainian custom) or **пан/пані** plus first name (West Ukrainian custom used by most emigrés):

Мико́ло! Чи ви́ зна́єте Марі́ю?
Па́не Мико́ло! Чи ви́ зна́єте па́ні Марі́ю?

A still more formal relationship requires the use of the first name plus a patronymic (East Ukrainian custom) or **пан/пані** plus the last name (traditional Ukrainian form of address used by all emigré Ukrainians):

Васи́лю Миха́йловичу! Тетя́но Миха́йлівно!
Па́не Гончаре́нко! Па́ні Гончаре́нко!

An unmarried woman may be formally addressed as **па́нна: Па́нно Лі́до!** But this form of address is considered oldfashioned. Instead **'па́ні'** is used for 'Miss'. **Па́н** also stands for 'master', as in master-slave relationship.

4. In spoken Ukrainian personal pronouns are often omitted, especially in asking and answering question and in listing a series of activities.

Хо́чеш диви́тися фі́льм? — Хо́чу.
Що́ ви́ ро́бите? — Чита́ємо, пи́шемо.

5. Note the construction:

Я́ хо́чу зна́ти про те́, я́к вони́ живу́ть.
I want to know about their life.

про те́, я́к literally means 'about that how'.

6. **Число́** is more common than **но́мер; бу́ква** is preferred to **лі́тера** by Western Ukrainians.

7. Beside **телеба́чення** the term **телеві́зія** is also used. A television (and radio) program is called **програ́ма** or **переда́ча** In colloquial speech, one even hears 'диви́тися телеві́зор' 'to watch TV'.

8. The particle **чи** beside its interrogatory function is also used with the meaning 'whether' ('if') and 'or'. For example:

Це́ по-украї́нському чи по-англі́йському?
Is it in Ukrainian or in English?

Я́ не зна́ю, чи ви́ все́ розумі́єте.
I don't know if you understand it all.

Чи це́ до́бре, чи пога́но — я́ не зна́ю.
I don't know whether it's good or bad.

9. The pronoun що́ may appear in different functions: 1. interrogative, 2. interrogative as relative, 3. conjunction, 4. interrogative idiom:

1. Що́ вона́ чита́є?	What is she reading?
2. Я́ не зна́ю, що́ вона́ чита́є.	I don't know what she's reading.
3. Я́ зна́ю, що вона́ чита́є.	I know that she's reading.
4. А що́?	Why do you ask?

To differentiate between що́ meaning 'what' (see the second example) and що meaning 'that' (see the third example) a stress mark is usually provided over the former in printed texts.

10. Another word for 'question' is запита́ння, and for the verb 'to ask' запи́тувати.

11.When speaking of an elderly person, the terms немолоди́й 'not young' and лі́тній 'advanced in years' are usedin addition to the affectionate старе́нький.

NOTES ON GRAMMAR

I. GENERAL OBSERVATIONS ON THE DECLENSION OF NOUNS

Most Ukrainian words consist of a stem* and an ending, e.g.

Stem	*Ending*	*Stem*	*Ending*
програ́м-	а	украї́нц-	і
дома́шн-	ій	істо́рі-	я
відповіда́-	ють	ба́чи-	ти

The substituting of one ending for another in nouns, pronouns, adjectives and participles is called declension (e.g. **програ́ма — програ́му**), and a set of all the possible forms of one word is called a *paradigm*. The declension provides information regarding gender, number and case. Ukrainian has six cases (nominative, accusative, genitive, locative, dative and instrumental), and an additional form (in the singular only) called vocative. The nominative case indicates the subject of the sentence or the predicate, in an equational statement (as we saw in Lesson 1).

---

* The stem itself may be further analyzable. It contains a root which may be accompanied by one or more affixes. Affixes are of two types: prefixes, which precede the root, and suffixes, which follow the root (e.g. **від-по-ВІД-а́й-те**).

Ukrainian has three main groups of nouns which we call *declension-types*, two feminine (those of feminine and masculine gender which end in **-а/-я**, the *-a type* and feminines with a zero ending or a bare stem which we will call consonant or *c-type*) and one masculine-neuter. A further subdivision of the *a-type* nouns and masculine-neuters is made on the basis of the quality of the stem-final consonant: in the *soft type*, the stem ends in a *soft* consonant or **й**; in the *hard type* the stem ends in a *hard* consonant.

Here are some examples of the two declension types:

FEMININE DECLENSION

a-type (-a ending)				*c-type* (zero ending)
Hard	Украї́н-а Мико́л-а	*Soft*	О́л-я (Ol'-a) істо́рі-я (istórij-a)	**ві́дповідь, любо́в**

MASCULINE-NEUTER DECLENSION

Hard (stem)	*Soft* (stem)
стіл	**Васи́ль, Андрі́й**
вікно́	мі́сц-е,* пита́нн-я

Here are some further details on the declension system (Note: read it for information only at this point):

(a) masculine-neuters with stems ending in **ж, ч, ш,** щ belong to the soft type. However, due to spelling requirements (see Sound System, p. xv) letters **а** and **у** are written in certain case endings instead of the expected **я** and **ю** (unless **ж, ч** or **ш** is doubled).

(b) masculine nouns ending in the consonant **р** may follow either hard or soft declension type or both. This will be indicated in the vocabularies.

(c) some neuter nouns which end in **-а** or **-я** receive an additional suffix **-ат/-ят** or **-ен** (we will call them the **ат/ен** type). Those which receive the suffix **-ат/-ят** designate baby animals (or humans) or diminutive things. Those with the suffix **-ен** are very few in number (only two are commonly used **-ім'я́** 'name' and **пле́м'я** 'tribe'). All these nouns follow a declension pattern which is partly like that of other neuters and partly like the feminine -a declension nouns.

II. VOCATIVE

The vocative form is used for an appeal or address. In practice it occurs chiefly with nouns designating human beings, although it is available for metaphorical address to inanimates as well.

* Before **е** the consonant is hard (see Sound System, p. xvi), however, in all cases but N/A neuter nouns like **місце** have soft stems and follow the soft-stem declension pattern.

Only masculine and feminine nouns in the singular have the vocative form. Otherwise the nominative form is used.

FEMININE DECLENSION VOCATIVE

-a type

Hard: -o	Оксáна — Оксáно!
Soft: -ю / -є /	Óля — Óлю!
	Марíя — Марíє! (mar'íj-e)

-c type

-e	любóв — любóве!

In the a-declension, the vocative ending is -o for hard-stems and -e for soft stems (nouns ending in a sibilant follow the soft-stem pattern). All the -c-type nouns have the vocative in -e. (see Sound System, pp. xviii).

MASCULINE DECLENSION VOCATIVE

Hard: -e	*Soft, sibilants, glides* and *-k-suffixed:* -у, -ю
студéнт — студéнте!	Васúль — Васúлю!
профéсор — профéсоре!	Михáйлович — Михáйловичу!
Михáйло — Михáйле!	Андрíй — Андрíю (andr'íj-u)
	Андрíйко — Андрíйку!

The vocative ending for masculine soft-stems and for those whose stem ends in a -к- which is part of a suffix is у/ю. All other hard stem masculines receive the ending -e. This general rule, however, admits exceptions, with nouns of either group having both variants, or hard stem nouns having the endings **-у (ю)** and soft stem nouns taking the ending **-е** (cf.: **швéць — шéвцю, шéвче** 'shoemaker'; **хлóпець — хлóпче** 'boy'; **стéльмах — стéльмаху, стéльмаше** 'cartwright').

Vocative stress

In the **a**-declension nouns and masculine nouns whose nominative ends in a stressed vowel, the stress in the vocative form shifts to the stem:

Петрó — Пéтре!	Хомá — Хóмо!
Левкó — Лéвку!	пáн головá — пáне гóлово!
Павлó — Пáвле!	(Mr. Chairman!)

Uses of vocative

The vocative form is often replaced by the nominative. This is especially true of foreign names, e.g. **Би́л! Бо́б! Мі́стер Ка́ртер!** The Ukrainian surnames also tend to remain in the nominative when used as a form of address, e.g.

Гончаре́нко! Па́не Гончаре́нко!

The Ukrainian first names, or first names followed by patronymics always take the vocative form when addressing people:

Васи́лю Миха́йловичу! Тетя́но Миха́йлівно!
Па́не Пе́тре! Па́ні Марі́є!

If the form of address contains a title preceded by the words **па́н** or **па́ні** the title is normally in the vocative (occasionally in the nominative) if the addressee is a man; with women feminine gender titles are in the vocative and masculine titles are in the nominative:

Па́не профе́соре! (Па́не профе́сор!) Па́не го́лово!
Па́ні профе́сор! Па́ні го́лово!

(Exercises 1, 2, 5)

III. FORMATION OF PATRONYMICS

Patronymics are derived from the father's name by adding suffixes **-івна/-ївна** for women, and **-ич/-ович** for men. The suffix **-ич** is reserved for the few bisyllabic a' stem names such as **Лука, Хома, Сава, Кузьма, Ілля** and also **Яків** (the latter can have parallel forms **Я́кович, Я́ківна** and **Я́ковлевич, Я́ковлівна**). Some patronymics have the suffix **-йович** although the corresponding names lack the **й**, cf.: **Мико́ла — Микола́йович, Оле́кса — Олексі́йович.** Actually they derive from the more formal variants of these names. **Микола́й, Олексі́й.**

Patronymics retain the stress of the original names (one exception: **Павло́ Па́влович**).

Here are some examples of the formation of patronymics:

Ві́ктор	Васи́ль	Андрі́й	Петро́
Ві́кторович	Васи́льович	Андрі́йович	Петро́вич
Ві́кторівна	Васи́лівна	Андрі́ївна	Петрі́вна

(Exercises 3, 4)

IV. PRESENT TENSE

The present tense of the Ukrainian verb has six forms, each of which expresses person and number. Like all verb forms, the present tense forms consist of a stem and an ending. The final stem vowel plays an important role in the classification of the patterns which different verbs follow in their conjugations. For example:

	I Conjugation			*II Conjugation*		
	Stem	*Vowel*	*Stem Ending*	*Stem*	*Vowel*	*Stem Ending*
Singular						
1st	пиш-	Ø[*] + ý	pyš-Ø-ú	бáч-	Ø + у	báč-Ø-u
	дýма-	Ø + ю	dúmaj-Ø-u	роб-л-	Ø + ю́	robl'-Ø-ú
2nd	жив-	é + ш	žyv-é-š	бáч-	и + ш	báč-y-š
	читá-	є + ш	čytáj-e-š	рóб-	и + ш	rób-y-š
3rd	знá-	Ø + є	znáj-e-Ø	бáч-	и + ть	báč-y-t'
	жив-	Ø + é	žyv-é-Ø	рóб-	и + ть	rób-y-t'
Plural						
1st	пи́ш-	е + мо	pýš-e-mo	бáч-	и + мо	báč-y-mo
	дýма-	є + мо	dúmaj-e-mo	рóб	и + мо	rób-y-mo
2nd	жив-	е + те	žyv-e-té	бáч-	и + те	báč-y-te
	читá-	є + те	čytáj-e-te	рóб-	и + те	rób-y-te
3rd	знá-	ю + ть	znáj-u-t'	бáч-	а + ть	báč-a-t'
	пи́ш-	у + ть	pýš-u-t'	рóб-л-	я + ть	róbl'-a-t'

Thus we observe that the ending pattern is as follows:

Present tense endings

	Singular		*Plural*	
1st	-у/ю	u	-мо	mo
2nd	-ш	š	-те	te
3rd	-ть/Ø	t' or Ø	-ть	t'

Further, we see that except for the 1st person singular, the endings are preceded by stem-vowels which fall into two groups: one where the predominant vowel is е (we call it the е verb or 1st conjugation) and the other where the predominant vowel is и (we call it the и verb or 2nd conjugation).

---

[*] Ø stands for 'zero'.

The key form is the third personal plural:

e- stem verbs have the stem-vowel *u* (spelled у or ю) and и- verbs have the stem-vowel *a* (spelled а or я). It is this form (and not the infinitive) from which we can predict the other forms of the present:*

When the 3rd pl. is -уть or -ють the other persons have the stem-vowel -е (є)
When the 3rd pl. is -ать or -ять the other persons have the stem-vowel -и (ї)

Here are some examples of both conjugations:

	I Conjugation		*II Conjugation*	
Singular				
1st	жив-ý	питá-ю	бáч-у	робл-ю́
2nd	жив-é-ш	питá-є-ш	бáч-и-ш	рóб-и-ш
3rd	жив-é	питá-є	бáч-и-ть	рóб-и-ть
Plural				
1st	жив-е-мó	питá-є-мо	бáч-и-мо	рóб-и-мо
2nd	жив-е-тé	питá-є-те	бáч-и-те	рóб-и-те
3rd	жив-ý-ть	питá-ю-ть	бáч-а-ть	рóбл-я-ть

Here is the complete distribution of the present tense stem-vowels and endings in each conjugation:

I CONJUGATION
(e- verbs)

Singular	*Stem-vowel*	*Ending*	*Plural*	*Stem-vowel*	Ending
1st	Ø	у/ю	1st	е/є	мо
2nd	е/є	ш	2nd	е/є	те
3rd	е/є	Ø	3rd	у/ю	ть

Note: The 3rd person singular ending of the e- verbs is Ø unless the verb has the particle -ся in which case the ending is -ть (ся) (see Note 4 of this section).

---

* The vocabulary list for this lesson contains the 3rd pl. forms of all the verbs we have encountered so far.

II CONJUGATION
(и - verbs)

Singular			*Plural*		
	Stem-vowel	*Ending*		*Stem-vowel*	Ending
1st	Ø	у/ю	1st	и/ї	мо
2nd	и/ї	ш	2nd	и/ї	те
3rd	и/ї	ть	3rd	а/я	ть

(1) Note on spelling. The stem-vowel and ending variants in the conjugation patterns given above are dictated by the spelling rules (see Sound System, p. xxvii–xxviii).

(2) Note on the stress. Some verbs keep their stress in the same position throughout the conjugation, others have a "mobile stress". cf .:

Stable stress	*Mobile stress*
ба́чать, ба́чу	ка́жуть, кажу́
хо́чуть, хо́чу	пи́шуть, пишу́

If the final vowel* of the 3rd plural is stressed, then the final vowel in all other persons will be stressed.

живу́ть — живу́, живемо́
боя́ться — бою́сь, боїте́ся

The patterns of the "mobile stress" will be discussed in further lessons. Until that time, the first person singular form will be provided for verbs with the mobile stress.

(3) Note on changes. It has been pointed out that the key form in verb conjugation is the 3rd pl. However, 2nd conjugation verbs whose stem ends in a labial consonant (**б, п, в, ф, м**) undergo a change of stem in the 3rd person plural as well as the 1st person singular (a soft l' is added after the stem-final consonant) but not in other forms:

ро́блять, роблю́; ро́биш, ро́бить
ди́вляться, дивлю́ся; ди́виться, ди́вимося

In the 1st conjugation the stem-final consonant remains the same in all forms of the present.

(4) Note on the particle **-ся**. The particle **-ся** is affixed to certain verbs.

For example: the present of **боя́тися** and **диви́тися** is:

бою́ся, бої́шся, бої́ться, боїмо́ся, боїте́ся, боя́ться
дивлю́ся, ди́вишся, ди́виться, ди́вимося, ди́витеся, ди́вляться

---

* Not counting the particle -ся.

Some verbs occur both with and without **-ся**, with a difference in meaning which will be discussed later cf .:

(to ask) питáти: питáє
(to ask permission) питáтися: питáється

In pronunciation the endings **-шся** and **-ться** become -s’s’a and -c’c’a, a phenomenon called ‘assimilation’ (see Appendix 3.)

(Exercises 6, 7, 8)

V. INFINITIVE

We have said that the key forms of the Ukrainian verb are the third person plural present and the infinitive.

(1) Infinitive stem. The infinitive stem has the ending **-ти***. The infinitive stem is the form minus **-ти**:

питá-ти, розумí-ти, роби́-ти, жи́-ти, дя́кува-ти, диви́-ти(ся)

Note that the infinitive stem is usually different from the present tense stem, cf.:

Infinitive stem: жи́-(ти), казá-(ти), говори́-(ти)
Present tense stem: жив-(у́ть), кáж-(уть), говóр-(ять)

This is one of the reasons why both forms must be memorized.

(2) Some uses of infinitive. One of the chief uses of the infinitive (which is ordinarily translated into English "to-") is as complement of such verbs as "want", "be able", "like". For example:

Я́ хóчу цé бáчити.	I want to see it.
Я́ люблю́ читáти.	I like to read.

It is also used as the complement of certain other forms (the translation may be "-ing"):

Читáти цікáво.	To read is fun. (Reading is fun).
Цé вáжко розумíти.	This is hard to understand.

* In poetry and in speech in many regions of Ukraine the infinitive form in **-ть** is used, e.g. **казáть, роби́ть.**

ВПРАВИ

I. Give the vocative form using the following model:

Дé **Івáн**? — **Івáне**, дé ти́?

(Микóла, Óля, профéсор Гончарéнко, пáні Лíда, Маркó, пáн профéсор, Тетя́на Михáйлівна, Оксáна, пáн Петрó, пáні Марíя)

II. Give the vocative form using the following model:

Щó **Івáн** рóбить? — **Івáне**, щó ти́ рóбиш?

(Васи́ль, Андрíй, Вíктор, Михáйло, Тетя́на, Васи́ль Михáйлович, пáні профéсор, Тетя́на Михáйлівна, Петрó, Маркó, пáн Микóла)

III. Give the first name and the patronymic using the model:

Її ім'я **Марíя**. Йогó ім'я **Васи́ль**.
Цé **Марíя Васи́лівна**.

1. Її ім'я Оксáна. Йогó ім'я Петрó. Цé . . . . .
2. Її ім'я Тетя́на. Йогó ім'я Андрíй. Цé . . . . .
3. Її ім'я Óльга. Йогó ім'я Вíктор. Цé . . . . .
4. Її ім'я Лíдія. Йогó ім'я Маркó. Цé . . . . .
5. Її ім'я Марíя. Йогó ім'я Микóла. Цé . . . . .
6. Її ім'я Оксáна. Йогó ім'я Михáйло. Цé . . . . .

IV. Give the first name and the patronymic using the model:

Йогó ім'я **Івáн**. А цé **Михáйло**.
Вíн **Івáн Михáйлович**.

1. Йогó ім'я Івáн. А цé Вíктор. Вíн . . . . .
2. Йогó ім'я Івáн. А цé Васи́ль. Вíн . . . . .
3. Йогó ім'я Івáн. А цé Петрó. Вíн . . . . .
4. Йогó ім'я Івáн. А цé Андрíй. Вíн . . . . .
5. Йогó ім'я Івáн. А цé Маркó. Вíн . . . . .
6. Йогó ім'я Івáн. А цé Микóла. Вíн . . . . .

V. Finish the greetings using vocative form as in the model:

Óсь **Васи́ль Михáйлович.** Добри́день, **Васи́лю Михáйловичу!**

(Андрíй Петрóвич, Óльга Петрíвна, Маркó Андрíйович, Марíя Андріївна, Васи́ль Миколáйович, Оксáна Миколáївна, Петрó Мáркович, Тетя́на Мáрківна, Вíктор Васи́льович, Лíдія Васи́лівна)

VI. Supply the necessary forms of the verbs in parentheses.

1. (говори́ти)

   Ми́ . . . . . по-украї́нському. Чи ви́ . . . . . по-украї́нському?
   Та́к, я́ . . . . . по-украї́нському. Чи ві́н . . . . . по-украї́нському?
   Ні́, ві́н не . . . . . , але́ вона́ вже́ до́бре . . . . . Чи вони́ . . . . . по-украї́нському?
   Ні́, не ду́же, але́ ти́ ду́же до́бре . . . . .

2. (розумі́ти)

   Чи ви́ все́ . . . . . ? Та́к, я́ . . . . . А ві́н? Ві́н те́ж усе́ . . . . .
   Чи вони́ до́бре . . . . . ? Та́к, вони́ . . . . . ду́же до́бре, але́ ми́ не все́ . . . . .
   Чи ти́ все́ . . . . . ? Ні́, я́ те́ж не все́ . . . . .

3. (ба́чити)

   Щó ти́ та́м . . . . . ? Ні́чо́го, а щó ви́ . . . . . ? Ми́ . . . . . журна́л.
   Чи ві́н те́ж . . . . . ? Та́к, але́ вони́ не́ . . . . . Я́ те́ж пога́но . . . . .

4. (люби́ти)

   Я́ . . . . . чита́ти. Чи ви́ те́ж . . . . . чита́ти? Ми́ всі́ . . . . . чита́ти, і вони́ те́ж. Чи вони́ . . . . . чита́ти? Ві́н . . . . . , а вона́ ні́.

5. (зна́ти)

   Чи ти́ . . . . де́ ві́н живе́? Та́к, я́ . . . . , а ви́ не́ . . . . ? Ми́ . . . . , але́ вона́ не . . . . Вони́ все́ . . . .

6. (боя́тися)

   Я́ . . . . ., щó це́ ду́же ва́жко. Чи ви́ не . . . . , щó це́ ва́жко? Ні́, ми́ не . . . . ., але́ ві́н . . . . Ти́ . . . . .? Вони́ всі́ . . . . , щó це́ ва́жко.

7. (писа́ти)

   Вони́ . . . . . повí́льно. Чи ти́ те́ж . . . . . повí́льно? Та́к, я́ . . . . . повí́льно, а вона́ . . . . шви́дко. Ви́ те́ж . . . . . ду́же шви́дко. Та́к ми́ . . . . шви́дко.

8. (роби́ти)

   Ми́ . . . . дома́шнє завда́ння. Чи ви́ те́ж . . . . . дома́шнє завда́ння? Я́ . . . . . , а вона́ ні́. Я́ не зна́ю, щó вона́ . . . . . Щó ти́ . . . . . ? Ні́чо́го. Вони́ . . . . дома́шнє завда́ння, а я́ не хо́чу.

9. (каза́ти)

   Що́ ти́ . . . . ? Нічо́го, а що́ ви́ . . . . . ? Те́ж нічо́го, а що́ вона́ . . . . . ? Вона́ . . . . . "до́бре". А що́ вони́ . . . . . ? Вони́ . . . . "непога́но". Я́ те́ж . . . . "непога́но". Ми́ всі́ . . . . . "непога́но".

10. (диви́тися)

   Він тепе́р . . . . програ́му, а ти́ не́ . . . . . ? Ні́, я́ . . . . . вве́чері. Чи ви́ те́ж . . . . вве́чері? Та́к, ми́ . . . . вве́чері, а вони́ . . . . тепе́р.

VII. Supply the appropriate verbs.

1. Я́ . . . . . , а вона́ . . . . . на пита́ння.
2. Ми́ . . . . . ціка́вий фі́льм.
3. Вона́ . . . . . дома́шнє завда́ння, а він . . . . . програ́му.
4. Що́ ти́ . . . . . ? Журна́л "Украї́на".
5. Чи ти́ . . . . . оліве́ць? — О́сь, про́шу. А що́ ти́ хо́чеш . . . . . ?
6. Я́ . . . . . говори́ти по-украї́нському.
7. Він . . . . . , що він усе́ розуміє.
8. Вона́ та́к шви́дко . . . . , що́ ва́жко . . . . .
9. Окса́на до́бре . . . . . Усі́ студе́нти . . . . . її́ відповідь.

VIII. Complete the sentences using the given verbs.

1. Вони́ це́ лю́блять. Я́ те́ж це́ . . . . . Чи ви́ це́ . . . . . ?
2. Вони́ це́ розумі́ють. Я́ те́ж це́ . . . . . Чи ти́ це́ . . . . . ?
3. Вони́ це́ ба́чать. Я́ те́ж це́ . . . . . Чи він це́ . . . . . ?
4. Вони́ це́ ма́ють. Я́ те́ж це́ . . . . . Чи вона́ це́ . . . . . ?
5. Вони́ це́ чита́ють. Я́ те́ж це́ . . . . . Чи ви́ це́ . . . . . ?
6. Вони́ це́ ка́жуть. Я́ те́ж це́ . . . . . Чи ти́ це́ те́ж . . . . . ?
7. Вони́ та́к пи́шуть. Я́ те́ж та́к . . . . . Чи вона́ та́к . . . . . ?
8. Вони́ та́к ро́блять. Я́ те́ж та́к . . . . . Чи він та́к . . . . . ?
9. Вони́ та́к живу́ть. Я́ те́ж та́к . . . . . Чи ви́ та́к . . . . . ?
10. Вони́ та́к відповіда́ють. Я́ та́к . . . . . Чи ти́ та́к . . . . . ?

IX. Read and translate (orally).

1. Марі́я студе́нтка. Вона́ украї́нка. Вона́ до́бре гово́рить по-украї́нському і по-англі́йському. Я́ пита́ю: "Марі́є, я́к по-англі́йському твоє́ ім'я́?" Вона́ відповіда́є, що́ її́ ім'я́ по-англі́йському "Ме́рі". Я́ знов пита́ю: "А я́к моє́ ім'я́?" Вона́ ка́же, що́ моє́ ім'я́ "Ма́рк". Я́ хо́чу зна́ти, я́к по-англі́йському "Миха́йло", і "Мико́ла", і "Петро́", але́ Марі́я ка́же, що́ тепе́р вона́ ма́є ле́кцію. "До поба́чення, Марі́є", — кажу́ я́. "До поба́чення, Ма́рку", — відповіда́є вона́.

2. Віктор ужé дóбре розуміє по-украї́нському. О́сь він тепéр читáє журнáл "Украї́на". Він лю́бить читáти про тé, я́к живу́ть украї́нці. "Ві́кторе!", — кáже Андрі́й. "Щó ти читáєш?" "О́сь, бáчиш?" — відповідáє Ві́ктор. "Цé украї́нський журнáл". Андрі́й ди́виться й кáже: "Цé цікáво. Алé я́ щé погáно читáю по-украї́нському". "Цé не вáжко," кáже Ві́ктор.

3. Пáні Лі́да лю́бить телебáчення, а пáн Микóла ні́. Він ужé старéнький і погáно бáчить. Пáні Лі́да лю́бить диви́тися всé: чи фі́льм стари́й, чи нови́й — вонá всé ди́виться. Сьогóдні фі́льм "Украї́на". Цé про тé, я́к живу́ть украї́нці, щó вони́ рóблять, щó ду́мають, я́к говóрять, щó лю́блять. Пáні Лі́да кáже, щó фі́льм ду́же дóбрий, і питáє, чи пáн Микóла хóче диви́тися. Він кáже "ні́". Вонá питáє, чи я́ хóчу диви́тися. Я́, звичáйно, відповідáю, щó тáк. Телебáчення — цé моя́ любóв.

X. Answer the following questions to the dialogues:

"Нови́й телеві́зор"

1. Щó Андрі́й питáє?
2. Щó Оксáна відповідáє?
3. Щó Андрі́й бáчить?
4. Щó хóче роби́ти Микóла сьогóдні ввéчері?
5. Чи Андрі́й лю́бить телебáчення?

"О́ля читáє"

1. Чи Ві́ктор знáє, щó О́ля рóбить?
2. Щó він думáє?
3. Микóла бáчить слóво "Украї́на". Щó він питáє?
4. Щó О́ля відповідáє?

"Вáжко читáти"

1. Щó Лі́да не розуміє?
2. Хтó відповідáє на її питáння?
3. Я́к пи́ше Тетя́на Михáйлівна?
4. За щó дя́кує Лі́да?

"Журнáл 'Украї́на' "

1. Про щó питáє профéсор Гончарéнко?
2. Щó відповідáють на йогó питáння?
3. Щó роби́ть пáн Петрó?
4. Чи він пéрший рáз цé бáчить?
5. Чи пáні Марі́я лю́бить телебáчення?
6. Щó про цé ду́має пáн Васи́ль?

XI. Answer the following questions (give complete answers, not just “yes” and “no”).

1. Чи ви́ любите телеба́чення?
2. Чи ви́ ма́єте телевізор?
3. Яки́й фільм ви́ ди́витеся?
4. Чи ви́ ро́бите дома́шнє завда́ння вве́чері?
5. Чи ви́ лю́бите чита́ти?
6. Чи ви́ до́бре пи́шете по-украї́нському?
7. Чи ви́ розумі́єте сло́во “відповідь”?
8. Чи ви́ зна́єте журна́л “Украї́на”?
9. Чи ви́ дума́єте, що це́ до́брий фільм?
10. Чи ви́ дума́єте, що ця́ істо́рія ціка́ва?

XII. Reconstitute questions or statements to which the following could be responses.

1. Ні, дя́кую. Я́ не люблю́ телеба́чення.
2. Я́ не зна́ю, я́к вони́ живу́ть.
3. Та́к, це́ нови́й телевізор.
4. Та́к, хо́чу.
5. Та́к, він ду́же ціка́вий.
6. Ні, це́ не ва́жко.
7. Ні, ми́ не ма́ємо.
8. Та́к, я́ зна́ю відповідь.
9. Я́ те́ж люблю́
10. Ніч́ого ново́го.

XIII. Translate into Ukrainian.

1. Oksana, what are you doing?
2. I'm watching television. It's an old movie. It's very interesting. Do you want to watch together?
3. No, thanks. I have an interesting magazine. I want to read.

1. Peter, what's new?
2. Nothing's new. But I see that you have a new television set.
3. Yes, Olja likes to watch it. I say, “Don't you think that reading is better than watching TV?” but she answers that television is her love. I'm afraid to say that watching television is not good. What do you think about it, Vasyl'?
4. You know, I like to watch an interesting movie too. How is your Olja, is she a good student?
5. Yes. How does she do it? She watches TV and does her homework. Both together. I don't know how she does it.

ТРЕТЯ ЛЕКЦІЯ

#5 Фотографія
A photograph

Dialogue Paticipants: Ма́рта - М, Павло́ - П
Marta - M, Pavlo - P

1. П- Ма́рто, подиви́сь на цю́ фотогра́фію. Кого́ ти́ ту́т зна́єш?
2. М- Я́ зна́ю Андрі́я, Ві́ктора Ме́льника і його́ бра́та Мико́лу, Га́лю та О́лю Прокопо́вич, Ле́сю Палі́й. А хто́ це́й хло́пець?
3. П- Це́ Ігор Ле́сів, на́ш нови́й студе́нт. А це́ його́ сестра́ Лю́ба. А цього́ хло́пця ти́ зна́єш? Це́ Марко́ Поліщу́к.
4. М- Ні́, я́ його́ не зна́ю. Хто́ ві́н, америка́нець чи кана́дець?
5. П- Ві́н америка́нець. І оця́ ді́вчина америка́нка, а ця́ кана́дка.

1. P- Marta, take a look at this photo.Whom do you know here?
2. M- I know Andrij, Viktor Mel'nyk and his brother Mykola, Halja and Olja Prokopovyč, Lesja Palij. And who is this fellow?
3. P- That's Ihor Lesiv, our new student. And this is his sister Ljuba. And do you know this fellow? It's Marko Poliščuk.
4. M- No, I don't know him. What is he, an American or Canadian?
5. P- He is an American. And so is this girl.This one is Canadian.

6 Цікава книжка
An interesting Book

Dialogue Paticipants:
Ле́ся Палі́й - Л, проф. Гончаре́нко - Г, Тетя́на Миха́йлівна - Т
Lesja Palij - L, Prof. Hončarenko - H, Tetjana Myxajlivna - T

1. Л- Добри́день, Тетя́но Миха́йлівно! Чи мо́жна ба́чити Василя́ Миха́йловича?
2. Т- Та́к, за́раз. Васи́лю! Ту́т тебе́ хо́че ба́чити Ле́ся Палі́й.
3. Г- Добри́день, Ле́сю. Ма́єш яке́сь пита́ння?
4. Л- Та́к. Ви́ сказа́ли, що є́ ціка́ва кни́жка про Кана́ду. Де́ її мо́жна діста́ти?
5. Г- Я́ її ма́ю. Хо́чеш подиви́тися?
6. Л- Та́к, будь ла́ска.
7. Т- Це́ стара́ і ду́же ціка́ва кни́жка. О́сь, про́шу.
8. Л- Ду́же дя́кую.

1. L- How are you, Tetjana Myxajlivna! May I see Vasyl' Myxajlovyč?
2. T- Yes, just a minute. Vasyl'! Lesja Palij is here to see you.
3. H- Hello, Lesja! You have a question?
4. L- Yes. You said that there was an interesting book on Canada. Where can I get it?
5. H- I have it. Would you like to see?
6. L- Thank you very much.
7. L- Yes, please.
8. T- It's an old and a very interesting book.Here you are.

7 Стара мапа
An old map

Dialogue Paticipants:
Богда́н -Б, Га́ля -Г   Bohdan -B, Halja -H

1. Г- Богда́не, що́ ти́ чита́єш?
2. Б- Істо́рію. О́сь, подиви́сь..
3. Г- Що́ це́? Кана́да чи Аме́рика?
4. Б- Аме́рика. Це стара́ ма́па. А о́сь подиви́сь на це́й малю́нок: "Індія́нець — спра́вжній америка́нець".
5. Г- Ціка́во. А о́сь ту́т які́йсь вели́кий буди́нок: "Готе́ль", а та́м ще́ оди́н, "Музе́й". Чому́ це́ вони́ ту́т?
6. Б- Бо це́ вже́ нова́ Аме́рика.

1. H- Bohdan, what are you reading?
2. B- History. Here. Look.
3. H- What is it? Canada or America?
4. B- America. It's an old map. Look at this drawing: "An Indian — a True American".
5. H- That's interesting. And here is a tall building."Hotel". And here another one, "Museum". Why are they here?
6. B- Because that is already the new America.

 # 8 Справжня любов
True Love

Dialogue Paticipants:
Петро́ - П, Марі́я - М   Petro - P, Marija - M

1. М- Пе́тре, подиви́сь у вікно́. Ба́чиш?
2. П- Що́ я́ ма́ю ба́чити?
3. М- Не "що́", а "кого́". Он та́м ба́чиш Марка́ й Га́лю?
4. П- Ну́ ба́чу. Чого́ я́ на ни́х ма́ю диви́тися?
5. М- О́т, яки́й! Така́ про́ста рі́ч — і не розумі́є. На́ш Марко́ лю́бить Га́лю, а вона́ його́. Вони́ лю́блять одне́ о́дного.
6. П- Чому́ ти́ та́к ду́маєш?
7. М- Я́ не ду́маю, я́ зна́ю. Ві́н та́к на не́ї ди́виться, а вона́ ті́льки про ньо́го гово́рить. Це́ спра́вжня любо́в.
8. П- Ну́, як ка́жеш, що спра́вжня, то спра́вжня.

1. M- Petro, look out the window. Can you see?
2. P- What am I supposed to see?
3. M- Not 'what' but 'whom'. Over there see Marko and Halja?
4. P- So I do. Why should I be looking at them?
5. M- What a man! Such a simple thing and he doesn't understand. Our Marko loves Halja and she loves him. They are in love.
6. P- You think so?
7. M- I don't just think so. I know. The way he looks at her, and she talks only about him. It's real love.
8. P- Well, if you say it's real love, then it (must be) real love.

СЛОВНИК

Аме́рика (f)	America
америка́нець (m)	American (m)
америка́нка (f)	American (f)
бо	because
бра́т (m)	brother
буди́нок (m)	house, building
вели́кий	big, large, great
готе́ль (m)	hotel

дівчина (f)	girl
діста́ти, діста́нуть	to get (= obtain, procure)
за́раз	right away, in a minute; just a moment
індія́нець (m)	Indian (Am.)
Кана́да (f)	Canada
кана́дець (m)	Canadian (m)
кана́дка (f)	Canadian (f)
ма́па (f)*	map
малю́нок (m)	drawing
мо́жна	may, can
музе́й (m)	museum
ну́	well (interj.)
оце́й, оця́, оце́	this
подиви́тися, подивлю́ся	to take a look
поди́вляться; подиви́ся! (-сь) на + A	take a look!
про́стий	simple
рі́ч (f)	thing
сестра́ (f)	sister
спра́вжній	real, genuine, true
та**	and
та́к	so, in such a way
таки́й, така́, таке́	such
тільки	only
то (conj.)	then, in that case
тре́тій, -я, -є	third
фотогра́фія (f)	photograph
хло́пець (m)	boy, guy, fellow
чого́	why, what for
чому́	why
у (+ A)	in, into
я́к	if
яки́йсь, яка́сь, яке́сь	some (sort of)

NAMES

Богда́н, Га́ля,*** Ігор (-я),**** Ле́ся, Ма́рта, Павло́, Лю́ба; Ме́льник, Палі́й (-я́), Поліщу́к (-а́), Прокопо́вич, Ле́сів (-ева)

---

* Today, ма́паis considered old fashioned in Ukraine. The word ка́рта is used instead.

** Used mostly between vowels, e.g.: Га́ля та О́ля.

*** The full name is **Гали́на**. cf . also Лю́ба — **Любо́в, О́ля — О́льга.**

**** Vocative of **І́гор** is **І́горю**!

IDIOMS

Люби́ти одне́ о́дного	to love one another
О́т яки́й...!	What a ...!

SUPPLEMENT

індія́нка(f)	Indian (Am.) (f)
коха́ний	beloved
коха́ння	love (romantic)
коха́ти, а́ю	to love (rom.)

EXPLANATORY NOTES

1. The correct Ukrainian terms for 'Canadian' are **кана́дець** for a man and **кана́дка** for woman, although Ukrainians in Canada use the words **кана́дієць** and **канаді́йка** as though from 'Кана́дія'.

2. The basic meaning of the adverb **за́раз** is "right away", "in a minute", e.g.:

Я́ за́раз подивлю́ся на це́й малю́нок.	I will take a look at that drawing in a minute.

It may be used alone in the sense of "just a minute":

Пе́тре, подиви́сь на це́й малю́нок.	Petro, look at this drawing.
— За́раз.	—Just a minute.

3. Note the idiomatic usage of **про́шу** as a formula of politeness when handing over some object:

Де́ словни́к?	Where is the dictionary?
— О́сь, про́шу.	— Here you are.

It is also used when answering a summoning call or when being addressed by name:

— Ма́рто!	— Marta!
— Про́шу!	— Yes (here I am). (Yes, I'm listening).

4. **Мо́жна** indicates a possibility or permission:

Чи мо́жна діста́ти цю́ кни́жку?	Is it possible to obtain this book?
Мо́жна подиви́тися?	Is it all right (permissible) to look? (May I/we ... take a look?)
— Та́к, мо́жна.	— Yes, it's all right (you may).
— Ні́, не мо́жна.	— No, it's not (you may not).

It is commonly used when asking permission to enter:

Мóжна?	May I come in?
— Тáк, прóшу.	— Please, do.

5. **Індіянець** is an American Indian. An Indian from India is called **індієць.**

6. The Ukrainian term for 'photograph' is **фотогрáфія** or **фóто** for short (West Ukrainians also use the word **світли́на**). There are also different words for 'snapshot': **знíмок** used in the eastern regions, and **зни́мка** common among the West Ukrainians.

7. Certain types of Ukrainian surnames are typical of certain regions.

For example:

Suffixes	Predominantly
– óвич (Прокопóвич)	– western regions
– ів (Лéсів)	– western regions
– ук (-чук, -щук) (Поліщýк)	– western and southern
– ій (Палíй)	– eastern
– енко (Гончарéнко)	– eastern (the most common type)

Names of animals, various objects, as well as professions also appear as surnames all over the Ukraine (cf. **Мéльник** = Miller).

First names are often given in accordance with a family tradition or a current vogue. But generally we can also speak of certain names being more typical of certain regions.

For example, the parents of **Мáрта** and **Богдáн** are probably from Galicia, while those of **Вíктор** are probably from farther East.

8. The interrogatives **чомý** and **чогó** can both be used with the meaning 'why', 'for what reason'. cf.:

Чомý ти́ боїшся цé сказáти? Чогó ти́ боїшся цé сказáти?	Why are you afraid to say it?

However, the interrogative **чогó** has slightly more coloquial coloring.

9. The prefix **о-** in the demonstrative pronoun **оцéй** has an intensifying function, i.e. 'this one over here'. This prefix is frequently added to other pronouns and adverbs, cf. **отóй, отаки́й, оцé, отó, отáк, отáм, отýт.**

10. The idiom **однé óдного** 'each other' is used on reference to a male and a female. When both are male the phrase is **оди́н óдного**, and when both are female it is **однá óдну**. Notice that only the second word is declined. The preposition is placed between the two words, e.g. **Вони́ диви́лися однé на óдного**. 'They looked at each other'. The forms are those of a pronoun. Notice the position of the stress in.

11. To designate romantic love Ukrainians use the word . The corresponding verbs are **кохáти** 'to love' and **покохáти** 'to fall in love'.

NOTES ON GRAMMAR

I. ACCUSATIVE SINGULAR OF NOUNS

1. In all neuter nouns, all feminine nouns of the **-c** type, and all nouns of masculine gender which refer to inanimate objects or abstract notions the accusative is identical with the nominative. cf.:

Nominative	*Accusative*
Це́ його́ **прі́звище.** (n)	Я́ зна́ю його́ **прі́звище.** (n)
This is his name.	I know his name.
Це́ його́ **ві́дповідь.** (f)	Я́ зна́ю його́ **ві́дповідь.** (f)
This is his answer.	I know his answer.
Це́ **журна́л.** (m)	Він чита́є **журна́л.** (m)
This is a magazine.	He is reading a magazine.

2. All **-a** type nouns take the ending *u* in the accusative. It is spelled **y** or **ю** depending on the stem-final consonant (**-y** corresponds to nominative **-a**, and **-ю** to nominative **-я**):

	Hard		*Soft*	
N.	Лі́да	Мико́ла	О́ля	Марі́я
A.	Лі́ду	Мико́лу	О́лю	Марі́ю
	(l'íd-u)	(mykól-u)	(ól'-u)	(mar'íj-u)

3. All masculine nouns of the masculine-neuter declension which designate living beings (this includes animals, birds, fish, sometimes also plants) have the accusative form ending in *-a*, spelled **-a** or **-я** depending on the stem-final consonant:

	Hard		*Soft*	
N.	студе́нт	Ві́ктор	Васи́ль	І́гор
A.	студе́нта	Ві́ктора	Василя́	І́горя
	(studént-a)	(v'íktor-a)	(vasyl'- á)	(íhor'-a)

Here, then, are the accusative endings in tabular form:

ACCUSATIVE SINGULAR OF NOUNS

Feminine declension		Masculine-Neuter declension		
a-type	*c-type*	*neuters*	*masculine*	
-у/-ю	= N	= N	*inanimate*	*animate*
(*-u*)			= N	-а/-я
				(*-a*)

Note 1: In the conversational language, and quite frequently in the written literary language as well, many inanimate masculine nouns receive the ending -a in the accusative singular, e.g. **Я́ ма́ю олівця́** 'I have a pencil'. However the student is advised not to use this ending for inanimate nouns until he/she is more thoroughly acquainted with the language.

Note 2: Some р- stem nouns follow the hard declension patterns (e.g. **Ві́ктор — Ві́ктора**) while others are soft-stem nouns (see Lesson 2, p. 30).

The nominative forms not indicate this distinction since r' must become r at the end of a word. Thus íhor' -Ø yields **І́гор** but íhor'-a is **І́горя**.

Note 3: Some nouns have end-stress throughout the declension, for examle **Васи́ль — Василя́**. We will mark all such stresses in the vocabularies.

Note 4: Many stems have an е or an о which appears before a zero-ending (as in the nominative) but is absent before any other ending (as in the animate accusative):

N.	кана́дець	хло́пець
A.	кана́дця	хло́пця

Note 5. The noun **па́ні** is not declined,* nor are the surnames of women when the ending is **-ко** or a consonant, e.g.:

Чи ви́ зна́єте па́ні Марі́ю Поліщу́к?	Do you know Mrs. Maria Poliščuk?
Чи ви́ зна́єте цю́ па́ні?	Do you know this lady?
Чи ви́ зна́єте па́ні Гончаре́нко?	Do you know Mrs. Hončarenko?

(Exercises 1, 2, 4)

II. ACCUSATIVE OF PERSONAL PRONOUNS.

Personal pronouns have special accusative forms:

		Nominative	*Accusative*	*Accusative with preposition*
Sg.	1st	я́	мене́	про ме́не
	2nd	ти́	тебе́	про те́бе
	3rd	ві́н	його́	про нього
	"	воно́	його́	про нього
	"	вона́	ї́ї	про неї
Pl.	1st	ми́	на́с	про на́с
	2nd	ви́	ва́с	про ва́с
	3rd	вони́	ї́х	про ни́х

* In the West Ukrainian usage **па́ні** was sometimes declined like a-type noun (by analogy with its variants **па́ня** and **па́нія**).

Note 1: Notice that the two-syllable forms **мене́, тебе́, його́** have stress on the first syllable when preceded by a preposition. This shift occurs in the bisyllabic forms of the following pronouns: personal, demonstrative, interrogative **хто́** and **що́**, the reflexive **себе́**, and the pronoun **уве́сь** in A and G; and in the demonstrative, interrogatives **хто́** and **що́**, and **уве́сь** in D and L as well.

Note 2: The third person pronoun in all non-nominative forms (both singular and plural) has a stem consisting only of the glide **й** (j): **його́** j-ohó, **її** j-ijí, **їх** j-íx. With prepositions this stem becomes a soft n': **ньо́го** n'óho. This n' becomes hard, however, before **е** (e) or **и** (y): **про не́ї** pró néji, **про ни́х** pro nýx (see The Sound System, p. xviii)

(Exercises 6, 7, 8, 9)

III. ACCUSATIVE OF INTERROGATIVE PRONOUNS ХТО AND ЩО

The accusative forms of the pronouns **хто** and **що** are:

N.	хто́	що́
A.	кого́ (про ко́го)	що́

Notice the shift in stress in **кого́** but **про ко́го** (see the rule, p. 49). Thus:

Хто́ це́?	Who is that?
Кого́ ви́ ба́чите?	Whom do you see?
Про ко́го ви́ гово́рите?	Whom are you talking about?
Що́ це́?	What is that?
Що́ ви́ ба́чите?	What do you see?

IV. ACCUSATIVE OF THE PRONOUNS ТОЙ, ЦЕЙ, УВЕСЬ, (ВВЕСЬ), ЧИЙ AND THE NUMERAL ОДИН

The accusative forms of the demonstrative pronouns **це́й, ця́, це́** and **то́й, та́, те́** as well as the pronouns **уве́сь (вве́сь), чи́й** and the numeral **оди́н** are as follows:

Masculine

N.	це́й	уве́сь/вве́сь	чи́й	оди́н	то́й
A.=N.	цього́	=N. усього́/всього́	=N. чийо́го	=N. одного́	=N. того́
	на цьо́го	в усьо́го/на всьо́го			про то́го

Feminine

N.	ця́	уся́/вся́	чия́	одна́	та́
A.	цю́	усю́/всю́	чию́	одну́	ту́

Neuter

N.	цé	усé/всé	чиé	однé	тé
A.=N.					

Note: The stress shift rule (p. 49) does not apply to the feminine form **усі́я: усю́ — в усю́**.

Notice the correspondences:

Когó ти́ знáєш?	Whom do you know?
— Я́ знáю **цьогó** хлóпця.	— I know this boy.
— Я́ знáю **йогó**.	— I know him.
— Я́ знáю **цю́** дíвчину.	— I know this girl.
— Я́ бáчу **всю́** кімнáту.	— I see the whole room.

Note 1: The numeral **оди́н** declines like **тóй** throughout the declension. The pronoun **увéсь (ввéсь)** is declined like **цéй** through most of its declension.

Note 2: As modifiers of masculine nouns these pronouns have two parallel forms, one agreeing with animate nouns another with inanimate:

Я́ бáчу **цéй** малю́нок.	I see this drawing.
Я́ бáчу **цьогó** хлóпця.	I see this boy.
Я́ знáю **тóй** журнáл.	I know that magazine.
Я́ знáю **тогó** студéнта.	I know that student.

Note 3: Notice that the palatalized consonant **ц** (c') in the pronouns **ця́, цю́, цьогó** becomes hard before the vowel **е** (e), **цé, цéй** (cé, céj). The same is true of the consonant s' in **увéсь, усьóго, усю́** which becomes s in **усé** usé. (See The Sound System, p. xviii).

Here are paradigms of nouns with modifiers in the accusative sg.

N=A (neuters, c-type feminine nouns, masculine inanimate)

N.	цé всé завдáння	ця́ вся́ вíдповідь	цéй увéсь журнáл
A.	цé всé завдáння	**цю́ всю́** вíдповідь	цéй увéсь журнáл

-у/-ю (a-type nouns)

N.	однá дíвчина	однá кімнáта	ця́ лéкція	чия́ Óля	чи́й Микóла
A.	однý дíвчину	однý кімнáту	цю́ лéкцію	чию́ Óлю	чийóго Микóлу

-а/-я (masculine animates of the masc./neut. declension)

N.	то́й студе́нт	це́й Васи́ль	чи́й Андрі́й	оди́н Марко́
A.	того́ студента	цього́ Василя́	чийо́го Андрі́я	одного́ Марка́

(Exercises 3, 5, 10, 11)

V. PRINCIPAL USES OF THE ACCUSATIVE

(1) As direct object of non-negated verbs. For example:

Чи ти́ ба́чиш ма́пу?	Do you see the map?
— Та́к, я́ ї́ї ба́чу.	— Yes. I see it.
Чи ти́ розумі́єш **Марка́**?	Do you understand Marko?
— Та́к, я́ **його́** розумі́ю.	— Yes, I understand him.

Note 1: Note the position of the pronoun as opposed to the noun. As a rule, an object expressed by a noun follows the verb, while an object expressed by a pronoun precedes the verb, unless it is emphasized.

(2) With certain prepositions:

Вона́ ди́виться **в** кни́жку.	She is looking in the book.
Подиви́ся **у** вікно́!	Look out the window!
Подиви́ся **на** це́.	Take a look at this.
Я́ говорю́ **про** цю́ кни́жку.	I am talking about this book.

Note 2: The preposition **у** has a variant **в** (see The Sound System, p. xxxi). **у** is normally used at the beginning of a sentence or after pauses in deliberate speech. In rapid speech it is used when the preceding word ends with a consonant and the following word begins with a consonant. The consonantal short **в** is used mostly between vowels. cf.:

У цю́ кімна́ту не мо́жна.	You may not go into that room.
Подиви́сь **у** вікно́.	Look out the window.
Вона́ все́ ди́виться **в** оце́ вікно́.	She keeps looking out this window.

When the preceding word ends with a vowel and the following begins with a consonant either **в** or **у** may be used:

Подиви́ся **в** це́ вікно́. Подиви́ся **у** це́ вікно́.	Look out this window.

В is also frequently found in the initial position, e.g.:

В цю́ кімна́ту не мо́жна.	You may not enter this room.

Thus to sum up:
1) **у** between consonants
2) **в** before a vowel
3) **у** or **в** before a consonant

Note 3: Most Ukrainian surnames are declined as either nouns or as adjectives. Thus, **Гуме́цька** is declined like the adjective **украї́нська**, while **Ме́льник** (if it designates a male) is declined like the noun **студе́нт**. Surnames belonging to women are not declined if they end in a consonant or in **-ко*** (see this lesson, section I, note 5).

Я́ зна́ю Андрі́я Палія́.	I know Andrij Palij.
Я́ зна́ю Га́лю Палі́й.	I know Halja Palij.
Чи ти́ зна́єш па́на Ме́льника?	Do you know Mr. Mel'nyk?
Чи ти́ зна́єш па́ні Ме́льник?	Do you know Mrs. Mel'nyk?
Де́ ти́ ба́чиш Гончаре́нка?	Where do you see Hončarenko?
Де́ ти́ ба́чиш па́ні Гончаре́нко?	Where do you see Mrs. Hončarenko?

ВПРАВИ

I. Put the bracketed words into the correct form.

1. Що́ ти́ чита́єш? (кни́жка)
2. Що́ ви́ чита́єте? (журна́л "Украї́на")
3. Що́ ти́ ма́єш? (оліве́ць)
4. Що́ ви́ ма́єте? (оце́й словни́к)
5. Що́ ти́ хо́чеш ба́чити? (кімна́та)
6. Що́ ви́ хо́чете чита́ти? (історі́я)
7. Що́ ти́ ба́чиш? (оце́ сло́во)
8. Що́ ви́ ба́чите? (оце́ завда́ння)
9. Що́ ти́ ро́биш? (оце́ завда́ння)
10. Що́ ви́ лю́бите? Я́ люблю́ (істо́рія)

II. Put the bracketed words into the correct form.

1. Кого́ ти́ пита́єш? (Ві́ктор)
2. Кого́ ви́ пита́єте? (Марко́)
3. Кого́ ти́ зна́єш? (студе́нт-індія́нець)**
4. Кого́ ви́ зна́єте? (І́гор)
5. На кого́ ти́ ди́вишся? На (Богда́н)
6. На кого́ ви́ ди́витеся? На (Андрі́й)
7. Кого́ ти́ ба́чиш? (студент-кана́дець)
8. Кого́ ви́ ба́чите? (студе́нт-америка́нець)
9. Кого́ ти́ лю́биш? (профе́сор Гончаре́нко)
10. Кого́ ви́ лю́бите? (па́н Поліщу́к)

---

* When speaking informally about an absent woman whose last name is of the undeclinable type Ukrainians sometimes change the name by adding the suffix **-ова/ева (єва)** which makes the surname declinable, for example, **Гончаре́нкова, Павліє́ва, Прокопо́вичева** (Declension of surnames will be discussed in Lesson 10.)

** Both parts of appositions are declined.

III. Ask questions according to the model.

Та́м яка́сь дівчина. Ви́ про цю́ дівчину гово́рите?
Та́м яки́йсь хло́пець. Ви́ про цього́ хло́пця гово́рите?

(яка́сь студе́нтка, яки́йсь америка́нець, яка́сь америка́нка, яки́йсь студе́нт, яка́сь украї́нка, яки́йсь украї́нець, яки́йсь індія́нець, яка́сь індія́нка, яки́йсь кана́дець, яка́сь кана́дка)

IV. Change the sentences according to the model.

Подиви́сь, де́ Га́ля. Подиви́ся на Га́лю.

(па́ні Лі́да, Марі́я Поліщу́к, О́ля Прокопо́вич, Ле́ся Палі́й, Лю́ба, Ма́рта, Тетя́на Миха́йлівна, Марі́я Васи́лівна, О́льга Па́влівна, Гали́на Миколаї́вна)

V. Give complete answers to the following questions.

1. Про ко́го вони́ гово́рять?
2. Що́ він ма́є?
3. Кого́ вона́ пита́є?
4. Кого́ вона́ ту́т зна́є?
5. Що́ він пи́ше?
6. Про що́ ви́ ду́маєте?
7. Що́ ви́ хо́чете діста́ти?
8. За що́ ви́ дя́куєте?
10. Про ко́го ви́ ду́маєте?

VI. Complete the sentences according to the model (use the appropriate prepositions)

О́н та́м украї́нська студе́нтка. Подиви́сь на цю́ студе́нтку. Подиви́сь на не́ї.

1. О́н та́м ма́па. Чи ти́ лю́биш диви́тися . . . . .
2. Це́ ціка́ве пита́ння. Хто́ зна́є ві́дповідь . . . . .
3. О́н та́м вікно́. Вона́ лю́бить диви́тися . . . . .
4. Це́ украї́нський словни́к. Подиви́сь . . . . .
5. Це́ ціка́ва книжка. Подиви́сь . . . . .
6. О́сь нови́й журна́л. Подиви́сь . . . . .
7. О́н та́м студе́нт. Ми́ гово́римо . . . . .
8. Це́ спра́вжня ві́дповідь. Я́ дя́кую . . . . .
9. Це́ ду́же стара́ істо́рія. Я́ ду́маю . . . . .
10. О́сь тре́тє пита́ння. Він відповіда́є . . . . .
11. О́сь тре́тя лі́тера. Подиви́сь . . . . .

VII. Supply the necessary form of personal pronouns.

1. Він ту́т. Павло́ . . . . . ба́чить.
2. Я́ ту́т. Павло́ . . . . . ба́чить.
3. Вони́ ту́т. Павло́ . . . . . зна́є.

4. Ми́ ту́т. Павло́ . . . . . зна́є.
5. Ви́ ту́т. Павло́ . . . . . пита́є.
6. Ти́ ту́т. Павло́ . . . . . пита́є.
7. Воно́ ту́т. Павло́ . . . . . ба́чить.
8. Вона́ ту́т. Павло́ . . . . . ба́чить.

VIII. Answer the questions using personal pronouns. Example:

Чи ти́ зна́єш **Іва́на**? Та́к, я́ **його́** зна́ю.

1. Чи ти́ ба́чиш Мико́лу?
2. Чи ти́ зна́єш відповідь?
3. Чи ти́ ди́вишся на Марі́ю?
4. Чи ти́ пита́єш про кни́жку?
5. Чи ти́ зна́єш його́ прі́звище?
6. Чи ти́ діста́неш зо́шит?
7. Чи ти́ розумі́єш це́ сло́во?
8. Чи ти́ гово́риш про дома́шнє завда́ння?
9. Чи ти́ лю́биш істо́рію?
10. Чи ти́ відповіда́єш на пита́ння?
11. Чи ти́ зна́єш цю́ бу́кву?

IX. Put the pronouns into the correct form

1. Студе́нти . . . . . ба́чать, вони́ на . . . . . ди́вляться.
(ти́) (ти́)
2. Студе́нти . . . . . ба́чать, вони́ на . . . . . ди́вляться.
(вона́) (вона́)
3. Студе́нти . . . . . ба́чать, вони́ на . . . . . ди́вляться.
(ми́) (ми́)
4. Студе́нти . . . . . ба́чать, вони́ на . . . . . ди́вляться.
(воно́) (воно́)
5. Студе́нти . . . . . ба́чать, вони́ на . . . . . ди́вляться.
(ви́) (ви́)
6. Студе́нти . . . . . ба́чать, вони́ на . . . . . ди́вляться.
(ві́н) (ві́н)
7. Студе́нти . . . . . ба́чать, вони́ на . . . . . ди́вляться.
(я́) (я́)
8. Студе́нти . . . . . ба́чать, вони́ на . . . . . ди́вляться.
(вони́) (вони́)

X. Change the sentences according to the model

Це́й журна́л ціка́вий. Я́ люблю́ **це́й журна́л.**
Це́ га́рне ім'я́. Я́ люблю́ **це́ ім'я́**.

1. Ця́ кни́жка ціка́ва.
2. Це́й фі́льм ціка́вий.
3. Ця́ істо́рія ціка́ва.

4. Це́й словни́к ціка́вий.
5. Ця́ програ́ма ціка́ва.
6. Це́й малю́нок ціка́вий.
7. Ця́ фотогра́фія ціка́ва.
8. Це́й музе́й ціка́вий.
9. Це́ до́бра річ.
10. Це́ до́бра кімна́та.
11. Це́ до́брий студе́нт.
12. Це́ до́бра студе́нтка.
13. Це́ до́брий профе́сор.
14. Це́ до́брий словни́к.
15. Це́ до́брий телевізор.
16. Це́ до́бре місце.

XI. Put the bracketed words into the correct form

Чи ти́ зна́єш **Іва́на**? Та́к, я́ **його́** зна́ю.

1. Чи ви́ ба́чите . . . . . ма́пу? (уве́сь)
2. Чи ви́ ба́чите . . . . . вікно́? (уве́сь)
3. Чи ви́ ба́чите . . . . . украї́нське сло́во? (оди́н)
4. Чи ви́ зна́єте . . . . . студе́нтку? (це́й)
5. Чи ви́ зна́єте . . . . . студе́нта? (то́й)
6. . . . . . прізвище ви́ ба́чите? (чи́й)
7. . . . . . кни́жку ви́ ма́єте? (чи́й)
8. . . . . . бра́та ви́ зна́єте? (чи́й)
9. Чи ви́ ма́єте ще́ . . . . . фотогра́фію? (оди́н)
10. Чи ви́ зна́єте . . . . . музе́й? (це́й)

XII. Read and translate

1. Я́ ма́ю сестру́. Її́ ім'я́ Ма́рта. Вона́ до́бра дівчина, але́ вона́ лю́бить усе́ мене́ пита́ти. Сього́дні вона́ ди́виться фільм. Це́ фільм про любо́в. Я́ ба́чу, що́ Ма́рта вже́ хо́че мене́ пита́ти і кажу́: "Ма́рто, чи ти́ ма́єш яке́сь пита́ння?". "Та́к", — відповіда́є вона́. "Я́ не розумію, чому́ Ві́ктор коха́є і Марію і О́льгу. Чи мо́жна коха́ти ра́зом і ту́ дівчину, і цю́? Чи це́ спра́вжнє коха́ння?" Я́ не зна́ю, що́ відповіда́ти. А я́к ви́ ду́маєте?*

2. Па́ні Поліщу́к ма́є кни́жку про Украї́ну. Це́ стара́ кни́жка, але́ ду́же ціка́ва. Па́ні Поліщу́к ка́же, що не мо́жна її́ чита́ти шви́дко. Це́ істо́рія. Я́ люблю́ чита́ти про Украї́ну, про її́ істо́рію, але́ я́ не все́ розумію. Чому́ та́м та́к ва́жко жи́ти? Але́ я́ ба́чу, що всі украї́нці лю́блять Украї́ну. Звича́йно, я́ хо́чу подиви́тися, я́к украї́нці живу́ть тепе́р.

---

* А я́к ви́ ду́маєте? And what do you think?

XIII. Answer the questions to the above passages

(1)

1. Хтó Мáрта?
2. Щó вонá рóбить сьогóдні?
3. Про щó цéй фільм?
4. Якé питáння мáє Мáрта?

(2)

1. Чи кни́жка пáні Поліщýк цікáва?
2. Про щó ця́ кни́жка?
3. Чи цéй хлóпець усé розуміє?
4. Щó він дýмає про Украї́ну?
5. Щó він хóче побáчити?

XIV. Follow the requests in the following sentences

1. Скажíть, якá цé лéкція.
2. Скажíть, якá цé кни́жка.
3. Скажíть, хтó ви́.
4. Скажíть, когó ви́ тáм бáчите.
5. Скажíть, якá цé річ.
6. Скажíть, на когó ви́ тепéр ди́витеся.
7. Скажíть, щó ви́ тепéр рóбите.
8. Скажíть, хтó ця́ дівчина.
9. Скажíть, я́к ви́ говóрите.
10. Скажíть, щó нóвого.

XV. Supply questions or reguests corresponding to the following statements

1. Ні, я вáс не знáю.
2. Я́ тебé не бáчу.
3. Ні, цé дýже прóсто.
4. Так, ї́ї мóжна дістáти.
5. Тáк, вонá дýже старá.
6. Зáраз подивлю́ся.
7. Я́ не знáю, хтó він.
8. Ні, вонá американка.
9. Тáк, він мíй брáт.
10. Тáк, вонá моя́ сестрá.

XVI. Translate into Ukrainian

1. They are in love.
2. Why do you look at me?
3. This exercise is so simple.
4. It's the third time I'm asking you if you want to see my drawing.
5. Where can I get this map?

6. May I take a look?
7. There is some boy asking for you.
8. Is he a real Indian?
9. I think she is either American or Canadian.
10. Excuse me for asking you all the time.

XVII. Answer the following questions

1. Чи ви́ ма́єте бра́та?
2. Чи ви́ хо́чете зна́ти, я́к живу́ть украї́нці?
3. Я́к ви́ ду́маєте, що́ кра́ще: чита́ти чи диви́тися програ́му?
4. Чи ви́ лю́бите Аме́рику?
5. Чи ви́ зна́єте, де́ мо́жна діста́ти ма́пу?
6. Кого́ ви́ зна́єте, хто́ ма́є словни́к?
7. Чи ця́ ді́вчина — ва́ша сестра́?
8. Чи ви́ кана́дець (кана́дка)?
9. Чи це́й хло́пець — індія́нець?
10. Чи я́ украї́нка (украї́нець)?

XVIII. Answer the questions to the dialogues

"Фотогра́фія"

1. На що́ ди́вляться Павло́ і Ма́рта?
2. Кого́ Ма́рта зна́є?
3. Про ко́го вона́ пита́є?
4. Хто́ Лю́ба й І́гор?
5. Чи Марко́ Поліщу́к кана́дець?

"Ціка́ва кни́жка"

1. Кого́ ба́чить Ле́ся Палі́й?
2. Кого́ вона́ хо́че ба́чити?
3. Яке́ вона́ ма́є пита́ння?
4. Чи Васи́ль Миха́йлович ма́є цю́ кни́жку?

"Стара́ ма́па"

1. Що́ Богда́н чита́є?
2. На що́ ві́н ди́виться?
3. Що́ Га́ля не розумі́є?
4. Що́ Богда́н відповіда́є?

"Спра́вжня любо́в"

1. На ко́го ди́виться Марі́я?
2. Чому́ ціка́во на ни́х диви́тися?
3. Чи Петро́ про це́ зна́є?
4. Чому́ Марі́я ду́має, що це спра́вжня любо́в?
5. Чи Петро́ тепе́р те́ж та́к ду́має?

ЧЕТВЕРТА ЛЕКЦІЯ

9 Нікого немає
No one is here

Dialogue Paticipants: Тетя́на Миха́йлівна - Т, Мико́ла - М
Tetjana Myxajlivna - T, Mykola - M

1.	Т-	Чи Окса́на сього́дні є́?	T-	Is Oksana in today?
2.	М-	Ні́. Окса́ни нема́є.	M-	No, Oksana is not in.
3.	Т-	Чи Миха́йло є́?	T-	Is Myxajlo in?
4.	М-	Ні́, Миха́йла те́ж нема́є.	M-	No, Myxajlo is not in either.
5.	Т-	А Марко́ Поліщу́к?	T-	What about Marko Poliščuk?
6.	М-	І Марка́ Поліщука́ нема́.	M-	Marko is not in either.
7.	Т-	Кого́ ще́ нема́?	T-	Who else is not in?
8.	М-	Нема́ Марії, О́лі Прокопо́вич і Андрія́.	M-	Marija is not in, Olja Prokopovyč and Andrij.
9.	Т-	Що́ це́? Ніко́го нема́є! Яка́ ж це́ бу́де шко́ла, якщо́ ніхто́ не бу́де прихо́дити?	T-	What is that? No one is here! What kind of school is this going to be if no one will be coming?

10 Нічого не має
He doesn't have anything

Dialogue Paticipants: Тетя́на Миха́йлівна - Т, Ві́ктор - В
Tetjana Myxajlivna - T, Viktor - V

1.	Т-	Ві́кторе, де́ тві́й зо́шит?	T-	Viktor, where is your notebook?
2.	В-	Я́ не ма́ю сього́дні зо́шита.	V-	I don't have a notebook today.
3.	Т-	Ма́єш яки́йсь папі́р?	T-	Do you have some paper?
4.	В-	Ні́, я́ не ма́ю папе́ру.	V-	No, I don't have any paper.
5.	Т-	А оліве́ць або́ ру́чку ма́єш?	T-	What about a pencil or a pen?
6.	В-	Ні́, я́ не ма́ю ні олівця́ ні ру́чки.	V-	No, I don't have either a pencil or a pen.
7.	Т-	Я́ цього́ не розумі́ю! Ти́ ні́чо́го не ма́єш! Я́к же ти́ бу́деш писа́ти?	T-	I don't understand it! You have nothing. How are you going to write?
8.	В-	Але́ ви́ вчо́ра сказа́ли, що за́втра ми́ не бу́демо писа́ти, ті́льки чита́ти.	V-	But you said yesterday that tomorrow we won't be writing, only reading.
9.	Т-	Та невже́? Я́ не пам'ята́ю. Ні́, ми́ бу́демо і чита́ти, і писа́ти. О́сь, на́ оліве́ць і папі́р.	T-	Really? I don't recall it. We'll both read and write. Here, take this pencil and paper.
10.	В-	Дя́кую.	V-	Thank you.

11 Літературний вечір
A literary evening

Dialogue Paticipants: І́гор - І, Богда́н - Б, Ма́рта - М
Ihor - I, Bohdan - B, Marta - M

1.	І-	Добри́день, Ма́рто! Це́ гово́рить І́гор Ле́сів. Чи Богда́н удо́ма?	I-	Hello, Marta! This is Ihor Lesiv speaking. Is Bohdan at home?
2.	М-	Ні́, його́ нема́, але́ він за́раз бу́де. А́, о́сь він! Богда́не, І́гор дзво́нить.	M-	No, he is not, but he will be right back. Oh, here he is. Bohdan, Ihor is calling.
3.	Б-	Добри́день, І́горю! Що́ ново́го?	B-	Hello, Ihor! What's new?
4.	І-	У цю́ субо́ту ми́ влашто́вуємо літерату́рний ве́чір. Бу́демо чита́ти ві́рші Тара́са Шевче́нка, Іва́на Франка́, Ле́сі Украї́нки. Я́, звича́йно, бу́ду говори́ти про життя́ й тво́рчість Шевче́нка. Всі ду́же хо́чуть тебе́ та́м ба́чити.	I-	We are having a literary evening this Saturday. We'll be reading poems by Taras Ševčenko, Ivan Franko, and Lesja Ukrajinka. I, of course, will be speaking about Ševčenko's life and work. Everyone wants to see you there.
5.	Б-	Коли́ це́? В субо́ту? Бою́ся, що в цю́ субо́ту я́ не бу́ду ма́ти ча́су.	B-	When is it? Saturday? I'm afraid I won't have any time this Saturday.
6.	І-	Прихо́дь, ду́же тебе́ про́шу.	I-	Please do come. I beg you.
7.	Б-	Ну́ до́бре.	B-	Well, all right.

СЛОВНИК

бу́ти, бу́дуть	to be
вдо́ма = удо́ма	at home
ві́рші (pl.)	poetry; poems
ві́рш (m)	poem
влашто́вувати = улашто́вувати	to arrange
вчо́ра = учо́ра	yesterday
дзвони́ти, дзвоню́, дзво́нять (+I; до +G; в +A)	to phone; to ring
до́бре	all right
ж (же)	emphatic particle ('but')
життя́ (n)	life
за́втра	tomorrow
і...і	both...and
коли́	when
літерату́рний	literary
на́!	here! take it!
невже́	really?
нема́ (нема́є)	is/are not there
ніхто́	nobody
ні...ні	neither ... nor
пам'ята́ти	to remember, to recall

прихóдити, прихóджу, прихóдять	to come
прихóдь!	come!
просúти, прошý, прóсять*	to ask; to beg
сказáти, скажý, скáжуть*	to say; to speak
субóта (f)	Saturday
твóрчість, -ости (f)	creativity; creative work
тéж	either
удóма	at home
улаштóвувати, улаштóвують	to arrange
учóра	yesterday
чác, чáсу or часý (m)	time
четвéртий	fourth
шкóла (f)	school
щé	else
якщó	if

NAMES

Тарáс Григóрович Шевчéнко
Івáн Франкó, Лéся Украї́нка

IDIOMS

Та невжé!	You don't say!

SUPPLEMENT

понеділок, -лка (m)	Monday
вівтóрок, -рка (m)	Tuesday
середá (f)	Wednesday
четвéр, -гá (m)**	Thursday
п'ятниця (f)	Friday
неділя (f)	Sunday
áні ... áні	neither ... nor
пáм'ять, -ті (f)	memory
поéт, -а (m)	poet
телефонувáти, телефонýють	to call (by phone)

* Verbs marked by an * appeared in the Introduction. The first person sg. of the verb **просúти** takes two different stresses, **прóшу** when making an invitation or thanking someone, and **прошý** when the meaning is "I beg you."

** Note the genitive of четвéр: четвергá.

EXPLANATORY NOTES

1. There are two variants of the expression of absence: **нема** and **немає.** The second is more formal, the first is more colloquial. Note that **немає** is spelled as one word as opposed to the negated verb 'to have' in the third person singular, **не має.** cf.:

Він нічóго не мáє.	He doesn't have anything.
Йогó тýт немáє.	He is not here.

2. The interjection **нá!** is equivalent in meaning to Прóшу! when it accompanies a gesture ("Here!", "Take it!"). It has a much more familiar tone and should be used only between close friends or relatives, even though it has a plural "polite" form **нáте.**

3. **Тарáс Шевчéнко** (1814–1861), **Івáн Франкó** (1856–1916) and **Лéся Украї́нка** (1871–1913) are the three most famous poets of Ukrainian literature.

4. The day on which something takes place appears in the accusative preceded by the preposition **у (в)**:

Коли́ бýде лéкція?	When will the lecture be?
У сéреду.	On Wednesday.

When preceeded by a modifier such as 'this', 'next', 'last', 'some', the noun indicating the day of an event is either in the accusative preceded by *у* or in the genitive:

Лéкція бýде в цю субóту.	The lecture will be this Saturday.
Лéкція бýде ціє́ї субóти.	

5. **Áні ... áні** is an emphatic variant of **ні ... ні** used very frequently:

Він не має áні олівця́ áні рýчки. Яки́й же він студéнт?

He has neither a pencil nor a pen. What kind of a student is he?

6. Today, in Ukraine when making an official phone call it is customary to introduce oneself by saying "Вáс турбýє таки́й-то/такá-то", "So-and-so is troubling/disturbing you".

NOTES ON GRAMMAR

I. GENITIVE SINGULAR OF NOUNS

FEMININE DECLENSION

1. a- *type*

Hard			*Soft*			
N. -а	кімна́та		-я	О́ля	-я	Марі́я
G. -и	кімна́ти		-і	О́лі	-ї	Марі́ї

c- *type*

N.	Ø	річ	любо́в	відповідь
G.	-і/-и	ре́чі	любо́ви	відповіді

Note 1: The genitive ending for the a- type nouns is **-и** when the stem consonant is hard, and **i** when the stem-final consonant is soft or a sibilant (**-ї** is writen to include the stem-final **j**).

Note 2: The c- type nouns take the ending -i in the genitive, except the following two groups which take **-и**:

(a) nouns whose stems end in two consonants (**тво́рчість — чости**)

(b) the nouns **Ру́сь, сіль, кро́в, любо́в, о́сінь** (**Ру́си, со́ли, кро́ви, любо́ви, о́сени**) 'Rus', 'salt', 'blood', 'love', 'autumn'.

2. The masculine-neuter declension has the endings **-а/-я** and -у/-ю. Their distribution is as follows:

NEUTER NOUNS

Hard stems			*Soft stems and* ж ч ш щ *stems*			
N. -о	сло́во	вікно́	-е -я	мі́сце	життя́	прі́звище
G. -а	сло́ва	вікна́	-я (а)	мі́сця	життя́	прі́звища

Note 1: All neuter nouns which have **-о** in the nominative have **-а** in the genitive. Those ending in **-е** or **-я** in the nominative have **-я** in the genitive.

Note 2: Remember that the spelling rule forbids writing -я after a single consonant **ж ч ш щ** and the letter **-а** must be written instead : **прі́звище — прі́звища** (Otherwise, such nouns follow a soft declension.)

Note 3: Neuter nouns of the **-ат/ен** type take the ending -и in the genitive singular, e.g. **ім'я́ — і́мени.**

MASCULINE ANIMATE NOUNS

	Hard stem			*Soft stem*			
N.	Ø /-o	Віктор	Маркó	Ø	Васúль	Íгор	Андрíй
A.	-a	Віктора	Маркá	-я	Василя́	Íгоря	Андрія
G.	-a	Віктора	Маркá	-я	Василя́	Íгоря	Андрія

Note 1: Note that the genitive form of masculine nouns denoting animate beings is identical with the accusative.

MASCULINE INANIMATE NOUNS

Group A

	Hard stem			*Soft stem*		
N.	Ø	стíл	зóшит	Ø	олівéць	стілéць
G.	-a	столá	зóшита	-я	олівця́	стільця́

Group B

	Hard stem						*Soft stem*		
N.	Ø	рáнок	папíр	чáс	журнáл	будúнок	Ø	музéй	готéль
G.	-y	рáнку	папéру	чáсу	журнáлу	будúнку	-ю	музéю	готéлю

Note 1: The ending **-a/-я** (Group A) is found mainly in nouns denoting concrete objects, certain types of measurements (such as time, size), certain geographical names and in the surnames ending in **-ів, -їв, -ськ, -ин, -ль, -ик, -ок.**

Note 2: All other masculine inanimate nouns take the ending **-y/-ю**. This group includes many more nouns than Group A. The nouns in Group B include those denoting abstract notions, institutions, buildings, collective nouns, nouns denoting substance or material, most foreign borrowings, including geographic names. Thus we see that the distribution of the masculine endings is dependent on both the form and meaning, and the guidelines are not always clear-cut. Dictionaries and grammars disagree on details, and there is great variation in the usage of different regions. However, the student is advised to follow the basic outline presented here.

3. Stem differences in the genitive and the nominative.

(1) In some masculine nouns the stem ends in a consonantal cluster which in the nominative (and accusative inanimate) is broken by inserting the so-called "fleeting" vowel **-o** or **-e:**

N. / A.		G.
будúнок	—	будúнку
рáнок	—	рáнку
олівéць	—	олівця́
дéнь	—	дня́

(2) The root vowel **-o** (more rarely **-e**) appears throughout the declension but is replaced by **-i** in the nominative and accusative, i.e. before a zero ending. The i automatically requires palatalization of the preceding consonant. (see The Sound System, p. xviii)

G.	стол-á	stol- á	папéр-у	papér-u	вéчор-а	véčor-a
N./A.	стíл-Ø	st'il-Ø	папíр-Ø	pap'ír-Ø	вéчір-Ø	véč'ir-Ø

(Compare the pronominal stems: **вонá** but **він**, i.e. von-á, von-Ø=v'ín; **моя́, моє́** but **мíй**, i.e. moj-á, moj-é, moj-Ø=m'ij)

(3) In some masculine nouns the stem does not possess stress. However, if the ending is zero, the stress must fall on the final syllable of the stem.

G.	стол-á	олівц-я́	стільц-я́
N./A.	стíл-Ø	олівéць-Ø	стілéць-Ø

Note 1: Note that the stem-final consonant in the genitive **стільця́** (s't'il'c' á) is soft while in the nominative before -e it is hard (see The Sound System, p. xviii).

4. Summary of the noun declension genitive endings.

The endings of the genitive singular of nouns may be summed up as follows:

	Feminine		*Masculine*		*Neuter*	
	Hard	*Soft*	*Hard*	*Soft*	*Hard*	*Soft*
N.	Ø, а	Ø, я	Ø	Ø	о	е, я
G.	и	і	а, у	я, ю	а	я

Here are some sample paradigms:

N.	студéнт	Васи́ль	журнáл	готéль	Маркó
A.	студéнта	Василя́	журнáл	готéль	Маркá
G.	студéнта	Василя́	журнáлу	готéлю	Маркá
V.	студéнте!	Васи́лю!	(журнáле!)	(готéлю!)	Мáрку!
N.	студéнтка	Óля	слóво	мíсце	питáння
A.	студéнтку	Óлю	слóво	мíсце	питáння
G.	студéнтки	Óлі	слóва	мíсця	питáння
V.	студéнтко!	/Óлю!	(слóво!)	(мíсце!)	(питáння!)

(Exercises 1, 2, 3, 4, 5)

II. GENITIVE OF THE PERSONAL PRONOUNS

The genitive case of the personal pronouns is identical with the accusative:

N.	я́	ти́	він/вонó	вонá	ми́	ви́	вони́
A.	менé	тебé	йогó	ї́ї	нáс	вáс	ї́х
	(на мéне)	(на тéбе)	(на ньóго)	(на неї̈)			
G.	менé	тебé	йогó	ї́ї	нáс	вáс	ї́х
	(у мéне)	(у тéбе)	(на ньóго)	(на неї̈)			

(Exercises 6, 7)

III. GENITIVE OF THE PRONOUNS ЦЕЙ, ТОЙ, ЧИЙ, УВЕСЬ AND THE NUMERAL ОДИН

Masculine

N.	це́й	уве́сь/вве́сь	чи́й	то́й	оди́н
G.	цьо́го́	усього́/всього́	чийо́го	того́	одного́
	(у цьо́го)	(у всьо́го)		(у то́го)	

Feminine

N.	ця́	уся́/вся́	чи́я	та́	одна́
G.	ціє́ї	усіє́ї/всіє́ї	чиє́ї	тіє́ї/то́ї	одніє́ї/одно́ї

Neuter

N.	це́	усе́/все́	чи́є	те́	одне́
G.	цього́	усього́/всього́	чийо́го	того́	одного́
	(у цьо́го)	(у всьо́го)		(у то́го)	

Note 1: Note that the masc./ntr. genitive is identical with the masculine animate accusative.

Note 2: Note that the palatalized consonant c' in the pronouns **ця́, цю́, цього́** becomes hard before the vowel **е: це́, це́й** (see The Sound System, p. xvi–xviii).

Note 3: Notice that the stem in **оди́н** is **одн-**. The vowel **-и-** is inserted in the N/A (inanimate) masculine forms. The feminine genitive of **то́й** and **оди́н** is either **тіє́ї, одніє́ї** or **то́ї, одно́ї**, both variants being equally common.

(Exercise 8, 9, 10)

IV. GENITIVE OF THE INTERROGATIVE AND THE NEGATIVE PRONOUNS

	Interrogative		*Negative*	
N.	хто́	що́	ніхто́	ніщо́
G.	кого́	чого́	ніко́го	нічо́го
	(у ко́го)	(у чо́го)		

Notice also the similarity in all pronominal endings, cf.: **його́, того́, кого́, нічо́го**. In colloquial speech, the genitive form **нічо́го** is often substituted for the nominative form **ніщо́.**

(Exercise 6)

V. USES OF THE GENITIVE

The genitive has a number of uses; only four will be mentioned here:

a) For possession and closely related attributive constructions:

Це́ місце Мико́ли.	This is Mykola's place.
Вона́ сестра́ профе́сора Гончаре́нка.	She is the sister of Prof. Hončarenko.
О́сь ма́па Кана́ди.	Here is a map of Canada.

Note 1: Note the difference in word order: in English 'Mykola's place', in Ukrainian **місце Мико́ли**.

b) As the direct object of a negated verb (the genitive of negation):

Я́ не ба́чу папе́ру.	I don't see any paper.
Я́ не зна́ю цього́ пое́та.	I don't know this poet.

c) To indicate absence or non-existence (notice that the genitive object of such constructions is the subject of statements of presence or existence), cf.:

Presence	*Absence*
Чи Окса́на ту́т?	**Окса́ни** ту́т нема́є.
(subject)	(object)
Existence	*Non-existence*
Він ка́же, що **Бо́г** є́.	Він ка́же, що **Бо́га** нема́є.
He says that there is a God.	He says that there is no God.

d) With certain verbs, for example **боя́тися, дзвони́ти (до...)**:

Усі́ боя́ться цього́ профе́сора.	Everyone is afraid of this professor.
Я́ дзвоню́ до університе́ту.	I am calling the university.

(Exercises 1, 2, 5, 7)

VI. NEGATIVE CONSTRUCTIONS

In Ukrainian negative pronouns and adverbs (like 'no one', 'nowhere') require a negated verb:

Ту́т ніко́го нема́є.	No one is here.
Ти́ ніко́ли нічо́го не зна́єш.	You never know anything.

Notice that negative constructions or the presence of a negated verb require a different translation in English of particles **те́ж** and **ще́**:

Positive sentence	*Negative sentence*
те́ж = also, too	те́ж = either
Це́ те́ж пога́но. This is bad too.	Це́ те́ж непога́но. This is not bad either.
Ві́н те́ж украї́нець. He is also Ukrainian.	Ві́н те́ж не украї́нець. He is not a Ukrainian either.
ще = more, still, else	ще = yet, still, else
Повторі́ть ще́ раз! Repeat once more.	Його́ ще́ нема́є. He is not here yet.
Ти́ ще́ пи́шеш? Are you still writing?	Ти́ ще не зна́єш? You still don't know?
Кого́ ти́ ще́ зна́єш? Who(m) else do you know?	Кого́ ще́ нема́є? Who else is not here? (or WHO isn't here yet?)

(Exercise 3)

VII. FUTURE TENSE

One type of future used in Ukrainian is the compound future consisting of the verb бу́ти 'to be' in its future tense form plus an infinitive* of another verb:

Я́ бу́ду чита́ти.	I will read.
Ми́ бу́демо писа́ти.	We will write.

(Exercises 11, 12).

ВПРАВИ

I. Change the sentences according to the model

Це́ **Марко́**, а це́ Іва́н. — Іва́н — бра́т **Марка́**.
Це́ **Богда́н**, а це́ Іва́н. — Іва́н — бра́т **Богда́на**.

(Васи́ль, Тара́с, Андрі́й, Петро́, Миха́йло, Мико́ла, І́гор, Андрі́йко, Павло́)

---

* Not all infinitives can be used, only those in the imperfective aspect (aspects will be discussed in Lesson 6).

II. Combine the sentences according to the model:

Óсь фотогрáфія. Цé **Лю́ба**. — Цé фотогрáфія **Лю́би.**

(Оксáна, Мáрта, Óля Прокопóвич, Тетя́на Михáйлівна, пáні Лíда, Марíя Поліщýк, Лéся Палíй, Гáля Гончарéнко, Óльга Миколáївна)

III. Answer the questions according to the model:

Чи **пáн профéсор** удóма? Ні, **пáна профéсора** немá вдóма.

(пáн Гончарéнко, пáн Палíй, пáн Поліщýк, пáн Лéсів, пáн Прокопóвич, цéй студéнт, тóй хлóпець, тá дíвчина, ця́ студéнтка, пáні Гочарéнко)

IV. Give the negative answers to the following questions:

Model: Чи ви́ мáєте **журнáл "Украї́на"**? Ні, я́ не мáю **журнáлу "Украї́на".**

(мáпу Канáди, папíр, буди́нок, стілéць, мíсце, телевíзор, сестрý, чáс, словни́к, кни́жку, зóшит, олівéць)

V. Give negative answers (use nouns).

1. Чи ти́ розумíєш лéкцію?
2. Чи ти́ лю́биш істóрію?
3. Чи ти́ пам'ятáєш йогó ім'я́?
4. Чи ти́ пам'ятáєш ї́ї прíзвище?
5. Чи ти́ розумíєш питáння?
6. Чи ти́ бáчиш музéй?
7. Чи ти́ пам'ятáєш йогó буди́нок?
8. Чи ти́ читáєш журнáл "Украї́на"?
9. Чи ти́ бáчиш йогó вікнó?
10. Чи ти́ знáєш вíдповідь?

VI. Put the bracketed pronouns into the correct form.

1. Когó він не пам'ятáє? (ти́)
2. Когó він не бáчить? (цé; ніщó)
3. Чогó він не знáє? (вони́)
4. Когó він не розуміє? (він)
5. Когó він не хóче бáчити? (вони́; ніхтó)
6. Чогó він не лю́бить? (тé; ніщó)
7. Когó він не питáє? (я́)
8. Когó він не прóсить? (ми́; ніхтó)

VII. Complete the sentences according to the model:

Я́ розумі́ю, але́ **мене́** не розумі́ють. 'I understand but they don't understand me'.

(ти́, він, вона́, ви́, ми́, вони́, воно́)

VIII. Complete the sentences according to the model:

Я́ зна́ю **це́й ві́рш**, а вона́ не зна́є **цього́ ві́рша**.

1. Я́ люблю́ цю́ мо́ву, а вона́ не . . . . .
2. Я́ діста́ну ту річ, а вони́ не . . . . .
3. Я́ ма́ю цю́ фотогра́фію, а він не . . . . .
4. Я́ розумі́ю це́й ві́рш, а вона́ не . . . . .
5. Я́ зна́ю всю́ його́ тво́рчість, а ви́ не . . . . .
6. Я́ розумі́ю це́ пита́ння, а він не . . . . .
7. Я́ зна́ю його́ життя́, а вона́ не . . . . .
8. Я́ ма́ю ча́с, а ви́ не . . . . .
9. Я́ розумі́ю цього́ індія́нця, а вони́ не . . . . .
10. Я́ люблю́ ту́ ді́вчину, а вона́ не . . . . .

IX. Answer the questions using the words in brackets.

1. Кого́ ти́ не пам'ята́єш? (То́й америка́нець)
2. Чого́ ти́ не пам'ята́єш? (То́й ве́чір)
3. Кого́ ти́ не лю́биш? (Та́ америка́нка)
4. Чого́ ти́ не лю́биш? (Одне́ сло́во)
5. Кого́ ти́ не зна́єш? (То́й кана́дець)
6. Чого́ ти́ не зна́єш? (Уве́сь ві́рш)
7. Кого́ ти́ не ба́чиш? (Та́ ді́вчина)
8. Чого́ ти́ не ба́чиш? (Та́ фотогра́фія)
9. Кого́ ти́ не розумі́єш? (То́й хло́пець)
10. Чого́ ти́ не розумі́єш? (Уся́ ле́кція)

X. Replace the pronoun **то́й** by the pronoun **це́й**.

1. Ніхто́ того́ не зна́є.
2. Я́ не розумі́ю того́ па́на.
3. Я́ не зна́ю тіє́ї па́ні.
4. Я́ не хо́чу того́ журна́лу.
5. Я́ не чита́ю тіє́ї кни́жки.
6. Я́ не ба́чу того́ мі́сця.
7. Я́ не люблю́ того́ малю́нка.
8. Я́ не ма́ю тіє́ї ма́пи.
9. Я́ не ба́чу того́ і́мени.
10. Я́ не зна́ю того́ прі́звища.

XI. Change the verbs to the future tense according to the model:

Я́ тепе́р **розумі́ю.** Я́ бу́ду **розумі́ти.**

1. Я́ тепе́р роблю́ дома́шнє завда́ння.
2. Ві́н тепе́р чита́є нови́й журна́л.
3. Ти́ тепе́р пи́шеш.
4. Вона́ тепе́р дзво́нить.
5. Я́ тепе́р відповіда́ю на ва́ше пита́ння.
6. Вони́ тепе́р ди́вляться програ́му.
7. Ми́ тепе́р ду́маємо про того́ індія́нця.
8. Ви́ тепе́р ма́єте ле́кцію.
9. Вона́ його́ ба́чить.
10. Вони́ тепе́р це́ пам'ята́ють.

XII. Supply the correct form of the verbs (give the present tense).

1. Чи мо́жна та́к жи́ти? Я́ та́к . . . . .
2. Чи мо́жна та́к ду́мати? Ві́н та́к . . . . .
3. Чи мо́жна та́к писа́ти? Ми́ та́к . . . . .
4. Чи мо́жна та́к відповіда́ти? Ти́ та́к . . . . .
5. Чи мо́жна та́к проси́ти? Я́ та́к . . . . .
6. Чи мо́жна та́к дзвони́ти? Вона́ та́к . . . . .
7. Чи мо́жна та́к каза́ти? Ми́ та́к . . . . .
8. Чи мо́жна та́к роби́ти? Вони́ та́к . . . . .
9. Чи мо́жна та́к говори́ти? Ві́н та́к . . . . .
10. Чи мо́жна та́к диви́тися? Я́ та́к . . . . .

XIII. Complete the sentences.

1. Студе́нти . . . . . літерату́рний ве́чір.
2. Ві́н бу́де говори́ти про . . . . . Франка́.
3. Моя́ сестра́ . . . . на це́ пита́ння.
4. Ві́н прихо́дить . . . . . або́ в четве́р.
5. Чому́ ти́ не ма́єш . . . . . ? Її́ не ва́жко діста́ти.
6. Ві́н ма́є . . . . . здоро́в'я.
7. У цю́ субо́ту я́ не . . . . . часу́.
8. Тепе́р вже́ та́м нема́ . . . . . Тепе́р та́м шко́ла.
9. Ві́н ка́же, що́ це́ спра́вжня . . . . . , а вона́ ка́же, що́ ві́н . . . . . не лю́бить.
10. Я́ люблю́ це́й . . . . . Ле́сі Украї́нки.

XIV. Translate into Ukrainian.

1. This building is not a hotel, it's a school.
2. I want to say it in Ukrainian, but I don't remember a word.
3. Don't you know this girl? She is Ihor's sister.

4. I'm afraid to ask her about this drawing.
5. Do you see that Canadian over there? He thinks this film is very interesting.
6. Mark! Look out the window, do you know that fellow?
7. It's a very difficult book. I don't understand it.
8. They are not Ukrainians and they don't know anything about Ukraine, about the way Ukrainians live and think.
9. What day is it tomorrow? Tuesday? No, it's Wednesday. Is the lecture on Wednesday? No, it will be on Thursday.
10. Life is so interesting and you are afraid of it, you are afraid to live.

XV. Answer the following questions:

1. Чи ви́ бу́дете вдо́ма сього́дні ввече́рі?
2. Чи ви́ ма́єте ча́с диви́тися фі́льм?
3. Чи ви́ лю́бите чита́ти ві́рші?
4. Чи ви́ пам'ята́єте це́й ві́рш Тара́са Шевче́нка?
5. Яки́й сього́дні де́нь? Яки́й де́нь бу́де за́втра?
6. Чи на́ш буди́нок — це́ готе́ль?
7. Що́ ви ду́маєте про ва́ше життя́?
8. Яки́й музе́й ви́ хо́чете ба́чити?

XVI. Answer the questions to the dialogues.

"Ніко́го нема́є"

1. Кого́ сього́дні нема́?
2. Що́ ка́же Тетя́на Миха́йлівна про шко́лу?

"Ні́чо́го не ма́є"

1. Чи Ві́ктор ма́є зо́шит, папі́р, оліве́ць або́ ру́чку?
2. Чому́ ві́н ї́х не ма́є?
3. Чи́ Тетя́на Миха́йлівна про це́ пам'ята́є?
4. Що вони́ бу́дуть роби́ти сього́дні?

"Літерату́рний ве́чір"

1. Що́ студе́нти влашто́вують?
2. Коли́ це́ бу́де?
3. Які́ ві́рші та́м бу́дуть чита́ти?
4. Про що́ бу́де говори́ти І́гор?
5. Чи Богда́н ма́є ча́с?
6. Чи Богда́н та́м бу́де?

REVIEW

I. Read and translate:

1. Сьогóдні ввéчері прихóдять студéнти Óля й Маркó. Вонú хóчуть бáчити новý книжку профéсора Гончарéнка, "Істóрія Україні". Профéсор Гончарéнко бýде відповідáти на питáння. Він ужé старéнький, йогó здорóв'я погáне, алé він ще пúше і любить, колú прихóдять студéнти і питáють йогó про українську мóву, українську істóрію.

2. Я́ хóчу дістати мáпу Україні. Я́ мáю англíйську мáпу, алé я́ хóчу мáти українську. Я́ хóчу тéж дістáти істóрію Україні по-українському. Мú мáємо українську істóрію, алé по-англíйському.

3. Цé нáша кімнáта. Óсь подивúся на мíй стіл. Оця́ фотогрáфія — цé моя́ дíвчина Óля. А óсь її малюнок. Оцé книжка профéсора Василя́ Михáйловича Гончарéнка. Цé істóрія Україні. Óн тáм словнúк української мóви, а це англíйський словнúк. Цé журнáл "Нáше здорóв'я".

4. Óсь нáш новúй телевізор. Я́ не дýже люблю йогó дивúтися, я́ люблю читáти, алé Оксáна, моя́ сестрá, дúвиться, колú рóбить домáшнє завдáння. Я́ цьогó не розумію, алé не хóчу нічóго казáти.

II. Translate into English.

1. Тú знóв нічóго не рóбиш.
2. Тáм немá нічóго новóго.
3. Я́ вжé четвéртий рáз прихóджу, і йогó немá вдóма.
4. Чи він спрáвжній індія́нець?
5. Я́ не пам'ятáю, я́к вáс по бáтькові.
6. Чи мóжна вáс просúти прийтú на нáш літератýрний вéчір?
7. Прóшу, говорíть повíльно, я́ щé не дýже дóбре розумію по-українському.
8. Я́к вáше здорóв'я? Дя́кую, непогáно.
9. Цéй журнáл не вáжко дістáти.
10. Цé прáвильно, щó він говóрить.

III. Translate into Ukrainian.

1. It will be a good day.
2. They love to talk about their health.
3. Take a look at this old thing.
4. Do you know this American girl?
5. Why do you write so slowly?
6. This assignment is hard.

7. Your place is over there.
8. What is her name and surname?
9. I don't like this drawing.
10. Look at my drawing.

IV. Put the bracketed words into the correct form (review of V/A).

1. На ко́го ти́ ди́вишся? На (Ле́ся). — (Ле́ся)!, я́ на (ти́) дивлю́ся!
2. Про (хто́) ти́ ду́маєш? Про (Андрі́й). — (Андрі́й)!, я́ про (ти́) ду́маю.
3. Чия́ це́ фотогра́фія? Це́ фотогра́фія(Марі́я). — (Марі́я)! Ця́ твоя́ фотогра́фія непога́на.
4. Кого́ ти́ бої́шся? Я́ боюся (Марко́). — Чого́ ти́ (він) бої́шся? — (Марко́)! Він (ти́) бої́ться.
5. Чи ти́ пам'ята́єш (Тетя́на Миха́йлівна)? Та́к, я́ (вона́) до́бре пам'ята́ю. (Тетя́на Миха́йлівна)! Він (ви́) до́бре пам'ята́є.
6. Про (що́) ви́ пи́шете? Ми́ пи́шемо про (Украї́на). — Я́ те́ж пишу́ про (вона́). О́сь мі́й ві́рш: "(Украї́на моя́)! Я́к я́ (ти́) люблю́!"
7. Кого́ ти́ та́м ба́чиш? Я ба́чу (Миха́йло й Окса́на). Чи ти́ (вони́) до́бре ба́чиш? — Та́к. — (Миха́йло й Окса́на!) Він (ви́) до́бре ба́чить.
8. Кого́ ти́ пита́єш? Я́ пита́ю (Ві́ктор). — Ві́ктор не зна́є, о́сь І́гор. (І́гор)! Чи ти́ зна́єш, де́ мі́й словни́к?
9. Кого́ ви́ хо́чете ба́чити? Я́ хочу́ ба́чити (па́ні Лі́да). (Вона́) тепе́р нема́є вдо́ма. Є її́ сестра́ Га́ля. — До́бре, чи мо́жна ба́чити (Га́ля)?
10. Кого́ ти́ ту́т не зна́єш? Я́ не зна́ю (оця́ ді́вчина). — Це́ О́ля Прокопо́вич. Невже́ ти́ не зна́єш (О́ля Прокопо́вич)? (Вона́) всі́ зна́ють.

V. Finish the sentences using the infinitives.

1. Говорі́ть го́лосно! — Він не хо́че . . . . . го́лосно.
2. Подиви́ся на це́! Чому́ ти́ не хо́чеш на це́ . . . . . . ?
3. Відповіда́йте на пита́ння! — Ми́ не хо́чемо . . . . .
4. Прихо́дь уве́чері! — Вона́ не хо́че . . . . .
5. Ду́же прошу́! — Кра́ще не . . . . .

VI Give the present tense of the verbs.

1. Чого́ ви́ (боя́тися)?
2. Чому́ ти́ не (дзвони́ти)?
3. Що́ вони́ (роби́ти)?
4. Про що́ ти́ (говори́ти)?
5. Що́ вони́ (влашто́вувати)?
6. Чого́ ви́ не (розумі́ти)?
7. Що́ ви́ (писа́ти)?
8. Про що́ ти́ (пита́ти)?
9. Де́ вони́ (жи́ти)?
10. Чи ти́ це́ (пам'ята́ти)?

П'ЯТА ЛЕКЦІЯ

12 Бібліотека
Library

Dialogue Paticipants:
Бібліоте́кар - Б, Студе́нт - С
Librarian - B, Student - S

1.	С- Яка́ це́ газе́та?	S- What kind of newspaper is this?
2.	Б- Це́ кана́дська газе́та. А ви́ яку́ хо́чете?	B- It's a Canadian newspaper. What kind do you want?
3.	С- Я́ хо́чу америка́нську, "Нью Йо́рк Та́ймс".	S- I want an American one, "The New York Times".
4.	Б- Ми́ ма́ємо, але́ тільки вчора́шню. О́сь, про́шу.	B- We have it, but it's yesterday's. Here you are.
5.	С- Ні, дя́кую. Вчора́шньої я́ не потребу́ю.	S- No, thank you. I don't need yesterday's.
6.	Б- Ви́бачте, сього́днішньої ще́ нема́.	B- Sorry, today's is not in yet.
7.	С- Це́ нічо́го. А який то́ журна́л, украї́нський?	S- It's all right. And what kind of magazine is that, Ukrainian?
8.	Б- Ні, росі́йський. Хо́чете подиви́тися?	B- No, it's Russian. Do you want to see it?
9.	С- Ні, дя́кую. Я́ по-росі́йському не чита́ю.	S- No, thanks. I don't read Russian.

13 Переклад
Translation

Dialogue Paticipants:
Ві́ра - В, па́ні Лі́да - Л
Vira - V, pani Lida - L

1.	В- Па́ні Лі́до, що́ ви́ друку́єте?	V- Pani Lida, what are you typing?
2.	Л- Пере́клад Мико́ли. Він перекладає одну́ кни́жку з украї́нської на англі́йську.	L- Mykola's translation. He is translating a book from Ukrainian into English.
3.	В- А́, та́к, я́ зна́ю: "Істо́рію украї́нської мо́ви". Ду́же ціка́ва.	V- Oh, yes, I know: "History of the Ukrainian Language". It's very interesting.
4.	Л- Для те́бе ціка́ва, а я́ ту́т ні о́дного сло́ва не розумі́ю.	L- For you perhaps, but I don't understand a word of it.

14 Лист
A Letter

Dialogue Paticipants:
Степа́н - С, Ві́ра - В
Stepan - S, Vira - V

1.	В-	Степа́не, чи ти́ не зна́єш адре́си Сергі́я, на́шого ново́го кана́дського студе́нта?	V-	Stepan, do you know the address of our new Canadian student Serhij?
2.	С-	Та́к, зна́ю. Він живе́ недале́ко від університе́ту.	S-	Yes, I do. He lives not far from the university.
3.	В-	А яки́й у нього но́мер телефо́ну?	V-	And what's his phone number?
4.	С-	Він ще́ не ма́є телефо́ну. Ма́тиме насту́пного ти́жня. А що́ таке́?	S-	He doesn't have a phone yet. He'll have it next week. Why do you ask?
5.	В-	Для нього є ли́ст від ма́тері з Монре́алю.	V-	There is a letter for him from his mother in Montreal.
6.	С-	Диви́сь! Сергі́й ту́т тільки ти́ждень, а вже́ ма́ти до нього пи́ше.	S-	Look at that! Serhij has been here only a week and his mother is already writing to him.
7.	В-	Пи́ше, бо ду́же його́ лю́бить.	V-	She's writing because she loves him dearly.
8.	С-	Звича́йно. Ну́, до́бре, я́ за́втра його́ ба́читиму й скажу́, що до нього є ли́ст.	S-	Sure. Well, I'll be seeing him tomorrow and I'll tell him that there is a letter for him.
9.	В-	Ду́же дя́кую.	V-	Thanks a lot.
10.	С-	Нема́ за́ що.	S-	Don't mention it.

15 Фільм
A Film

Dialogue Paticipants:
Степа́н - С, Ві́ра - В, Мико́ла - М
Stepan - S, Vira - V, Mykola - M

1.	С-	Мико́ло, зна́єш, сього́дні йде́ ціка́вий фі́льм про стару́ Росію. Хо́чеш подиви́тися?	S-	Mykola,you know,there is an interesting film about Old Russia playing today. Want to see it?
2.	М-	Ні́, дя́кую. Я́ не ма́ю ча́су, роблю́ пере́клад.	M-	No, thanks. I don't have the time. I'm working on a translation.
3.	С-	Ві́ро, а ти́ що́ роби́тимеш уве́чері?	S-	And you Vira, what are you doing tonight?
4.	В-	Я́ писа́тиму листи́.	V-	I'll be writing letters.
5.	С-	Уве́сь ве́чір?	S-	The whole evening?
6.	В-	Та́к. Оди́н ли́ст до моє́ї сестри́, оди́н до мого́ бра́та, оди́н до ма́ми і оди́н до ба́тька.	V-	Yes. One to my sister, one to my brother, one to Mom, and one to my father.
7.	М-	Ми́ писа́тимемо, а ти́ йди́ диви́ся сві́й фі́льм без на́с.	M-	We will be writing and you go and watch your movie without us.
8.	С-	До́бре.	V-	O.K.

СЛОВНИК

адре́са (f)	address
америка́нський	American
англі́йський	English
ба́тько (m)	father
бе́з (+ G)	without
бібліоте́ка (f)	library
бібліоте́кар, -я (m)	librarian (m)
від (+ G)	from
вчора́шній, -я, -є	yesterday's
газе́та (f)	newspaper
до (+G)	to; for
для (+ G)	for
з (+ G)	from
іти́, іду́ть (іди́!)	to go, to come (go!), walk
кана́дський	Canadian
ли́ст, -а́ (m)	letter
листи́ (pl.)	letters
ма́ма (f)	Mom
ма́ти, ма́тері (f)	mother
насту́пний	next
недале́ко	not far
пере́клад, -у (m)	translation
перекладáти, перекладáють	to translate
по-російському	in Russian
потребува́ти, потребу́ють (+ G)	to need
п'ятий	fifth
російський	Russian
Росія (f)	Russia
свій	one's own
сього́днішній, -я, -є	today's
телефо́н, -у (m)	telephone
ти́ждень, ти́жня (m)	week
у (+G)	at
у (+ G) + є́	to have
університе́т, -у (m)	university

NAMES AND PLACES

Віра, Степа́н, Сергі́й
Монреа́ль, -я/ -ю, Нью Йо́рк, -а/-у*

---

* See The Explanatory Notes.

SUPPLEMENT

бібліоте́карка (f)	librarian (f)
жо́дний	none
іти́ на фі́льм	to go to a movie (to go see a movie)
отри́мати	to receive

IDIOMS

іде́ фі́льм	a film is playing
Нема́ за́ що! (= Нема́ за що́ дя́кувати)	Don't mention it! (= Nothing to thank for)
ні о́дного/о́дної*	not one, not a (single)
Це́ нічо́го!	It's all right!
А що́ таке́?	Why (do you ask)?
Що́ таке́? Що́ це́ таке́?	What's that (thing)?
Що́ та́м таке́?	What's going on? What's the matter?

EXPLANATORY NOTES

1. Beside **газе́та**, there is another word **часо́пис** which is widely used by emigré Ukrainians and less frequently in Ukraine.

2. Most geographical names which end in a consonant have the genitive ending **-а**. However, in colloquial Ukrainian they often appear with the ending **-у**, especially names of foreign cities:

Монреа́ль — Монреа́лю/Монреа́ля
Нью Йо́рк — Нью Йо́рку/Нью Йо́рка

Notice that the official name for Montreal follows the French pronunciation, without t: Monreal. Most Ukrainians outside Ukraine follow the English pronunciation and accordingly write **Монтреа́ль**.

3. In making an inquiry one often uses a negated verb as a form of politeness (cf. the English "Would you..." "Perhaps you could...")

Чи ви́ не хо́чете подиви́тися на цю́ фотогра́фію?
Would you like to take a look at this photograph?

Чи ти́ не зна́єш його́ адре́си?
Would you happen to know his address?

* Note the position of the stress.

4. Note that the noun **ти́ждень** 'week' loses the consonant **-д** in the genitive and in all other cases:

ти́ждень — ти́жня, ти́жнем, ти́жні ...

'Next week' is **насту́пного ти́жня** (the preposition **у** plus accusative may not be used).

5. **Телефонува́ти** is identical in meaning and function with **дзвони́ти**. **Дзвони́ти** is sometimes followed by **по телефо́ну** or **телефоно́м**, 'by phone'. Both verbs can be used with either the dative or **до** + G of the animate object, or **у/в/до** of the inanimate, cf.:

Кому́/До ко́го ти дзво́ниш?	Whom are you calling?
Куди́ ти́ дзво́ниш?	Where are you calling?
— В Украї́ну	— Ukraine.

6. **Ні о́дного/о́дної** may be replaced by **ані** or simply **ні** or by **жо́дний** (none):

Я́ (а)ні сло́ва не розумі́ю. Я́ жо́дного сло́ва не розумі́ю.
I don't understand a word.

7. To receive a letter is **отри́мати ли́ст(а́)** as well as **діста́ти** (more colloquial).

NOTES ON GRAMMAR

I. ADJECTIVAL DECLENSION

Adjectives, many pronouns, ordinal numerals and some other words belong to a single declension we will call adjectival.

Here we will consider two cases, accusative and genitive, of adjectives, possessive pronouns, ordinals and the numeral **оди́н**.

1. Accusative and genitive singular of adjectives.

Ukrainian has only one adjectival declension with regular spelling variations connected with the distinction between hard and soft stems. For example:

HARD STEMS: добрий

	Masculine	*Neuter*
A.	Я́ ма́ю до́бр-**ий** словни́к. Ми́ ма́ємо до́бр-**ого** бібліоте́каря.	Я́ ма́ю до́бр-**е** мі́сце.
G.	Я́ не ма́ю до́бр-**ого** словника́. Ми́ не ма́ємо до́бр-**ого** бібліоте́каря.	Я́ не ма́ю до́бр-**ого** мі́сця.

Feminine
Я́ ма́ю до́бр-**у** кімна́ту
Я́ не ма́ю до́бр-**ої** кімна́ти.

SOFT STEMS: справжній

	Masculine	*Neuter*
A.	Я́ ма́ю спра́вжн-**ій** словни́к.	Я́ ма́ю спра́вжн-**є** завда́ння.
	Ми́ ма́ємо спра́вжнь-**ого** бібліоте́каря.	
G.	Я́ не ма́ю спра́вжнь-**ого** словника́.	Я́ не ма́ю спра́вжнь-**ого** мі́сця.
	Ми́ не ма́ємо спра́вжнь-**ого** бібліота́каря.	

Feminine
Я́ ма́ю спра́вжн-**ю** бібліоте́ку.
Я́ не ма́ю спра́вжнь-**ої** бібліоте́ки.

Thus the endings are:*

	Masculine	*Neuter*	*Feminine*
N.	-ий, -ій	-е/-є	-а/-я
A.	-ий, -ий/-ого	-е/-є	-у/-ю
G.	-ого	-ого	-ої

Note 1: There are very few adjectives with the stem-final consonant j, cf. **безкра́їй** (bezkráj-ij) 'endless'. They follow the soft stem spelling, i.e. **безкра́-їй, безкра́-я, безкра́-є.**

Note 2: Notice the presence of a soft sign after the stem-final consonant -н in the genitive to indicate n' before o (see The System, p. xvii-xviii). (Exercises 1, 4, 5, 7)

2. Accusative and genitive of the ordinal numerals.

The ordinal numerals follow the adjectival declension. The numeral **тре́тій** 'third' follows the soft-stem pattern (see The Sound System, p. xviii, Note 5), and all the other ordinals take the hard-stem endings.

	Masculine		*Neuter*		*Feminine*	
N.	тре́тій	четве́ртий	тре́тє	четве́рте	тре́тя	четве́рта
A.=	N. or G.	N.=N. or G.	=N.	=N.	тре́тю	четве́рту
G.	тре́тього	четве́ртого	тре́тього	четве́ртого	тре́тьої	четве́ртої

(Exercises 7, 8)

* Formerly, feminine, neuter, and plural nominative and accusative forms also had longer forms, e.g. **важка́я, важку́ю, важке́є, важкі́ї.** These form have been preserved in poetry until quite recently, while oral speech may use them for ironic effect.

3. Accusative and genitive singular of possessives

The pronouns **на́ш** and **ва́ш** follow the hard-stem pattern and the pronoun **ї́хній** follows the soft-stem pattern. In the declension of **мі́й, тві́й, сві́й** the expected sequence **-ойо-** is reduced to **-о-**:

N.	на́ш	мі́й	ї́хній
	на́ше	моє́	ї́хнє
	на́ша	моя́	ї́хня
A.	на́ш/на́шого	мі́й/моґо́	ї́хній/ї́хнього
	на́ше	моє́	ї́хнє
	на́шу	мою́	ї́хню
G.	на́шого	моґо́	ї́хнього
	на́шого	моґо́	ї́хнього
	на́шої	моє́ї	ї́хньої

The stems of the pronouns **мі́й, тві́й, сві́й** are moj, tvoj, svoj. The **-о-** becomes an **-і-** before a zero ending (cf. Lesson 4, p. 61).

The possessive pronouns **сві́й** refers to the subject of the clause in which it stands and can be used with any subject singular or plural:

Я́ ма́ю своє́ завда́ння.	I have my (own) assignment.
Ти́ ма́єш сво́є завда́ння	You have your assignment.
Ми́ ма́ємо своє́ завда́ння.	We have our assignment.

Сві́й may not be used in any clause where it does not refer to the logical subject:

Ві́н іде́ до **свого́** бра́та, але́ **його́** бра́та нема́ вдо́ма.
He goes to ric brother but his brother is not home.

(Exercises 2, 3, 6)

II. FURTHER USES OF THE GENITIVE CASE

1. The genitive of possession and indication of place with the preposition **у.** The genitive with the preposition **у** has two basic meanings. One indicates someone's place:

Ві́н у своє́ї сестри́.	He is at his sister's place.
Ві́н живе́ в ни́х.	He lives at their place.

The other expresses possession, and is synonymous with the one which employs the verb 'to have' and the direct object. Possessive construction with the preposition **у** requires the use of **є**. cf.:

Я́ ма́ю словни́к. У ме́не є́ словни́к.	I have a dictionary.
Ві́н ма́є сестру́. У нього є́ сестра́.	He has a sister.

Note that the expressions with **у** have the object of possession as the grammatical subject, so that literally the above sentences read 'There is a dictionary in my possession', 'There is a sister with/by him'. Note also the similarity between these expressions and the expressions of existence or presence both of which require the use of the verb **є**:*

Presence/Absence		*Possession/Lack of possession*	
Чи ту́т є́ ма́па?	Та́к, є́. Та́к, ту́т є́ ма́па. Ні́, нема́ (нема́є). Ні́, ту́т нема́ ма́пи.	Чи в те́бе є́ ма́па?	Та́к є́. Та́к, у ме́не є́ ма́па. Ні́, нема́ (нема́є). Ні́, у ме́не нема́ ма́пи.

(Exercise 6)

It may be useful to compare the different expressions dealing with possession.

Statement of possession:	*Identification of the object:*
У ме́не є́ словни́к. I have a dictionary.	У ме́не **словни́к**. (це́ у ме́не **словни́к**). That's a dictionary which I have.

Identification of the possessor or place:

Словни́к **у ме́не**.
I have the dictionary.
(or: The dictionary is at my place)

2. The preposition **до**. This preposition indicates the direction of an action:

Я́ йду́ до університе́ту.	I am going to the university.
Я́ йду́ до не́ї.	I am going to her place. (or: I am walking toward her.)
До кого́ ти́ гово́риш?	Who are you talking to?

* The verb **є** is omitted in expressions dealing with some activity, such as a concert, a lecture, etc. **У на́с тепе́р ле́кція. Ту́т ле́кція.** We are having a class now. There is a class (lecture) here.

It also is used in the sense "until":

Я та́м бу́ду до субо́ти.	I will be there till Saturday.
До поба́чення.	Good-bye! (lit. "Till I see you")

До is used with many verbs, e.g. **дзвони́ти, писа́ти, говори́ти**.

3. The preposition **з** (also **зі** or **із**) when used with the genitive case indicates a place of origin (action originates within) and means "from" or "out":

Вона́ йде́ з університе́ту.	She is coming from the university.
Він дзво́нить з університе́ту.	He is calling from the university.
Вони́ з Кана́ди.	They are from Canada.
Це́ з Украї́ни.	This is from Ukraine.
З цьо́го ніч́ого не бу́де.	Nothing will come of it.

Its other meaning is "off", as in **зі стола́** 'off the table' indicating motion off a surface.*

The two variants **зі** and **із** occur before a consonant cluster, **зі** before **мн-** and clusters beginning with **з, с, ж, ш, щ** and **із** in all other cases: **зі шко́ли, із кни́жки, зі мно́ю**.

4. The preposition **від** indicates motion 'away from', from a position beside, as in pacing a room **від вікна́ до стола́** 'from the window to the desk', or in measuring the distance **від Нью-Йо́рку до Монреа́лю** 'from New York to Montreal'.

On the other hand, the preposition **від** must be used when referring to the person from whose place one is coming:

Він іде́ від Ле́сі.	He is coming from Les'a's place.
Він іде́ від не́ї.	He is coming from her place.

Від is commonly used to indicate a sender:

Це́ ли́ст від О́лі.	This is a letter from Ol'a.
Це́ завда́ння від університе́ту.	This is an assignment from the university.
Це ли́ст з Ки́єва, з університе́ту, від профе́сора Гончаре́нка.	This is a letter from Kyiv, from the university from Prof. Honcharenko.

Note: Note the constructions: **до О́лі до Ки́єва, від О́лі з Ки́єва**. ('to Ol'a in Kyiv', 'from Ol'a in Kyiv').

* Note that Ukrainian **з** corresponds both to Russian **из** and Russian **с**.

	Where to	*Where*	*Where from*
To, up to	до		від
To, into	до	у	з
Letter to a person	до		від
Letter to a place	до	у	від

(Exercises 9, 10)

III. DECLENSION OF THE NOUN МАТИ

The noun **мáти*** has the stem **мáтер-** except in nominative and vocative. Before the Ø ending of accusative, е is replaced by і (see Lesson 4, p. 63). The declension is that of the that of the c-type feminine nouns.

N. мáти
A. мáтір
G. мáтері
V. мáти!

IV. FUTURE TENSE (NON-COMPOUND IMPERFECTIVE)

We have seen that future may be expressed by the future of the verb **бýти** 'to be' plus infinitive:

Я́ бýду перекладáти.	I will be translating.
Я́ бýду потребувáти словникá.	I will need a dictionary.

We may call this compound future the "**бýду** — form".

Another future formation consists of the infinitive form of an imperfective verb plus a suffix **-м-** and the first conjugation endings (the 3rd sg. of the **ся-** verbs has the ending **-ме + ть + ся: боя́ти-ме-ть-ся** (see Lesson 2, pp. 32). We may call this form "м-form".

---

* In solemn style the archaic N/A form **мáтір** is still used. In religious contexts in reference to the Divine Mother the accusative form **мáтер** may be found, as in Ševčenko's poem "Iržavec'":

> Як покидáли запорóжці велúкий Лýг і мáтір Січ,
> Взялú з собóю Мáтер Бóжу...
>
> When the Zaporožci were leaving the Great Meadow and mother Sič,
> They took with them (the image of) the Mother of God...

Роби́ти: ми́ роби́тимемо, вони́ роби́тимуть
Дя́кувати: він дя́куватиме, ти́ дя́куватимеш
Чита́ти: ви́ чита́тимете, я́ чита́тиму
Диви́тися: диви́тимуся, вона́ диви́тиметься

The two forms, the "бу́ду-form" and the "м-form" are absolutely identical in meaning and in function.* Thus:

Я́ бу́ду переклада́ти = Я́ переклада́тиму
I will be translating.

Я́ бу́ду потребу́вати словника́ = Я́ потребува́тиму словни́ка
I will need a dictionary.

The only verb which does not have the "м-form" is бу́ти. The stress remains as in the infinitive.

(Exercises 11, 12)

ВПРАВИ

I. Finish the sentences according to the model:

Дé **сього́днішня газе́та**? Я́ потребу́ю **сього́днішньої газе́ти**.

(америка́нський журна́л, англі́йський словни́к, росі́йська кни́жка, до́брий папі́р, нова́ ма́па, вчора́шня газе́та, ціка́вий малю́нок, до́брий оліве́ць, тре́тій сті́л)

II. Finish the sentences according to the model:

Це́ його́ **сестра́**. Він боі́ться **своє́ї сестри́**.

(бра́т, ба́тько, ма́ти, профе́сор, пе́рша ле́кція)

III. Change the sentences according to the two models:

О́сь **на́ша фотогра́фія**. (1) Подиви́сь на **на́шу фотогра́фію.**
(2) Я́ не ба́чу **на́шої фотогра́фії**.

(на́ш телефо́н, її́ хло́пець, його́ ді́вчина, і́хній малю́нок, мі́й сті́ле́ць, на́ш телеві́зор, тві́й ли́ст, моя́ ру́чка, на́ше вікно́, її́ ма́ти).

---

* The "м- form" is used less frequently by speakers from the West Ukrainian regions.

IV. Give the response according to the model:

Я́ люблю́ украї́нську істо́рію. — А я́ не люблю́ украї́нської істо́рії.

1. Я́ зна́ю цю́ річ.
2. Ми́ ма́ємо важке́ завда́ння.
3. Я́ пишу́ англі́йський пере́клад.
4. Я́ розумі́ю це́ украї́нське сло́во.
5. Я́ пам'ята́ю це́ прі́звище.
6. Ми́ ро́бимо дома́шнє завда́ння.
7. Я́ друку́ю сві́й літерату́рний пере́клад.
8. Я́ перекладаю англі́йську кни́жку.
9. Я́ чита́ю сього́днішню газе́ту.
10. Ми́ влашто́вуємо літерату́рний ве́чір.

V. Put the bracketed words into the correct form (genitive or accusative).

1. Вона́ дзво́нить до (на́ш бібліоте́кар)
2. Я́ потребу́ю (звича́йний папі́р)
3. Ми́ йдемо́ до (украї́нський студе́нт Гончаре́нко)
4. Ви́ сказа́ли (одна́ ціка́ва річ)
5. Вона́ отри́мала листа́ від (своя́ старе́нька ма́ти)
6. Ми́ гово́римо про (росі́йська істо́рія)
7. Я́ не пам'ята́ю (та́ стара́ фотогра́фія)
8. Це́ фотогра́фія (на́ша студе́нтка Марі́я)
9. Вони́ живу́ть у (ця́ стара́ па́ні)
10. Я́ пита́ю (то́й украї́нський хло́пець)

VI. Finish the sentences using the pronouns **сві́й.**

Model: Це́ його́ бра́т Андрі́й. Ві́н живе́ у **свого́ бра́та Андрі́я.**

(сестра́ Ві́ра, ма́ти, ба́тько, профе́сор; ма́ти, Тетя́на Миха́йлівна; ба́тько, Васи́ль Миха́йлович; профе́сор, па́н Поліщу́к; сестра́, Ле́ся Палі́й; бра́т, Мико́ла Ме́льник).

VII. Supply the missing endings and stresses:

1. Це́ ціка́в..... фі́льм, але́ я́ не ма́ю часу́ диви́тися ц..... ціка́в..... фі́льм.
2. У нього стар..... украї́нськ..... прі́звище, але́ я́ не пам'ята́ю ц..... стар..... украї́нськ.... прі́звища.
3. Я́ чита́ю ї́хн..... англі́йськ.... пере́клад. Як..... пога́н..... пере́клад! Я́ не потребу́ю так..... пога́н..... пере́кладу.
4. О́сь сього́днішн..... газе́та. Я́ чита́ю сього́днішн..... газе́ту, але́ я́ не ба́чу та́м ніч..... ціка́в..... Я́ не хо́чу чита́ти та́к..... нецiка́в..... газе́ти.
5. Це́ п'ят.... ле́кція. Я́ чита́ю п'ят..... ле́кцію, але́ я́ вже́ не пам'ята́ю ні четве́рт.... ле́кції, ні тре́т....., ні дру́г..... Я́ пам'ята́ю ті́льки одн..... пе́рш.....!

6. У ме́не вели́к..... вікн..... Я́ уве́сь де́нь дивлю́ся в мо....... вели́к..... вікно́. Як..... нецікав..... життя́! Я́ не люблю́ сво..... житт.....
7. Це́ адре́са на́ш..... нов..... готе́л....., а це́ адре́са бібліоте́к..... на́ш..... університе́т.....
8. Лі́да телефон.... до сво.... ба́тьк....., а я́ бу́ду телефон..... до мо..... ма́т.....
9. Моя́ сестра́ пи́ше до одн.... росі́йськ.... ді́вчини. Вона́ пи́ше про сво..... любо́в до на́ш..... украї́нськ..... бібліоте́каря Степа́на. Вона́ друку́є його́ пере́клад з росі́йськ..... мо́ви на англі́йськ....
10. Це́й профе́сор дя́кує за ва́ш...... відповід....., але́ він пи́ш...., що він пога́но розуміє по-украї́нс..... Його́ студе́нт І́гор переклад..... ва́ш..... листи́ з украї́н..... мо́в..... на англі́й.....

VIII. Answer the questions according to the model:

Сього́дні вже́ **понеділок**. Коли́ бу́де літерату́рний ве́чір?
- Насту́пного **понеділка.**

(вівто́рок, середа́, четве́р, п'я́тниця, субо́та, неді́ля)

IX. Write the sentences according to the model:

Це́й ли́ст від Іва́на зі шко́ли.

(Степа́н — Кана́да, Га́ля — Аме́рика, Гончаре́нко — Монреа́ль, Ві́ктор — Росі́я, Андрі́й — Нью Йо́рк, Марі́я — Украї́на.)

X. Select the appropriate preposition (**до, для, на, з, за, від, у**).

1. Марі́я живе́ . . . . . ни́х.
2. Я́ це́ роблю́ . . . . . ва́с.
3. Вони́ ду́же дя́кують . . . . . листа́.
4. Степа́н прихо́дить . . . . . на́с.
5. Ми́ живемо́ недале́ко . . . . . музе́ю.
6. На́ш профе́сор . . . . . Кана́ди.
7. Бібліоте́кар іде́ . . . . . бібліоте́ки.
8. Ві́ра ди́виться . . . . . фотогра́фію.
9. Звича́йно, ... ме́не є́ зо́шит.
10. Це́ до́бра відповідь . . . . . моє́ пита́ння.

XI. Give the non-compound imperfective future (the **м**-form).

1. Ми́ бу́демо переклада́ти.
2. Він бу́де до на́с прихо́дити.
3. Студе́нти бу́дуть це́ пита́ти.
4. Ти́ бу́деш боя́тися це́ пита́ти.
5. Я́ бу́ду пам'ята́ти це́й ві́рш.
6. Ви́ бу́дете до́бре жи́ти.
7. Ця́ ді́вчина бу́де тебе́ люби́ти.
8. Це́й хло́пець бу́де тебе́ розумі́ти.

XII. Change the present tense to the non-compound imperfective future (the м-form).

1. Я́ це́ зна́ю.
2. Вони́ пи́шуть листи́.
3. Я́ роблю́ пере́клад.
4. Ви́ ка́жете, що це́ нічо́го.
5. Ми́ потребу́ємо телефо́ну.
6. Вони́ ди́вляться телевізі́йну програ́му.
7. Він іде́ шви́дко.
8. Ти́ хо́чеш це́ ба́чити.
9. Я́ перекладаю́ цю́ кни́жку.
10. Вона́ друку́є мі́й пере́клад.

XIII. Give appropriate answers to the following questions.

1. Про яку́ газе́ту ви́ гово́рите?
2. Яку́ газе́ту ви́ лю́бите чита́ти?
3. Яку́ студе́нтку ви́ зна́єте?
4. До яко́го профе́сора ви́ пи́шете?
5. Яко́го профе́сора ви́ не розумі́єте?
6. Яко́го готе́лю ви́ не лю́бите?
7. Про яку́ ді́вчину ви́ гово́рите?
8. У яко́го студе́нта бу́де ве́чір?
9. Яки́й пере́клад ви́ друку́єте?
10. Яко́го сло́ва ви́ не розумі́єте?

XIV Translate into Ukrainian.

1. I don't have a telephone. How will I call her? — If you can't call her, go to her.
2. I love that poem by Taras Ševčenko where he speaks about his mother.
3. Our professor, pani Hončarenko, has an old map of Canada. I like to look at it. — I think you like to look at pani Hončarenko and not at the map.
4. They love each other and they write letters to each other all the time. — But they see each other on Monday, and on Tuesday, and on Wednesday, Thursday, Friday and Saturday. — Yes, but not on Sunday.
5. There will be a movie next week about Old Russia. I want to see it but I'm afraid that I won't have the time.
6. We have a new Canadian student Marko. He has a sister. Her name is Oksana. — What kind of a name is that? — It's a real Ukrainian name. Marko and Oksana are Ukratnians.
7. Next Saturday there will be a literary evening. The students will read poetry. Ihor will read some poem by Ševčenko, Vita will read a poem by Les'a Ukrainka, Taras will read a poem by Ivan Franko. They all ask me, what I'm going to read. I say that I'm not going to read anything. I don't remember a single poem.
8. My telephone rings all day. My sister calls and talks about her homework, my mother calls and asks about my health, my brother calls and talks about his girl Hal'a. Now you see why I can't read at home.

9. I am reading a Russian newspaper. I don't understand everything. I need a Russian-English dictionary.
10. I think I know today's lesson very well. It's not very hard. Here is our assignment: Exercise 5, to answer questions and to translate.

XV. Read and translate.

1. У нác є дýже дóбра бібліотéка. Я́ люблю тáм читáти, перéкладáти. Я́ прихóджу ввéчері, читáю сьогóднішню газéту, читáю журнáл "Нáше життя́". Для перéкладу я́ потребýю англíйсько-украї́нського словникá. Тýт є й англíйсько-украї́нський і украї́нсько-англíйський. Я́ пишý, дивлю́ся в словни́к, дýмаю. Тýт дóбре перекладáти, алé не мóжна друкувáти. Та цé нічóго, я́ друкувáтиму вдóма.

2. Я́ з Канáди, з Монреáлю. Тепéр я́ живý недалéко від Нью Йóрку. Я́ живý тýт ужé ти́ждень. Я́ хóчу подзвони́ти* до моéї мáтері, алé я́ щé не мáю телефóну. Кáжуть, що телефóн бýде настýпного ти́жня. Сьогóдні прихóдить до мéне оди́н студéнт-канáдець і кáже, щó для мéне є ли́ст. "Я́ дýмаю", — кáже він, — "щó цé ли́ст від твоéї мáтері. Прíзвище тéж Мéльник. Óсь, подиви́ся". Я дивлю́ся: тáк, цé від мáтері. Вонá в мéне** дýже дóбра, усé про мéне дýмає, всé для мéне рóбить.

3. Я́ читáю кни́жку про старý Росíю. Тáм є про Украї́ну, є мáпа Украї́ни, тíльки немáє слóва "Украї́на", а є "Малорóсія".*** Я́ не знáю цьогó слóва, дивлю́ся в словни́к. Але мій словни́к нови́й, тáм цьогó слóва немáє. Я́ йдý до бібліотéки, тáм є стари́й словни́к. Тáм є цé слóво.

XVI. Answer the questions to the reading passages.

(1)

1. Щó читáє студéнт?
2. Щó він пи́ше?
3. Щó він для цьóго потребýє?
4. Чи тáм мóжна друкувáти?

(2)

1. Чи цéй студéнт канáдець?
2. Дé він тепéр живé?
3. Чомý він не дзвóнить до свéї мáтері?
4. Щó дýмає студéнт-канáдець?

---

* подзвонити perfective of дзвони́ти to make a phone call

** в мéне = моя́ (=Моя́ мáти дýже дóбра) See note 6 to Lesson 7.

*** Малорóсія (Little Russia) was the official name of Ukraine under the tsarist regime.

(3)

1. Яка́ та́м ма́па?
2. Яко́го сло́ва він не зна́є?
3. Яко́го словника́ він потребу́є?

XVII. Answer the questions to the dialogues.

"Бібліоте́ка"

1. Яку́ газе́ту ба́чить студе́нт?
2. Яку́ газе́ту він хо́че?
3. Чи бібліоте́ка має́ таку́ газе́ту?
4. Яки́й він ба́чить журна́л?
5. Чому́ він не хо́че чита́ти це́й журна́л?

"Пере́клад"

1. Що́ друку́є па́ні Лі́да?
2. З які́ї мо́ви на яку́ переклада́є Мико́ла?
3. Про що́ ця́ кни́жка?
4. Чи па́ні Лі́да її́ розуміє?
5. Для ко́го вона́ ціка́ва?

"Ли́ст"

1. Про чию́ адре́су пита́є Ві́ра?
2. Чому́ вона́ хо́че ма́ти цю́ адре́су?
3. Від ко́го це́й ли́ст?
4. Де живе́ Сергі́й?
5. Чи він ма́є телефо́н?
6. Що́ Ві́ра ка́же про ма́тір Сергі́я?
7. Чи Степа́н ба́читиме Сергі́я сьо́годні?
8. Що́ він ска́же?

"Фі́льм"

1. Про яки́й фі́льм гово́рить Степа́н?
2. Чому́ Мико́ла не ма́є часу́ дивитися фі́льм?
3. Що́ Ві́ра хо́че роби́ти вве́чері?
4. До ко́го вона́ писа́тиме?

ШОСТА ЛЕКЦІЯ

16 Вірші треба надрукувати
The poems must be published

Dialogue Paticipants:
Микóла - М, Лéся - Л; Mykola - M, Lesja - L

1. Л- Микóло, чи ти́ перекладáтимеш усí вíрші Франкá?	L- Mykola, are you going to translate all of Franko's poems?
2. М- Ні́, не всí, тíльки дéкілька. Я́ тепéр перекладáю шóстий вíрш.	M- No, not at all, only a few. I'm now translating the sixth poem.
3. Л- Ти́ тáк гáрно перекладáєш. Чи ти́ дýмаєш ї́х надрукувáти?	L- You translate so beautifully. Are you thinking of publishing them?
4. М- Не знáю, я́ подýмаю. Побáчимо, щó скáже профéсор Гончарéнко, коли́ ї́х прочитáє.	M- I don't know, I'll think about it. We'll see what Prof. Hončarenko will say when he reads them.
5. Л- Я́ пéвна, що він не тíльки скáже, що вони́ дóбрі, алé й допомóже ї́х надрукувáти.	L- I'm sure he will not only say that they are good, but will also help with their publishing.
6. М- Побáчимо.	M- We'll see.

17 Треба гарно попросити
One must ask nicely

Dialogue Paticipants:
Вíра - В, Степáн - С; Vira - V, Stepan - S

1. С- Вíро, до кóго ти́ дзвóниш?	S- Vira, whom are you calling?
2. В- До Гáлі. А щó?	V- Halja. Why?
3. С- Я́ хóчу подзвони́ти до могó товáриша.	S- I want to call a friend of mine.
4. В- Дóбре, я́ тíльки спитáю Гáлю, чи вонá при́йде до нáс у субóту.	V- O.K. I'll just ask Halja if she will come to our place on Saturday.
5. С- Я́ твою́ Гáлю дóбре знáю. Вонá не захóче і відповíсть, щó не мáє чáсу.	S- I know Halja well. She won't feel like coming and will answer that she has no time.
6. В- Побáчиш, що ні. Трéба тíльки гáрно попроси́ти. Óсь диви́сь: Гáлю! Прихóдь, сердéнько, до нáс у цю́ субóту. Дýже тебé прошý! При́йдеш? Чудóво!... Бáчиш?	V- You'll see that she won't. One should just ask nicely. Here, watch: Halja, darling, do come to our place this Saturday. Please do. Will you come? Wonderful!... See?
7. С- Бáчу. Щó ж я́ мáю казáти?	S- I see. What can I say?
8. В- Мáєш подя́кувати за наýку.	V- You have to thank me for the lesson.
9. С- Дя́кую.	S- Thank you.

18 У нас завтра іспит
We have an exam tomorrow

Dialogue Paticipants:
Богда́н - Б, Ма́рта - М; Bohdan - B, Marta - M

1.	М- Богда́не, куди́ ти́ йде́ш?	M- Bohdan, where are you going?
2.	Б- До бібліоте́ки. А ти́ куди́?	B- I'm going to the library. And you?
3.	М- Я́ до гурто́житку. Кра́ще поспіша́й, бо за́раз пі́де до́щ.	M- I'm going to the dorm. Better hurry up, because it's going to rain now.
4.	Б- Це́ нічо́го, я́ не бо́юся дощу́. У на́с за́втра і́спит, і я́ хо́чу взя́ти одну́ кни́жку про Шевче́нка.	B- It's all right, I'm not afraid of rain. We have an exam tomorrow and I want to take out a book about Ševčenko.
5.	М- Ма́буть, "Життя́ Тара́са Григо́ровича Шевче́нка" профе́сора Палія́?	M- Probably "Life of Taras Hryhorovyč Ševčenko" by Professor Palij.
6.	Б- Та́к. Чи ти́ її́ взяла́?	B- That's right. Did you take it out?
7.	М- Ні́, я́ хоті́ла взя́ти, але́ її́ не мо́жна бра́ти додо́му.	M- No, I wanted to, but they won't let you take it out (home).
8.	Б- Шкода́. Ну́, то я́ піду́ і та́м прочита́ю.	B- Too bad. In that case I will go and read it there.

#19 Коли полюбиш
When you fall in love

Dialogue Paticipants:
Ві́ра - В, Га́ля - Г; Vira - V, Halja - H

1.	В- Га́лю, що́ ти́ ро́биш?	V- Halja, what are you doing?
2.	Г- Дома́шнє завда́ння. А ти́? Вже зроби́ла?	H- Homework. And you? Are you done yet?
3.	В- Ще ні́. Ще́ є́ до́сить часу́. На́м ті́льки тре́ба написа́ти шо́сту впра́ву і відпові́сти на пита́ння. А що́ ти́ роби́тимеш уве́чері?	V- Not yet. There is still plenty of time. We only have to write exercise six and to answer the questions. And what will you be doing tonight?
4.	Г- Я́ хо́чу піти́ на фі́льм "Коли́ полю́биш".	H- I want to go and see the movie "When you fall in love".
5.	В- А́, я́ зна́ю це́й фі́льм, і як това́ришка, скажу́: він не для те́бе.	V- Oh yes, I know that movie, and as a friend I'll say this: it's not for you.
6.	Г- Чому́ ти́ та́к ду́маєш? Бої́шся, що я́ його́ не зрозумі́ю?	H- Why do you think so? Are you afraid that I won't understand it?
7.	В- Ні́, не тому́, а тому́, що та́м таке́ гово́рять!...	V- No, it's not that, it's because they say such things there.
8.	Г- Це́ нічо́го, ка́жуть, що це́й фі́льм ціка́вий.	H- It's all right, they say the movie is interesting.
9.	В- Ну́ диви́ся, якщо́ хо́чеш.	V- Well, go ahead, if you insist.

СЛОВНИК

бра́ти, беру́ть I*	to take
взя́ти, ві́зьмуть P	
га́рний	nice, fine, pretty
гурто́житок, -тку (m)	dormitory
де́кілька	some, a few
до́брі (pl.)	good
додо́му	home, homeward
допомага́ти, допомага́ють, I	to help
допомогти́, допомо́жуть P	
до́сить (+ G)	enough
до́щ, -у́ (m)	rain
і́спит, -у (m)	examination
куди́	where (w. to)
ма́буть and мабу́ть	probably
нау́ка (f)	lesson, science
пе́вний (+G)	sure, certain (of)
пе́вно	certainly, surely, probably
поспіша́ти, поспіша́ють I	to hurry
поспіши́ти, поспіша́ть P	
поспішай!	hurry!
серде́нько (n)	darling ("little heart")
това́риш (m)	friend, comrade (m)
това́ришка (f)	friend, comrade (f)
тому́	why, the reason
тому́ що	because
тре́ба	it is necessary, one must, has to
чудо́во, чудо́вий	wonderful, wonderful (adj)
шкода́	too bad, sorry
шо́стий	sixth
ще	still

IDIOMS

іде́ до́щ/пі́де до́щ	it's raining, it will rain
ще ні	not yet

* I = imperfective aspect, P = perfective aspect (see grammar notes to this lesson). Aspects of the verbs found in lessons 1–4 are listed on pp. 91–92.

SUPPLEMENT

іспит з (+ G)	exam in
іспит з украї́нської мо́ви	a Ukrainian Language exam
склада́ти іспит (склада́ти, склада́ють I)	to take an exam
скла́сти іспит (скла́сти, складу́ть P)	to pass an exam
оці́нка	grade
товари́ство	company, society, association

List of all the verbs encountered so far in both aspects

IMPERFECTIVE

ба́чити, ба́чать	to see
боя́тися, боя́ться	to be afraid
бра́ти, беру́ть	to take
вибача́ти, вибача́ють	to excuse, to forgive
виправля́ти, виправля́ють	to correct
відповіда́ти, відповіда́ють	to answer
влашто́вувати, влаштову́ють	to arrange
говори́ти, гово́рять	to speak, to talk
дзвони́ти, дзво́нять	to phone
дістава́ти, дістаю́ть	to get
диви́тися, ди́вляться	to look
допомага́ти, допомага́ють	to help
друкува́ти, друку́ють	to type, to print
ду́мати, ду́мають	to think
дя́кувати, дя́кують	to thank
жи́ти, живу́ть	to live
запи́тувати, запи́тують	to ask
зва́ти, звуть	to call, to name
знайо́митися, знайо́мляться	to become acquainted
зна́ти, зна́ють	to know (no perfective)
іти́, іду́ть	to go; to walk
каза́ти, ка́жуть	to say
коха́ти, коха́ють	to love
люби́ти, лю́блять	to love
ма́ти, ма́ють	to have (no perfective)
отри́мувати, отри́мують	to receive
пам'ята́ти, пам'ята́ють	to remember
переклада́ти, переклада́ють	to translate
писа́ти, пи́шуть	to write
питати, пита́ють	to ask
помиля́тися, помиля́ються	to err, to make a mistake
поспіша́ти, поспішають	to hurry

потребува́ти, потребу́ють	to need (no perfective)
почува́ти себе́, почува́ють себе́	to feel (no perfective)
прихо́дити, прихо́дять	to come
проси́ти, про́сять	to ask (a favor)
повто́рювати, повто́рюють повторя́ти, повторя́ють	to repeat
роби́ти, ро́блять	to do, to make
розумі́ти, розумі́ють	to understand
склада́ти, склада́ють (іспит)	to take (an exam)
телефону́вати, телефону́ють	to call (by phone)
турбува́ти, турбу́ють	to trouble, to disturb
хоті́ти, хо́чуть	to want
чита́ти, чита́ють	to read

PERFECTIVE

поба́чити, поба́чать	to catch sight of
побоя́тися, побоя́ться	to be afraid
узя́ти, візьму́ть	to take
ви́бачити, ви́бачать	to excuse, to forgive
ви́правити, ви́правляти	to correct
відпові́сти, відповідя́ть	to answer
влаштува́ти, влашту́ють	to arrange
поговори́ти, погово́рять	to have a talk
подзвони́ти, подзво́нять	to give a call
діста́ти, діста́нуть	to get, to obtain
подиви́тися, поди́вляться	to take a look
допомогти́, допоможуть	to help
надрукува́ти, надруку́ють	to type, to print
поду́мати, поду́мають	to think, to give a thought
подя́кувати, подя́кують	to thank
пожи́ти, поживу́ть	to live for a while
назва́ти, назву́ть	to name, to call
познайо́митися, познайо́мляться	to get acquainted
піти́, пі́дуть	to go to, to begin walking
сказа́ти, ска́жуть	to say, to tell
покоха́ти, покоха́ють	to fall in love
полюби́ти, полю́блять	to fall in love
запам'ята́ти, запам'ята́ють	to remember, to memorize
перекла́сти, перекладу́ть	to translate
написа́ти, напи́шуть	to write
отри́мати, отри́мають	to receive
поспіши́ти, поспіша́ть	to hurry
спита́ти, спита́ють запита́ти, запита́ють	to ask
помили́тися, поми́ляться	to err, to make a mistake
прийти́, при́йдуть	to come
попроси́ти, попро́сять	to ask (a favor)

повтори́ти, повто́рять	to repeat
зроби́ти, зро́блять	to do, to make
зрозумі́ти, зрозумі́ють	to understand
скла́сти, складу́ть	to pass (an exam)
потурбува́ти, потурбу́ють	to trouble, to disturb
потелефонува́ти, потелефону́ють	to phone
захоті́ти, захо́чуть	to want, to get a desire
прочита́ти, почита́ють	to read through

EXPLANATORY NOTES

1. The verb **влашто́вувати (влаштува́ти)** means 'to arrange' in various senses:

Студе́нти влашто́вують ве́чір.	The students are arranging a party.
Вона́ влашту́є його́ в бібліоте́ку.	She'll get him a job at the library. (She'll arrange that he gets a job at the library)

2. The words **това́риш** and **това́ришка** (abbreviation **тов.**) besides the meaning 'friend', 'companion' have a second meaning 'comrade' and were used in reference to members of the communist party.

3. The diminutive **серде́нько** (lit. 'little heart') is used as a form of endearment in reference to both men and women. It is frequently heard in folk songs.

4. The adverb **куди́** 'where' (where to) is used with verbs implying some direction, such as verbs of motion, 'looking at', 'writing to' or 'calling a place' etc. For example:

Куди́ ти́ йде́ш? Куди́ ти́ ди́вишся? Куди́ ти́ дзво́ниш?
Where are you going? Where are you looking? Where are you calling?

NOTES ON GRAMMAR

I. FURTHER OBSERVATIONS ON VERB CONJUGATION

1. Substitutive softening.

II conjugation verbs whose present tense 3rd plural stems are soft (spelled with **-ять**) undergo a stem-final consonant alternation in the first person singular. This alternation is called substitutive softening:

Stem-final consonant:	т	д	с	з	ст	зд
is replaced by:	ч	дж	ш	ж	щ	ждж

For example:

(проси́ти): про́сять — **прошу́** — про́сиш, про́сить, про́симо, про́сите
(прихо́дити): прихо́дять — **прихо́джу** — прихо́диш, прихо́дить, прихо́димо

Other examples: плати́ти (to pay) пла́тять — **плачу́** — пла́тиш, пла́тить ...
носи́ти (to carry) но́сять — **ношу́** — но́сиш, но́симо...
вози́ти (to drive) во́зять — **вожу́** — во́зиш, во́зить...
чи́стити (to clean) чи́стять — **чи́щу** — чи́стить, чи́стите...
і́здити (to ride) і́здять — **і́жджу** — і́здиш, і́здить...

2. Spelling rules. The ending of the 1st person singular is normally spelled **-у** if the 3rd plural is **-уть** or **-ать**, and **-ю** if the 3rd plural is **-ють** or **-ять**. However, when the stem of the 1st singular ends in **ж, ч,** ш or щ as a result of substitutive softening, then the spelling convention requires that -у be written instead:*

про́сять — прошу́ прихо́дять — прихо́джу

3. *Accentuation.*

Accentuation of the present (and future perfective) follows one of three patterns:

(1) The stress is constant, remaining (a) on the stem, or (b) on the last syllable of the stem-final syllable in all other persons.

For example:

	Type I *Constant stress*		*Type II* *Mobile stress*	
Singular	(a) stem	(b) ending		
1st	ба́чу	беру́	кажу́	говорю́
2nd	ба́чиш	бере́ш	ка́жеш	годо́риш
3rd	ба́чить	бере́	ка́же	гово́рить
Plural				
1st	ба́чимо	беремо́	ка́жемо	гово́римо
2nd	ба́чите	берете́	ка́жете	гово́рите
3rd	ба́чать	беру́ть	ка́жуть	гово́рять

ACCENTUATION RULE

All forms of the present tense follow the accent of the 3rd person plural (type I, either a or b) unless the stress in the 3rd plural is one syllable closer to the beginning of the word than in the infinitive, in which case we have type II. Thus:

	Type I (consonant Stress)			*Type II (Mobile Stress)*		
(a)	ба́чи-ти	ба́ч-ать	ба́чу	говори́-ти	гово́р-ять	говор-ю́
	дя́кува-ти	дя́ку-ють	дя́ку-ю	сказа́-ти	ска́ж-уть	скаж-у́
(b)	жи́-ти	жив-у́ть	жив-у́			

---

* Remember that by the general spelling rule the letters **ю** and **я** are not permitted after щ or single **ж, ч,** ш; they do occur in noun-stems with **жж,** шш and **чч**. (see The Sound System p. xxix).

4. Exceptions*.

(a) Verbs with infinitive in stressed **-ува́ти / -юва́ти** always have 3rd plural in **-у́ють / -ю́ють** i.e. one syllable closer to the beginning of the word than in the infinitive, yet they have a fixed stress throughout the present, including 1st person singular. Thus this group constitutes an important exception to the rule for mobile stress:

влаштува́ти: влашту́ють, влашту́ю, влашту́єш, влашту́є
друкува́ти: друку́ють, друку́ю, друку́єш, друку́є
потребува́ти: потребу́ють, потребу́ю, потребу́єш, потребу́є

(b) Two important verbs have fixed stem-stress throughout the present **хоті́ти** and **могти́** 'to be able' (see Lesson 7):

хо́чу, хо́чеш, хо́чуть, мо́жу, мо́жеш, мо́жуть.

(c) The verb **проси́ти** has both the expected **прошу́** and the anomalous **про́шу** (probably a Polish influence) with a difference in meaning (the 1st means "I beg you", the 2nd means "please" or "you are welcome").

II. PAST TENSE

1. The past tense forms express number — singular and plural — and gender (in the singular). They do not express person.

я́ пита́ла	I was asking. (female speaking)
ти́ розумі́ла	You understood. (female being addressed)
ми́ відповіда́ли	We were answering.
каза́ли	They / we / you / "people" were saying.

2. The past tense is formed by adding past-tense suffixes to the infinitive stem:**

-в	for masculine singular
-ло	for neuter singular
-ла	for feminine singular
-ли	for all plurals

Thus:

пита́-ти	пита́в	пита́ло	пита́ла	пита́ли
хоті́-ти	хоті́в	хоті́ло	хоті́ла	хоті́ли
сказа́-ти	сказа́в	сказа́ло	сказа́ла	сказа́ли
боя́тися	боя́вся	боя́лося	боя́лася	боя́лися.

* From now on only infinitives and 3 rd. pl. will be given in the vocabularies.

** The position of the stress is treated in section IV.

Note 1. The infinitive stem of most verbs ends in a vowel, but there are exceptions. Certain verbs whose present-stems end in **-т** or **-д** have infinitives in **-сти;** the т or д has been replaced by **с** before the infinitive ending **-ти** past tense, the т or д is lost before the past-endings. Thus:

Present stem	*Infinitive*	*Past*
переклад-у́ть	перекла́сти	перекла́в, перекла́ла
відповід-я́ть	відповісти́	відповів, відповіла́

Note 2. The particle **-ся** is added after the past-tense suffixes, e.g. **диви́вся, диви́лася, диви́лися.**

Note 3. Recall that the word-final **в** in the masculine is pronounced as a glide w (see The Sound System, p. xxvii).

Note 4. Note that the past tense may be translated into English in several ways:

я́ писа́ла	I wrote, I have written, I was writing I used to write, I have been writing

Note 5. The past tense of the verb (п)іти is (п)ішо́в, (п)ішла́, (п)ішло́, (п)ішли́, of допомогти́ — допомі́г, допомогла́, -ло́, -ли́ (see Lesson 4 on o/i alternation)

(Exercises 3, 5)

III. STRESS IN THE PAST TENSE

1. The past tense accent is normally that of the infinitive.

роби́ти -	роби́в,	роби́ла,	роби́ли
подиви́тися-	подиви́вся,	подиви́лася,	подиви́лися
пам'ята́ти -	пам'ята́в,	пам'ята́ла,	пам'ята́ли

In a few verbs, like **бу́ти** and **жи́ти** (usually with monosyllabic roots) the past endings are stressed:

бу́ти -	бу́в,	була́,	було́,	були́
жи́ти -	жи́в,	жила́,	жило́,	жили́

2. The infinitive of the verb 'to answer' admits two different stresses **відпові́сти** and **відповісти́**. In the past, the stress is always on the ending:

відпові́сти: відпові́в, відповіла́, відповіли́

Note. The end stress in the infinitive and the past tense of this verb is recommended by grammars and dictionaries. In actual speech the stem stress is used by most speakers.

3. The verb узя́ти has mobile stress in the present and end-stress in the past:

узя́ти: візьму́, ві́зьмеш, ві́зьме, ві́зьмемо, ві́зьмете, ві́зьмуть
узя́в, узяла́, узяли́

The initial у- of the infinitive and past tense becomes в- (pronounced w) when a vowel precedes:

він узя́в	v'in uz'aw
хто́ взя́в?	xto wz' aw

cf. similar u — w alterations in Ми́ всі студе́нти (ws'i), see The Sound System, p. xxviii but Я вас усе́ пита́ю (use), Lesson 2, p. 00.

IV. ASPECTS OF THE VERB

Every Ukrainian verb necessarily belongs to one of two classes called aspects: perfective and imperfective. This is a question of meaning and grammatical function. The perfective aspect denotes a concrete single action with a specific "marked" meaning of completion. The imperfecrive aspect is "unmarked": this means that it does not make a specific reference to completion of an act but presents it as a process in its duration at a given moment or as a habitual occurence. Most verbs come in aspectual pairs.

1. The perfective aspect: meaning and function. In most cases the perfective aspect refers to the result* or the desired end of an action:

Я́ прочита́в це́й журна́л.
I read this magazine. (= read it all, read it through)

Я́ за́втра напишу́ до нього́ листа́.
I will write him a letter tomorrow. (= will definitely finish it)

Вона́ надрукува́ла листа́.
She typed a letter. (= finished typing)

The idea of completion expressed in the perfective verb is found also in references to a definite start of a single action or to an instantaneous action:

Він пішо́в до мі́ста.	He went to town. (= set our for)
Вона́ захоті́ла чита́ти.	She suddenly felt like reading.
Він на не́ї подиви́вся.	He took a look at her.
Він ї́ї поба́чив.	He (suddenly) saw her.

Many perfectives (usually with the prefix по-) carry the idea of completion of an action of short duration:

Він почита́в журна́л і пішо́в додо́му.	He read a magazine for a while and went home. (= finished reading, but did not read the whole magazine)

* Many linguists consider this the only true perfective.

Perfective verbs have no present tense. Their conjugation, which is formally identical with the present tense conjugation of the imperfective verbs, refers to future. We shall call it perfective future.

прочита́ти: прочита́ю 'I will read', прочита́ємо 'We will read'
надрукува́ти: надруку́ють 'They will type', надруку́єш 'You will type'

2. The imperfective aspect: meaning and function. The idea of duration may be expressed by an imperfective in any tense, cf.:

Я́ пишу́ листа́.	I am writing a letter.
Я́ писа́ла листи́.	I wrote letters (= used to write/ was writing)
Я́ писа́тиму (бу́ду писа́ти) листи́.	I will be writing letters.

In its habitual function the imperfective is often reinforced by various adverbs and phrases expressing frequency.

Ввечері він **звича́йно** ди́виться яку́сь програ́му.
He usually watches some TV program in the evening.

Вдо́ма вона́ **всé** диви́лася яку́сь програ́му.
At home she always watched some TV program.

Насту́пного ти́жня вони́ **з ра́нку до ве́чора** диви́тимуться телеві́зор.
Next week they are going to watch TV from morning till evening.

Another example of use of the imperfective is found in generalized statements of "timeless" or permanent validity:

Всі зна́ють, що мо́жна ду́мати одне́, а говори́ти і́нше.
Everybody knows that one can think one thing and say another.

Чита́ти ціка́во.
It is fun to read.

In many cases a Ukrainian may choose not to specify the totality or completion of the act and will use an imperfective. For example:

Ми́ вже́ ба́чили це́й фі́льм.	We have already seen this film.
Я́ до ни́х писа́в, але́ вони́ не відпові́ли.	I wrote to them but they didn't answer.
Вона́ вже́ дзвони́ла до сестри́.	She already called her sister.
Я́ вже про це́ ду́мала.	I already thought about it.
Чи ти́ вже́ пита́в проф. Гончаре́нка, де́ ця́ ма́па?	Did you ask Prof. Hončarenko where that map is?
Я́ тебе́ проси́ла в понеді́лок зроби́ти це́ для ме́не.	I asked you on Monday to do it for me.

In each case the action is single and concrete. By choosing the imperfective instead of perfective (a possibility in all but the 1st of the examples above) the speaker omits specific reference to completion in favor of a general statement of the fact that an action did indeed take place. It is not the verbal aspect which tells us that it was a single action, but the whole context. We might label this type of imperfective "factual".

Let us compare the following sentences* where the verbs appear in different aspects.

Perfective	*Imperfective*
Я́ прочита́в газе́ту. (= read through) (completion)	Я́ чита́в газе́ту. (= was reading) (process)
Я́ подиви́вся на не́ї. (= took a look) (single instant)	Я́ диви́вся на не́ї. (kept looking) (process)
Я́ напишу́ листи́. (= will write) (completion)	Я́ писа́тиму листи́. (=will write) (process — at one time/habitual)
Ві́н допомо́же. (will help) (single occurrence)	Ві́н допомага́тиме. (= will be helping) (process — at one time/habitual)
Вона́ діста́не від ни́х папі́р. (= will get — single occurrence)	Вона́ дістава́тиме від ни́х папі́р. (= will be getting; habitual)
Вона́ його́ полюби́ла. (= fell in love) (beginning)	Вона́ його́ люби́ла. (= loved; used to love) (state — no ref. to beginning or end)
Ми́ її́ про це́ спита́ли. (= asked) (completion)	Ми́ її́ про це́ пита́ли. (= kept asking or asked) (factual/process)
Чи мо́жна взя́ти це́й папі́р? (= take) (single occurrence)	Чи мо́жна бра́ти це́й папі́р? (= take) (generalized)
Тре́ба відпові́сти на цьо́го листа́. (concrete)	Тре́ба відповіда́ти го́лосно. (generalized)

We may sum up the basic distinctions between the aspects as follows:

Perfective	*Imperfective*
Specific (marked)	Non-specific (unmarked)
Tenses: past and future	Tenses: past, present, future
Denotes: a) completed action	Denotes: a) action in the process of unfoldment
b) one time action	b) habitual, repeated action
c) limited action	c) "factual" action; truism

3. Basic formal distinctions between the aspects.

The verbs of aspect-pairs are normally closely related in form. The usual types of relationship are:

---

* Since these sentences are given out of context the particular shades of meaning could receive other interpretation inherent in the "unmarked" nature of the imperfective verbs.

Type A. The imperfective has no prefix while the perfective does have a prefix:*

роби́ти,	ро́блять	зроби́ти,	зро́блять
ба́чити,	ба́чать	поба́чити,	поба́чать
пита́ти,	пита́ють	спита́ти,	спита́ють

Type B. The imperfective has a different suffix than perfective:

вибача́ти,	вибача́ють	ви́бачити,	ви́бачать
влашто́вувати,	влашто́вують	влаштува́ти,	влашту́ють

It is not uncommon for two imperfectives, synonymous in meaning but with different suffixes, to appear in standard Ukrainian, cf:

Imperfective		*Perfective*
повто́рювати,	повто́рюють	повтори́ти
повторя́ти,	повторя́ють	

Two synonymous perfectives also occur but less frequently.

Type C. The imperfective and perfective stems are different. cf.:

бра́ти	беру́ть	узя́ти	ві́зьмуть

Note 1: Addition of a prefix to an imperfective verb besides changing the aspect almost always results in some change in meaning as well. cf.:

ба́чити	'to see'	поба́чити	'to catch sight of'
хоті́ти	'to want'	захоті́ти	'to get a desire'

Addition of the prefix по- often results in changing the meaning to one with a time limitation. cf.:

жи́ти	'to live'	пожи́ти	'to live/reside s. where for a while'
чита́ти	'to read'	почита́ти	'to read for a while'

Strictly speaking, all such perfectives should not be considered aspectual pairs to the non-prefixed imperfectives. However, for practical purposes we shall list them together, except the temporal **по-** perfectives. These will not be listed at all unless they occur in the dialogues. However, it will be assumed that the student is familiar with their formation and will recognize them in the drills.

Note 2: A fairly large group of verbs have only the imperfective aspect due to their meanings which stress the continuing nature of the action or state they express, e.g.:

боя́тися, зна́ти, ма́ти, потребува́ти, почува́ти себе́, пам'ята́ти

---

* The most common prefixes in this function are **з (с), по-, за-, вид-, ви-, у (в)-.**

All such verbs will be marked accordingly in the vocabularies.

In the vocabularies, verbs will be given in both aspects, the imperfective (marked 'I' and the perfective (marked P), wherever possible.

4. Conjugation of perfective verbs. The perfective future has the same conjugation pattern as the imperfective present, following either 1st or 2nd conjugation, and adhering to the same spelling and phonetic rules (see section I of this lesson).

	1st conjugation		*2nd conjugation*	
Sg.				
1st	влаштýю	поживý	побáчу	подзвоню́
2nd	влаштýєш	поживéш	побáчиш	подзвóниш
3rd	влаштýє	поживé	побáчить	подзвóнить
Pl.				
1st	влаштýємо	поживемó	побáчимо	подзвóнимо
2nd	влаштýєте	поживетé	побáчите	подзвóните
3rd	влаштýють	поживýть	побáчать	подзвóнять

Note: The verb **відповíсти** belongs to a very small group of verbs with a special conjugation. Its forms are:

відповíм, відповісú, відповíсть, відповімó, відповістé, відповідя́ть

Some Ukrainians avoid the 3rd plural form, substituing instead the phrase **дадýть вíдповідь** 'they will give an answer'.

(Exercises 1, 2, 4, 6, 8)

ВПРАВИ*

I. Change the infinitives to future perfective.

Model: Трéба цé **сказáти. Я́ скажý.**

1. Трéба допомогтú. — Я́ . . . . .
2. Трéба взя́ти словнúк. — Тú . . . . .
3. Трéба цé запам'ятáти.. — Мú . . . . .
4. Трéба гáрно попросúти. — Вíн . . . . .
5. Трéба цé надрукувáти. — Вонá . . . . .

* In most of these exercises stress marks are left out on purpose. The student should supply them.

6. Тре́ба до не́ї подзвони́ти. — Я́ . . . . .
7. Тре́ба на це́ відповісти. — Ви́ . . . . .
8. Тре́ба його́ влаштува́ти. — Вони́ . . . . .
9. Тре́ба це́ діста́ти. — Я́ . . . . .
10. Тре́ба поду́мати. — Ми́ . . . . .

II. Change the verbs to the imperfective aspect as in the model:

Чи мо́жна **поговори́ти**? Чи можна **говори́ти**?

(подиви́тися, це́ взя́ти, допомогти́, та́к сказа́ти, це́ перекла́сти, це́ влаштува́ти, відповісти, спита́ти, прийти́, повтори́ти)

III. Change present to past.

1. Вона́ не любить цього гуртожитку.
2. Він цього не розуміє.
3. Вони́ не бояться іспиту.
4. Вона́ живе у брата.
5. Я́ цього не кажу.
6. Ми́ за це не відповідаємо.
7. Вона́ не хоче дивитися на цей малюнок.
8. Він читає сьогоднішню газету.
9. Вони́ перекладають вірші Лесі Українки.
10. Ти не маєш справжнього товариша.
11. Хто́ до нього телефонує?

IV. Answer the questions according to the model:

Хто́ хо́че це́ **надрукува́ти**? Я́ це́ **надруку́ю.**

(допомогти́, це перекла́сти, це прочита́ти, це повтори́ти, це зроби́ти, це сказа́ти, це взя́ти, подиви́тися, спита́ти)

V. Change future to past.

Model: Ви́ це́ **надруку́єте?** Ви́ це **надрукува́ли?**

1. Ви́ це́ напишете?
2. Ти́ його́ попросиш?
3. Вони́ дістануть її фотографію?
4. Вони́ захочуть піти до музею?
5. Вони́ це зрозуміють?
6. Ви́ про це́ подумаєте?
7. Ви́ за це́ подякуєте?
8. Вони́ подзвонять додо́му?
9. Вони́ влаштують ве́чір?
10. Вони́ візьмуть вели́ку валізку?

VI. Select the appropriate aspect. In cases where either aspect is possible, write in both.

1. Я́ ____________________ його́ сього́дні вве́чері, коли́ бу́ду в них.
   ба́чити/поба́чити
2. Він уве́сь ча́с ____________________ це́ сло́во.
   повтори́ти/повто́рювати
3. Хто́ ______________ мі́й словни́к?
   бра́ти/взя́ти
4. Куди́ ви́ ______________ насту́пного ти́жня?
   іти́/піти́
5. Я́ ________________ говори́ти про це́, але́ ви́ не ма́єте часу́.
   хоті́ти/схоті́ти
6. Чи ви́ до́бре __________________, коли́ він говори́в?
   розумі́ти/зрозумі́ти
7. Я́ до ва́с __________________ в четве́р.
   дзвони́ти/подзвони́ти
8. Чому́ він до те́бе не ________________________?
   говори́ти/поговори́ти
9. Я́ хо́чу ______________________ ще оди́н ли́ст.
   писа́ти/написа́ти
10. Вона́ ____________________ на нього один раз і __________________ .
    диви́тися/подиви́тися кохáти/покоха́ти

VII. Put the accent marks over all the verbs. Translate. Put the verbs in the past tense and provide the accent marks.

1. Ми́ беремо це́й журна́л.
2. Чи ви́ та́м живете?
3. Я́ те́ж це́ кажу.
4. Чого́ ви́ боїтеся?
5. Куди́ вона́ дзвонить?
6. Що́ вони́ відповідають?
7. Вони́ люблять допомагати.
8. Я́ матиму кімна́ту.
9. Де́ ви́ це́ дістаєте?
10. Коли́ вони́ це́ перекладуть?
11. Коли́ ви́ цього потребуватимете?
12. Шкода́, що́ він не пам'ятає її́ імени.
13. Він пе́вний, що ти́ це́ влаштуєш.
14. Коли́ вони́ приходять?
15. Коли́ вже́ вони́ підуть додо́му?
16. Він усе́ вибачає.
17. Я́ це́ зроблю для ва́с.
18. Вони́ люблять одне́ о́дного.
19. Чого́ вони́ потребують?
20. Що́ ви́ відповісте?
21. Хто там телефонує?

VIII. Give the correct form of the verbs.

1. Це́ га́рний журна́л. Чи ту́т (print) ві́рші?
2. Я́ ще́ не зна́ю. Я́ хо́чу (think).
3. Я́ не розумі́ю, що́ вони́ (say).
4. Я́ ду́маю, що та́м (ring) телефо́н.
5. Вони́ тепе́р та́м (live).
6. Я́ (come) сього́дні вве́чері.
7. Я́ (ask) її прийти́, а вона́ не хо́че.
8. Чого́ ти́ (afraid)?
9. На кого́ ви́ (look)?
10. Кого́ вона́ (fall in love)?

IX. Say what you are asked in the following requests.

1. Скажі́ть, хто́ це́ написа́в.
2. Скажі́ть, куди́ ви́ йдете́.
3. Скажі́ть, яка це́ ле́кція.
4. Скажі́ть, до ко́го ви́ дзво́ните.
5. Скажі́ть, що́ тре́ба зроби́ти.
6. Скажі́ть, що́ ви́ ду́маєте.
7. Скажі́ть, чи ви́ перекла́ли всі́ ві́рші.
8. Скажі́ть, що ви́ лю́бите чита́ти.
9. Скажі́ть, що́ ви́ пи́шете.
10. Скажі́ть, до ко́го ви́ пи́шете листа́.

X. Supply the appropriate vocabulary.

1. Учо́ра я́ . . . . . . ціка́вий фі́льм. Ві́н бу́в про . . . . . Я́ його́ . . . . . ті́льки . . . . . ра́з, а Га́ля його́ . . . . вже́ шо́стий ра́з. Я́ пе́вний, що вона́ . . . . . . та́м не зрозумі́ла і тому́ ввесь ча́с . . . . мене́, що́ це́ таке́.
2. Га́ля ду́же . . . . . ді́вчина. Вона́ ма́є до́бру . . . . . . О́лю. О́ля . . . . . студе́нтка, вона́ знає . . . . ві́рші Шевче́нка, ... і Франка́. За́втра у них бу́де і́спит. О́ля ду́же . . . . . цього́ . . . . . , але́ Га́ля пе́вна, що О́ля його́ . . . . . . ду́же до́бре.

XI. Answer the questions.

1. Чи ви́ вже́ зроби́ли ва́ше завда́ння?
2. На яки́й фі́льм ви́ йдете́?
3. Чи ви́ маєте на це́ ча́с?
4. Чи́ ви́ хочете допомогти́ влаштува́ти літературний вечі́р?
5. Чи́ ви́ при́йдете до на́с у наступну субо́ту?
6. Яки́й це́ журна́л ви́ чита́єте?
7. За що́ ти́ дя́куєш?
8. Що́ ти́ на це́ ска́жеш?
9. Хто́ влашту́є насту́пний вечі́р?
10. Хто́ це́ перекла́в?

XII. Translate into Ukrainian.

1. Next week I am going to help translate this poem from English into Ukrainian.
2. I think she knows lesson six very well but she says that she doesn't remember a single word.
3. What did you say? I'm sorry, I didn't understand what you said.
4. May I ask where you got this book?
5. Are you the friend of Mykola Mel'nyk?
6. I don't know Les'a Palij. Is she a friend of Ol'a Prokopovyč?
7. What will you say when they ask us to come to their place Sunday evening?
8. I remembered a beautiful hotel there. I wanted to live there. But you say it's no longer there. What a pity!
9. - One must forgive
   - Who says so?
   - An old book. It's a wonderful book. I'm sure you have read it.
   - Who, me? I never read anything.
   - Don't say that, I know you do. (= 'I know that you read')
10. Would you please look out the window. Who is that talking so loud?

XIII. Read and translate.

1. Сього́дні я́ вдо́ма. Моя́ това́ришка друку́є і ка́же, що в не́ї вже́ нема́ папе́ру. Я́ йду́ діста́ти папе́ру. Я́ пе́вна, що́ мі́й това́риш ма́є папі́р і допомо́же.
2. Мі́й това́риш Сергі́й пи́ше ві́рші. Ві́н написа́в уже́ де́кілька. Учо́ра ві́н подзвони́в до ме́не і сказа́в, що ві́рш чудо́вий і його́ тре́ба надрукува́ти. Я́ спита́в, чи профе́сор Гончаре́нко вже́ його́ ба́чив. Сергі́й відпові́в, що ні. Ві́н бої́ться, що профе́сор Гончаре́нко не захо́че чита́ти його́ ві́рш, але́ я́ пе́вний, що захо́че і, якщо́ тре́ба, допомо́же його́ надрукува́ти.
3. Я́ вже́ шо́стий ра́з дзвоню́ до Га́лі, але́ її́ нема́ вдо́ма. Я́ хоті́в спита́ти Га́лю, чи вона́ не хо́че піти́ в субо́ту до університе́ту на літерату́рний ве́чір. Та́м бу́де літерату́рне чита́ння, бу́де фі́льм про життя́ Тара́са Шевче́нка. Але́ що́ роби́ти? Га́лі нема́ вдо́ма. У Га́лі є това́ришка Окса́на. Я́ зна́ю, що́ вона́, звича́йно, захо́че піти́. Вона́ га́рна ді́вчина і моя́ до́бра това́ришка, але́ не така́, як Га́ля. Га́лю я́ люблю́, і вона́ мене́ те́ж. У на́с спра́вжня любо́в.

XIV. Rewrite passage 2 above in the form of a dialogue and answer the following questions to passages 1 and 3.

(1)

1. Що́ ро́бить това́ришкаціє́ї ді́вчини?
2. Чого́ в не́ї нема́є?
3. До кого́ йде́ ця́ ді́вчина?

(2)

1. Чого́ це́й хло́пець дзвони́в до Га́лі?
2. Що́ бу́де в субо́ту?
3. Чи Га́ля була́ вдома́?
4. Хто́ Окса́на?
5. Що́ ві́н ду́має про Окса́ну?

XV. Answer the following questions to the dialogues.

"Вірші тре́ба надрукува́ти"

1. З які́ї мо́ви перекладáв Мико́ла?
2. Чи він хо́че переклáсти всі вірші?
3. Що́ ду́має Ле́ся про пере́клад?
4. Чи Мико́ла хо́че надрукува́ти свій пере́клад?
5. Чого́ пе́вна Ле́ся?

"Тре́ба гáрно попроси́ти"

1. Що́ Степáн питáє у Віри?
2. До ко́го він хо́че подзвони́ти?
3. Про що́ Віра хо́че спитáти Гáлю?
4. Що́ ду́має Степáн?
5. Я́к тре́ба проси́ти?
6. Що́ відповіла Гáля?
7. Що́ Степáн мáє зроби́ти?

"Я́ хо́чу взя́ти одну́ кни́жку"

1. Куди́ Богдáн іде́?
2. Що́ він тáм хо́че роби́ти?
3. Чого́ шкодá?

"Коли́ полю́биш"

1. Чи Віра і Гáля вже́ зроби́ли домáшнє завдáння?
2. Що́ Віра ще́ мáє зроби́ти?
3. Що́ Гáля роби́тиме вве́чері?
4. Що́ Віра ду́має про фільм?
5. Чому́ вонá тáк ду́має?
6. Що́ відповідáє Гáля?

СЬОМА ЛЕКЦІЯ

20 Інженер з України
An engineer from Ukraine

Dialogue Paticipants:
Степáн - С, Михáйло - М
Stepan - S, Myxajlo - M

1.	М- Степáне, чи тú пам'ятáєш тогó інженéра з Кúєва, що приїздúв на нáшу конферéнцію в Нью Йóрку, колú ще не булó незалéжної Украї́ни?	M- Steve, do you remember that engineer from Kyiv who came to our conference in New York when Ukraine was not yet independent?
2.	С- Тáк, дóбре пам'ятáю: Івáн Дмитрóвський. Симпатúчний такúй. Здаéться, він до тéбе писáв?	S- Yes, I remember him well: Ivan Dmytrovs'kyj A nice fellow. I believe he was writing to you?
3.	М- Тáк, і щé пúше. Ось йогó остáнній лúст до мéне.	M- Yes, he still does. Here is his last letter to me.
4.	С- Цікáво. А чомý тýт стої́ть "Львів", а не "Кúїв"?	S- Interesting. But why does it say here "L'viv" and not "Kyiv"?
5.	М- Томý що він тепéр живé у Львóві. Бáчиш йогó новý адрéсу: Украї́на, Львів, вýл. Івáна Франкá, 7, кв.1.*	M- It's because he now lives in L'viv. See his new address: Ukraine, L'viv, 7 Ivan Franko str., apt. 1.**
6.	С- Тáк бáчу. А щó він пúше?	S- Yes, I see. And what does he say?
7.	М- Пúше, що працюé на завóді, прáця крáща, ніж булá в ньóго в Кúєві.	M- He says that he works at a plant and that the job is better than the one he had in Kyiv.
8.	С- Цé добре. Між іншим, як тú до ньóго звертáєшся: "пáне Івáне" чи "пáне Дмитрóвський?	S- That's good. By the way, how do you address him? "Pan Ivan" or "Pan Dmytrovs'kyj"?
9.	М- Та ні, прóсто "Івáне Семéновичу". Він волíє, щоб до ньóго звертáлися по-бáтькові. Він тáк звúк.	M- Neither way. I simply say "Ivan Semenovych." He prefers to be called by his patronymic. He is used to that.
10.	С- Розумію.	S- I understand.

* вул. = вýлиця
кв. 1 = квартúра одúн (квартúра нóмер одúн)

** The English spelling of the country is UKRAINE, although on Ukrainian stamps the name is UKRAINA. The name of the capital city is now spelled KYIV rather than the previously used Russian spelling 'Kiev'.

21 Івась в університеті
Ivas' is at the university

Dialogue Paticipants:
Пáні Лíда - Л, пáн Петрó - П
pan Petro - P, pani Lida - L

1.	П- Пáні Лíдо, Óля Прокопóвич щé хóдить до шкóли чи вжé скінчи́ла?	P- Pani Lida, is Olja Prokopovyč still going to school or has she already graduated?
2.	Л- Ні́, вонá щé вчи́ться в шкóлі, цьогó рóку кінчáє сьóму кля́су.	L- No, she's still in school, she'll be finishing 7th grade this year.
3.	П- А Івáсь ужé, мáбуть, в університéті?	P- And Ivas' probably is already at the university?
4.	Л- Тáк, вивчáє медици́ну.	L- Yes, he's studying medicine.
5.	П- Медици́ну? Алé ж він, здаéться, дýмав про профéсію інженéра.	P- Medicine? But I thought he was considering the engineering profession.
6.	Л- Цé прáвда, та ви́ знáєте, йогó бáтько — лíкар і хóче, щоб си́н тéж вивчáв медици́ну.	L- That's true, but you know, his father is a doctor and he also wants his son to study medicine.
7.	П- Агá, розумíю.	P- Oh, I see.

22 Тато спить
Dad is asleep

Dialogue Paticipants:
Мáрта - М, Богдáн - Б
Marta - M, Bohdan - B

1.	М- Богдáне, чи не крáще бýде постáвити цé крíсло бíля вікнá?	M- Bohdan, will it not be better to put this armchair by the window?
2.	Б- Чомý? Вонó тáк дóбре стоі́ть. Якщó постáвимо бíля вікнá, будé незрýчно ходи́ти.	B- Why? It's alright where it is. If we put it by the window it will be in the way.
3.	М- Мáєш рáцію. Чогó ти́ шукáєш?	M- You're right. What are you looking for?
4.	Б- Газéту. Куди́ ти́ її́ поклáла?	B- The newspaper. Where did you put it?
5.	М- На стíл, як звичáйно. Знайшóв?	M- On the table as usual. Did you find it?
6.	Б- Ні́, немá. Мóже, її́ тáто взя́в почитáти?	B- No, it's not there. Maybe dad took it to read?
7.	М- Мóже, взя́в. Подиви́ся у ньóго в кімнáті.	M- Maybe he did. Look in his room.
8.	Б- Звичáйно! Тáто лежи́ть на лíжку і спи́ть, а газéта на підлóзі.	B- Of course: dad is lying on his bed asleep and the newspaper is on the floor.

СЛОВНИК

ага́	oh, aha
б, би	(conditional particle)
бі́ля (+ G)	near, next to
вивча́ти, вивча́ють I (+ A)	to study, to learn
ви́вчити, ви́вчать P	
волі́ти, волі́ють (по P)	to prefer
ву́лиця (f)	street
заво́д, -у (m)	plant, factory
зверта́тися, зверта́ються I (до + G)	to address s.one
зверну́тися, зве́рнуться P	
звика́ти, звика́ють I (до + G)	to get used to
зви́кнути, зви́кнуть P	
звик, -ла, -ло, -ли past t.	
здає́ться	it seems
знахо́дити, знахо́дять I	to find
знайти́, зна́йдуть P	
інжене́р (m)	engineer
і́нший	other different
кварти́ра (f), кв.	apartment, apt.
кінча́ти, кінча́ють I	to finish
скінчи́ти, скінча́ть P	
кла́с see кля́са	
кла́сти, кладу́ть I	to put, to place
покла́сти, покладу́ть P	
кля́са (f)	grade, class
конфере́нція (f)	conference
крі́сло	armchair
лежа́ти, лежа́ть I	to lie (down)
лі́жко (n)	bed
лі́кар, -я (m)	doctor
медици́на (f)	medicine (science)
мину́лий	past, last
мо́же	maybe, perhaps
на (+ L)	on; at
незале́жний	independent
незру́чно	inconvenient; awkward, uncomfortable
оста́нній	last
підло́га (f)	floor
почита́ти, почита́ють P	to read a little (for a while)
пра́вда (f)	truth; true
працюва́ти, працю́ють I	to work
пра́ця	work, job
приїзди́ти, приїздя́ть I	to come, to arrive
приї́хати, приї́дуть P	
профе́сія (f)	profession
рік, ро́ку (m)	year

симпати́чний	nice, likeable
си́н (m); voc. си́ну!	son
ста́вити, ста́влять I	to put, to stand
поста́вити, поста́влять P	
сто́	hundred
стоя́ти, стоя́ть I	to stand; to be written
сьо́мий	seventh
та	but, and
та́то, -а (m)	father
тоді́	then; in that case
у (+ Loc)	in; at
учи́тися, у́чаться I	to study, to learn
навчи́тися, навча́ться P	
ході́ти, ходжу́, хо́дять I	to walk, to go
шука́ти, шука́ють I	to look for
пошука́ти, пошука́ють P	
щоб	that; in order to
якби́	if (only)

NAME AND PLACES

Іва́сь diminutive of Іва́н	Ivas' diminutive of Ivan
Іва́н Семе́нович Дмитро́вський	Ivan Semenovych Dmytrovskyj
Ки́їв, Ки́єва; Льві́в, Льво́ва	Kyiv; Lviv

IDIOMS

до то́го ще́ й	on top of it; in addition
ма́ти ра́цію	to be right
між і́ншим	by the way
ході́ти до шко́ли	to attend school
Це́ пра́вда	it's true

SUPPLEMENT

ви́сіти, ви́шу, ви́сять	to hang (be hanging)
губи́ти, гу́блять I	to lose
загуби́ти, загу́блять P	
зру́чно	convenient
карти́на (f)	picture, painting
ля́мпа (f)	lamp
ме́шкати, ме́шкають I	to live, to reside
поме́шкання (n)	apartment
со́н, сну́; сни́ (m)	dream, sleep

EXPLANATORY NOTES

1. To address someone using the first name is звертáтися до кóгось на ім'я́. Likewise, "to be on familiar terms", i.e. to address s.one using the pronoun ти is бýти на "ти́" as opposed to бýти на "ви́".

2. There is more than one verb in Ukrainian with the meaning 'to study'. In this lesson we have two verbs, **вивчáти** and **учи́тися (вчи́тися)**. Both these verbs can be used with an object, cf.:

Я́ вчýся украї́нської мóви. (G)	I am studying Ukrainian.
Я́ вивчáю украї́нську мóву. (A)	

The verb **вчýся** in the first example indicates a general process of study such as might take place in a high school, while **вивчáю** in the second example implies a more thorough and comprehensive study, scholarly research or investigation such as one expects at the university level. Compare the perfective aspect of these verbs:

Він навчи́вся украї́нської мóви.	He has learned Ukrainian.
Він ви́вчив украї́нську мóву.	He has mastered Ukrainian.

While both these verbs can be used with an object, only **учи́тися** can appear in the sense of 'studying' in general, i.e. without naming the object of study:

Він лю́бить учи́тися.	He loves to study.
Він дóбре вчи́ться.	He studies well.

In addition to the verb **учи́тися** there is a more formal term **навчáтися**:

Вонá навчáється в університéті.	She is studying at the university.

3. Likewise, for the verb **кінчи́ти (скінчи́ти)** there is a more formal variant **закíчувати (закінчи́ти)**:

Чи вон вже закíнчила школу?	Has she finished school yet?
Ні, закíнчує цього року.	No, she is finishing it this year.

4. Current practice in Ukraine is to replace **кля́са** with **клáс** i.e. masculine with a hard л, as in Russian.

5. Note the order in which the information appears in addresses: Украї́на, Львів, вýлиця Івáна Франкá, 100, кв. 1, i.e. first the country, then the city (or the administrative region), then the street, the house, and the apartment. A person's name appears last (in the dative case). Some Ukrainians use '**б.**' for **буди́нок** house (number), and 'пом.'for **помéшкання**, apartment (number).

6. Note the expression **у ньóго в кімнáті**. It means the same as **в йогó кімнáті**, however the possessive pronouns are more directly related to the notion of 'possession' or 'ownership', so that the phrase **в йогó кімнáті** means 'in his own room' while **у ньóго в кімнáті** may indicate that he is merely staying in that room as a guest; however this can only be deducted from context. cf.: other expressions of close relationship: **У мéне мáти дýже дóбра** and **моя́ мáти дýже дóбра**. Here the first emphasis the relationship (= 'This mother of mine...'), while the second merely indicates it, placing the emphasis on the other person (see the reading passage for Lesson 5).

7. Another word for armchair is **фоте́ль** (a Polish word ultimately from French 'fauteuil'). In West Ukrainian usage the noun **крі́сло** stands for any chair and **стіле́ць** refers to a (foot) stool.

NOTES ON GRAMMAR

I. LOCATIVE SINGULAR OF NOUNS

The locative of nouns usually has the ending **-і**, but **у/ю** and **ові/еві (-)ві)** also occur. As was the case with the genitive, the distribution of the locative forms is subject to a good deal of fluctuation.

The general distribution of endings is as follows:

1. The ending -і (-ї) occurs with:

(a) all nouns of the feminine **c**-type.*
(b) all neuter nouns (except those with a suffix ending in -к)**
(c) all nouns of the -**a** type
(d) most unsuffixed masculine nouns*** (especially monosyllabic)

For example:

(a)	N.		відповідь		любо́в		
	L.	(у)	відповіді	(у)	любо́ві		
(b)	N.		вікно́		мі́сце		пита́ння
	L.	(у)	вікні́	(на)	мі́сці	(у)	пита́нні
(c)	N.		кімна́та		Мико́ла		істо́рія
	L.	(у)	кімна́ті	(на)	Мико́лі	(в)	істо́рії
(d)	N.		зо́шит		ли́ст		музе́й, готе́ль
	L.	(у)	зо́шиті	(у)	листі́	(у)	музе́ї, готе́лі

2. The endings **-у/-ю** occur with masculine and neuter nouns with a **-к-** suffix **(-(о)к, -ик, -ник, -ак, -ко)** and masculine monosyllabic stem nouns whose genitive ending is **-у**. In the latter case, the gen. ending is unstressed, while the locative **-у́** receives a stress.

---

* The locative of **ма́ти** is **ма́тері**.

** The locative of **ім'я** is **і́мені**.

*** Many such nouns have parallel forms in і and in у́, cf.: **у лісі- у лісу́, у са́ді- у саду́, на краї́- на краю́**.

For example:

-к-	N.	словни́к	малю́нок	се́рденько
	L.	(у) словнику́	(на) малю́нку	(у) се́рденьку
-у-	N.	сте́п*	сні́г	бі́й
	G.	сте́пу	сні́гу	бо́ю
	L.	(у) степу́	(на) сніѓу	(у) бою́
		(steppe)	(snow)	(battle)

3. The endings **-ові/-еві/-єві** are typical for masculine animate nouns of the masculine declension, although occasionally names of animals and even inanimate objects take this ending.

N.	Васи́ль	Андрі́й	това́риш	Іва́н
L.	(на) Василе́ві	(на) Андрієві	(на) това́ришеві	(на) Іва́нові

4. Consonant and vowel alternations.

(a) Before the ending -і the stem-final consonants **г, к, х** become **з, ц, с** respectively.

N.	О́льга	до́шка	ру́х 'motion'
L.	(на) О́льзі	(на) до́шці	(у) ру́сі

(b) The stem vowel **-о** or **-е** which appears before a zero ending (see Lesson 4 p. 63) in the nominative (accusative) alternates with Ø in the locative.

N.-A.	буди́нок	де́нь	стіле́ць
L.	(у) буди́нку	(у)дні́	(на) стільці́ (stem: st'il'c'-)

(Exercises 1, 2, 3, 4, 5)

II. LOCATIVE OF PERSONAL PRONOUNS

The locative forms of personal pronouns are as follows:

	Singular			
N.	я́	ти́	вона́	він, воно́
L.	(на) мені́	(на) тобі́	(на) ній	(на) ньо́му / (на) ні́м
	Plural			
N.	ми́	ви́	вони́	
L.	(на) на́с	(на) ва́с	(на) ни́х	

Thus, the locative forms of the plurals **ми́, ви́, вони́** are identical with their genitive forms. The masculine **він** and the neuter **воно́** ordinarily have (на) **ньо́му** but a less frequent variant (на) **ні́м**, with no semantic or stylistic distinction, also occurs. (Exercices 5, 6)

**** cf.: however, ча́с, ча́су — (у) ча́сі.

III. USES OF THE LOCATIVE

The locative case occurs only with certain prepositions which specify location chiefiy **у/в** 'in, inside, at' and **на** 'on, on top of, at'.

Вона́ вчи́ться в університе́ті.	She is studying at the university.
Він працю́є на заво́ді.	He works at the factory.
Папі́р на столі́.	The paper is on the desk.
На ньо́му ва́жко писа́ти.	It's hard to write on it.

1. Generally **на** is used with nouns denoting surfaces and open spaces, while **у/в** indicates location within a space, cf.

Що́ в цьо́му буди́нку?	What's in this building?
Що́ це́ на цьо́му буди́нку?	What's that on (top of) that building?

There are notable exceptions as with the nouns **по́ле** 'field' or **сте́п** 'steppe' which are normally used with the preposition **у.** On the other hand **на** is frequently used to indicate an official building or institution, such as a post office, railroad station, or a factory (in the West Ukrainian usage this includes the university as well, i.e. **на університе́ті**). There are also instances where a choice between the two prepositions is possible, but the meaning will be different. For example:

у го́рах	'in the mountains' (= in the mountain area) but
на го́рах	'on mountain slopes, on mountain tops' (= surface).

IV. CONDITIONS

Ukrainian makes a grammatical distinction between conditions which are believed possible of fulfillment and those which are viewed as doubtful or impossible to fulfil because the condition is improbable or contrary to fact.

The realizable condition is expressed by **якщо́** and the future tense. E.g.:

Якщо́ я́ ма́тиму ча́с, я́ прийду́.	I will come if I have the time.
Якщо́ ви́ бу́дете в Ки́єві, про́симо до на́с.	If you are in Kyiv, please come to see us.

It may also be expressed by **як** with present or future tense, e.g.:

А що́, я́к вона́ спита́є?	What if she should ask?
Я́к ка́жеш до́бре, то до́бре.	If you say it's O.K., it's O.K.

The unlikely or unrealizable condition is expressed by **якби́** plus the past tense (in the condition clause) and past tense plus the particle **б (и)** (in the result clause). Past tense must be used in both the condition and the consequence clauses regardless of the time of the speech event or the time of the condition:

Якби́ я ма́в ча́с, я́ б пішо́в, але́ я не ма́в часу́.	If I had the time, I would have gone, but I didn't have the time.
Якби́ я ма́в ча́с, я́ пішо́в би, але́ я не ма́ю часу́.	If I had the time, I would go, but I don't have the time.
Якби́ я ма́в ча́с, я́ б пішо́в, але́ я не ма́тиму часу́.	If I had the time, I would go, but I won't have the time.

Note 1: The consequence clause may or may not be introduced by то or тоді́. cf.: **Якби́ я бу́в у Ки́єві, (то, тоді́) я́ б до ни́х подзвони́в.**

'If I had been in Kyiv, (then, in that case) I would have called them'.

Note 2: The particle **би** which appears in the consequence clause is shortened to **б** when the preceding word ends in a vowel. This particle is usually placed after the subject or the predicate — it may never appear in the position immediately preceding either of them (unless, of course, it is placed between them as in the above examples). It may not begin a clause.

Note 3: The realizable condition which is projected into the future must have a future tense verb in its 'if' clause. It may not have a present, as is common in English 'if' clauses, cf. 'If I see him tomorrow I'll ask him' — Якщо́ я його́ за́втра **поба́чу**, я́ його́ спита́ю.

(Exercises 7,8)

V. THE CONJUNCTION ЩОБ

One of the functions of the conjunction щоб is to introduce the request or wish clause (cf. the English 'I want you to...'):

Я́ хо́чу, щоб ви́ туди́ пішли́.	I want you to go there.
Ві́н про́сить, щоб ми́ до нього писа́ли.	He asks that we write to him.

Such constructions require the use of the past tense in the clause which begins with щоб.

(Exercises 12, 13)

VI. VERBS OF PUTTING

Ukrainian has two sets of verbs to describe the motion of putting, one for 'standing something up' **ста́вити**, and another for 'laying something down' **кла́сти**. cf.:

СТА́ВИТИ	КЛА́СТИ
Вона́ ста́вить стіле́ць бі́ля вікна́.	Вона́ кладе́ газе́ту на сті́л.
She is putting the chair by the window.	She is putting the newspaper on the table.

Note the correspondence between the motion verbs **покла́сти** and **поста́вити** and the position verbs **лежа́ти** and **стоя́ти:**

Куди́ ти́ поста́вила стіле́ць?	Куди́ ти́ покла́ла газе́ту?
Я́ його́ поста́вила біля вікна́.	Я́ її́ покла́ла на сті́л.
Він стої́ть біля вікна́.	Вона́ лежи́ть на столі́.
Де́ він стої́ть? — Біля вікна́.	Де́ вона́ лежи́ть? — На столі́.

Note also the difference in the adverbs: **куди́** for motion and **де́** for location.

(Exercises 9, 10)

VII. PAST TENSE OF THE VERB ІТИ

The verb **іти́** 'to go' has an irregular past tense:

іти́:	ішо́в (йшо́в)	ішла́ (йшла́)	ішли́ (йшли́)
піти́:	пішо́в	пішла́	пішли́

Similarly the past tense of **прийти́** is прийшо́в, прийшла́, прийшли́.

Note the position of the stress.

ВПРАВИ

I. Ask the questions according to the model:

Подиви́ся на **ма́пу**. Що́ ти́ ба́чиш на **ма́пі?**

(вікно́, підло́гу, фотогра́фію, лі́жко, до́шку, малю́нок, стіле́ць, буди́нок, ву́лицю, папі́р)

II. Answer the questions using the words in brackets.

1. Де́ ви́ працю́єте? (музе́й)
2. Де́ він пра́цює? (бібліоте́ка)
3. Де́ він у́читься? (шко́ла)
4. Де́ вона́ вчи́ться? (університе́т)
5. Де́ працю́є це́й інжене́р? (заво́д)
6. Де́ ви́ жили́? (гурто́житок)
7. Де́ ти́ тепе́р живе́ш? (його́ поме́шкання)
8. Де́ вони́ тепе́р? (Нью Йо́рк)
9. Де́ вона́ тепе́р? (Льві́в)
10. Де́ бу́де конфере́нція? (Украї́на, Ки́їв)

III. Change the sentences according to the model:

Він з Кана́ди. Він живе́ в Кана́ді.

(з Аме́рики, з Украї́ни, з Ки́єва, зі Льво́ва, з Нью Йо́рку, з Монреа́лю, з Росії́)

IV. Ask the questions according to the model:

Подиви́ся на О́лю. Що́ це́ на О́лі?
Look at Ol'a. What's that she is wearing?

(Іва́на, Василя́, О́льгу, Марка́, Андрі́я, його́ ма́тір, її́ бра́та, її́ сестру́, Павла́, Марі́ю)

V. Rephrase the following statements according to the model:

Я́ ма́ю важке́ завда́ння. **На ме́ні** лежи́ть важке́ завда́ння.

(ми́, ти́, вони́, він, ви́, вона́)

VI. Put the bracketed words into the correct form.

1. У ме́не в (кімна́та) стої́ть вели́кий сті́л. На (сті́л) лежи́ть журна́л. Це́ журна́л "Украї́на". У (він) пи́шуть про життя́ в (Украї́на). О́сь фотогра́фія (вели́кий буди́нок). Це́ готе́ль "Украї́на". Ту́т в (готе́ль "Украї́на") бу́де вели́ка конфере́нція.
2. О́сь оста́ння фотогра́фія Іва́на, си́на (ліка́р Дмитро́вський). Він навча́ється (університе́т) і́мени Тара́са Шевче́нка. Він вивча́є (украї́нська мо́ва). Він до́бре пи́ше. Він пи́ше ві́рші. Я́ люблю́ його́ (ві́рш "Украї́на"). У (він) Іва́н гово́рить про (своя́ любо́в до Украї́ни).
3. Це́ ціка́ва кни́жка. Її́ написа́в мі́й това́риш Іва́н. У (вона́) Іва́н пи́ше про те́, що́ він ба́чив в (Украї́на). Він бу́в на (конфере́нція) у (Львів). Іва́н інжене́р і, звича́йно, хоті́в ба́чити, я́к украї́нці працю́ють на (заво́д), але́ він на ма́в на це (ча́с).

VII. Change the "true" conditions to the "hypothetical" conditions.

1. Якщо́ ви́ допомо́жете, то ми́ скінчимо́ це́ до четверга́.
2. Якщо́ він захо́че, він піде.
3. Якщо́ вона́ цього́ потребува́тиме, вона́ ска́же.
4. Якщо́ я діста́ну цю́ кни́жку, я її́ прочита́ю.
5. Якщо́ ти́ поспіши́ш, ти́ напи́шеш пере́клад до вівто́рка.
6. Якщо́ я пам'ята́тиму, я подзвоню́.
7. Якщо́ ми́ попро́симо, він це́ влашту́є.
8. Якщо́ ти́ спита́єш, вона́ відпові́сть.
9. Якщо́ ви́ ска́жете, вони́ це́ зро́блять.
10. Якщо́ ти́ це́ ви́вчиш, ти́ діста́неш "Ду́же до́бре".
11. Якщо́ ви́ потелефону́єте, то отри́маєте ві́дповідь.
12. Якщо́ ви́ до ни́х зве́рнетеся, вони́ допомо́жуть.
13. Якщо́ ти при́йдеш сього́дні, ми́ ще́ будемо́ вдо́ма.

VIII. Change the "true" conditions to the "hypothetical" conditions. Model:

Я́ це́ **зроблю́,** якщо́ тре́ба.
Я́ **б** це́ **зроби́в**, якби́ було́ тре́ба.

1. Я́ це́ кінчу́, якщо́ тре́ба.
2. Я́ це́ покладу́, якщо́ тре́ба.
3. Я́ це́ поста́влю, якщо́ тре́ба.
4. Я́ це́ ві́зьму, якщо́ тре́ба.
5. Я́ пошука́ю, якщо́ тре́ба.
6. Я́ це́ надруку́ю, якщо́ тре́ба.
7. Я́ це́ напишу́, якщо́ тре́ба.
8. Я́ це́ перекладу́, якщо́ тре́ба.
9. Я́ це́ скажу́, якщо́ тре́ба.
10. Я́ подивлю́ся, якщо́ тре́ба.
11. Я́ потелефону́ю, якщо́ тре́ба.
12. Я́ прийду, якщо́ тре́ба.

IX. Ask questions using the appropriate verbs of 'putting'. Then answer them using appropriate prepositions and the words in brackets. Model:

О́сь журна́л. Куди́ покла́сти цей журна́л? Це́й журна́л мо́жна покла́сти на сті́л.

1. О́сь газе́та.. Куди́...? (крі́сло)
2. О́сь лі́жко. Куди́...? (вікно́)
3. О́сь телефо́н. Куди́...? (сті́л)
4. О́сь телеві́зор. Куди́...? (та́ кімна́та)
5. О́сь папі́р. Куди́ ...? (стіле́ць)
6. О́сь сті́л. Куди́ ...? (до́шка)
7. О́сь словни́к. Куди́ ...? (журна́л)
8. О́сь стіле́ць. Куди́ ...? (підло́га)
9. О́сь ма́па. Куди́ ...? (зо́шит)
10. О́сь оліве́ць. Куди́ ...? (сті́л)

X. Change the sentences using the appropriate verbs. Model:

Я́ кладу́ ли́ст на сті́л. Ли́ст лежи́ть на столі́.

1. Я́ кладу́ газе́ту на вікно́.
2. Я́ ста́влю телефо́н на сті́л.
3. Я́ ста́влю крі́сло на підло́гу.
4. Я́ кладу́ малю́нок на крі́сло.
5. Я́ ста́влю кни́жку на мі́сце.
6. Я́ ста́влю сті́л у його́ кімна́ту.
7. Я́ ста́влю телеві́зор на підло́гу бі́ля вікна́.
8. Я́ кладу́ ві́рш на стіле́ць.
9. Я́ кладу́ ру́чку на папі́р.
10. Я́ ста́влю фотогра́фію на телеві́зор.

XI. Answer the following questions

1. Дé ви́ живетé?
2. Дé ви́ вчитéся?
3. Чогó ви́ шукáєте?
4. Дé працює вáш бáтько?
5. Дé працює вáша мáти?
6. Щó ви́ вивчáєте?
7. Дé ви́ жили́, коли́ ходи́ли до шкóли?
8. Куди́ ви́ поклáли вáш зóшит?
9. Чи ви́ спитé?
10. Чи ви́ тепéр у кля́сі?
11. До кóго ви зверну́лися?

XII. Change these statements to indirect commands according to the model:

Я́ хóчу **читáти**. Я́ хóчу, **щоб ти́ читáв**.

1. Я́ хóчу поспáти.
2. Я́ хóчу попрацювáти.
3. Я́ хóчу цé скінчи́ти.
4. Я́ хóчу цé зроби́ти.
5. Я́ хóчу подя́кувати за нау́ку.
6. Я́ хóчу подзвони́ти додóму.
7. Я́ хóчу цé влаштувáти.
8. Я́ хóчу побáчити цю́ телевізíйну прогрáму.
9. Я́ хóчу в ни́х жи́ти
10. Я́ хóчу цé переклáсти на украї́нську мóву.
11. Я́ хóчу заадресувáти цéй ли́ст до університéту.

XIII. Change the statements to indirect command according to the model:

Він ду́має, що Óля це **зрóбить.**
Він хóче, щоб Óля цé **зроби́ла.**

1. Він ду́має, що Óля цé постáвить.
2. Він ду́має, що Óля цé покладé.
3. Він ду́має, що Óля цé візьме.
4. Він ду́має, що Óля бу́де вдóма.
5. Він ду́має, що Óля пошукáє.
6. Він ду́має, що Óля лежи́ть у лíжку.
7. Він ду́має, що Óля почувáє себé дóбре.
8. Він ду́має, що Óля допомóже.
9. Він ду́має, що Óля пíде додóму.
10. Він ду́має, що Óля надрукýє цьогó листá.
11. Він ду́має, що Óля при́йде зáвтра.

REVIEW

XIV. Put the bracketed words into the correct form.

1. Це́ його́ нове́ поме́шкання. Ві́н живе́ в (своє́ нове́ поме́шкання). Чи ви́ вже́ бачили (це́ нове́ поме́шкання)? Ні, я́ ще не ба́чив (це́ нове́ поме́шкання).
2. Це́ лікар Дмитро́вський. Чи ви́ зна́єте (лі́кар Дмитро́вський)? Я́ бою́ся (це́й лі́кар), він, ка́жуть, не ду́же до́брий лі́кар.
3. О́сь моє́ лі́жко. Біля (моє́ лі́жко) стіл, а на (стіл) лежи́ть кни́жка "Що́ ка́же медици́на про любо́в". Я́ дивлю́ся на (своє́ лі́жко), на (ця́ ціка́ва кни́жка) і ду́маю: чи йти́ спа́ти чи почита́ти?
4. О́ля потребу́є (украї́нський словник). Вона́ ма́є (оди́н словни́к), але́ в її́ (словни́к) нема́ (сло́во "клас"). Це́ стари́й словни́к.
5. Дмитро́вський пи́ше до (лі́кар Ме́льник) про Ки́їв. Він з (Ки́їв), але́ тепе́р живе́ не в (Ки́їв), а біля (Ки́їв).
6. Ми́ чита́ли про (тво́рчість) Шевче́нка. Я́ ду́же люблю́ його́ ві́рші про (ма́ти). У (тво́рчість) Шевче́нка я́ ба́чу (вели́ка пра́вда) і (спра́вжня любо́в).
7. Ві́ра ма́є (одне́ пита́ння). З її́ (пита́ння) я́ ба́чу, що́ вона́ не розуміє (сьо́ма ле́кція). У її́ (пита́ння) є́ непра́вильне сло́во: вона́ сказа́ла "па́ні Дмитро́вський", а тре́ба "па́ні Дмитро́вська".
8. О́н та́м буди́нок №.7. Чи ви́ ба́чите (буди́нок №.7)? У (буди́нок №.7) бібліоте́ка. Бі́ля (буди́нок) стоїть вели́ка до́шка. На (до́шка) ми́ чита́ємо: "Бібліоте́ка і́мени Іва́на Франка́".
9. Я́ читаю (газе́та "Пра́вда"). О́сь фотогра́фія (заво́д), де працю́є інжене́р Дмитро́вський. Я́ зна́ю від (інжене́р Дмитро́вський), що це́й заво́д уже́ стари́й, але́ на (фотогра́фія) я́ ба́чу (нови́й буди́нок).
10. Моя́ това́ришка — сестра (лі́кар). Я питала (моя́ това́ришка), чи вона́ лю́бить (медици́на). Вона́ ка́же, що не ду́же, але її́ бра́т ка́же, що праця лі́каря — ду́же ціка́ва.

XV. Supply the correct forms of the names:

1. Це́ О́ля. Я́ ма́ю до . . . . . пита́ння. Я́ хо́чу спита́ти . . . . . про Украї́ну. Я́ кажу́: . . . . . . ! Чи Украї́на га́рна?
2. Це́ Мико́ла Ме́льник. Я́ ма́ю до . . . . пита́ння. Я́ хо́чу спита́ти . . . . про Украї́ну. Я́ кажу́: . . . . . ! Де́ ти́ бу́в на Украї́ні?
3. Це́ Андрі́й. Я́ ма́ю до . . . . . пита́ння. Я́ хо́чу спита́ти . . . . . . про Украї́ну. Я́ кажу́ . . . .! Де́ ти́ жи́в на Украї́ні?
4. Це́ Марі́я Поліщу́к. Я́ ма́ю до . . . . пита́ння. Я́ хо́чу спита́ти . . . . . . про Украї́ну. Я́ кажу: . . . .!Де ти жила на Украї́ні?
5. Це́ Василь Гончаренко. Я маю до . . . . . . питання. Я хочу спитати . . . . про Украї́ну. Я́ кажу́: . . . . . . що́ ти́ ба́чив на Украї́ні?
6. Це́ па́ні Лі́да. Я́ ма́ю до . . . . пита́ння. Я́ хо́чу спита́ти . . . . . про Украї́ну. Я́ кажу́: . . . . де́ ви́ були́ на Украї́ні?
7. Це́ Марко́ Поліщу́к. Я́ ма́ю до . . . . пита́ння. Я́ хо́чу спитати . . . . . . про Украї́ну. Я́ кажу́: . . . . . що ти́ ду́маєш про Украї́ну?

XVI. Change future to present. Model:

Я́ бу́ду чита́ти. Я́ чита́ю.

(вчи́тися, спа́ти, писа́ти, це́ бра́ти, про це́ ду́мати, це́ роби́ти, це́ потребува́ти, шука́ти пра́вди, кінча́ти, це́ вивча́ти, телефонува́ти)

XVII. Change present to non-compound imperfective future. Model:

Що́ вони́ пи́шуть? Що́ вони́ **писа́тимуть**?

1. Чого́ вони́ шука́ють?
2. За що́ вони́ дя́кують?
3. Що́ вони́ ро́блять?
4. Що́ вони́ пита́ють?
5. Що́ вони́ вивча́ють?
6. Що́ вони́ беру́ть?
7. Що́ вони́ відповіда́ють?
8. Що́ вони́ пам'ята́ють?
9. Чого́ вони́ про́сять?
10. Чого́ вони́ боя́ться?
11. До ко́го вони́ зверта́ються?

XVIII. Read and retell.

1. Мину́лого ро́ку я́ бу́в на конфере́нції в Нью Йо́рку. Та́м були́ украї́нці: Іва́н Семе́нович Дмитро́вський, інжене́р, і його́ това́риш Іва́н Іва́нович Ме́льник, лі́кар. Дмитро́вський працю́є в Ки́єві на заво́ді, а його́ това́риш живе і працю́є у Льво́ві. Ми́ говори́ли про те́, яке́ тепе́р життя́ в Украї́ні. Іва́н Семе́нович каза́в, що тепе́р кра́ще, ні́ж було́. Ві́н ма́є до́бру кварти́ру, до́бру працю, його́ си́н навча́ється в університе́ті. Ме́льник те́ж каза́в, що ві́н до́бре живе, але́ ві́н ду́має, що ми́ ту́т в Аме́риці ма́ємо кра́ще життя́. Його́ това́риш сказа́в: "Та́м кра́ще, де́ на́с нема́. Та́к усі́ ду́мають, чи не пра́вда?" Ме́льник відпові́в: "Мо́же всі́, а мо́же й не всі́. О́сь за́раз спита́ємо па́на Поліщука́. "Що́ ви ду́маєте, па́не Поліщу́к?" Я́ не зна́в, що́ каза́ти. Поду́мав і кажу́: "Я́ в Ки́єві не бу́в, я америка́нець. Ви́ з Украї́ни, ви́ кра́ще зна́єте, яке́ у ва́с та́м життя́. Якщо́ Іва́н Іва́нович ду́має, що ту́т кра́ще, мо́же він ма́є ра́цію. Я́ не ма́ю відповіді на ва́ше пита́ння". "Я́к не ма́єте?" сказа́в Ме́льник. "Ва́ша відповідь була́ ду́же до́бра і пра́вильна".

2. Я́ ма́ю старе́, але́ вели́ке поме́шкання бі́ля університе́ту. Я́ потребу́ю мі́сця для моєї бібліоте́ки. Я́ поста́вив та́м сті́л — на ньо́му я́ пишу́, друку́ю. Я́ ма́ю зру́чне крі́сло, лі́жко, щоб спа́ти, стіле́ць, телеві́зор. Чого ще́ потребу́є студе́нт? Я́ все́ ма́ю.

3. Я́ отри́мала листа від това́риша з Монреа́лю. Він пи́ше, що цього́ ро́ку закі́нчує університе́т і ду́має йти́ працюва́ти. Він хо́че отри́мати працю інжене́ра, але́ не зна́є, коли́ це́ бу́де. Тепа́р він бу́де працюва́ти на заво́ді. Він живе́ у ма́тері. У ни́х гарне поме́шкання неда́ле́ко від заво́ду, але́ та́м нема́ мі́сця для його́ бібліоте́ки, і він шука́є і́ншого поме́шкання.

XIX. Answer the following questions to the above passages.

(1)

1. Кого́ Поліщу́к зустрів у Нью Йорку?
2. Я́к живе́ Іва́н Семе́нович?
3. Що́ каза́в Ме́льник про Аме́рику?
4. Що́ відповів Поліщу́к?

(2)

1. Де́ ме́шкає цей студе́нт?
2. Що́ він ма́є в своїй кімна́ті?
3. Чого́ він ще́ потребу́є?

(3)

1. Звідки це́й ли́ст?
2. Від ко́го це́й ли́ст?
3. Що́ це́й хло́пець тепе́р ро́бить?
4. Що́ він хо́че роби́ти?
5. Що́ він пи́ше про своє поме́шкання?

XX. Answer the following questions to the dialogues.

"Інжене́р з України"

1. Де́ Миха́йло і Степа́н зустріли Дмитро́вського?
2. Де́ Дмитро́вський тепе́р і що́ він ро́бить?
3. Яка́ його́ адре́са?
4. Як Миха́йло до нього́ зверта́ється: "па́не Іва́не" чи "па́не Дмитро́вський"?

"Іва́сь в університе́ті"

1. Чи О́ля Прокопо́вич уже́ скінчи́ла шко́лу?
2. А її бра́т Іва́сь закінчи́в чи ні?
3. Про яку́ профе́сію він говори́в?
4. Чому́ він вивча́є медици́ну?

"Та́то спи́ть"

1. Куди́ Ма́рта хо́че поста́вити крісло?
2. Що́ про це́ ду́має Богда́н?
3. Куди́ Ма́рта звича́йно кладе́ газе́ту?
4. Чому́ газе́ти нема́ та́м, куди́ Ма́рта її покла́ла?

XXI. Translate into Ukrainian.

1. - I thought you were going to study medicine.
   - I was, but my father wants me to be an engineer.
2. - Where did you put my notebook?
   - I put it by the telephone. Isn't it there?
   - No, it isn't.
3. - Where should I put the seventh chair? By the window perhaps?
   - No, I think it would be better to put it by the table.
   - You are right.
4. - Where is your brother?
   - I think he went to take a nap.
   - Didn't he go to the plant?
   - I don't think so. I will go and look in his room.
   - Is he there?
   - Yes. He is asleep.
5. - Who took the newspaper? I put it here by the telephone.
   - I believe Martha did.
   - I thought she went to bed.
   - Yes, but she is not sleeping. You know, she likes to read in bed.
6. - By the way, when is your brother arriving from New York?
   - He called and said he will arrive tomorrow.
7. - How do you address Professor Honcharenko?
   - I think it's best to address him "Mister Honcharenko"
   - And why not say "mister" (pan) and "professor" together?
   - That would be alright too.
8. - What grade is she in?
   - Seventh. It's the last grade.
   - So, this year she is graduating from school (=finishing school)?
   - Yes. It's wonderful.
9. - I'm not used to address her by her first name and patronymic.
   - And how do you address her?
   - Simply "Martha" We are on familiar terms.
   - That's nice. She is a nice (likable) girl.

ВОСЬМА ЛЕКЦІЯ

23 Вірш Шевченка

Окса́на студе́нтка пе́ршого ку́рсу Ки́ївського університе́ту.
Вона́ вчи́ться на філологі́чному факульте́ті, вивча́є украї́нську мо́ву й літерату́ру.
Сього́дні вони́ чита́ли ві́рші Шевче́нка.
В одно́му ві́рші було́ ре́чення:

> Учі́теся, брати́ мої́,
> ду́майте, чита́йте,
> і чужо́го научა́йтесь,
> й свого́ не цура́йтесь.

Профе́сор підкре́слив це́ ре́чення й сказа́в:
"Неха́й усі́ студе́нти ви́вчать це́ напа́м'ять."

A poem by Sevcenko

Oksana is a Freshman at the Kyiv university.
She is in the Department of Philology, studying Ukrainian language and literature.
Today they were reading Ševčenko's poetry.
In the poem there was a sentence:

> Study, my brothers,
> think and read,
> learn from the others, (lit. 'foreign things')
> but don't forsake your own.

The professor underlined the sentence and said:
"I want all the students to learn it by heart."

24 Важко знайти помешкання

Окса́на живе́ в старо́му поме́шканні. Ту́т усе́ старе́: сті́л, лі́жко, крі́сло. Коли́ до Окса́ни прихо́дять го́сті, вона́ ка́же: "Не сіда́йте на це́ крі́сло. На цьо́му крі́слі незру́чно сиді́ти. Ми́ мо́жемо сиді́ти на моє́му лі́жку." Го́сті сіда́ють. Хто́сь пита́є, чи мо́жна відчини́ти вікно́. Окса́на ка́же: "Ні́, про́шу, не відчиня́йте вікна́. Пот́ім його́ не мо́жна бу́де зачини́ти." Това́ришка Окса́ни слу́хає й ка́же: "Якби́ я́ була́ на твоє́му мі́сці, я́ б шука́ла і́ншого поме́шкання." "Я́ вже́ шука́ла", відповіда́є Окса́на, "але́ в на́шому мі́сті та́к ва́жко знайти́ поме́шкання".

It's hard to find an apartment

Oksana lives in an old apartment. Everything is old here: the table, the bed, the armchair. When people come to see Oksana she says: "Don't sit in this armchair. It's uncomfortable. We can all sit on my bed." The guests sit down. Someone asks if it's all right to open the window. Oksana says: "No, please don't open the window. If you do you won't be able to shut it." Oksana's friend listens and says: "If I were you I would look for another apartment." "I have already looked," answers Oksana, "but it's so hard to find an apartment in our town."

25 Слава Богу! Thank God!

Dialogue Paticipants:
Ю́рій Володи́мирович - Ю, Га́нна Сергі́ївна - Г
Jurij Volodymyrovyč - Ju, Hanna Serhijivna - H

1. Г- Ю́рку, не забу́дь, що в цю́ п'я́тницю в на́с бу́дуть го́сті.
2. Ю- Го́сті? А я́ ду́мав, що в п'я́тницю ми́ йдемо́ на конце́рт.
3. Г- Ні! Ти́ зно́ву все́ забу́в. Запам'ята́й до́бре або́ кра́ще візьми́ олівця́ та́ напиши́: у п'я́тницю в на́с го́сті, у субо́ту ми́ йдемо́ в го́сті, а в неді́лю бу́де конце́рт.
4. Ю- А що́ в понеді́лок, вівто́рок і та́к да́лі? Те́ж хто́сь прихо́дить чи ми́ куди́сь ідемо́?
5. Г- Ні́, не бі́йся. Ми́ ніку́ди не пі́демо, бу́демо сиді́ти вдо́ма.
6. Ю- Сла́ва Бо́гу!

1. H- Jurko, don't forget that we are having guests at our house this Friday.
2. Ju- Guests? I thought we were going to a concert on Friday.
3. H- No, you forgot everything again. Remember well or better still take a pencil and write down: on Friday we're having guests, on Saturday we are going out, and on Sunday there will be a concert.
4. Ju- What about Monday, Tuesday and so forth? Is someone coming over or are we going out again someplace?
5. H- No, relax. We're not going anywhere, we'll stay at home.
6. Ju- Thank God!

СЛОВНИК

Бо́г, Бо́же!; боги́ (m)	God
відчиня́ти, відчиня́ють I	to open (to open up)
відчини́ти, відчи́нять P	
во́сьмий	eighth
гість, го́стя (m)	guest
го́сті (pl.)	guests
забува́ти, забува́ють I	to forget
забу́ти, забу́дуть P	
зачиня́ти, зачиня́ють I	to close (to shut)
зачини́ти, зачи́нять P	
і́нший	other, different
ки́ївський	Kyiv(an)
конце́рт, -у (m)	concert
на конце́рт	to the concert
куди́сь	somewhere
ку́рс, -у (m)	course
слу́хати ку́рс	to take a course
на ... ку́рсі	to be in ... year
літерату́ра (f)	literature
мі́сто (n)	city, town
могти́, мо́жуть I	to be able
змогти́, змо́жуть P	
(мі́г, могла́, -о́)	(Past t.)
навча́тися, навча́ються I*	to study, to learn
навчи́тися, навча́ться P (+ G or inf.)	
напа́м'ять	by heart, by memory
неха́й	let
підкре́слювати, підкре́слюють I	to underline
підкре́слити, підкре́слять P	
ре́чення (n)	sentence
сиді́ти, сиджу́, сидя́ть I	to sit
сіда́ти, сіда́ють I; сі́сти, ся́дуть P	to sit down
сла́ва (f); сла́ва!	glory, fame; hail!
слу́хати, слу́хають I (+A)	to listen (to)
послу́хати, послу́хають P	
факульте́т, -у (m)	department, school
філологі́чний	philological
хто́сь	someone
цура́тися, цура́ються I (+ G)	to shun
відцура́тися, відцура́ються P	
чужи́й	strange, foreign; someone else's

* The verb **науча́тися** (in the poem) spelled with an **у** is a less frequent variant of the verb **навча́тися.**

NAMES AND PLACES

Володи́мир Volodymyr (Walter)
Га́нна (Ann) Га́нна Сергі́ївна
Ю́рі́й (George) Ю́рій Володи́мирович.
Юрко́ (diminutive)

IDIOMS

і та́к да́лі (і т.д.)	and so forth (etc)
іти́ в го́сті до ... (+ G)	to go visiting someone
у на́с го́сті	we have guests
на твоє́му мі́сці	if I were you (lit. 'in your place')
сиді́ти вдо́ма	to stay at home
сла́ва Бо́гу!	thank God!
учи́ти напа́м'ять	to learn by heart

SUPPLEMENT

запро́шувати/запроси́ти (в го́сті)	to invite (as a guest)
запам'ята́ти (pfv. only)	to remember, memorize

EXPLANATORY NOTES

1. The noun ку́рс has several meanings: a course or subject one takes at the university level, or the year of the student's enrollment. In Ukrainian one does not 'take' a course but 'listens' to it:

> Я́ слу́хаю ку́рс істо́рії украї́нської літерату́ри.
> I am taking a course in the History of Ukrainian Literature.

The professor does not 'give' a course, he 'reads' it:

> Проф. Гончаре́нко чита́є ку́рс істо́рії украї́нської літерату́ри.
> Prof Hončarenko gives a course in the History of Ukrainian Literature.

To ask about a student's status at the university, one uses the expression:

На яко́му ти́ ку́рсі?	What year are you in?
На пе́ршому.	I am a freshman.

2. The term **факульте́т** refers to the department such as 'History Department' or 'Department of Linguistics':

Вона́ на істори́чному факульте́ті.	She is in the History Department.
Він на літерату́рному факульте́ті.	He is in the Department of Literature.

3. Note the use of the preposition **на** and **в** with the Locative:

на	в
на ку́рсі	в університе́ті
на факульте́ті	
на ле́кції	
на конфере́нції	
на іспиті	
на конце́рті	
на фільмі	
на заво́ді	в Росії, Кана́ді, Аме́риці

With the noun **Украї́на** both prepositions may be used, preposition **на** being more common (some linguists insist that **в Украї́ні** is more correct, paralleling such phrases as **в Росії, в Аме́риці**, etc.).

4. We have encountered several adjectives with the suffix -ський: **Украї́на — украї́нський, Кана́да — кана́дський, Ки́їв — ки́ївський.**

Such adjectives often appear in titles, place names and names of various institutions:

Це́ Нью-Йо́ркська бібліоте́ка.	This is the New York Library.
Це́ університе́тська біблітéка.	This is the university library.

Names of universities traditionally include **-ський** adjectives:

У Га́рвардському університе́ті є ку́рс украї́нської мо́ви.	Harvard University is offering a course in Ukrainian language.
Вона́ вчи́ться в Колумбійському університе́ті.	She is studying at Columbia University.

5. It may surprise students to learn that Ukrainian does not have a specific word for 'party' or an informal gathering (**вечі́рка** listed in the dictionaries is becoming less frequent today). The expressions 'to have guests' and 'to pay a visit' are more formal:

У на́с сього́дні го́сті.	We are having guests today.
Ми́ йдемо́ в го́сті.	We are going to visit some friends.

Other expressions one may hear in colloquial Ukrainian (here and in Ukraine) are 'to get together', 'to have people over':

До нáс сьогóдні прихóдять (лю́ди).	People are coming over tonight.
Ми́ сьогóдні збирáємося у Олі.	We are meeting at Ol'a's tonight.

In addition, there is a term **прийóм**, borrowed from Russian, which stands for a formal reception (used in Ukraine). The corresponding term used by emigré Ukrainians (mostly from the West Ukraine) is **прийня́ття**. A dancing party is called **забáва** (a Polish borrowing used by West Ukrainians) or **тáнці** (more common among those from the Eastern regions). A formal ball is **бáл** (or **бáль**).

NOTES ON GRAMMAR

I. LOCATIVE SINGULAR OF ADJECTIVES, ORDINALS, DEMONSTRATIVE PRONOUNS, УВЕСЬ AND ОДИН

The locative case endings for all feminine adjectives, demonstratives, and the numeral **однá** is **-ій**. Masculine and neuter endings are **-ому** or, less frequently, **-ім**. Thus:

Adjectives

	Masculine and neuter		*Feminine*	
N.	чужи́й, чужé	вчорáшній, вчорáшнє	чужá	вчорáшня
L.	(на) чужóму	(на) вчорáшньому	(на) чужíй	(на) вчорáшній
	(на) чужíм	(на) вчорáшнім		

The pronouns **яки́й, таки́й** and ordinal numerals follow the same pattern.

(Exercises 1, 2, 3, 6)

Demonstratives and **оди́н**

	Masculine and neuter			
N.	увéсь, усé	цéй, цé	тóй, тé	оди́н, однé
L.	(на) усьóму	(на) цьóму	(на) тóму	(на) однóму
	(на) усíм	(на) цíм	(на) тíм	(на) однíм

Feminine	
ця́, уся́	тá, однá
(на) цíй, усíй	тíй, однíй

(Exercises 2, 7)

II. LOCATIVE SINGULAR OF POSSESIVE PRONOUNS

These pronouns also follow the adjectival pattern with one important diffirence: the masculine / neuter locative ending of **мíй, твíй** and **свíй** is **-єму** instead of **-ому***. They do have the variant **-ім**:

Possessives

	Masculine and neuter		
N.	мíй моє́	нáш нáше	ї́хній ї́хнє
L.	(на) моє́му	(на) нáшому	(на) ї́хньому
	(на) мої́м	(на) нáшім	(на) ї́хнім
	Feminine		
	моя́	нáша	ї́хня
	(на) мої́й	нáшій	ї́хній

The pronouns **твíй, свíй** are declined like **мíй**, and **вáш** is declined like **нáш**.

(Exercises 4, 5, 6)

The possessive interrogative **чи́й** follows the adjectival pattern but in addition the masculine / neuter forms **чи́й, чиє́** also have the **-єму** ending which is characteristic of the possessive pronouns **мíй, твíй** and **свíй**, so that **чи́й, чиє́** have three possible variants for the locative case.**

N.	чи́й чиє́	чия́
L.	(на) чийóму	(на) чиї́й
	(на) чиє́му	
	(на) чиї́м	

III. THE LOCATIVE OF THE INTERROGATIVE PRONOUNS

The personal interrogative pronouns хтó and щó take adjectival endings in the locative.

N.	хтó	щó
L	(на) кóму	(на) чóму
	(на) кíм	
	(на) чíм	

---

* The forms **мойóму, твойóму, свойóму** are considered dialectal by some linguists and admissible in the standard language by others.

** All the variants are acceptable in contemporary standard Ukrainian. In this as in all other cases where there are several variants the student should learn the first form listed and simply make a note of the other forms. Any stylistic or semantic distinctions between the various form will be mentioned, if no such mention appears it means that the forms are synonymous for all practical purposes.

IV. THE IMPERATIVE

The imperative has three forms: second person singular, first person plural and second person plural. The second singular imperative is directed to a person addressed as **ти** while the second plural is directed to a person addressed **ви** or to a group of people. The first person plural imperative is an exhortation which includes the speaker. For example:

2nd sg.	Спита́й його́!	Ask him!
2nd pl.	Спита́йте його́!	Ask him!
1st pl.	Спита́ймо його́!	Let's ask him!

The imperative stem is the same as the present (or perfective future) stem, i.e. 3rd plural minus **-уть/-ють** or **-ать/-ять** (except that in labial-stems the **л** of **-лять** must also be removed). The endings are zero or **-и** for the second singular, **-іть** or **-те** for the second plural and **-ім (о)** or **-мо** for the first plural.

	Stem	*Ending*	
2nd sg.	говор-	и́	
	роб-	и́	(róbl' -at' rob-)
	чита́-й-	Ø	(čytáj -ut' čytáj-)
	бач-	Ø	
2nd pl.	говор-	і́ть	
	роб-	і́ть	
	чита́-й	те	
	діста́нь-	те	
lst pl.	говор-	і́м (о)	
	роб-	і́м (о)	
	чита-й-	мо	

1. Formation of the imperative.

Two factors play a role in the formation of the imperative: 1. the stem-final consonant(s), 2. the position of the stress in the 1st person singular present / future perfective. To form the imperative, apply these rules in order:

Rule 1. If the stem-final consonant is **j**, add nothing for the singular and -**мо** and **-те** for the plural. (In terms of spelling such stems end in a vowel to which one adds **-й, -ймо, -йте**).

Rule 2. Otherwise check the position of the stress in the 1st person singular present / future perfective.

- a. If the ending is stressed, add stressed **-и́** for the singular, **-і́м** or **-і́мо** for 1st plural and **-і́ть** for 2nd plural.
- b1. If the stem ends in two consonants, add unstressed **-и, -ім(о), -іть**.
- b2. If the stem ends in a consonant, add nothing for the singular, **-мо** and -**те** for the plural. Note: If the consonant is **т, д, с, з, н** or **л** it becomes palatalized, so that the endings will be spelled **-ь, -ьмо, -ьте**.

For example:

Rule 1.

Infinitive	imp. stem	1 sg. pres. /future	sg. imp.	1 pl. imp.	2nd pl. imp.
пита́ти	пита́-ють	пита́-ю	пита́й	пита́ймо	пита́йте
	pytáj-ut’	pytáj-u	pytáj-	pytáj-mo	pytáj-te
працюва́ти	працю́-ють	працю́-ю	працю́й	працю́ймо	працю́йте
	prac’új-ut’	prac’új-u	prac’új	prac’-új-mo	prac’új-te

Rule 2a.

бра́ти	бер-у́ть	бер-у́	бер-и́	бер-і́мо (о)	бер-і́ть
узя́ти	візьм-уть	візьм-у́	візьм-и́	візьм-і́м (о)	візьм-і́ть
сказа́ти	ска́ж-уть	скаж-у́	скаж-и́	скаж-і́м (о)	скаж-і́ть
роби́ти	ро́б(л)-ять	робл-ю́	роб-и́	роб-і́м(о)	роб-і́ть
спа́ти	сп(л)-я́ть	спл-ю́	сп-и́	сп-і́м (о)	сп-і́ть

Rule 2b (1).

підкре́слити	підкре́сл-ять	підкре́сл-ю	підкре́сл-и	підкре́сл-ім	підкре́сл-іть

Rule 2b (2).

ба́чити	ба́ч-ать	ба́ч-у	ба́ч	ба́ч-мо	ба́ч-те
ста́вити	ста́в(л)-ять	ста́вл-ю	ста́в	ста́в-мо	ста́в-те
прихо́дити	прихо́д-ять	прихо́дж-у	прихо́дь	прихо́дь-мо	прихо́дь-те
	pryxód’-at’				
забу́ти	забу́д-уть	забу́д-у	забу́дь	забу́дь-мо	забу́дь-те
діста́ти	діста́н-уть	діста́н-у	діста́нь	діста́нь-мо	діста́нь-те

Note 1: Verbs with infinitives in **-АВА-**, which drop **-ВА-** in the present, retain it in the imperative. cf.: **дАВА́-ти, да-ють, дАВА́й, дістАВА́-ти, дістА-ю́ть, дістАВА́й.**

Note 2: If the root-vowel in verbs with the stem-final consonant j is -o it usually changes to i in the imperative. cf.: **стоя́ти**, сто-я́ть stoj-át’ -сті́й, сті́ймо, сті́йте; **боя́тися**, бо-я́ться boj-ác’c’a — бі́йся, бі́ймося, бі́йтеся.

Note 3: The imperative of the verb ‘to be’ is бу́дь, бу́дьмо, бу́дьте.

Note 4: The particle **-ся** may be reduced to **-сь** in the imperative just in the other forms* (cf. the quotation from Ševčenko in the passage 'A poem by Ševčenko' in this lesson). Note also that the verb **учітеся** in that quotation does not follow rule 1, as it should and has an **-е** in place of **-ь (учіться)**.

This is an older form which was preserved in poetry for some time (cf. another famous quote from Ševčenko: "Борíтеся — побóрете, вáм Бóг помагáє..." 'Fight and you will overcome, God is helping you').

2. Indirect command.

To express a wish or indirect command that a third party perform an act, **нехáй** or **хáй** is used with the present or future perfective 3rd person singular or plural.** For example:

Хáй він читáє.	Let him read.
Хáй вонá прочитáє.	Let her read (it through).
Нехáй скáжуть по-украї́нському.	Let them say it in Ukrainian.

This construction is often used in slogans with the verb **жи́ти** to mean 'Long live'.

3. Negative commands.

The general rule is that the perfective imperative is used in commands and the imperfective imperative is used in prohibitions. cf:

Зачини́ вікнó!	Shut the window!
Не зачиня́й вікнá!	Don't shut the window!

However, speaker may choose the imperfective for a positive command when the focus of attention is on the process itself:

Зачиня́й шви́дко!	Hurry up and shut it!

On the other hand, the perfective may be used in a negative imperative when a warning is sounded or the focus is upon completion of one single instant.

Не забýдь подзвони́ти!	Don't forget to call!
Прóшу, не зрозумíйте менé непрáвильно.	Please, don't misunderstand me.

(Exercises 7, 8, 9, 10)

---

* The current handbooks prescribe that -**ся** be written. However, authors of belles lettres often disregard this rule.

** Compare this with the **щоб** construction which also expresses an indirect command or a wish, but requires the past tense and may refer to any person (see Lesson 7, p. 117).

V. INDEFINITE PRONOUNS AND ADVERBS IN -СЬ

Interrogative pronouns and adverbs can be changed to indefinite prononns and adverbs by adding the particle **сь**, cf.:

Interrogatives		*Indefinite pronouns and adverbs*	
хтó	who	хтóсь	someone
дé	where	дéсь	somewhere (location)
щó	what	щóсь	something
куди́	where	куди́сь	somewhere (direction)
чогó	why	чогóсь	for some reason
чомý	why	чомýсь	for some reason
яки́й	which	яки́йсь	some kind
чи́й	whose	чи́йсь	someone's
я́к	how	я́кось	somehow*

Note that addition of the particle **-сь** not only changes the meaning to indefinite ('some') but in some cases changes the basic meaning as well.

Indefinite pronouns are declined the same way as their definite counterparts, the particle **-сь** being preserved thoughout the declension.

N.	хтóсь	щóсь	яки́йсь
A.	когóсь	щóсь	яки́йсь / якóгось
G.	когóсь	чогóсь	якóгось
L.	(на) кóмусь	(на) чóмусь	якóмусь
	(на) кíмсь	(на)чíмсь	(на) якíмсь

VI. REPORTED SPEECH

The indirect (reported) speech or thought preserve the verb tense of the original:

Original	*Reported*
"Вони́ йдýть на концéрт", — сказáла вонá.	Вонá сказáла, що вони́ йдýть на концéрт.
"Чи ти́ йдéш на концéрт?" — спитáв він.	Він спитáв, чи я́ йдý на концéрт.
"Вонá не пíде на концéрт", — подýмав він.	Він подýмав, що вонá не пíде на концéрт.

Note the word order in identifying the speaker / thinker: **сказáв (подýмав) він.**

---

* The old form of **я́к** was **я́ко**. The **-о-** is kept in **я́кось**.

ВПРАВИ

I. Give the locative case of the nouns and adjectives in the following sentences:

1. Та́м бу́в ціка́вий конце́рт. Ми́ булú на . . . . . .
2. Та́м була́ велúка конфере́нція.
3. Та́м бу́в літерату́рний ве́чір.
4. То бу́в старúй фі́льм.
5. Та́м бу́в велúкий заво́д.
6. Та́м була́ нова́ ву́лиця.
7. Та́м бу́в ціка́вий ку́рс.
8. Та́м бу́в літерату́рний факульте́т.

II. Finish the sentences:

1. Це́ до́брий готе́ль. Ми́ живемо́ в . . . . . .
2. Це́ стара́ шко́ла. Ві́н навча́ється у . . . .
3. Це́ пога́на кімна́та. Ти́ живе́ш у . . . . . .
4. Це́ старúй стіле́ць. Ви́ сидите́ на . . . . . .
5. Це́ новúй будúнок. Ві́н працю́є в . . . . .
6. Це́ університе́тська бібліоте́ка. Вона́ сидúть в . . . . .
7. Це́ Га́рвардський університе́т. Ми́ навча́ємо́ся в . . . .
8. Це́ украї́нська шко́ла. Ви́ вчите́ся в . . .
9. Це́ ціка́вий музе́й. Ми́ бу́ли в . . . . . .

III. Write out numerals in both parts of the exercise.

1. Вона́ студе́нтка 1-го ку́рсу. Вона́ навча́ється на . . . . . .
2. Вона́ студе́нтка 2-го ку́рсу.
3. Вона́ студе́нтка 3-го ку́рсу.
4. Вона́ студе́нтка 4-го ку́рсу.
5. Вона́ кінча́є 5-у кля́су. Вона́ в . . . .
6. Вона́ кінча́є 6-у кля́су.
7. Вона́ кінча́є 7-у кля́су.
8. Вона́ кінча́є 8-у кля́су.

IV. Give the response according to the model:

Чи це́ твоє́ пита́ння? Я́ нічо́го не розумію в твоє́му пита́нні.

(тві́й пере́клад, твоє́ ре́чення, твоя́ ві́дповідь, тві́й лúст, твоє́ завда́ння, тві́й ві́рш, тві́й малю́нок, твоя́ тво́рчість)

V. Answer the questions using the possessive pronouns, incl. **свій**

1. На чийо́му стільці ти́ сиді́в?
2. На чийо́му мі́сці ти́ сиді́в?
3. У чиї́й кімна́ті ти́ жи́в?
4. У чийо́му зо́шиті ти́ писа́в?
5. На чийо́му крі́слі ти́ сиді́ла?
6. На чийо́му мі́сці ти́ працюва́ла?
7. У чийо́му поме́шканні ти́ ме́шкав?
8. У чиї́й кварти́рі ти́ жила́?

VI. Finish the sentences using the correct form of nouns, pronouns and adjectives.

1. Це́ мі́й папі́р! Ти́ сиди́ш на . . . .
2. Це́ сього́днішня газе́та! .
3. Це́ на́ш ли́ст!
4. Це́ ї́хній журна́л!
5. Це́ моя́ мапа!
6. Це́ тві́й малю́нок!
7. Це́ моя́ фотогра́фія!
8. Це́ мі́й пере́клад!
9. Це́ моя́ украї́нська кни́жка!
10. Це́ англі́йський словни́к!

VII. Give the correct form of the words in brackets.

1. Де́ ви́ сиді́ли? На (це́й стіле́ць).
2. На чо́му ви писа́ли? На (ця́ до́шка).
3. Де́ ви́ лежа́ли? На (те́ лі́жко).
4. Де́ ви́ це́ прочита́ли? В (одна́ кни́жка).
5. Де́ ви́ це́ ба́чили? В (яки́йсь журна́л).
6. Де́ ви́ це́ знайшли́? В (оди́н словни́к).
7. Де́ ви́ чита́ли про сла́ву Шевче́нка? У (ця́ кни́жка).
8. Де́ словни́к? На (то́й сті́л).

VIII. Give the 2nd sg. imperative.

Model: **Я́ чита́ю. —** До́бре, **чита́й.**

(лежу́, вчу́ся, працю́ю, дзвоню́, стою́, дивлю́ся, кінча́ю, сиджу́)

IX. Give the 2nd pl. imperative.

Model: **Я́ знайду́.** До́бре, **знайді́ть.**

(покладу́ це́ на лі́жко, поста́влю це́ на сті́л, надруку́ю це́й пере́клад, підкре́слю це́ ре́чення, зачиню́ две́рі, його́ спита́ю, ї́ї попрошу́, повторю́ ще́ раз)

X. Change the positive commands to prohibitions:

Model: **Зроби́ це́! — Не роби́ цього́!**

1. Відчини́ це́ вікно́.
2. Прочита́й цю́ кни́жку.
3. Підкре́сли це́ сло́во.
4. Напиши́ це́ ре́чення.
5. Ви́вчи це́й ві́рш.
6. Зроби́ це́ завда́ння.
7. Послу́хай цю́ ві́дповідь.
8. Скажи́ це́ сло́во.

XI. Answer the following questions:

1. На яко́му ви́ ку́рсі?
2. На яко́му ви́ факульте́ті?
3. У яко́му ви́ університе́ті?
4. На чиє́му стільці́ ви́ сидите́?
5. У яко́му поме́шканні ви́ живете́?
6. У які́й ти́ кля́сі?
7. На які́й ви́ ле́кції?
8. У яко́му ви́ буди́нку?
9. Коли́ в те́бе і́спит?

XII. Translate into Ukrainian:

1. I am afraid to sit (down) on this old chair.
2. I want your friend Oksana to come on Monday.
3. How can you lie in bed all day long?
4. How can you stay at home on such a wonderful day?
5. Are you afraid of this little girl?
6. Let him do it for you.
7. Are you sure she wants us to memorize this poem?
8. It's too bad you can't go to the concert.

XIII. Translate into Ukrainian:

Peter is studying at a Canadian university. He studied medicine but now he is taking a course in Ukrainian literature. He loves Ševčenko's poems and has learned a few of them by heart. In his room he has a drawing by Ševčenko.

XIV. Reading exercise.

1. Я́ живу́ у своє́ї сестри́ Ві́ри. Вона́ працю́є в бібліоте́ці, а я́ ходжу́ до шко́ли. Ві́ра все́ ка́же: "Вчи́ся до́бре, якщо́ не хо́чеш усе́ життя́ працюва́ти в які́йсь бібліоте́ці, я́к я́". Я́ не ба́чу ту́т нічо́го пога́ного. Я́ ду́маю, що працюва́ти в бібліоте́ці ціка́во.

2. Мій товáриш Юркó навчáється на дрýгому кýрсі Гáрвардського університéту. Він лю́бить істóрію і вивчáє істóрію Украї́ни, алé він хóче тéж знáти й украї́нську мóву і літератýру. У цьóму університéті мóжна всé цé дóбре ви́вчити, алé трéба вчи́тися і в понеділок, і у вівтóрок, і в сéреду, і в четвéр, і в п'ятницю, і в субóту, і в неділю. Немá часý диви́тися телевізíйну прогрáму, трéба абó слýхати лéкції, абó сидíти в бібліотéці і читáти.

3. Я́ дýже люблю́ вíрші. Я́ ї́х вивчáю напам'ять, і коли́ студéнти влаштóвують літератýрний вéчір, вони́ менé прóсять прийти́ і прочитáти дéкілька. Зáвтра бýде Дéнь Мáтері. Студéнти хóчуть, щоб я́ продеклямувáв* яки́йсь вíрш. У Шевчéнка є оди́н чудóвий вíрш про мáтір:

У нáшім рáї, на землí**
Нічóго кращóго немáє,
Я́к тáя мáти молодáя
З своḯм дитя́точком мали́м ... і т.д.

Я́ дýмаю, що я́ прочитáю цéй вíрш.

XV. Answer the following questions to the above passages:

(1)

1. Дé живé ця́ дівчина?
2. Щó кáже ї́ї сестрá?
3. Чи ця́ дівчина тéж тáк дýмає?

(2)

1. Дé вчи́ться Юркó?
2. Щó він тáм вивчáє?
3. Чи він багáто вчи́ться?

(3)

1. Щó студéнти прóсять цьогó хлóпця зроби́ти?
2. Яки́й зáвтра дéнь?
3. Щó цéй хлóпець дýмає прочитáти?

---

* деклямувáти, продеклямувáти — to recite

** рáй — paradise
землí — earth
молоди́й — young (the long form used here is archaic)
дитя́точко — baby
мали́й — little

XVI. Ansver the following questicns to the dialogues:

"Вірш Шевчéнка"

1. На якóму кýрсі Оксáна?
2. На якóму вонá факультéті?
3. Про щó говóрить Шевчéнко у своéму вíрші?
4. Щó профéсор хóче, щоб студéнти зробúли?

"Вáжко знайтú квартúру"

1. Чомý Оксáна боїться, щоб гóсті сідáли на крíсло?
2. Чомý не мóжна відчиняти вікнó?
3. Щó кáже товáришка Оксáни?
4. Щó відповідáє Оксáна?

"Слáва Бóгу"

1. Щó бýде в п'ятницю?
2. А щó дýмав Ю́рій Володúмирович?
3. Чи вонú йдýть купúсь у понедíлок?

ДЕВ'ЯТА ЛЕКЦІЯ

26 Я голодний
I am hungry

Dialogue Paticipants:
Віктор Ме́льник - В, Мико́ла Ме́льник - М
Viktor Mel'nyk - V, Mykola Mel'nyk - M

1. В- Мико́ло, чи в на́с є щоне́будь ї́сти? Я́ таки́й голо́дний!	V- Mykola, do we have anything to eat? I am so hungry.
2. М- Подиви́ся в холоди́льнику. Здає́ться, та́м ще́ було́ тро́хи борщу́ й ка́ші.	M- Check in the refrigirator. I think there was still some borsht and kasha there.
3. В- Ні, дя́кую. Ми́ вже́ цю́ ка́шу й бо́рщ ці́лий ти́ждень ї́мо́ — і на снідáнок, і на обі́д, і на вече́рю.	V- No, thanks. We have been eating that kasha and borsht all week long, for breakfast, lunch and supper.
4. М- Ну́ то з'ї́ж яйце́. Там є я́йця, я́ вчо́ра купи́в.	M- Well, have an egg then. There are eggs in there, I bought them yesterday.
5. В- Чудо́во! З'ї́м яйце́ й шмато́к хлі́ба і ви́п'ю гаря́чої ка́ви.	V- Wonderful! I'll have an egg and a slice of bread and some hot coffee.
6. М- Ка́ви у на́с нема́. Є́ ча́й.	M- We don't have any coffee. We have tea.
7. В- Ну́ то неха́й бу́де ча́й. Мо́жна й ча́ю ви́пити, аби́ гаря́чий.	V- OK, let it be tea. I can drink tea as long as it's hot.

27 Мова — це душа народу
Language is the soul of the people

Dialogue Paticipants:
Тетя́на Миха́йлівна -Т, Ната́лка, ї́ї дочка́ - Н
Tetjana Myxajlivna - T, Natalka - N (her daughter)

1. Т- Ната́лко, чи ти́ ще́ бу́деш користува́тися словнико́м?	T- Natalka, will you still be using the dictionary?
2. Н- Ні, я його́ вже́ не потребу́ю. Я́ тільки заціка́вилася сло́вом "ра́ція" і хоті́ла дізна́тися, зві́дки воно́ похо́дить.	N- No, I don't need it any more. I was just curious about the word 'racija' and wanted to find out from where it came.
3. Т- Я́ ду́же ра́да, що ти́ ціка́вишся мо́вою. Мо́ва, ка́жуть, — це́ душа́ наро́ду.	T- I am so glad that you are interested in the language. Language, they say, is the soul of the people.
4. Н- Та́к, я згі́дна, і я те́ж ду́же ра́да, що вивча́ю украї́нську мо́ву. Я́ давно́ хоті́ла ї́ї до́бре ви́вчити, але́ в ме́не все́ не було́ часу́.	N- Yes, I agree, and I'm also very happy that I am studying the Ukrainian language. I have been wanting to learn it well for a long time but I never had the time.

28 Дмитро Іванович працює вчителем
Dmytro Ivanovyc works as a teacher

Я́ похо́джу з мало́го села́ недале́ко від Ха́ркова. Коли́ я́ бу́в ще́ мали́м, то ви́рішив, що бу́ду вчи́телем. Спочáтку я́ вчи́вся в шко́лі у на́с в селі́, по́тім у Ха́рківському інститу́ті. Тепе́р я́ закінчи́в інститу́т і працю́ю вчи́телем у шко́лі. Моя́ жі́нка ще́ вчи́ться. Вона́ хо́че ста́ти лі́карем.

I come from a small village not far from Kharkiv. When I was still little I decided that I will be a teacher. I first went to school in our village and later I studied at the Kharkiv institute. Now I have granduated from the institute and am working as a school teacher. My wife is still in school. She wants to become a doctor.

СЛОВНИК

аби́	as long as; in order that
бо́рщ, -у́ (m)	borsht
вече́ря (f)	supper
вирі́шува́ти, вирі́шують I (вирішáти, вирішáють)* ви́рішити, ви́рішать P	to decide
голо́дний	hungry
гаря́чий	hot
давно́	for a long time; long ago
дочка́ (f)	daughter
дев'ятий	ninth
дізнава́тися, дізнаю́ться I дізна́тися, дізнаються P	to find out
душа́ (f)	soul
жі́нка (f)	woman; wife
звідки	from where
згі́дний (з+I)	to agree
інститу́т, -у (m)	institute

* Less frequent

ї́сти, їдя́ть I, з'ї́сти, з'їдя́ть P *	to eat
ка́ва (f)	coffee
ка́ша (f)	cooked cereal
користува́тися, -у́ються I	to use (+ I);
скористува́тися, -у́ються P	to take advantage of
корист́атися, -ються I (з + G)	
скорист́атися, -ються P**	
купува́ти, купу́ють I (у + G; в + L)	to buy (from; at)
купи́ти, ку́плять P	
мо́жна	one can; possible
мали́й	small; little
наро́д, -у	people; nation
обі́д, -у (m)	lunch; dinner
пи́ти, п'ють I	to drink
ви́пити, ви́п'ють P	
(ви́)пий! (-те, -мо)	
похо́дити, похо́джу,	to come from, to originate
похо́дять I (no perf.)	
почина́ти, почина́ють I	to begin
поча́ти, почну́ть P	
ра́дий, -а, -е, -і (за + A)	glad, happy (for)
село́ (n)	village
сніда́нок, -нку (m)	breakfast
спочатку	at first
става́ти, стають I	to become
ста́ти, ста́нуть P	
тро́хи	a little, some (what)
учи́тель (m)	teacher
ха́рківський	Kharkiv (adj.)
хлі́б, -а (m)	bread
холоди́льник, -а (m)	refrigerator
ці́лий	entire; whole
ціка́витися, ціка́вляться I (+ I)	to be interested in
зацікавитися, -вляться P	to become
ча́й, ча́ю (m)	tea
шмато́к, шматка́ (m)	piece, slice
щоне́будь	anything
яйце́, -я́ (n)	egg
я́йця (pl.)	eggs

* Irregular (see Grammar notes, p. 151)

** Less frequent

NAMES AND PLACES

Ната́ля (Natalie),
Ната́лка (informal)
Дмитро́ Іва́нович
Ха́рків, -кова (m) Kharkiv (Xarkiv)

IDIOMS

на сніда́нок (обі́д, вече́рю)	for breakfest (dinner, supper)

SUPPLEMENT

лі́карка (f)	doctor (female)
ліка́рня (f)	hospital
селяни́н (m), селя́нка (f), селя́ни (pl.)	villager, farmer

EXPLANATORY NOTES

1. We have seen that the verb **диви́тися** implies a direction (cf.: in English 'to throw a glance in the direction of...'). Consequently the object at which one is looking appears in the accusative case:

Куди́ я́ ма́ю диви́тися?	Where should I look?
- На вчи́теля.	- At the teacher.
- У кни́жку.	- In the book.

However, the verb **диви́тися** may also be used in the sense of 'looking for', 'searching'. Then the noun designating the place where one is looking (searching) appears in the locative case:

Подиви́ся уньо́го в кімна́ті.	Look in his room.
Подиви́ся в холоди́льнику	Look (cheek) in the refrigerator.

2. **Обі́д** is a 'midday meal', according to the dictionary. Some speakers use this term in reference to a meal in late afternoon (5:00 or 6:00 P. M.).

3. **Ка́ша** is any cooked cereal. The favorite Ukrainian cereal is buckwheat, **греча́на ка́ша**.

4. **Бóрщ** is a traditional Ukrainian soup, whose distinctive ingredient is beets. There are many different ways to prepare it (one cookbook lists 22 varieties, including one which is called 'Polish'). A meatless **бóрщ** is traditionally included in the Christmas Eve evening meal. One particular variety called '**Украї́нський бóрщ**' can often be found on the menu in Ukrainian restaurants.

5. In addition to universities, there are in Ukraine institutes and schools of technology (**тéхнікум**). In Dmytro Ivanovyč's biography we learn that he graduated from an **інститýт**, i.e. from a Teachers College. It is a four year college and upon graduation one receives a teacher's certificate which entitles one to teach high school.

6. Female physicians are called either **лíкар** (m.) or **лíкарка** (f.).

7. The verb **(с)корист(ув)áтися** has two meanings, 'to use' and 'to take advantage of'. In the first case it is followed by instrumental, in the second case by the preposition **з** plus genitive. For example:

Я́ користáюся словникóм.	I use the dictionary.
Трéба скористáтися з тогó, що він тепéр тýт.	We should take advantage of the fact that he is here now.

8. Collective farmer is **колгóспник (колгóспни́ця́)** from **колгóсп (колекти́вне господáрство)** collective farm.

NOTES ON GRAMMAR

I. INSTRUMENTAL SINGULAR OF NOUNS

Each declension has its characteristic endings.

(1) The feminine a-declension has **-ою** for hard stems and **-ею (-єю)** for soft stems or stems ending in **ж, ч, ш, щ**.

a-declension

N.	Микóла	Гáля	Марíя	кáша	душá
I.	Микóлою	Гáлею	Марíєю	кáшею	душéю

(2) The feminine c-declension has the ending u spelled **ю**. The stem-final consonant is lengthened by doubling and becomes soft, if not already soft. Doubling does not occur if the stem ends in two consonants:

річ -	річчю	*r'ič'č'u* (see Sound System p. xvi)
відповідь -	відповіддю	*v'idpovidd'u*
твóрчість -	твóрчістю	*tvorč'is't'u*

The c-type nouns with stems ending in a labial (p, b, f, v, m) or in r have the instrumental ending ju spelled **'ю**. There is no doubling nor softening of the stem-final consonant:

любо́в	любо́в'ю	*l'ubów'ju*
ма́ти	ма́тір'ю	*m át'ir'ju*
(G. **ма́тер-і**)		

Note 1: For all practical purposes this rule is applicable to only four nouns:

любо́в'ю, кро́в'ю, ма́тір'ю, ве́рф'ю

Note 2: In nouns whose stems have **-e/-o** before vowel-ending but **-i** before the zero ending (as in the nominative and the accusative) **-i** also appears before the instrumental ending, cf.: **річ** — **ре́чі** — **річчю**, **ма́тері** — **ма́тір** — **ма́тір'ю**

c-declension

N.	відповідь	річ	ма́ти	любо́в
L.	відповіддю	річчю	ма́тір'ю	любо́в'ю

(3). The masculine-neuter declension has **-ом** for the hard stems and **-ем (-єм)** for the soft stems and those ending in **ж, ч, ш, щ**. All neuter nouns have the ending **-м**.

Masculine-neuter deslension

Masculine

N.	сті́л	гість	Андрі́й	това́риш
I.	столо́м	го́стем	Андрі́єм	това́ришем

Neuter

N.	село́	місце	прізвище	життя́
I.	село́м	місцем	прізвищем	життя́м

Note 4: The instrumental of the noun **ім'я́** is either **ім'я́м** or **і́менем**.

(4). Stress. The stress is in the same position in the instrumental as it is in the genitive. For example:

N.	олівець	ли́ст	бо́рщ	хло́пець	пра́вда
G.	олівця́	листа́	борщу́	хло́пця	пра́вди
I.	олівце́м	листо́м	борще́м	хло́пцем	пра́вдою

(Exercises 6, 7, 8, 9)

II. INSTRUMENTAL OF PERSONAL PRONOUNS

The instrumental form of the personal pronouns are:

N.	я́	ти́	він/воно́	вона́	ми́	ви́	вони́
I.	мно́ю	тобо́ю	ни́м	не́ю	на́ми	ва́ми	ни́ми

Note: Unlike the genitive which differentiates between the forms **його́** and **нього́, її** and **не́ї** depending on the presence or absence of a preceding preposition, the instumental knows only the forms with **н-** (ним, з ним, нею, з нею).

(Exercise 8)

III. USES OF THE INSTRUMENTAL

Some uses of the instrumental are (a) predicative, (b) instrument, (c) complement (object) of certain verbs.

(a) Predicative use. In statements which describe a temporal or new condition (usually with the verbs 'to be' and 'to become'):

Я́ тоді́ бу́в мали́м хло́пцем.	I was a small boy at the time.
Вона́ ста́ла ма́тір'ю.	She became a mother.

(b) Instrument:

Я́ пишу́ олівце́м.	I am writing with a pencil.

Note: That Ukrainian uses no preposition when 'with' is an equivalent of 'by means of (an instrument or tool)'.

(c) Object:

Я́ користу́юся словнико́м.	I am using a dictionary.
Я́ ціка́влюся літерату́рою.	I am interested in literature.
Я́ говорю́ украї́нською мово́ю.	I speak Ukrainian.

(Exercises 6,7,8)

IV. PARTITIVE GENITIVE

The genitive of nouns denoting divisible substances may be used as the object of some perfective verbs to indicate an indefinite quantity.

Ми́ купи́ли хлі́ба.	We bought some bread.

This usage, called the partitive genitive, may be found with the verbs **купи́ти, узя́ти, з'ї́сти** (among others):

Я́ куплю́ хлі́ба.	I'll buy some bread.
Ві́н узя́в борщу́.	He took some borsht.
Вона́ ви́пила ча́ю.	She had (drank) some tea.
З'ї́ж хлі́ба!	Eat some bread!

The imperfective equivalents of these verbs almost always take an accusative object:

Чому́ ти́ бере́ш мі́й папі́р?	Why are you taking my paper?
Ми́ пи́ли ча́й, коли́ ти́ подзвони́в.	We were having tea when you called.
Я́ ту́т купу́ю хлі́б.	I buy bread here.

With the imperfective **ї́сти** and **пи́ти** the accusative object is obligatory (i.e. only the substance is indicated, not the quantity):

З'ї́ж кашу!	Eat your cereal!*
Пи́й ка́ву!	Drink your coffee!
Я́ вже́ пила́ ка́ву.	I already had coffee.
Що́ ти́ ї́си́, ка́шу?	What are you eating, cereal?
Я́ п'ю ча́й.	I'm having tea.
Кра́ще пи́ти ча́й, а не ка́ву.	It's better to drink tea and not coffee.

The imperfective verb **хоті́ти**, on the other hand, is normally used with the partitive genitive when reference is made to an indefinite quantity. For example:

Я́ хо́чу ка́ви.	I want some coffee.
Хо́чеш хлі́ба?	Do you want some bread?

The genitive is required after quantitative expressions such as **тро́хи** 'a little, some small quantity of', **ма́ло** 'little, very little', **бага́то** 'much, a lot of':

Ві́н узя́в тро́хи хлі́ба.	He took some bread.
Ми́ ма́ємо тро́хи борщу́.	We have some borsht.
У ме́не є́ бага́то папе́ру.	I have a lot of paper.
Ту́т ма́ло хлі́ба.	There is very little bread there.

Thus, partitive genitive alone indicates an indefinite (usually small) quantity, in combination with **тро́хи** it means 'a little' and with **ма́ло** it means 'very little' or even 'too little'. cf.:

Чи ти́ купи́в **хлі́ба?**	Did you buy some bread?
-Та́к, я́ купи́в **тро́хи** хлі́ба.	Yes, I bought a little bread.
Але́ це́ ма́ло. Чому́ ти́ купи́в та́к **ма́ло хлі́ба?**	But that's too little. Why did you buy so little bread?
Це́ не ма́ло. Це́ доси́ть.	It's not little. It's enough.

* Ukrainian does not use the possesive modifiers in such expressions as 'Drink your tea' or 'Eat your cereal'. To use a possessive here would either carry a touch of annoyance ('Drink your miserable tea') or actually indicate that you should eat your own cereal and not someone else's.

Note 1: The partitive genitive must be accompanied by some quantitive modifier when used with the verbs **бу́ти** and **ма́ти:**

Ту́т є **тро́хи** папе́ру.	There is some paper here.
У на́с є **тро́хи** борщу́.	We have a little borsht.
Я́ ма́ю **ма́ло** часу́.	I have very little time.

(Exercises 1,3,4)

V. PREDICATION IN EXPRESSIONS OF LIMITATION, PRESENCE AND ABSENCE

1. When the quantitative modifier **тро́хи** is the grammatical subject of a sentence, it is treated as a neuter noun; the verb, therefore must be 3rd singular, and, if past, neuter.*

Та́м лежи́ть тро́хи хлі́ба.	There is some bread lying there.
Та́м лежа́ло тро́хи хлі́ба.	There was some bread lying there.

2. We have seen that **є** is used in statements about existence, presence or possession (limited or unlimited).

Студе́нти вже́ та́м є́?	Are the students already there?
Та́м є́ бібліоте́ка.	There is a library there.
У ме́не є́ словник.	I have a dictionary.
У ме́не є́ тро́хи папе́ру.	I have some paper.

In the past and future tenses the verb 'to be' in such expressions agrees with the subject (unless it is accompanied by a quantitative modifier — see rule V.1. above).

Студе́нти та́м бу́дуть.	The students will be there.
У на́с бу́дуть го́сті.	We will have company.
Бу́в конце́рт.	There was a concert.

However, when the positive statements of this sort are made negative (absence, lack of possession) the verb automatically changes to 3rd singular (neuter in the past) and the noun appears in the genitive:

Конце́рту не було́.	There was no concert.
У ме́не не було́ часу.	I didn't have any time.
Мене́ не бу́де.	I won't be there.

(Exercise 2)

* The same is true of other nondeclinable parts of speech and phrases, e.g. **Твоє́ "дя́кую" ("ні дя́кую") було́ до́сить холо́дне.** Your 'thank you' ('no, thank you') was rather cool.

VI. THE VERBS ЇСТИ AND ВІДПОВІСТИ

The verbs **(з')ї́сти** 'to eat' and **відпові́сти** 'to answer' are quite irregular. The future tense of the perfective verb **відпові́сти** has been give in Lesson 6 (p. 103) but we repeat it here for the sake of comparison.

Present / Future Perfective

	Singular		*Plural*	
1st	(з')ї́м	відпові́м	(з')їмо́	відповімо́
2nd	(з')їси́	відповіси́	(з')їсте́	відповісте́
3rd	(з')ї́сть	відпові́сть	(з')їдя́ть	відповідя́ть

Imperative

(з')ї́ж, (з')ї́мо, (з')ї́жте

Past

(з')ї́в, (з')ї́ла, (з')ї́ло, (з')ї́ли — відпові́в, відповіла́, відповіло́, відповіли́ (see p. 98)

(Exercise 5)

VII. THE INDEFINITE PRONOUNS AND ADVERBS IN -НЕБУДЬ

The indefinite pronouns and adverbs in **-не́будь** have the meaning any-:

хтоне́будь	anyone
щоне́будь	anything
дене́будь	anywhere (location)
кудине́будь	anywhere (direction)
якне́будь	carelessly, sloppily, in any way
якийне́будь	any kind
чийне́будь	anyone's
чогоне́будь	for any reason

The stress is always on **-не́будь** and the declension is the same as with the definite pronouns: **кого-не́будь, кому-не́будь, ким-не́будь**, etc.

ВПРАВИ

I. Change the sentences using partitive genitive.

Ми́ ма́ємо ча́с. Ми́ ма́ємо тро́хи ча́су.

(хлі́б, на обі́д бо́рщ, на сніда́нок ка́шу, ча́й, ка́ву, папі́р)

II. Change the sentences from positive to negative.

Та́м була́ ле́кція. Та́м не було́ ле́кції.

(шмато́к папе́ру, яйце́, ціка́вий ку́рс, вчора́шня газе́та, літерату́рний факульте́т, спра́вжня шко́ла, до́брий лі́кар, вели́ке село́, до́бра ліка́рня, "Істо́рія Украї́ни")

III. Put the bracketed words into the correct form (give both genitive and accusative where possible).

1. Чого́ ти́ хо́чеш? (папі́р)
2. Що́ ти́ взя́в? (шмато́к хлі́ба)
3. Що́ ви́ бу́дете пи́ти? (ча́й)
4. Чи ви́ щоне́будь ї́ли? (ка́ша)
5. Чи ми́ ма́ємо щоне́будь пи́ти? (ка́ва)
6. Що́ ти́ з'ї́в? (одне́ яйце́)
7. Що́ ти́ п'є́ш? (ча́й)
8. Що́ ти́ діста́в? (папі́р)
9. Чого́ ві́н про́сить? (хлі́б)
10. Що́ ти́ їси́? (бо́рщ)

IV. Change the sentences so that the object will be in the genitive (use different verb aspects and quantitative modifiers where necessary).

1. Я́ ви́п'ю ча́й.
2. У на́с є́ хлі́б.
3. Ми́ беремо́ ка́шу.
4. Ми́ діста́ли папі́р.
5. Тре́ба взя́ти бо́рщ.
6. Ми́ з'ї́ли вве́сь хлі́б.
7. О́сь ча́й.
8. Ту́т є́ ка́ва.
9. Я́ ма́ю ча́с.
10. У ме́не є́ папі́р.

V. Supply the necessary present tense forms of the verb **їсти.**

1. Ми́ . . . . . . до́брий обі́д, а вона́ . . . . . . пога́ний.
2. Ти́ . . . . ду́же шви́дко.
3. Вони́ . . . . . . ура́нці в ці́й кімна́ті.
4. Я́ . . . . .хлі́б, а ві́н . . . . . . ка́шу.
5. Окса́но, що́ ти́ . . . . . . ?
6. Чому́ ви́ вже́ тепе́р . . . . . . вече́рю?
7. Коли́ ти́ . . . . . . сніданок?

VI. Change the sentences using the instumental case.

Вона́ студе́нтка. Вона́ ста́ла студенткóю.

(профе́сор, його́ жі́нка, америка́нка, ма́ти, лі́кар, інжене́р, її́ това́ришка, лі́карка, учи́телька)

VII. Change the sentences using the instrumental case.

Ві́н її́ студе́нт. Ві́н бу́в її́ студе́нтом.

(її́ вчи́тель, її́ това́риш, її́ профе́сор, її́ лі́кар, її́ ба́тько, її́ си́н, її́ бра́т, її́ па́н і бо́г)

VIII. Answer the questions according to the model:

Чи́й це́ словни́к? — Мі́й. Я́ користу́юся словнико́м. Я́ ни́м користу́юся.

(сті́л, оліве́ць, ма́па, крі́сло, стіле́ць, лі́жко, ру́чка, бібліоте́ка, кімна́та)

IX. Put the bracketed words into the correct form.

Ві́н ціка́виться (О́ля). Ві́н ціка́виться О́лею.

(літерату́ра, життя́ в Украї́ні, медици́на, фотогра́фія, істо́рія, тво́рчість Шевче́нка, ця́ ле́кція, нова́ лі́карня, молода́ вчи́телька, на́ша лі́карка, його́ здоро́в'я, твоя́ дочка́, Марі́я, Андрі́й)

REVIEW

X. Supply the correct prepositions.

1. Я́ дзвоню́ . . . . Ві́ри.
2. Дя́кую . . . . . .фотогра́фію.
3. . . . . . . неді́лю ми́ пі́демо . . . . . села́.
4. Коли́ ви́ та́м були́? . . . . . субо́ту.
5. Вона́ навчи́лася украї́нської мо́ви . . . . . університе́ті.
6. Ми́ поспіша́ємо . . . . . . конце́рт.
7. Хто́сь уже́ перекла́в це́ . . . . . . украї́нської мо́ви. . . . . . . англі́йську.
8. Я́ чита́ю листа́ . . . . .Монреа́лю . . . .мого́ това́риша.
9. Я́ тепе́р живу́ . . . . . . своє́ї сестри́. Це́ . . . . університе́ту.
10. Ві́н усе́ роби́в . . . . . . своє́ї сла́ви.

XI. Change the following conditionals to **якби́** conditionals.

1. Якщó я́ тáм бýду, ми́ працювáтимемо рáзом.
2. Якщó він змóже, він подзвóнить.
3. Якщó він відповість, ми будемо знати, що робити.
4. Якщó вони́ подзвóнять, я́ бýду дýже рáда.
5. Якщó немá кáви, то мóжна взя́ти чáй.
6. Якщó ти́ знáйдеш йогó адрéсу, я́ напишý до ньóго.
7. Якщó ти́ кýпиш папір, я́ надрукýю твій перéклад.
8. Якщó піде дóщ, ми́ сидітимемо вдóма.
9. Якщó вони́ цьогó потребýють, вони́ скáжуть.
10. Якщó я́ забýду цé слóво, я́ подивлюся в словни́к.

XII. Translate into Ukrainian.

1. I would like some tea, if possible.
2. He did live in this town but it was a long time ago.
3. We will listen to your story if it is interesting.
4. He is not at home, he went somewhere.
5. What were you doing last night when I called?
6. Would you like me to buy some bread?
7. Last year we lived in a real Ukrainian village not far from Kyiv.
8. We were studying the life of the Ukrainian people. What a wonderful soul these people have.
9. I found out that he went to a Kharkiv institute, graduated and is now teaching school somewhere.
10. That was a bad year: we had nothing to eat.

XIII. Read and translate.

1. Учóра в нáс булú гóсті — Ю́рій Володи́мирович і йогó жíнка Гáнна Сергíївна. Ю́рій Володи́мирович стари́й товáриш могó Дмитрá, вони́ рáзом учи́лися в університéті, а я́ і Гáнна Сергíївна працю́ємо рáзом в інститýті. Коли́сь ми́ жили́ на однíй вýлиці, в однóму буди́нку, а тепéр вони́ живýть далéко від нáс. Ми́ ї́х ужé давнó не бáчили, і я́ булá дýже рáда, що вони́ до нáс прийшли́.

2. Моя́ Натáлка цíлий дéнь щóсь ї́сть: абó хліб, абó кáшу, абó щé щóсь. Я́ кажý: "Натáлко! Не ї́ж увéсь чáс! Цé недóбре для твогó здорóв'я". Вонá відповідáє:"Але ж, мамо, що я мáю роби́ти, коли́ я ввесь час голóдна?" Я кажý: "Піди́ до лíкаря, мóже він допомóже." Я́ дýмаю: "Мóже вонá й мáє рáцію, алé що роби́ти?" Я́ дзвоню́ до своéї товáришки Лíди, кажý всю́ істóрію й питáю: "Лíдо, щó б ти́ зроби́ла на моéму мíсці?" Лíда відповідáє: "Чомý ти́ щóсь мáєш роби́ти. Нехáй Натáлка щóсь зрóбить. Алé якщó хóчеш, мóжеш óсь що зроби́ти: прóсто не купýй нíчóго ї́сти". Я́ дýмаю й кажý: "Тáк, цé дýже прóсто, алé що я́ тоді бýду ї́сти?"

XIV. Answer the following questions to the above passages.

(1)

1. Чи Ю́рі́й Володими́рович бра́т Дмитра́?
2. Де́ працю́є Га́нна Сергі́ївна?
3. Чи ви́ ме́шкаєте в одно́му буди́нку?

(2)

1. Що́ Ната́лка лю́бить ї́сти?
2. Чому́ вона́ вве́сь ча́с ї́сть?
3. Чи вона́ ходи́ла до лікаря?
4. Що́ ка́же Ліда?
5. Чи ви́ ду́маєте, що вона́ ма́є ра́цію?

XV. Answer the following questions to the dialogues.

"Я́ голо́дний"

1. Чи є́ ще́ бо́рщ і ка́ша?
2. Чому́ Віктор не хо́че цього́ ї́сти?
3. Що́ Мико́ла вчо́ра купи́в?
4. Що́ Віктор ви́рішив з'ї́сти?
5. Що́ він пи́тиме?

"Мо́ва — це́ душа́ наро́ду"

1. Для чо́го Ната́лка потребува́ла словника́?
2. Яке́ сло́во вона́ шука́ла?
3. Чи Ната́лка давно́ ціка́виться мо́вою?

"Дмитро́ Іва́нович працю́є вчи́телем"

1. Звідки похо́дить Дмитро́ Іва́нович?
2. Де́ він учи́вся?
3. Де́ він працю́є?
4. Що́ вивча́є його́ жі́нка?

ДЕСЯТА ЛЕКЦІЯ

29 Перевір ще раз
Check it once more

Dialogue Paticipants:
Катери́на Сковорода́ - К, Рома́н, її чолові́к - Р
Kateryna Skovoroda - K, Roman, her husband - R

1. К- Ро́мку, де́ ти́ бу́в та́к до́вго?
2. Р- В університе́ті. Я́ хоті́в поговори́ти з профе́сором Ле́севим пі́сля ле́кції, але́ ві́н му́сив бу́ти на засі́данні, а пі́сля то́го ще́ ма́в розмо́ву з доце́нтом Івани́шиним; о́тже, для ме́не вже́ не лиши́лося ча́су.
3. К- Шкода́. Коли́ ж ти́ з ни́м тепе́р поба́чишся?
4. Р- За́втра вра́нці, до ле́кції.
5. К- Ну́ то до́бре. Ти́ кра́ще переві́р ще́ раз свою́ дисерта́цію.
6. Р- Я́ вже́ ці́лу ні́ч переві́ря́в, сиді́в аж до тре́тьої ра́нку.

1. K- Romko, where were you so long?
2. R- At the university. I wanted to talk to professor Lesiv after the lecture, but he had to be at a meeting and after that he also had a talk with docent Ivanyšyn so that there was no time left for me.
3. K- It's too bad. So now when will you see him?
4. R- Tomorrow morning before the lecture.
5. K- It's all right then. You better check your thesis once more.
6. R- I have been checking it all night; I was up till three A.M.

30 Ромко закінчив дисертацію
Romko finished his dissertation

Dialogue Paticipants: Катери́на - К, Рома́н -Р
Kateryna - K, Roman - R

1. К- Я́ така́ ра́да, Ро́мку, що ти́ вже́ закінчи́в свою́ дисерта́цію. Я́к до́вго ти́ над не́ю працюва́в?
2. Р- Ці́лий рік. Я́ поча́в рік тому́, якра́з перед ти́м, як ми́ одружи́лися.
3. К- Зна́єш, на мою́ ду́мку, рік — це́ зо́всім не до́вго. Не ко́жний мо́же написа́ти дисерта́цію за оди́н рік.
4. Р- Мо́же, якщо́ сиді́тиме над не́ю і вде́нь і вночі́ і ма́тиме тако́го керівника́, як профе́сор Ле́сів. Під його́ керівни́цтвом усі́ студе́нти шви́дко пи́шуть.
5. К- Мо́же й шви́дко, але́ не та́к як ти́. І в усякому ра́зі не та́к до́бре, як ти́. Ти́ не ті́льки працьови́тий, але́ ти́ ще й ду́же зді́бний.
6. Р- Дя́кую за компліме́нт, але́, пра́вду ка́жучи, якби́ не Ле́сів, я́ б тако́ї дисерта́ції не написа́в.
7. К- А я всé ж таки ду́маю, що в те́бе вели́кі зді́бності і ві́рю, що через рі́к ти́ вже́ бу́деш доце́нтом.
8. Р- За такі́ слова́ вже́ ма́ло сказа́ти "дя́кую", му́шу тебе́ поцілува́ти.

1. K- Romko, I am so glad you already finished your dissertation. How long have you been working at it?
2. R- A whole year. I started a year ago, just before we got married.
3. K- You know, in my opinion, a year is not long at all. Not everyone can write a dissertation in one year.
4. R- Yes he can, if he works at it day and night and has such a director as Prof. Lesiv. All the students who work under him write fast.
5. K- Maybe they do, but not as fast as you. And in any case, not as good as you. You are not only hard working, you are also very talented.
6. R- Thanks for the compliment, but to tell the truth, if it hadn't been for Lesiv I wouldn't have written such a dissertation.
7. K- And I still think that you have great abilities and I am convinced that within a year you will be a docent.
8. R- For such words it is not enough to say "thank you", I must give you a kiss.

30 Марко одружився
Marko got married

Dialogue Paticipants:
Наталка - Н, Катерина - К
Natalka - N, Kateryna - K

1.	Н- Катрю, чи ти чула, що Марко Поліщук одружився?	N- Katrja, have you heard: Marko Poliščuk got married?
2.	К- Ні. З ким?	K- No, I haven't. To whom?
3.	Н- З нашою Галею Палій. Тиждень тому, якраз перед Новим Роком.	N- To our Halja Palij. A week ago, just before the New Year.
4.	К- Дивися! Він же з нею зовсім недавно познайомився.	K- Look at that! He only met her a short while ago.
5.	Н- Так, але на такі речі не треба багато часу.	N- Yes, but these things don't take long.
6.	К- Маєш рацію. Чи ти думаєш, що в них справжня любов?	K- You are right. Do you think there is a true love between them?
7.	Н- Не знаю, але їхні батьки кажуть, що вони дуже люблять одне одного. Хочу вірити, що це так.	N- I don't know, but according to their parents they love each other very much. I want to believe that.

СЛОВНИК

аж	so that, even
багато	much, many
батьки	parents
бачитися, бачаться I	to see each other
побачитися, побачаться P	
великі (pl.)	great, big, large
вірити, вірять I	to believe (trust)
повірити, повірять P	
десятий	tenth
вранці = уранці	
дисертація (f)	dissertation, thesis
до (+ G)	before, (until) till
довго	for a long time
довгий	long
доцент (m)	docent (M.A.)
думка (f)	thought, idea, opinion
з (+ I)	with
за (+ A)	in, within (time)

засідання (n)	meeting; conference
здібний	gifted, capable
здібність (f) здібності (pl.)	ability
знайо́митися, знайо́мляться I	to meet
познайо́митися, познайо́мляться P	(get acquainted)
зо́всім	completely, quite; at all
керівни́к, -á (m)	director, in charge
керівни́цтво (n)	leadership; direction
ко́жний	every
компліме́нт (m)	compliment
лиша́тися, лиша́ються I	to remain, to stay
лиши́тися, ли́шаться P	
ма́ло	little, few, not enough
му́сити, му́шу, му́сять I (no P.)	must
над (+ I)	over
неда́вно	not long ago
ніч, но́чі (f), но́че!	night
одру́жуватися, одру́жуються I (з + I)	to get married (to)
одружи́тися, одру́жаться P	
о́тже [ódže]	so, therefore
перевіря́ти, перевіря́ють I	to check
(переві́рювати, переві́рюють) I	
переві́рити, переві́рять P	
пе́ред (+ I)	before, just before
пе́ред ти́м я́к	before, just before
під (+ I/A)	under
після (+G)	after
після то́го	afterwards
працьови́тий	hard working
ре́чі (pl. of річ)	things
розмо́ва (f)	conversation, talk
слова́ (pl. of сло́во)	words
такі́ (pl. of таке)	such
тому́	ago
рік тому́	a year ago
уде́нь	in the day
уночі́	in the night
ура́нці	in the morning
цілува́ти, цілу́ють I	to kiss
поцілува́ти, поцілу́ють P	to give a kiss
че́рез (+ A)	after, at the end of
чолові́к (m)	man, husband
чу́ти, чу́ють I; почу́ти, почу́ють P	to hear; to smell
якра́з	just, exactly

SUPPLEMENT

весíлля (n)	wedding
корóткий	short
ознайóмлюватися, -юються I	to familiarize oneself
ознайóмитися, -ляться	
розмовля́ти, -ють I	to talk to
порозмовля́ти, -ють P	to converse

NAMES

Katери́на, Кáтря Catherine, Cathy
Ромáн, Ромко, Roman
Сковородá

IDIOMS

в уся́кому рáзі	in any case
на мою́ дýмку	in my opinion
прáвду кáжучи	to tell the truth
працювáти над	to work on
трéба часý(+ A)	it takes time to
(усé) всé ж таки	still, nevertheless
якби́ не (+ N)	if it weren't for

EXPLANATORY NOTES

1. A student must complete five years of study and write a degree thesis called **диплóмна прáця** before he may be accepted to graduate school, i.e. become an **аспірáнт.** Towards the end of his graduate studies which last 2,3, or even 4 years the student takes comprehensive exams called **кандидáтський мíнімум** and submits another thesis **кандидáтська прáця**. A successful defence of the thesis makes him a **кандидáт** of a particular science (an approximate equivalent to the American Ph. D. — there is no B.A. in the Ukrainian university system). The candidate then may proceed to apply for the position of **доцéнт** by submitting his credentials to a special committee. If approved, the applicant receives the title **доцéнт** and the right to teach at the university level (there are two lower level teaching positions similar to instructors and lecturers). To become a professor, one must write a doctoral thesis and do much scholarly research.

2. The verb **бáчитися** differs from **бáчити** in both form and meaning. The former refers to a meeting between two or more individuals, i.e. it stresses a reciprocal action. The latter is not marked for reciprocity — it may or may not occurr —but it is used to mean the physical ability or the act of "seeing" per se.

Ми́ давно́ не ба́чилися.	We have not seen each other for a long time.
Я́ з ни́м ба́чився вчо́ра.	I saw him (met with him) yesterday.
Я́ його́ ба́чив учо́ра.	I saw him (at a distance) yesterday.
	(or: I met with him yesterday.)
Я́ його́ ба́чив, а він мене́ ні.	I saw him but he didn't see me.
Я́ ба́чив його́ дисерта́цію.	I saw his dissertation.

3. Ukrainians consider the day as the 12 hour stretch between 8 A.M . and 8 P.M., the rest being the night (together they are called **доба́**). On the other hand, morning is generally considered to begin around 4 A. M. and lasts till noon, the day is the time after 12 P.M. until about 5 P.M. when evening sets in. The evening lasts till 11 P.M. 12 A.M. is when night begins. When quoting time by clock, one uses the expressions **ра́нку, ве́чора, но́чі** and **дня́**.

4. **Сковорода́** means 'frying pan'. It was the surname of the famous Ukrainian philosopher and poet who lived in the 18th century.

5. The noun **керівни́цтво** 'leadership', 'direction' can also be used to designate those in command, the leaders themselves, e.g.

Там сиді́ло все керівни́цтво.	All the bosses sat there.

6. The verb **одружи́тися** "to get married" can be applied to a man, or a woman, or both together, cf.:

Він одружи́вся з Га́лею.	He married Hal'a.
Вона́ одружи́лася з Марко́м.	She married Marko.
Вони́ одружи́лися.	They got married.

On the other hand, 'to marry someone' is **ви́йти заміж** (**за** + A) is for women, and **ожени́тися** (**з** + I) for men:

Вона́ ви́йшла за ньо́го за́між.	She married him.
Він з не́ю ожени́вся.	He married her.

7. The verbs **лиша́тися/лиши́тися** have a set of parallel forms **залиша́тися/залиши́тися** (the first is more conversational).

8. Instead of **любити одне одного** one can use the verb **любитися** or **кохатися**.

9. **Знайомитися** refers to people, **ознайомлюватися** to objects or abstract notions.

10. Instead of **че́рез** one can also use **за** when speaking of time span:

Я за годи́ну прийду́.	I'll be back in an hour (within an hour).

NOTES ON GRAMMAR

I. INSTRUMENTAL SINGULAR OF THE INTERROGATIVE PRONOUNS ХТО AND ЩО.

The interrogative pronouns **хтó** and **щó** have the following forms in the instrumental:

N.	хтó	щó
I.	ки́м	чи́м

II. INSTRUMENTAL SINGULAR OF ADJECTIVES

All feminine adjectives, both hard-stem and soft-stem, have the instrumental ending **-ою**. Masculine and neuter hard-stem adjectives have the instrumental ending **-им**, and these with soft stems have the ending **-ім**.

Feminine

	Hard-stem	*Soft-stem*
N.	пéвна	домáшня
I.	пéвною	домáшньою (domašn'-oju)

Masculine/neuter

	Hard-stem	*Soft-stem*
N.	пéвний, пéвне	домáшній, домáшнє
I.	пéвним	домáшнім

Note 1: In a small number of adjectives the stem-final consonant is (j): **безкрáїй** (bezkraj-ij). These adjectives have the instrumental endings **-їм, -єю: безкрáїм, безкрáєю**.

Note 2: Ordinal numerals follow the adjectival declension. The numeral **трéтій** 'third' has a soft stem, while the rest have hard stems. Thus the instrumental endings are:

N.	пéрший, пéрше, пéрша	трéтій, трéтє, трéтя
I.	пéршим, пéршою	трéтім, трéтьою

(Exercises 1, 3)

III. INSTRUMENTAL SINGULAR OF THE DEMONSTRATIVE PRONOUNS ОДИН AND УВЕСЬ

N.	тóй, тé, тá	оди́н, однé, однá	цéй, цé, ця́	увéсь, усé, уся́
I.	ти́м, ти́м, тóю (тіéю)	одни́м, одни́м, однóю (одніéю)	ци́м, ци́м, ціéю	усíм, усíм, усіéю

Note 1: The pronoun **увéсь** has the instrumental ending **-ім** instead of **-им** (otherwise it declines like **цéй**).

Note 2: The two variants for **та** and **однá** have no stylistic or semantic difference.

(Exercises 1, 2, 3)

IV. INSTRUMENTAL SINGULAR OF THE POSSESSIVE PRONOUNS AND THE PRONOUN ЧИЙ

The possessive pronouns and the interrogative чи́й follow basically the adjectival declension: the pronouns на́ш and ва́ш follow the hard-stem pattern; the pronoun ї́хній follows the soft-stem pattern; мі́й, тві́й, сві́й, чи́й take the same endings as the (j) -stem adjectives.

N.	на́ш, на́ше, на́ша	ї́хній, ї́хнє, ї́хня	мі́й, мо́є, моя́	чи́й, чиє́, чия́
I.	на́шим, на́шою	ї́хнім, ї́хньою	мої́м, моє́ю	чи́м чиє́ю

(Exercises 4,5)

V. FURTHER USES OF THE INSTRUMENTAL

1. The instrumental is used with the preposition з to indicate accompaniment or interaction:

Я́ вже́ з ни́м поговори́в.	I have talked to him already.
Я́ йду́ зі свої́м това́ришем.	I am going with my friend.
Ві́н ї́в бо́рщ з ка́шею*.	He was eating borsht with cereal.

Note 1: The student must be careful not to use the preposition з when indicating a tool or an instrument:

Я́ писа́в ра́зом з ни́м.	I was writing with him.
but	
Я́ писа́в олівце́м.	I was writing with a pencil.

Note 2: The preposition з has several variants: із, зі, зо, ізі, ізо.

The following basic rules of usage are applied (whether з is followed by the instrumental or the genitive):

(a) Use з before words which begin with a vowel:

з О́лею, з університе́том з Аме́рикою

(b) Use з or із before words which begin with a consonant, especially з, с, ж, ч, ш, щ.

з (із) села́ з доце́нтом із засі́дання

(c) Use зі before words which begin with two consonants, in particular мн, лв, ст, сп:

зі мно́ю зі Льво́ва зі сто́лу

* One way to eat borsht is to put in it hard-cooked buckwheat cereal.

(d) **ізі** or **ізо** are used when the preceding word ends in a consonant cluster and the following word begins with a cluster, especially **мн, лв, ст, сп**:

гість ізі (ізо) мнóю

However, such usage is rare today and the prepositions **зі** and **зо** are used instead.

2. The instrumental is also used with certain prepositions indicating place:

Він стоя́в за на́ми.	He was standing behind us.
Він ішóв перед на́ми.	He was walking before us.
Ли́ст бу́в під столóм.	The letter was under the table.

The most frequent prepositions of this kind are:

за, між, над, перед, під

(Exercise 6)

VI. PREPOSITIONS WHICH MAY BE FOLLOWED BY MORE THAN ONE CASE

Some prepositions are used with more than one case with a difference in meaning. For example:

(a) **за** can be used with either the accusative (motion to a place) or instrumental (location):

Сіда́йте за стіл! (motion)	Come to the table!
Ми́ сиді́ли за столóм. (location)	We were sitting at the table.

(b) **під** can also be used with either the accusative (motion) or instrumental (location):

Подиви́ся під стіл!	Look under the table.

(direction)

Кни́жка лежи́ть під столóм.	The book is under the table.

(location)

(c) **з** is used either with the genitive (from, of, out of) or the instrumental (with):

Я́ йду́ з бібліоте́ки.	I am coming from the library.
Я́ йду́ з ва́ми.	I am coming with you.

(d) **в** and **на** can be used with either the accusative or the locative, depending on whether direction or location is indicated. cf.:

Він на заво́ді.	He is at the plant.
Він іде́ на заво́д.	He is going to the plant.
Вона́ в ті́й кімна́ті.	She is in that room.
Іди́ в ту́ кімна́ту.	Go into that room.

(Exercise 6)

VII. DECLENSION OF SURNAMES IN THE SINGULAR

Ukrainian surnames have declensions corresponding to their forms, most being straightforward nouns (like **Сковорода́**)* or adjectives (like **Дмитро́вський, Гуме́цька**):

	Male		*Female*	
N.	Сковорода́	Дмитро́вський	Сковорода́	Дмитровська
A.	Сковороду́	Дмитро́вського	Сковороду́	Дмитро́вську
G.	Сковороди́	Дмитро́вського	Сковороди́	Дмитро́вської
L.	(на) Сковороді	Дмитро́вському	(на) Сковороді́	Дмитро́вській
I.	Сковородо́ю	Дмитро́вським	Сковородо́ю	Дмитро́вською

Last names in **-ів, -їв, -ов, -ин** and the corresponding feminine forms **-ева, -єва, -ова, -ина** are substantivized possessive adjectives (see Lesson 14, p. 248–9) but only the feminine forms follow the adjectival declension. Masculine surnames of this type are declined as nouns in the singular with the exception of the instrumental, where surnames in **-ів, -їв, -ов,** and **ин** have the ending **-им** rather than **-ом**:**

	Male		*Female*	
N.	Ле́сів	Івани́шин	Ле́сева	Івани́шина
A.	Ле́сева (-іва)	Івани́шина	Ле́севу	Івани́шину
G.	Ле́сева (-іва)	Івани́шина	Ле́севої	Івани́шиної
L.	(на) Ле́севі(-іві)	Івани́шині (-ові)	Ле́севій	Івани́шиній
I.	Ле́севим (-івим)	Івани́шиним	Ле́севою	Івани́шиною

Note 1. Womens' surnames which end in **-ко** or in a consonant are not declined. For the West Ukrainian speakers this rule includes also the names in **-ів, їв, -ов, -ин**, i.e. they do not use forms **-ева, -єва, -ова, -ина**. Thus, **Я́ зна́ю Марі́ю Івани́шину** (E. Ukr.), **Я́ зна́ю Марі́ю Івани́шин** (W. Ukr.).

Note 2. Names in -ів have variant forms in oblique cases without the vowel alternation.

Note 3. Fot the dative case sg. endings see lesson XII p. 208.

(Exercise 7)

---

* Гончаре́нко declines like **ба́тько**

** These rules apply only to surnames. Geographic names, such as **Льві́в** follow noun declension throughout, e.g. **Львовом**.

VIII. TIME EXPRESSIONS*

1. The accusative case is used to indicate time duration ("for a certain period"), e.g.:

Ми́ ту́т живемо́ рік.	We have been living here for a year.
Я́ працю́ю над ци́м оди́н ти́ждень.	I have been working on it for a week.

Note that the Ukrainian equivalent of the English progressive continuous form "have been -ing" is simply imperfective present.

2. "Ago" is rendered by **тому́** which follows the accusative time expression :

Це́ було́ рік тому́.	It was a year ago.
Я́ та́м була́ годи́ну тому́.	I was there an hour ago

"A long time ago" is **давно́** (without **тому́**):

Я́ давно́ та́м бу́в.	I was there a long time ago.

3. The end of a period in the future is expressed by the prepositions **за** or **че́рез** plus accusative:

Я́ подзвоню́ за (через) ти́ждень.	I will call in a week.
Я́ почну́ чита́ти за (через) ти́ждень.	I will start reading within a week.

4. Completion within a limited time period is expressed by the preposition **за** plus accusative. The verb must be perfective. E.g.:

Вона́ це́ прочита́ла за тиждень.	She read it in one week.
Вона́ це́ зро́бить за ти́ждень.	She will do it in one week.

Compare the following examples:

Duration	*Completion within a certain time*
Я́ це́ чита́в ти́ждень.	Я́ це́ прочита́в за ти́ждень.
I read it for a week.	I read it in a week.
Він це́ роби́тиме ти́ждень.	Він це зробить за тиждень.
He'll be doing it for a week.	He'll do it in a week.
	(= finish it in a week's time)
End of a period	*Time ago*
Я́ це́ прочита́ю через ти́ждень.	Я́ це́ чита́в ти́ждень тому́.
I'll read it in a week from now.	I was reading it a week ago.

---

* Genitive of time (e.g. мину́лого ро́ку, цього́ ро́ку) was introduced in Lesson 7.

Я́ це́ прочита́ю за ти́ждень.	Я́ це́ прочита́в ти́ждень тому́.
I'll read it a week from now.	I read it a week ago.

Note that the expression **Я́ це́ прочита́ю за ти́ждень** could mean either "I'll read it a week from now" or "I'll read it in a week" (= it will take me a week to read it).

5. The adverbs of time corresponding to the nouns designating time of the day are:

ра́нок — ура́нці (вра́нці)	'in the morning'
де́нь — уде́нь (вде́нь)	'during the day'
ве́чір — уве́чері (вве́чері)	'in the evening'
ні́ч — уночі́ (вночі́)	'during the night'

Combined with the adverbs **сього́дні, за́втра** or **учо́ра** they produce the equivalents to the English 'this morning', 'yesterday morning', 'tomorrow morning', etc.:

сьогодні	вра́нці	'this morning'
	вве́чері	'tonight', 'this evening'
	вночі́	'tonight', 'this coming night' or 'last night', 'this past night'
завтра	вра́нці	'tomorrow morning'
	вве́чері	'tomorrow evening'
	вночі́	'tomorrow night'
учо́ра	вра́нці	'yesterday morning'
	вве́чері	'yesterday evening', 'last night'
	вночі́	'last night', 'this past night'

Notice that **сього́дні вночі́** may refer to either the past or the coming night, since **сього́дні** 'today' begins at midnight the previous night and ends at midnight the following night, so that both 'nights' in a way are related to 'today'. Usually it is clear from the context which 'night' is being referred to, however, to avoid ambiguity one usually speaks of the past night as **учо́ра вночі́** and of the coming night as **сього́дні вночі́.**

6. When reference is made to the time just prior an event the preposition **пе́ред** (+ I) is used. The preposition **до** (+ G) refers to some time before the event, cf.

Я́ це́ скінчу́ до обі́ду.	I will finish it before dinner.
Ви́пий це́ перед обі́дом.	Drink this just before dinner.

When the event is described by a phrase rather than a noun the prepositions **пе́ред** and **пі́сля** are followed by **ти́м як** and **то́го як** respectively.*

* The combinations **пе́ред ти́м я́к** and **пі́сля то́го я́к** are considered as compound conjunctions. Comma is placed either before the compound or before **як**.

Ми́ поїли перед ти́м, як пішли́ на конце́рт.
We ate before we went to the concert. (= before going)

Ми́ пішли на конце́рт, після то́го як поїли.
We went to the concert after we ate. (= after eating)

(Exercise 8)

IX. ЯКБИ НЕ FOLLOWED BY A NEGATED NOUN

Якби́ не plus a noun in the nominative case functions as a clause meaning 'If it weren't for' or 'If it hadn't been for'.

Якби́ не чолові́к, я́ б не пішла́ на конце́рт.	If it weren't for my husband I wouldn't go to the concert.
Якби́ не це́й словни́к, я б цьо́го не переклала.	If it hadn't been for this dictionary I wouldn't have translated it.

X. THE -СЯ VERBS INDICATING RECIPROCITY

The particle **-ся** is a positive marker of intransitivity, i.e. **-ся** verbs cannot have an accusative object. However there are many **-ся** verbs which are reciprocal in meaning and require a plural subject. For example:

Ми́ вже́ ба́чилися.	We already saw each other.
Чи ви́ давно́ зна́єтеся?	How long have you known each other?
Вони́ одружи́лися.	They got married. (= to each other)
Вони́ поцілува́лися.	They kissed. (= each other)
Вони́ вже́ давно́ лю́бляться (коха́ються).	They have been in love for a long time.
Коли́ ви́ познайо́милися?	When did you meet each other?

ВПРАВИ

I. Put the words in brackets into the correct form.

1. З ки́м вона́ та́к го́лосно розмовля́ла? (мі́й керівни́к)
2. З ки́м він ба́чився? (одна́ америка́нка)
3. З ки́м він одружи́вся? (одна́ кана́дка)
4. З ки́м вона́ цілува́лася? (один украї́нець)
5. З ки́м ви́ зна́лися? (один індія́нець)
6. З ки́м вона́ залиши́лася? (стара́ ма́ти)
7. З ки́м ти́ познайо́мився? (один стари́й чолові́к)
8. З ки́м ви́ згі́дні? (ва́ш нови́й доце́нт)
9. З ки́м ви́ пі́дете? (одна́ моя́ това́ришка)
10. З ки́м ви́ це́ переві́рите? (оди́н мі́й това́риш)

II. Change the sentences according to the model:

Я́ кладу́ ре́чі на те́ лі́жко. — Ре́чі лежа́ть на то́му лі́жку.

(на то́й стіле́ць, на підло́гу, за те́ крі́сло, у ту́ кімна́ту, під ту́ до́шку, в то́й холоди́льник, на те́ мі́сце, за те́ вікно́, під то́й стіле́ць, під то́й телеві́зор)

III. Continue the sentences according to the model:

Він ма́є а́нгло-украї́нський словни́к. Але́ він ма́ло користу́ється ци́м а́нгло-украї́нським словнико́м.

(до́бре поме́шкання, чудо́ву ма́пу, ціка́ву бібліоте́ку, непога́ну па́м'ять, нови́й телеві́зор, стари́й холоди́льник, чудо́вий папі́р, нови́й сті́л, одну́ до́бру рі́ч)

IV. Follow the three-step conversation according to the model:

Він говори́в з дочко́ю. — З чие́ю дочко́ю? — Мо́же зі свое́ю, а мо́же з ва́шою. — Він говори́в з чие́юсь дочко́ю.

(з бра́том, з ма́тір'ю, з това́ришем, з това́ришкою, з сестро́ю, з ба́тьком, з учи́телем, з учи́телькою, з жі́нкою, з сино́м, зі студе́нткою)

V. Change the following sentences according to the model:

Це́ Марко́. Хо́чеш познайоми́тися з на́шим Марко́м?

(доце́нт Івани́шин, профе́сор Ле́сів, профе́сор Тетя́на Гончаре́нко, інжене́р Дмитро́вський, на́ш дома́шній лі́кар Андрі́й Ме́льник, інжене́р Ві́ра Ме́льник, на́ш керівни́к па́н Поліщу́к, студе́нтка Палі́й, учи́тель Іва́н Прокопо́вич, учи́телька О́льга Ле́сева)

VI. Supply the appropriate prepositions and open the brackets.

1. Ми́ жили́ . . . . . . (Ки́їв) і . . . . . . (Ха́рків).
2. Вона́ ду́же працьови́та і до́бре працюва́ла . . . . . .його́ керівни́цтвом.
3. Я́ дя́кую . . . . . (ва́ша га́рна фотогра́фія).
4. Її́ дочка́ стоя́ла . . . . . (вікно́) і диви́лася . . . . . . (ву́лиця).
5. . . . . . . (ми́) була́ ціка́ва розмо́ва . . . . . (конце́рт).
6. Ми́ поба́чили малю́нок, а . . . . . (малю́нок) ще́ одну́ фотогра́фію.
7. Ба́тько бу́в згі́дний . . . . . (си́н) і щі́сь го́лосно говори́в.
8. Ма́ти йшла . . . . . . (Ка́тря) і проси́ла її́ не йти та́к шви́дко.
9. На́ш буди́нок стої́ть . . . . . . (ву́лиця Іва́на Франка́). Це́ . . . . . (готе́ль "Украї́на") і (бібліоте́ка).
10. Інжене́р Дмитро́вський уже́ давно́ працю́є . . . . (це́ пита́ння).

VII. Change the questions according to the model:

Чи ви́ зна́єте О́лю Прокопо́вич? Чи ви́ познайо́милися з О́лею Прокопо́вич?

(на́шого профе́сора Ле́сева, на́шого лі́каря Володи́мира Прокопо́вича, на́шу студе́нтку Лю́бу Ле́севу, її́ чолові́ка Ві́ктора Ме́льника, на́шого інжене́ра Іва́на Семе́новича Дмитро́вського, його́ жі́нку Ві́ру Іва́нівну Дмитро́вську, Ю́рія Семе́новича Івани́шина, Гали́ну Петрі́вну Івани́шину, на́шого вчи́теля па́на Палія́, мою́ ма́тір Тетя́ну Миха́йлівну, доце́нта Рома́на Сковороду́ і його́ жі́нку Катери́ну Сковороду́, на́шого студе́нта Василя́ Гончаре́нка)

VIII. Translate into Ukrainian

1. - Where were you? I have been looking for you.
   - I went to Lesiv's to check his work.
   - Did he finished it yet?
   - Yes, today. He stayed up all night till three in the morning.
2. - We have a little time left. What would you like to do? 'Want to take a look at the newspaper?
   - No, thanks. Let's just (= simply) sit and talk a little.
   - Yes, it's much better.
3. - When will you see docent Ivanyšyn?
   - We already saw each other last week at the conference.
   - What did he say?
   - He was very pleased to hear that in a year I too will be a docent.
4. - Mykola has been working on his translation for a month now. I wonder how he is doing (= It's interesting how his work is going).
   - Already a month? So long?
   - That's not long at all. He must check every word.
   - Why? Doesn't he know Ukrainian?
   - He does, but this is old Ukrainian.
   - Oh, I didn't know that.
5. - Oksana, may I kiss you?
   - I don't know. I have to think.
   - What is there to think about? Just say "yes".
   - But we have only met a short while ago.
   - So what? Such things as love don't take long.
   - Don't talk (to me) about love. This can't be true love.
   - You'll see.
6. -Whom did he marry?
   -His student Luba Leseva.
7. -Whom did she marry?
   -My old friend Semen Lesiv.

REVIEW

IX. Give the imperatives according to the model:

Я́ ва́с прошу́ сіда́ти. Про́шу, сіда́йте!
Я́ ва́с прошу́ це́ зроби́ти. Про́шу, зро́біть це́!

(слу́хати до́бре, не забува́ти цього́, купи́ти це́ для ме́не, почина́ти, знайти́ це́ для нього́, ви́вчити це́ напа́м'ять, переві́рити це́ ще́ раз, не повто́рювати цього́, це́ пам'ята́ти, поспіша́ти)

X. Finish the sentences using both nouns and adjectives.

1. Та́м було́ зру́чне мі́сце. Він сиді́в на . . . . .
2. Та́м було́ вели́ке крі́сло. Він сиді́в у . . . . .
3. Та́м було́ старе́ лі́жко. Він лежа́в на . . . . .
4. Та́м була́ вели́ка до́шка. Він стоя́в бі́ля . . . . .
5. Та́м був мали́й стіле́ць. Він сиді́в на . . . . .
6. Та́м був стари́й буди́нок. Він ко́жного ве́чора ходи́в до . . . . .
7. Та́м була́ стара́ ву́лиця. Він жи́в на . . . . .
8. Та́м була́ до́бра бібліоте́ка. Він працюва́в у . . . . .
9. Та́м був до́брий університе́т. Він чу́в про . . . . .
10. Та́м була́ нова́ шко́ла. Він учи́вся в . . . . .

XI. Supply the appropriate adjectives.

1. Споча́тку ви́п'ємо . . . . . ча́ю.
2. Ми́ вже́ повтори́ли сьо́му ле́кцію, тепе́р ми́ повто́рюємо . . . . , ... і . . . . .
3. Це́й папі́р не до́брий, чи у ва́с нема́є . . . . . папе́ру?
4. Він похо́дить з . . . . . . села́, а вона́ з . . . . . мі́ста.
5. Вона́ навча́лася в Ха́ркові, в . . . . . університе́ті, а він зі Льво́ва, закінчи́в . . . . . університе́т.
6. Ма́ти була́ ду́же . . . . . мене́ ба́чити.
7. Я́ . . . . . ве́чір сиді́в удо́ма і диви́вся на . . . . . фі́льм.
8. Не бери́ . . . . . словника́, користу́йся свої́м.

XII. Change the verbs aspects.

1. Я́ користу́юся словнико́м.
2. Він зацікав́ився ціє́ю нау́кою.
3. Вони́ почали́ ї́сти.
4. Я́ все́ та́м купу́ю.
5. Вона́ відчиня́ла всі две́рі.
6. Я́ шука́в у ці́й кімна́ті.
7. Ми́ вчи́лися друкува́ти.
8. Вони́ пили́ ча́й.
9. Він ї́ї слу́хав.
10. Ми́ тоді́ вже́ кінча́ли шко́лу.

XIII. Give the imperatives.

1. Не (пи́ти) таку́ гаря́чу ка́ву!
2. Про́шу (купи́ти) для ме́не я́йця.
3. (Ста́ти) лі́карем!
4. (Допомогти́) це́ перекла́сти.
5. (Підкре́слювати) такі́ слова́.
6. (Покла́сти) це́ на мі́сце.
7. (Ви́вчити) це́ напа́м'ять!
8. (Знахо́дити) це́ мі́сце в кни́жці.
9. (Поспа́ти) тро́хи!
10. (Поле́жати) ще́ тро́хи!
11. (Не боя́тися) дощу́!

XIV. Read and translate

1. Якби́ не це́й і́спит, я́ б пішо́в у го́сті до свого́ това́риша Івани́шина. Ми́ з Івани́шиним* навча́лися ра́зом на філологі́чному факульте́ті, але́ пі́сля того́, як ві́н закінчи́в університе́т і поча́в працюва́ти в шко́лі вчи́телем, я́ його́ зо́всім не ба́чу. Ві́н ду́же бага́то працю́є, ці́лий ти́ждень, і в субо́ту, і в неді́лю. Я́ те́ж му́шу ці́лий де́нь чита́ти. Я́ пишу́ дисерта́цію про тво́рчість Ле́сі Украї́нки. Я́ давно́ ціка́влюся її́ тво́рчістю; ще коли́ я́ бу́в мали́м хло́пцем, я́ вивча́в напа́м'ять її́ ві́рші.

2. Я́ йду́ до буди́нку, де живу́ть Богда́н і Ма́рта. Я́ йду́ пові́льно, ма́ю бага́то ча́су. О́сь я́ вже́ ба́чу ї́хній буди́нок, о́н ї́хнє вікно́. Я́ стою́ пе́ред вікно́м і дивлю́ся. Ма́рта сиди́ть за столо́м і що́сь пи́ше. Я́ зна́ю, що вона́ працю́є над своє́ю дисерта́цією, але́ вона́ пи́ше на мало́му шматку́ папе́ру — це́ не дисерта́ція. Мо́же, це́ вона́ пи́ше листа́? А о́н Богда́н сиди́ть у крі́слі і що́сь чита́є. Ві́н уве́сь ча́с чита́є — і вра́нці, і вве́чері, і вде́нь, і вночі́. Я́ його́ зна́в, ще бу́в — ві́н усе́ ходи́в з кни́жкою. Я́ розумі́ю, чому́ ві́н ста́в бібліоте́карем. О́сь Ма́рта йде́ до вікна́, відчиня́є його́ і ба́чить мене́: "Іва́не! До́брий ве́чір! Чого́ ти́ ту́т стої́ш під вікно́м? Іди́ до кімна́ти!" Я́ дя́кую і йду́. Ма́рта відчиня́є две́рі й ка́же: "Я́ якра́з пита́ла Богда́на, коли́ ти́ до на́с при́йдеш. Про́шу, сіда́й. Мо́же хо́чеш ви́пити чо́гось гаря́чого? Ми́ ма́ємо і ча́й, і ка́ву." "Дя́кую, я́ ви́п'ю тро́хи ка́ви". До́бре ма́ти тако́го това́риша, як Богда́н і таку́ това́ришку, як Ма́рта.

3. Ми́ з Ма́ртою і Богда́ном говори́ли про ду́шу украї́нського наро́ду. Богда́н каза́в: "Чи мо́жна говори́ти про такі́ ре́чі? Хто́ мо́же зна́ти ду́шу ці́лого наро́ду?" Ма́рта відпові́ла, що ко́жний украї́нець зна́є, що́ таке́ бу́ти украї́нцем. Хто́ вивча́є украї́нську істо́рію, чита́є украї́нську літерату́ру, знайо́миться з тво́рчістю Шевче́нка, Ле́сі Украї́нки, Іва́на Франка́, то́й зна́є, чи́м живе́ украї́нський наро́д, яка́ в нього душа́. Я́ ду́маю, що Ма́рта ма́є ра́цію.

---

* Ivanyšyn and I.

XV. Answer the questions to the above passages.

(1)

1. Чому́ це́й студе́нт не мо́же йти́ в го́сті?
2. Зві́дки він зна́є Івани́шина?
3. Чи він його́ ба́чить ко́жного дня́?
4. Чи́м він ціка́виться?

(2)

1. До ко́го Іва́н іде́?
2. Що́ ро́блять Ма́рта і Богда́н?
3. Що́ Богда́н лю́бить?
4. Що́ Ма́рта ка́же, коли́ відчиня́є две́рі?

(3)

1. Про що́ вони́ говоря́ть?
2. Що́ каза́в Богда́н?
3. Яка́ була́ ду́мка Ма́рти?
4. Хто́ ма́є ра́цію?

XVI. Answer the questions to the dialogues.

"Перевір ще́ раз"

1. З ки́м Ро́мко хоті́в поговори́ти?
2. Чому́ він не змі́г поговори́ти?
3. Коли́ він змо́же це́ зроби́ти?
4. Що́ на це́ ка́же Катери́на?
5. Що́ відповіда́є Рома́н?

"Дя́кую за компліме́нт"

1. Чому́ Катери́на така́ ра́да?
2. Я́к до́вго Рома́н писа́в дисерта́цію?
3. Чи Катери́на ду́мае, що це́ ду́же до́вго?
4. Під чиї́м керівни́цтвом Рома́н працю́є?
5. У що́ Катери́на ві́рить?
6. Я́к Рома́н хо́че подя́кувати за її́ слова́?

"Марко́ одружи́вся"

1. Коли́ Марко́ одружи́вся?
2. З ки́м він одружи́вся?
3. Чи вони́ ходи́ли ра́зом до шко́ли від пе́ршої кля́си?
4. Що́ Ната́лка ду́мае про любо́в?
5. Чи це́ спра́вжня любо́в?

ОДИНАДЦЯТА ЛЕКЦІЯ

32 Ми їдемо в Карпати
We are going to the Carpathians

Dialogue Paticipants:
Га́нна Сергіївна - Г, Оле́на Макси́мівна - О
Hanna Serhijivna - H, Olena Maksymivna - O

1. Г- Оле́но Макси́мівно, чи ви́ куди́сь ї́дете влі́тку?
2. О- Та́к, ми́ з чолові́ком хо́чемо пої́хати в го́ри. Ви́ зна́єте, ми́ за́вжди ї́здимо на мо́ре, але́ цьо́го ро́ку ви́рішили пої́хати в Карпа́ти. Ми́ ще та́м ніко́ли не були́.
3. Г- Ка́жуть, що та́м чудо́во.
4. О- Та́к. На́ші дру́зі були́ та́м мину́лого лі́та й розповіда́ли, я́к та́м га́рно.
5. Г- Чи ви́ пої́дете свої́м нови́м а́втом?
6. О- Ні́, авто́бусом. Я́ ще не вмі́ю керува́ти а́втом, а туди́ ї́хати дале́ко. Я́ не хо́чу, щоб чолові́к уве́сь ча́с керува́в са́м.

1. H- Olena Maksymivna, are you going somewhere this summer?
2. O- Yes, my husband and I want to go to the mountains. You know, we always go to the sea, but this year we decided to go to the Carpathians. We have never been there.
3. H- They say it's wonderful out there.
4. O- Yes. Our friends were there last summer and told us how beautiful it is there.
5. H- Are you going in your new car?
6. O- No, we are going by bus. I don't know how to drive yet and it's a long drive. I don't want my husband to drive alone all the time.

33 Ми спізнилися на автобус
We are late for the bus

Dialogue Paticipants: Леся - Л, Віра, її пóдруга - В
Lesja - L, Vira, her girlfriend - V

1. В- Лéсю, ти не знáєш, котрá годúна?
2. Л- Ужé шóста.
3. В- Óй, трéба бíгти, бо спізнюся на автóбус.
4. Л- Не біжú, тú вжé спізнúлася. Автóбус тепéр хóдить тíльки до п'ятої.
5. В- Та невжé? Я́ й не знáла. Щó ж тепéр робúти?
6. Л- Ідú пíшки... Абó чекáй! Здáється, Максúм ї́здить з робóти цíєю вýлицею. Мóже, він тебé підвезé.
7. В- Чудóва дýмка! А до котрóї він працює?
8. Л- До сьóмої. Тú крáще подзвонú до ньóго на робóту пóки не пíзно.
9. В- Зáраз підý подзвоню. Скажý, що ходúтиму по вýлиці пéред бібліотéкою і чекáтиму на ньóго. А тú щé не йдéш додóму?
10. Л- Ні, ще рáно, я́ тýт посúджу до вóсьмої.

1. V- Lesja, do you know what time it is?
2. L- It's already six.
3. V- Oh no! I must run, otherwise I will be late for the bus.
4. L- Don't run, you are already late. The bus only runs till five now.
5. V- Really? I didn't even know. What am I to do now?
6. L- Walk or... Wait! I think Maksym drives from work this way. Perhaps he could give you a ride.
7. V- An excellent idea! Till what time does he work ?
8. L- Till seven. You better call him at work before it's too late.
9. V- I'm going right now and call him. I'll tell him that I will be walking in front of the library waiting for him. And what about you? Aren't you going home yet?
10. L- No, it's too early. I'll stay here till eight.

34 Я люблю ходити
I like to walk

Dialogue Paticipants: Макси́м - М, Оле́на - О
Maksym - M, Olena - O

1. О- Макси́ме, куди́ ти́ ходи́в?
2. М- До Євге́на Гуме́цького. Це́ мі́й да́вній дру́г, ві́н тепе́р сюди́ приї́хав зі Льво́ва.
3. О- Та́к, ти́ вже́ розповіда́в про ньо́го. Але́ чека́й, ві́н, здає́ться, живе́ за мі́стом. Невже́ ти́ ходи́в пі́шки?
4. М- Та́к, це́ не та́к дале́ко звідси, як здає́ться. Крі́м то́го, я́ ж люблю́ ходи́ти.
5. О- Ду́же до́бре, але́ ж тепе́р зима́, хо́лодно.
6. М- Це́ нічо́го, ходи́ти тре́ба і взи́мку, і влі́тку. Лікарі́ ка́жуть, що найкра́ща рі́ч для здоро́в'я люди́ни — це́ ходи́ти.
7. О- Пра́вильно, але́ я́ тебе́ зна́ю: ти́ не хо́диш, ти́ бі́гаєш. Ду́маєш, що ти́ ще́ молоди́й?
8. М- Звича́йно. Люди́на тоді́ молода́, коли́ в не́ї молоде́ се́рце й душа́.

1. O- Maksym, where did you go?
2. M- To see Jevhen Humec'kyj. He is an old friend of mine, he came over here from L'viv.
3. O- Yes, you told me about him. But wait, doesn't he live out of town? Don't tell me you walked there?
4. M- Yes, I did. It's not so far from here as it might seem. Besides, I do love to walk.
5. O- That's fine, but it's winter now, it's cold.
6. M- It doesn't matter, one should walk both in the winter and in the summer. Doctors say that walking is the best thing for a person's health.
7. O- True, but not the way you do. You don't walk, you run. Do you think you are still young?
8. M- Of course I am. A person is young as long as he is young at heart and in spirit.

СЛОВНИК

áвто (n)*	car
автóбус (m)	bus
бíгати, бíгають I (M)**	to run (around)
бíгти, біжáть I (U)	to run
побíгти, побіжáть P (U)	to start running
взи́мку (узи́мку)	in the winter
влíтку (улíтку)	in the summer
вмíти = умíти	
годи́на (f)	hour, o'clock
котрá годи́на?	what time is it?
до котрóї годи́ни?	till what time?
горá, -и́ (f)	mountain; hill
у гóри (pl)	to the mountains
дáвній	old
далéко	far
дрýг (m)	friend
дрýзі (pl.)	friends
зáвжди	always
звíдси	from here
зимá (f)	winter
і (й)	even
ї́здити, ї́жджу, ї́здять I (M)	to ride (around)
	to go, to drive
ї́хати, ї́дуть I (U)	to go, to drive (to)
поїхати, пої́дуть P (U)	to set out (for)
керувáти, керýють I (+I)	to drive; to direct
котри́й	which, what
крім	besides
крім тóго	besides
лікарí (pl. of лíкар)	doctors
лíто (n)	summer
люди́на (f)	person, human being
молоди́й	young
мóре (n)	sea
найкрáщий	best
нікóли	never
одинáдцятий	eleventh
óй!	Oh no!
підвóзити, підвóжу, підвóзять I	to give a ride
підвезти́, підвезýть P	
підвíз, підвезлá, підвезли́ (past tense)	

* Some dictionaries mark it as indeclinable with the stress on o.

** (M) = multidirectional, (U) = uniderectional. See grammar notes p. 181–183.

пізно (пізній)	late; too late
пішки	on foot
по (+ L)	along
пóдруга (f)	girlfriend
пóки	while; until
пóки не	before; until
посúдіти, -джу, -дять P	to stay/sit a while
рáно (рáнній)	early
робóта (f)	work; job
на робóті	at work
розповідáти, розповідáють I*	to tell (a story)
розповíсти, розповідя́ть P	
сáм, самá, самé**	oneself, alone
самí (самú pl.)	
сéрце (n)	heart
спізня́тися, спізня́ються I	to be late (for...)
спíзнюватися, спíзнюються (на + A) I***	
спізнúтися, спізнюся, спíзняться P	
сюдú	this way; here
тудú	that way; there
умíти, умíють I	to know how
зумíти, зумíють P	to be able
хóлодно	cold
чáсто	often
чекáти, чекáють (+ gen. or [на] + A) I	to wait
почекáти, почекáють P	

NAMES AND PLACES

Євгéн (Eugene) Гумéцький, Максúм, Олéна (Helen) Максúмівна; (гóри) Карпáти, Карпáт Carpathian mountains

IDIOMS

за містом	beyond city limits

* **Розповíсти** is conjugated like **відповíсти** (cf. Lesson 9, p. 151)

** **Сáм** is declined like the hard stem adjectives.

*** This verb has several other variants, equally frequent. We will mention only **запізнюватися/запізня́тися** I, **запізнúтися** P.

SUPPLEMENT

автóбусна зупи́нка	bus stop
веснá (f), навесні́	spring, in the spring
зупиня́тися, зупиня́ються I	to stop
зупини́тися, зупиню́ся, зупи́няться P	
гуля́ти, гуля́ють	to walk (for pleasure)
надвóрі	outside, outdoors
(двір)	(yard, backyard)
óсінь, óсени (f), восени́	fall, in the fall
погóда	weather
рі́дко	rarely
робітни́к; -и́ (m), робітни́ця (f)	worker
сві́тло	light
сóнце	sun
тéмно	dark
тéпло	warm
ти́хо	quiet
хвили́на (f)	minute
я́сно	clear; bright

EXPLANATORY NOTES

1. Note the difference in the choice of prepositions: у гóри but на мóре (see Lesson 7, p. 116). Here are more examples of the use of the two prepositions:

НА	В
Ми́ були́ на концéрті. We were at the concert.	Вонá булá в шкóлі. She was at school.
Ми́ були́ на робóті. We were at work.	Вонá працю́є в бібліотéці. She was at the library.
Ми́ були́ на засі́данні. We were at a meeting.	Вонá вчи́ться в інститу́ті. She is studying at the institute.
Ві́н на пéршому ку́рсі. He is in his first year (at the university).	Ві́н у пéршій кля́сі. He is in the first grade.
Ві́н на філологі́чному факультéті. He is in the Philology department.	Ві́н (навчá‌ється) в університéті. He is (studying) at the university.

When referring to a trip to a body of water, such as a sea, lake or river, both prepositions на and до are used, i.e. на мóре and до мóря, the first being considered more colloquial.

With some nouns the choice of the preposition **у** or **на** depends on the context.

Воний жили́ у вели́кому селі́.	Вони́ жили́ на селі́.
They lived in a large village.	They lived in the country.

With the name of the country — **Україна** — both prepositions were used until recently. Today, however, **в** is preferred, cf.:

Я́ живу́ в Украї́ні.	I live in Ukraine.
Я́ ї́ду в Украї́ну.	I'm going to Ukraine.

2. The Carpathians are a favorite vacation spot. Tourism is a popular and well organized activity among the Ukrainians, although it does not compare with the North American mobility, since private cars are a luxury few can afford.

3. Beside **керува́ти** other expressions for driving a car are currently used in Ukraine, **керува́ти а́втóм води́ти автó** (lit. 'to direct a machine'). It is not used by emigre Ukrainians who prefer to say **їздити (ї́хати) а́втóм**. Since, however, the same expression means 'to ride (in) a car' it can be ambiguous and should be avoided.

4. The English 'to be late for' must be translated by the verb **спізня́тися** plus **на** + accusative: **Він спізни́вся на робóту**. The time by which one is late is also expressed by **на** plus accusative: **Він спізни́вся на годи́ну**. The present tense is normally used to indicate an habitual lateness:

Ти́ всé спізнюєшся.
You are always late.

It may also be used in situations where one is about to be late or in the process of 'being late':

Немá часу́ ї́сти, трéба бігти. Ми́ спізнюємося.
There is no time to eat, we must run. We are being late.

When tardiness is an established fact Ukrainians use past tense perfective **спізни́вся (спізни́лася, спізни́лося, спізни́лися)**:

Ми́ спізни́лися.
We are late.

Note: Do not translate the English 'late' in the sense of 'tardy' as **пізно**.

5. The nouns **дру́г** and **товáриш** are almost synonymous and are often used interchangeably:

Цé мій дóбрий товáриш.	This is a good friend of mine.
Цé мій дóбрий дру́г.	

However, **товáриш** may also mean simply a school mate, a colleague, etc, whereas **дру́г** always indicates a close personal relationship. Note, that while **товáриш** has a feminine counterpart **товáришка** the noun **дру́г** is applied to both men and women. In the latter case the relationship is not of a romantic nature but that of confidence, trust, respect:

Вона́ мі́й спра́вжній дру́г.	She is my true friend.

The noun по́друга, on the other hand, means a 'girlfriend' usually implying romantic attachment in a male-female relationship. **По́друга життя́** is a poetic phrase used to describe a wife.

6. Even though the verbs **іти́, ходи́ти, прохо́дити** etc. indicate walking they are often used with the adverb **пішки** 'on foot':

Чи ти́ приї́хав а́втом?	Did you drive a car?
Ні́, я́ прийшо́в пі́шки.	No, I came on foot (I walked).

7. When the preposition **по** is used with masculine or neuter singulars the ending **-у** (rather than **-і**) is preferred: **по мі́сту (мі́сті), по селу́** (селі́). One can also use adverbial forms **мі́стом, село́м** etc.

NOTES ON GRAMMAR

I. VERBS OF MOTION ('GOING VERBS')

In Ukrainian verbs of motion differ from other verbs by having two sets of imperfectives, one set is called unidirectional and the other multidirectional.*

1. Unidirectional vs. multidirectional verbs. The difference between the two sets is basically one of expressed or implied destination (unidirectional) as opposed to round trip or motion per se with no implied destination (multidirectional.) For example:

Unidirectional	*Multidirectional*
Ві́н іде́ по ву́лиці (ву́лицею). He is walking along the street.	Ві́н хо́дить по ву́лиці (ву́лицею). He is walking up and down the street.
Ві́н ішо́в шви́дко. He was walking fast. (= heading in some direction).	Ві́н ходи́в шви́дко. He used to walk fast. (or: He walked fast = walking around)
Ві́н ішо́в до мі́ста. He was going downtown.	Ві́н ходи́в до мі́ста. He went downtown (He has been downtown and returned) or He used to go downtown (made many round trips).

* Some grammarians call them "determined" (or "determinate") and "indetermined" (or "indeterminate").

2. Aspects of motion verbs.

The unidirectional verbs have a set of **по-** prefixed perfectives:*

Тепе́р я́ піду́ шви́дко.	I will walk fast now.
Я́ піду́ до мі́ста.	I will go to town.
Вона́ пішла́ до мі́ста.	She went to town.

These unidirectional **по-**perfectives focus on the start of the motion (past or future). They specify the departure without indicating what happened (will happen) next. In fact the statement **Вона́ пішла́ до мі́ста** may be followed by another describing some accident or interference which prevented her from reaching her destination. In order to indicate that the end or goal was reached, one must use another perfective with the prefix **при-** which means 'to come' or 'to arrive'.

Де́ Макси́м?	Where is Maksym?
- Ві́н уже́ пішо́в додо́му. Пі́шки.	- He already went home. On foot.
То ві́н до́вго бу́де йти́.	In that case it will take him long (he will be walking for a long time).
Та́к, ві́н каза́в, що при́йде додо́му пі́зно.	Yes, he said he will arrive home late.

Thus, the two aspects of the going-verbs can be presented as follows:

Imperfective		*Perfective*
Unidirectional	*Multidirectional*	*(Unidirectional)*
іти́, іду́ть	ходи́ти, хо́дять	піти́, пі́дуть
ї́хати, ї́дуть	ї́здити, ї́здять	пої́хати, пої́дуть

The imperfective multidirectional verbs are normally used as factual imperfectives to indicate a round trip:

Ми́ ходи́ли до мі́ста.	We went to town (and came back).

This means that:

Ми пішли́ до мі́ста.	We went to town (set out for).
Ми́ йшли́ до мі́ста.	We went to town (walked , were on our way).
Ми́ прийшли́ до мі́ста.	We came to town.
Ми́ ходи́ли по мі́сту.	We walked around town.
Ми́ пішли́ додо́му.	We went home.
Ми́ прийшли́ додо́му.	We came home.
= Ми́ ходи́ли до мі́ста.	= We made a trip to town.

* The multidirectional verbs when prefixed by **по-** also produce perfectives but they are temporal in meaning, e.g.: **походи́ти** 'to walk around for a while', **пої́здити** 'to ride around for a while'. Such temporal perfectives have a limited function and will not be considered here for the moment.

Here are more illustrations of the use of the motion verbs:

1. - Дé ти́ бу́в? - Я́ ходи́в до міста. - А куди́ ти́ тепéр ідéш? - До бібліотéки.	1. - Where have you been? - I went downtown. - And where are you off to now? - To the library.
2. - Хтó цé тáм тáк швидко йдé? - Цé нáш профéсор Гончарéнко. Він зáвжди тáк швидко хóдить.	2. - Who is that walking so fast? - It's our Professor Hončarenko. He always walks so fast.
3. - Куди́ ти́ йдéш? - Я́ хóчу піти́ до міста. Хóчеш, пíдемо рáзом? - А щó ми́ бýдемо тáм роби́ти? - Нічóго, ходи́ти, диви́тися. - Дóбре, я́ вжé йдý.	3. - Where are you going? - I want to go downtown. Want to come along? - And what will we do there? - Nothing much, just walk and look around. - OK, I am coming.
4. - Чи Макси́м удóма? - Ні, йогó немá. Він пішóв до бібліотéки. - Чи він ужé давнó пішóв? - Годи́ну томý. Він завжди́ хóдить врáнці до бібліотéки.	4. - Is Maksym home? - No, he isn't. He went to the library. - How long ago did he leave? - An hour ago. He always goes to the library in the morning.
5. - Óлю, ти́ вжé йдéш до шкóли? - Тáк, вжé сьóма годи́на. - А Мáрко тéж ідé? - Ні, він ще мали́й, він не хóдить до шкóли. Він пíде настýпного рóку.	5. - Ol'a, are you off to school already? - Yes, it's already seven o'clock. - Is Marko going (coming) too? - No, he is still little, he doesn't go to school. He will start (going to) school next year.

3. Tense of motion verbs.

As in English, the present tense of the verbs of motion may be used in reference to the future time:

Я́ йдý туди́ зáвтра.
I'm going there tomorrow. (= implied future)

However, the perfective future is just as common:

Я́ пiдý туди́ зáвтра.
I'll go there tomorrow. (= true future)

The imperfective future of the unidirectional verbs of motion is used only to indicate the manner of the process of motion itself:

Я́ бýду йти́ повíльно.	I will walk slowly.
Коли́ ви́ бýдете ї́хати до міста, тó побáчите нови́й готéль.	When you go downtown you will see the new hotel.

The imperfective future of the multidirectional verbs is used to indicate the manner of motion or a habitual motion. It may not refer to a single round trip as the past tense does. E.g.:

Я́ бу́ду ходи́ти пові́льно.	I will walk slowly (= from now on)
Ми́ бу́демо ї́здити до міста.	We will go downtown. (= more than once).

4. The verb **іти́** may mean either 'to go or' 'to come' depending on the context. cf.:

О́сь іде́ Іва́н. Він іде́ додо́му.	There goes lvan. He is going home.
О́сь іде́ Іва́н. Він іде́ до на́с.	Here comes lvan. He is coming to see us.

The verb **піти́** in the past tense is used in the sense of 'leaving' when no destination is indicated:

Він уже́ пішо́в.	He has already left.
Я пішла́.	I'm off.

When the idea of leaving is only contemplated it is expressed by the verb **іти́** rather than **піти́** if no destination is indicated:

Я́ му́шу йти́.	I must leave. (I have to go.)

5. The imperative of motion verbs.

The imperative 'Come!' as in 'Come here!' may be expressed by using either verb **іти́** or **ходи́ти.**

Іди́ (іді́ть) сюди́!	Come here!
Ходи́ (ході́ть) сюди́!	

The same is true of commands 'Go!' as in 'Go there!', especially when the command is a prohibition, 'Don't go there!'

Не йди́ туди́!	Don't go there!
Не ходи́ туди́!	

Both forms of the negative command may be applied to a single instance, however **Не ходи́ туди́!** may also be an all-inclusive prohibition meaning. 'Don't go there any more' or 'Don't ever go there'.

Certain forms are preferred when the verbs **іти́** and **ходити** are used as positive or as negative commands. In the table below verbs accompanied by the adverb **туди́** are to be translated as 'go' and those with the adverb **сюди́** mean 'come!':

	Positive commands		*Negative commands*	
	ІТИ́	**ХОДИ́ТИ**	**ІТИ́**	**ХОДИ́ТИ**
2nd sg.	Іди́ сюди́!	Ході́ сюди́!	Не йди́ сюди́!	Не ході́ сюди́!
Іди́ туди́!	—	Не йди́ туди́!	Не ході́ туди́!	
2nd pl.	Іді́ть сюди́!	Ході́ть сюди́!	Не йді́ть сюди́!	Не ході́ть сюди́!
Іді́ть туди́!	—	Не йді́ть туди́!	Не ході́ть туди́!	
1st pl.	—	Ході́м(о) туди́!		

The perfective imperatives are employed mostly in commands which involve an errand (= go and do something):

Піди́ до ньо́го й попроси́ у ньо́го словника́. Go to him and ask him for a dictionary.

6. The verbs 'riding' and 'walking'

There are two sets of verbs in Ukrainian which correspond to the English verb 'to go', **іти́ / ходи́ти** which describe self-locomotion (such as people walking, cars coming or going) and **ї́хати / ї́здити** which describe riding in some type of transportation (such as going by bus or a car). In colloquial speech, movement of a vehicle may also be referred to by the verb **ї́хати**.

ІТИ́ / ХОДИ́ТИ	Ї́ХАТИ / Ї́ЗДИТИ
Я́ йду́ на ле́кцію. I'm going to class.	Я́ ї́ду на робо́ту. I'm going to work (by car, bus, etc.)
Я́ до ни́х ходжу́ ціє́ю ву́лицею. I take this street when I go to their place.	Я́ до ни́х ї́жджу авто́бусом. I take a bus when I go to see them.
О́сь іде́ авто́бус. Here comes the bus.	О́сь авто́бус, а в ньо́му ї́де Га́нна. There goes the bus and Hanna is riding in it.

7. The general usage of the verb **ї́хати** corresponds to that of the verb **іти́**, while **ї́здити** behaves like **ходи́ти**. Likewise, **пої́хати** corresponds to **піти́** and **пої́здити** to **походи́ти**. To reinforce the idea of walking the adverb 'on foot' is often added. cf.:

ІТИ́	Ї́ХАТИ
Ми́ йдемо́ на мо́ре (до мо́ря). We are going to the sea (= walking)	Ми́ ї́демо на мо́ре (до мо́ря). We are going to the sea (= driving)
Ми́ йдемо́ село́м. We walk through the village.	Ми́ ї́демо село́м. We ride through the village.
Ми́ йшли́ додо́му ціє́ю ву́лицею. We walked home down this street.	Ми́ ї́хали додо́му ціє́ю ву́лицею. We rode home down this street.

ПІТИ́	ПОЇХАТИ
Чи ми́ підемо туди́ пішки? Are we going there on foot?	Чи ми́ поїдемо туди́ а́втом? Are we going there by car?
Вони́ пішли́ до міста. They went to town. (= walked)	Вони́ поїхали до міста. They went to town. (= drove)
Вони́ вже́ пішли́. They have already left. (= on foot)	Вони́ вже́ поїхали. They have already left. (= by car)
ХОДИ́ТИ	**ЇЗДИТИ**
Ми́ ко́жного ра́нку хо́димо до мо́ря. Every morning we go down to the sea. (= we walk)	Ми́ ко́жного ра́нку їздимо до мо́ря. Every morning we go down to the sea. (=we drive)
Він хо́дить повільно. He walks slowly.	Він їздить повільно. He drives slowly.
Ми́ сього́дні ходи́ли (містом) по місту. We walked today all around town.	Ми́ сього́дні їздили (містом) по місту. We drove today all around town.
ПОХОДИ́ТИ	**ПОЇЗДИТИ**
Ми́ тро́хи походи́ли по місту (містом). We walked around town a bit.	Ми́ тро́хи поїздили по місту (містом). We drove around town a bit.

The same is true of the verbs **бігти** (cf. **іти́**) and **бігати** (cf. **ходи́ти**), and **побігти** (cf. **піти́**) and **побігати** (cf. **походи́ти**).

(Exercises 1-12, 14)

II. THE VERBS МОГТИ, УМІТИ, ЗНАТИ

There are three verbs in Ukrainian to translate 'can, know' in their various meanings: **могти́** 'to be (physically) able', 'can', **уміти** 'to have some skill', 'can', 'know how to', and **зна́ти** 'to know (intellectually)'.

Могти́ — Змогти́

This verb must be followed by an infinitive (perfective or imperfective). It indicates ability or possibility (usually physical):

Чи ти́ мо́жеш купи́ти це́ для ме́не?	Can you buy it for me?
Він нічо́го не мо́же ї́сти.	He can't eat anything. (= he is ill)
Я́ не мо́жу спа́ти.	I can't sleep.
Чи ти́ мо́жеш це́ прочита́ти?	Can you read this?
Я́ мо́жу чита́ти голосні́ше, якщо́ хо́чеш.	I can read louder if you wish.

The past tense of the imperfective **могти́** merely states that something could (or couldn't) be done, while the perfective indicated that a definite effort was made to achieve the result. cf.:

Він не міг цьо́го зроби́ти.
He couldn't do it. (was physically unable or had no chance) or
He couldn't have done it (was incapable of doing it).

Він не зміг цьо́го зроби́ти.
He was unable to do it. (tried unsuccessfully)

Він не міг цього́ перекла́сти.
He couldn't translate it. (didn't know the language or was unable due to circumstances) or
He couldn't have translated it (was not capable of it)

Він не зміг цього́ перекла́сти.
He couldn't (was unable to) translate it (but tried)

Умі́ти — Зумі́ти

The imperfective **умі́ти** indicates an acquired or 'know how', while the perfective **зумі́ти** indicates the successful application of the skill ('to manage', 'to succed'). They are followed by an infinitive.

Умі́ти	**Зумі́ти**
Чи він уміє говори́ти по-украї́нському? Can he speak Ukrainian? (Does he know how to...)	Чи він зуміє це́ зроби́ти пра́вильно? Can he (will he be able to) do it right?
Він умів зроби́ти стіле́ць. He knew how to make a chair.	Він зумів зроби́ти стіле́ць. He succeeded in making a chair.

Зна́ти

The verb **зна́ти** indicated mental awareness or knowledge. It has no perfective and must be followed by an accusative object or a clause.

Я́ зна́ю, що він украї́нець.	I know that he is Ukrainian.
Я́ зна́ю це́ сло́во.	I know this word.
Я́ його́ зна́ю.	I know him.
Я́ зна́ю, я́к це́ ва́жко.	I know how difficult it is.

Note the difference between зна́ти and умі́ти:

> Ві́н не зна́в украї́нської мо́ви, але́ ви́вчив.
> He didn't know the Ukrainian language but he learned it.
>
> Ві́н не вмі́в говори́ти украї́нською мо́вою, але́ навчи́вся.
> He didn't know how to speak Ukrainian but he learned.
>
> Я́ зна́ю, я́к це́ відчини́ти. Я́ ба́чив, я́к О́ля це́ відчиня́ла.
> I know how to open it. I saw Ol'a open it. (= theoretical knowledge)
>
> Я́ вмі́ю це́ відчиня́ти. Я́ вже́ відчиня́в.
> I know how to open it. I opened it (once). (= practical know-how)

(Exercises 18, 19)

III. ADVERBS OF DIRECTION AND LOCATION

We have seen that the idea of location as opposed to motion can be expressed in the adverbs as in де́ versus куди́ (see Lesson 7, p. 118). Here are a few more such adverbs:

Location		*Motion*	
та́м	there	туди́	where (to)
удо́ма	at home	додо́му	home (homeward)
де́сь	somewhere	куди́сь	(to) somewhere
дене́будь	anywhere	кудине́будь	(to) anywhere
ту́т	here	сюди́	here (this way)
		звідси	from here
		звідти	from there
		звідки	where from

IV. INDEFINITE ADVERBS AND PRONOUNS СЬ AND -НЕБУДЬ.*

(Difference in meaning and usage). The indefinite pronouns and adverbs in -сь are used when the speaker knows the fact but lacks specific information:

Ві́н живе́ де́сь у цьо́му мі́сті.	He lives somewhere in this town.
Вона́ куди́сь пішла́.	She went somewhere.

---

* In spoken Ukrainian the forms with -сь are often used in place of those -небудь, for example:
Are you going somewhere? **Чи ти́ куди́сь іде́ш?**

The pronouns and adverbs in **-небудь** indicate existence of several possibilities or refer to a hypothetical fact, i.e. one which may or may not happen:

Хтоне́будь мо́же це́ зроби́ти.	Anybody can do it (several choices).
Я́ хо́чу поі́хати кудине́будь, де́ не та́к хо́лодно.	I want to go somewhere where it's not so cold. (=several choices)
Чи ти́ кудине́будь іде́ш сього́дні вве́чері?	Are you going anywhere tonight? (hypothetical fact)
Compare: Чи хтоне́будь дзвони́в?	Did anyone call? (hypothetical fact)
Та́к, хто́сь дзвони́в.	Yes, someone did call. (known fact, specifics missing)

(Exercises 15, 16, 17)

V. MORE USES OF THE INSTRUMENTAL

1. When the subject of a sentence is expressed by two nouns (or a noun and a personal pronoun, or two pronouns) the conjunction **і** ('and') is often replaced by the preposition **з** ('with') and the second noun / pronoun changes to instrumental of accompaniment. cf.:

Оле́на та її́ чолові́к уже́ пішли́. Olena and her husband already left.	Оле́на з чолові́ком уже́ пішли́.

Furthermore, a singular pronoun joined to a noun or another pronoun by **і** may change to plural when the construction is changed to instrumental of accompaniment (this is especially common for the pronouns **я** and **ти**). cf.:

Я́ і вона́ були́ на одно́му ку́рсі. Ми́ з не́ю були́ на одно́му ку́рсі. Я́ з не́ю бу́в на одно́му ку́рсі.	She and I were in the same year.
Ти́ і О́ля почека́йте ту́т. Ти́ з О́лею почека́й ту́т. Ви́ з О́лею почека́йте ту́т.	You and Ol'a wait here.

If the subject is a singular pronoun (+ з +I) the verb is in the singular. If the subject is a singular noun (+ з +I) the verb may be either in the singular or in the plural. This depends on the point of view of the speaker: if the first component is considered more important the verb is in the singular, if both are viewed as equal, the verb is in the plural. cf.:

Мáти з си́ном пішлá до лíкаря.	Мáти з си́ном пішли́ до лíкаря.
Mother took her son to the doctor.	Mother and son went to the doctor.

When the word order is shifted to produce a sentence like: Мáти пішлá з си́ном до лíкаря. the instrumental is no longer considered part of the compound subject justifying a plural verb.

2. The instrumental is regularly used to indicate means of travel:

Я́ ї́ду áвтом.	I am going by car.

Certain nouns are used in the instrumental to denote the area through which locomotion occurs:

Ми́ ї́хали мóрем.	We were going by sea.
Вонá йшлá вýлицею.	She was walking down the street.

Note: The latter usage of the instrumental is much more frequent in Ukrainian than in modern Russian.

(Exercise 22)

VI. MORE TIME DESIGNATIONS

1. The word for 'hour' is **годи́на**

Ми́ чекáли цíлу годи́ну.	We waited for a whole hour.
Булá пíзня годи́на.	The hour was late.

The same word stands for 'o'clock' when referring to time by the clock. The hour is designated by an ordinal numeral.

Котрá годи́на? Котрá тепéр годи́на?*	What time is it? What time is it now?
- Одинáдцята (годи́на).	- It's eleven (o'clock).
До котрóї годи́ни ви́ чекáли?	Until what time did you wait?
- Ми́ чекáли до одинáдцятої годи́ни.	-We waited till eleven o'clock.

2. The adverbs for 'early' **рáно** and 'late' **пíзно** are often combined with the words for 'morning' and 'evening' to produce 'early in the morning' and 'late at night':

Цé булó рáно врáнці.	This was early in the morning.
Цé булó пíзно ввéчері.	It was late in the evening.

The expressions **ще рáно** and **вжé пíзно** may be translated as 'still early' or 'too early' and 'already late' and 'too late' respectively.

---

* In modern Ukrainian usage the adverb зáраз rather than тепéр would be found in such time expressions. However, тепéр is used for wider time spans such as seasons, years, etc. cf.:

Тепéр зимá.	It's winter now.
Тепéр двáдцять пéрше столíття.	It is the 21st century now.

3. To indicate the seasons of the year Ukrainian uses the following expressions:

N.	*Modifier + G.*		*Adverb*	
Winter	зима́:	—зими́	взи́мку	зимо́ю
Spring	весна́:	— весни́	навесні́	весно́ю
Summer	лі́то:	— лі́та	влі́тку	лі́том
Autumn	о́сінь:	— о́сени	восени́	—

(1) The genitive is used only in conjunction with modifiers 'last', 'next', 'this', and 'that', e.g.:

Ми́ пої́демо туди́ насту́пного лі́та.	We will go there next summer.
Ми́ та́м були́ мину́лої зими́.	We were there last winter.

The demonstrative **це́й** may refer to either 'this coming' or 'past', cf.:

Де́ ви́ були́ цього́ лі́та?	Where were you this (past) summer?
Де́ ви́ бу́дете цього́ лі́та?	Where will you be this summer?

The pronoun **то́й**, on the other hand, is used in a narrative style after the time in the past has been specified.

Це́ бу́в рік, коли́ ти́ скінчи́в шко́лу. Була́ весна́. Тіє́ї весни́ було́ ду́же хо́лодно, пам'ята́єш?	It was the year you graduated from school. It was spring. It was very cold that spring, do you remember?

(2) The instrumental is used without modifiers, except 'late' and 'early':

Це́ було́ ра́нньою весно́ю.	It was early in the spring.

The instrumental of the noun **о́сінь** is not used for this purpose, the adverbial form **восени́** is used instead.

Восени́ ти́ пі́деш до шко́ли.	In the fall you will go to school.

(3) The adverbs are used to indicate seasons in general, i.e. 'in the summertime', 'in the winter time', etc. and may not be accompanied by a modifier.

Я́ люблю́ ї́здити туди́ влі́тку.	I love to go there in the summer.
Я́ люблю́ ї́здити туди́ взи́мку.	I love to go there in the winter.
Та́м та́к га́рно навесні́!	It's so beautiful there in the spring.
Та́м та́к га́рно восени́!	It's so beautiful there in the fall.

Unless the year is specified, the adverbs can be used interchangeably with the instrumental forms: **Це́ було́ взи́мку/зимо́ю** 'It was in the winter'. With the exact year the instrumental form must be used: Це́ було́ зимо́ю 1976 р. 'It was in the winter of 1976'.

Note: Since the use of modifiers in all these time expressions is strictly limited, there is really no Ukrainian equivalent to the English 'In the good old summer-time'. One must say **Цé булó давнó, влíтку.** Лíто **тоді булó дýже гáрне.** 'It was a long time ago, in the summer. The summer was beautiful.'

(Exercise 24)

ВПРАВИ

I. Make a choice between the verbs **ітú** and **ходúти.**

1. Кудú тú тепéр . . . . . .? Я́ . . . . . . в гóсті до Максúма.
2. Вонá ще малá, вонá не . . . . . . до шкóли.
3. Узúмку вонá рíдко . . . . . . до нáс, алé тепéр . . . . . дýже чáсто.
4. Чомý тú . . . . . тáк повíльно? Чи тú завждú тáк повíльно . . . . . . ?
5. Чи тú вжé . . . . . . на лéкцію? — Ні, почекáй ще трóхи.
6. Вчóра, колú мú . . . . . додóму, мú бáчили Мáрту.
7. Чи тú вжé . . . . . до мíста? — Тáк, я́ вжé тáм бýв.
8. Чи цé вíн . . . . . до нéї в гóсті кóжного вéчора? — Тáк, вíн.
9. Не . . . . . . тáк швúдко, малúй Максúм не мóже щé тáк швúдко . . . . . .
10. Скажíть, бýдь ласка, кудú . . . . . . цéй автóбус?

II. Make a choice between the verbs **ітú** and **пітú**

1. Сьогóдні я́ хóчу . . . . . . на концéрт.
2. Вíн приї́хав, колú вú вжé . . . . . . додóму.
3. Дé Микóла? — Вíн . . . . . . до мíста.
4. Кудú тú вчóра . . . . ., колú я́ тебé бáчив?
5. Чи тú . . . . . . з нáми? Тáк, я́ . . . . .
6. Чи мú . . . . . пíшки? — Ні, мú ся́демо на автóбус.
7. Чи цé тú . . . . . . і сказáв, що менé немá вдóма?
8. Вíн чýв, я́к вú . . . . . і говорúли про ньóго.
9. Вíн посúдів трóхи і . . . . . додóму.
10. Вíн . . . . . і ввéсь чáс дýмав про нéї.

III. Make a choice between the verbs **ї́хати** and **ї́здити.**

1. Минýлого рóку мú . . . . . на Украї́ну.
2. Я́ не хóчу ввéсь чáс . . . . . áвтом, я́ бýду ходúти пíшки.
3. Якщó тú бýдеш . . . . . . тáк повíльно, то мú спíзнимося на робóту.
4. Тú ж усé . . . . . . до мíста, а тепéр знóв . . . . . ?
5. Вíн погáно себé почубáє і мýсить . . . . . повíльно.
6. Вíн зáвжди . . . . свої́м старúм áвтом, а новúм не хóче . . . .
7. Я́ не люблю́ . . . . . . автобýсом.
8. Дивúсь, óн Костю́к . . . . . . свої́м новúм áвтом.
9. Я́ бáчив, як вонá вчóра . . . . . з нúм до мíста.
10. Цé áвто вжé такé старé, що нúм не мóжна . . . .

IV. Make a choice between **іти́, піти́** and **ходи́ти.**

1. - Я́ вже́ . . . . . До побачення.
Чека́й, куди́ ти́ . . . . ?
- Я́ ду́мала . . . . . до Люби. А що́?
- Ми́ якра́з хотіли диви́тися телеба́чення. Бу́де ціка́ва програ́ма. Кра́ще . . . . до на́с.
- До́бре, ... до ва́с.

2. - Диви́сь, он та́м . . . . . О́ля.
- Яка́ О́ля? Я́ її не зна́ю.
- Та невже́! . . . . . . до не́ї. О́лю! Це́ Ма́рта.
- Добри́день.

3. - Чого́ ти́ ту́т . . . . .?
- Я́ чека́ю на Окса́ну. Вона́ каза́ла, що . . . . . зі мно́ю на конце́рт.
- Та вона́ вже́ . . . . . з Марко́м.
- Вона́ ж каза́ла, що не хо́че з ни́м ніку́ди . . . . . .
- Не зна́ю, але́ я́ ба́чив, як вона́ з ни́м . . . . .

4. - Я́ вже́ . . . . , а ти́?
- Почека́й хвили́ну, я́ за́раз те́ж . . . . .

V. Make a choice between **ї́здити** and **поїхати.**

1. - Куди́ ви́ . . . . . . мину́лого ти́жня?
- Пе́рше ми́ . . . . . . до Нью Йо́рку, а тоді до Монреа́лю.
- А куди́ ви́ хо́чете . . . . . . насту́пного ти́жня?
- Ми́ вже́ ніку́ди не хо́чемо . . . . . . Бу́демо сиді́ти вдо́ма.

2. - Я́ хо́чу . . . . . . до мі́ста. Хто́ . . . . . . зі мно́ю?
- Юрко́. Він ду́же лю́бить . . . . . . а́втом.
- Але́ я́ не а́втом . . . . , а авто́бусом.
- Це́ нічо́го. Він ка́же, що і авто́бусом . . . . . з тобо́ю.

3. - Де́ моє́ а́вто? Чи Марко́ зно́в . . . . . куди́сь мої́м а́втом?
- Та́к. Він . . . . . до Євге́на. Він ко́жної субо́ти до нього . . . . . .
- До́бре, але́ чому мої́м а́втом? Ма́є своє́, мо́же . . . . . . свої́м.

VI. Make a choice between **ї́хати** and **поїхати.**

1. - З ки́м ти́ вчо́ра . . . . . коли́ я́ тебе́ ба́чила?
- Це́ бу́в профе́сор Гончаре́нко. Він мене́ проси́в . . . . . . з ни́м до лі́каря.
- А́, це́ тому́ ти́ так пові́льно . . . .?
- Та́к. Профе́сор Гончаре́нко хоті́в, щоб я́ . . . . . пові́льно.

2. - Чи Михáйло вдóма?
   - Ні, він . . . . . . до університéту.
   - Чи він . . . . . . áвтом?
   - Ні, автóбусом. Áвтом сьогóдні . . . . . . я́.

3. - Я́к цé ти́ . . . . ?
   - Я́ дóбре . . . . . ., не шви́дко.
   - Я́ не про тé, як ти́ . . . . . . , алé якóю вýлицею.
   - Пéрше . . . . . . цією вýлицею, а тоді ми́ . . . . . тією вýлицею áж до університéту. Дóбре?
   - Дóбре.

VII. Make a choice between **поїхати, поїздити** and **їздити.**

1. - Ми хóчемо трóхи . . . . . по місту. Хóчеш з нáми . . . . . . ?
   - Дóбре, я люблю́ . . . . . . áвтом.

2. - Я́ чýв, що ти́ вжé вмієш керувáти áвтом. Чи ти́ вжé ни́м . . . . . .?
   - Тáк, вчóра я́ . . . . . . до міста і цілу годи́ну тáм . . . .
   - Хóчеш сьогóдні щé раз . . . . . .?
   - Дóбре, тільки в мéне мáло часý.
   - Цé нічóго, ми́ трóхи . . . . . . і . . . . додóму.

3. - Чи ти́ щé . . . . . . своїм стари́м áвтом?
   - Тáк, я́ люблю ни́м . . . . . Минýлої óсени я ни́м . . . . . . áж до Монреáлю. Цьогó рóку знóву хóчу туди́ . . . . . .

VIII. Make a choice between **бігати** and **бігти.**

1. - Хтó цé до нáс . . . . . . ?
   - Цé мали́й Юркó. Він недáвно навчи́вся . . . . .
   - Диви́сь, як він шви́дко . . . . . .!

2. - Почекáй на мéне! Чомý ти́ тáк шви́дко . . . . . . ?
   - Лікар кáже, що . . . . . цé дóбре для здорóв'я.
   - Мóже для твогó, алé не для могó. Я́ вжé не мóжу . . . . . !
   - Нý, то не . . . . тáк шви́дко.

3. - Микóла вміє дóбре . . . . .
   - Тáк, я́ бáчив, як він . . . . . .
   - Я́ їхав áвтом, а він . . . . біля áвта.

IX. Make a choice between the verbs **їхати/їздити, поїхати.**

1. Йогó немá, він куди́сь . . . . . .
2. Він тепéр у місті, ... туди́ своїм нови́м áвтом.
3. Минýлого літа ми́ . . . . . на мóре.

4. Восени́ ві́н . . . . . . до Ки́єва і тепе́р навча́ється та́м в університе́ті.
5. У мі́сті не мо́жна . . . . . . та́к шви́дко.
6. Я́ бою́ся, щоб ти́ сама́ . . . . . . та́к дале́ко.
7. Ві́н звича́йно . . . . . на робо́ту авто́бусом, але́ сього́дні його́ хто́сь підві́з.
8. Ми́ тепе́р у Євге́на, а за́втра . . . . . да́лі.
9. Ві́н уже́ давно́ . . . . . додо́му.
10. Куди́ ви́ хо́чете . . . . . насту́пної весни́?

X. Make a choice between the verbs **іти́/ходи́ти, піти́.**

1. Її́ дочка́ ще мала́, вона́ ще́ не . . . . . до шко́ли.
2. Ще́ ті́льки одина́дцята годи́на, куди́ ти́ . . . . . . ?
3. Я́ не розумі́ю, чому́ ти́ сього́дні . . . . . та́к пові́льно, ти́ ж лю́биш . . . . . шви́дко.
4. Якщо́ ти́ . . . . . та́к пові́льно, ми́ спі́знимося на авто́бус.
5. Ко́жного ве́чора вона́ . . . . . по ву́лиці ці́лу годи́ну.
6. Подиви́ся у вікно́: до на́с хто́сь . . . . .
7. Оле́ни нема́є, вона́ вже́ . . . . . на робо́ту.
8. Якби́ ви́ . . . . . з на́ми в субо́ту на конце́рт, я́ була́ б ду́же ра́да.
9. Я́ вже́ не хо́чу . . . . . , кра́ще тро́хи поси́дьмо.
10. Ва́с підвезти́? — Ні дя́кую, я́ люблю́ . . . . . пі́шки.

XI. Make a choice between the verbs **бі́гати/бі́гти, побі́гти.**

1. Лі́кар сказа́в, щоб ві́н улі́тку . . . . . . ко́жного дня́ годи́ну.
2. Чека́й, куди́ ти́ . . . . . ?
3. Якщо́ ти́ . . . . . та́к бага́то, це́ бу́де недо́бре для твого́ се́рця.
4. Вони́ поба́чили, що́ лиши́лася ті́льки одна́ хвили́на і шви́дко . . . . . , щоб не спізни́тися на авто́бус.
5. Мали́й хло́пець поча́в . . . . . бі́ля шко́ли.
6. Про́шу, ... за ни́м і скажи́, що ві́н забу́в зателефонува́ти на робо́ту.
7. А́вто ї́хало пові́льно, а за ни́м . . . . . якась люди́на.
8. Чого́ ти́ вве́сь ча́с . . . . . ? Поси́дь тро́хи.
9. Де́ ти́ бу́в? — Я́ . . . . . подиви́тися на мо́ре.
10. Ві́н лю́бить . . . . . , але́ тепе́р ві́н уже́ не . . . . . та́к бага́то, як тоді́, коли́ бу́в молоди́м.

XII. Supply the approrpiate verbs of motion.

1. До ко́го ти́ вчо́ра . . . . . .?
2. Куди́ ти́ . . . . . сього́дні вве́чері?
3. Куди́ ви́ . . . . . мину́лого ро́ку?
4. Куди́ ви́ . . . . . насту́пного ро́ку?
5. Куди́ ви́ ви́рішили . . . . . ко́жного лі́та?
6. З ки́м ти́ . . . . . , коли́ я тебе́ ба́чив?
7. До ко́го ти́ . . . . . ко́жного ве́чора?
8. Чому́ ти́ . . . . . та́к пові́льно?
9. Хо́чеш . . . . . ра́зом?
10. Чи ва́ш си́н уже́ . . . . . до шко́ли?

XIII. Change the sentences so that location becomes destination. Model:

Ми́ були́ на мо́рі. Ми́ пої́хали на мо́ре.

1. Оле́на в нього́.
2. Євге́н на робо́ті.
3. Вони́ живу́ть у Льво́ві.
4. Авто́бус стої́ть перед університе́том.
5. Макси́м ході́в по кімна́ті.
6. Ми́ були́ на конце́рті у вівто́рок уве́чері.
7. Ми́ цілу годи́ну ї́здили по селу́.
8. Ми́ були́ на ле́кції.
9. Вони́ тепе́р удо́ма.
10. Вони́ на засі́данні.

XIV. Supply the appropriate verbs of motion.

1. Мину́лого ро́ку ми́ . . . . . в Украї́ну і . . . . . по всій Украї́ні.
2. Ко́жного ра́нку, коли́ я́ . . . . . на робо́ту, я́ ба́чу, як він . . . . . по ву́лиці.
3. Сього́дні він ви́рішив не . . . . . пішки, а . . . . . а́втом.
4. Ми́ вже́ весно́ю . . . . . в го́ри, тепе́р ми́ хо́чемо . . . . . на мо́ре (до мо́ря).
5. Ко́жного лі́та ми́ . . . . . в село́ до на́шого дру́га Макси́ма, а цього́ лі́та ми́ не змо́жемо до нього . . . . .
6. Інжене́р Дмитро́вський ча́сто . . . . . по мі́сту своі́м нови́м а́втом. О́сь і сього́дні він . . . . . до мі́ста.
7. Вчо́ра ми́ . . . . . за мі́сто. Ми́ . . . . . туди́ авто́бусом.
8. Вона́ вже́ вдо́ма, вона́ . . . . . до своє́ї ма́тері.
9. Я́ його́ вчора́ ба́чив, коли́ . . . . . з робо́ти.
10. Коли́ вона́ вчо́ра . . . . . на робо́ту, Оле́на була́ вже́ та́м: вона́ тепе́р ма́є а́вто і . . . . . на робо́ту а́втом.

XV. Answer the following questions using indefinite adverbs and pronouns.

1. Куди́ він пішо́в?
2. Де́ ти́ про це́ чита́в?
3. Куди́ ти́ хо́чеш, щоб я́ диви́вся?
4. Де́ ти́ хо́чеш сі́сти?
5. Звідки ти́?
6. Куди́ вони́ ї́дуть?
7. Де́ вони́ були́?
8. Куди́ ти́ хо́чеш піти́ сього́дні вве́чері?
9. Де́ ту́т мо́жна купи́ти журна́л "Украї́на"?
10. Де́ вона́ працю́є?

XVI. Translate into Ukrainian.

1. Let's go home.
2. Don't go there.
3. Come here.

4. Where do you come from?
5. I don't want to move from here. (= go from)
6. Let's eat somewhere.
7. He lives somewhere in the country.
8. The doctor is at home now.
9. I don't know where he is. He went somewhere.
10. I can sit anywhere.

XVII. Select between the indefinite adverbs and pronouns in **-сь** and **-нéбудь.**

1. Вонú живýть . . . . . у місті.
2. Цьогó рóку мú хóчемо . . . . . поїхати, алé щé не вúрішили кудú.
3. Я́ . . . . . поклáв свíй олівéць. Дé вíн?
4. Вíн не хóче мéшкати . . . . . , хóче тíльки у велúкому дорогóму помéшканні.
5. Вíн . . . . . пішóв, алé не сказáв кудú.
6. Чи вú мáєте . . . . . кнúжку про Украї́ну?
7. Тáм . . . . . прийшóв, здаéться . . . . . студéнт.
8. Не кладú тудú свої́ рéчі, ї́х . . . . . мóже взя́ти.
9. Я́ хóчу . . . . . поїсти. Щó мú мáємо?
10. Вонú про . . . . . говорúли, алé я́ не чýла.

XVIII. Translate into Ukrainian.

1. Can you see anything from here?
2. Can you give me a ride?
3. I can't understand it.
4. You know Ukrainian, you can read it.
5. Can you help me with my homework?
6. He goes to school and already knows how to write.
7. Do you know how to spell (= write) this word?
8. You can go home.
9. Do you know how to get (= go) there? — Yes, we can take a bus.
10. Why can't we go there now?

XIX. Supply the appropriate verbs (**могтú, знáти, умíти**).

1. Чи вú . . . . . керувáти áвтом?
2. Чи тú . . . . . , я́к по-украї́нському пúшуть адрéсу?
3. Я́ не . . . . . сьогóдні з вáми говорúти, бо мáю багáто робóти.
4. Тú не . . . . . дóбре розповідáти.
5. Нáш учúтель . . . . . , якé цé важкé завдáння.
6. Під йогó керівнúцтвом усí . . . . . дóбре працювáти.
7. Щоб перекладáти, трéба дóбре . . . . . мóву, з якóї перекладáєш, а щé крáще тý мóву, на якý перекладáєш.
8. Вíн не . . . . . дóбре говорúти по-украї́нському.
9. Я́ . . . . . розповíсти, я́к усé булó.
10. Тú . . . . . , я́к цé відчинúти?

XX. Supply the appropriate adverbs (**сюди́, туди́, та́м, де́**).

1. . . . . . ви́ ходи́ли?
2. Біжи́ . . . . . до ме́не.
3. Я́ не зна́ю, ... це́ покла́сти.
4. Про́шу, сіда́йте . . . . . , на це́й стіле́ць.
5. . . . . . це́ мо́жна поста́вити?
6. Не ї́дь . . . . . , уже́ пі́зно.
7. Покладі́ть це́ . . . . .
8. . . . . . ти́ йде́ш?
9. Ві́н . . . . . пішо́в.
10. . . . . . не мо́жна диви́тися.

XXI. Select the correct preposition (**у** or **на**).

1. Ми́ вже́ були́ . . . . . мі́сті.
2. . . . . . ва́шому мі́сці, я́ б цього́ не каза́в.
3. Вони́ ї́дуть . . . . . Карпа́ти.
4. Його́ мати́ живе́ . . . . . селі́.
5. Його́ си́н навча́ється . . . . . інститу́ті.
6. Її́ дочка́ вже́ . . . . . дру́гому ку́рсі університе́ту.
7. Її́ ба́тько ви́рішив працюва́ти . . . . . заво́ді.
8. Сестра́ вчи́ться . . . . . шко́лі, ... одина́дцятій кля́сі.
9. Оди́н бра́т живе́ . . . . . Украї́ні, а дру́гий . . . . . Аме́риці.
10. Подиви́сь, що це́ та́ке та́м . . . . . ву́лиці?

XXII. Translate into Ukrainian.

1. He came late in the evening around (near) eleven o'clock.
2. In the summer my friend and I usually go to the mountains.
3. She was saying how wonderful it would be to go to sea for the whole summer.
4. We were afraid to miss the bus, so we ran as fast as we could.
5. You don't know how to ask.
6. He said he would give us a ride if we could wait a little.
7. He is our best teacher and a very nice person besides.
8. We will drive from here to there and then we will go on foot.
9. I want to tell this story myself.
10. You will be late for class (= lecture).

XXIII. Change the subject to include the instrumental of accompaniment.

1. Я́ і Євге́н — да́вні дру́зі.
2. Оле́на і Макси́м живу́ть за мі́стом.
3. Ти́ і брат — студе́нти?
4. Я́ і мі́й това́риш — лікарі́.
5. Ви́ і ва́ша жі́нка пої́дете а́втом, а я́ і чолові́к пої́демо авто́бусом.
6. Чи ти́ і твоя́ сестра́ гово́рите по-украї́нському?

7. Гончаре́нко і Гуме́цький — украї́нці.
8. Ти́ і О́ля му́сите почека́ти.
9. Ти́ і я́ пі́демо ра́зом.
10. Дмитро́вський і його́ жі́нка поі́дуть в Карпа́ти.

XXIV. Translate into Ukrainian.

1. Run, otherwise you will be late for class.
2. The bus was one hour late.
3. He will come late in the evening.
4. What are you doing at such a late hour?
5. Where were you last summer?
6. Every winter they go to the Carpathians.
7. In the winter they live in the city.
8. Next spring we will go to Montreal.
9. It's very cold there in the winter, but very nice in the summer and in the spring.
10. We will leave in the fall.

XXV. Read and translate.

1. Неда́вно ми́ з бра́том поі́хали додо́му в Карпа́ти. Ми́ лю́бимо Карпа́ти, ми́ ту́т жили́ все́ своє́ життя́. Для на́шого се́рця го́ри — це́ найкра́ще, що мо́же бу́ти. Ми́ і́здили й на мо́ре, були́ у вели́кому Ки́єві, у на́шому старо́му Льво́ві — і та́м га́рно, й ту́т, але́ нема́ ні́чо́го кра́щого, я́к Карпа́ти.

2. Мі́й дру́г Євге́н і́здив мину́лого ро́ку по всі́й Украї́ні. Ві́н розповіда́є бага́то ціка́вого. Бу́в ві́н і в мі́сті і в селі́, і́здив на мо́ре і в Карпа́ти. Це́ вже́ дру́гий ра́з ві́н і́здив на Украї́ну. Пе́рший ра́з ві́н поі́хав са́м. Взя́в своє́ а́вто й і́здив ни́м по ці́лій Украї́ні. А цьо́го ра́зу ві́н поі́хав з жі́нкою, си́ном і дочко́ю. А́вто в ни́х мале́, було́ б незру́чно і́хати, тому́ вони́ ви́рішили і́здити авто́бусом. Це́ була́ до́бра ду́мка. З авто́буса мо́жна було́ все́ до́бре ба́чити і роби́ти фотогра́фії. Насту́пного лі́та я́ те́ж ду́маю туди́ поі́хати.

3. Про́шу, познайо́мтеся з мої́м найкра́щим дру́гом, Оле́ною Макси́мівною. Я́ з не́ю мо́жу говори́ти про все́, розповіда́ю про свою́ робо́ту, про те́, що́ я́ чита́ю, що ду́маю. Я́ не бою́ся, що вона́ мене́ не зрозумі́є, вона́ лю́бить мене́, як ма́ти. Усе́ своє́ життя́ вона́ працюва́ла в бібліоте́ці. У не́ї нема́ чолові́ка, не ма́є вона́ ні си́на, ні дочки́, але́ вона́ до́бре зна́є життя́ і в не́ї чудо́ве се́рце. Я́ від не́ї бага́то навчи́вся. Вона́ для ме́не кра́щий учи́тель, ні́ж шко́ла та університе́т. Вона́ закінчи́ла шко́лу життя́, а це́ до́бра шко́ла.

XXVI. Answer the following questions to the above passages.

(1)
1. Куди́ і́здили брати́?
2. Чи вони́ та́м вже́ коли́сь були́?
3. Де́ вони́ були́ пе́ред ти́м?
4. Чому́ вони́ лю́блять Карпа́ти?

(2)
1. Куди́ ї́здив Євге́н мину́лого ро́ку?
2. Що́ він ба́чив?
3. Чи він їздив са́м?
4. Чи́м він ї́здив?
5. Чому́ не а́втом?

(3)
1. Чи Оле́на Макси́мівна ма́ти цього́ хло́пця?
2. Про що́ він з не́ю лю́бить говори́ти?
3. Чому́ вона́ живе́ сама́?
4. Чи́м вона́ є́ для цього́ хло́пця?
5. Чому́ вона́ бага́то зна́є?

XXVII. Answer the questions to the dialogues.

"Ми́ ї́демо в Карпа́ти"

1. Куди́ Оле́на Макси́мівна з чолові́ком звича́йно ї́здять?
2. Чому́ вони́ ви́рішили пої́хати в Карпа́ти?
3. Що́ розповіда́ли дру́зі?
4. Чому́ вони́ поїдуть авто́бусом?

"Ми́ спізни́лися на авто́бус"

1. До котро́ї годи́ни хо́дить авто́бус?
2. А котра́ тепе́р?
3. Чи тре́ба бі́гти?
4. Хто́ мо́же допомогти́?
5. Що́ тре́ба зроби́ти?
6. Де́ Ві́ра бу́де чека́ти?

"Я́ люблю́ ходи́ти"

1. Хто́ Євге́н Гуме́цький?
2. Де́ він живе́?
3. Чи Макси́м до нього пої́хав авто́бусом?
4. Що́ ка́жуть лікарі́?
5. Коли́ люди́на молода́?

ДВАНАДЦЯТА ЛЕКЦІЯ

 # 35 Вареники готові
The dumplings are ready

Dialogue Paticipants:

Тетя́на Миха́йлівна (ма́ти) - Т,
Ната́лка - Н (дочка́), Сла́вко - С (си́н)
Tetjana Myxajlivna (the Mother) - T,
Natalka - N (her daughter), Slavko - S (her son)

1. Т- Ді́ти, варе́ники вже́ гото́ві. Кому́ покла́сти?
2. Н- Мені́ ні́, дя́кую. Да́й Сла́вкові, він за́вжди голо́дний.
3. Т- Сла́вку, тобі́ да́ти?
4. С- До́бре да́й. А з чи́м вони́?
5. Т- Є́ з карто́плею, з си́ром і з капу́стою. Скі́льки тобі́ да́ти?
6. С- Да́й мені́ два́ з карто́плею, три́ з капу́стою і чоти́ри з си́ром.
7. Т- Чи ти́ ду́маєш, що тобі́ цього́ бу́де до́сить?
8. С- Як не бу́де до́сить, даси́ ще́.
9. Н- А́х ти́, порося́ мале́! А ти́ не забу́в ма́мі що́сь сказа́ти?
10. С- Дя́кую, ма́мо.

1. T- Children, the dumplings are ready. Who would like some?
2. N- Not me, thank you. Give some to Slavko, he is always hungry.
3. T- Slavko, can I give you some?
4. S- O.K. What's the filling?
5. T- Some are with potatoes, others with cheese and with cabbage.
   How many can I give you?
6. S- Give me two with potatoes, three with cabbage, and four with cheese.
7. T- Are you sure this will be enough for you?
8. S- If it isn't, you will give me more.
9. N- You little piggie! Aren't you forgetting to say something to your mother?
10. S- Thank you, mother.

36 Що ти везеш? What are you bringing?

Dialogue Paticipants:
Катери́на - К, Рома́н - Р; Kateryna - K, Roman - R

1. К- Чи це́й годи́нник пра́вильно йде́? Він пока́зує пів на двана́дцяту.	K-	Is that clock right? It shows half past eleven.
2. Р- Ні, він запізнюється на чве́рть го́дини. Тепе́р за чве́рть двана́дцята.	R-	No, it's 15 minutes slow. It's quarter to twelve now.
3. К- Тобі вже́ тре́ба ї́хати.	K-	You should be going.
4. Р- Та́к, я обіця́в Тетя́ні Миха́йлівні, що бу́ду в не́ї о двана́дцятій.	R-	Yes, I promised Tetjana Myxajlivna that I'll be at her place at twelve.
5. К- Що́ ти́ з собо́ю бере́ш?	K-	What are you taking along?
6. Р- О́сь цю валізку.	R-	This suitcase over here.
7. К- Да́й я тобі понесу́.	K-	Let me carry it for you.
8. Р- Дя́кую, але́ вона́ до́сить важка́.	R-	Thanks, but it's rather heavy.
9. К- Ого́! Що́ це́ ти́ таке́ везе́ш?	K-	Hey!! What's that you are taking?
10. Р- Я́блука з на́шого са́ду. Це́ подару́нок Тетя́ні Миха́йлівні.	R-	Apples from our orchard. It's a present for Tetjana Myxajlivna.
11. К- Я́ пе́вна, що ї́й бу́де приємно оде́ржати таки́й подару́нок.	K-	I am sure she will appreciate such a present.

35 Лист від колишнього учня A letter from a former pupil

Dialogue Paticipants:
Тетя́на Миха́йлівна - Т, Васи́ль Миха́йлович - В
Tetjana Myxajlivna - T, Vasyl' Myxajlovyč - V

1. Т- Васи́лю, я́ хо́чу показа́ти тобі листа́, яко́го я́ сього́дні оде́ржала. О́сь на́, прочита́й.	T-	Vasyl', I want to show you a letter I received today. Here, read it.
2. В- Дорога́ Тетя́но Миха́йлівно! Я́ хо́чу Вам подя́кувати від усьо́го се́рця за все́, що́ ви́ для ме́не зроби́ли. Ви́ мені сті́льки допомогли́, ви́ навчи́ли мене́, я́к жи́ти. Коли́ я́ ва́с зустрів, я́ бу́в ци́ніком, ніко́му не ві́рив, не ві́рив і в Бо́га. Ви́ зроби́ли з ме́не люди́ну. Тепе́р я́ працю́ю, ма́ю роди́ну. Моя́ дружи́на очі́кує дити́ну — якщо́ бу́де дівчинка, ми́ хо́чемо назва́ти її́ Тетя́ною. Ще́ раз спаси́бі за все́. Ваш коли́шній учень Роман.	V-	Dear Tetjana Myxajlivna! I want to thank you from the bottom of my heart for everything you have done for me. You have helped me so much, you have taught me how to live. When I met you I was a cynic, I didn't trust anyone, I didn't believe in God either. You made me a human being. Today I have a job, and a family. My wife is expecting a baby. If it's a girl we want to name her Tetjana. Once again, thanks for everything. Your former pupil Roman.

СЛОВНИК

А́х!	Oh! Ah!
важки́й	heavy
валі́зка (f)	suitcase
варе́ник (m)	dumpling
варе́ники (pl.)	dumplings
везти́, везу́ть I (U)	to carry, to drive, to take
повезти́, повезу́ть P (U)	
вози́ти, во́зять I (M)	to carry, to drive
годи́нник (m)	watch, clock
гото́вий	ready
дава́ти, даю́ть I	to give (to let)
да́ти, даду́ть P	(A + D)
два́ (+ m/n), дві́ (+ f)	two
двана́дцятий	twelfth
дити́на (f)	child, baby
ді́ти (pl.)	children
ді́вчинка (f)	little girl (baby girl)
дороги́й	dear; expensive
дружи́на (f)	spouse
запі́знюватися, запі́знюються I	to be late; to be slow (clocks)
запізни́тися, запі́зняться P	
(спі́знюватися I, спізни́тися P)	
зустріча́ти, зустріча́ють I	to meet (someone, something)
зустрі́ти, зустрі́нуть P	
зустрі́нути, зустрі́нуть P	
капу́ста (f)	cabbage
карто́пля (f)	potatoes
коли́шній	former
навча́ти, навча́ють I	to teach
навчи́ти, навча́ть P	
назива́ти, назива́ють I	to name
назва́ти, назву́ть P	
нести́, несу́ть I (U)	to carry
понести́, понесу́ть P (U)	
носи́ти, но́сять I (M)	to carry; to wear
о (+ L)	at (time)
обіця́ти, обіця́ють I	to promise
пообіця́ти, пообіця́ють P (+ D)	
ого́!	hey!

одéржувати, одéржують I	to receive
одéржати, одéржать P	
очíкувати, очíкують (I only)	to expect
пів	half
подарýнок, -нка (m)	gift, present
покáзувати, покáзують I	to show
показáти, покажý, покáжуть P	(+ A + D)
поросÿ, поросÿти; поросÿта (n)	piglet
приéмно	pleasant
роди́на (f)	family
сáд, -у (m)	garden
себé	oneself
си́р, -у (m)	cheese; cottage cheese
скíльки	how much, how many
стíльки	so much, so many
спаси́бі	thank you
три́	three
ýчень, ýчня (m)	pupil, student (grade/high school)
ци́нік (m)	cynic
чвéрть (f)	quarter
чоти́ри	four
я́блуко (n)	apple
я́блука (pl.)	apples

NAMES

Слáвко — short for many names:
Ростислáв, Ярослáв, Святослáв

IDIOMS

від усьóго сéрця	from the bottom of (my) heart
годи́нник ідé	the watch is running
годи́нник запíзнюється	the watch is slow

SUPPLEMENT

годи́нник поспіша́є	the watch is fast
зустріча́ти(ся), зустріча́ють(ся) I	to meet (each other)
зустрі́тися, зустрі́нуться P	
пів на (чве́рть на) + A	half past (quarter past)
півгоди́ни	half an hour
плати́ти, плачу́, пла́тять I	to pay (for) (s. one) (with)
заплати́ти, заплачу́, запла́тять P	
(за + A) (D) (I)	
Прие́мно познайо́митися!	Pleased to meet you
свиня́ (f)	pig
учени́ця (f)	pupil; student (grade and highschool) (f)

EXPLANATORY NOTES

1. **Варе́ники** is the favorite Ukrainian dish. These are dumplings with some filling such as potatoes, sauerkraut, cottage cheese, cherries. They are cooked in boiling water for a few minutes and then eaten with sour cream, melted butter, or bits of bacon. West Ukrainians call this dish **пироги́** (cf.: Polish 'pierogy'). In East Ukrainian usage **пирі́г** means a pie. **Капу́ста** means 'cabbage' while **ки́сла капу́ста** means 'sauerkraut', but in the popular speech the shorter form is often used in the sense of 'sauerkraut', so that when one is offered **варе́ники з капу́стою** one should expect to get dumplings with the sauerkraut filling. The word **капу́ста** has no plural form. **Карто́пля** even though it is singular does not mean 'a potato' but 'potatoes', so that to ask for 'one potato' in Ukrainian one must use a different term, **картопли́на.** The word **си́р** is used for any kind of cheese, including cottage cheese. Dumplings are filled with cottage cheese.

2. The verb **навча́ти (навчи́ти)** means to teach, to instruct how to do something. It is normally used with an infinitive, but can also take a genitive object. The person taught appears in the accusative.

Він навчи́в мене́, я́к зроби́ти стіле́ць.	He taught me how to make a chair.
Вона́ навчи́ла мене́ чита́ти.	She taught me how to read.
Він навча́є украї́нської мо́ви.	He teaches Ukrainian.

Another verb which has the same meaning and function is **учи́ти (I), навчи́ти (P)**. Note that the perfective of the two verbs is identical: **Вона́ навчи́ла мене́ украї́нської мо́ви** "She taught me the Ukrainian language".

The above verbs may not be used in the sense of 'teaching school' i.e. without specifying the subject or skill taught. The verb **учителюва́ти** means 'to be a teacher' in schools below college level, and the verb **виклада́ти** is used for any institution of learning. cf.:

Вона́ вчителю́є в шко́лі.	She teaches school.
Вона́ виклада́є в університе́ті.	She teaches at the university.

Let us summarise the various verbs with the meaning 'to study', 'to learn' and 'to teach'.

To teach

учи́ти / навча́ти (I) — **навчи́ти** (P) + A (animate) + G/infin.

Учи́тель навча́є (вчи́ть) на́с украї́нської мо́ви.
The teacher teaches us the Ukrainian language.

Вона́ шви́дко навчи́ла ї́х чита́ти.
She quickly taught them to read.

To study, to learn.

учи́тися, навча́тися (I), навчи́тися (P) + G + infin.

Ми́ вчимо́ся украї́нської мо́ви.
We are studying Ukrainian.

Ді́ти навча́ються в шко́лі.
The children are studying at school.

Ми́ бага́то чого́ навчи́лися за це́й рік.
We learned a lot this year.

Ми́ вчимо́ся чита́ти по-украї́нському.
We are learning to read Ukrainian.

(see also Lesson, 7, p. 113)

3. The numeral 'two' has two forms, one which is used with feminine nouns, **дві́** and another which is used with masculine and neuter nouns, **два́**:

О́н та́м два́ студе́нти і дві́ студе́нтки.
Over there are two students (male) and two students (female).

4. The verb **вірити** when it means 'to believe, to trust' takes the dative object:

Я́ тобі́ ві́рю.	I trust you/I believe you.
Йому́ не мо́жна ві́рити.	He cannot be trusted.
Я́ не ві́рю ні одному твоє́му сло́ву.	I don't believe a word you are saying.

When **вірити** is used in the sense of 'to believe in', it is followed by the preposition **в** + accusative or a clause:

Я́ ві́рю в Бо́га.	I believe in God.
Я́ ві́рю, що ви́ ста́нете до́брим учи́телем.	I believe that you will become a good teacher.

In English 'to believe' is also used in the sense of 'to think', 'to have an opinion', as in 'I believe he is a teacher'. Ukrainian does not use вірити in this sense.

5. The noun дружи́на is synonymous with жі́нка 'wife' but has a somewhat more dignified flavor. Observe that the same root appears in the word дру́г 'friend' and in the verb одружи́тися 'to get married'. Formerly, дружина could be applied to a man as well in the sense of 'husband', 'spouse'.

6. Instead of дя́кую a Ukrainian may say спаси́бі. Ethymologically this word comes from a phrase Спаси́ Бі́г 'May God save you' (Бі́г is another form of the word Бо́г). Спаси́бі may be used as a noun (neuter) with different modifiers (see Lesson 9, p. 150). The person being thanked is in the dative:

Вели́ке ва́м спаси́бі!	Thank you very much. (Many thanks).

7. У́чень is the word for a high school or an elementary school student. It also means pupil, disciple, or anyone who receives instruction, especially private.

8. In official correspondence and in private letters to people to whom one wants to show respect the pronouns 'you', 'yours' are capitalized, e.g. Я́ Ва́м відповіда́ю на Ва́шого листа́ 'I'm answering your letter'. To capitalize the second singular ти́, тві́й is no longer customary.

9. The verb плати́ти 'to pay' is used with the payee in the dative, the commodity being paid for in the accusative (with the preposition за), and the payment in the accusative (or instrumental if mode of payment is indicated), e.g.

Скільки́ ти йому́ за цю́ валі́зку заплати́ла?	(Одну) ти́сячу.
How much did you pay him for the suitcase?	One thousand.
Я́к ти́ запла́тиш?	Готі́вкою.
How will you pay?	In cash.

10. The verbs оде́ржати and отри́мати (see Vs) are near synonyms e.g. оде́ржати/ отри́мати листа́ 'to receive a letter'.

NOTES ON GRAMMAR

I. DATIVE SINGULAR OF NOUNS

1. (a) All feminine nouns and a-stem masculines have identical forms in the dative and the locative singular, i.e. -і/-ї:

Скажи́ це́ О́лі і Марі́ї.	Tell this to Ol'a and Marija.
Да́йте це́ Любо́ві Микола́ївні.	Give this to L'ubov Mykolajivna.
Подзвони́ Мико́лі.	Call Mykola.

(b) Dative of ма́ти is ма́тері.

2. Neuter nouns have three types of ending **-у/-ю, -ові/-еві** and **-і**. The distribution is as follows:

(a) The majority of neuters have the ending **-у/-ю**:

Місту дали́ нове́ ім'я́: Іва́но-Франкі́вськ.	The city was given a new name, Ivano-Frankivs'k.

(b) Diminutives in **-к (о)** and two nouns **се́рце** 'heart' and **ли́хо** 'misfortune' have doublets, i.e. **-у/-ю** as well as **-ові/-еві**:

N.	се́рденько	порося́тко, (dim. of порося́)	се́рце
D.	се́рденьку / се́рденькові	порося́тку/ порося́ткові	се́рцю/ се́рцеві

(c) Neuters with the suffixes **-ат/-ят/-ен** have the dative ending **-і** (for complete declension of such nouns see this lesson, section IX):

Порося́ті тре́ба було́ бі́гти.	The piglet had to run.

3. Masculine nouns of the masculine-neuter declension have two dative singular endings **-ові -еві/-єві** and **-у/-ю**. They occur with any nouns, both animate and inanimate, however the ending **-ові/-еві/єві** is more typical of animate nouns. The ending **-ові** is used for hard stems, **-еві/-єві** is used for soft stems and stems ending in **ж, ч, ш, щ, ц**:

Да́й це́ Богда́нові.	Give it to Bohdan.
Да́й це́ Гончаре́нкові.	Give it to Hončarenko.
Напиши́ това́ришеві листа́.	Write a letter to your friend.
Напиши́ вчи́телеві листа́.	Write a letter to the teacher.

Note 1: The variant ending **-у/-ю** is used in nouns with the suffixes **-ов/-ев/-ів** and **-ин**:

Це́ подару́нок місту Льво́ву.	This is a gift to the city of L'viv.
Скажі́ть це́ Ле́севу.	Tell it to Lesiv.
Напиші́ть Івани́шину.	Write to Ivanyšyn.

Note 2: In sequences involving people's names and titles only one, rarely two, will take the ending **-ові/-еві** and the rest have **-у/-ю**:

Це́ Гончаре́нкові Василю́ Маха́йловичеві.
This is for Hončarenko Vasyl' Mychajlovyč.

Да́йте це́ профе́сорові Гончаре́нку.
Give this to Professor Hončarenko.

О́сь ли́ст Василе́ві Миха́йловичу.
Here is a leter to Vasyl' Mychajlovyč.

Він написа́в пое́тові Тара́су Григоро́вичу Шевче́нкові.
He wrote to the poet Taras Hryhorovyč Ševčenko.

Note 3: Remember that stems in **г, к, х** change the stem final consonant to **з, ц, с** respectively, e.g. **О́льга — О́льзі, жінка́ — жінці́** (see Lesson 7, p. 115). Remember also that all consonants are hard before the vowel **е** (see the Sound System, p. xvi), so that Vasyl' becomes Vasylem, xlopec' — xlopcem, etc.

Note 4: The dative has the same stress as the genitive.

Here are paradigms of the dative singular:

1. *Feminine declension*

N.	О́ля	Микола	Марі́я	любо́в	па́м'ять	Аме́рика
D.	О́лі	Мико́лі	Марі́ї	любо́ві	па́м'яті	Аме́риці

2. *Neuters*

N.	вікно́	мо́ре	прі́звище	пита́ння	се́рденько	порося́
D.	вікну́	мо́рю	прі́звищу	пита́нню	се́рденьку /-ові	порося́ті

3. *Masculines of the masculine-neuter declension*

N.	профе́сор	сті́л	Васи́ль	гі́сть	де́нь
D.	профе́сорові	столу́/о́ві	Василе́ві	го́стеві	дн-ю́/-е́ві
N.	Андрі́й	това́риш	кана́дець	Льві́в	
D.	Андрі́єві	това́ришеві	кана́дцеві	Льво́ву	

(Exercises 1, 3, 4)

II. DATIVE OF PERSONAL PRONOUNS AND THE INTERROGATIVES ХТО, ЩО

The personal pronouns in the dative case are generally identical with the locative forms in the singular, but differ in the plural.

N.	я́	ти́	ві́н / воно́	вона́	ми́	ви́	вони́
D.	мені́	тобі́	йому́	ї́й	на́м	ва́м	ї́м
L.	на мені́	на тобі́	на ньо́му	на ні́й	на на́с	на ва́с	на ни́х

N.	хто́	що́
D.	кому́	чому́
L.	на ко́му	на чо́му

(Exercises 2, 5)

III. USES OF THE DATIVE CASE

1. The dative case is used to express the object to which or toward which action is directed. Typically the object is animate and the action is mental rather than physical, e.g.:

Я́ ва́м відпові́м.	I will answer you.
Я́ тобі́ допоможу́.	I will help you.
Я́ тобі́ кажу́.	I'm telling you.
Я́ тобі́ не ві́рю.	I don't believe you.
Ви́бачте мені́!	Excuse me!

2. A dative object is often used in combination with another object in a different case or with a clause, e.g.:

Да́й мені́ си́ру, будь ла́ска.	Give me some cheese, please.
Ві́н показа́в мені́ ціка́ву рі́ч.	He showed me an interesting thing.
Дя́кую ва́м за кни́жку.	Thank you for the book.
Про́шу, ви́бачте мені́ (за те́), що я́ не прийшла́ на засі́дання.	Please forgive me for not coming to the meeting.

Notice that in many instances a parallel construction with the preposition **до** or **для** followed by the genitive may be used, cf.:

Dative	*Genitive*
Це́ тобі́. This is for you.	Це́ для те́бе. This is for you.
Ві́н мені́ написа́в. He wrote to me.	Ві́н до ме́не написа́в. He wrote to me.
Вона́ мені́ подзвони́ла. She called me.	Вона́ до ме́не подзвони́ла. She called me.
Я́ діста́в вам ма́пу. I got you a map.	Я́ діста́в для вас ма́пу. I got a map for you.
Я́ тобі́ купи́ла подару́нок. I bought a present for you.	Я́ купи́ла для те́бе подару́нок. I bought you a present.
Тобі́ цього́ ще́ не до́сить? Is this still not enough for you?	Для те́бе цього́ ще́ не до́сить? Is this still not enough for you?

Stylistically, **для** + genitive expresses a greater degree of individualization (approximately "especially for you") than the dative. However there is no clear difference between the dative and **до** + genitive.

3. The dative is required with certain adverbs:

Ва́м не мо́жна цього́ ї́сти.	You may not eat this.
Тобі́ тре́ба це́ ще́ раз переві́рити.	It is necessary for you to check it once more.

IV. THE REFLEXIVE PRONOUN СЕБЕ

The pronoun **себе́** (self) has no gender or number and can refer to any person appearing as the subject of the sentence:

Я́ себе́ завжди́ перевіря́ю.	I always check myself.
Ти́ себе́ не мо́жеш ба́чити.	You can't see yourself.
Вони́ тільки себе́ лю́блять.	They love only themselves.

This pronoun lacks a nominative form, its other forms are as follows:

A.G.	себе́	(на се́бе, у се́бе)
L.	(на) собі́	
I.	собо́ю	
D.	собі́	

1. As a substitute for the possessive pronoun **свій** it can appear in constructions with the prepositions **у/до** which refer to someone's place, cf.:

СВІ́Й	СЕБЕ́
Вона́ в свої́й кімна́ті.	Вона́ в се́бе в кімна́ті.
She is in her room.	She is in her room.
Він пішо́в до своє́ї кімна́ти.	Він пішо́в до се́бе в кімна́ту.
He went to his room.	He went to his room.

Stylistically the possessive **свій** is felt as expressing a higher degree of belonging or ownership (= one's own room) as opposed to simply a designation of a place where one is staying or living at the moment. The distinction is similar to that between such phrases as **В мої́й кімна́ті** and **У мене́ в кімна́ті** (see Lesson 7, Explanatory Note 6, p. 113).

3. The emphatic pronoun **са́м (сама́, саме́, самі́)** 'self' follows the adjectival declension and agrees with the word which it modifies. It is often used to reinforce the reflexive **себе́**:

Вона́ сама́ себе́ не розуміє.	She does not understand herself.
Він говори́ть са́м до се́бе.	He is talking to himself.

In generalized statements 'self' is masculine:

Само́го себе́ ва́жко зрозумі́ти.	It's hard to understand oneself.
З сами́м собо́ю ле́гко говори́ти.	It's easy to talk to oneself.

Otherwise, **са́м** generally means 'alone', 'by onself':

Вона́ тепе́р сама́.	She is alone now.
Він са́м зроби́в цей стіле́ць.	He made this chair by himself.

(Exercises 6, 7)

V. VERBS OF MOTION НЕСТИ AND ВЕЗТИ

Here are two more verbs of motion:

нести́ / носи́ти: понести́	'carry (on one's person)'
везти́ / вози́ти: повезти́	'convey, transport (in a vehicle)'

The two sets of the uni- and the multi-directional forms are:

unidirectional	multidirectional
НЕСТИ́ (to carry) (ПОНЕСТИ́)	НОСИ́ТИ (to carry; to wear habitually)
Що́ ти́ несе́ш? What are you carrying?	Що́ ви́ но́сите? What are you carrying back and forth?
Я́ це́ понесу́. I will carry it.	Вчо́ра вона́ носи́ла дити́ну до лі́каря. She took the baby to the doctor yesterday.
Я́ несу́ кни́жку до бібліоте́ки. I am taking the book to the library.	Ко́жного ти́жня вона́ ході́ла до вчи́теля і носи́ла з со́бою словни́к. Every week she went to the teacher carrying her dictionary with her.
	Чому́ ти́ за́вжди но́сиш цю́ су́кню?* Why do you always wear this dress?

* The verb 'носити' in the sense of 'wearing' is used only in its imperfective aspect, 'to wear habitually'.

ВЕЗТИ́ (to carry) (**ПОВЕЗТИ́**)	**ВОЗИ́ТИ** (to carry; to wear habitually)
Що́ ти́ везе́ш? What are you carrying?	Ві́н во́зить я́блука до мі́ста. He carries apples to town.
Куди́ ти́ на́с везе́ш? Where are you taking us?	Ві́н на́с вози́в по місту. He was driving us around the city.
Я́ повезу́ ва́с до мі́ста. I will take (drive) you to town.	Ві́н на́с вози́в до мі́ста. He drove us to town (and back)

1. In Lesson 6, p. 98, we discussed the past tense of certain verbs whose infinitive stem-final consonant **-с** (ти) which in the present/future stems alternates with д or т (e.g. переклас-ти, переклад-у) drop the stem-final consonant in the past (**перекла́в, перекла́ла, перекла́ли).**

If the infinitive stem-final consonant is other than с as in the verb **вез-ти**, or it is an с which does not alternate with т or д in the present/future stems as in the verb **нести́, несу́ть** the stem-final consonant is preserved in the past. Furthermore, the past-ending **-в** of the masculine form is dropped and its root vowel о or е changes to і:

Infinitive	*Present*	*Past*
нести́	несу́ть	ні́с, несла́, несло́, несли́
везти́	везу́ть	ві́з, везла́, везло́, везли́

(Exercises 8, 9)

VI. TIME BY THE CLOCK

1. Expressions dealing with the exact hour are:

1. Котра́ годи́на? - Одина́дцята. - Тре́тя.	1. What time is it? - It's eleven (o'clock). - It's three (o'clock).
2. О котрі́й годи́ні? - Об одина́дцятій. - О тре́тій.	2. At what time? - At eleven. - At three.

Note: The preposition об (+ L) is used only with the eleventh hour, **об одина́дцятій.**

2. Different expressions are used for the time between the hour and half past the hour and for the other half of the dial.

1. Котрá годи́на?	1. What time is it?
-Однá хвили́на на вóсьму.	-(It's) one minute after seven.
-Дéсять на вóсьму.	-(It's) ten after seven.
-Дéсять по сьóмій.	-(It's) ten after seven.
-Сьóма дéсять.	-(It's) seven ten.
-Чвéрть на вóсьму.	-(It's) quarter after seven.
-Чвéрть по сьóмій.	-(It's) quarter after seven.
-Пів на вóсьму.	-(It's) half past seven.
-Пів до вóсьмої.	-(It's) half past seven.
2. Котрá годи́на?	2. What time is it?
-За чвéрть вóсьма.	-Quarter to eight.
-За однý хвили́ну вóсьма.	-One minute to eight.
3. О котрíй годи́ні?	2. At what time?
-Дéсять на вóсьму.	-At ten after seven.
-Дéсять по сьóмій.	-At ten after seven.
-О сьóмій дéсять.	-At seven ten.
-(О) пів на вóсьму.	-At half past seven.
-За чвéрть вóсьма.	-At a quarter to eight.

Note 1: The expressions which come closest to English, such as **сьóма дéсять** (7:10) and **о сьóмій дéсять** (at 7:10) belong to the official rather than conversational style.

Note 2: Note that the expression with **на** (+A) and **до** (+G) name the next hour, while those with **по** (+ L) name the past hour. The last two are preferred by the West Ukrainians. Those without any prepositions like **пів вóсьмої** and **полови́на вóсьмої** are also used in colloquial speech (they are Russisms).

Note 3: The preposition **о**, 'at', is used with the exact hour, with the half hour (optional), and in expressions of the **о сьóмій дéсять** type. Otherwise, with fractions of an hour the time given and 'at what time' are expressed in the same way.

Note 4: Official timetables use the numbers 13, 14, 15 , etc. for 1:00 P.M., 2:00 P.M., 3:00 P.M., etc. Since WWII the usage of 13, 14, 15 etc. has become standard among speakers in Ukraine. In writing, the hour and the minutes are separated by a period: 7.10, 7.30, 7.15, etc., while the exact hour may be indicated by a numeral plus the abbreviation **-ій: о 10-ій (о деся́тій), об 11-ій (об одина́дцятій).**

Note 5: The expressions for A.M. are **рáнку** (from 3:00 A.M. to 11:00 A.M.) and **нóчі** (from 1:00 A.M. to 2:00/3:00 A.M.); P.M. is either **дня́** (from 12:00 noon till about 4:00 P.M.) or попóлудні (West Ukrainian usage) or **вéчора** (from 5:00 P.M. till 11:00 P.M.) — see note 3 to Lesson 10, p. 161.

3. When referring to time in the past, expressions stating the exact hour have the verb in the feminine gender to agree with the noun **годи́на**. In all other instances the verb is in the neuter. E.g.:

Булá сьóма годúна.	It was seven o'clock.
Булó пів на вóсьму.	It was half past seven.
Булó за чвéрть сьóма.	It was quarter to seven.

(Exercises 12, 15)

VII. THE VERB ДАТИ

The verb дáти is another verb in the special group of verbs (дáти, íсти, відповíсти). Its forms are as follows:

Future perfective

1st sg. дáм	1st pl. дамó
2nd sg. дасú	2nd pl. дастé
3rd sg. дáсть	3rd pl. дадýть

Imperative
дáй! дáйте!

Past
дáв, далá, далó, далú

VIII. NEUTER NOUNS WITH SUFFIXES -AT (-ЯТ) -ЕН (THE COMPLETE DECLENSION)

Here is the complete declension of the -ат/-ен nouns in the singular.

N.	поросÿ	ім'ÿ
A.	поросÿ	ім'ÿ
G.	поросÿти	íмени
L.	поросÿті	íмені
I.	поросÿм	ім'ÿм (íменем)
D.	поросÿті	íмені
V.	поросÿ	ім'ÿ

Note: The parallel instrumental form in -ен (íменем) is bookish and not typical for spoken Ukrainian.

ВПРАВИ

I. Continue the sentences according to the model:

Цé від Маркá. Трéба Маркóві подÿкувати.

(Слáвка, йогó дружúни, доцéнта Іванúшина, профéсора Гончарéнка, її́ ýчня, її́ сестрú, йогó лíкаря, Ю́рія Володúмировича, йогó вчúтеля, її́ вчúтельки, йогó жíнки, її́ бáтька, Василÿ, Андрíя та Íгоря)

II. Change the sentences according to the model:

Чого́ **він** хо́че? Чого́ **йому́** тре́ба?

(ти́, вона́, я́, вони́, воно́, ми́, ви́)

III. Change the sentences according to the model:

Марко́ лю́бить варе́ники. ***Марко́ві*** одно́го варе́ника ма́ло.

(О́льга, Марі́я, чолові́к, ма́ти, її́ гі́сть, си́н, її́ дочка́, його́ учени́ця, його́ това́риш, її́ това́ришка)

IV. Give the dative of the nouns contained in the questions:

1. Де́ Іва́н Семе́нович? Пока́жіть це́. . . . .
2. Де́ вчи́тель? Скажі́ть це́. . . . .
3. Де́ інжене́р? Да́йте це́ . . . . .
4. Де́ лі́кар? Подзво́ніть . . . . .
5. Де́ вчи́телька? Напиші́ть . . . . .
6. Де́ па́н Поліщу́к? Подя́куйте . . . . .
7. Де́ профе́сор Ле́сів? Покажі́ть це́ . . . . .
8. Де́ його́ у́чень? Да́йте це́ . . . . .
9. Де́ її́ ді́вчинка? Скажі́ть це́ . . . . .
10. Де́ її́ хло́пець? Подзво́ніть . . . . .

V. Replace the words in bold face by dative of the corresponding pronouns.

1. Я́ куплю́ **для ньо́го** подару́нок.
2. Він **до те́бе** напи́ше.
3. **Для ме́не** цього́ не до́сить.
4. Ми́ **до ва́с** подзво́нимо.
5. Це́ бу́де **для ни́х** подару́нок.
6. Я́ **до не́ї** говорю́.
7. **Для ва́с** цього́ до́сить.

VI. Supply the correct form of the pronouns **са́м себе́.**

1. Ти́ му́сиш спита́ти . . . . .
2. Вона́ му́сить подя́кувати . . . .
3. Я́ це́ обіця́ю . . . . .
4. Він не розуміє . . . . .
5. Вона́ не ві́рила . . . . .
6. Я́ це́ купи́в . . . . . для . . . . .
7. Вона́ ціка́виться ті́льки . . . . .
8. Він слу́хає ті́льки . . . . .
9. Ти́ му́сиш це́ сказа́ти . . . .
10. Хто́ лю́бить . . . . .?

11. Подивíться . . . . . на . . . . .
12. Вонá забýла . . . . за . . . .
13. Він ніко́ли не дýмає . . . . . . про . . . .
14. Ле́гко подо́батися . . . . .
15. Тре́ба вміти сміятися з . . . . .

VII. Supply the correct form of the pronoun **себé.**

1. Вони́ самí . . . . . не вíрили.
2. Я́ взялá . . . . . трóхи си́ру.
3. Він сáм з . . . . говори́в.
4. Вонá цé . . . . надрукýє.
5. Спитáй . . . .
6. Лиши́ . . . . трóхи картóплі.
7. Я́ покладý . . . . капýсти.
8. Перевір . . . . . .
9. Ти́ мóжеш . . . . купи́ти порося́.
10. Він сáм . . . . . не пам'ятáє.
11. Вонá самá . . . . бої́ться.
12. Я́ за . . . . не відповідáю.
13. Він не знáє, щó з . . . . роби́ти.
14. Вонá почувáє . . . . . недóбре.
15. Він називáє . . . . . профе́сором, а він тíльки вчи́тель.

VIII. Give the appropriate forms of the verbs **вози́ти, везти́, повезти́.**

1. Куди́ цé ти́ вчóра ї́здив? Я́ . . . . . свою́ мáтір до лíкаря.
2. Настýпної весни́ я́ хóчу вáс . . . . . в Украї́ну.
3. Вчóра він цíлий дéнь нáс . . . . . і покáзував мíсто.
4. Чи ти́ мóжеш менé . . . . . до бібліотéки?
5. Я́ зáраз ї́ду до мíста і . . . . . Мáрту з собóю.
6. Куди́ вáс . . . . .? — Прóшу, ... менé на вýлицю Шевченка, буди́нок 12.
7. Не . . . . дити́ну ввéсь чáс, тáк вонá нікóли не навчи́ться ходи́ти.
8. Минýлої óсени нáшу клясу . . . . . . на завóд.
9. Почекáйте трóхи, я́ вáс зáраз . . . . своїм áвтом.
10. Я́ . . . . з собóю тíльки однý валíзку.

IX. Give the appropriate forms of the verbs **носи́ти, нести́, понести́.**

1. Вонá вжé двá рáзи . . . . дити́ну до лíкаря.
2. О́сь вонá знóв . . . . . її́.
3. Я́ бáчу що ви́ . . . . . . щóсь важкé. Хóчете я́ вáм цé . . . . .?
4. Прóшу, не . . . . свою́ валíзку туди́-сюди́.
5. Чогó ти́ . . . . ці я́блука з мíсця на мíсце?
6. Щó цé ти́ . . . . .? — Цé словни́к, я́ йогó . . . . до бібліотéки.
7. Я́ зáвтра . . . . свою́ робóту показáти профéсорові.
8. Вчóра він . . . . йомý вíрші своє́ї сестри́.
9. Я́ не хóчу бíльше . . . . йомý ї́сти. Нехáй сáм собí . . . .

X. Choose the appropriate verb from the following: **(по)везти́, вози́ти.**

1. Я́ хо́чу ва́с . . . . . . сього́дні в на́ш са́д.
2. Куди́ ти́ ї́здив? Я́ . . . . . . Сла́вка до лі́каря.
3. Я́ ба́чила вра́нці, я́к вона́ . . . . . свою́ ді́вчинку по ву́лиці.
4. Мину́лого лі́та ві́н . . . . . свою́ роди́ну в го́ри.
5. О 12-ій годи́ні ми́ . . . . ї́х до інститу́ту.
6. Ко́жного лі́та вона́ . . . . . сво́ю ма́тір на мо́ре.
7. Подиві́ться, що́ ві́н . . . . . .?
8. Я́ не мо́жу ніко́го . . . . . , я́ не ма́ю а́вта.
9. О́сь іде́ на́ш авто́бус. Ві́н . . . . на́с до мі́ста.
10. Вона́ . . . сво́ю дочку́ до шко́ли ко́жного ра́нку.

XI. Choose the appropriate verb: **(по)нести́, носи́ти.**

1. Вона́ вже́ вміє ходи́ти, чому́ ти́ її́ вве́сь ча́с . . . . . .?
2. Куди́ це́ ти́ . . . . мою́ валі́зку?
3. Ві́н лежи́ть у лі́жку. Тре́ба йому́ . . . . ї́сти.
4. Ві́н за́вжди . . . . з собо́ю словни́к.
5. Вона́ взяла́ кни́жку й . . . . . її́ до бібліоте́ки.
6. О́сь я́блука. Про́шу, ...ї́х та́тові.
7. Я́ візьму́ цю́ валі́зку, а ти́ . . . . оту́.
8. Його́ ві́рші . . . . наро́дові пра́вду.
9. Ді́ти му́сять . . . . . до шко́ли зо́шит, ру́чку й оліве́ць.
10. Чому́ ти́ . . . . . свою валі́зку туди́ й сюди́?

XII. Give the time (both A.M. and P.M.).

1. За́раз 1:30.
2. За́раз 2:30.
3. За́раз 3:30.
4. За́раз 4:30.
5. За́раз 5:30.
6. За́раз 6:30.
7. За́раз 7:30.
8. За́раз 8:30.
9. За́раз 9:30.
10. За́раз 10:30.
11. За́раз 11:30.
12. За́раз 12:30.

XIII. Write the time, giving both constructions, with **на** and **по.**

Тепе́р пе́рша. Че́рез чве́рть годи́ни бу́де чве́рть по пе́ршій.
Тепе́р пе́рша. Че́рез чве́рть годи́ни бу́де чве́рть на дру́гу.

(п'я́та, во́сьма, одина́дцята, дру́га, дев'я́та, шо́ста, деся́та, двана́дцята, тре́тя, сьо́ма, четве́рта).

XIV. Translate into Ukrainian (use both types of time expression where applicable).

1. It was 3:00 A.M.
2. I will come at 6:30 P.M.
3. It was 8:45.
4. We will leave at a quarter to eight.
5. At what time do you eat your supper?
6. Breakfast is at eight.
7. It was 11:15.
8. He called me at seven in the morning.
9. I will come in the evening around nine.
10. Be there at 10:00 A.M.

XV. Translate into Ukrainian.

1. When did you see him? Last night at six.
2. When will you talk to her? Tomorrow morning at eleven.
3. When are you going to see your friend Eugene? Tonight.
4. When will you get the watch? Next week.
5. When did she graduate from the university? Last year.
6. When did she tell you this? Last Wednesday.
7. Where were you all night? At the plant. We had a lot of work.
8. What time is it? It's either five or quarter past five. I'm not sure.
9. What day is today? Today is Thursday.
10. When is she coming? She is coming Monday evening.

XVI. Make a choice between the verbs meaning 'to teach', **навча́ти — навчи́ти.**

1. До́брий учи́тель мо́же та́к бага́то . . . . .
2. Хо́чеш, я́ тебе́ . . . . керува́ти а́втом?
3. Вона́ за́вжди́ . . . . всíх, що́ роби́ти, а сама́ нíчо́го не вмíє.
4. Хто́ тебе́ . . . . . так га́рно спíва́ти?
5. Чого́ ва́с та́м у тíй шко́лі . . . . . ?
6. Він ї́х до́вго . . . . . росíйської мо́ви, але́ та́к і не . . . .

XVII. Make a choice between the verbs meaning 'to study', **навча́тися—навчи́тися, учи́тися, вивча́ти—ви́вчити.**

1. Це́й америка́нський профе́сор . . . . . істо́рію Украї́ни.
2. Він коли́сь . . . . . . в цьо́му університе́ті.
3. Марко́ . . . . . . в двана́дцятій кля́сі.
4. Де́ ви́ та́к до́бре . . . . говори́ти по-украї́нському?
5. Бо́б . . . . украї́нської мо́ви в одно́го вчи́теля-украї́нця.
6. Шевче́нко каза́в, щоб ми́ бага́то . . . ., щоб . . . . . чужо́го, але́ й свого́ не цура́лися.

XVIII. Read and translate.

1. Дорогий Богдáне! Пишý тобі зі Львóва. Прáвду кáжуть, що побáчити — цé повірити. Я́ багáто чýв про цé старé украї́нське місто, про тé, що тýт усі говóрять по-украї́нському, не тáк, як у Ки́єві. Я́ зустрів тýт однý дýже гáрну дівчину. Її́ ім'я Мáрта. Я́ з нéю вчóра ходи́в на концéрт. Я́ ще не мáю її́ фотогрáфії, мені булó незрýчно проси́ти її́ з пéршого рáзу, алé сьогóдні я її́ знóв побáчу й тоді попрошý. В настýпному листі дістанéш. Напиши́, щó ти́ про неї́ дýмаєш. У Мáрти є товáришка Óля. Тéж дýже гáрна дівчина. Мóже, ти́ візьмеш своé áвто й прии́деш сюди́? Скáжеш мені спаси́бі.
   Нý, на сьогóдні дóсить. Пиши́.
   Твій дрýг Микóла.

2. Нáш телефóн не працює, і я мýсив піти́ до пáні Поліщýк, щоб подзвони́ти Слáвкові. Я́ хотів розповісти йомý про тé, щó булó на сьогóднішній лéкції, я́к Мáрко спав, а вчи́тель цé побáчив і сказáв йомý йти́ додóму. Я́ розповів цю історію пáні Поліщýк, алé мені здаєтся, щó вонá мені не повірила. Нехáй не вірить, алé цé прáвда.

3. Коли́ я прийшóв, пáні Поліщýк пилá чай. Вонá дóбра жінка, мáє дóбре сéрце. Вонá зáвжди́ даé мені щóсь ї́сти. Óсь і цьогó рáзу вонá спитáла менé, чи я не хóчу капýсти, абó картóплі, абó борщý. Я́, звичáйно, зáвжди голóдний, алé сказáв ї́й, що я вжé ї́в. Мені незрýчно стільки в неї́ ї́сти. Алé вонá не хотіла й слýхати, пішлá до другої кімнáти й бáчу: несé варéники з капýстою і з картóплею! Тýт я вжé не міг сказáти "ні" і з'ї́в цілу гóру.

XIX. Answer the questions to the dialogues.

"Варéники готóві!"

1. Комý мáти даé варéники?
2. З чи́м вони́?
3. Які варéники ї́сть Слáвко і скільки?
4. Щó він забýв зроби́ти?

"Щó ти́ везéш?"

1. Котрá тепéр годи́на?
2. Куди́ ї́де Ромáн?
3. Коли́ він тáм мáє бýти?
4. Щó він везé?

"Ли́ст від коли́шнього ýчня."

1. До кóго пи́ше Ромáн?
2. За щó він дя́кує?
3. Яки́м він бýв коли́сь?
4. Я́к він тепéр живé?

ТРИНАДЦЯТА ЛЕКЦІЯ

 # 38 Співатиме хор
A choir will be singing

Dialogue Paticipants:
На́дя - Н, Семе́н - С
Nadja - N, Semen - S

1.	С-	На́дю, ви́ зна́єте, сього́дні свя́то. У на́с у це́ркві бу́де конце́рт.	S-	Nadja, you know, today is a holiday. We are having a concert at our church.
2.	Н-	Та́к, я́ чу́ла. Співа́тиме хор це́ркви св. Миха́їла.* Та́м співа́є мій знайо́мий, Оре́ст Тарнове́цький.	N-	Yes, I heard. St. Michael's church choir will be singing. A fellow I know sings there, Orest Tarnovec'kyj.
3.	С-	Я́ його́ те́ж зна́ю, чудо́вий ба́с. Мо́же, хо́чете піти́ послу́хати?	S-	I know him too, a beautiful basso. Perhaps you would like to go and hear them?
4.	Н-	А о котрі́й годи́ні поча́ток?	N-	At what time do they start?
5.	С-	У програ́мі пи́шеться, що то́чно о во́сьмій, але́ в на́с ніко́ли нічо́го то́чно не почина́ється.	S-	It says in the program that they start at eight sharp but nothing ever begins on time with us.
6.	Н-	Та́к, а кінчи́ться, ма́буть, де́сь об одина́дцятій або́ на́віть о двана́дцятій. Це́ для́ ме́не ду́же пі́зно.	N-	Yes, and it will probably end around 11 or even 12. It's too late for me.
7.	С-	Але́ ми́ не му́симо сиді́ти до кінця́. То я́к, пі́демо?	S-	But we don't have to stay till the end. How about it, shall we go?
8.	Н-	Я́ не зна́ю. Мені́ хоті́лося б піти́, але́ не хо́чу пі́зно ляга́ти спа́ти.	N-	I'm not sure. I would like to go but I don't want to go to bed late.
9.	С-	За́втра ж неді́ля, ви́ мо́жете спа́ти хо́ч до по́лудня. В це́ркві є́ слу́жба Бо́жа пі́сля по́лудня о 12:30.	S-	Tomorrow is Sunday, you can sleep till noon, if you wish. There is a church service in the afternoon at 12:30 at the church.
10.	Н-	Це́ пра́вда. Ну́ до́бре, ході́м.	N-	That's true. Well, O.K. let's go.

---

* Pronounced: свято́го Миха́їла.

 # 39 Що мені вдягнути?
What shall I wear?

Dialogue Paticipants:
пáні Миросла́ва - М, Оле́кса - О, Да́рка - Д
pani Myroslava - M, Oleksa - O, Darka - D

1. М-	Оле́ксо, яка́ це́ на тобі́ соро́чка?	M- Oleksa, what's that shirt you have on?
2. О-	Та́това. Мені́ вона́ подоба́ється, а то́бі?	O- It's dad's. I like it. Do you?
3. М-	Та́к, тобі в ні́й га́рно. Блаки́тна, я́к твої́ о́чі. Це́ та́то тобі́ да́в?	M- Yes, you look nice in it. It's blue like your eyes. Did dad give it to you?
4. О-	Та́к, він мені́ її́ подарува́в.	O- Yes, he gave it to me as a present.
5. М-	Це га́рно. Да́рко, чому́ ти́ ще́ не́ вдя́гнена?	M- That's nice. Darka, why you are not dressed yet.
6. Д-	Я́ нія́к не мо́жу ви́рішити, яку́ су́кню вдягну́ти: жо́вту чи блаки́тну?	D- I just can't make up my mind what dress to wear: the yellow or the blue one.
7. М-	Я́ б одягну́ла жо́вту. Вона́ на тобі́ кра́ще сиди́ть.	M- I would put on the yellow one. It fits you better.
8. Д-	Я́ те́ж волію жо́вту, а о́т моє́му Андрі́єві більше подо́бається блаки́тна.	D- I too prefer the yellow one, but my Andrij likes the blue one better.
9. М-	Слу́хай, я́ не помилю́ся, коли́ скажу́, що твоє́му Андрі́єві не сама́ су́кня подо́бається а ти́ в ні́й. Чи не та́к?	M- Listen, I won't be wrong if I say that it's not the dress itself that your Andrij likes but you in that dress. Am I right?
10. Д-	Ну́, звича́йно, ма́мо. Андрі́й мені́ на́віть сказа́в, що йому́ взагалі́ байду́же, я́к я́ вдя́гнена — бо я́ в будьяко́му о́дязі га́рна.	D- Yes, of course, mom. Andrij even told me that he doesn't care at all what I wear. I am pretty in any clothes.
11. М-	О́т ба́чиш. Вдягни́ жо́вту, і тоді́ ви́ з Оле́ксою бу́дете жо́вто-блаки́тна па́ра.	M- See? Put on the yellow one and then you and Oleksa will make a yellow-and-blue pair.
12. О-	Як на́ш украї́нський пра́пор? Лиша́ється тільки причепи́ти значо́к з тризу́бом, і тоді́ ми́ виглядатимемо вже́ цілко́м патріоти́чно.	O- Like our Ukrainian flag? It remains only to clip on a badge with the trident sign and then we will look fully patriotic.
13. М-	Ну́, до́сить жартува́ти, одяга́йся шви́дше, бо вже́ сьо́ма годи́на.	M- Well, enough joking. Get dressed fast, it's already seven o'clock.
14. Д-	Вже́ біжу́.	D- I'm off.

СЛОВНИК

байду́же and байдуже	no matter
мені байду́же	I don't care
ба́с, -у; -и́ (m)	basso
бі́к, бо́ку (m); з його́ бо́ку	side; on his part
блаки́тний	light blue
Бо́жий	God's, divine
будь-яки́й	any kind, whichever
вдяга́ти, вдяга́ють I вдягну́ти, вдягну́, вдя́гнуть P	to put on, to dress

вдяга́тися, вдяга́ються I	to get dressed
вдягну́тися, вдягну́ся, вдя́гну́ться P	
вдя́гнений (в + A)	dressed (in)
взагалі́	in general; at all
дарува́ти, дару́ють I	to give as a present
подарува́ти, подару́ють P	
дівча́та (pl.)	girls
жо́втий; жо́вто-блаки́тний	yellow; yellow-and-blue
знайо́мий	familiar; an acquaintance
значо́к, значка́ (m)	badge, pin
кіне́ць, кінця́ (m)	end
кінча́тися, кінча́ються I*	to end
кінчи́тися, кінча́ться P	
ляга́ти, ляга́ють I	to lie down
лягти́, ля́жуть P	
лі́г, лягла́, -о (past. pfv.)	
на́віть	even
на жа́ль	unfortunately
нія́к	in no way
нія́кий	none, no
о́дяг	clothes, garment
о́ко, -а (n); о́чі (pl.)	eye
па́ра (f)	pair, couple
патріоти́чно	patriotic
писа́тися, пи́шуться I	to be written
написа́тися, напи́шуться P	
подо́батися, подо́баються I	to like
сподо́батися, сподо́баються P	(+ D)
по́лудень, по́лудня (m)	noon
and полу́день, полу́дня	
пі́сля по́лудня	(in the) afternoon
поча́ток, поча́тку (m)	beginning
почина́тися, почина́ються I	to begin
поча́тися, почну́ться P	
пра́пор, -а; -и́ (m)	flag
причіпля́ти, -ля́ють I	to fasten on, to pin
причепи́ти, приче́плять P	
святи́й (св.)	holy; saint (St.)
свя́то (n)	holiday
сиді́ти (про о́дяг) (на +L)	to fit (of clothes)
слу́жба (f)	service
слу́жба Бо́жа	liturgy
соро́чка (f)	shirt
співа́ти, співа́ють I	to sing (+ A/ G)
заспіва́ти, заспіва́ють P	to begin singing

* This verb has only 3rd sg. and pl. forms.

су́кня (f)	dress
та́тів, та́това, та́тове	dad's
твої́ (pl.)	your
то́чно	exactly
тризу́б (m)	trident (Ukr. natl. emblem)
хіба́ (= чи, невже́)	really (in a question)
хо́р, -у (m)	choir
хоті́тися, хо́четься* I	to feel like
захоті́тися, захо́четься P	
хоч (хоча́)	if you wish; at least; although
це́рква (f)	church
цілко́м	fully, completely

NAMES

Да́рка (Ода́рка) — short for Да́рія
Мирosла́ва (Сла́ва for short)
На́дя (short for Наді́я) — Hope
Оле́кса (conversational for Олексі́й = Alex)
Оре́ст Тарнове́цький, Семе́н
Михаї́л = Миха́йло

IDIOMS

ляга́ти (лягти́) спа́ти	to go to bed
То́ як?	how about it ?

SUPPLEMENT

по́милка and поми́лка -и́ (f)	mistake
свяще́ник (m)	priest
штани́ (pl)	pants, slacks

EXPLANATORY NOTES

1. **Михаї́л** is the traditional church spelling of the name of the archangel and of several saints, while in the ordinary language the name is **Миха́йло.**

2. Unspecified time in the afternoon is referred to as **після по́лудня, по по́лудні, після півдня (південь** is a variant of **полу́день**):

* 3rd sg. only

Я́ прийду́ пі́сля по́лудня. Я́ прийду́ попо́лудні.	I will come in the afternoon.

A specific time in the afternoon is usually left without the designation 'P.M.', unless an ambiguity can arise, in which case all the above expressions may be used in addition to **вде́нь, дня́** and **по обі́ді**, plus the hour.

3. The expressions for church service or liturgy are **богослу́ження, слу́жба Бо́жа**.One may also say **(свята́) літургі́я.**

4. There is a variety of ways in which to express the notion of 'wearing' in Ukrainian.

a) The verb **вдяга́тися**, which alternates with **одяга́тися** and the less frequent **удяга́тися**, means to 'get dressed', 'dress in', or 'to be dressed' and the article of clothes one wears or puts on is in the accusative with the preposition **у/в**:

Вона́ за́вжди вдяга́ється в штани́.	She always wears slacks.
Він вдягну́вся в нову́ соро́чку.	He put on a new shirt.
Одяга́йся!	Get dressed!
- Я́ вже́ одягну́вся.	- I am already dressed.

(b) The participle **вдя́гнений** (or its variant **вдя́гнутий**) stands for 'dressed (in)', 'to be wearing'. The article one is wearing is in the accusative with **у/в**:

Вона́ ще́ не вдя́гнена.	She is not dressed yet.
Він бу́в вдя́гнений у нову́ соро́чку.	He was dressed in (was wearing) a new shirt.

(c) The verb **носи́ти** (in its multidirectional form only) stands for 'wearing always', i.e. indicates iterative action. The object is in the accusative:

Чому́ ти́ но́сиш такі́ штани́?	Why do you (always) wear such pants?
Він за́вжди но́сить стару́ соро́чку.	He always wears an old shirt.

(d) The verb **ходи́ти** also means 'to wear', 'to walk around in'. The object is in the locative with **у/в:**

Вона́ за́вжди хо́дить у ці́й су́кні.	She always walks around in this dress.

(e) The idea of 'having s. thing on' or 'to be in s. thing' is expressed by the verb **бу́ти + на +** locative (the wearer is in the loc., the object worn is in the nom.) and **бу́ти + в +** locative (the wearer is in the N., apparel is in the L.) E.g.:

На ні́й (була́) га́рна су́кня.	She has (had) a nice dress on.
Вона́ була́ в до́вгій су́кні.	She wore (was in) a long dress.

5. The official name of the Ukrainian flag is си́ньо-жо́втий (lit. 'dark blue and yellow).

6. Note the masculine nominative singular form of the denominal possessive adjective **та́тів**. Such adjectives decline like regular adjectives (see further discussion in Lesson 14).

7. The verb кінча́тися has a more formal variant закі́нчуватися I (закінчи́тися P):

Коли́ закі́нчується навча́льний рік? When does the school year end?

NOTES ON GRAMMAR

I. DATIVE SINGULAR OF ADJECTIVES

The dative endings of the adjectives are exactly like those of the locative:

N.	коли́шній коли́шнє	тяжки́й тяжке́	коли́шня	тяжка́
D.	коли́шньому	тяжко́му	коли́шній	тяжкі́й
L.	(на) коли́шньому	тяжко́му	коли́шній	тяжкі́й

Ordinals follow the same declension.

(Exercises 3, 6)

II. DATIVE SINGULAR OF THE DEMONSTRATIVE PRONOUNS, ОДИН AND УВЕСЬ

In the dative case the demonstrative pronouns and the numeral оди́н have the same form as in the locative but a different stress in the masculine and the neuter forms.

N.	то́й/те́	оди́н/одне́	це́й/це́	уве́сь/усе́	та́/одна́	ця́	уся́
D.	тому́	одному́	цьому́	усьому́	ті́й/одні́й	ці́й	усі́й
L.	(на) то́му	одно́му одні́м	цьо́му ці́м	усьо́му усі́м	ті́й/одні́й	ці́й	усі́й

Note: In the phrase 'one another' (see Lesson 3, p. 49) the stress in the second word always falls on the first syllable, i.e.

оди́н о́дному, одне́ о́дному, одна́ о́дній (оди́н о́дного, одна́ о́дну; оди́н з о́дним, одна́ з о́дною; оди́н до о́дного, одна́ до о́дної; etc.)

(Exercises 1, 3)

III. DATIVE SINGULAR OF THE POSSESSIVE PRONOUNS AND THE PRONOUN ЧИЙ

The dative case forms of the possessive pronouns and the pronoun чи́й are exactly like the -ому/-єму locative forms, including the position of the stress.

N.	мі́й моє́	ї́хній ї́хнє	чи́й чиє́	моя́ ї́хня	чия́
D.	моє́му	ї́хньому	чийо́му (чиє́му)	мої́й ї́хній	чиї́й
L.	(на) моє́му	(на)ї́хньому	(на) чийо́му (на) чиє́му	(на) мої́й (на) ї́хній	(на) чиї́й

The dative case endings of the pronouns **твій** and **свій** are the same as those of the pronoun **мій**. **На́ш**, **ва́ш** follow the hard stem pattern:

N.	на́ш/на́ше	на́ша
D.	на́шому	на́шій
L.	(на) на́шому	(на) на́шій
	(на) на́шім	

(Exercises 2, 3, 4, 5, 6)

IV. USES OF DATIVE (CONTINUED)

1. The verb **хоті́ти** has a parallel **-ся** form with the meaning 'to feel like having / doing something'. The person is in the dative, the object of desire is in the genitive. cf.:

ХОТІ́ТИ	ХОТІ́ТИСЯ
Я́ хо́чу ка́ші. I want some cereal.	Мені́ хо́четься ка́ші. I feel like having some cereal.
Я́ не хоті́ла ї́сти. I didn't want to eat.	Мені́ не хоті́лося ї́сти. I didn't feel like eating.

There is a number of other verbs which have a parallel **-ся** form which are used in constructions with the dative.

Я́к ва́м працю́ється?	How is the work going?
Мені́ сього́дні не працю́ється.	I can't (don't feel like) working today.
Я́к тобі́ спа́лося?	How did you sleep?
Мені́ не спи́ться.	I can't sleep* (= I have insomnia).

Note that in all such constructions the verb is in the 3rd person singular (neuter in the past).

2. The verb **подо́батися** 'to like', 'to appeal', 'to please' takes the dative object of the person who experiences these feelings, while the person or object liked is in the nominative.

Вона́ подо́бається мені́, а я́ ї́й.	I like her and she likes me.
Мені́ подо́бається ця́ ду́мка.	This idea appeals to (pleases) me.

---

* cf.: a folk song:

І не спи́ться й не лежи́ться і со́н мене́ не бере́.
Я́ пішо́в би до ми́лої, та не зна́ю, де́ живе́.

I can't sleep and can't lie down and sleep doesn't come to me,
I would go see my darling but I don't know where she lives.

Note: The verb **люби́ти** indicates not only a strong liking (or love) but also a feeling of long standing, so that one may not use it immediately upon encountering a person or getting the first impression of something. cf.:

ЛЮБИ́ТИ	ПОДО́БАТИСЯ
Вона́ полюби́ла Ки́їв. She fell in love with Kyiv. (= after spending some time there)	Ї́й сподо́бався Ки́їв. She liked Kyiv. (= after one visit)
Вона́ люби́ла це́й ві́рш. She used to love this poem. (or She loved that poem)	Ї́й подо́бався це́й ві́рш. She used to like this poem. (or She liked that poem.)
Я́ люби́ла це́й фі́льм. I loved that movie. (= saw it many times)	Мені́ сподо́бався це́й фі́льм. I liked that movie. (= saw it once)

3. In expressions dealing with emotional states and physical conditions, such as 'I am happy', 'I am cold', the experiencer is in the dative case, e.g.:

Мені́ до́бре (= Я́ почува́ю себе́ до́бре)	I'm fine.
Мені́ пога́но (недо́бре).	I feel sick.
Мені́ прие́мно з ва́ми познайо́митися.	I'm pleased to meet you.
Мені́ байду́же.	I don't care (= I feel indifferent)
Мені́ незру́чно його́ пита́ти.	I am embarassed to ask him.
Мені́ незру́чно ту́т сиді́ти.	I'm uncomfortable sitting here.

(Exercises 1, 2, 5, 6, 7)

V. THE REFLEXIVE VERB AND OTHER VERBS IN -СЯ

1. There are verbs with the particle **-ся** which indicate that the action is directed towards the subject or self. They are called reflexive verbs. cf.:

Non-reflexive	*Reflexive*
Вона́ вдяга́є дити́ну. She is dressing the child.	Вона́ вдяга́ється. She is dressing herself. (She is getting dressed.)

2. Another group of **-ся** verbs is not truly self-oriented but still refers to the subject. cf.:

Я́ влаштува́в його́ на робо́ту. I got him a job.	Я́ влаштува́вся на робо́ту. I got myself a job.
Я́ ї́х лиши́в удо́ма. I left them at home.	Я́ лиши́вся вдо́ма. I stayed home.

Я́ йому́ ви́бачив. I forgave him.	Я́ ви́бачився. I excused myself.
Я́ його́ вчи́в. I taught him.	Я́ вчи́вся. I studied.

Note: Some verbs in this group may be made reflexive in meaning by adding the reflexive pronoun **себе́** usually accompanied by **са́м**:

Я́ са́м собі́ ви́бачив.	I forgave myself.
Ві́н са́м себе́ навчи́в чита́ти.	He taught himself how to read.

3. **-ся** verbs in passive constructions. In such constructions the direct object of the transitive verb becomes the grammatical subject, as was the case with the verb **подо́батися**. cf.:

Active	*Passive*
Я́к написа́ти це́ сло́во? How do you write this word?	Я́к пи́шеться це сло́во? How is this word written?
Я́к ви́ назвете́ таку́ літерату́ру? How would you call this type of literature?	Я́к назива́ється така́ літерату́ра? How is this type of literature called?
Я́к прочита́ти це́ пр́ізвище? How do you read (pronounce) this name?	Я́к чита́ється це́ пр́ізвище? How is this name pronounced?
Та́к не гово́рять (ка́жуть). They don't say it this way.	Це́ та́к не гово́риться (ка́жеться). That's not the way it's said.
Я́к ви́ ро́бите варе́ники? How do you make the dumplings?	Я́к ро́бляться варе́ники? How are dumplings made?
Я́ давно́ забу́в цю́ істо́рію. I forgot that story long ago.	Це́ істо́рія давно́ забу́лася. This story is long forgotten.

To indicate the performer of the action in these and other passive constructions is rather bookish. The use of personal pronouns in this function is actually foreign to the spirit of the Ukrainian language and should be avoided. When named, the performer is in the instrumental and the verb must be imperfective. E.g.:

Дома́шня робо́та перевіря́ється вчи́телем.
The homework is checked by the teacher.

With perfective verb passive constructions of this type are either impossible or the action is viewed as happening by itself. cf.:

Imperfective	*Perfective*
Усі пита́ння вирі́шувалися ба́тьком. All questions were decided by the father.	Пита́ння ви́рішилося само́ собо́ю. The question resolved itself.
Завда́ння роби́лося ці́лою кля́сою. The assignment was carried out by the entire class.	Це́ зроби́лося само́ собо́ю. It happened by itself.

4. The verbs **кінча́тися, почина́тися** and **відчиня́тися, зачиня́тися.**. The verbs **кінча́тися** 'to end', 'to come to an end', **почина́тися** 'to begin', 'to have a beginning', **відчиня́тися** 'to open up' and **зачиня́тися** 'to shut' all denote a self-contained action, i.e. they are intransitive. cf.:

Transitive	*Intransitive*
Кінчі́м цю́ розмо́ву. Let's end this conversation.	Розмо́ва кінчи́лася. The conversation ended.
Ві́н кінчи́в ле́кцію. He finished his lecture.	Ле́кція кінчи́лася. The lecture is over.
Ми́ почина́ємо засі́дання. We begin the meeting.	Засі́дання почина́ється. The meeting begins.
Я́ зачини́в две́рі. I closed the door.	Две́рі зачини́лися. The door shut (by itself).
Я́ відчини́в вікно́. I opened the window.	Вікно́ відчини́лося. The window opened.
Ми́ почина́ємо нову́ впра́ву. We are beginning a new exercise.	Нова́ впра́ва почина́ється ту́т. The new exercise begins here.
—	Поча́вся пе́рший де́нь у шко́лі. The first day of school began.
—	До́вгий де́нь скінчи́вся. The long day is over.

(Exercises 7, 8)

VI. NEGATIVE PRONOUNS AND ADVERBS WITH THE PARTICLE НІ

A group of pronouns and adverbs is formed from the interrogative pronouns and adverbs by adding the prefix **ні-**. Semantically they are the counterpart of positive indefinite pronouns and adverbs. cf.:

Indefinite	*Interrogative*	*Negative*
хтóсь	хтó?	ніхтó
щóсь	щó?	ніщó
я́кось	я́к?	нія́к
яки́й	яки́й?	нія́кий
дéсь	дé?	нідé
коли́сь	коли́?	нікóли
куди́сь	куди́?	нікýди

Note 1: Prepositions are placed between ні and the pronouns: **ні з ки́м, ні до чóго, ні в я́кому.**

Note 2: In the negative forms, stress is always on the second syllable, cf.: **яки́й** but **нія́кий, куди́** but **нікýди.**

Note 3: To review the declension of pronouns, adjectives and numerals see Appendix 4.

ВПРАВИ

I. Change the sentences according to the model:

Цéй хлóпець кáже, що тýт дóбре. **Цьомý хлóпцеві** тýт дóбре.

1. Ця́ дíвчина кáже, що тýт незрýчно сидíти.
2. Цéй студент кáже, що тýт цікáво вчи́тися.
3. Ця́ дити́на кáже, що ї́й хóлодно.
4. Цéй чоловíк кáже, що йомý погáно чýти.
5. Ця́ жíнка кáже, щó ї́й приємно тýт жи́ти.
6. Цéй ýчень кáже, що йомý нецікáво цé читáти.
7. Ця́ америкáнка кáже, що ї́й недóбре.
8. Цéй пан кáже, що йомý байдýже, дé спáти.
9. Ця́ дíвчинка кáже, що ї́й недóбре.
10. Ця́ студéнтка кáже, що ї́й неприéмно про цé говори́ти.

II. Change the sentences according to the model.

Мíй си́н любить істóрію. **Моéму си́нові** подóбається істóрія.

1. Моя́ знайóма лю́бить кáву.
2. Мíй знайóмий лю́бить істóрію.
3. Твоя́ учени́ця лю́бить цю́ сýкню.
4. Твíй брáт лю́бить цю́ робóту.
5. Вáш чоловíк лю́бить цю́ прогрáму.
6. Уся́ нáша кля́са лю́бить йогó вíрші.
7. Ї́хній бáтько лю́бить такý слýжбу.
8. Йогó жíнка лю́бить дóбру розмóву.
9. Нáш товáриш лю́бить літератýру.
10. Нáша товáришка лю́бить медици́ну.

III. Put the bracketed words into the correct form.

1. Я́ пишу́ листа́ (одна́ моя́ до́бра знайо́ма).
2. Я́ ма́ю подзвони́ти (оди́н кана́дський профе́сор).
3. Я́ хо́чу це́ подарува́ти (мі́й коли́шній учи́тель).
4. Ми́ хо́чемо подя́кувати (ці́ла деся́та кля́са).
5. Тре́ба відповісти (то́й ха́рківський інжене́р).
6. Ти́ кра́ще дай ї́сти (твій голо́дний си́н).
7. Тре́ба допомогти́ (ця́ стара́ жі́нка).
8. Да́й папе́ру (то́й нови́й студе́нт).
9. Покажі́ть це́ (ці́ла сьо́ма кля́са).
10. Скажи́ це́ (коли́шній та́тів у́чень).

IV. Put the bracketed words into the correct form.

1. (Яка́ дити́на) хо́лодно. (Нія́ка).
2. (Чия́ дити́на) хо́лодно? (Моя́).
3. (Котри́й хло́пець) це́ сказа́ти? (Тре́тій від вікна́).
4. (Яки́й хло́пець) це́ сказа́ти? (О́н то́й).
5. (Чи́й си́н) да́ти ка́ші? (Мі́й).
6. (Чия́ дочка́) да́ти ка́ші? (Твоя́).
7. (Котра́ ді́вчинка) це́ показа́ти? (Четве́рта від вікна́).
8. (Чия́ ма́ти) це́ байду́же? (На́ша).
9. (Чий ба́тько) це́ байду́же? (Ва́ш).
10. (Яка́ учени́ця) незру́чно? (О́н та́).

V. Change the sentences according to the model:

Я люблю́ варе́ники. Да́йте мені́ кі́лька (тро́хи).

1. На́ш Сла́вко лю́бить бо́рщ.
2. На́ша Да́рка лю́бить си́р.
3. Чи ва́ш Оле́кса лю́бить карто́плю?
4. Чи ва́ша На́дя лю́бить ка́шу?
5. Мі́й Семе́н лю́бить капу́сту.
6. Моя́ Миросла́ва лю́бить ка́ву.
7. Мі́й Сла́вко лю́бить холо́дний ча́й.
8. Чи твоя́ Оле́на лю́бить варе́ники?
9. Чи твій Євге́н лю́бить варе́ники?
10. Чи твій Андрі́й лю́бить жо́вті я́блука?

VI. Change the sentences so that the transitive verb **хоті́ти** becomes intransitive **хоті́тися.**

1. Ця́ мала́ дити́на хо́че ї́сти.
2. Ця́ жі́нка хо́ченам щó́сь розповісти.
3. Ця́ мала́ ді́вчинка хо́че побі́гати.
4. То́й молоди́й чолові́к хо́че співа́ти.
5. Уся́ на́ша кля́са хо́че це́ послу́хати.
6. Ї́хній това́риш хо́че це́ послу́хати.
7. Ї́хній това́риш хо́че ї́хати на мо́ре.

8. Ва́ша старе́нька ма́ти хо́че спа́ти.
9. Тві́й голо́дний чолові́к хо́че ї́сти.
10. Ця́ га́рна ді́вчина хо́че купи́ти собі́ су́кню.
11. Це́й га́рний хло́пець хо́че купи́ти собі́ соро́чку.

VII. Change the sentences using the verb **почина́тися, кінча́тися (поча́тися, кінчи́тися).**

1. Сього́дні ми́ почина́ємо нову́ програ́му.
2. Уже́ поча́ли дру́гий но́мер програ́ми.
3. Учо́ра ми́ закінчи́ли ку́рс швидко́го чита́ння.
4. Че́рез ти́ждень бу́де поча́ток лі́та.
5. Учо́ра бу́в кіне́ць зими́.
6. Вони́ почали́ розмовля́ти.
7. Ми кінча́ємо робо́ту.
8. Усе́ ма́є сві́й кіне́ць.
9. За́втра поча́ток конфере́нції.
10. Ми́ почали́ чита́ти.
11. Ми́ вже́ зва́ри́ли обі́д.

VIII. Change the sentences so that the verbs in bold face become **-ся** verbs (retain the same tense).

1. Ві́н **влашту́є** ва́с на це́ мі́сце.
2. Вона́ **вдяга́є** дити́ну.
3. Ві́н ва́м **ви́бачить.**
4. Ві́н **вдягну́в** нову́ соро́чку.
5. Вона́ мене́ всього́ **вчи́ла.**
6. Ві́н пока́зує, я́к **писа́ти** це́ сло́во.
7. Вони́ розповіда́ли, я́к вони́ **ро́блять** варе́ники.
8. Ві́н не зна́є, я́к це́ **зачини́ти.**
9. Вона́ не розумі́є, я́к це́ **відчини́ти.**
10. Ми́ **лишимо́** дити́ну вдо́ма з ма́мою.

IX. Translate into Ukrainian.

1. What do you expect from me?
2. Unfortunately the program was already over when we got there.
3. He promised that he would take me into his choir.
4. I would like very much to sing in that choir.
5. I slept till noon and was late for the church service.
6. Every year he sends a present to his family in Ukraine.
7. If I were you I wouldn't walk there, he lives way out of town.
8. When she graduated from school her father gave her a watch as a present.
9. I made a mistake and called her 'panna Hal'a', I forgot that she and Marko got married and she is now called 'pani Poliščuk'.
10. Our choir sang in the Ukrainian laguage. Orest sang with his beautiful basso — everybody liked it very much.

X. Rewrite the dialogues in the narrative form.

REVIEW

XI. Change the sentences according to the model:

Я́ і мі́й бра́т ї́демо в го́ри. Ми́ з мої́м бра́том ї́демо в го́ри.

1. Я́ і моя́ дружи́на ї́демо в го́ри.
2. Я́ і моя́ това́ришка ї́демо в го́ри.
3. Я́ і мі́й дру́г ї́демо на мо́ре.
4. Я́ і мі́й си́н ідемо́ до мо́ря.
5. Я́ і моя́ учени́ця ї́демо до міста.
6. Я́ і моя́ сестра́ ї́демо до міста.
7. Я́ і мі́й учи́тель ї́демо до бібліоте́ки.
8. Я́ і мі́й у́чень ї́демо до бібліоте́ки.
9. Я́ і мі́й това́риш ї́демо в село́.
10. Я́ і моя́ до́чка ї́демо в село́.

XII. Supply the appropriate prepositions (за, перед, над, під, з, після, по, крім)

1. Авто́бус стої́ть . . . . . готе́лем чве́рть годи́ни.
2. Пої́дуть усі́, ... О́лі.
3. Ми́ пі́демо пе́рші, а ви́ йді́ть . . . . . на́ми.
4. Авто́бус при́йде . . . . . пів годи́ни.
5. Ми́ скінчимо́ на́шу розмо́ву . . . . . засі́дання.
6. Він шви́дко йшо́в . . . . . ву́лиці.
7. Твоя́ валі́зка стої́ть . . . . . столо́м.
8. З'ї́ж шмато́к хлі́ба . . . . . си́ром.
9. Він працю́є . . . . . свое́ю дисерта́цією.
10. Вона́ розмовля́ла . . . . . учи́телем ці́лу годи́ну.

XIII. Open the brackets.

1. Нeда́вно ми́ познайо́милися з (профе́сор Ле́сів та його́ дружи́на).
2. Ми́ йдемо́ в го́сті до (Івани́шин та його́ бра́т).
3. Чи ви́ знайо́мі з (Васи́ль Гончаре́нко та його́ у́чень Андрі́й)?
4. Вона́ одружи́лася з (Івани́шин) і тепе́р її́ прі́звище . . . . .
5. Учо́ра ми зустрі́ли (Васи́ль Гончаре́нко).
6. Я́ поговорю́ з (Петро́ Полішу́к і його́ жі́нка).
7. Подзвоні́ть (Дмитро́вський або́ Богда́н Палі́й).
8. Ми́ ба́чилися з (Іва́н Прокопо́вич).
9. Він розповіда́в про (Степа́н Палі́й та його́ сестра́ Марі́я).
10. Він до́брий знайо́мий мого́ ба́тька (Івани́шин).

XIV. Give the correct form of the pronoun **себе́**.

1. Про́шу, візьмі́ть . . . . . ще́ борщу́.
2. Ти́ му́сиш працюва́ти над . . . . .
3. Обіця́й . . . . . , що ти́ до́бре ви́вчиш украї́нську мо́ву.

4. Подиви́ся на . . . . .
5. Не ду́май про . . . . .
6. Він до́бре . . . . . зна́є.
7. Подя́куй . . . . . за це́.
8. Він тільки . . . . . лю́бить.
9. Він розмовля́є са́м з . . . . .
10. Скажи́ . . . . . "до́сить!"

XV. Give the imperatives of the verbs in brackets.

1. Не (спізнюва́тися) на ле́кцію.
2. Про́шу, (знайти́) поча́ток цього́ ві́рша!
3. Про́шу, (познайо́митися)!
4. Не (ві́рити) йому́!
5. Не (пока́зувати) йому́ подару́нка!
6. Про́шу, (перекла́сти) це́ ре́ченння!
7. Про́шу, (підвезти́) мене́!
8. Про́шу, не (почина́ти) без ме́не!
9. Про́шу, (поси́діти) ще́ тро́хи!
10. Про́шу, (да́ти) мені́ цю соро́чку.

XVI. Change the aspects.

1. Вона́ йому́ не ві́рила.
2. Вона́ га́рно вдяга́лася.
3. Ми́ ї́м розповіда́ли про се́бе.
4. Вони́ зустрілися пі́сля робо́ти.
5. Я́ спізню́ся на робо́ту.
6. Програ́ма кінча́ється ци́м но́мером.
7. Конце́рт поча́вся о 8-ій.
8. Ми́ купи́ли та́м я́блука.
9. Він сі́в на крі́сло,
10. Я́ чека́ю його́.

XVII. Supply the appropriate verbs of motion.

1. Я́ му́шу . . . . . до Нью Йо́рку на конфере́нцію, але́ мені́ та́к не хо́четься туди́ . . . . . !
2. Куди́ це́ ти́ вже́ зно́в . . . . . ?
   Я́ му́шу подзвони́ти до това́ришки.
3. Він . . . . . по ву́лиці й на все́ диви́вся.
4. Ко́жного дня́ вона́ . . . . . по ву́лиці й во́зить свою́ дити́ну.
5. Звідки ти́ . . . . . ? — Я́ . . . . . з мі́ста.
6. Куди́ ви́ вчо́ра . . . . . ? — Ми́ були́ за мі́стом.
7. Я́ не люблю́ бага́то . . . . .
8. Вони́ завжди́ . . . . . на робо́ту авто́бусом.
9. А я́ люблю́ . . . . . пі́шки.

XVIII. Read and translate.

1. Учóра мú ходúли на концéрт. Співáв хор нáшої украї́нської шкóли. Прогрáма булá дóсить цікáва і всім дýже сподóбалася. У цьóму хóрі співáє моя́ знайóма дíвчина Нáдя. Ї́ї брат тéж дóбре співáє. Він ужé студéнт університéту і співáє в університéтськім хóрі. Минýлого рóку ї́хній хóр ї́здив в Украї́ну. Цé пéрший рáз украї́нці почýли, що америкáнський хóр співáє по-украї́нському.

2. Вчóра мú з чоловíком ляглú пíзно спáти. У нác булú гóсті, сиділи áж до дрýгої годúни нóчі. Булó дýже приéмно — цé всé молоді студéнти, нáші дóбрі дрýзі. Сьогóдні неділя, мú моглú поспáти до полýдня. О 12:30 мú пішлú до цéркви на слýжбу Бóжу. У нáшій цéркві чудóвий хóр, алé він співáє тíльки о 7-ій і об 11-ій, óтже мú йогó не чýли.

3. Зáвтра мú з дружúною йдемó в гóсті. Вонá хóче, щоб я́ вдягнýв новý сорóчку й штанú, які вонá мені купúла. Прáвду кáжучи, мені ця́ сорóчка і штанú не дýже подóбаються, алé я́ не хóчу ї́й цьогó казáти, щоб ї́й не булó неприéмно. Я́ швúдко вдягáюся і чекáю. Моя́ дружúна вдягáється дóвго, томý що ніяк не мóже вúрішити, якý сýкню вдягнýти. Я́ чекáю чвéрть годúни, півгодúни. Та óсь моя́ Гáля кáже, що вонá вжé готóва. Слáва Бóгу! Мú сідáємо в áвто і ї́демо. Нáші дрýзі живýть далéко, тудú трéба ї́хати півгодúни. Вонú просúли, щоб мú прийшлú о вóсьмій, алé мú, як звичáйно, спізнимося на півгодúни. Та нáші дрýзі нác дóбре знáють. Вонú вúбачать.

XIX. Answer the questions to the dialogues.

Співáтиме хóр

1. Щó бýде зáвтра?
2. Якúй хóр співáтиме?
3. Колú почнéться прогрáма?
4. Колú вонá скінчúться?
5. Чи Нáдя хóче пітú?
6. Щó кáже Степáн про богослýження?
7. Щó Нáдя вúрішила?

Щó мені вдягнýти?

1. Щó вдягнýв Олéкса?
2. Звідки він цé взя́в?
3. Чомý Дáрка щé не вдя́гнена?
4. Щó пáні Мирослáва ї́й кáже вдягнýти?
5. Щó вонá питáє про Андрія́?
6. Щó відповідáє на цé дочкá?
7. Чи мáти цьóму вíрить?
8. Щó дочкá кáже про штанú?
9. Хтó мáє рáцію?

ЧОТИРНАДЦЯТА ЛЕКЦІЯ

40 Лист від Богдана

Дорогí дрýзі! Пишý вáм із Київа. Цé чудóве мíсто: ширóкі вýлиці, пáрки, гáрні велúкі будúнки, приéмні симпатúчні люди. Мú бáчили íнші містá й сéла Украї́ни, алé Кúїв, менí здáється, найкрáще мíсто не тíльки в Украї́ні, а й взагалí якé я бýдьколú бáчив. Усí мої́ товариші тéж тієї дýмки. Нáш провіднúк розповíв нáм, що Кúїв — цé найстарíше мíсто на нáшій землí. Хтось із нáшої грýпи зауважив, що вíн чýв, як росіяни кáжуть, що Кúїв — цé російське мíсто, "мáть городóв рýсских"*. Нáш провіднúк пояснúв, що тýт "рýський" не знáчить "російський", що в старí часú украї́нці називалú себé "рýські люди", а нáша землá називáлася "Рýсь". Між íншим, він говорúв чудóвою украї́нською мóвою, приéмно булó йогó слýхати.

Богдáн

P.S. Чéрез двá дні мú летимó до Львóва.

A letter from Bohdan

Dear friends, I am writing to you from Kyiv. This is a wonderful city: wide streets, parks, beautiful tall buildings, pleasant, friendly people. We have seen other cities and villages of Ukraine but Kyiv, it seems to me, is the best not only in Ukraine but of all the cities I have ever seen. All my friends are of the same opinion. Our guide told us that Kyiv is the oldest city in our land. One of our group made a remark, that he heard Russians claim that Kyiv was a Russian city, "mother of ruski cities". Our guide explained that "ruskyj" here does not mean "Russian", that in the old times Ukrainians called themselves "ruski people" and our land was called "Rus'". Incidentally, he spoke beautiful Ukrainian, it was a pleasure to listen to him.

Bohdan

P.S. In two days we are flying to L'viv.

---

* Read it as mát' garadóf rúsk'ix.

41 Лист від Марти

Лю́ба ма́мо! Ми́ живемо́ в готе́лі "Дніпро́". Ту́т у ме́не до́бра кімна́та: вели́кі ві́кна, до́брі зру́чні ме́блі. З вікна́ ви́дно ма́йже ціле́ мі́сто. Пам'ята́єш, ти́ мені́ чита́ла, я́к коли́сь у Ки́єві скрізь були́ церкви́, і тому́ він назива́вся "золотове́рхим"? Тепе́р не те́. За́втра Вели́кдень, і ми́ сказа́ли на́шому провідникові́, що хо́чемо піти́ на слу́жбу Бо́жу. Ві́н обіця́в, що поведе́ на́с у Володи́мирський собо́р — та́м ми́ мо́жемо почу́ти чудо́вий хо́р, а по́тім огля́немо найстарі́шу це́ркву в Украї́ні — Софі́йський собо́р 11-го столі́ття. Ну́, я тепе́р кінча́ю, бо мене́ вже́ кли́чуть: ми́ йдемо́ на Дніпро́, хо́чемо скупа́тися й попла́вати човно́м, а вве́чері йдемо́ до рестора́ну. Я́ тобі́ по́тім опишу́ всі́ свої́ вра́ження. Цілу́ю.
Твоя́ Ма́рта

P.S. Пришли́ мені́, будь ла́ска, О́лину адре́су.

A letter from Marta

Dear Mom, we are staying at the hotel "Dnipro". I have a nice room here, large windows, nice, comfortable furniture. From my window I can see almost the entire city. Remember, you used to read to me how at one time there were churches all over Kyiv so that it was called "the gold-domed" city? It's different now. Tomorrow is Easter and we told our guide that we wanted to go to a church service. He promised to take us to the St. Volodymyr cathedral where we can hear a beautiful choir, and then we will visit the oldest church in Ukraine, the St. Sophia cathedral of the 11th century. Well, I've got to finish now, they are calling me. We are going to the Dnipro, we want to go swimming and take a boat, and in the evening we are going to a restaurant. I will later tell you all my impressions. Love and kisses.
Your Marta

P.S. Please send me Olja's address.

СЛОВНИК

бу́дьколи	ever, at any time
Вели́кдень, Велико́дня (m)	Easter
вести́, веду́ть I (U)	to lead, to take
повести́, поведу́ть	
(ві́в, вела́, вело́, вели́)	past tense
води́ти, воджу́, во́дять (M) I	to take around
взагалі́	in general

ви́дно	one can see
вра́ження (n)*	impression
гру́па (f)	group
зауважувати, зауважують I**	to remark, to note
зауважити, зауважать P	
земля́ (f)	land, earth
зна́чити, зна́чать I	to mean, to signify
золотове́рхий	gold-domed
(золоти́й ве́рх)	(golden top)
кли́кати, кли́чуть I	to call
покли́кати, покли́чуть P	to summon
купа́тися, купа́ються I	to swim, to take a bath
скупа́тися, скупа́ються P	
леті́ти, лечу́, летя́ть I (U)	to fly
полеті́ти, полечу́, полетя́ть P (U)	
літа́ти, літаю, літа́ють I (M)	to fly, to fly around
політати, політаю, політають P (M)	
лю́бий	dear, beloved
лю́ди (pl. of люди́на)	people
ма́йже	almost
ме́блі (pl. only)	furniture
між (+ I)	among, between
назива́тися, назива́ються I	to be called
найстаріший	the oldest (most ancient)
огляда́ти, огляда́ють I	to visit, to inspect
огля́нути, огля́нуть P	
опи́сувати, опи́сують I	to describe
описа́ти, опишу́, опи́шуть P	
па́рк, -у (m)	park
пла́вати, пла́вають I (M)	to swim, to sail
попла́вати, попла́вають P (M)	to swim, to sail for a while
пливти́, пливу́ть I (U)***	to swim, to sail
попливти́, попливу́ть P	
пли́в, пливла́, пливли́ (past imfv.)	
по́тім	then, next
присила́ти, присила́ють I	to send
присла́ти, пришлю́ть P	
поя́снювати, поя́снюють I	to explane
поясни́ти, поясню́, поя́снять P	
провідни́к, -а́ (m)	guide
рестора́н -у (m)	restaurant
росія́нин (m)	Russian m.

* Variant: вражіння (W. Ukr.)

** Variant: завва́жувати/завва́жити

*** Variant: плисти́ (W. Ukr.)

росія́ни (pl.)	Russians
ру́ський	Rus' (adj.)
симпати́чний	nice, likable, pleasant
скрізь	everywhere
собо́р, -у (m)	cathedral
столі́ття (n)*	century
чо́вен, човна́, човни́ (m)	boat
широ́кий	wide

NAMES AND TITLES

Володи́мирський собо́р	St. Volodymyr Cathedral
Дніпро́ (m)	the Dnipro river
Ру́сь, -и (f)	Rus'
Софі́йський собо́р	St. Sophia Cathedral

IDIOMS

бу́ти яко́їсь ду́мки	to be of a certain opinion
між і́ншим	among other things, incidentally, by the way
не то́й	different, not the same as it was; wrong
те́ж тіє́ї ду́мки	of the same opinion

SUPPLEMENT

воді́й	driver
зо́лото (n)	gold
корабе́ль	ship
літа́к, -а́; -и́ (m)	airplane
паропла́в	steamship
пливти́ паропла́вом/кораблє́м (на паропла́ві/кораблі́)	to go by boat
провідни́ця	guide (female)
росія́нка(f)	Russian (f)
(вельми) шано́вний	(most) honorable
(Вельми) шано́вні па́(ʼ)ні й пано́ве!	Ladies and gentelmen!

---

* Variant: сторі́ччя

EXPLANATORY NOTES

1. Note that the seeming cognate **симпати́чний** does not mean 'sympathetic' but rather 'likable' (the same as in French, German, Italian, Spanish).

2. The recent archeological findings in and around Kyiv prove that man has inhabited this area even before the stone age. The city itself existed in some form as far back as the first century A.D. (see M.Ju. Brajčevs'kyj, *Koly i jak vynyk Kyjiv*, Academy of Sciences of the Ukrainian SSR, Kyiv, 1963). According to a legend, it was founded by three brothers, the oldest of whom was called **Ки́й**.

3. The phrase concerning Kyiv comes from an 11th century chronicle where it says that when Prince Oleh ascended the throne he spoke of the city Kyiv, the seat of Great Princes, saying "this will be the mother to all the Rus' cities", thus asserting his dominion over all the Kyivan principalities.

4. The epithet **золотове́рхий** which was applied to Kyiv had its origin in the fact that church cupolas were traditionally covered with sheet gold (gold leaf). (Today where certain churches are being restored this tradition is kept).

5. The noun **столі́ття** is often abbreviated to **ст.** For example:

> Істо́рія украї́нської літерату́ри 19-го (XIX) ст.
> History of Ukrainian literature of the 19th century.

6. St. Volodymyr's cathedral **Володи́мирський собо́р** was built in the late 19th century. Its style is pseudo-Byzantine showing the Russian influence upon the Ukrainian architecture which became dominant in the 19th century. The cathedral is known for its icons, some painted by famous painters such as Vasnecov. It has been the favourite church among the citizens of Kyiv who enjoy good singing. Today one can hear opera stars joining the church choir.

7. The famous St. Sophia cathedral was built during the reign of Prince Jaroslav the Wise in 1037. It has undergone restorations in the 17th century, in the 18th century, and again in this century. The cathedral has beautiful mosaics and frescoes and now is a national monument, i.e. a museum. It may soon become a house of worship once again.

8. There are several ways to express the idea 'to be called by name' in Ukrainian. In order of frequency they are:

Я́к тебе́ зва́ти? Я́к тебе́ зву́ть? Я́к ти́ зве́шся?	What do they call you?	Ма́рта (Ма́ртою).	Marta.

In the answer the name is usually in the nominative but can also be put in the instrumental case. The verb **кли́кати**, and less frequently **зва́ти**, also means 'to call, to summon'.

> Іди́, ма́ти тебе́ кли́че.
> Go, mother is calling you.

Remember that 'to call by phone' is **дзвони́ти (телефонува́ти) + до + G** (or D).

9. The verb **купа́тися** can mean either 'to take a bath' or 'to take a swim', depending on the context. Its transitive form **купа́ти** means 'to give a bath'. cf:

Ми́ йдемо́ до Дніпра́ купа́тися.	We are going to the Dnipro for a swim.
Вона́ купа́є дити́ну.	She is bathing the baby.

The verb **пла́вати** as opposed to **купа́тися** is more specific with regard to the movements involved: купа́тися could mean just splashing around while **пла́вати** is definitely swimming (multi-linear motion).

10. While both adverbs **тоді́** and **по́тім** may be used in the sense of 'then', the first is usually reserved to indicate a specific point in time (at that time) while the second serves as link in a sequence of events, one coming after another ('next'):

Він тоді́ ще бу́в дити́ною.
At the time he was still a baby.

Він попрацюва́в, по́тім попла́вав, по́тім зно́в сі́в за робо́ту.
He worked a little, then took a swim, then went back to work.

Тоді́ is also used to connect a given situation or an intention with the resultant action:

А якщо́ я́ не піду́, що́ ти́ тоді́ ска́жеш?
What if I didn't go, what would you say then?

Він до́вго ду́мав, а тоді́ сказа́в: "До́бре".
He thought for a long time and then said: "All right".

Compare, however, the following case where either adverb would be appropriate:

Пе́рше зроби́ дома́шне завда́ння, а тоді́ мо́жеш іти́ купа́тися.
First do your homework, and then (= only then, in that case) you may go swimming.

Пе́рше зроби́ дома́шне завда́ння, а по́тім мо́жеш іти́ купа́тися.
First do your homework and then (= after that, late) you can go swimming.

11. P.S. is pronounced 'postskriptum'.

12. The verb води́ти (+A) is also used in the sense of 'driving a vehicle', and the noun **водій** means 'driver'.

NOTES ON GRAMMAR

I. NOUNS WHICH HAVE ONLY SINGULAR

As in English, certain nouns are used only in the singular in Ukrainian. These are mostly abstract nouns such as **тво́рчість** 'creativity', **здоро́в'я** 'health', **па́м'ять** 'memory', etc.

A number of abstract nouns which in English can be pluralized are used only in the singular in Ukrainian. Among them are: **любо́в** 'love', **життя́** 'life'.

II. NOUNS WHICH HAVE ONLY PLURAL (PLURALIA TANTUM)

Among nouns which have only plural are those which come in pairs, like **штани́** 'trousers, pants'. Others pluralia tantum which we encountered include **Карпа́ти** 'Carpatians', **ме́блі** (from the French 'les meubles') 'furniture' — note that the English uses only singular here, and **две́рі** 'doors'.

III. NOMINATIVE PLURAL OF NOUNS

Nominative plural is identical with the accusative plural of all inanimate nouns.There is no special vocative form in the plural, the nominative being used in vocative function.

All feminine nouns and all masculine nouns have nominative plural ending **-и** for hard stems and **-і/-ї** for soft stems and stems ending in **ж, ч, ш, щ**. Neuters have the ending **-а** for hard stems and **-я** for soft stems (stems ending in **ж, ч, ш, щ** take the ending **-а**).

NOMINATIVE PLURAL OF NOUNS

Feminine	Masculine	Neuter
кімна́та — кімна́ти	заво́д — заво́ди	село́ — се́ла
ву́лиця — ву́лиці	готе́ль — готе́лі	мо́ре — моря́
річ — ре́чі	вірш — ві́рші	пі́звище — прі́звища
істо́рія — істо́рії	музе́й — музе́ї	пита́ння — пита́ння

1. Feminine nouns.

(a) The noun **ді́вчина** has the same plural as its neuter diminitive variant **дівча́**: **дівча́та** (see Neuter nouns, Lesson 2, p. 29).

(b) Plural of **ма́ти** is **матері́**.

(c)The nouns **люди́на** 'person' and **дити́на** 'child' lose the suffix **-ин** in all their plural cases. Their nominative plurals are **лю́ди** and **ді́ти** respectively.

2. Masculine nouns.

(a) The noun **па́н** has both the regular plural **пани́** and the special **пано́ве** which is commonly used as a form of address: **Шано́вні (Вельмишано́вні, Дорогі́) па́ні й пано́ве**! Ladies and gentlmen!

(b) Nouns with the suffix **-а (-я) нин** which indicate a member of a group lose **-ин** in all cases in the plural: **росія́нин** (N.sg.) — **росія́ни** (N.pl.)

(c) The noun **дру́г** which follows the hard stem declension pattern in the sigular has the plural form **дру́зі** with a soft stem (druz'-) and follows the soft declension pattern throughout the plural.

(d) The plural of **ба́тько** is **батьки́**. It has two meanings: 'fathers' and 'parents'.

3. Neuter nouns.

(a) The plural of **óко** is **óчі**.

(b) The nominative plural of neuters whose stems end in two consonants is identical with the nominative singular, e.g. **питáння** (N.sg.) **питáння** (N.pl.).

(c) The nominative plural of **-ат/-ен** neuters, is **-áта/-енá, поросń — поросńта, ім'ń — іменá**.

Note. Instead of чаї 'teas' and сирń 'cheeses' the expression сортń чáю/сńру 'sorts of tea/cheese' can be used.

IV. STRESS IN THE NOMIMATIVE PLURAL OF NOUNS

Most nouns have the stress on the same stem-syllable throughout all declensional forms, singular and plural; a small group (masculine only) has the stress on the ending throughout. Stem-stress in the singular and end-stress in the plural is very productive and general in a lot of important Ukrainian nouns. The reverse phenomenon, i.e. end-stress in the singular and stem-stress in the plural is extremely rare.

The key form is genitive singular. In the great majority of instances the nominative plural stress is identical with that of the genitive singular. In the vocabularies we provide genitive singular stress where it differs from the nominative singular or where the monosyllabic form gives no clue to the stress pattern (cf. **пáрк, пáрку** but **бóрщ, борщý; провіднńк, провідникá** but **годńнник, годńнника**).

1. Here are some examples of stable stress pattern throughout the declension (singular and plural).

MASCULINE

(1) Stem-stressed

N.sg.	G.sg.	N.pl.	N.sg.	G.sg.	N.pl.
вірш	вірша	вірші	студéнт	студéнта	студéнти
пáрк	пáрку	пáрки	папíр	папéру	папéри
хóр	хóру	хóри	готéль	готéлю	готéлі
			завóд	завóду	завóди

(2) End-stressed

N.sg.	G.sg.	N.pl.	N.sg.	G.sg.	N.pl.
стíл	столá	столń	кінéць	кінцń	кінцí
лńст	листá	листń	олівéць	олівцń	олівцí
дéнь	днń	днí	стілéць	стільцń	стільцí
бóрщ	борщý	борщí	шматóк	шматкá	шматкń
			словнńк	словникá	словникń
			провіднńк	провідникá	провідникń

FEMININE
Stem-stressed

N.sg.	G.sg.	N.pl.	N.sg.	G.sg.	N.pl.
чвéрть	чвéрті	чвéрті	кáша	кáші	кáші
любóв	любóви	—	мóва	мóви	мóви
відповідь	відповіді	відповіді	кімнáта	кімнáти	кімнáти
			американка	американки	американки
			істóрія	істóрії	істóрії
			газéта	газéти	газéти

NEUTER
Stem-stressed

N.sg.	G.sg.	N.pl.
питáння	питáння	питáння
засідання	засідання	засідання
я́блуко	я́блука	я́блука
свя́то	свя́та	свя́та
ліжко	ліжка	ліжка
крісло	крісла	крісла
порося́	порося́ти	порося́та

2. Mobile stress. The mobile stress pattern is found among nouns of all three genders:

MASCULINE
Stem-stress in the singular, end-stress in the plural

N.sg.	G.sg.	N.pl.	N.sg.	G.sg.	N.pl.
брáт	брáта	брати́	лікар	лікаря	лікарі
сáд	сáду	сади́	вéчір	вéчора	вечори́
си́н	си́на	сини́	бáтько	бáтька	батьки́

FEMININE

Stem-stress (sg.)		end-stress (pl.)	End-stress (sg.)		stem-stress (pl.)
N.sg.	G.sg.	N.pl.	N.sg.	G.sg.	N.pl.
мáма	мáми	мами́ (or мáми)*	сестрá	сестри́	сéстри
кни́жка	кни́жки	книжки́	земля́	землі	зéмлі
цéрква	цéркви	церкви́	веснá	весни́	вéсни

* Some speakers feel that the end-stressesed form мами́ can be perceived as disrespectful and prefer to use the form мáми with the stress on the initial syllable.

NEUTER

Stem-stress (sg.)		end-stress (pl.)	End-stress (sg.)		stem-stress (pl.)
N.sg.	G.sg.	N.pl.	N.sg.	G.sg.	N.pl.
мо́ре	мо́ря	моря́	вікно́	вікна́	ві́кна
сло́во	сло́ва	слова́	село́	села́	се́ла

These patterns simply have to be memorized.

(Exercises 1, 2, 3, 4, 5, 6, 7, 8)

LIST OF NOUNS WHOSE NOMINATIVE PLURAL STRESS IS DIFFERENT FROM THE SINGULAR*

N.sg.	G.sg.	N.pl.	N.sg.	G.sg.	N.pl.
ба́с	ба́са	баси́	мо́ре	мо́ря	моря́
ба́тько	ба́тька	батьки́	па́н	па́на	пани́ (пано́ве)
бра́т	бра́та	брати́	поча́ток	поча́тку	початки́
ве́чір	ве́чора	вечори́	профе́сор	профе́сора	профе́сори
вікно́	вікна́	ві́кна	рі́к	ро́ку	роки́
гора́	гори́	го́ри	са́д	са́ду	сади́
дочка́	дочки́	до́чки	село́	села́	се́ла
до́шка	до́шки	дошки́	се́рце	се́рця	серця́
ду́мка	ду́мки	думки́	сестра́	сестри́	се́стри
душа́	душі́	ду́ші	си́н	си́на	сини́
жі́нка	жі́нки	жінки́	си́р	си́ру	сири́**
земля́	землі́	зе́млі	сло́во	сло́ва	слова́
зима́	зими́	зи́ми	това́риш	това́риша	товариші́
кни́жка	кни́жки	книжки́	учи́тель	учи́теля	учителі́
лі́кар	лі́каря	лікарі́	хлі́б	хлі́ба	хліби́ (хліба́)
ма́ма	ма́ми	мами́ (ма́ми)	це́рква	це́ркви	церкви́
ма́ти	ма́тері	матері́	ча́й	ча́ю	чаї́**
мі́сто	мі́ста	міста́	ча́с	ча́су	часи́
мі́сце	мі́сця	місця́	чо́вен	чо́вна (човна́)	човни́

V. NOMINATIVE PLURAL OF ADJECTIVES, PRONOUNS, ORDINALS, AND ОДИН

There is only one plural form for all three genders. All adjectives, pronouns and ordinal numerals have the nominative plural ending -і (the stem final consonant automatically becomes palatalized before -і) e.g.:

* The list includes all nouns given in lessons 1–14.

** See note on p.224.

мали́й (мала́, мале́)	—	малі́
коли́шній (коли́шня, -є)	—	коли́шні
четве́ртий (четве́рта, -е)	—	четве́рті
тре́тій (тре́тя, -є)	—	тре́ті

1. The plural ending **-і** is added to the basic stem which as you recall may differ from the nominative masculine singular form normally listed in dictionaries (the feminine of neuter forms are more indicative). cf.:

Nominative sg.,	*Basic stem*	*Nominative pl.*
то́й, та́, те́	т-	ті́
це́й, ця́, це́	ц- (c')	ці́
оди́н, одна́, одне́	одн-	одні́
мі́й, моя́, моє́	мо- (moj-)	мої́ (mojí)
сві́й, своя́, своє́	сво- (svoj-)	твої́ (svojí)
тві́й, твоя́, твоє́	тво- (tvoj-)	твої́ (tvojí)
уве́сь, уся́, усе́	ус- (us'-)	усі́ (us'í)
чи́й, чия́, чиє́	чи- (čuj-)	чиї́ (čují)

2. Note that after a vowel letter the plural ending **-і** must be spelled **-ї** (actually it's the stem-final sound *-j* + which give *ї*, see Sound System, p. xxvii).

3. The numeral **оди́н** 'one' has the plural **одні́** which means 'some', 'certain ones', i.e. it is an indefinite pronoun:

Одні́ ї́ли, і́нші пили́.	Some where eating, others were drinking.

4. Like all adjectives, surnames in **-ський (-ська), -цький (-цька), -зький (-зька)** take **-і** in the nominative plural:

Дмитро́вський	Дмитро́вська	— Дмитро́вські
Гуме́цький	Гуме́цька	— Гуме́цькі

Surnames in **-ин (-ина)** and **-ів (-ева), -їв (-єва)** have the form of possessive adjective (see below), however their nominative plural ending is -**и** rather than **-і**, e.g.:

Іва́нишин	Івани́шина	— Івани́шини
Ле́сів	Ле́сева	— Лесе́ви

(Exercises: adjectives — 1, 4, 5, other — 2, 3, 7, 8).

VI. POSSESSIVE ADJECTIVES

Possessive adjectives are formed from people's names, first and last,* as well as from other nouns designating human beings. The suffix **-ов/-ев** is added to masculine nouns of the masculine-neuter declension, and the suffix **-ин** is added to nouns of the feminine declension. For example:

Suffix **-ов/-ев**,	Suffix **-ин**
бра́т — **бра́тів**, бра́това, -ове, -ові	Лі́да — Лі́дин, -ина, -ине, -ині
ба́тько — **ба́тьків, ба́тькова,** -ове, -ові	Мико́ла — Мико́лин, -ина, -ине, -ині
Шевче́нко — Шевче́нків, **-ова**, -ове, -ові	сестра́ — сестри́н, -ина́, -ине́, -ині́
Васи́ль — **Василі́в, -е́ва**, -е́ве, -е́ві	О́ля — О́лин, -ина, -ине, -ині**
Андрі́й — **Андрі́їв, -єва**, -єве, -єві	Марі́я — Марі́їн, -їна, -їне, -їні
вчи́тель — **вчи́телів, -ева**, -еве, -еві	ма́ти — ма́терин, -ина, -ине, -ині

Note 1: The suffix **-ов** is added to masculine nouns which end in hard consonant or **-о**, the suffix **-ев (-єв)** is added to those with soft stems and stems in **j**. Before a zero ending, i.e. in the nominative and the accusative inanimate of the masculine gender possessive adjectives, the suffix **-ов/-ев/(-єв)** becomes **-ів/(-їв)**:

Де́ ба́тьків ли́ст?	Чи ти́ ба́чив ба́тьків ли́ст?	Ні, я́ не ба́чив ба́тькового листа́.
Василі́в	Василі́в	Василе́вого
Андрі́їв	Андрі́їв	Андрі́євого
Де́ ба́тьків бра́т?	...ба́тькового брата	...ба́тькового брата

Note 2: The stress in possessive adjectives depends on the suffix. Those with the suffix **-ов** have the same stress as the genitive singular of the corresponding noun, i.e. stem-stress or end-stress.

ба́тько, ба́тька — ба́тьків, ба́тькова, ба́тькове
Петро́, Петра́ — Петрі́в, Петро́ва, Петро́ве

The adjectives with the suffix **-ин** preserve the stress of the nominative singular of the corresponding noun, i.e. they are either stem-stressed or end-stressed:

Га́ля — Га́лин, Га́лина, Га́лине
Марі́я — Марі́їн, Марі́їна, Марі́їне
сестра́ — сестри́н, сестрина́, сестрине́. сестрині́

Note 3: The consonants **г, к, х** change to **ж, ч, ш** before the suffix **-ин**:

Да́рка — Да́рчин
О́льга — О́льжин
дочка́ — доччи́н, -а́, -е́

---

* Last names in **-ів, -ин** already have the form of possessive adjectives and do not lend themselves to formation of further possessives.

** In today's speech, it is more common to hear the soft ending -ін in adjectives of this type, i.e. those derived from the soft stem nouns.

Note 4: Possessive adjectives follow the hard-stem adjectival declension (the declension of surnames of this type was discussed in Lesson 10; it is further discussed in Lesson 15).

Note 5: Some geographic names have the form of possessive adjectives:

Ки́їв — the city founded by **Ки́й**
Льві́в — the city of **кня́зь Ле́в** (Prince Leo).

Note 6: Possessive adjectives are used mostly in the conversational language and in the language of literature, as well as in folklore. The scientific, the business and the newspaper styles avoid this form and use the genitive instead, e.g. **ли́ст Григоре́нка** rather than **Григоре́нків ли́ст** (this "officialese" is a Russian influence).

(Exercises 9, 10).

VII. ACCUSATIVE PLURAL OF INANIMATE NOUNS AND THEIR MODIFIERS

The accusative plural of all nouns denoting inanimate objects or abstract notions and their modifies is identical with their nominative plural forms, e.g.:

Nominative plural	*Accusative plural*
Це́ твої́ думки́. These are your thoughts.	Я́ зна́ю твої́ думки́. I know your thoughts.
Де́ Рома́нові ре́чі? Where are Roman's things?	Чи ти́ ба́чив Рома́нові ре́чі? Did you see Roman's things?
О́сь олівці́. Here are the pencils.	Я́ ма́ю олівці́. I have pencils.

Note: We have seen that some inanimate nouns have parallel forms in the accusative singular, one identical with the nominative and another identical with the genitive singular, e.g.: **Я́ ма́ю оліве́ць / Я́ ма́ю олівця́** (see Lesson 3, Note 1, p. 48). In the plural the accusative of inanimate nouns is always identical with the nominative.

(Exercises 11, 12, 13).

VIII. EXPRESSIONS OF QUALITY WITH NUMBERS 2, 3, 4

1. The noun following the numbers 2, 3, 4 (or any numeral which ends in **два́, три́, чоти́ри**) is in the nominative plural when the numeral-noun combination is the subject or the inanimate accusative object of a sentence. For example:

Ці́ два́ дні́ були́ га́рні.	Those two days were nice.
Че́рез два́ дні́ ми́ бу́демо вдо́ма.	In two days we will be home.
Дві́ студе́нтки чита́ли ві́рші.	Two students read poetry.
Сто́ два́ а́вта були́ блаки́тні.	One hundred and two cars were blue.

Note 1: Remember that number 2 has two forms, **дві** wich is used with the feminine nouns, and **два́** which is used with masculines and neuters (see Lesson 12, p. 199–200).

> О́н та́м на столі́ два́ олівці́ і дві́ ру́чки.
> Over there on the desk are two pencil and two pens.

2. The stress of the noun following 2, 3, 4 when the numeral-noun combination is the subject or the accusative (inanimate) object of a sentence, is that of the genitive singular:

2, 3, 4 + noun	G.sg. (stress)	N.pl. (form)
О́сь ті́ три́ вікна́. Here are the three windows.	Ту́т нема́є вікна́. There is no window here.	Ту́т вели́кі ві́кна. There are large windows here.
Я́ ма́ю ті́льки дві́ руки́. I have only two hands.	Ві́н не ма́є руки́. He doesn't have an arm.	У ва́с га́рні ру́ки. You have pretty hands.
О́сь його́ три́ бра́ти. Here are his three brothers.	Ві́н не ма́є бра́та. He doesn't have a brother.	О́сь його́ брати́. Here are his brothers.

Note 1: A number of nouns have both the genitive singular stress and form when in combination with numbers 2, 3, 4 they appear as the subject of a sentence. These are:

(a) Masculine nouns with the suffix **-ин** which is dropped in the plural, e.g.

2, 3, 4 + noun	G.sg.	N.pl.
О́н та́м чоти́ри росія́нина. Over there are four Russians.	Я́ не ба́чу росія́нина. I don't see the Russians.	Де́ росія́ни? Where are the Russians?

(b) The nouns **ді́вчина, о́ко** and **плече́** 'shoulder':

2, 3, 4 + noun,	G.sg.	N.pl.
Ці́ три́ ді́вчини — украї́нки. These three girls are Ukrainian.	Я́ не зна́юціє́ї ді́вчини. I don't know this girl.	Де́ дівча́та? Where are the girls?
Ту́т до́бре ви́дно два́ о́ка. You can clearly see the two eyes.	У ньо́го нема́є одного́ о́ка. He doesn't have one eye.	У не́ї блаки́тні о́чі. She has blue eyes.

3. The modifier in the phrase "2, 3, 4 + modifier + noun" when the phrase is the subject or the accusative object of a sentence is normally in the nominative plural, e.g.:

О́сь два́ вели́кі я́блука.	Here are two large apples.
З'ї́ж ці́ два́ вели́кі я́блука.	Eat these two large apples.

Note 1: Genitive plural of the modifier is also permissible, especially with masculine and neuter nouns: два́ вели́ких я́блука, три́ стари́х буди́нки.

(Exercises 13, 14).

IX. MORE VERBS OF MOTION: "TO SWIM" AND "TO FLY" (ПЛАВАТИ, ЛІТАТИ) AND VERBS OF TAKING/LEADING (ВОЗИТИ, ВОДИТИ)

1. The unidirectional verbs **(по)пливти** indicate motion in a specific direction, either swimming or sailing, thus presenting a parallel to such verbs as **(п)ітй** and **(по)їхати**.

Вона́ попливла́ до на́с.	She swam toward us.
Чо́вен шви́дко пли́в.	The boat sailed fast.

The multidirectional **пла́вати** is similar to **ходи́ти** and **їздити** in that it indicates motion as such (no direction specified) or motion of varied direction such as 'swimming around', or a 'round trip':

До́сить ва́м уже́ пла́вати.	You have had enough swimming around.
Він уже́ два́ ра́зи туди́ пла́вав свої́м човно́м.	He already made two trips there in his boat.

2. For the verb 'to fly' the unidirectional pair is **летіти** (imperf.) and **полетіти** (perf.). The multidirectional verb is **літа́ти**:

Це́й літа́к лети́ть до Ки́єва.	This airplane flies to Kyiv.
Він полетів до Монреа́лю.	He flew to Montreal.
Літа́к літа́в над містом.	The airplane was flying (circling) over the city.

3. The verbs (по)**вести́** (U), **води́ти** (M) mean 'to lead', 'to show the way (walking)' and **(по)везти́** (U), **вози́ти** (M) mean 'to convey', 'to transport', 'to take (in a vehicle)'. cf.:

(ПО)ВЕСТИ́, ВОДИ́ТИ	(ПО)ВЕЗТИ́, ВОЗИ́ТИ
Я́ піду́ з ва́ми і поведу́ ва́с туди́. I will walk with you and take you, there.	Я́ поі́ду а́втом і повезу́ ва́с туди́. I will drive the car and take you there.
Він ході́в і води́в ї́х по місту. He was walking and showing them around the town.	Він вози́в ї́х по місту. He was driving them around the town.

(Exercises 15, 16, 17)

X. PREDICATIVE ВИДНО

Ви́дно is used to indicate visibility and is usually translated as 'can see'.

Чи ти́ ба́чиш то́й буди́нок? Do you see that building?	Чи тобі ви́дно то́й буди́нок? Can you see that building?

The object is in the accusative (or the genitive of negation) and the viewer is in the dative:

Мені не було́ ви́дно.	I couldn't see (it).
Мені не ви́дно вікна́.	I can't see the window.
Звідси тобі бу́де до́бре ви́дно.	You can see well from here.

Or it may be used with an accusative (the genetive of negation) object without naming the viewer in the sense of 'to be in sight', 'to be visible', 'it is possible/one can see'.

З вікна́ було́ ви́дно шко́лу.
From the window one could see the school.
(The school could be seen from the window.)

Ту́т ніч́ого не ви́дно.
You can't see anything here.
(= It's impossible to see anything here.)

(Exercise 18)

ВПРАВИ

I. Put the bracketed words into plural.

1. У Ки́єві є (га́рний буди́нок).
2. У Льво́ві є (до́брий ресторя́н).
3. В Украї́ні є (стари́й собо́р).
4. У Ки́єві (широ́ка ву́лиця).
5. У Льво́ві (чудо́вий па́рк).
6. В Украї́ні є (університе́т та інститу́т).
7. В Украї́ні є (украї́нська й росі́йська шко́ла).
8. В цьо́му мі́сті є (вели́кий заво́д і готе́ль).
9. В цьо́му селі́ є (золотове́рха це́рква).
10. В цьо́му ре́ченні є (по́милка).

II. Change the nouns and the pronouns to their plural forms.

О́сь на́ше вікно́. О́сь на́ші ві́кна.

(мі́й олі́ве́ць, ва́ш керівни́к, ва́ше мі́сце, на́ша валі́зка, ва́ш у́чень, ї́хня дити́на, ї́хня ма́ти, ї́хній сті́л, твоє́ я́блуко, мі́й словни́к)

III. Change the nouns and the pronouns to plural (for 'his' and 'her' give 'their').

Це́ її́ вчи́телька. Це́ ї́хні вчительки́.

(його́ сестра́, її́ бра́т, мі́й дру́г, на́ш профе́сор, його́ това́риш, її́ това́ришка, його́ вчи́тель, її́ дочка́, на́ш си́н, ї́хній гі́сть)

IV. Change the adjective and the nouns to plural.

1. Чи це́ украї́нське сло́во?
2. Чи це́ чужа́ ду́мка?
3. Чи це́ яке́сь нове́ свя́то?
4. Чи це́ ціка́ва профе́сія?

5. Чи це́ пра́вильна ві́дповідь?
6. Чи це́ америка́нська гру́па?
7. Чи це́ ціка́вий ку́рс?
8. Чи це́ ха́рківський лі́кар?
9. Чи це́ яка́сь і́нша конфере́нція?
10. Чи це́ спра́вжній індія́нець?

V. Change all the words to plural.

1. Ві́н симпати́чний чолові́к.
2. Вона́ га́рна ді́вчина.
3. Ти́ до́бра жі́нка.
4. Я́ молода́ люди́на.
5. Ві́н стари́й у́читель.
6. Вона́ чудо́ва вчи́телька.
7. Ти́ спра́вжній дру́г.
8. Вона́ моя́ да́вня знайо́ма.
9. Ві́н ще мала́ дити́на.
10. Ві́н ще молоди́й хло́пець.

VI. Put the bracketed words into plural.

1. В ці́й кімна́ті (золоти́й стіле́ць).
2. В цьо́му готе́лі (старе́ лі́жко).
3. В цьо́му буди́нку (вели́ке вікно́).
4. В то́му літако́ві (зру́чне крі́сло).
5. В ті́й кімна́ті (нови́й сті́л).
6. В на́шому поме́шканні (нови́й холоди́льник).
7. В ї́хньому гурто́житку (до́брий телеві́зор).
8. В тому́ готе́лі (стари́й телефон).
9. В ці́й бібліоте́ці (ціка́ва кни́жка).
10. В ці́й бібліоте́ці (стари́й журна́л).

VII. Put the following questions into plural.

1. Де́ то́й оліве́ць?
2. Чи́й це́ чо́вен?
3. Де́ вве́сь пере́клад?
4. Де́ та́ земля́?
5. Я́к назива́ється ця́ гора́?
6. Де́ тві́й знайо́мий?
7. Де́ то́й провідни́к?
8. Куди́ лети́ть то́й літа́к?
9. Де́ вве́сь папі́р?
10. Чи це́ ва́ша золота́ ру́чка?

VIII. Put both questions and answers into plural.

1. Чиє́ це́ ім'я́? Її́.
2. Чиє́ це́ вра́ження? Моє́.
3. Чия́ це́ ду́мка? Твоя́.
4. Чи́й це́ чо́вен? Його́.
5. Чиє́ це́ пита́ння? Моє́.
6. Чия́ це́ земля́? Моя́.
7. Чия́ це́ дружи́на? Його́.
8. Чи́й це́ ба́тько? Її́.
9. Чия́ це́ дити́на? Твоя́.
10. Чиє́ це́ я́блуко? Твоє́.

IX. Provide the possessive adjectives of the given nouns.

1. Це́ . . . . .зо́шит.
 (Мико́ла)
2. Це́ . . . . профе́сія.
 (бра́т)
3. Це́ . . . . вра́ження.
 (ма́ма)
4. Це́ . . . . лі́жко.
 (та́то)
5. Це́ . . . . .мі́сце.
 (Миха́йло)
6. Це́ . . . . гру́па.
 (Гончаре́нко)

X. Replace the bracketed nouns by the corresponding possessive adjectives.

1. Чиї́ це́ книжки́? (Чолові́к).
2. Чиї́ це́ ре́чі? (Жі́нка).
3. Чия́ це́ кімна́та? (Дочка́).
4. Чий це́ годи́нник? (Ба́тько).
5. Чия́ це́ фотогра́фія (Ма́ма).
6. Чия́ це́ ду́мка? (Сестра́).
7. Чия́ це́ валі́зка? (Учи́тель).
8. Чиє́ це́ мі́сце? (Та́то).
9. Чиї́ це́ листи́? (Ма́рта).
10. Чиє́ це́ а́вто? (Лі́кар).

XI. Change the nouns and their modifiers from the accusative singular to the accusative plural.

1. Де́ поста́вити це́й сті́л?
2. Подиви́сь на то́й чо́вен.
3. Де́ ви́ купи́ли таку́ ціка́ву кни́жку?
4. Яки́й і́спит ви́ скла́ли?

5. Ми́ оглядáли нову́ квартúру.
6. Вони́ закінчи́ли яки́йсь інститу́т.
7. Я́ читáю твíй перéклад.
8. Я́ люблю́ цé старé крíсло.
9. Вíн ведé нáшу гру́пу.
10. Ти́ зроби́в яку́сь пóмилку.

XII. Change the nouns and their modifiers from singular to plural.

1. Бáчите отóй вели́кий буди́нок?
2. Я́ пам'ятáю ї́хній літерату́рний вéчір.
3. Ви́вчіть напáм'ять цéй вíрш.
4. Ми́ говори́ли про мину́лий рíк.
5. Чи ти́ зроби́в усé завдáння?
6. Подивíться на нáше вікнó.
7. Хтó взя́в мíй стілéць?
8. Хтó знáє цé украї́нське слóво?
9. Вони́ забу́ли про тóй ти́ждень.
10. Вонá лю́бить свою́ украї́нську су́кню.

XIII. Provide the stresses over the nouns and change the sentences according to the model:

Тáм є новí столи́. Тáм є два новí (нови́х) столи́.

1. Тáм є дóбрі олівці.
2. Тáм є гáрні парки.
3. Тáм є старí човни.
4. Тáм є дóбрі місця.
5. Тáм є непогáні баси.
6. Тáм є цікáві думки.
7. Тáм є вели́кі яблука.
8. Тáм є гáрні сади.
9. Тáм є старí церкви.
10. Тáм є дорогí сири.

XIV. Change the questions according to the model:

Дé тóй студéнт? Дé тí три́ студéнти?

1. Дé тóй профéсор?
2. Дé тá вчи́телька?
3. Дé тóй росія́нин?
4. Дé тóй хлóпець?
5. Дé тá дíвчина?
6. Дé тóй провідни́к?
7. Дé тóй у́чень?
8. Дé тóй товáриш?
9. Дé тá учени́ця?
10. Дé тóй учи́тель?

XV. Complete the sentences using verbs of 'flying'.

1. Тепе́р ми́ . . . . . над Нью Йо́рком.
2. Мину́лої зими́ ми́ . . . . . до Монреа́лю.
3. У це́й понеді́лок він . . . . . додо́му.
4. Він у́читься . . . . . .літако́м.
5. Його́ нема́, він . . . . . на конфере́нцію.
6. Чи ви́ колине́будь . . . . . літако́м?
7. Здає́ться, що ми́ . . . . . ду́же пово́лі.
8. Це́й літа́к сьогóдні ще ніку́ди не . . . . .
9. Коли́ ви́ . . . . . пе́рший ра́з літако́м, чи ви́ боя́лися?
10. Він ча́сто . . . . . до Ки́єва.

XVI. Complete the sentences using verbs of "swimming/sailing".

1. Я́ нікóли ще не . . . . . у мо́рі.
2. Не . . . . . та́к шви́дко.
3. Куди́ . . . . . он то́й чо́вен?
4. Чи ви́ вмієте . . . . . ?
5. Вона́ за́вжди . . . . . пові́льно.
6. Ми́ хо́чемо за́втра . . . . . дале́ко по Дніпрі́.
7. Ко́жної неді́лі він . . . . . своі́м човно́м.
8. Тепе́р на́ш чо́вен . . . . . .зо́всім пові́льно.
9. Я́ бою́ся туди́ . . . . . , це́ ду́же дале́ко.
10. Лікарі́ ка́жуть, що . . . . . це́ ду́же до́бре для здоро́в'я.

XVII. Complete the sentences using verbs of 'leading', 'driving'.

1. У ме́не є а́вто. Хо́чете, я́ ва́с . . . . . до мі́ста?
2. Куди́ ви́ на́с . . . . . ? Ми́ не хо́чемо туди́ йти́.
3. У субо́ту він . . . . . її на конце́рт до Монреа́лю.
4. О́сь іде́ на́ш авто́бус. Він . . . . . на́с до мо́ря.
5. У на́с були́ го́сті, і ми́ . . . . . і́х по мі́сту на́шим а́втом.
6. За́втра ми́ пі́демо до музе́ю, і я́ . . . . . ва́с до одно́ї ду́же ціка́вої кімна́ти.
7. Ма́ти йшла́ ву́лицею й . . . . . свого́ мало́го си́на до па́рку.
8. Ва́ша дочка́ вже́ не мала́, чого́ ви́ її уве́сь ча́с . . . . . ?
9. Її чолові́к тепе́р не працю́є, ма́є бага́то часу́ і скрі́зь її . . . . .
10. З села́ і́хало вели́ке а́вто і . . . . . я́блука.

XVIII. Change the sentences using **ви́дно**. For example:

Я́ її ба́чу. Мені́ її ви́дно.

1. Ма́ти тебе́ ба́чить.
2. Провідни́к ва́с не ба́чить.
3. Ця́ жі́нка на́с не ба́чить.
4. Це́й росія́нин мене́ не ба́чить.

5. Я́ ба́чив вели́кий паропла́в.
6. Ти́ зві́дси ні́чо́го не бу́деш ба́чити.
7. З гори́ мо́жна було́ ба́чити все́ село́.
8. З літака́ поба́чите ве́рх гори́.
9. Зві́дти поба́чимо усю́ на́шу Зе́млю.
10. З вікна́ мого́ готе́лю я́ ба́чу ці́лий Ки́їв.

XIX. Translate into Ukrainian.

1. - Do you know Halja's address?
   - No, I don't, but I have her phone number.
2. - Did you notice their furniture?
   - Yes, it's beautiful. I took a good look at it (='inspected it').
3. - How did you like those people?
   - They made a good imperession on me.
4. - What is your opinion about their program?
   - It could be better.
5. - Have you ever been to Kyiv?
   - No, but my father has described it to me. He comes from Kyiv.
6. - Lida, your mother is calling you.
   - I'll be right over.
7. - Incidentally, did he explain to you what the words "Rus'" and "rus'kyj" meant?
   - Yes, he did. Our guide is a very likable fellow.
8. - It's about twelve o'clock. Time to go home.
   - Please stay. We will sing new Ukrainian songs.
   - All right. We'll stay, but not till three in the morning like last time.
9. - Do you want to have a swim in the Dnipro river?
   - I don't know how to swim.
   - That's too bad.
10. They were sailing their boat for a long time without seeng any land.
11. - Good evening, ladies and gentlemen! Our plane is about to take off.

XX. Read and translate.

1. На́дя вже давно́ зsavва́жила, що вона́ подо́бається Семе́нові: ві́н за́вжди запро́шує ї́ї піти́ з ни́м на конце́рт або́ до рестора́ну. За́втра свя́то, і Семе́н спита́в, чи На́дя не хо́че піти́ в па́рк над Дніпро́м, а по́тім скупа́тися й попла́вати човно́м. На́дя не вміє пла́вати і бої́ться йти́, але́ Семе́н ка́же, що навчи́тися пла́вати зо́всім не ва́жко, і що ві́н навчи́ть ї́ї пла́вати за оди́н де́нь. О́сь уже́ 10-а годи́на, а Семе́н каза́в, що при́йде об 11-ій і щоб На́дя була́ вдя́гнена. На́дя вже́ гото́ва — ї́й не тре́ба до́вго вирі́шувати, у що́ вдягну́тися легка́ про́ста су́кня — і о́сь вона́ вже́ гото́ва.

2. Мину́лого ти́жня ми́ літа́ли до Льво́ва. Ми́ ма́ли ті́льки оди́н де́нь на те́, щоб огля́нути це́ чудо́ве мі́сто, але́ ми́ поба́чили собо́р св. Ю́рія, що ту́т зву́ть "Ю́ром", ба́чили старі́ ву́лиці, буди́нки. Були́ в до́брому рестора́ні, а вве́чері на конце́рті. У нас лиши́лися ду́же прие́мні вра́ження. В насту́пному листі́ опишу́, як ми́ ходи́ли в го́ри, ходи́ли по землі́, де́ жили́ твої́ батьки́.

3. О́сь уже́ дру́гий де́нь на́ша гру́па хо́дить по Ки́єву й огляда́є його́. Ки́їв — це́ се́рце Украї́ни, але́ чому́ ту́т не чу́ти украї́нської мо́ви? Невже́ ту́т живу́ть самі́ росія́ни? Ні́, ту́т живу́ть украї́нці, які́ не хо́чуть, а де́які вже́ й не вмі́ють говори́ти своє́ю мо́вою. Та я́ ві́рю, що й у ни́х украї́нське се́рце. Коли́ я́ з ни́ми почина́ю розмовля́ти по-украї́нському, вони́ ра́до відповіда́ють мені́ украї́нською мо́вою. Ми́ говоримо про ті́ книжки́, які́ ми́ чита́ли, про життя́ в Аме́риці й Украї́ні, і взагалі́ на на́шій Землі́. Я́ ба́чу, що хо́ч думки́ в на́с не за́вжди однако́ві*, ми́ всі́ хо́чемо, щоб лю́ди не були́ голо́дні, щоб життя́ було́ га́рне й прие́мне скрі́зь, для ко́жної люди́ни.

4. Я́ ту́т познайо́мився з одніє́ю симпати́чною молодо́ю студе́нткою Ві́рою. Вона́ навча́ється в Ки́ївському університе́ті, вивча́є мо́ви, а крі́м то́го працю́є як провідни́ця. Вона́ води́ла на́шу гру́пу огляда́ти Софі́йський собо́р та і́нші церкви́ Ки́єва. Я́ її́ спита́ла, чи вона́ ві́рить у Бо́га, і була́ пе́вна, що вона́ відпові́сть "ні́". Але́ вона́ сказа́ла, що її́ ціка́вить іде́я Бо́га, і вона́ бага́то над ци́м ду́має, але́ ще не ви́рішила для се́бе цього́ пита́ння. Її́ товаришки́, звича́йно, не ві́рять, і її́ батьки́ теж, але́ лю́ди, які́ живу́ть у селі́, де́ вона́ була́ влі́тку, ві́рять. У ни́х вона́ поба́чила спра́вжню ві́ру, і це́ ї́й сподо́балося. І лю́ди ці́ сподо́балися: про́сті, симпати́чні, з до́брим се́рцем і душе́ю. Це́, звича́йно, ще не зна́чить, що вона́ гото́ва повірити, заува́жила вона́, а я́ собі́ поду́мала: "Але́ це́ вже́ поча́ток".

XXI. Answer the following questions to the above passages.

(1)

1. Чому́ На́дя ду́має, що вона́ подо́бається Семе́нові?
2. Куди́ Семе́н її́ запро́шує?
3. Чого́ він мо́же її́ навчи́ти?
4. Коли́ Семе́н при́йде?
5. Я́к На́дя вдягну́лася?

(2)

1. Що́ вони́ огля́нули у Льво́ві?
2. Де́ вони́ були́ вве́чері?
3. Що́ ця́ ді́вчина опи́ше в насту́пному листі́?

(3)

1. Що́ його́ заціка́вило в Ки́єві?
2. Чому́ це́ та́к, на його́ ду́мку?
3. Про що́ вони́ розмовля́ли?
4. Чого́ всі́ хо́чуть?

---

* однако́ві — the same, alike, identical

(4)

1. Хтó Віра і щó вонá рóбить?
2. Куди́ вонá ї́х води́ла?
3. Щó ця́ дівчина її́ спитáла?
4. Щó вонá ї́й відповіла?
5. Щó вонá розповіла про селó?
6. Які тáм люди?

XXII. Answer the following questions to the basic text.

"Ли́ст від Богдáна"

1. Звідки Богдáн пи́ше?
2. Щó він тáм бáчив?
3. Яке́ йогó врáження?
4. Щó сказáв провідни́к?

"Ли́ст від Мáрти"

1. Дé Мáрта тепéр живé?
2. Якá в нéї кімнáта?
3. Чогó вонá не бáчить з вікнá?
4. Куди́ вони́ підуть зáвтра?
5. Щó обіця́в провідни́к?
6. Куди́ Мáрту кли́чуть?
7. Якá в ни́х прогрáма на ве́чір?

П'ЯТНАДЦЯТА ЛЕКЦІЯ

42 На базарі все свіже
Everything is fresh at the market

Dialogue Paticipants:
Дмитро́ Іва́нович Костю́к - Д, Іри́на Бори́сівна Костю́к - І
Dmytro Ivanovych Kostjuk - D, Iryna Borysivna Kostjuk - I

1. І- Дми́тре, за́раз бу́демо сні́дати. Я́ купи́ла яє́ць і молока́, за́раз зроблю́ яє́шню.
2. Д- До́бре. А я́блук і ви́шень ти́ не купи́ла?
3. І- Ні́, в крамни́ці не було́ до́брих. Я́ за́втра пої́ду на база́р, та́м усе́ сві́же, хоч і дороге́.
4. Д- Я́ зна́ю, в крамни́ці не ва́рто купува́ти. Пам'ята́єш ті́ ви́шні, що ти́ купи́ла мину́лого ти́жня, а вони́ на дру́гий де́нь зіпсува́лися?
5. І- До́бре пам'ята́ю. Ти́ зна́єш, я́ ча́сом шкоду́ю, що ми́ пере́їхали на це́ поме́шкання. Тепе́р на база́р тре́ба ї́хати а́ж на дру́гий кіне́ць мі́ста.
6. Д- Та́к, але́, з дру́гого бо́ку, ту́т для діте́й кра́ще, і до твої́х батькі́в зві́дси бли́жче.
7. І- Це́ пра́вда. І до пра́ці мені́ тепе́р зовсі́м близе́нько.
8. Д- О́сь ба́чиш.

1. I- Dmytro, we will have breakfast in a minute. I bought milk and some eggs. I will make an omelette.
2. D- That's fine. But didn't you buy any apples or cherries?
3. I- No, they didn't have any good ones at the store.Tomorrow I'll go to the market. Everything is fresh there, although it's expensive.
4. D- I know, it's not worth shopping at the store. Remember those cherries you bought last week, how they spoiled the very next day?
5. I- I sure do. You know, sometimes I feel sorry we moved to this apartment. Now, to get to the market I have to ride all the way across town.
6. D- Yes, but on the other hand, it's better here for the children, and it's closer from here to your parents' place.
7. I- That's true. And it's very close to where I work.
8. D- There, you see!

43 Ой, не ходи, Грицю
Hey, Hrуc', don't go

Dialogue Paticipants:
О́ля - О, Гри́ць - Г; Olja - O, Hryc' - H

1.	О-	П'я́ть, ші́сть, сі́м, ві́сім, де́в'ять, де́сять...	O-	Five, six, seven, eight, nine, ten...
2.	Г-	О́лю, що́ ти́ раху́єш? Гро́ші?	H-	Olja, what are you counting? Money?
3.	О-	Не заважа́й мені́! Одина́дцять, двана́дцять, трина́дцять. чотирна́дцять, п'ятна́дцять. О́сь: це́ 15 квитків на сього́днішній конце́рт, які́ я́ ма́ю прода́ти. Хо́чеш купи́ти? Три́ за до́ляр, оди́н за п'ятдеся́т це́нтів. Це́ ду́же де́шево.	O-	Don't interrupt! Eleven, twelve, thirteen, fourteen, fifteen. Here, there are the 15 tickets I have to sell for tonight's concert. Want to buy some? They are three for a dollar, one for fifty cents. It's a real bargain.
4.	Г-	Та чека́й, яки́й конце́рт? Я́ нічо́го не зна́ю.	H-	But, wait a minute, what concert? I don't know anything about it.
5.	О-	Сього́дні бу́де конце́рт на́шого хо́ру. У програ́мі бага́то га́рних украї́нських пісе́нь, включа́ючи твою́ улю́блену "Садо́к вишне́вий ко́ло ха́ти".	O-	Tonight our choir is giving a concert. In the program we have many beautiful Ukrainian songs, including your favorite, "A cherry orchard by the house".
6.	Г-	До́бре, але́ наві́що мені́ аж три́ квитки́? Я́ ж сам-оди́н.	H-	That's fine, but what do I need three tickets for? I'm just by myself.
7.	О-	Це́ нічо́го, купи́ для дівча́т. О́сь хоча́ б для сесте́р Тарнове́цьких. Пі́дете ра́зом: ти́ і а́ж дві́ ді́вчини.	O-	That's all right, buy some for the girls, perhaps for the Tarnovec'ki sisters. You can all go together, two girls and yourself.
8.	Г-	Чи це́ не забага́то для одного́ хло́пця? Щоб не ви́йшло та́к, я́к у ті́й пі́сні: "О́й, не ходи́, Гри́цю..."	H-	Isn't this a bit too many for one guy? It may end up as in that song "Hey, Hryc', don't go..."
9.	О-	Не бі́йся, все́ бу́де в поря́дку.	O-	Don't worry, everything will be all right.

СЛОВНИК

База́р, -у (m)	market
бі́к, бо́ку; боки́ (m)	side, way
бли́жче	closer, nearer
близе́нько (бли́зько)	very closer (closer, near)
ва́рто	worth while
вихо́дити, вихо́джу, вихо́дять I	to go out; to turn out
ви́йти, ви́йдуть P	
вишне́вий	cherry (adj.)
ви́шня (f); ви́шні, ви́шень	cherry (fruit & tree)
ві́сім	eight
включа́ючи	including
гро́ші, гро́шей (pl.)	money

дванáдцять	twelve
дéв'ять	nine
дéсять	ten
дéшево; дешéвий	cheap
дóляр, -а (m)	dollar
забагато	too much, too many
заважáти, заважáють I	to bother, to interfere (+D)
завáдити, -джý, -дять P (+D)	
квитóк, -кá; -ки́ (m)	ticket
крамни́ця (f)	store
кóло (+G)	near, around
молокó (n)	milk
навíщо	what for
одинáдцять	eleven
переїзди́ти, -їджý, -їздя́ть I	to move
переїжджáти, переїжджáють I	
переїхáти, переї́дуть P	
пíсня; піснí; пісéнь (f)	song
порядок, -ку (m)	order
прáця; прáці (f)	work, job
на прáці	at work
продавáти, продаю́ть I (+D, за +A)	to sell (to, for)
продáти, продадýть P	
псувáтися, псую́ться I	to spoil; to break down
зіпсувáтися, зіпсую́ться P	
(попсувáтися, попсую́ться) P	
п'ятдеся́т (pjades'át)	fifty
п'ятнáдцятий	fifteenth
п'ятнáдцять	fifteen
п'ять	five
рахувáти, рахýють I	to count
порахувáти, порахýють P	
садóк, -кá; -ки́ (m)	little garden; kindergarten
сам-оди́н	alone
свíжий	fresh
сíм	seven
снíдати, снíдають I	to have breakfast
поснíдати, поснíдають P	
тринáдцять	thirteen
улю́блений	favorite
хáта; -и́ (f)	house (in a village)
цéнт, -а (m)	cent
чáсом	at times
чотирнáдцять	fourteen
шíсть	six
шкодувáти, шкодýють I	to regret
пошкодувáти, пошкодýють P	
яéшня (f)	omelette

NAMES

Гри́ць (Грицько́) short for Григо́рій / Григі́р (Gregory)
Ірúна (Irene) / Ірúна Борúсівна Костю́к
(Ярúна — colloquial for Ірúна)

IDIOMS

ви́йшло	it turns out
все́ в поря́дку	everything is in order
з дру́гого бо́ку	on the other hand

SUPPLEMENT

працівни́к	worker

EXPLANATORY NOTES

1. Beside the word крамни́ця West Ukrainians use the word скле́п, which is a Polish borrowing, and the Easterners use магази́н, which is a Russism (Russians, in their turn, borrowed it from French).

2. The noun база́р which is known to the English speakers as 'bazaar' (usually a charity affair), comes from Persian and is an equivalent to what we would call a 'farmers' market'. In Ukraine collective farmers bring their goods and sell them to the customers at prices higher then those in the government owned stores.

3. The noun бі́к has two meanings, 'side' and 'direction', 'way':

В яки́й бі́к він побі́г?	Which way did he go?
Чи ти́ на на́шому бо́ці?	Are you on our side?
На то́му бо́ці ву́лиці була́ крамни́ця.	On the other side of the street was a store.
По то́й бі́к ву́лиці була́ крамни́ця.	Across the street was a store.

The last example with по + acc. is more idiomatic and common than на + loc. The adjective потойбі́чний means 'otherworldly', i.e. 'on the other side'.

4. The noun пра́ця is often synonymous with робо́та, cf:

Це́ ціка́ва пра́ця.	This is an interesting work (paper).
Це́ ціка́ва робо́та.	

However, manual labor is робо́та and intellectual work is пра́ця.

5. The song about the cherry orchard is a poem by Ševčenko written in 1847 which became like so many other of his lyrics, a popular song. The full text is given bellow.

Ве́чір	**An Evening**
Садо́к вишне́вий ко́ло ха́ти. Хрущі́ над ви́шнями гуду́ть, Плугатарі́ з плуга́ми йду́ть, Співа́ють, ідучи́, дівча́та, а матері́ вече́рять жду́ть.	A cherry orchard grows near the house, May-beetles hum above the trees, The ploughmen walk behind their ploughs, The girls are singing as they walk, And the mothers wait, their supper ready.
Сім'я́ вече́ря ко́ло ха́ти, Вечі́рня зі́ронька встає́, Дочка́ вече́рять подає́, А ма́ти хо́че навча́ти, Так солове́йко не дає́.	The family is having supper outside, The evening star is rising, The daughter is serving supper As her mother tries to teach her how, But the nightingale doesn't let her.
Покла́ла ма́ти ко́ло ха́ти Мале́ньких ді́точок свої́х, Сама́ засну́ла ко́ло ї́х. Зати́хло все́ ... Ті́льки дівча́та Та солове́йко не зати́х.	The mother has put to sleep Her little children near the house, And she herself has fallen asleep near them. Everything has became quiet... except for the girls and the nightingale.

6. The songs about Hryc' is a typical folk ballad about a young girl who found out that her boyfriend was two-timing her and so she 'did him in'. This song has attracted many Ukrainian dramatists, the best known version being the play by Myxajlo Staryc'kyj ("Oj ne hody, Hryc'u", 1890). According to the popular legend, the authorship of this song belongs to a talented Cossack girl from Poltava, Marus'a Čuraj. Here are the words and the music:

О́й, не ходи́ Гри́цю, та й на вечорни́ці, Бо на вечорни́цях дівки́ чарівни́ці! Одна́ ді́вчина чорнобри́вая Та й чарівни́ченька справедли́вая.	Don't go, Hryc', to the evening parties, For the girls there are enchantresses, The one with the dark eyebrows That one is a true enchantress.
У неді́лю ра́но зі́лля копа́ла, А у понеді́лок переполоска́ла, А у вівторо́к зі́лля вари́ла, А в се́реду ра́но Гри́ця отруї́ла.	Early Sunday morning, she dug up some herbs, On Monday she washed them well, On Tuesday she cooked the herbs, And Wednesday morning she poisoned Hryc'.
Прийшо́в четве́р — та вже́ Гри́ць уме́р, Прийшла́ п'я́тниця — похова́ли Гри́ця, А в субо́ту ра́но ма́ти дочку́ би́ла: "Нащо́ ти́, до́чко, Гри́ця отруї́ла?"	Thursday came and Hryc' was already dead, Friday came, they buried him, And Saturday morning her mother was beating her "Why did you poison Hryc', my daughter?"
"О́й, ма́ти, ма́ти, жа́ль ваги́ не ма́є, Неха́й же́ Гри́ць ра́зом та дво́х не коха́є! Неха́й він не бу́де ні ї́й, ні мені́, Неха́й доста́неться він сирі́й землі́!"	"O, mother, mother, you can't measure my grief, Hryc' shouldn't have loved two girls at once, Let him belong neither to her nor to me, Let the damp earth take him!"

"Оцé тобí, Грúцю, я́ тáк ізробúла,	"This is what I have done to you, Hrys',
Що чéрез тéбе менé мáти бúла!	And because of you my mother beat me,
Оцé ж тобí, Грúцю, за тéє заплáта —	this is what you get, for it, Hrys'—
Із чотирьóх дощóк дубóвая хáта!"	An oak house made of four boards!"

7. The noun грóші is used only in the plural in modern Ukrainian, although the singular гріш is preserved in saying and proverbs, such as 'it's not worth a penny' — 'це не варто ламаного гроша' (in the old times there was a coin called гріш worth half a copeck or half a penny).

8. The interrogative word навíщо "what for" is close in meaning to the expression для чóго 'what for'. The difference lies in the greater emotional coloring of навíщо ('what could possibly be the reason for/the purpose of') and its greater degree of abstraction (it inquires about the purpose). Для чóго, on the other hand, is more practical and concrete ('what is this designed for', 'what does it do'), although it may be used to inquire about the purpose of an action as well (minus emotional coloring). cf.:

Навíщо тú цé зробúв?	What did you do that for? (annoyance)
Для чóго тú цé зробúв?	What did you do that for? (matter of fact)
Навíщо вчúтися? Цé не вáрто.	Why study? It's not worth it.
Для чóго він ýчиться?	Why does he study?
Щоб отрúмати дóбру прáцю.	To get a good job.

NOTES ON GRAMMAR

1. GENITIVE PLURAL OF NOUNS

There are 3 types of endings in the genitive plural: **-ів, -ей** and Ø (zero). Their distribution is as follows:

1. Most masculine nouns of the masculine-neuter declension have the ending **-ів**:

Nominative sg.	*Nominative pl.*	*Genitive pl.*
собóр	собóри	собóрів
кінéць	кінці́	кінці́в
дéнь	дні́	дні́в
провіднúк	провідникú	провідникíв
музéй	музéї	музéїв

Note 1: Masculine nouns with the suffix **-ин** have a zero ending in the genitive plural (the suffix **-ин** is lost in the plural, see Lesson 14, p. 245)

Nominative sg.	*Nominative pl.*	*Genitive pl.*
росія́н-ин	росія́н-Ø-и	росія́н-Ø

Note 2: The nouns рáз and дéнь admit two endings in the genitive plural, **-ів** and zero (the latter is rare):

Порахýй щé кíлька разíв (раз).	Count a few more times.
За кíлька днів (дéнь) побáчимося.	I will see you in a few days.

Note 3: The noun **чоловік** besides the regular genitive in **-ів** has another form with a zero ending with a difference in meaning: **чоловіків** = men, **чоловік** = persons. cf.:

Та́м було́ бага́то чолові́ків.	There were many men (=males) there.
В кімна́ті було́ кі́лька чолові́к.	There were several people in the room.

2. Most neuters and the a-declension nouns have a zero ending in the genitive plural.

Zero ending

Nominative plural		*Genitive plural*	
Stem	*Ending*	*Stem*	*Ending*
кімна́т-	и	кімна́т	Ø
міст-	á	мі́ст	Ø
ле́кці-	ї	ле́кцій	Ø
(lekcij	i)		
порос-я́т-	а	порося́т	Ø
ім-ен-	á	іме́н	Ø
поба́чен-н	я	поба́чень	Ø

Note 1: The noun **до́шка** has the genitive plural **дощо́к** with a щ rather than ш.

Note 2: Neuters with the suffixes **-ат-/-ен-** follow the Ø ending pattern.

Note 3: A number of neuter and a-declension nouns have the ending **-ів** in the genitive plural (in most instances a parallel zero-ending form also exists):

Nominative sg.	Nominative pl.	Genitive pl.
мо́ре	моря́	морі́в
по́ле	поля́	полі́в and пі́ль
ма́ма	мами́	ма́м and мамі́в
ба́ба	баби́	ба́б and бабі́в 'grandmothers'
губа́	гу́би	гу́б and губі́в 'lips'

3. All feminine nouns of the C-type as well as some a-declension, neuter and soft-stem masculine nouns have the ending **-ев** in the genitive plural:

-ей

(a) C-type feminine nouns

Nominative sg.	*Nominative pl.*	*Genitive pl.*
рі́ч	ре́чі	рече́й
відповідь	відповіді	відповідей

(b) a-type nouns

Nominative sg.	*Nominative pl.*	*Genitive pl.*
сім'я́	сі́м'ї	сіме́й 'families'
стаття́	статті́	стате́й 'articles'
свиня́	сви́ні	свине́й 'pigs'

(c) neuters and soft-stem masculines

Nominative sg.	*Nominative pl.*	*Genitive pl.*
о́ко	о́чі	оче́й
плече́	пле́чі	плече́й 'shoulders'
гість	го́сті	госте́й
кінь	ко́ні	ко́ней 'horses'

Note 1: The nouns **дити́на** and **люди́на** have the genitive plural ending **-ей**: **дити́на — ді́ти — діте́й; люди́на — лю́ди — люде́й**

Note 2: The noun **ма́ти** which belongs to the c-type declension has the genitive plural in **-ів** rather than **-ей**: **матері́в**. However, the form **матере́й** was considered standard until quite recently.

4. Pluralia tantum. These nouns may have three types of endings:

(a)	-ів	—	ме́блі — ме́блів, штани́ — штані́в
(b)	-ей	—	две́рі — двере́й, гро́ші — гро́шей
(c)	zero	—	Карпа́ти — Карпа́т

SUMMARY

Let us now sum up all the possible genitive plural endings.

The ending **-ів**

1. Most masculine nouns of the masc./neuter declension (собо́р — собо́рів).
2. Some neuter nouns (мо́ре — морі́в).
3. Some feminine a-declension nouns (ма́ма — мамі́в) and the noun **ма́ти** (ма́ти — матері́в).
4. Some pluralia tantum nouns (ме́блі — ме́блів).

The ending **-ей**

1. All feminine c-type nouns (річ — рече́й).
2. Some nouns of the masc./neuter declension (гість — госте́й, о́ко — оче́й).
3. Some feminine a-declension nouns (свиня́ — свине́й).
4. Some pluralia tantum nouns (гро́ші — гро́шей).

Zero ending

1. Most neuter nouns (місто — міст).
2. Most feminine a-declension nouns (гру́па — гру́п).
3. Masculine nouns with the suffix **-ин** which lose this suffix in nom. pl. (росія́нин — росія́ни — росія́н).
4. Some pluralia tantum nouns (Карпа́ти — Карпа́т).

(Exercises 1, 2, 3)

II. SPELLING CONVENTIONS AND STRESS IN THE GENITIVE PLURAL

1. The zero ending genitive plural of feminine and neuter nouns may have two or more stem-final consonants, e.g. **студе́НТК-, віКН-**. In such clusters a vowel is usually inserted before the final consonant:

(a) In the feminine nouns the vowel **е** is inserted before the final consonants **л, ль, н, нь, м, п** and in the neuter nouns before the final consonants **л, ц, р, н** (**н** must not be preceded by **к**):

Stem	Stem				
земл-я́	/zeml'-/	земе́ль	крі́сл-о	/kr'isl-/	крі́сел
весн-а́	/vesn-/	ве́сен	яйц-е́	/jajc-/	яе́ць
ви́шн-я	/vyšn'/	ви́шень	се́рц-е	/ser(d)c'/*	серде́ць
сестр-а́	/sestr-/	сесте́р			

(b) The vowel **о** is inserted before the final consonant-suffix **-к-**, before the final **в** which is not preceded by **ст** or **цт**, and between **к** and the final /n/, /n'/:

кни́жк-а	книжо́к	вікн-о́	ві́кон
лі́жк-о	лі́жок	су́кн-я	су́конь
це́ркв-а	церко́в	до́шк-а	дощо́к

In all other cases no vowel is inserted as a rule, cf.: **а́вто — а́вт, слу́жба — слу́жб, місто — міст.** Genitive plural of **місце** is **місць.**

2. The stem final vowel **-о** changes to **-і** before the genitive plural zero ending of neuter and feminine nouns (cf. Lesson 4, p. 62).

шко́ла — шкіл
гора́ — гір
сло́во — слів

The stem final vowel **е** under these circumstances normally undergoes no change (cf. **перо́ — пе́р** "feathers", **о́зеро — озе́р** "lakes"). However, there are exeptions, cf. **село́ — сіл.**

---

* A simplification rule removes the /d/ in the cluster /rdc/.

Note: The **-о** to **-і** mutation rule has many exceptions, e.g. **мóва — мóв, водá — вóд**. It is normally absent in foreign borrowings, e.g. **мóда — мóд** "fashion", **нóта — нóт** 'note'.

3. Neuter nouns which have a double stem-final consonant lose one of the consonants in the genitive plural:

Stem	*Genitive plural*
засíданн-(я)	засíдань
/zas'ídan' n'-a/	/zas'ídan'/
питáнн-(я)	питáнь
/pytán' n'-a/	/pytán'/

4. Stress position in the genitive plural of most nouns is the same as in the nominative plural, cf.:

Nominative sg.	Nominative pl.	Genitive pl.
лúст	листú	листíв
жíнка	жінкú	жінóк
завдáння	завдáння	завдáнь
вíдповідь	вíдповіді	вíдповідей
	грóші	грóшей

Some feminine C-type nouns with a stem stress in the nominative sg. and pl. have their genitive plural ending **-ей** stressed. Pluralia tantum nouns with the **-ей** genitive may also follow this pattern. cf.:

Nominative sg.	Nominative pl.	Genitive pl.
píч	péчі	речéй
ніч	нóчі	ночéй
	двéрі	дверéй
	лю́ди	людéй

In some nouns the inserted vowel **-о/-е** attracts the stress:

Nominative sg.	*Nominative pl.*	*Genitive pl.*
землЯ́	зéмлі	земéль
яйцé	я́йця	яéць
сестрá	сéстри	сестéр

III. GENITIVE PLURAL OF ADJECTIVES, PRONOUNS, ORDINALS, ADJECTIVAL SURNAMES AND ОДИН

1. All hard-stem adjectives, pronouns, ordinal numerals and **одúн** have the genitive plural ending **-их**. All soft-stem adjectives, pronouns, and ordinals have the genitive plural ending **-іх (-їх)**.

Hard stems							
N. sg.	малúй	нáш	п'ятий	одúн	цéй	тóй	якúйсь
G. pl.	малúх	нáших	п'ятих	однúх	цúх	тúх	якúхось (якúхсь)

Soft stems						
N. sg.	домáшній	ї́хній	увéсь	мі́й	чи́й	трéтій
G. pl.	домáшніх	ї́хніх	усі́х	мої́х	чиї́х	трéтіх

Note: Remember that the letter ї in spelling actually indicates two sounds, the "soft" consonant /j/ of the stem plus the ending /i/: /moj-ix/, /čyj-ix/.

2. All adjectival surnames have adjectival endings in the genitive plural, e.g. **Дмитрóвських, Лéсевих, Івани́шиних**. There is no gender distinction in the plural.

(Exercises 4, 6)

IV. ACCUSATIVE PLURAL OF ANIMATE NOUNS AND THEIR MODIFIERS

The accusative plural of the nouns and their modifiers which refer to animate beings is identical with the genitive plural:

Genitive plural	*Accusative plural*
Я́ не знáю ци́х студéнтів.	Я́ знáю ци́х студéнтів.
I don't know these students.	I know these students.
Я́ не знáю ци́х студéнток.	Я́ знáю ци́х студéнток.
I don't know these students.	I know these students.

Note 1: Nouns referring to animals in the accusative plural can have parallel forms, one identical with the genitive plural and the other identical with the nominative plural, as in inanimate nouns. The nominative plural form is more frequent, e.g.:

Ми́ бáчили поросятá (поросят)	Він продáв кóні (кóней)
We saw the piglets.	He sold the horses.

Note 2: Occasionally the nouns, especially feminine nouns referring to people, in the accusative case can have the form identical with the nominative plural, particularly when preceded by a numeral:

Вони́ лиши́ли жінки́ і діти.	Він зустрів три́ жінки.
They left their wives and children.	He met three women.

Since this usage is not too frequent the student is advised to abide by the rule for the animate nouns given above.

Note 3: In the idiomatic expression **іти́ в гóсті** 'to go visiting' (see Lesson 8) the animate noun in the accusative case has the form of the nominative plural.

(Exercises 5, 7)

V. GENITIVE PLURAL IN EXPRESSIONS OF QUANTITY

1. Numerals 5 and up (excluding those ending in **оди́н, два́, три́, чоти́ри**) are followed by the genitive plural of nouns and their modifiers when the numeral (+modifier)+ noun phrase is the subject or the accusative object of a sentence.

Ще́ є сто́ п'ять деше́вих квиткі́в.	There are still 105 cheap tickets.
Ми́ купи́ли п'ятна́дцять деше́вих квиткі́в.	We bought 15 cheap tickets.
Та́м де́сять дівча́т і де́сять хло́пців.	There are 10 girls and 10 boys there.
Ми́ повеземо́ де́сять дівча́т і де́сять хло́пців.	We will drive 10 girls and 10 boys.

2. The quantitative adverbs **бага́то** and **ма́ло** when followed by the genitive plural translate as 'many' and 'few'.

Чи та́м бага́то люде́й? Ні́, ма́ло.	Are there many people there? No, few.
(However: У ме́не бага́то/ма́ло гро́шей.	I have a lot of/little money.)

3. The numeral-noun phrase and the quantitative adverb+noun combination when they appear as subject of a sentence require the 3rd person singular verb (neuter in the past):

Скі́льки та́м бу́де (було́) люде́й?	How many people will be (were) there?
-Та́м було́ (бу́де) сто́ люде́й.	-There were (will be) a hundred people.
Чи та́м було́ бага́то люде́й?	Were there many people there?
-Та́к, де́сять люде́й на́віть стоя́ло.	-Yes, ten people were even standing.

(Exercises 8, 9, 10)

VI. PREFIXED VERBS OF MOTION

1. Verbs of motion can receive various prefixes with special meaning. The most frequent of them are:

ви- motion out or from s. thing	ви́нести	to carry out
в-, до-, під-, при- motion to, toward, into	вбі́гти	to run into
	допливти́	to swim as far as
	під'ї́хати	to drive up to
	прийти́	to arrive, to come
	приї́хати	"
від-, з- motion away from	від'ї́хати	to drive away
	знести́	to carry down
пере- motion across, over	перейти́	to cross over
про- motion through	проїхати	to drive through

2. The basic uni- and multidirectional verbs lose the directional juxtaposition when they become prefixed. Instead they function as regular pairs, with the former multidirectional verb remaining imperfective and the former unidirectional verb becoming perfective:

Prefix+multi=Imperfective

в-	ходи́ти	вхо́дити
ви-	ї́здити	виїзди́ти (виїжджа́ти)
під-	носи́ти	підно́сити
при-	вози́ти	приво́зити
до-	води́ти	дово́дити
про-	бі́гати	пробіга́ти
пере-	пла́вати	перепліва́ти

Prefix+uni=Perfective

в-	іти́	ввійти́ (увійти)	to enter
ви-	ї́хати	ви́їхати	to drive out, to leave
під-	нести́	піднести́	to lift, to raise
при-	везти́	привезти́	to bring (transp.)
до-	вести́	довести́	to lead to, to drive to, to reduce to
про-	бі́гти	пробі́гти	to run (through, by)
пере-	пливти́	перепліва́ти	to swim across

The difference between the perfective and the imperfective prefixed verbs of motion is the same as with any other aspectual pair. cf.:

Imperfective	*Perfective*
Вони́ вже́ перехо́дять (через) ву́лицю. They are already crossing the street.	Вони́ перейшли́ (че́рез) ву́лицю. They crossed the street.
Я́ завжди́ перехо́джу ву́лицю ту́т.	I always cross the street here.

The former multidirectional verbs when prefixed can no longer be used to indicate a round trip.

3. The stem of the motion verbs remains the same under prefixation with the exception of **плава́ти** 'to swim' which changes to **-плива́ти**, i.e. **перепліва́ти** 'to swim across'. The verb **ї́здити** when prefixed has two parallel forms **в'їзди́ти** and **в'їжджа́ти** 'to drive in', 'to move in'.

4. The root vowel in the verb **іти́** changes to **й** when a prefix (other than **по-**) is added to it. Prefixes ending in a consonant require an insertion of the vowel **і** between them and **-йти**. Prefix **до-** changes to **ді-**, and instead of **в-** the prefix **вві-** or **уві-** is used. Thus:

ви́йти	дійти́
прийти́	зійти́
перейти́	підійти́
пройти́	відійти́
увійти́	

The past tense of these verbs is **ви́йшов, ви́йшла, ви́йшло, ви́йшли; дійшо́в, дійшла́, дійшло́, дійшли́**, etc.

5. The stress in the **ви-** prefixed perfectives is always on the prefix. In all other perfective motion verbs the stress remains the same as in their basic imperfective forms:

везти́	—	провезти́	but	**ви́везти**
нести́	—	віднести́		**ви́нести**
бі́гти	—	прибі́гти		**ви́бігти**
вести́	—	довести́		**ви́вести**
пливти́	—	перепливти́		**ви́пливти**

The stress in the prefixed imperfectives depends on the position of the stress in its non-prefixed form. If the initial syllable was stressed the stress moves to the next syllable, otherwise it moves to the preceding syllable. cf.:

бі́гати	—	перебіга́ти
пла́вати	—	переплива́ти
ї́здити	—	виїзди́ти
ходи́ти	—	підхо́дити
носи́ти	—	прино́сити
вози́ти	—	приво́зити

6. Certain prefixed verbs of motion require the use of certain prepositions.*

For example:

до- + до (+G.)
Я́ ва́с довезу́ до бібліоте́ки. — I will drive you to the library.

від- + від (+G.) in verbs indicating motion away from s.th.
Вона́ відійшла́ від вікна́. — She walked away from the window.

Verbs with the prefixes **про-** and **пере-** may be followed by a direct object or by the preposition **че́рез** (+A.) to indicate the area travelled:

Ми́ перейшли́ (че́рез) ву́лицю. — We crossed (went across) the street.
Ми́ проі́хали (че́рез) село́. — We drove through the village.

(Exercises 12, 13)

---

* For a complete list of verb government see Appendix 3.

ВПРАВИ

I. Change the sentences according to the model:

Ту́т нема́є ні о́дного **прі́звища.** Ту́т нема́є **прі́звищ.**

1. У на́с нема́є ні о́дного квитка́.
2. У селі́ нема́є жо́дної крамни́ці.
3. У ме́не нема́є ні о́дного це́нта.
4. На база́рі нема́є ні о́дного я́блука.
5. У крамни́ці нема́є ні о́дної ви́шні.
6. У бібліоте́ці нема́є жо́дної газе́ти.
7. Та́м нема́є жо́дного журна́лу.
8. У поме́шканні нема́є ні о́дного крі́сла.
9. У кімна́ті нема́є вікна́.
10. У цьо́му мі́сті нема́є жо́дного музе́ю.

II. Change the statements from positive to negative.

1. Я́ зна́ю ві́дповіді.
2. Я́ зна́ю адре́си.
3. Вони́ ма́ють гро́ші.
4. Вони́ ма́ють до́ляри.
5. Ми́ купи́ли подару́нки.
6. Ми́ купи́ли стільці́.
7. Ві́н продає́ ре́чі.
8. Ві́н продає́ а́вта.
9. Ти́ слу́хаєш пісні́.
10. Ти́ слу́хаєш програ́ми.

III. Change the words in parenthesis from N.pl. to G.pl.

1. Ти́ не ба́чив (її́ валі́зки)?
2. Ви́ не чу́ли (його́ слова́)?
3. Вона́ не потребу́є (су́кні).
4. Вони́ не слу́хають (ле́кції).
5. Ві́н не розуміє (пита́ння).
6. Ми́ не лю́бимо (і́спити).
7. Вона́ бої́ться (хло́пці).
8. Ми́ ще не зустрі́ли (студе́нтки-кана́дки).
9. Вони́ ще не зроби́ли (впра́ви).
10. Вони́ ще не зроби́ли (завда́ння).

IV. Give the negative answers to the following questions.

1. Чи ві́н опи́сував моря́?
2. Чи вона́ купи́ла ті дорогі́ ме́блі?
3. Чи ти́ забу́в свої ре́чі?

4. Чи ви́ пам'ята́єте вчора́шні розмо́ви?
5. Чи ви́ лю́бите малі́ кімна́ти?
6. Чи вони́ ба́чили нові́ се́ла й міста́?
7. Чи ви́ огляда́ли ті́ церкви́?
8. Чи ти́ зачини́ла две́рі?
9. Чи ти́ відчини́в ві́кна?
10. Чи ви́ ба́чили Карпа́ти?

V. Change the nouns and their modifiers to plural.

1. Я́ зна́ю цього́ провідника́.
2. Вона́ розуміє цього́ росія́нина.
3. Ми́ зустрі́ли одного́ інжене́ра.
4. Ві́н не пам'ята́є нія́кого старо́го чолові́ка.
5. Я́ не люблю́ ціє́ї люди́ни.
6. Вона́ слу́хала яку́сь жі́нку.
7. Я́ кли́чу оту́ дити́ну.
8. Ми́ чека́ємо на на́шого вчи́теля.
9. Я́ не ба́чив ва́шого у́чня.
10. Я́ зна́ю твою́ учени́цю.
11. Вони́ зустрі́ли свою́ вчи́тельку.

VI. Open the brackets.

1. Чиї́ це́ су́кні? (ці́ га́рні дівча́та)
2. Чиї́ це́ човни́? (на́ші дру́зі)
3. Чия́ це́ пра́ця? (ті́ украї́нські студе́нти)
4. Чиє́ це́ пита́ння? (ті́ америка́нські студе́нтки)
5. Чи́й це́ сніда́нок? (ті́ малі́ ді́ти)
6. Чиї́ це́ чолові́ки? (ті́ молоді́ жінки́)
7. Чиї́ це́ а́вта? (ті́ англі́йські професори́)
8. Чия́ це́ ха́та? (ті́ старі́ лю́ди)
9. Чиї́ це́ книжки́? (ці́ малі́ хло́пці)
10. Чиє́ це́ пр́ізвище? (ті́ се́стри)

VII. Change the sentences according to the model:

Це́ його́ студе́нти. **Вона́ зна́є його́ студе́нтів.**

(украї́нські студе́нтки, ї́хні товаришки, мої́ батьки́, ки́ївські лікарі́, ха́рківські дівча́та, америка́нські індія́нці, росі́йські жінки́, ї́хні матері́, мої́ бра́ти, мої́ се́стри)

VIII. Complete the sentences.

У ме́не ті́льки оди́н сті́л, а у ни́х **бага́то столі́в.**
У ме́не ті́льки оди́н това́риш, а у ни́х бага́то. . . . .

(одне́ крі́сло, одне́ лі́жко, одна́ поли́ця, одна́ кімна́та, одна́ ле́кція, одне́ пита́ння, одна́ ві́дповідь, одне́ ім'я́, оди́н словни́к, одна́ кни́жка)

IX. Answer the questions using the given numbers.

1. Скільки у ва́с браті́в? (2)
2. Скільки у ва́с до́ларів і скільки це́нтів? (3, 15)
3. Скільки у ва́с українських книжо́к? (4)
4. Скільки у ва́с англійських словників? (1)
5. Скільки у ва́с а́вт? (2)
6. Скільки у ва́с сорочо́к? (12)
7. Скільки у ва́с я́блук? (5)
8. Скільки у ва́с су́конь? (11)
9. Скільки у ва́с іспитів? (3)
10. Скільки у ва́с дру́зів? (2)

X. Translate into Ukrainian.

1. They have 4 cheap chairs and 2 old armchairs.
2. My room has 3 large windows.
3. She has 2 jobs.
4. He has 6 pupils.
5. Here are 10 apples.
6. We were there (for) 15 days.
7. They sold the 12 chairs.
8. He ate 6 eggs.
9. There are 5 stores on this street.
10. She already went to Kyiv 7 times.
11. I gave you 13 dollars.
12. We bought it for a dollar and a half.
13. They ate 9 potato dumplings.
14. There were 11 cherry trees in their garden.
15. These 14 cars are broken.
16. Look at those three guests.

XI. Translate into Ukrainian.

1. Have you had your breakfast yet?
2. Don't spoil it!
3. He keeps bothering me all the time.
4. When are you moving?
5. I saw him when he was just leaving the house.
6. How much are you selling it for?
7. Please, count your money.
8. Do you regret coming here?
9. Nothing will come out of it.
10. What a beautiful song!

XII. Supply the appropriate prefixes to the given verbs.

1. Вони́ . . . . .ї́хали з Нью Йо́рку до Чіка́ґо.
2. Про́шу, ...везі́ть мене́ додо́му.
3. Та́м до те́бе хто́сь . . . . .йшо́в.
4. Стара́ ма́ти . . . . .йшла з ха́ти.
5. Куди́ ви́ . . . . .ї́дете насту́пного лі́та?
6. А́вт нема́, мо́жна . . . . .йти́ ву́лицю.
7. Ї́х . . . . .везли з Украї́ни.
8. Коли́ ві́н . . . . .ї́хав до Аме́рики?
9. Ми́ диви́лися, я́к лю́ди . . . . .хо́дять з це́ркви.
10. Вони́ ввє́сь ча́с . . . . .ї́здять з мі́сця на мі́сце.
11. Вони́ . . . . .летіли з Ки́єва вчо́ра вве́чері.

XIII. Supply the appropriate verbs of motion.

1. Богда́н якра́з ї́де до мі́ста, він тебе́ мо́же під. . . . .
2. Здає́ться, ви́ неда́вно пере. . . . . на нове поме́шкання.
3. Коли́ ми́ ви. . . . . з буди́нку, ми́ поба́чили Мико́лу.
4. Авто́бус уже́ при. . . . .
5. Її́ по. . . . . до ліка́ря.
6. До на́с при. . . . . го́сті з Монреа́лю.
7. Його́ нема́, він якра́з ви. . . . . з кімна́ти.
8. Про́симо, при. . . . . до на́с у го́сті!
9. Тепе́р вони́ якра́з пере. . . . . на дру́гий бі́к ву́лиці.
10. Ви́. . . . . з кімна́ти!

XIV. Read and translate.

1. Сього́дні вра́нці ми́ ходи́ли купува́ти я́блука. Я́блук ми́ не купи́ли, бо не було́ таки́х, які́ я́ люблю́, але́ купи́ли сві́жі ви́шні. Хоч вони́ до́сить дорогі́, тому́ що ї́х приво́зять з дале́ких сіл, але́ мені́ ду́же хотілося поі́сти тро́хи сві́жих ви́шень. Чолові́к хоті́в, щоб я́ звари́ла* варе́ники, але́ ци́х ви́шень не до́сить для варе́ників. Я́ ви́рішила, що зроблю́ варе́ники з си́ром, а ви́шні бу́демо ї́сти та́к.

2. Моя́ сестра́ лю́бить украї́нські пісні́. Вона́ ї́х мо́же співа́ти ці́лий де́нь, а коли́ до не́ї прихо́дять товари́шки, вони́ співа́ють ра́зом. У ни́х спра́вжній хо́р і непога́на програ́ма. Насту́пного ти́жня вони́ влашто́вують конце́рт для всі́х своі́х знайо́мих, дру́зів, для діте́й і ї́хніх батькі́в. Вони́ не хо́чуть бра́ти гро́ші, але́ я́ кажу́ сестрі́, щоб вони́ бра́ли хоча́ б до́ляра за квито́к. Та сестра́ не хо́че й слу́хати, ка́же, що це́ ж не для чужи́х люде́й, а для своі́х, і що взагалі́ ї́х гро́ші не ціка́влять. Пра́вду ка́жучи, мені́ це́ подо́бається.

---

* вари́ти I, звари́ти P — to cook.

XV. Answer the following questions to the reading passages.

(1)

1. Щó робúла жíнка сьогóдні врáнці?
2. Щó вонá купúла?
3. Чомý вонú дорогí?
4. Чогó хотíв чоловíк?
5. Чомý жíнка цьогó не зробúла?
6. Щó вонá вúрішила?

(2)

1. Щó любить сестрá цієї дівчини?
2. Щó вонú з товáришкою влаштóвують?
3. Когó вонú клúчуть?
4. Щó цá дíвчина дýмає про грóші?
5. Якóї дýмки її сестрá?

XVI. Answer the following questions to the dialogues.

"На базáрі всé свíже"

1. Щó купúла Ірúна Борúсівна?
2. Чомý вонá хóче пітú на базáр?
3. Щó булó минýлого тúжня?
4. За чúм шкодýє Ірúна Борúсівна?
5. Чомý у новóму помéшканні крáще?

"Óй не ходú, Грúцю"

1. Щó Óля рахýє?
2. Скíльки в нéї квиткíв?
3. Скíльки вонú кóштують?
4. Якá бýде прогрáма?
5. Для кóго Гриць мáє купувáти квиткú?
6. Чогó вíн боїться?
7. Щó відповідáє Óля?

ШІСТНАДЦЯТА ЛЕКЦІЯ

44 Козацькому роду нема переводу
The Cossack stock will never cease to be

Dialogue Paticipants:
Марти́н - М, На́стя - Н
Martyn - M, Nastja - N

1. М- Зна́єш, На́сте, сього́дні де́нь наро́дження моє́ї бабу́ні. Ї́й уже́ сімдеся́т п'я́ть ро́ків.
2. Н- Що́ ти́ ка́жеш! Вона́ вигляда́є бага́то моло́дшою.
3. М- Якби́ ти́ ба́чила мого́ ді́да! Ото́ бу́в коза́к! До са́мої сме́рти ходи́в з на́ми в го́ри, ї́здив коне́м. Ві́н поме́р, коли́ йому́ було́ ві́сімдеся́т ро́ків.
4. Н- Я́ зна́ю, у ва́шій роди́ні всі до́вго живу́ть, всі такі́ здоро́ві, си́льні, висо́кі. О́т що́ зна́чить коза́цький рі́д.
5. М- Звича́йно! "Коза́цькому ро́ду нема́ переводу."

1. M- You know, Nastja, today is my grandmother's birthday. She is already seventy five years old.
2. N- You don't say! She looks much younger.
3. M- You should have seen my grandfather. That was a real Cossack. Right up to his death he would go hiking to the mountains with us and ride horses. He died when he was eighty years old.
4. N- I know, everyone in your family lives long, they are all so heathly, and strong and tall. That's what I call a real Cossack clan.
5. M- Of course: "The Cossack stock will never cease to be".

45 Коли ти народився?
When were you born?

Dialogue Paticipants:
Зі́на - З, Бори́с - Б; Zina - Z, Borys - B

1. З- Бори́се, в котро́му мі́сяці ти́ народився?
2. Б- В сі́чні, тридця́того сі́чня. А ти́?
3. З- Я́ в бе́резні. Тре́тього бе́резня.
4. Б- Підожди́, яке́ сьо́годні число́?
5. З- Два́дцять во́сьме лю́того.
6. Б- То скоро бу́де твій де́нь наро́дження! А ти́ нічо́го не ка́жеш.
7. З- Ти́ са́м пови́нен спита́ти.
8. Б- Ну́, о́сь я́ пита́ю: скі́льки тобі́ бу́де ро́ків?
9. З- Це́ нече́мне пита́ння, але́ тобі́, як това́ришеві, скажу́: три́дцять оди́н рі́к.
10. Б- А мені́ три́дцять два́ ро́ки. То вихо́дить, що я́ на рі́к ста́рший за те́бе, на́віть більше — на рі́к і два́ мі́сяці.
11. З- Ну́, це́ невели́ка різни́ця.
12. Б- Помиля́єшся: я́ ста́рший, і тому́ ти́ по́винна мене́ слу́хатися.
13. З- Що́-о? Які́ в те́бе старосві́тські по́гляди! Тепе́р скрі́зь рівнопра́вність.
14. Б- Та́к, але́ у на́с в наро́ді зберіга́ють стару́ до́бру тради́цію поша́ни до ста́рших.
15. З- Пра́вильно, але́ ж ста́рші — це́ діди́ й батьки́, а не такі́, як ти́.
16. Б- Ну́, до́сить. Я́ ж пожартува́в.
17. З- Я́ не ма́ю нічо́го про́ти жа́ртів. Коли́ жарту́єш, веселі́ше і ле́гше жи́ти.

1. Z- Borys, in what month were you born?
2. B- In January, on the thirtieth of January. And you?
3. Z- I was born in March. March third.
4. B- Wait, what date is today?
5. Z- February twenty eight.
6. B- So your birthday is coming soon. And you are not saying anything.
7. Z- You are the one who should ask.
8. B- So I am asking now: how old will you be?
9. Z- That's not a polite question, but to you as a friend I'll give an answer: I'll be thirty one.
10. B- And I'm thirty two. That makes me a year older than you, or even more, a year and two months.
11. Z- Well, that's not much of a difference.
12. B- Wrong: I am older and you should obey me as one older than yourself.
13. Z- What? You have some old-fashioned ideas.Today there is equality for everyone.
14. B- Yes, but our people preserve a good old tradition of respect for elders.
15. Z- True, but elders are the fathers and the grandfathers, not such as you.
16. B- Well, enough of that. I was joking.
17. Z- I have nothing against jokes. When one is joking, life is brighter and easier.

СЛОВНИК

бабу́ня (f)	granny
бі́льше	more
веселі́ше	merrier
ве́село	merry
висо́кий; ви́соко	tall, high
виглядáти, -ють I (no perf) (+I)	to look like
ді́д, ді́ду! (m)	grandfather
діди́ (pl.)	ancestors
жа́рт, -у (m)	joke
жартува́ти, -ють I	to joke
пожартува́ти, -ють P	
жда́ти, -у́ть I	to wait
підожда́ти, -у́ть P	
зберіга́ти, -ють I	to preserve
зберегти́, -жу́ть P	
зберіг, зберегла́ (past. t.)	
здоро́вий	heathly
і	emphatic particle
кі́нь, -коня́, ко́ню!; ко́ні (m)	horse
коза́к, -а́, коза́че!; -и́ (m)	Cossack
коза́цький	Cossack (adj.)
ле́гше	easier
ле́гко (легки́й)	easy
мі́сяць; -і (m)	month; moon
моло́дший /molódžšyj/	younger
наро́д, -у	people; nation
наро́дження (n)	birth
наро́джуватися, -ються I	to be born
народи́тися, -джуся, -яться P	
нече́мний	impolite
о́т, ото́	that is/those are
пови́нен, пови́нна, -е, -і	must, obligated
по́гляд, -у (m)	look, glance, viewpoint
помира́ти, -ють I	to die
поме́рти, помру́ть P	
поме́р, поме́рла (past. t.)	
поша́на (f)	respect
про́ти (+G)	against
рі́д, ро́ду; роди (m)	descent, family
різни́ця (f)	difference
са́мий	the very
си́льний	strong

скóро	soon
слýхатися, -ються I	to obey
послýхатися, -ються (+G) P	
смéрть (f) gen. смéрти	death
старосвíтський	old-fashioned
стáрший	older, elder
числó, -á; -а (n)	number; date

NAMES

Бори́с, Зíна (short for Зінаї́да), Марти́н, Нáстя (short for Анастáсія)

IDIOMS

ї́хати конéм	to ride a horse
"Козáцькому рóду немá перевóду"	"The Cossack stock will never cease to be"

SUPPLEMENT

низьки́й, ни́зько	low; short (height)
ни́жчий, ни́жче	lower, shorter
Різдвó (n); на Р.	Christmas; at (for) Christmas
рíзні (pl.)	different, various
свíт, -у; -и́ (m)	world
слабки́й (and слаби́й)	weak
чéмний	polite

Months

сíчень, сíчня	January
лю́тий, -ого	February
бéрезень, бéрезня	March
квíтень, квíтня	April
трáвень, трáвня	May
чéрвень, чéрвня	June
ли́пень, ли́пня	July
сéрпень, сéрпня	August
вéресень, вéресня	September
жóвтень, жóвтня	October
листопáд, -а	November
грýдень, грýдня	December

Numerals

шістна́дцять, -тий	sixteen, -th
сімна́дцять, -тий	seventeen, -th
вісімна́дцять, -тий	eignteen, -th
дев'ятна́дцять, -тий	nineteen, -th
два́дцять, двадця́тий	twenty, -ieth
три́дцять, тридця́тий	thirty, -ieth
со́рок, сороко́вий	forty, -ieth
п'ятдеся́т, -ий	fifty, -ieth
шістдеся́т, -ий	sixty, -ieth
сімдеся́т, -ий	seventy, -ieth
вісімдеся́т, -ий	eighty, -ieth
дев'яно́сто, -тий (дев'ятдеся́т, -ий)	ninety, -ieth
сто́, со́тий	hundred, -th

EXPLANATORY NOTES

1. The noun **бабу́ня** 'granny' is a diminutive or affectionate for **ба́ба** 'grandmother'. Since, however, **ба́ба** is also used to designate a peasant woman as well as, in certain circumstances, a vulgar or rude woman, a 'wench', the diminutives **бабу́ня** or **бабу́ся** are usually the terms used for 'grandmother' (**ба́бця** may also be found, but it is dialectal).

2. The historical Cossacks were a brave breed, so the term **коза́к** is used today in describing any brave or gallant man, or simply a stocky, strong fellow. The proverb about the Cossack never dying out is often used by Ukrainians in a wider sense of the entire Ukrainian nation persevering to the end.

3. The expression **ї́хати коне́м** may mean either to ride a horse or to drive a horse. If one wants to be specific, one uses the adverb **ве́рхи** "horseback" (cf. **пішки** for walking 'on foot').

4. The verb **жда́ти** is synonymous with **чека́ти**. Both verbs can be used with the preposition **на**+A. (unrestricted usage), or with direct object (mostly people's designations), or with genitive (mostly abstract notions).

5. The verb (по)**слу́хатися** takes a genitive object:

Він послу́хався сестри́ і пішо́в додо́му.	He listened to his sister and went home.

6. The verb **народи́тися** 'to be born' is also used in the sense 'to have a child':

У не́ї народи́лася дити́на.	She had a baby.

7. The compound adjective **старосві́тський** has two parts, **стари́й** 'old' and **сві́т** 'worldly', 'secular'. The compound noun **рівнопра́вність** consists of the adjective **рі́вний** 'equal', 'straight' and **пра́во** 'law', 'right' with the suffix **-ість** added to it. Compounds are particularly characteristic of bookish and scientific language.

8. The noun нарóд has a parallel form нáрід, with the first being the literary norm and the second reflecting the West Ukrainian speech pattern (this word, like the word Бóг*, собóр, and a few others of Church Slavic origin, does not undergo the o/i alternation). The meaning of the word is rather complex. It may be used as a synonym for лю́ди, i.e. 'a crowd of people'. It may stand for a 'nation' as a national entity, or 'simple folk', 'common people' as opposed to the elite.

9. The traditional respect for older people among the Ukrainians goes back to the ancient times when there was a cult of the ancestors or ancestor worship. Linguistically, this respect shows up in the form of address — one uses the 'plural' polite form ви́ when addresing an older person (among villagers this includes one's own parents).

10. The numeral 90 has two forms, дев'янóсто and дев'ятдеся́т. Today the latter is gaining popularity.

11. Although both слабки́й and слаби́й can be used in the sense of 'weak', the first term is preferred since слаби́й also stands for 'sick' (there is also a verb заслáбнути 'to get sick').

NOTES ON GRAMMAR

I. ADJECTIVAL ADVERBS IN -O

1. Most adjectives have parallel adverbial forms in **-o**. Usually the basic meaning is the same in both, sometimes, however, it is different. cf.:

Identical meaning

Adjective	*Adverb*	*Meaning*
пові́льний	пові́льно	slow — slowly
тóчний	тóчно	exact — exactly
чудóвий	чудóво	wonderful — wonderfully

Different meaning

Adjective	*Adverb*	*Meaning*
рáдий	рáдо	happy — willingly
дóвгий	дóвго	long — for a long time

2. (a) In the majority of cases the stress falls on the same syllable in the adjective and the corresponding **-o** adverb. For example:

цікáвий	—	цікáво
гáрний	—	гáрно
далéкий	—	далéко

2. (b) If the adjective has an end stress the corresponding -o adverb has stress on the first syllable (with the exeption of давнó the final -o is never stressed in adverbs). Thus:

---

* The variant Біг also exists in such expressions as бігмé "by God", пáн Біг "Lord God" (all W.Ukr.), cf. also спаси́бі (see Lesson 12).

близькúй	—	блúзько
важкúй	—	вáжко
голоснúй	—	гóлосно
дорогúй	—	дóрого
легкúй	—	лéгко
молодúй	—	мóлодо
м'якúй	—	м'якo
тяжкúй	—	тя́жко
швидкúй	—	швúдко

2. (c) Some trisyllabic adjectives with the stress on the second syllable have the corresponding adverbs with the stress on the initial syllable. For example:

весéлий	—	вéсело
висóкий	—	вúсоко
дешéвий	—	дéшево
здорóвий	—	здóрово
холóдний	—	хóлодно
ширóкий	—	шúроко

3. The adjective **велúкий** 'great, big, large' has no adverbial **-o** form with the same root. The adverb 'greatly', 'much' is **багáто**.

II. ADJECTIVAL ADVERBS IN -E

Adjectival adverbs in **-e** are much less frequent than those in **-o**. The **-e** forms is standard after sibilants:

байдýжий	—	байдýже
дýжий	—	дýже
гаря́чий	—	гáряче

III. COMPARISON OF ADJECTIVES AND ADVERBS

1. Comparative forms indicate a greater degree of quality* expressed by an adjective or an adverb beginning with the 1st or positive form (the basic non-compared form such as **дóбре** 'good'), 2nd or comparative degree (**крáще** 'better') and 3rd or superlative degree (**найкрáще** 'best').

2. There are two types of comparative forms, simple and compound. The first is formed by suffixation and prefixation and the second by combining the adverbs **більш** 'more' and **найбільш** 'most' with the positive forms.

---

* Comparison can also indicate a lesser degree by means of the adverbs **мéнш** "less" and **наймéнш** "least". Structurally such "negative comparatives" parallel those with the adverbs **більш** "more" and **найбільш** "most".

3. Comparative degree. The great majority of adjectives and adverbs form their comparative degree by means of the suffix -іш- which usually attracts the stress. The ending for the adverbs is -е, the adjective endings remain the same. Thus:

прóстий	—	простíший	прóсто	—	простíше
холóдний	—	холоднíший	хóлодно	—	холоднíше
весéлий	—	веселíший	вéсело	—	веселíше

Note 1: A considerable number of adjectives and adverbs keep the original stress in their comparatives, especially those with the suffixes **-ат-**, **-аст-**, **-ист-**, **-ічн-** (**-ичн-**), **-овит-**. For example: **симпатúчний — симпатúчніший, талановúтий** "talented" — **талановúтіший**. A few comparatives admit both stresses, cf.: **щаслúвий** "happy", — **щаслúвіший** and **щасливíший**, **смілúвий** "bold" — **смілúвіший** and **сміливíший**.

Note 2: In the adjective **рáдий** an -н- is inserted before the suffix **-іш-**: **раднíший**. Comparative of the adverb **рáдо** is **рáдше** (more rarely **раднíше**).

Note 3: An emphatic comparative is formed by adding **ще** before the comparative form: **щé крáще** 'even better'.

4. A limited group of adjectives and adverbs with the root ending in one consonant receives the suffix -ш-. The stress is always on the syllable preceding -ш-:

старúй	—	стáрший (but also старíший)*			
дешéвий	—	дешéвший	дéшево	—	дешéвше
молодúй	—	молóдший	мóлодо	—	молóдше

5. The suffix -ш- is normally added form the comparative of adjectives and adverbs with the suffix **-к-** (**-ок-**, **-ек-**) replacing the latter. E.g.:

лéг-к-о	лег-к-úй	лéг-ше	лéг-ший
шúр-ок-о	шир-óк-ий	шúр-ше	шúр-ш-ий
дал-éк-о	дал-éк-ий	дáлі (дáль-ше)**	дáль-ш-ий
швúд-к-о	швид-к-úй	швúд-ш-е	швúд-ш-ий

Note 1: In adjectives whose stem-final consonant is **з, ж, г** the addition of the suffix -ш- results in the combination **жч**:

блúзь-к-ий	—	блúжчий	блúзь-к-о	—	блúжче
важ-к-úй	—	вáжчий	вáж-к-о	—	вáжче
тяж-к-úй	—	тя́жчий	тя́ж-к-о	—	тя́жче
дорог-úй	—	дорóжчий	дóрог-о	—	дорóжче
дýж-ий	—	дýжчий	дýж-е	—	дýжче
(But лéг-к-о	—	лéгше)			

---

* The first is used in comparing any age, the second only in comparing old age. (see III.8.)

** Some dictionaries list **дáльше** as conversational and **дáлі** as the literary norm.

Note 2: In the adjectives with the stem-final consonant **с** the comparative suffix becomes -щ-:

вис-óк-ий	—	вúщий	вúс-ок-о	—	вúще

Note 3: In the adjectives **дóвгий** and the adverb **дóвго** the stem-final consonant -г is dropped in the comparative form:

дóвг-ий	—	дóвший	дóвго	—	дóвше

6. A small number of adjectives and adverbs has a different root in their comparative degree. These are:

велúкий	—	більший	багáто	—	більше
малúй	—	мéнший	мáло	—	мéнше
погáний	—	гірший	погáно	—	гірше
дóбрий	—	крáщий*	дóбре	—	крáще
(‘good’)	—	(also лíпший)		—	(also лíпше)
гáрний	—	крáщий	гáрно	—	крáще

7. The final -е in adverbial comparatives formed by means of the suffix -іше- may be dropped:

скóро	—	скорíше and скорíш
рáно	—	ранíше and ранíш
вéсело	—	веселíше and веселíш

In adverbial comparatives formed by means of the suffix **-ше** the final -е- may be dropped only if the stem-final consonant preceding the suffix -ш- is **р, л (ь)** or **н**:

пéрший	—	пéрше or пéрш
погáно	—	гірше or гірш
багáто	—	більше or більш
мáло	—	мéнше or мéнш

8. The adjective старúй has two comparative forms, стáрший (‘older’ comparing people of any age) and старíший (‘older’ comparing old people, buildings, etc.).

9. The compound comparative consists of the adverb plus the positive form of the adjective or the adverb. It is identical in meaning to the simple form but is more typical of the written rather than the conversational language.** Both forms are declined, e.g.:

Я́ читáю цікавíшу (більш цікáву) книжку.
I am reading a more interesting book.

---

* **Дóбрий** in its other meaning “kind” has a regular comparative **добрíший**.

** Some linguists are opposed to using such compound forms considering them non-Ukrainian in origin (a Russian influence).

10. The superlative or the highest comparative degree is formed by adding the prefix **най-** to the comparative degree:

кра́щий	—	найкра́щий	кра́ще	—	найкра́ще
бі́льший	—	найбі́льший	бі́льше	—	найбі́льше
ме́нший	—	найме́нший	ме́нше	—	найме́нше

The compound superlative consists of the adverb **найбі́льш** (or **найме́нш** in "negative comparison") plus the positive form of the adjective:

Це́й профе́сор мені́ найбі́льш симпати́чний.
This professor appears to me best of all.

Ця́ робо́та найме́нш ціка́ва.
This job is the least interesting.

The two-word superlatives are typical for official or scientific style, while the simple superlative belongs to belles-lettres and to the conversational language.

11. Use of comparatives.

(a) In making a comparison several types of constructions are used in Ukrainian. In order of frequency they are:

(1) від + G
(2) за + A
(3) ніж (аніж) + N*
(4) як + N.

For example:

(1) Він ста́рший від На́сті.
He is older than Nast'a.

(2) Він ста́рший за На́стю.
He is older than Nast'a.

*** **Аніж** is an emphatic variant of **ніж**.

(3) Вона́ вчи́ться кра́ще, ніж (аніж) він.
She studies better than he.

(4) Вона́ вчи́ться кра́ще, як він.
She studies better than he.

Note 1: In bookish or scientific style type (3) is prefered. In conversational style type (3) is used mostly in comparing inanimate objects. Type (4) has a conversational flavor and is used mostly in adverbal comparisons. Types (1) and (2) are usually found in comparisons of animate beings, though not exclusively.

Note 2: The adjectives **ви́щий, ни́жчий, ста́рший, моло́дший** in combination with certain nouns are used as terminological units without comparative meaning. E.g.: **ви́ща шко́ла** "school of higher learning", **ни́жчий со́рт** "low grade", **ста́рший лейтена́нт** "senior lieutenant", **моло́дший науко́вий працівни́к (робітни́к)** "junior research assistant".

Constructions involving superlatives can also be of several types. For example:

(1) з, серед + G. ('of', 'among')
(2) між + I. ('among')
(3) за, від + усе́ (усі́х) ('of all')

For example:

(1) Він найкра́щий з на́ших студе́нтів.
He is the best of our students.

Він найви́щий серед ни́х.
He is the tallest among them.

(2) Він найста́рший між ни́ми.
He is the oldest among them.

(3) Вона́ кра́ща за (від) всі́х дівча́т.
She is the prettiest of all the girls.

Note: Many comparatives can occur in constructions of type (3) above **(за всі́х, все́, від усі́х)** thus acquiring the meaning of superlatives:

На́стя моло́дша від усі́х у кля́сі.
Nast'a is the youngest one in class.

Більш за все́ він любив плава́ти.
Most of all he loved swimming.

The comparative **кра́щий** can have the superlative meaning not only in such constructions but also in combination with various nouns, e.g.: **кра́щий студе́нт факульте́ту, кра́щий у мі́сті готе́ль.**

(Exercises 1-6)

IV. MASCULINE SHORT ADJECTIVES

Certain masculine adjectives besides the regular **-ий** ending can have a zero form. These are:

ва́ртий/ва́рт	worthy
ви́нний/ви́нен	guilty; owes (owing)
гото́вий/гото́в	ready
зго́дний/зго́ден	willing
здоро́вий/здоро́в	well, healthy; greetings!
ко́жний/ко́жен	every, each
ла́дний/ла́ден	ready, capable
ласка́вий/ласка́в	kind
пе́вний/пе́вен	sure, certain
по́вний/по́вен	full
пови́нний/пови́нен	must, obliged
потрі́бний/потрі́бен	needed, necessary
ра́дий/ра́д	glad, happy

Note: If the root ends in two consonants, the vowel -е- is inserted before **н** and -о- before **в**.

Most of these adjectives, namely: **ва́рт, ви́нен, гото́в, зго́ден, ла́ден, пе́вен, по́вен, пови́нен, потрі́бен, ра́д** function as predicates. For example:

Кому́ він потрі́бен?	Who needs him?
Я́ пе́вен, що він тобі́ ви́нен гро́ші.	I am sure he owes you money.
Ти́ пови́нен зна́ти, чи він зго́ден ї́хати.	You should know whether he is willing to go.

Ко́жен is used in the sense of "anyone", "everyone", or as a modifier:

Ко́жен тобі́ це́ ска́же.	Anyone will tell you that.
Ко́жен де́нь ти́ пови́нен тро́хи відпочива́ти.	Every day you should take some rest.

Здоро́в and **ласка́в** are used mostly in set expressions such as **Бу́дь здоро́в!** "Good-bye" (or "Greetings") and **Бу́дь ласка́в, зроби́ це́.** "Be so kind and do it".

Note: A number of other adjectives appear in the short form in poetry and in folklore both in the predicative function and as modifiers (in N. and A.).

1. The short form is regular for masculine possessive adjectives. Their nominative endings are **-ин (-їн), -ів (-їв)**. The other case forms are the same as with the regular masculine adjectives and they function as modifiers or predicates. For example:

Це́й кі́нь ба́тьків, а то́й Андрі́їв.
This horse is father's and that one is Andrij's.

На́стин ли́ст до́вгий, а Марі́їн ще́ до́вший.
Nast'a's letter is long and Marija's still longer.

V. NUMERALS 11 TO 100. FORM AND SPELLING

1. All numbers from 11 through 19 end in **-на́дцять** with the stress on **-а**

оди́н	+	надцять	=	одина́дцять
два́	+	надцять	=	двана́дцять
три́	+	надцять	=	трина́дцять
чоти́ри	+	надцять	=	чотирна́дцять
п'я́ть	+	надцять	=	п'ятна́дцять
ші́сть	+	надцять	=	шістна́дцять
сі́м	+	надцять	=	сімна́дцять
ві́сім	+	надцять	=	вісімна́дцять
де́в'ять	+	надцять	=	дев'ятна́дцять

Note the spelling of **одина́дцять** (one **н**), **чотирна́дцять** (no **и** after **р**), and **п'ятна́дцять, шістна́дцять, дев'ятна́дцять** where the /t'/ becomes hard before **-на́дцять**.

2. Numbers 50, 60, 70, 80 end in **-craft**. The /t'/ before **-деся́т** becomes hard:

п'ятдеся́т
шістдеся́т
сімдеся́т
вісімдеся́т

3. Ninety is **дев'яно́сто** and hundred is **сто́**.

Note: The form **дев'ятдеся́т** for 90 is more typical for W. Ukr.

VI. DATES: MONTHS AND DAYS

1. All the names of the months in Ukrainian are nouns except the name for February **лю́тий** which is an adjective. The vowel **-е-** of the last syllable in all these nouns appears only in the nominative and the accusative but is absent in all other cases (the so-called "fleeting vowel"): **сі́чень — сі́чня, бе́резень — бе́резня, кві́тень — кві́тня**, etc. The first letter is not capitalized.

2. When quoting the date, the day or the month are given in the nominative if they are quoted separately. If they are given together, the day is in the nominative and the month is in the genitive:

Яки́й тепе́р мі́сяць?	What is the month now?
Тепе́р жо́втень.	It's October.
Котре́ сього́дні число́?	What's the date today?
Сього́дні шістна́дцяте.	Today is the sixteenth.
Сього́дні шістна́дцяте жо́втня.	Today is the sixteenth of October.

Note 1: The word order may not be reversed in the day and month dates as in English (October 16th).

Note 2: In the past tense the verb is either in the neuter or masculine depending on the subject:

Бу́в жо́втень.	It was October.
Вчо́ра було́ шістна́дцяте (число́).	Yesterday was the 16th.
Вчо́ра було́ шістна́дцяте жо́втня.	Yesterday was October 16th.

Note 3: In writing out dates when numbers are used instead of words the following abbreviations are common:

Сього́дні 16-е	Today is the 16th.
Сього́дні 12.X (12-е/X).	Today is 10.12.

3. The date of an event is expressed by the genitive of the numeral indicating the day (**пе́ршого** "on the first") and by the preposition **в + L.** of the name of the month, if either the day or the month are quoted alone:

Котро́го числа́ він приї́хав?	What day did he come?
Він приї́хав пе́ршого.	He came on the first.
У яко́му мі́сяці він приї́хав?	What month did he come?
Він приї́хав у тра́вні.	He came in May.

If the date of an event includes both the day and the month they are given in the genitive:

Коли́ це́ було́?	When was it?
Це́ було́ пе́ршого тра́вня.	It was on the first of May.

Note: The date on a letter is also given in the genitive: **пе́ршого тра́вня** (or **1-го тра́вня**, or 1.V., or 1/V).

(Exercises 9-12).

VII. TELLING AGE

1. The question "How old are you?" is expressed by **скі́льки ро́ків** plus dative of the noun or pronoun (literally "How many years /are/ to you?", with omission of the present-tense of the verb "to be"):

Скі́льки тобі́ ро́ків?	How old are you?
Мені́ шістна́дцять.	I am sixteen.
А скі́льки ро́ків твої́й сестрі́ О́лі?	And how old is your sister Ol'a?
Ї́й чотирна́дцять ро́ків.	She is fourteen years old.

When asking the age of a baby the expression **скільки місяців** is used instead:

Скільки місяців цій дити́ні?	How old is this baby? (= How many months...)
Ї́й два́ місяці.	It's two months old.

Note: A baby's age may be expressed in terms of months only up to eleven months.

2. In the past tense and in the future tense such questions require the use of the verb "to be" (**було́** in the first case and **бу́де** in the second).

Скільки йому́ було́ ро́ків (місяців)?	How old was he?
Скільки йому́ бу́де ро́ків (місяців)?	How old will he be?

3. A statement about a person's age involves the dative of the noun or pronoun designating the person. The quantity expression is the subject, and the verb is either zero (in the present tense), or **бу́де** in the future. In the past tense the verb is **бу́в** if the ages is "one" (**оди́н рік, місяць**) or a number ending in **оди́н** (**два́дцять оди́н рік**); otherwise it is **було́:**

Йому́ оди́н рік, а ї́й два́ ро́ки.
He is one and she is two years old.

Йому́ бу́де оди́н рік, а ї́й бу́де два́ ро́ки.
He will be one and she will be two years old.

Йому́ бу́в оди́н рік, а ї́й було́ два́ ро́ки.
He was one and she was two years old.

Йому́ бу́в два́дцять оди́н рік, а ї́й було́ два́дцять два́ ро́ки.
He was twenty one and she was twenty two years old.

4. The idea of "turning" a certain age or being "passed" a certain age is expressed by the dative of the noun/pronoun referring to the person, and an ordinal numeral indicating the age. The verbs are **іти́** for being "in the year" and **мину́ти/мина́ти** for the year that has passed (or is about to end). In the past tense the verbs are in the masculine agreeing with the subject **рік**:

Ї́й іде́ (ішо́в) шістна́дцятий рік.	She is (was) in her sexteenth year.
Ї́й мина́є (мину́в) шістна́дцятий рік.	She is almost (just turned) seventeen.

5. Formerly the noun **лі́то** was used in the sense of "year". Today, the plural form **лі́та** (G. **лі́т**) may be used to refer to age or a period of time, as an equivalent of **роки́**. It has a poetic flavor but can be heard in colloquial speech also. The expression **Мно́гії лі́та!** (or its Church Slavic equivalent **Мно́гая лі́та!**) is used when wishing someone a long life, "many happy returns".

ВПРАВИ

I. Give the comparative forms of adjectives according to the model:

Вона́ **до́бра.** А він **добрі́ший** за не́ї.

(весе́ла, стара́, молода́, висо́ка, че́мна, здоро́ва, симпати́чна, пога́на, про́ста)

II. Give the comparative forms of adverbs according to the model:

Це́ ду́же **дале́ко.** А це ще **да́лі.**

(до́бре, пога́но, га́рно, ма́ло, ви́соко, бли́зько, ва́жко, де́шево, до́рого, га́ряче)

III. Give the comporative forms of adjectives according to the model:

Ця́ дівчина **висо́ка.** А та́ дівчина ще **ви́ща.**

1. Ця жінка молода́.
2. Це́й кінь си́льний.
3. Це́ завда́ння важке́.
4. Це́й рід стари́й.
5. Це́ крісло зру́чне.
6. Ці́ ви́шні сві́жі.
7. Ця́ пра́ця пога́на.
8. Ці́ квитки́ дорогі́.
9. Це́ пита́ння про́сте.
10. Це́й по́гляд пра́вильний.

IV. Change the sentences replacing adverbs and adjectives by corresponding comparatives:

1. Ту́т ма́ло місця.
2. У не́ї бага́то ене́ргії.
3. Тре́ба до́вго чека́ти.
4. Це́ дале́ко від на́с.
5. Ту́т Дніпро́ широ́кий.
6. Ва́м бу́де ва́жко зрозуміти.
7. Це́й літа́к лети́ть шви́дко.
8. Це́ ле́гко діста́ти.
9. Я ляга́ю спа́ти пізно.
10. Вона́ виглядає мо́лодо.

V. Provide the questions supplying the superlatives.

Ту́т усі́ **си́льні.** Хто ту́т **найсильні́ший?**

(молоді́, весе́лі, че́мні, низькі́, голо́дні, висо́кі, здоро́ві, старі́, пога́ні, га́рні)

VI. Replace the compound superlatives by their non-compound equivalents.

1. Це́ найбільш про́сте завда́ння.
2. Це́ найбільш че́мний ли́ст.
3. Це́ найбільш до́вга ву́лиця.
4. Це́ найбільш широ́ка ву́лиця.
5. Це́ найбільш висо́кий буди́нок у світі.
6. Це́ найбільш ціка́ві вірші.
7. Це́ найбільш дороги́й готе́ль.
8. Це́ найбільш деше́ве місце.
9. Це́ найбільш легка́ валізка.
10. Це́ найбільш тяжке́ пита́ння.

VII. Give the complete answers using the numbers in brackets.

1. Скільки йому́ ро́ків? (55)
2. Скільки тобі ро́ків? (24)
3. Скільки ї́й ро́ків? (60)
4. Скільки ї́м ро́ків? (1)
5. Скільки ва́м ро́ків? (19)
6. Скільки йому́ ро́ків? (32)
7. Скільки ї́й ро́ків? (4)
8. Скільки ї́м ро́ків? (11)
9. Скільки ва́м ро́ків? (16)
10. Скільки йому́ ро́ків? (14)

VIII. State the difference in age according to the model.

1. Йому́ 11, а ї́й 10. Він ста́рший від не́ї на оди́н рік.
2. Йому́ 12, а ї́й 8. Він . . . . .
3. Йому́ 70, а ї́й 30. Він . . . . .
4. Йому́ 50, а ї́й 20. Він . . . . .
5. Йому́ 91, а ї́й 90. Він . . . . .
6. Йому́ 100, а ї́й 80. Він . . . . .
7. Йому́ 29, а ї́й 19. Він . . . . .
8. Йому́ 38, а ї́й 18. Він . . . . .
9. Йому́ 47, а ї́й 17. Він . . . . . .
10. Йому́ 56, а ї́й 16. Він . . . . .

IX. Name the required months.

1. Тепе́р пе́рший мі́сяць ро́ку. Тепе́р сі́чень.
2. Тепе́р шо́стий мі́сяць ро́ку. Тепе́р . . . . .
3. Тепе́р тре́тій мі́сяць ро́ку. Тепе́р . . . . .
4. Тепе́р деся́тий мі́сяць ро́ку. Тепе́р . . . . .
5. Тепе́р во́сьмий мі́сяць ро́ку. Тепе́р . . . . .

6. Тепéр дванáдцятий мíсяць рóку. Тепéр . . . . .
7. Тепéр сьóмий мíсяць рóку. Тепéр . . . . .
8. Тепéр дев'ятий мíсяць рóку. Тепéр . . . . .
9. Тепéр дрýгий мíсяць рóку. Тепéр . . . . .
10. Тепéр четвéртий мíсяць рóку. Тепéр . . . . .
11. Тепéр одинáдцятий мíсяць рóку. Тепéр . . . . .
12. Тепéр п'ятий мíсяць рóку. Тепéр . . . . .

X. Answer the questions giving the following month.

1. Чи ти́ народи́вся в сíчні? Ні́, в лю́тому.
2. Чи ти́ народи́вся в жóвтні? Ні́, ...
3. Чи ти́ народи́вся в ли́пні? Ні́, ...
4. Чи ти́ народи́вся в сéрпні? Ні́, ...
5. Чи ти́ народи́вся в квíтні? Ні́, ...
6. Чи ти́ народи́вся в грýдні? Ні́, ...
7. Чи ти́ народи́вся в лю́тому? Ні́, ...
8. Чи ти́ народи́вся в трáвні? Ні́, ...
9. Чи ти́ народи́вся в вéресні? Ні́, ...
10. Чи ти́ народи́вся в чéрвні? Ні́, ...

XI. Write out the dates.

1. Сьогóдні 21.X
2. Сьогóдні 3.II
3. Сьогóдні 16.IX
4. Сьогóдні 2.III
5. Вчóра булó 30.I
6. Вчóра булó 28.XII
7. Вчóра булó 1.XI
8. Вчóра булó 19.VIII
9. Зáвтра бýде 20.IV
10. Зáвтра бýде 12.VII

XII. Write out the dates.

1. Котрóго числá він при́йде? 18.XI
2. Котрóго числá ви́ при́йдете? 22.II
3. Котрóго числá вони́ при́йдуть? 31.I
4. Котрóго числá ти́ при́йдеш? 17.VIII
5. Котрóго числá вонá при́йде? 5.V
6. Котрóго числá ви́ цé одéржали? 15.X
7. Котрóго числá вони́ переї́хали? 4.IV
8. Котрóго числá ви́ йогó очíкуєте? 14.XII
9. Котрóго числá вони́ одружи́лися? 7.VII
10. Котрóго числá ви́ ї́м написáли? 27.III
11. Котрóго числá починáються íспити? 19.VI
12. Котрóго числá ви́ летитé до буди́нку відпочи́нку? 20.IX

XIII. Read and translate.

1. Скóро бýде дéнь нарóдження моєї сестри́ Зіни, а я́ не знáю, щó ї́й подарувáти. Вонá народи́лася 1-го сíчня, якрáз на Нови́й рік, і я́ вжé подарувáла ї́й сýкню і тепéр не мóжу ви́рішити, щó ї́й щé подарувáти. Щé однý сýкню? Цé бýде забагáто, і, крім тóго, я́ знáю, що взагалі Зíну бíльше цікáвлять книжки́, ніж сýкні. Куплю́ кни́жку. Алé якý? Трéба щóсь про Украї́ну, алé щó сáме?*. Зíна лю́бить украї́нські пíсні. Я́ недáвно бáчила в крамни́ці новý кни́гу** "Козáцькі пíсні і дýми"***. Ця́ кни́жка дóсить дорогá, алé дешéвша за тý, якý Нáстя подарувáла своі́й мáтері, про сéла й мíста Украї́ни.

2. Зáвтра 22-е сíчня, вели́ке украї́нське свя́то: 22-е сíчня украї́нський нарóд гóлосно сказáв усьóму свíту, що хóче жи́ти свої́м життя́м на своі́й землí, бýти "сáм собí пáн". Ми́ в шкóлі з нáшим учи́телем Василéм Михáйловичем Гончарéнком ви́вчили кíлька вíршів про 22-е сíчня. Нáш хóр співáтиме кíлька пісéнь, а я́ мáю сказáти декíлька слíв про цé вели́ке свя́то. Я́ люблю́ такí свя́та набагáто**** бíльше, ніж усякí днí смéрти. Чомý нáш нарóд тáк лю́бить дáти***** смéрти свої́х герóїв?******. І пісéнь стíльки співáють про смéрть козакá, я́к він помирáв абó помéр. Ви́дно,******* такá вжé в нáс істóрія, що ми́ не мóжемо не дýмати про ти́х, хтó помéр за свíй нарóд. Трéба ї́х пам'ятáти.

3. Нáші студéнти говори́ли про рівноправність жінóк. Чи мóже бýти спрáвжня рівноправність між жінкою і чоловíком? Мáйже всí казáли, що тáк, а хтóсь заввáжив, що на Украї́ні давнó булá і є тради́ція рівноправности жінóк, про цé говóрить уся́ нáша істóрія. Бори́с відповíв, що, на йогó дýмку, спрáвжньої рівноправности щé не булó нідé, включáючи Украї́ну, алé тепéр часи́ інші і рівноправности бíльше, ніж булó ранíше. Профéсор Гончарéнко, яки́й прийшóв нас послухáти, сказáв, що він бáчить, я́к молоді лю́ди тепéр інáкше ди́вляться на ці рéчі, ніж нáвіть ї́хні батьки́, не кáжучи вжé про дідíв.

REVIEW

XIV. Translate into Ukrainian.

1. You must have supper with us.
2. We saw a cathedral with a golden dome.
3. He told us about his father's cherry orchard.
4. I left the money at home.
5. Sit close to me.

---

* що сáме = exactly what

** кни́га = кни́жка

*** дýма = a kind of historical song

**** набагáто = much, by far

***** дáта = date

****** герóй; герóї = hero

******* ви́дно = it seems

6. Unfortunately, I was late for the concert and didn't hear the first song.
7. It's almost 12:30 and he still isn't here. We have been waiting for almost an hour.
8. She is sorry she decided to take that course.
9. This morning we went swimming and later took a boat and went to the other side.
10. When does the program start?

XV. Answer the question using the words in brackets.

1. Кому́ ти́ прода́в своє́ а́вто? (О́льжин бра́т).
2. Кому́ ти́ дзвони́ла? (Гри́ців ді́д).
3. Кому́ ти́ пи́шеш? (Семе́нів учи́тель).
4. Кому́ ти́ купи́ла цю́ су́кню? (Ната́лчина дочка́).
5. Кому́ ти́ подару́єш цю́ кни́жку? (Оре́стів си́н).
6. Кому́ ти́ обіця́в написа́ти? (Оле́ксин ба́тько).
7. Кому́ ти́ ви́рішила подзвони́ти? (Ле́сина ма́ти).
8. Кому́ ти́ розповів про це́? (Сла́вків това́риш).
9. Кому́ ти́ заважа́єш писа́ти? (Євге́нова това́ришка).
10. Кому́ ти́ це́ поясни́в? (Богда́нів у́чень).

XVI. Supply the appropriate objects (nouns or pronouns).

1. Він не слу́хається . . . . .
2. Вона́ жде́ . . . . .
3. Вони́ зберіга́ють . . . . .
4. Я́ кли́чу . . . . .
5. Ми́ огляда́ли . . . . .
6. Ти́ пришле́ш . . . . .
7. Про́шу, поясні́ть . . . . .
8. . . . . . хо́четься . . . . .
9. Тре́ба порахува́ти . . . . .
10. Ви́ мо́жете повезти́ . . . . .

XVII. Supply the appropriate verbs.

1. Ми́ . . . . . ви́шні.
2. Вони́ . . . . . до рестора́ну.
3. Діти́ . . . . . у Дніпрі.
4. Вони́ . . . . . в нови́й буди́нок.
5. Він . . . . . життя́ на Украї́ні.
6. Чо́вен . . . . . в інший бік.
7. Коза́к . . . . . коне́м.
8. Вона́ . . . . . як стара́ ба́ба.
9. Ця́ дити́на . . . . . в гру́дні.
10 З ха́ти . . . . . стари́й ді́д.

XVIII. Supply the demonstrative pronouns and appropriate adjectives.

1. Ми́ оглядáли . . . . . собóр.
2. Йомý подарувáли . . . . . годи́нник.
3. На ні́й булá . . . . . сýкня.
4. Ми́ познайóмилися з . . . . . студéнткою.
5. Вони́ співáли . . . . . пісні́.
6. Вонá називáла йогó . . . . . íменем.
7. Ві́н вдягнýвся в . . . . . сорóчку.
8. Лягáйте на . . . . . ліжко.
9. Сідáйте на . . . . . крíсло.
10. Ми́ були́ на . . . . . концéрті.

XIX. Write out the numbers and supply the noun endings.

1. У мéне 4 дол. . . . . , а у тéбе 14 дол. . . . .
2. У ни́х 2 квит. . . . . , а у нáс 12 квит. . . . .
3. Я́ з'ї́в 3 варéник. . . . . , а вони́ з'ї́ли 13 варéник. . . . .
4. Я́ взя́в 15 я́блук. . . . . , а ти́ 5 я́блук. . . . .
5. Ві́н прислáв 2 книж. . . . . , а вонá прислáла 6 книж. . . . .
6. Ви́ заспівáєте 1 пісн. . . . . , а ми́ заспівáємо кі́лька . . . . .
7. Я́ мáю 1 завдáн. . . . . , а ти́ мáєш 11 завдáн. . . . . .
8. Ми́ мáємо 1 чóвен, а вони́ мáють 3 . . . . .
9. Звíдси ви́дно 1 церкв. . . . . , а звíдти ви́дно 2 . . . . .
10. Ві́н описáв 2 міст. . . . . , а вонá описáла 4 міст. . . . .

XX. Continue the dialogues as in the model:

- Вони́ не співáють.
Скажíть, щоб вони́ співáли.
- Співáйте!

(не купáються, не вдягáються, не слýхаються, не сíдають, не вихóдять, не плáвають, не лягáють спáти, не вечéряють, не починáють, не кінчáють)

XXI. Continue the dialogues as in the model:

Вони́ не хóчуть цé зроби́ти.
- Скажíть, щоб вони́ цé зроби́ли.
Зробíть цé!

(ї́х покли́кати, ї́х повести́ туди́, цé прислáти, туди́ переї́хати, цé продáти, цé порахувáти, підождáти, ви́йти, цé показáти, цé поясни́ти)

XXII. Answer the following questions to the reading passages.

(1)

1. Щó скóро бýде?
2. Чогó не мóже ви́рішити сестрá Зіни?
3. Яки́й подарýнок дістáла Зіна на Нови́й рік?
4. Щó Зіну цікáвить?
5. Якá кни́жка дешéвша?

(2)

1. Якé свя́то 22-го сíчня?
2. Щó ви́вчили ýчні?
3. З ки́м вони́ цé ви́вчили?
4. Щó щé бýде в прогрáмі?
5. Які свя́та лю́бить нарóд?
6. Які пісні співáють в нарóді?
7. Чомý ї́х лю́блять співáти?

XXIII. Answer the following questions to the dialogues.

"Козáцькому рóду немá перевóду"

1. Скíльки бабýні рóків?
2. Я́к вонá виглядáє?
3. Яки́й у Марти́на бýв дíд?
4. Щó Нáстя кáже про Марти́нову роди́ну?

"Коли́ ти́ народи́вся?"

1. Коли́ народи́вся Бори́с?
2. Коли́ народи́лася Зіна?
3. Скíльки ї́й бýде рóків?
4. Чомý вонá мáє слýхатися Бори́са?
5. Чи цé прáвильний пóгляд?
6. Про якý тради́цію кáже Бори́с?
7. Прóти чóго Зіна нічóго не мáє і чомý?

СІМНАДЦЯТА ЛЕКЦІЯ

46 Страшна спека
Terrible heat

Dialogue Paticipants:
Марі́я - М, Петро́ - П; Marija - M, Petro - P

1.	П-	До́брий ве́чір, ми́ла! Я́к у те́бе пройшо́в де́нь?	P-	Hi, dear! How did your day go?
2.	М-	Втоми́лася, як звича́йно. Ці́лий де́нь на нога́х, ні хвили́ни не відпочива́ла. А ту́т ще́ й ця́ страшна́ спе́ка.	M-	I'm tired as usual. I was on my feet all day long, didn't rest for a minute. And on top of everything there is that terrible heat.
3.	П-	Спра́вді, у на́с у ха́ті нема́ чи́м ди́хати. Хо́чеш, пі́демо вве́чері в кіно́? Там охоло́джене пові́тря.	P-	Really, you can't breathe in this house. Would you like to go to the movies tonight? It's air-conditioned.
4.	М-	До́бра ду́мка. Подиви́сь, що́ сього́дні йде́.	M-	Good idea. Check what's playing tonight.
5.	П-	За́раз подивлю́ся. Ту́т на ро́зі то́й са́мий фі́льм, що й мину́лого ти́жня, а в університе́ті що́сь про Кана́ду: "По го́рах, річка́х та озе́рах Кана́ди".	P-	Just a moment, I'll check. Here at the corner they have the same movie as last week, and at the university there's something about Canada, "Along the Mountains, Rivers and Lakes of Canada".
6.	М-	Чудо́во! Повече́ряємо й пі́демо.	M-	Wonderful! We will have supper and go.

47 Помий руки
Wash your hands

Dialogue Paticipants:
Тетя́на Миха́йлівна - Т, Сла́вко - С
Tetjana Myxajlivna - T, Slavko - S

1. С- Ма́мо, чого́ в те́бе на оча́х сльо́зи?
2. Т- Це́ тому́, що я́ кра́яла цибу́лю.
3. С- А я́ ду́мав, що ти́ пла́чеш.
4. Т- Ні́, це́ лише́ вигляда́є, ні́би я́ пла́чу. О́сь ба́чиш: я́ сміюся.
5. С- Це́ до́бре. А що́ ти ва́риш?
6. Т- Бо́рщ, а на дру́ге я́ сма́жу котле́ти.
7. С- А що́ це́ та́м у печі́?
8. Т- Це́ я́ печу́ пиріжки́ з м'я́сом.
9. С- Вони́ та́к сма́чно вигляда́ють. Мо́жна мені́ оди́н?
10. Т- За́раз ні́, ско́ро бу́демо обі́дати. Підожди́! Покажи́ мені́ свої́ ру́ки. І пра́ву, й лі́ву. Звича́йно, брудні́. Ма́йже чо́рні.
11. С- Ма́мо, вони́ не брудні́, вони́ чи́сті. Це́ в ме́не на рука́х фа́рба.
12. Т- І фа́рба, і бру́д. Іди́ за́раз поми́й гаря́чою водо́ю з ми́лом.
13. С- Ну́, до́бре.

1. S- Mom, why do you have tears in your eyes?
2. T- It's because I was slicing onions.
3. S- And I thought you were crying.
4. T- No, it just looks as if I'm crying. See, I'm laughing.
5. S- That's fine. What are you cooking?
6. T- Borsht, and for the second course I'm frying some meat patties.
7. S- And what's that in the oven?
8. T- I'm baking some meat pies.
9. S- They look so tasty. May I have one?
10. T- Not now, we'll soon have dinner. Wait! Show me your hands. Both the left and the right. Dirty, of course. Almost black.
11. S- Mom, they are not dirty, they are clean. That's paint on my hands.
12. T- Paint and dirt. Go and wash them right away with soap and hot water.
13. S- O.K.

48 Батько пам'ятає війну
Father remembers the war

Dialogue Paticipants:
Васи́ль Миха́йлович - В, Ма́рта - М
Vasyl' Myxajlovyč - V, Marta - M

1.	М- Васи́лю Миха́йловичу, чи ви́ пам'ята́єте Дру́гу світову́ війну́?	M- Vasyl' Mychajlovyč, do you remember World War II?
2.	В- Ні, Ма́рто. Я́ ж народи́вся в ти́сяча дев'ятсо́т со́рок п'я́тому ро́ці. Це́ бу́в оста́нній рік війни́. О́сь мі́й ба́тько, то́й мо́же тобі́ бага́то розповісти.	V- No, Marta. I was born in 1945. That was the last year of the war. But my father, he could tell you a lot.
3.	М- А коли́ він народи́вся?	M- When was he born?
4.	В- Ти́сяча вісімсо́т дев'яно́сто дев'я́того ро́ку. Він пам'ята́є не тільки оста́нню війну́, але́ й пе́ршу світову́ і громадя́нську. Тоді на на́ших зе́млях було́ спра́вжнє пе́кло: і бі́лі, і черво́ні, і украї́нці, і поля́ки, і росія́ни, і ні́мці — усі́ пролива́ли кро́в, свою́ й чужу́.	V- 1899. He remembers not only the last war but also the First World War and the civil war. That's when there was real hell in our land: the Whites, and the Reds, Ukrainians and Poles, Russians and Germans, they all spilled blood, other's and their own.
5.	М- Та́к, я́ чита́ла про це́, але́ мені́ було́ б ду́же ціка́во послу́хати кого́сь, хто́ це́ ба́чив на вла́сні о́чі.	M- Yes, I have read about it but it would be interesting to hear someone who saw it with his own eyes.

СЛОВНИК

бі́лий	white
брýд, -у (m)	dirt
брудни́й	dirty
вари́ти, вáрять I	to cook/boil
звари́ти, звáрять P	
вечéряти, -ють I	to supper
повечéряти, -ють P	
відпочивáти, -ють I	to rest
відпочи́ти, -нуть P	
війнá; вíйни, вóєн (f)	war
вісімсóт	800
влáсний	own
водá, вóду, вóди, вóд (f)	water
громадя́нський	civil
дев'ятсóт	900
ди́хати, -ють I	to breath
кінó, -á; кíна (n)	movie(s)
котлéта (f)	meat patty
кráяти, -ють I	to slice
покráяти, -ють P	
крóв, -и (f)	blood
лишé	merely, just
лíвий	left
ми́лий	sweet (heart)
ми́ло (n)	soap
ми́ти, -ють I	to wash
поми́ти, -ють P	
м'я́со (n)	meat
нíби	as if
нíмець, нíмця (m)	German (m)
ногá, нóгу; нóги, нíг (f)	foot; leg
обíдати, -ють I	to dine; to have lunch
пообíдати, -ють P	
óзеро; озéра (n)	lake
на óзері	at the lake
остáнній	last (in a series)
охолóджений	cooled
охолóджене повітря	air condition
пéкло (n)	hell
пекти́, -чýть I	to bake, to roast
спекти́, -чýть P	
пíч, пéчі, у печí;	stove, oven
пéчі, печéй, у пéчах (f)	

пиріжóк, -жкá; -жки́ (m)	small pie
плáкати, -чуть I	to cry (pfv. to begin/
заплáкати, -чуть P	to burst out crying)
пові́тря (n)	air
поля́к (m)	Pole
прáвий	right
прохóдити, -жу, -ять I	to pass
пройти́, прóйдуть P	
проливáти, -ють I	to spill
проли́ти, -люють P	
ріг, рóгу, на рóзі; роги́ (m)	corner, horn
рі́чка; рі́чки́ (f)	river
на рі́чці (r'ič͡c'i)	at the river
рукá, рýку; рýки (f)	hand; arm
світови́й	world (adj.)
сльозá; сльози́, слíз (f)	tear
смáжити, -ать I	to fry
посмáжити, -ать P	
смачни́й	tasty
смія́тися, -ються з + G	to laugh
засмія́тися, -ються P	(pfv. to begin to laugh)
спéка (f)	heat
спрáвді	indeed
страшни́й	terrible
ти́сяча; тисячí, ти́сяч (f)	thousand
тóй сáмий	same
утóмлюватися, -ються I	to tire
утоми́тися, -ляться P	
фáрба (f)	paint
цибýля (f) (collective)	onion
червóний	red
чи́стий	clean
чóрний	black

IDIOMS

бáчити на влáсні óчі	to see with one's own eyes
бýти на ногáх	to be on one's feet
ідé фільм	a film is playing
ні + gen.	not a
тóй, хтó	he who

SUPPLEMENT

громадя́нин; громадя́ни	citizen (m)
громадя́нка	citizen (f)
грома́да (f)	community
ли́ти, ллю́, ллю́ть I	to pour
налива́ти, налива́ють I	
нали́ти, наллю́, наллю́ть P	
до Хр. (до Христа́)	B.C.
по Хр. (по Христі́)	A.D.
рр. (роки́; років, рока́х і т.д.)	years
кінотеа́тр (m)	movie theater
ми́р, -у (m)	peace
німе́цький	German (adj)
Німе́ччина (f)	Germany
ні́мка (німке́ня) (f)	German (f)
по́лька (f)	Polish woman
по́льський	Polish (adj)
По́льща (f)	Poland
теа́тр (m)	theater
For #s 200, 300 . . . 1,000,000	see pp. 307-308

EXPLANATORY NOTES

1. The noun спе́ка 'heat' has the same root as пе́кло 'hell', and пекти́ 'to bake', 'to roast'.

2. The noun кіно́ 'cinema', like а́вто 'car', is a foreign borrowing which is declined by emigré Ukrainians who preserve the tradition established in the 1920's (see the Holoskévyč dictionary of 1929). Current Ukrainian dictionaries, however, list these two words as 'indeclinable', which may or may not reflect the actual usage in Ukraine.

3. The verb втоми́тися (perfective aspect) means 'to be tired', i.e. it indicates the result of the process of 'getting tired'. For this reason the past tense of this verb is used to indicate the past or the present situation (depending on the context), cf.:

> Я́ до́вго ходи́в і втоми́вся.
> I walked around for a long time and was (got) tired.
>
> Якщо́ ти́ втоми́лася, іди́ спа́ти.
> If you are tired go to sleep.

The imperfective aspect вто́млюватися indicates a repetitive or habitual situation of getting tired:

> Ві́н шви́дко вто́млюється.
> He tires quickly.

4. The expression на дру́ге means 'as a second course'. Correspondingly, на пе́рше means 'as a first/main course', and на тре́тє or на десе́рт means 'for dessert'.

5. The term **котлéта** in the East Ukrainian usage stands for a kind of hamburger or meat patty, while for the West Ukrainians it means a chop or veal cutlet. On the other hand, when the West Ukrainians say **шнúцель** they mean a meat patty but to the East Ukrainian it stands for a pork or veal chop.

6. The adjective **остáнній** 'last' refers to the last of a series. It may not be used in the sense of 'past':

Минýлий рік бýв його́ остáннім рóком в університéті.
Last year was his last year at the university.

7. **Цибýля** like **картóпля** is a collective noun. One onion is **цибулúна.**

8. The noun for 'taste' is **смáк**, and the verb **смакувáти** refers to the way something tastes, as in 'Мені́ цé смакýє', 'It tastes good to me'. However, the verb 'to taste, to try' is **куштувáти (по-)** 'Ось покуштуй цього хліба', 'Here, taste this bread'.

NOTES ON GRAMMAR

I. LOCATIVE PLURAL OF NOUNS

The locative plural ending of all hard stem nouns is **-ах** and of all the soft stem nouns is **-ях**:

N. pl.	столú	хвилúни	істóрії	хлóпці	відповіді	сéла
L. pl.	столáх	хвилúнах	істóріях	хлóпцях	відповідях	сéлах

Note: The nouns **лю́ди** and **діти** follow the soft declension.

1. The stress in the mobile-stress group (see Lesson 14, p. 247) is the same as in the nominative plural:

Masculine	*Neuter*	*Feminine*	*Pluralia tantum*
братú — братáх	сéла — сéлах	сéстри — сéстрах	лю́ди — лю́дях
синú — синáх	мóря — морях	зéмлі — зéмлях	двéрі — двéрях
лікарі — лікарях	вíкна — вíкнах	книжкú — книжкáх	штанú — штанáх*
батькú — батькáх	словá — словáх	пéчі — пéчах	грóші — грóшах
			діти — дітях

Note: Feminine **c**-type nouns with the stem stress in nominative plural and end stress in the genitive plural keep the end stress throughout the plural declension:

N. pl.	G. pl.	L. pl.
нóчі	ночéй	ночáх
рéчі	речéй	речáх

(Exercises 1, 2, 3, 4, 5)

---

* This noun has a variant **штáнях** with the stress on **а** and a soft /n'/.

II. LOCATIVE PLURAL OF PRONOUNS, ADJECTIVES, ORDINAL NUMERALS AND ОДИН

The locative plural ending for all the above categories is **-их** for hard stems and **-іх** for soft stems; /-j/ stems receive the ending **-їх**:

	(smačn-)	(ost án͡’ n’-)	(t-)	(c-)	(moj-)	(čyj-)
N.sg.	смачн-и́й	оста́нн-ій	т-о́й	ц-е́й	м-і́й	чи́й
N.pl.	смачн-і́	оста́нн-і	т-і́	ц-і́	мо-ї́	чи-ї́
L.pl.	смачн-и́х	оста́нн-іх	т-и́х	ц-и́х	мо-ї́х	чи-ї́х

	(četvért-)	(trét-)	(odn-)	(vs’-)	(jak-)
N.sg.	четве́рт-ий	тре́т-ій	оди́н	уве́сь(вве́сь)	яки́йсь
N.pl.	четве́рт-і	тре́т-і	одн-і́	усі́(вс-і́)	які́сь
L.pl	четве́рт-их	тре́т-іх	одн-и́х	ус-і́х(вс-і́х)	яки́хось

(Exercises 1, 2, 3, 5, 7, 8)

III. THE NUMERALS 200 AND HIGHER

Numbers 200 and higer are as follows: **дві́сті** (200), **три́ста** (300), **чоти́риста** (400), **п’ятсо́т** (500), **шістсо́т** (600), **сімсо́т** (700), **вісімсо́т** (800), **дев’ятсо́т** (900), **ти́сяча** (1,000), **мільйо́н** (1,000.000), **мілья́рд (більйо́н)** (1,000,000.000).

Note 1: Note the spelling of **дві́сті** as opposed to **три́ста** and **чоти́риста**. Note also the hard /t/ of the first part of the compounds **п’ятсо́т, шістсо́т, сімсо́т, вісімсо́т** (800) and **дев’ятсо́т**.

Note 2: Ukrainians (like most Europeans) use the comma for a decimal point and the period to set off thousands. For example:

Ukrainian	**English**
1.000	1,000
1.000.000	1,000,000
10,5	10.5

IV. THE ORDINALS 200th AND HIGHER

The ordinals for numbers 200 to 900 are as follows:

дві́сті	—	двохсо́тий
три́ста	—	трьохсо́тий
чоти́риста	—	чотирьохсо́тий
п’ятсо́т	—	п’ятисо́тий
шістсо́т	—	шестисо́тий
сімсо́т	—	семисо́тий
вісімсо́т	—	восьмисо́тий
дев’ятсо́т	—	дев’ятисо́тий

The ordinals for a thousand, a million, a billion, etc. are formed by adding the suffix **-н-(ий)**:

ти́сяча	—	ти́сячний
мільйо́н	—	мільйо́нний (мільйно́вий —W. Ukr.)

Note: The abbreviations **-ий, -е, -а** (or **-тий, -те, -та**) are used with ordinals in the nominative/accusative cases, in other cases the abbreviations are identical with the corresponding case endings. In the locative plural **-х** is used. For example:

О́сь 200-те мі́сце.	Ві́н на 200-му мі́сці.	Це́ було́ в 20-х рока́х.
Here is seat No. 200.	He is in the 200th place.	It was in the twenties.

(Exercises 6, 9)

V. DATES (YEAR)

To indicate the year the nominative case of cardinal numerals is used for all components except the last, not counting zeroes. The last component is an ordinal number of masculine gender (agreeing with the noun 'year' **рік**):

Бу́в ти́сяча вісімсо́т п'ятдеся́т шо́стий рік	It was the year 1856.
Бу́в ти́сяча вісімсо́т п'ятдеся́тий рік	It was the year 1850.
Бу́в ти́сяча вісімсо́тий рік	It was the year 1800.

1. As with other dates involving the days and the months, the designation of the year is in the nominative case for simple identification without reference to any events which took place within that year.

2. The expressions 'in the year...' may be rendered in two ways as was demonstrated in our dialogues: one is with the preposition **у** followed by the prepositional case of the ordinal numeral (the last digit of the year), or the ordinal is put into the genitive without any preposition. The first is more typical for the spoken language, the second — for the written narrative style. For example:

Вона́ народи́лася в ти́сяча дев'ятсо́т п'ятдеся́т дру́гому ро́ці.
She was born in 1952.

Ти́сяча дев'ятсо́т чотирна́дцятого ро́ку почала́ся Пе́рша світова́ війна́.
In the year 1914 the First World War began.

3. Abbreviation **рр.** stands for 'years', **до Хр. (до Христа́)** means B.C. and **по Хр. (по Христі́)** is A.D. In Ukraine they use **до н.е. (до на́шої е́ри)** for B.C. and **н.е. (на́шої е́ри)** for A.D. For example:

Це́ було́ в 20-х рр. по Хр. (= в двадця́тих рока́х по Христі́)
This was in the 20's A.D.

(Exercises 10, 11)

ВПРАВИ

I. Answer the questions according to the model:

Ба́чите ті нові́ буди́нки? Вони́ живу́ть **у ти́х нови́х буди́нках.**

(оті́ старі́ хати́, ті висо́кі го́ри, ці́ брудні́ кімна́ти, ті нові́ гурто́житки, ї́хні кварти́ри, ті га́рні ву́лиці, ті чудо́ві озе́ра, оті́ малі́ се́ла)

II. Provide the questions according to the model:

О́сь нові́ газе́ти. Що́ ціка́вого **в ци́х нови́х газе́тах**?

(німе́цькі журна́ли, росі́йські книжки́, нові́ словники́, його́ нові́ ві́рші, по́льські фі́льми, ї́хні ві́дповіді, ї́хні пита́ння, оста́нні ле́кції)

III. Answer the questions according to the model:

Чи ви́ були́ в ті́й кімна́ті? Ми́ були́ **в усі́х кімна́тах.**

(на то́му фі́льмі, в ті́й це́ркві, в то́му собо́рі, в то́му поме́шканні, на то́му заво́ді, в ті́й бібліоте́ці, на то́му база́рі, на то́му засі́данні, на ті́й ле́кції)

IV. Change the prepositional phrase to plural.

1. Ді́ти бі́гали по ву́лиці.
2. Вони́ ї́здили по селі́.
3. Ми́ ба́чили таке́ м'ясо лише́ в найкра́щій крамни́ці.
4. Ві́н ходи́в по кімна́ті.
5. Човни́ плили́ по рі́чці.
6. Хло́пці купа́лися в чи́стому о́зері.
7. Ми́ обі́дали в спра́вжньому по́льському рестора́ні.
8. У садку́ га́рні ви́шні.
9. Студе́нти були́ на ва́шій ле́кції.
10. Ні́мці прохо́дили че́рез украї́нське село́.
11. Ми́ були́ на німе́цькому заво́ді.

V. Answer the following questions using the words in brackets.

1. Де́ вони́ сиді́ли? На (ті́ чо́рні стільці́).
2. Де́ вони́ жили́? На (свої́ вла́сні зе́млі).
3. Де́ вони́ лежа́ли? На (які́сь до́брі до́шки).
4. У чо́му вони були́? У (га́рні си́ні сорочки́).
5. На ко́му були́ га́рні сорочки́? На (всі́ ї́хні ді́ти).
6. Де́ вони́ стоя́ли? На (свої́ місця́).

7. На чо́му вони́ спа́ли? На (ці м'які́ ліжка́).
8. На чо́му вони́ писа́ли? На (якісь шматки́ папе́ру).
9. Де́ ви́ це́ знайшли́? У (якісь старі́ словники́).
10. Де́ вони́ навча́лися? На (ви́щі ку́рси).
11. Де́ вони́ це́ пекли́? У (якісь старі́ пе́чі).

VI. Copy the following sentences writing out the numerals.

1. Це́ було́ в 20-х чи́слах мину́лого мі́сяця.
2. Це́ було́ пі́сля війни́, у 50-х рока́х.*
3. Це́ бу́де в 90-х рока́х цього́ столі́ття.
4. Це́ бу́де в 40-х рока́х насту́пного столі́ття.
5. Це́ було́ в 900-х рока́х.**
6. У 60-х рока́х в Украї́ні була́ ду́же ціка́ва літерату́ра.***
7. У 30-х рока́х в Украї́ні бу́в страшни́й го́лод.****
8. У 70-х рока́х мину́лого столі́ття в Украї́ні не мо́жна було́ нічо́го друкува́ти украї́нською мо́вою.*****
9. Громадя́нська війна́ в Украї́ні закінчи́лася в 20-х рока́х.
10. Оста́ннім коза́цьким ге́тьманом бу́в Кири́ло Розумо́вський, у 50-х рока́х XVIII столі́ття. Він бу́в ге́тьманом до 1764-го ро́ку.******

VII. Change to plural everything which can be changed.

1. На́ ва́шій дити́ні га́рна су́кня.
2. На́ твоє́му бра́тові брудні́ штани́.
3. На́ твої́й сестрі́ бі́ла соро́чка.
4. У ньо́го на руці́ дороги́й золоти́й годи́нник.
5. У її́ се́рці спра́вжня любо́в.
6. У ва́шій ду́мці є ло́гіка.
7. На моє́му годи́ннику пе́рша годи́на.
8. У її́ дисерта́ції ціка́ві думки́.
9. На до́шці були́ ма́пи По́льщі та Німе́ччини.
10. На ці́й фотогра́фії на́ші знайо́мі.
11. Чо́рне порося́ бі́гало по ву́лиці.

---

* When the century is understood, it may be omitted.

** This means in the first decade of the XX century (1901, 1902... etc.)

*** The brief renaissance of Ukrainian letters occured in the 1960's. Its representatives were called **шестидеся́тники,** i.e. 'people of the 60's'.

**** **Го́лод** = famine. This was an artificial famine brought on by the government's policy of collectivization.

***** Those were the years of the so-called 'Ems decree' (1876) which forbade Ukrainians to use their native tongue in print, on the stage, in schools.

****** **Ге́тьман** = Hetman (Head of the Cossack state). The Hetmanate was abolished by the decree of Catherine II.

VIII. Answer the questions using the words in brackets

1. У чиї́х ти́ ходи́в штана́х? (ба́тькові)
2. На яки́х ви́ сиділи місця́х? (оста́нні)
3. У яки́х журна́лах ви́ це́ ба́чили? (росі́йські)
4. У чиї́х хата́х вони́ живу́ть? (свої́ вла́сні)
5. На яки́х ві́йнах він бу́в? (усі́)
6. У яки́х су́княх вони́ були́? (бі́лі та блаки́тні)
7. У яки́х книжка́х ви́ це́ чита́ли? (украї́нські та німе́цькі)
8. У яки́х словника́х ви́ це́ знайшли́? (старі́ англі́йські)
9. У яки́х газе́тах ви́ це́ ба́чили? (сього́днішні)
10. На яки́х ме́блях вони́ сиділи? (дорогі́)

IX. Write out the dates.

1. Це́ було́ в 200-ому ро́ці до Хр.
2. Це́ було́ в 300-ому ро́ці по Хр.
3. Це́ було́ у 500х рр. по Хр.
4. Це́ було́ між 100-им і 150-им рока́ми до Хр.
5. Це́ було́ 400-го ро́ці по Хр.
6. Це́ було́ пе́ред 600-им ро́ком до Хр.
7. Це́ було́ пі́сля 700-го ро́ку по Хр.
8. Це́ було́ у 800-х рр. до Хр.
9. Це́ було́ у 900-х рр. по Хр.
10. Бу́в 1.000-ий рі́к по Хр.

X. Write out the dates (see the answers at the bottom of this and the next page)

1. Чи ви́ зна́єте, що́ було́ в Украї́ні у 1187 р.?

(2. у 1918 р. 3. у 1242 р. 4. у 1861 р. 5. у 988 р. 6. 1596 р. 7. у 1709 р. 8. у 1340 р. 9. у 1654 р. 10. у 1035 р. 11. у 1991 р.)*

---

* 1187 - Prince Ihor's famous campaign against the Polovcians
1918 - proclamation of Ukrainian independence by the Ukrainian National Republic (on January 22nd)
1242 - the siege and the destruction of Kyiv by the Tatars.
1861 - liberation of peasants in Ukraine (abolition of serfdom).
988 - Christianization of Rus' by Prince Volodymyr.
1596 - acceptance of Catholicism by some Ukrainian people and clergymen (Union of Brest)
1709 - the battle of Poltava.
1340 - the end of King Danylo's dynasty and of the Galician-Volynian State.
1654 - the Perejaslav treaty with Muscovy (signed by Xmel'nyc'kyj)
1035 - building of the St. Sofia Cathedral in Kyiv under Prince Jaroslav the Wise
1991 - over 90% of Ukraine's citizens vote for independence from the USSR

XI. Write out the dates.

1. 1675-го ро́ку вони́ пере́їхали до Киє́ва.
2. 1530-го ро́ку вони́ пере́їхали до Льво́ва.
3. 1920 ро́ку вони́ пої́хали в Кана́ду.
4. 1880 ро́ку вони́ пої́хали в Аме́рику.
5. 1740 ро́ку вони́ прии́хали до Ха́ркова.
6. 1490 ро́ку вони́ ви́їхали з цього́ мі́ста.
7. 1200 ро́ку вони́ ви́йшли з ци́х зе́мель.
8. 1300 ро́ку вони́ прийшли́ в Украї́ну.
9. 1100 ро́ку вони́ прийшли́ на ці́ землі́.
10. Що бу́де в 2000-му ро́ці?

XII. Translate into Ukrainian.

1. Do you have air-conditioning in your apartment?
2. Yesterday we visited some friends and had the most delicious dumplings with cheese.
3. I am very tired and would like to lie down and get some rest but I still have to type this letter.
4. I don't feel like reading all those German and Polish books.
5. Germans don't like the Poles, the Poles don't like the Germans, and both don't like Ukrainians — how can there be peace on earth?
6. Your hands are dirty. Here is some soap, go and wash your hands.
7. Your eyes are red, have you been crying?
8. If you want to be healthy you must get some fresh air every day.
9. Are you joking, or did you really see it with your own eyes?
10. What's the difference between a civil war and an ordinary war?
11. These pies are with fresh cabbage and those with meat.
12. Do you want your meat patties with potatoes or without?
13. Last month we were at the lake for two weeks.
14. What year were you born?

XIII. Read and translate.

1. Сього́дні така́ спе́ка, що ва́жко ди́хати. У ха́ті га́ряче, як у пе́клі. Я́ відчини́в усі́ ві́кна й две́рі, ду́мав, що бу́де хоч тро́хи свіжі́ше пові́тря — та де́ та́м! На ву́лиці ще гарячі́ше, ні́ж у кімна́тах. Я́ зно́в зачини́в ві́кна — тепе́р уже́ зо́всім нема́ чим ди́хати. Щ́о роби́ти? О́т якби́ було́ а́вто, сі́в би й пої́хав куди́сь на рі́чку або́ на о́зеро. Купа́вся б ці́лий де́нь, сиді́в у воді́ й не вихо́див би́ а́ж до са́мого ве́чора. Але́ а́вта я́ не ма́ю, бо я́ ще сту́дент, і всі́ мої́ гро́ші йдуть на книжки́ і на те́, щоб ма́ти що́ з'ї́сти і в що́ вдягну́тися. Таке́ вже́ життя́. Та це́ не бу́де до́вго, ско́ро закінчу́ університе́т і почну́ працюва́ти — тоді́ й по рестора́нах бу́ду ходи́ти, і дороги́м а́втом ї́здити. А сього́дні, щоб де́нь я́кось шви́дше пройшо́в, піду́, ма́буть, у кіно́: хоч ні́чо́го ціка́вого та́м не поба́чу, поси́джу в холо́днім мі́сці й поди́хаю охоло́дженим пові́трям.

2. Мі́й ді́д зо́всім стари́й, але́ в нього чудо́ва па́м'ять. Він пам'ята́є, як почала́ся війна́ 1914-го ро́ку. Він тоді́ бу́в молоди́м хло́пцем і му́сив іти́ на війну́. По́тім він пам'ята́є, як у 1918-му ро́ці війна́ скінчи́лася і почала́ся громадя́нська. Ота́к у всі́х ци́х ві́йнах пройшло́ усе́ його́ молоде́ життя́. Ді́д лю́бить про це́ розповіда́ти, а ми́ лю́бимо його́

слу́хати. Ми́ йому́ ка́жемо, щоб він описа́в це́ все́ в кни́жці, але́ ді́д не хо́че, ка́же, що він не вміє до́бре писа́ти, о́сь розповіда́ти — це́ і́нша річ. На мою́ ду́мку, він не ма́є ра́ції: то́й, хто́ вміє до́бре розповіда́ти, пови́нен і писа́ти ціка́во.

XIV. Answer the following questions to the above passages.

(1)

1. Чому́ студе́нт відчини́в усі ві́кна?
2. Чому́ не ста́ло кра́ще?
3. Що́ він зроби́в би, якби́ ма́в а́вто?
4. Чому́ в нього́ нема́ а́вта?
5. Що́ він роби́тиме, коли́ закі́нчить університе́т?
6. Що́ він ви́рішив зроби́ти сього́дні?

(2)

1. Що́ ді́д роби́в у 1914 р.?
2. А у 1918 р.?
3. Що́ ка́жуть ді́дові?
4. Що́ він відповіда́є?
5. Хто́ ма́є ра́цію?

XV. Answer the following questions to the dialogues.

"Страшна́ спе́ка"

1. Я́к у Петро́вої дружи́ни мину́в де́нь?
2. Яка́ у Петра́ ду́мка?
3. Що́ сього́дні йде́ в кінотеа́трі?
4. Що́ вони́ ви́рішили?

"Поми́й ру́ки"

1. Чи ма́ти пла́че?
2. Що́ бу́де на обі́д?
3. Що́ Сла́вко хоті́в би з'ї́сти?
4. Чому́ ма́ти ка́же "ні"?
5. Що́ вона́ ба́чить?
6. Що́ Сла́вко поя́снює?
7. Що́ ма́ти відповіда́є?

"Ба́тько пам'ята́є війну́"

1. Чому́ Васи́ль Миха́йлович не пам'ята́є війни́?
2. Коли́ народи́вся його́ ба́тько?
3. Що́ тоді́ було́ в Украї́ні?
4. Які́ ві́йни він пам'ята́є?
5. Що́ було́ б ціка́во?

ВІСІМНАДЦЯТА ЛЕКЦІЯ

 # 49 Ми будемо вишивати
We are going to embroider

Dialogue Paticipants:
Остáп - О, Вáля - В; Ostap - O, Valja - V

1. О- Вáлю, щó тú збирáєшся робúти з усімá цúми ниткáми?
2. В- Вишивáти. Мú з дівчáтами вúрішили вúшити собі сорочкú. Тепéр якрáз вакáції, мáємо багáто часý.
3. О- Прекрáсно, алé у вáс якíсь дúвні кóльори. Невжé вú хóчете вишивáти зелéними ниткáми?
4. В- Ні, ні, зелéні — для тітки Олéни, вонá тепéр вишивáє подýшку, а мú вишивáтимемо за традúцією червóними і чóрними ниткáми.
5. О- Як у пíсні "Двá кóльори"? А я люблю, колú вúшите сúнім, óсь як ті рушникú, що тú вúшила.
6. В- Тáк, я тéж люблю сúній кóлір, алé дівчáта хóчуть мáти спрáвжні полтáвські сорочкú.
7. О- Хóчуть виглядáти Натáлками-полтáвками. Нý, що ж, цé непогáно.

1. O- Valja, what do you intend to do with all that yarn?
2. V- Embroider. The girls and I decided to embroider our shirts. It's vacation now, we have plenty of time.
3. O- Splendid, but you've got some strange colors. Don't tell me you want to embroider with green yarn?
4. V- No, no, the green ones are for aunt Olena, she's embroidering a pillow. We will embroider with red and black yarn, according to tradition.
5. O- Like that song "Two colors"? And I like when it's embroidered in blue, like those towels and the table cloth which you embroidered.
6. V- I know, I like blue too, but the girls want to have genuine Poltava shirts.
7. O- They want to look like Natalka Poltavka. Well, that's fine.

50 Полиці для книжок
Book shelves

Dialogue Paticipants:
Остáп - О, Вáля - В; Ostap - O Valja - V

1. В- Остáпе, щó тú збирáєшся робúти з цúми дошкáми?
2. О- Хóчу зробúти полúці для книжóк.
3. В- Тú ж хотів купúти готóві.
4. О- Тáк, алé я́ передýмав. Хóчу спрóбувати зробúти сáм. Знáєш, приéмно мáти річ, зрóблену влáсними рукáми.
5. В- Звичáйно, і бýде знáчно дешéвше.
6. О- Цьогó я́ не пéвний, бо дошкú кóштували 12 грúвень 75 копíйок, а щé порахýй мíй чáс, днів 3–4 щонаймéнше.
7. В- Нý, чáс не рахýй, тú ж тепéр на вакáціях.
8. О- Тáк, і, мáбуть, роблю́ дурнúцю, що займáюсь такúми речáми під чáс вакáцій, зáмість відпочивáти абó зайня́тися сáдом і горóдом.
9. В- Так для тéбе ж такá робóта — цé і є відпочúнок. І на горóд, і на сáд бýде чáс, óсь побáчиш. Не журúся. Тú занáдто всíм жýришся.
10. О- Дóбре, не бýду журúтися.

1. V- Ostap, what do you intend to do with those boards?
2. O- I want to make some bookshelves.
3. V- But you were going to buy ready made ones.
4. O- Yes, but I changed my mind. I want to try to make them myself. You know, it's gratifying to have something made with your own hands.
5. V- Of course, and will be considerably cheaper.
6. O- I'm not sure of that. See, the boards cost 12 hryvnias 75 copecks and then consider my time, at least 3 or 4 days.
7. V- Well, don't count the time, you're on vacation now.
8. O- That's right, and I'm probably being foolish occupying myself with such things instead of getting some rest or getting busy with the orchard and the vegetable garden.
9. V- But this type of work is your way of relaxing. And there will be enough time instead for gardening too, you will see. Don't worry. You worry too much about everything.
10. O- All right, I won't worry.

51 Книжки треба повертати
The books should de returned

Dialogue Paticipants:
Остáп - О Вáля - В; Ostap - O, Valja - V

1. В- Остáпе, дзвони́в Мико́ла і казáв, щоб ти́ обов'язково поверну́в йому́ книжки́, які ти́ в нього позичив.
2. О- Я́к він мені набри́д із ти́ми книжкáми! Щоти́жня дзвóнить.
3. В- Пéвно. А ти́ я́к ду́мав, що пози́чені книжки́ не трéба повертáти? По-мóєму, не поверну́ти пози́чену кни́жку — цé тé сáме, що її вкрáсти.
4. О- О́т знóв ти́ зі своїми прóповідями! Я́ після вечéрі піду́ й віднесу́ йому назáд йогó нещáсні книжки́.
5. В- Цé не книжки́ нещáсні, а ти́ бу́деш нещáсний, якщó жи́тимеш за таки́ми при́нципами.
6. О- Але ж ти́ знáєш, що я́ щасли́вий, бо я одру́жений з тобóю.
7. В- Яки́й ти́ дипломáт!

1. V- Ostap, Mykola called and said that you must return the books which you borrowed from him.
2. O- I'm sick of him and his books! He keeps calling every week.
3. V- Sure. And what did you think, that borrowed books don't have to be returned? In my opinion a book that's not returned is the same as stolen.
4. O- Here you go again with your sermons. After supper I'll go and take him back his miserable books.
5. V- It's not the books that are miserable but you if you live by such principles.
6. O- But you know that I am happy because I'm married to you.
7. V- What a diplomat!

СЛОВНИК

вакáції (pl. only)	vacation (school)
вишивáти, -ють I	to embroider
ви́шити, -ють P	
ви́шитий	embroidered
віднóсити, -шу, -сять I	to take (carry) back
віднести́, -уть P	
відпочи́нок, -нку (m)	rest
горóд, -у (m)	veg. garden
гри́вня	hryvnia (monetary unit)
ди́вний	strange

диплома́т (m)	diplomat
дурни́ця (f)	foolishness; trifle
жури́тися, жу́ряться I	to worry (about)
зажури́тися, зажу́ряться P (+ I / за + I)	
за (+ I)	according to
займа́тися, -ються I	to engage in, to occupy oneself with
зайня́тися, займу́ся, за́ймуться P (+ I)	
за́між (+ G)	instead of
зана́дто	too, excessively
зеле́ний	green
зна́чно	considerably
зро́блений (з + G)	made (of); done
ко́лір, -льору (m)	color
копі́йка; копійки́ (f)	copeck
копійо́к (g.pl.)	
ко́штувати, -ють I (no perf.) + A	to cost
кра́сти, -дуть I (+ G)	to steal (from)
вкра́сти, -дуть P	
кра́в, кра́ла, -ло, -ли	
набрида́ти, -ють I	to bore, to be fed up with
набри́днути, -уть P	
набри́д, -ла, -ло, -ли (+ D)	
наза́д	back
неща́сний	unhappy, miserable
ни́тка; нитки́ (f)	thread, yarn
обов'язко́во	by all means, absolutely
одру́жений (з + I)	married (to)
переду́мати, -ють (no imperf.) P	to change one's mind
поверта́ти, -ють I	to return s. thing
поверну́ти, -уть P	
поду́шка, подушки́ (f)	pillow
позича́ти, -ють I	to borrow, to lend
пози́чити, -ать P	(+ D = to) (у + G = from)
пози́чений	borrowed
поли́ця (f)	shelf
полта́вка (f)	native of Poltava (f)
полта́вський	Poltava (adj)
по-мо́єму	in my opinion; my way
прекра́сно	excellent, splendid, beautiful
при́нцип, -у (m)	principle
про́бувати, -ють I	to try, to attempt
спро́бувати, -ють P	
про́повідь (f)	sermon
рушни́к, -а́; -и́ (m)	towel
си́ній	dark blue

тíтка; тíткú (f)	aunt
традúція (f)	tradition
щаслúвий	happy
щонайменше	at least
щотúжня	weekly, every week

NAMES

Вáля (Валентúна); Остáп

IDIOMS

зробúти дурнúцю	to do a foolish thing
під чáс	during

SUPPLEMENT

замíжня	married (woman)
карбóванець, -нці	karbovanec (monetary unit)
Полтáва	Poltava
по-твóєму, по-її́, по-йогó по-нашóму, по-вáшому, по-ї́хньому	in your (her/his/our/your/their) opinion/way
повертáтися, -ються I повернýтися, -нýся, -вéрнуться P	to return, to come back

EXPLANATORY NOTES

1. The shirts which the girls are going to embroider are traditional Ukrainian peasant blouse-slip outfits with richly embroidered long sleeves. Different regions have their own unique designs. Roses in red and black are representative of the Poltava district. Embroidered towels of fine linen are used in house decorations, particularly around icons, and are traditionally used in wedding ceremonies. Embroidered pillow cases (referred to as вишúвані подýшки, 'embroidered pillows') are equally popular.

2. The song **"Двá кóльори"** goes as follows:

Двá кóльори

Як я́ малúм збирáвся навеснí
Ітú у свíт незнáними шляхáми,
Сорóчку мáти вúшила менí
Червóними і чóрними ниткáми.

Двá кóльори моï, двá кольорú!
Обá на полотні, в душí моïй обá,
Двá кóльори моï, двá кольорú:
Червóне — цé любóв, а чóрне — цé жýрба!

Менé водúло в бéззісті життя́,
А я́ вертáвся на своï порóги.
Переплелúсь, як мáмине шиття́,
Щаслúві і сумні́ моï дорóги.

Двá кóльори моï... і т.д.

Two colors

When I was young and it was spring
I set out into the world along the unfamiliar paths.
My mother embroidered for me
a shirt in red and black.

Those two colors of mine, my two colors,
Both on the linen and in my heart,
Those two colors of mine, my two colors,
The red is for love and the black is for sorrow.

Life took me to lands unknown,
But I kept returning to my own.
My paths were interwoven like Mom's embroidery,
Those happy and those sad paths of mine.

Those two colors of mine, my two colors ... etc.

The words are by a well known Ukrainian poet D. Pavlyčko and the music by O. Bilaš. The song became very popular in the late sixties both in Ukraine and abroad.

3. Natalka Poltavka is the heroine of the Ukrainian opera by the same name. Written by Ivan Kotlarevs'kyj in 1819 it has gained national popularity and is still performed today.

4. The name **карбóванець** appeared on Soviet paper money along with the Russian official name **рýбль** 'ruble' and its equivalent in other languages of the USSR. The last time Ukraine had its own currency was during the brief existence of the Ukrainian independent state in 1918–1920. It included **карбованець** as the first Ukrainian paper money ever printed. Another denomination was **грúвна** which equalled 0.50 **карбованець**. Today, **грúвня** has been re-introduced (with a new spelling), and **карбóванець** is out.

5. The term **вакáції** is labeled as 'old-fashioned' in Soviet dictionaries, and another term, also of Latin origin, is recommended instead: **канíкули** (the same term is used in Russian). Emigré Ukrainians prefer the older term. **Відпýстка** is a vacation from the job.

6. The verb **займáтися** means to pursue any occupation or activity, or to direct one's attention to some subject. Note the change in the stem final consonant of the perfective infinitive зайН-я́тися. The perfective future retains the same stem consonant as the imperfective stem: зайМ-у́ся, зáйМ-ешся, etc.

7. The noun **сáд** designates an orchard or a flower garden while **горóд** stands for a vegetable garden. In the West Ukrainian usage **горóд** stands for both types of garden.

8. The verb **жури́тися** is used with the instrumental object (with or without the preposition **за**), e.g.:

Вонá жури́лася за си́ном.	She was worried about her son.
Не жури́ся ци́м!	Don't worry about it.

When **жури́тися** is used alone it stands for being 'sad':

Чогó ти́ зажури́лася?	Why are you sad?

9. The verb **набридáти** requires the dative case for the one who is bored while the thing or person that is boring is in the nominative (cf. the same construction with the verb **подóбатися**). The imperfective has the meaning of 'becoming bored' and the perfective indicates the state of 'having become bored'. This is why the past perfective **набри́д, -ла, -ли** can be used in the sense of 'being bored' now or in the past (cf.: a similar use of the past perfective forms of the verb **втомити́ся — втоми́вся, втоми́лася, -лося, -лися** in the sense of 'being tired' now or in the past — see Lesson 17, p. 302). Thus:

Вонá мені́ набри́дла.	She bores (bored) me. I am (was) tired of her.
Цé мені́ вжé набридáє.	I'm getting tired of it. (It begins to bore me.)

10. The verb **повертáти/поверну́ти** in the sense of 'returning' is transitive and is used with direct object. The recipient is in the dative if it is animate or it is in the genitive with the preposition **до** if it is a place or an inaminate object. E.g.:

Ві́н поверну́в мені́ книжки́.	He returned the books to me.
Ві́н поверну́в книжки́ до бібліотéки.	He returned the books to the library.

The use of this verb in the sense of 'coming back' is substandard. One must use the reflexive verb **повертáтися/поверну́тися** instead. E.g.:

Я́ скóро поверну́ся.	I'll be back soon.
Козаки́ повертáлися з війни́.	The Cossacks were returning from the war.

11. The verb **позичáти/пози́чити** means either 'to lend' or 'to borrow'. The object lent or borrowed is in the accusative, the recepient is in the dative, and the person from whom something is borrowed is in the genitive with the preposition **у**. Thus:

Ві́н пози́чив мені́ кни́жку.	He lent me a book.
Ві́н пози́чив у мéне кни́жку.	He borrowed a book from me.

To borrow books from the library is **позичáти книжкú в бібліотéці** (also **брáти книжкú в бібліотéці**).

The object may also appear in the genitive (cf. the use of the genitive in place of the accusative (see Lesson 3, p. 48). E.g.:

Позúч мені дóляра.	Lend me a dollar.

Genitive may also indicate a limited quantity (partitive genitive):

Вонá в мéне позúчила хлíба.	She borrowed some bread from me.

12. **Обов'язкóво** (from **обов'язкóвий** 'obligatory', 'binding') is used as an equivalent to 'must', 'make sure':

Обов'язкóво прочитáй цю́ книжку.	You must read this book. Make sure you read this book.

NOTES ON GRAMMAR

I. INSTRUMENTAL PLURAL OF NOUNS

The regular ending for all hard stem nouns in the instrumental plural is **-ами** and for those with soft stems is **-ями**:

N.	столú	лікарí	місцЯ́	прíзвища	вíдповіді
I.	столáми	лікарЯ́ми	місцЯ́ми	прíзвищами	вíдповідями

1. A group of nouns besides the regular instrumental plural endings **-ами, -ями** have parallel forms which end in (-ь)**мú** with the root vowel **о** changing to **і**. E.g.:

1. (a) certain feminine nouns of the a-declension, e.g.:

сльóзи — слізьмú (слíзьми and сльозáми)

1. (b) certain nouns of the masculine-neuter declension, e.g.:

гóсті — гістьмú (and гостЯ́ми)
кóні — кіньмú (and кóнями)

1. (c) the noun **кість** ('bone') of the c-type

кість — кістьми́ (and костя́ми)

1. (d) pluralia tantum nouns, e.g.:

лю́ди — людьми́
ді́ти — ді́тьми
штани́ — штаньми́ (also штана́ми and шта́нями)
две́рі — дверми́ (and двери́ма, see 2 below)

Note 1: For most of the nouns which admit the parallel form in **-ми́** the regular ending is preferred and is used more frequently (e.g. **сльоза́ми, гостя́ми, ко́нями, штана́ми**).

Note 2: The ending **-ми́** is normally stressed (but ді́тьми, грі́шми).

2. A number of nouns of the masculine-neuter declension and some pluralia tantum have still another type of the instrumental plural ending, namely **-и́ма.**

о́чі — очи́ма (and оча́ми)
пле́чі — плечи́ма (and плеча́ми) 'shoulders'
у́ші — уши́ма (but ву́ха — ву́хами)* 'ears'
две́рі — двери́ма (and дверми́)
гро́ші — гроши́ма (and грі́шми)

Note: The ending **-и́ма** is considered the norm for these nouns.

3. The stress pattern in the instrumental plural follows the stress of the locative plural (see Lesson 17, p. 309).

II. INSTRUMENTAL PLURAL OF ADJECTIVES, PRONOUNS, ORDINALS AND ОДИН

The soft stem adjectives, pronouns and ordinal numerals take the ending **-іми (-їми)** in the instrumental plural, while those with the hard stems and **оди́н** take the ending **-ими.** This rule applies to adjectival surnames also.

N.sg.	зеле́ний	дру́гий	оди́н	чий	си́ній	тре́тій
I.pl.	зеле́ними	дру́гими	одни́ми	чиї́ми	си́німи	тре́тіми

The pronoun **уве́сь** has the instrumental plural form **усіма́**.

(Exercises, 1, 2, 3, 4)

---

* The variant у́ші is less frequent than ву́ха.

III. ADVERBIAL MODIFIERS AND PREFIXES OF INTENSIFICATION

1. Comparison is often emphasized by various intensifiers. For example:

бага́то (набага́то)	—	Це́ бага́то кра́ще. It's much better.
дале́ко	—	Це́ дале́ко гі́рше. It's far worse.
зна́чно	—	Це́ зна́чно бли́жче. It's considerably closer.
ще́	—	Це́ ще́ кра́ще. It's still better.

Many intensifiers indicate a gradual increase.

все́ — Става́ло все́ холодні́ше. Става́ло все́ холодні́ше й холодні́ше.
= It was getting colder.

cf.: also чимра́з, щора́з, деда́лі.

2. Superlatives can be intensified by adding particles що- or як-:

Зробі́ть це́ якнайскорі́ше.	Do it as fast as you can.
Ту́т щонайме́нше шістна́дцять до́ларів.	There are at (the very) least sixteen dollars here.

3. When the degree of intensity is viewed as excessive the intensifiers used are на́дто or зана́дто:

Ча́й на́дто гаря́чий.	The tea is too hot.
Ти́ зана́дто жу́ришся.	You worry too much.

Another way to express this idea of excessive intensity is to add the prefix за- to the corresponding adjective or adverb:

Ця́ соро́чка на ме́не завели́ка.	This shirt is too large for me.
Це́ вже́ запі́зно.	This is too late.

Most of the за- prefixed adjectives and adverbs refer to time and space (in the speech of West Ukrainians such forms are more common).

4. Still another way of expressing a high degree is by adding the prefix пре-:

Це́ була́ прега́рна ді́вчинка з вели́кими си́німи очи́ма.
She was a most pretty little girl with large dark blue eyes.

This type of prefixation is rather limited.

(Exercise 6)

IV. PASSIVE PARTICIPLES

1. Participles are adjectives formed from verbs which have certain properties of the verb such as government and aspectual differentiation, but whose form and function is that of adjectives.

2. Passive participles are formed from transitive verbs of both aspects. They do not have tenses but can refer to past, present and future time when used in conjunction with auxiliary verbs such as 'to be', 'to become', 'to turn':

Робóта (булá) зрóблена.	The work is (has been) done.
Робóта бýде зрóблена.	The work will be done.

3. Passive participles are formed from the infinitive stems by way of suffixation. The suffixes may be **-н-**, **-ен-** or **-т-**:

(на)писáти	—	(на)пи́са-н-ий
(з)роби́ти	—	(з)рóбл-ен-ий
(по)ми́ти	—	(по)ми́-т-ий

3. (a) Most verbs whose infinitive stems end in **-а, -я** receive the suffix **-н-** keeping the stem-final vowel. The stress moves back one syllable if the infinitive stress was on the penultimate syllable. E.g.:

-Н- suffixed participles
(from **-а, -я** stem verbs)

сказá-ти	—	скáза-н-ий
читá-ти	—	чи́та-н-ий
обіця́-ти	—	обíця-н-ий
співá-ти	—	спíва-н-ий
преслá-ти	—	при́сла-н-ий
дá-ти	—	дá-н-ий

Note: In verbs with the stressed suffix **-ува** participles are formed by dropping this suffix and replacing it with a stressed **-о-**. E.g.:

куп-увá-ти	—	купóваний
друк-увá-ти	—	друкóваний

3. (b) A number of verbs* form their participles with the suffix **-т-**. The verbs with the suffix **-ну-** are included in this group:

---

* The rules are rather complex and the student need not learn them at this stage. However, here they are just for your reference: verbs with stems ending in **и, і, у, р** and without suffixes; verbs with stems ending in **-а, -я** which in their present tense is replaced by **м** or **н**; verbs with stems in **-оро-**, **-оло-** (the latter have parallel form in **-ен**). E.g.: **ви́шити — ви́шитий, грíти — грíтий** ('warmed'), **забýти — забýтий, подéрти — подéртий** ('torn'); **жáти (жнý) — жáтий** ('reaped').

ми́ти	—	ми́тий
забу́-ти	—	забу́тий
ви́ши-ти	—	ви́шитий
зайня́-ти	—	зайня́тий
узя́-ти	—	узя́тий
ви́пи-ти	—	ви́питий
вдяг-ну́-ти	—	вдя́гнутий
огля́-ну-ти	—	огля́нутий

Note: The **-ну-** suffixed verbs have doublet forms with the suffix **-ен-**: **вдя́гнений, огля́нений**. The **-т-** forms are becoming more frequent in modern Ukrainian. The stress in **-т-** suffixed participles falls on the syllable preceding the **-т-** (except in **-оро-**, **-оло-*** verbs). In participles which are formed from the **-ну-** suffixed verbs the stress is on the syllable preceding the suffix **-ну-**. All participles from perfective verbs with a stressed prefix **ви́-** retain the stress on the prefix.

3. (c) All other verbs form their participles with the suffix **-ен-** (**-єн-** for those whose stems end in /j/). The stem-final vowel is dropped and the stress is moved back one syllable if it was on the penultimate syllable in the infinitive. For example:

-ен- suffixed participles

зачини́-ти	—	зачи́н-ен-ий		
повтори́-ти	—	повто́р-ен-ий		
кінчи́-ти	—	кі́нч-ен-ий		
навчи́-ти	—	на́вч-ен-ий		
втоми́-ти	—	вто́мл-ен-ий		
роби́-ти	—	ро́бл-ен-ий		
купи́-ти	—	ку́пл-ен-ий		
знай-ти́	—	(знайд-у́)	—	зна́йд-ен-ий
вес-ти́	—	(вед-у́)	—	ве́д-ен-ий
покла́с-ти	—	(поклад-у́)	—	покла́д-ен-ий
зберег-ти́	—	(збереж-у́)	—	збере́ж-ен-ий

Note 1: 2nd conjugation verbs with a stem-final vowel **-и-** preceded by a labial (**б, п, в, м, ф**) add the consonant **л** after it (**роби́ти — ро́блений**).

Note 2: Verbs with stems ending in a consonant which undergoes a change in the present (or future perfective) show the same change in their participles (**ве́сти — веду́ — ве́дений**). Consonant mutation in **-и-** stem verbs (**народи́ти — народжу́**) is also preserved in participles: **наро́джений**.

3. (d) The irregular verb **відпові́сти** has no participles. The perfective of **ї́сти — з'ї́сти** has a participle **з'ї́дений** 'eaten'.

* **поборо́ти — побо́ротий (побо́рений)** ('conquered'); **моло́ти — мо́лотий (ме́лений)** ('ground').

4. Many participles have lost their verbal characteristics such as governing a case or appearing in passive constructions with an agent in the instrumental case. For example:

улю́блений 'favorite'	Це́ моя́ улю́блена пісня. This is my favorite song.
варе́ний 'cooked', 'boiled'	Візьміть варе́ної карто́плі. Take some boiled potatoes.
вто́млений 'tired'	Ви́ виглядаєте вто́мленою. You look tired.

Note: Frequently there is a difference in stress between the participle and its adjectival counterpart, e.g. **ва́рений** = participle, **варе́ний** = adjective, **пе́чений** 'baked' = participle, **пече́ний** = adjective. E.g.:

Якої карто́плі ви́ хо́чете, пече́ної чи варе́ної?
What kind of potatoes would you like, baked or boiled?

Ця́ карто́пля пе́чена в печі́, а та́ ва́рена у воді́.
These potatoes were baked in the oven and those were boiled in water.

5. Certain participles are correlated with intransitive verbs with **-ся**, e.g.:

одружи́тися	—	одру́жений	'married'
народи́тися	—	наро́джений	'born'
вдягну́тися	—	вдя́гнений	'dressed'
втоми́тися	—	вто́млений	'tired'

Note that the **-ся** is not included in these participles.

6. Formerly there existed present tense passive participles in **-м(ий)**. Today there is a number of adjectives with this suffix which have lost their verbal characteristics, e.g. **знайо́мий** 'known', 'familiar' (from the verb **зна́ти**).

7. Passive participles may appear in passive constructions with the agent in the instrumental case, e.g.:

Його́ по́слано туди́ університе́том. — He was sent there by the university.

However, this type of syntax is normally avoided and in the above case Ukrainians would be more likely to use the active voice, i.e.:

Його́ посла́в туди́ університе́т. — The university sent him there.

In general, English uses passive constructions much more freely than Ukrainian.

8. Ukrainian has a special impersonal passive construction used both in speech and in writing. It employs a special verbal form in **-но-, -то** which is derived from transitive verbs of perfective aspect the same way as participles. The object is in the accusative and an agent in the instrumental case may but need not be present. E.g.:

Коли́ збудо́вано цю́ це́ркву?
When was this church built?

Ці́ го́ри вигляда́ють та́к, ні́би ї́х побудо́вано людськи́ми рука́ми.
These mountains look as if they were buit by human hands.

(Exercises 7-10)

V. EXPRESSIONS OF APPROXIMATION

There are various ways to express approximation in Ukrainian. Some of them are:

(a) Giving the numbers and placing a hyphen between them to indicate that the actual number is somewhere between or one of the two (in English this is expressed by numbers separated by the word 'or').

Я́ прийду́ че́рез 3-4 дні́.	I'll come in three or four days.

(b) Reversing the word order, putting the numeral after the noun. The noun then must be used in genitive plural regardless of the number.

Це́ ко́штує копі́йок де́сять.	It costs about ten copecks.
Ми́ на це́ чека́ли мі́сяців три́.	We waited for it about three months.

(c) Using a combination of the above methods:

Ми́ чека́ли мі́сяців три́-чоти́ри.	We waited for about there or four months.

(Exercise 5)

VI. MORE TIME EXPRESSIONS: DURATION, RECURRENCE

1. The idea of duration ("at the time", "during") may be expressed by the phrase **під ча́с** followed by the genitive.

Ві́н народи́вся під ча́с війни́.	He was born during the war.
Під ча́с війни́ вона́ працюва́ла на за́воді.	During the war she worked at the factory.

2. Recurrence. To render "every" + time expression, two constructions are available:

(1) кóжний + noun, both in the genitive, e.g.:

Кóжного рóку вонú ї́здили на мóре.
Every year they went to the sea.

Кóжної хвилúни дéсь нарóджується дитúна.
Every minute a child is born somewhere.

(2) що prefixed to nouns in the genitive, or що followed by a numeral + noun phrase in the accusative. E.g.:

Щосубóти покáзували якúйсь фíльм.
A movie was shown every Saturday.

Що дві́ хвилúни вонú перевíря́ли, чи всé в порядку.
Every two minutes they checked if everything was in order.

ВПРАВИ

I. Change the instrumental singulars to plurals.

1. Вонú приї́хали свої́м влáсним áвтом.
2. Вонá прийшлá зі своéю дочкóю.
3. Остáп прийшóв зі свої́м провідникóм.
4. Вáля прийшлá зі своéю товáришкою.
5. Вонú прийшлú зі своéю мáтір'ю.
6. Студéнти розмовля́ли зі свої́м керівникóм.
7. Цéй дипломáт прийшóв з громадя́нкою України.
8. Профéсор прийшóв з однúм поля́ком.
9. Інженéр прийшóв з однúм росія́нином.
10. Мú мáли дóвгу розмовý з цúм лíкарем.

II. Finish the sentences providing the instrumental forms of nouns and adjectives.

1. Óсь золоті́ ниткú. Вúший цé . . . . .
2. Тýт зелéні й сúні кóльори. Цé вúшите . . . . .
3. Óсь чóрні та червóні олівці́. Напишú цé . . . . .
4. У тéбе бруднí рýки. Не берú цьогó . . . . .
5. У тéбе такí дúвні прúнципи. Я́к тú живéш за . . . . . ?
6. Цé такí погáні ýчні. Щó мені́ робúти з . . . . . ?
7. Бáчиш отúх гáрних полтáвок? Мої́ братú одрýжені з . . . . .
8. Цé такí нецікáві рéчі. Я́ не хóчу займáтися . . . . .
9. Вонú спрáвжні дипломáти. Хóчеш познайóмитися з . . . . .
10. Ці́ нíмки і пóльки — нáші студéнтки. Мú ходúли до кінá з . . . . .

III. Change the sentences according to the model.

Це́ брати́ Ме́льники. Познайо́мся з брата́ми Ме́льниками.

(се́стри Тарнове́цькі, інжене́ри Гончаре́нки, учителі́ Івани́шини, лікарі́ Палії́, на́ші кана́дські студе́нтки Поліщуки́, на́ші америка́нські студе́нти Ле́севи, мої́ товариші́ Дмитро́вські, мої́ товаришки́ Прокопо́вичі, ї́хні знайо́мі Гуме́цькі)

IV. Answer the question using the words provided in brackets.

Чи́м ви́ ціка́витеся? (ва́ші думки́) — Ва́шими думка́ми.

(украї́нські журна́ли, спра́вжні тради́ції, старі́ про́повіді, коза́цькі пісні́, ї́хні по́гляди, ру́ські при́нципи пра́ва, наро́ди Росії́, поря́дки в старі́й Росії́, ві́рші Шевче́нка, ва́ші ле́кції)

V. Change the numbers to approximate amounts.

1. Я́ ма́ю лише́ 10 дол.
2. Вона́ ма́є 18 гривень.
3. Ві́н ма́є 3 ро́ки.
4. Я́ ма́ю 20 коп.
5. Ми́ ма́ємо ще 2 або́ 3 місяці.
6. Це́ було́ 3-4 століття тому́.
7. Ї́й 23 ро́ки.
8. Та́м було́ 3 чи 4 ха́ти.
9. Та́м стоя́ло 2 чи 3 столи́.
10. Було́ ви́дно 3-4 човни́.

VI. Answer the questions using the superlative forms with **що-, як-.**

1. Чи до́вго туди́ ї́хати? Щонай . . . . . 2 годи́ни.
2. Чи це́ дале́ко звідси? Що . . . . . 3 км.
3. Чи ця́ гора́ висо́ка? Що . . . . . 1000 м.
4. Чи це́ вели́ка ене́ргія? Що . . . . . 50 квт.
5. Чи це́ бага́то ко́штує? Що . . . . . 5 дол.
6. Чи ві́н це́ до́бре зроби́в? Якнай . . . . .
7. Чи ві́н до́бре поми́в но́ги? Якнай . . . . .
8. Чи туди́ беру́ть тільки молоди́х? Та́к, як . . . . .
9. Я́к бли́зько ти́ хо́чеш сиді́ти? Як . . . . .
10. Ти́ хо́чеш купи́ти деше́ві ме́блі? Та́к, як . . . . .

VII. Answer the questions using the appropriate participles.

1. Чи ві́н уже́ скінчи́в про́повідь?
2. Чи ти́ вже́ прочита́в газе́ту?
3. Чи ти́ вже́ охолоди́в пові́тря в поме́шканні?
4. Чи зеле́не а́вто хто́сь укра́в?

5. Чи та німка зачини́ла две́рі?
6. Чи хто́сь звари́в це́ яйце́?
7. Чи ви́ вже́ покра́яли хліб?
8. Чи воні́ зберегли́ всі ре́чі?
9. Чи ви́ вже́ спекли́ пиріжки́?
10. Чи хто́сь купи́в ми́ло?

VIII. Change the sentences according to the model:

Це́ тре́ба ска́зати. Тре́ба, щоб це́ було́ ска́зане.

1. Полта́ву тре́ба га́рно описа́ти.
2. Тре́ба шви́дко надрукува́ти листа́.
3. Тре́ба поверну́ти гро́ші.
4. Якра́з це́ тре́ба підкре́слити.
5. Це́ тре́ба до́бре переві́рити.
6. Ці́ ві́рші обов'язково тре́ба ви́вчити напа́м'ять.
7. Це́ тре́ба ско́ро прода́ти.
8. Рушни́к тре́ба ви́шити.
9. Це́ тре́ба до́бре огля́нути.
10. Це́ тре́ба охолоди́ти.

IX. Supply the appropriate participles.

1. Я́к ти́ міг це́ чу́ти, коли́ две́рі були́ . . . . . ? (зачини́ти)
2. Ми́ ї́ли ви́шні, ... на база́рі. (купи́ти)
3. Не бери́ хлі́ба . . . . . рука́ми! (не ми́ти)
4. У ресторані було́ . . . . . пові́тря. (охолоди́ти)
5. Дисерта́ція вже́ . . . . . профе́сором. (переві́рити)
6. Це́ подару́нки . . . . . з Украї́ни. (присла́ти)
7. Ми́ були́ на ве́чорі . . . . . студе́нтами (влаштува́ти).
8. Ця́ кни́жка . . . . . на зна́чно кра́щому папе́рі. (надрукува́ти)
9. По-на́шому, це́й ли́ст . . . . . непога́ною украї́нською мо́вою. (написа́ти)
10. Це́ ще не . . . . . пробле́ма. (ви́рішити)

X. Translate into Ukrainian.

1. These copecks were found in Ukraine.
2. They were brought to Ukraine in the 11th century from foreign lands.
3. The long awaited day arrived.
4. They have been married for ten years.
5. Don't leave your work unfinished.
6. This towel was embroidered by my aunt.
7. Don't cry over the spilled milk.
8. On her desk I saw a poem which she had started.
9. This is a forgotten tradition.
10. The program was carried out with a great success.

XI. Read and translate.

1. Сього́дні я́ ходи́ла по всі́х крамни́цях і шука́ла поли́ць для книжо́к. У на́с сті́льки ти́х книжо́к, що вже́ нема́ для ни́х ніде́ мі́сця. Вони́ лежа́ть і стоя́ть і на поли́ці, і на столі́, і на вікні́. Оста́п давно́ обіця́в купи́ти або́ зроби́ти ще́ поли́ці, та все́ забува́є. Мину́лого ти́жня сказа́в, що вже́ тепе́р обов'язко́во зро́бить, але́ ти́ждень мину́в, а поли́ць ще нема́є. Тоді́ я́ ви́рішила не чека́ти більше і пішла́ до мі́ста. Ходи́ла, ходи́ла і нічо́го не знайшла́ — усе́ або́ зана́дто вели́ке, або́ задороге́. Чи не спро́бувати мені́ самі́й зроби́ти? До́шки в на́с є. Неха́й Оста́п поба́чить, що жінки́ змі́ють і поли́ці зроби́ти, коли́ тре́ба.

2. Я́ щоти́жня ба́чу на Оста́пові нову́ соро́чку: то си́ню, то зеле́ну, то вишне́ву. І де́ ві́н ї́х бере́? Невже́ купу́є щоти́жня нову́? Я́ що́сь не ві́рю, це́, ма́буть, його́ Ва́ля йому́ купу́є. Якби́ я́ бу́в на його́ мі́сці, я́ б ї́й сказа́в, що не хо́чу носи́ти таки́х сорочо́к і вигляда́ти, як манеке́н у крамни́ці. Я́ б таки́х сорочо́к не носи́в, але́ мо́же Оста́пові такі́ ко́льори подо́баються? Я́ ж не зна́ю його́ смаку́. І взагалі́, мо́же, це́ ті́льки я́, стари́й, за тради́цією ношу́ бі́лі виши́вані сорочки́, а молоді́ хло́пці вже́ вважа́ють це́ за старосві́тське? Ні́, не всі́, є́ й такі́, що лю́блять на́ші тради́ції, о́сь я́к Оста́пів си́н і його́ това́риш.

3. Сього́дні я́ оде́ржав листа́ з Ки́єва від мого́ знайо́мого інжене́ра Дмитро́вського. Ві́н розповіда́є, що бу́в з дружи́ною в буди́нку відпочи́нку на Чо́рному мо́рі і зустрі́вся та́м зі свої́ми знайо́мими Івани́шиними. Вони́ ра́зом га́рно прове́ли ча́с, ма́ли все́, чого́ душа́ бажа́є: ї́ли, спа́ли, нічи́м не жури́лися, купа́лися в мо́рі, ходи́ли в го́ри — коро́тше, займа́лися усіма́ ти́ми реча́ми, про які́ ду́мали під ча́с до́вгої зими́. Коли́ прийшо́в ча́с поверта́тися додо́му, всі́ зажури́лися — але́ робо́та це́ робо́та, коли́ обо́в'язок кли́че, тре́ба ї́хати.

XII. Answer the following questions to the above passages.

(1)
1. Чого́ шука́ла жі́нка?
2. Де́ в ни́х стоя́ть книжки́?
3. Що́ Оста́п обіця́в?
4. Чому́ Оста́пова жі́нка ви́рішила піти́ до мі́ста?
5. Чому́ вона́ нічо́го не купи́ла?

(2)
1. Які́ сорочки́ но́сить Оста́п?
2. Зві́дки в нього́ такі́ сорочки́?
3. Я́к вигляда́є Оста́п?
4. Яки́й у нього́ сма́к?
5. Що́ ду́мають молоді́ хло́пці?

(3)

1. Щó цéй чоловíк сьогóдні одéржав?
2. Дé був Дмитрóвський з дружи́ною?
3. Когó вони́ тáм зустріли?
4. Я́к вони́ провели́ чáс?
5. Чомý всí зажури́лися?

XIII. Answer the following questions to the dialogues.

"Ми́ бýдемо вишивáти"

1. Для чóго Вáля потребýє нитки́?
2. Щó ви́рішили дівчáта?
3. Для кóго зелéні нитки́ і для чóго?
4. Які кóльори традиційні?
5. Щó подóбається Остáпові?
6. Я́к дівчáта хóчуть виглядáти?

"Поли́ці для книжóк"

1. Щó Остáп збирáється роби́ти?
2. Чомý він передýмав?
3. Скільки кóштували дошки́?
4. Чомý не трéба рахувáти чáсу?
5. Чи́м Остáп міг би зайня́тися?
6. Щó про цé кáже Вáля?

"Книжки́ трéба повертáти?"

1. Чомý дзвони́в Микóла?
2. Щó Остáп про ньóго кáже?
3. Щó Вáля дýмає про пози́чені книжки́?
4. Якá відповідь Остáпа?
5. Коли́ Остáп бýде нещáсним?
6. Чомý він не є нещáсний?

ДЕВ'ЯТНАДЦЯТА ЛЕКЦІЯ

 # 52 Максим захворів
Maksym got sick

Dialogue Paticipants:
Макси́м - М, Оле́на - О; Maksym - M, Olena - O

1. О- Макси́ме, ти́ що́сь пога́но вигляда́єш. Чи ти́ не захворі́в?
2. М- Здає́ться, що та́к. У ме́не вже́ два́ дні́ боли́ть голова́ і го́рло.
3. О- Чи ти́ мі́ряв температу́ру?
4. М- Та́к, що́йно помі́ряв: бі́ля 38° (тридцяти́ восьми́).
5. О- Це́ недо́бре. Мо́же, я́ покли́чу до́ктора Прокопо́вича?
6. М- Ні́, ні́, не тре́ба. О́сь я́ ви́п'ю горі́лки, піду́ до лі́жка і все́ про́йде.
7. О- Мо́же б ти́ за́мість пи́ти горі́лку взя́в аспіри́ну?
8. М- Ні́, я́ про́ти аспіри́ни. Я́ бі́льше ві́рю наро́дним лі́кам. Вони́ до́бре допомага́ли на́шим діда́м і пра́дідам, то́ й мені́ допомо́жуть.
9. О- Не бу́дь таки́м старосві́тським. А що́ як це́ серйо́зна хворо́ба?
10. М- Не бі́йся. Таки́м козака́м, як я́ ні́яка хворо́ба не страшна́.
11. О- Ну́ до́бре, роби́, як зна́єш. Я́ за́раз подзвоню́ Палія́м і скажу́, що ти́ хво́рий, і ми́ не при́йдемо за́втра гра́ти в ка́рти.
12. М- По́ки що ні́чо́го не кажи́. Мо́же, я́ до за́втра ви́дужаю.
13. О- Ти́ невиліко́вний оптимі́ст.

1. O- Maksym, you don't look well somehow. You are not ill, are you?
2. M- I might be. I have had a headache for two days, and my throat is sore.
3. O- Did you take your temperature?
4. M- Yes, I just did. It's around 38° (100.4°F).
5. O- That's not good. Perhaps I should call Dr. Prokopovyč?
6. M- No, don't bother. I'll just have some horilka, go to bed, and everything will pass.
7. O- Perhaps instead of horilka you should take aspirin?
8. M- No, I am against aspirin. I have more faith in folk medicine. It helped our ancestors and it will help me also.
9. O- Don't be so old-fashioned. What if it's a serious illness?
10. M- Don't worry. Cossacks like myself are not afraid of any sickness.
11. O- Well, do as you see fit. I'm going to call the Palijs and tell them you are ill and we won't come tomorrow to play cards.
12. M- Don't tell them anything yet. Maybe by tomorrow I'll be all right.
13. O- You are an incurable optimist.

53 Наталка на дієті
Natalka is on a diet

Dialogue Paticipants:
Натáлка - Н, Слáвко - С
Natalka - N, Slavko - S

1. Н- Слáвку, хóчеш щé варéників?
2. С- Ні, дякую. Я́ вжé з'ї́в біля десяти́.
3. Н- Цé нічóго. Усíм молоди́м здорóвим хлóпцям трéба багáто ї́сти.
4. С- І всíм молоди́м здорóвим дівчáтам тéж трéба ї́сти. Чомý ж ти́ собí і Гáлі поклáла тíльки по два нещáсні варéники?
5. Н- Нáм дóсить двóх, бо ми́ на дієті.
6. С- Óх, я́ й забýв, що тобí й твої́м товаришкáм тепéр тíльки дієта в головí. Скíльки ти́ вáжиш?
7. Н- Біля вісімдесяти́ кілогрáмів, а Óля й Гáля вжé дійшли́ до дев'янóста. Ми́ хóчемо вáжити не бíльше сімдесяти́.
8. С- Бажáю вáм усíм ýспіху.

1. N- Slavko, do you want more varenyky?
2. S- No, thanks. I already ate around ten.
3. N- That's nothing. All young healthy boys should eat a lot.
4. S- And so should all young healthy girls. How come you and Halja took only two miserable varenyky each?
5. N- Two is enough for us because we are on a diet.
6. S- Oh, I forgot that all you and your friends have on your minds nowadays is the diet. How much do you weigh?
7. N- Around eighty kilograms and Olja and Halja have already reached ninety. We want to weigh no more than seventy.
8. S- I wish you all luck.

54 Заграй на бандурі
Play the bandura

Dialogue Paticipants:
Макси́м - М, Олéна - О
Maksym - M, Olena - O

1. О- Макси́ме, заграй нáм на бандýрі. Нáшим америкáнським гостя́м цікáво послýхати украї́нських пісéнь. Вони́ чýли, що украї́нці дýже співýчий нарóд.
2. М- Тáк, співýчий і живýчий. Як кáжуть: "Козáцькому рóду немá перевóду". Мóжеш цé переклáсти нáшим дороги́м гостя́м?
3. О- Спрóбую... А ти́ тим чáсом грáй.
4. М- Дóбре, тíльки щó? Я́ не знáю, щó америкáнцям подóбається. Нý, хібá оцю́:
   Взя́в би я́ бандýру,
   Тá й заграв, що знáв.
   Чéрез тý бандýру
   Бандури́стом стáв. ...Ну я́к, подобáється?
5. О- І питáти не трéба, дóсить на ни́х подиви́тися. Співáй дáлі, я́ потíм перекладý ї́м словá.

1. O- Maksym, play the bandura for us. Our American guests are curious to hear some Ukrainian songs. They have heard that Ukrainians are a song-loving people.
2. M- Yes, we are a singing and a tough nation. As they say, "The Cossack stock will never cease to be". Can you translate this for our dear guests?
3. O- I'll try. In the meantime you go on and play.
4. M- All right, but what? I don't know what the Americans like. Well, perhaps this one:

   I would take the bandura
   And play what I know.
   Because of that bandura
   I became a bandurist. ...Well, do they like it?

5. O- No need to ask: enough to look at them. Keep on singing, I'll translate the words for them afterwards.

СЛОВНИК

аспіри́на (f)	aspirin
бажа́ти, -ють I (+ G + D)	to wish (s.th. to s.one)
побажа́ти, -ють P	
банду́ра (f)	bandura
бандури́ст (m)	bandura player
біля (+ G)	around, ca.
болі́ти, боли́ть, боля́ть I	to ache
заболі́ти, -и́ть, -я́ть P	(3rd sg. & pl. only)
ва́жити, -ать I (no pfv)	to weigh (= to have a certain weight)
виду́жувати, -ють I	to get well
ви́дужати, -ать P	
голова́, го́лову, го́лово;	head
го́лови, голі́в (f)	
горі́лка (f)	horilka (vodka)
го́рло (n)	throat
гра́ти, -ють I	to play
загра́ти, -ють P	
гра́ти в (+ A)	to play a game
гра́ти на (+ L)	to play an instrument
діє́та (f)	diet
на діє́ті	on a diet
до́ктор, -а; -и́ (m)	doctor
дохо́дити, -жу, -ять I	to reach
дійти́, ді́йдуть P	
(до + G)	
живу́чий	tough, of great vitality
ка́рта (f)	card
кілогра́м, -а (m); кг; кіло́ (н)	kilogram; kg; kilo
лі́ки (pl)	medicine, drugs

міряти, -ють I	to measure
поміряти, -ють P	
народний	folk (adj.)
невиліковний	incurable
оптиміст (m)	optimist
по (+ A or L of a numeral)	(so much) each
проти (+ G)	against; opposed to
поки що	so far, for the time being
прадід (m)	great-grandfather
прадіди	forefathers
серйозний	serious
співучий	fond of singing
температура (f)	temperature
усміхатися, -ються I	to smile
усміхнутися, -уться P	
успіх, -у (m)	success
хворий	sick; patient
хворий на (+ A)	sick with
хворіти, -ють I	to be sick
захворіти, -ють P	(pfv. 'to become sick')
на (+ A) with	
хвороба (f)	sickness
хіба	perhaps
через (+ A)	because of
щойно	just now

IDIOMS

діди й прадіди	ancestors
у голові	on one's mind
у мене болить голова	I have a headache
у мене болить горло	I have a sore throat
тим часом	meantime
що як	what if
як знаєш	as you wish

SUPPLEMENT

градус (о) m.	degree (o)
грам (м); гр.	gram, gr.
успішний	successful

EXPLANATORY NOTES

1. **Хвóрий** means 'sick' either seriously or slightly. **Хворíти** usually denotes a long or chronic illness. **Захворíти** means 'to get sick' with no indication of the seriousness of illness or the ailment. Cf.:

Чи вонá тя́жко хвóра?	Is she gravely ill?
-Ні́, цé скóро прóйде.	-No, it will soon pass.

Коли́ він бу́в дити́ною, він бaгáто хворíв.
When he was a child he used to get sick a lot.

Він захворíв на якýсь хворóбу.	He came down with some kind of disease.

Хвóрий has another variant typical of the West Ukrainian speech, **хóрий** (cf.: also хорíти, хорóба).

2. **Аспіри́на** and similar medical terms such as **вазелíна, пеніцилíна, хинíна** (vaseline, penicillin, quinine) are traditionally feminine gender in Ukrainian. In the current usage in Ukraine such terms are masculine (as in Russian), **вазелíн, пеніцилíн, хинíн.** The expression 'to take medicine' uses the verb 'узя́ти' or 'вживáти/вжи́ти + A: вжи́й аспірини'. 'take some aspirin'.

3. The verb 'to ache' **болíти** has only the 3rd sg. and the 3rd pl. forms since it refers to the part(s) of the body which ache, not to the person experiencing pain. Therefore, to render into Ukrainian the English expression 'I ache all over' one must say **У мéне всé боли́ть** (literally 'Everything aches with me'). Besides у+ G this verb can also be used with the Dative case: мене́ боли́ть.

4. According to the centigrade system used in Ukraine a normal body temperature is considered to be 36.6 (written as 36,6° and spelled as **три́дцять шíсть і шíсть (деся́тих).** Anything above 37° is a high temperature with 38° being an equivalent of 100° F.

5. **Лíкар** signifies physician and is not used as a title; thus one says **Óсь дóктор Прокопóвич**, but **Микóла Прокопóвич — дýже дóбрий лíкар**. As in English, the title 'doctor' is usually reserved for physicians but may refer to anyone holding a doctoral degree, e.g. **Івани́шин ужé дóктор наýк** 'Ivanyshyn is already a doctor of sciences'.

Іти́ (ходи́ти) до лíкаря or **Бýти в лíкаря** means 'to (go to) see a doctor'. E.g.:

Чи ти́ вжé бýв у лíкаря?	
Чи ти́ вжé ходи́в до лíкаря?	Have you seen the doctor yet?

To examine a patient is **оглядáти (+ A)**, to see one is **при́ймати**:

Лíкар огля́нув хвóрого.	The doctor examined the patient.
Дóктор вáс зáраз при́йме.	The doctor will see you now.

6. Bandura is a Ukrainian folk instrument dating back to the 16th century. It has about sixty strings which are diatonically tuned. Traditionally, the bandura players were blind wandering musicians whose repertory included historical songs called **дýми**. The song about the love-lorn bandurist probably dates from the 19th century for it has definite Romantic overtones. The words are as follows:

ВЗЯВ БИ Я БАНДУРУ

1. Взя́в би я́ банду́ру
та й загра́в, що зна́в.
Через ту́ банду́ру
Бандури́стом ста́в.

1. I would take up the bandura
And play what I know
Because of that bandura
I became a bandurist.

2. А всé чéрез óчі,
Коли́ б я́ ї́х ма́в,
За ті ка́рі óчі
Ду́шу б я́ відда́в.

2. And it's all because of those eyes,
If only they were mine,
For those brown eyes
I would give my soul.

3. Маруси́но, сéрце,
Пожалі́й менé.
Візьми́ моє́ сéрце,
Да́й мені́ своє́.

3. Marusyna, sweetheart,
Have pity on me.
Take my heart
And give me yours.

4. Мару́ся не чу́є
Сéрця не дає́,
З дру́гими жарту́є,
Жа́лю завдає́.

4. Marus'a doesn't hear
Doesn't give me her heart,
She flirts with others.
Causing me pain.

5. Дé Кри́м за гора́ми,
Дé сóнечко ся́є,
Та́м моя́ голу́бка
З жа́лю завмира́є.

5. Beyond the mountains, in Crimea,
Where the sun is shining,
There my sweet love
Is pining away.

6. Взя́в би я́ банду́ру,
Та й загра́в, що зна́в.
Чéрез ту́ банду́ру
Бандури́стом ста́в.

6. I would take up the bandura
And play what I know
Because of that bandura
I became a bandurist.

NOTES ON GRAMMAR

I. DATIVE OF PLURAL NOUNS

All nouns which have hard stems receive the ending **-ам** in the dative plural, and all those with the soft stems receive the ending **-ям**:

N.	столи́	лікарі́	місця́	прізвища	відповіді	рéчі
D.	стола́м	лікаря́м	місця́м	прізвищам	відповідям	реча́м

1. The stress pattern is the same as for the locative plural (Lesson 17, p. 309).

2. Dative plural of **люди** and **діти** is **людям** and **дітям** respectively (see Lesson 17, p. 308).

(Exercises 1-5)

II. DATIVE PLURAL OF ADJECTIVES, PRONOUNS, ORDINAL NUMERALS, ОДИН

The dative plural ending for soft stem adjectives, pronouns, and ordinal numerals is **-ім (-їм)**, and for those with the hard stems and for **оди́н** it is **-им**:

N.	хво́рий	оста́нній	чи́й	сві́й	дру́гий	тре́тій	оди́н	усі́
D.	хво́рим	оста́ннім	чиї́м	свої́м	дру́гим	тре́тім	одни́м	усі́м

(Exercises 3, 4)

III. ACTIVE PARTICIPLES

In discussing the passive participles (see Lesson 18, p. 326) we have pointed out that many of them have lost their verbal characteristics and have become simple adjectives. The same is true to even a greater degree of the active participles. Actually, all the old forms of active participles of the present tense i.e. those with the suffixes **-уч(ий), -ущ(ий), -ач(ий), -ащ(ий)** have been lost. There remain only de-verbal adjectives with these suffixes and their number is rather small e.g.:

FORMER ACTIVE PARTICIPLES TURNED ADJECTIVES

Suffix

-уЧ(ИЙ)	співу́чий	(fond of singing)	живу́чий	(enduring; long-lived)

Suffix

-уЩ(ИЙ)	невмиру́щий	(undying)	невсипу́щий	(vigilant)

Suffix

-АЧ(ИЙ)	лежа́чий	(lying)	лю́блячий	(loving)

Suffix

-АЩ(ИЙ)	трудя́щий	(toiling)	пропа́щий	(lost)

For example:

У́ся ї́хня роди́на ду́же співу́ча.	Their whole family is fond of singing.
У неї́ лю́бляче се́рце.	She has a loving heart.
Він шука́є лежа́чої робо́ти.	He is looking for an easy job (i.e. the kind you do lying down).
Ба́тько бу́в трудя́ща люди́на.	Father was a hardworking man.

Note 1. **Трудя́щий, трудя́щі** in Soviet terminology stood for 'worker(s)'.

Note 2. Active participles have been artificially re-introduced into the Ukrainian language today and may be found in publicistic writing and in belles lettres in Ukraine (e.g. **керу́ючий гру́пою** instead of **керівни́к гру́пи** 'group leader', or **заві́дуючий магази́ном**, a calque from Russian **заве́дующий магази́ном**, "store manager"). Such constructions are foreign to the spirit of the Ukrainian language.

2. Former active participles of the past tense, i.e. those with suffixes **-ш(ий), -вш(ий)** have been lost almost completely and replaced by forms with the suffix **-л**: **мину́-вш-ий — мину́-л-ий, поме́р-ш-ий — поме́р-л-ий.**

Note: The student will encounter two active participles, one present and the other past, in the speech of many emigré Ukrainians (and in their press); **бу́вший** 'former' and **слі́дуючий** 'the following, next'. These forms are not considered a literary norm and should be replaced by **коли́шній** and **насту́пний** respectively.

IV. DECLENSION OF NUMERALS 1 THROUGH 100 AND ADVERBS OF QUANTITY

All cardinal numbers are declined in Ukrainian.

1. Number 'one' **оди́н** is declined like the pronoun **то́й**.

2. Numbers 2, 3, 4 follow the same type of declension. The adverbs **бага́то, небага́то** decline like 3, the adverbs **скі́льки, сті́льки, кі́лька, декі́лька** 'several' decline like 2.

N.	два́, дві́	кі́лька	три́	чоти́ри	бага́то
A.	= N or G	= N or G	= N or G	= N or G	= N or G
G.	дво́х	кілько́х	трьо́х	чотирьо́х	багатьо́х
L.	(на) дво́х	кілько́х	трьо́х	чотирьо́х	багатьо́х
I.	двома́	кількома́	трьома́	чотирма́	багатьма́
D.	дво́м	кілько́м	трьо́м	чотирьо́м	багатьо́м

3. Numbers 5 through 20 and the numbers 30, 50, 60, 70 and 80 follow another type of declension:

	5	6
N.	п'я́ть	ші́сть
A.	= N or п'ятьо́х (G)	= N or шістьо́х (G)
G.	п'яти́ (п'ятьо́х)	шести́ (шістьо́х)
L.	(на) п'яти́ (п'ятьо́х)	(на) шести́ (шістьо́х)
I.	п'ятьма́ (п'ятьома́)	шістьма́ (шістьо́ма)
D.	п'яти́ (п'ятьо́м)	шести́ (шістьо́м)

	7	8
N.	сі́м	ві́сім
A.	= N or сімо́х (G)	= N or вісьмо́х (G)
G.	семи́ (сімо́х)	восьми́ (вісьмо́х)
L.	(на) семи́ (сімо́х)	(на) восьми́ (вісьмо́х)
I.	сьома́ (сімома́)	вісьма́ (вісьмома́)
D.	семи́ (сімо́м)	восьми́ (вісьмо́м)

	9
N.	де́в'ять
A.	= N or дев'ятьо́х (G)
G.	дев'яти́ (дев'ятьо́х)
L.	(на) дев'яти́ (дев'ятьо́х)
I.	дев'ятьма́ (дев'ятьома́)
D.	дев'яти́ (дев'ятьо́м)

	15	50
N.	п'ятна́дцять	п'ятдеся́т
A.	= N or п'ятнадцятьо́х (G)	= N or п'ятдесятьо́х (G)
G.	п'ятна́дцяти (п'ятнадцятьо́х)	п'ятдесяти́ (п'ятдесятьо́х)
L.	(на) п'ятна́дцяти (п'ятнадцятьо́х)	(на) п'ятдесяти́ (п'ятдесятьо́х)
I.	п'ятнадцятьма́ (п'ятнадцятьома́)	п'ятдесятьма́ (п'ятдесятьома́)
D.	п'ятна́дцяти (п'ятнадцятьо́м)	п'ятдесяти́ (п'ятдесятьо́м)

Note 1. The variant forms in **-ьóх, -ьóм** given in parantheses are as frequent as the other forms.

Note 2. Note the softening of the stem consonant before a vowel in numbers 3 and 4 and in all the oblique cases in the adverb **бага́то**: /tr'ox, čotyr'ox, bahat'ox, bahat'ma/. The adverb **де́кілька** is usually stressed on the first syllable, other adverbs of quantity have end stress in oblique cases.

Note 3. The two forms in the accusative represent the familiar distinction between animate and inanimate categories (see the next section V.). For the animate category only the **-ох** (not **-и**) genitive forms are used. For example:

Ми́ ба́чили п'я́ть фі́льмів.	We saw five films.
Ми́ ба́чили п'ятьо́х хво́рих.	We saw five patients.

Note 4. In numbers ending in **-дцять** and **-десят** such as **одина́дцять, шістдеся́т** the first part of the compound **один-, шіст-** etc. remains unchanged. The stress in numbers 11 through 19 is on the stem (on the syllable **-на́д-**) in all the **-и** forms but moves to the last syllables in all other forms. In numbers 20, 30, 50, 60, 70, 80, 90 the stress is consistently on the last syllable (where N.=A. the stress is as in the N.).

4. The numbers **со́рок, дев'яно́сто, сто́** follow the same declension pattern:

N.	со́рок	дев'яно́сто	сто́
A.	= N	= N	= N
G.	сорока́	дев'яно́ста	ста́
L.	сорока́	дев'яно́ста	ста́
I.	сорока́	дев'яно́ста	ста́
	(сорокма́)	(дев'яностома́)	(стома́)
D.	сорока́	дев'яно́ста	ста́

The variant forms of the instrumental are rare today.

(Exercises 6, 7, 9, 11)

V. NUMERAL + MODIFIER + NOUN PHRASES IN A SENTENCE

1. We have discussed the numeral + modifier + noun phrases when they function as the subject or the accusative object (see Lessons 14 and 15). Here are further remarks on such phrases.

2. When the numeral + modifier + noun phrase appears as an indirect object all three components agree, e.g.:

Нема́ п'ятьо́х на́ших хло́пців.	Five of our boys are missing.
Подзвони́ ци́м п'ятьо́м хло́пцям.	Call those five boys.

3. The distinction between animate and inanimate nouns in the accusative is made for both feminines and masculines with noncompound numbers 2 through 100, e.g.:

Inaminate	*Animate*
A = N	**A = G**
Я́ ба́чив дві́ кімна́ти.	Я́ ба́чив дво́х дівча́т.
I saw two rooms.	I saw two girls.
Я́ ба́чив два́ квитки́.	Я́ ба́чив дво́х хло́пців.
I saw two tickets.	I saw two boys.
Я́ ба́чив два́дцять а́вт.	Я́ ба́чив двадцятьо́х дівча́т (хло́пців).
I saw twenty cars.	I saw twenty girls (boys).

With compound numbers this distinction usually disappears because of the general tendency not to decline the compounds, expecially those with three or more components, or to decline only the last component, e.g.:

Я́ ба́чив два́дцять трьо́х дівча́т/два́дцять три́ ді́вчини.
I saw twenty-there girls.

Я́ ба́чив три́ста три́дцять три́ хло́пці.
I saw three hundred thirty-three boys.

4. Here are some paradigms involving numbers:

N. два́ нові́ (нови́х) столи́; два́ нови́х (нові́) студе́нти, дво́є нови́х студе́нтів
A. два́ нові́ столи́; дво́х нови́х студе́нтів
G. дво́х нови́х столі́в/студе́нтів
L. двох нови́х стола́х/студе́нтах
I. двома́ нови́ми столами/студе́нтами
D. дво́м нови́м стола́м/студе́нтам

N. два́дцять нови́х столі́в; два́дцять нови́х студе́нтів
A. = N.; двадцятьо́х нови́х студе́нтів
G. двадцятьо́х нови́х столі́в/студе́нтів
L. двадцятьо́х нови́х стола́х/студе́нтах
I. двадцятьма́ нови́ми стола́ми/студе́нтами
D. двадцятьо́м нови́м стола́м/студе́нтам

N. два́дцять оди́н нови́й сті́л; два́дцять оди́н нови́й студе́нт
A. = N; два́дцять одного́ ново́го студе́нта
G. двадцяти́ одного́ ново́го стола́/студе́нта
L. двадцяти́ одному́ ново́му столі́/студе́нтові
I. два́дцять одни́м нови́м столо́м/студе́нтом
D. двадцяти́ одному́ ново́му столу́/студе́нтові

N. два́дцять два́ нові́ (нови́х) сто́ли; два́дцять два́ нови́х студе́нти
A. = N; два́дцять дво́х нови́х студе́нтів
G. двадцяти́ дво́х нови́х столі́в/студе́нтів
L. двадцяти́ дво́х нови́х стола́х/студе́нтах
I. двадця́ть дво́ма нови́ми стола́ми/студе́нтами
D. двадцяти́ дво́м нови́м стола́м/студе́нтам

(Exercises 8, 10)

ВПРАВИ

I. Change the sentences according to the model.

Він сказáв, щоб студéнти булú готóві.
Він сказáв студéнтам, щоб вонú булú готóві.

1. Він сказáв, щоб дíти йшлú спáти.
2. Він сказáв, щоб ýчні булú готóві до íспитів.
3. Він сказáв, щоб учителí навчáли дітéй грáти на бандýрі.
4. Він сказáв, щоб інженéри всé перевíрили.
5. Він сказáв, щоб диплома́ти булú готóві летíти до Канáди.
6. Він сказáв, щоб хвóрі бíльше дúхали свíжим повíтрям.
7. Він сказáв, щоб жінкú спеклú картóплю.
8. Він сказáв, щоб бандурúсти заграли щóсь весéле.
9. Він сказáв, щоб дівчáта помíряли температýру.
10. Він сказáв, щоб козáки сідáли на кóні.

II. Change the sentences according to the model.

Я́ не вíрю, що цí студéнти кáжуть прáвду.
Я́ не вíрю цúм студéнтам.

(цí бабýсі, цí дідú, цí тіткú, цí лю́ди, Мéльники, Палії́, Гончарéнки, Дмитрóвські, Лéсеви, Іванúшини)

III. Change all singulars to plurals.

1. Трéба допомогтú цьомý симпатúчному нíмцеві.
2. Трéба цé сказáти твоє́му новóму товáришеві.
3. Трéба помíряти температýру томý старóму дíдові.
4. Трéба подзвонúти вáшому молодóму вчúтелеві.
5. Трéба подя́кувати нáшому гáрному бандурúстові.
6. Трéба показáти дитúні твою́ золотý рýчку.
7. Трéба цé заграти твої́й канáдській товáришці.
8. Трéба побажáти ýспіху цьомý невилікóвному оптимíстові.
9. Трéба цé заспівáти вáшому знайóмому поля́кові.
10. Трéба цé переклáсти цьомý хвóрому росія́нинові.

IV. Change singular to plural.

1. Чийóму сúнові купúли бандýру?
2. Якóму хлóпцеві стáло погáно від тúх лíків?
3. У якóї дíвчини болúть ногá?
4. Одномý ýчневі далú подарýнка, а дрýгому ні.

5. Вона́ принесла́ я́блуко свої́й дити́ні.
6. Ці́й люди́ні стра́шно.
7. Ва́шій ма́тері ва́с шкода́.
8. Цьо́му лі́кареві ба́йдуже, яки́й поря́док у нього в ліка́рні.
9. Які́й жі́нці це́ не на́бридне?
10. Вона́ усміхну́лася англі́йському диплома́тові.

V. Change the sentences according to the model.

Ці́ пісні́ ніко́ли не скінча́ться.
Ци́м пісня́м ніко́ли не бу́де кінця́.

(вака́ції, ле́кції, про́повіді, програ́ми, конце́рти, ві́йни, свя́та, засі́дання, розмо́ви, конфере́нції)

VI. Change the sentences according to the model.

Йому́ три́ ро́ки. — Йому́ **біля трьо́х ро́ків.**

(три́дцять ро́ків, дев'яно́сто, шістдеся́т, шістна́дцять, сто́, два́дцять, со́рок, п'ятдеся́т, п'ятна́дцять, два́ ро́ки)

VII. Answer the questions according to the model.

Яка́ температу́ра? 10°? — Ні́, ви́ще десяти́ гра́дусів.

(11°, 22°, 33°, 44°, 55°, 66°, 77°, 88°, 99°, 100°)

VIII. Put the bracketed words into the correct form.

1. Я́ не хо́чу залиша́тися з (шість мали́х діте́й)
2. Звари́ вече́рю для (де́в'ять люде́й)
3. П'ять козаків їхало на (п'ять до́брих коне́й)
4. Прийшли́ листи́ від (чоти́ри студе́нтки)
5. Лі́кар це́ пора́див (усі́ три́ си́ни)
6. Він прийшо́в з (свої́ два́ това́риші)
7. Книжки́ на (ті́ дві́ поли́ці)
8. Да́йте аспіри́ну (ті́ сі́м хво́рих)
9. Вона́ диви́лася на ньо́го (свої́ два́ вели́кі си́ні о́ка)
10. Яка́ різни́ця між (ці́ два́ по́гляди)?
11. Бажа́ю (ва́ші три́ сини́) успі́шно закінчи́ти інститу́т.

IX. Give a response, as indicated. Write out all the numerals.

(In the request — accusative, and in the answer — genitive)
Пози́ч мені́ 2 крб. — Я́ не ма́ю . . . . .

(2 крб., 12 крб., 20 коп., 100 дол., 30 дол., 50 коп., 40 дол., 80 дол., 90 крб., 60 це́нтів, 3 це́нти)

X. Put the bracketed words into the correct form.

1. Горíлка стоя́ла на (3 вели́кі поли́ці)
2. Папéри лежáли на (2 вели́кі столи́)
3. Гóсті сидíли на (4 вели́кі крíсла)
4. Вони́ жили́ в (5 вели́ких кімнáт)
5. Автóбуси хóдять по (ці 20 ву́лиць)
6. Трéба дáти ліки (ці 10 хвóрих)
7. Цéй хліб вáжить біля (6 кг)
8. Нáші у́чні вчáться в (10 кля́с)
9. Студéнти вжé були́ на (8 йогó лéкцій)
10. Ми́ були́ в (30 міст і сіл Украї́ни)

XI. Answer the questions using the words in brackets.

1. Кому́ він подóбається? (Багáто дівчáт)
2. З ки́м ви́ познайóмилися? (Дéкілька людéй)
3. До кóго він усміхáвся? До (ті дві́ студéнтки)
4. Я́к надóвго ви́ ї́дете? На (декíлька ти́жнів)
5. Над чи́м ви́ працю́єте? Над (кíлька питáнь)
6. З ки́м ви́ говори́ли? З (багáто студéнтів)
7. Дé ви́ про цé чу́ли? На (багáто конферéнцій)
8. Від кóго ви́ цé чу́ли? Від (дéкілька товаришів)
9. Кому́ він цé казáв? (Багáто хлóпців)
10. До кóго він ходи́в у гóсті? До (багáто знайóмих)

XII. Translate into Ukrainian.

1. He has an incurable disease.
2. His great-grandfather has never been sick in his entire life and he lived to be a hundred.
3. If you have a headache take some aspirin.
4. You drink too much vodka.
5. What's aching you?
6. Let's play cards.
7. He plays the bandura like a real bandurist.
8. How much does your bandura weigh?
9. I think it weighs at least ten kilograms.
10. I wish you good health.
11. Why are you smiling?
12. We have reached Lesson 19.
13. I wish you luck.
14. Try this shirt.
15. He gave us five dollars each.
16. The doctor can see you on Monday.
17. Because of you we will be late for the concert.
18. Are you serious (= do you ask seriously) or are you joking?

19. Play something for us.
20. I have a sore throat.
21. What do you have against him?
22. The bandura player gave a successful concert.

XIII. Read and translate.

1. Учóра бýв дéнь нарóдження Микóли і в нáс булú гóсті. Прийшлú мáйже всí нáші знайóмі, тільки Мéльник не зміг прийтú, бо захворíв. Грúць прuнíс своЮ бандýру і цілий вéчір грáв і співáв. Він чудóво співáє украї́нські нарóдні пісні. І сáм він такúй гáрний, симпатúчний хлóпець. Я́ знáю, що він подóбається багатьóм дівчáтам, особлúво* сéстрам Тарновéцьким. Кóжна хотíла б, щоб він з нею одружúвся, алé він усміхáється й кáже, що з двомá одружúтися не мóже, то крáще зóвсім не одрýжуватися. Він цé всім дівчáтам кáже, і вонú не знáють, чи вíрити йомý чи ні. Чи мóжна взагалí вíрити такúм хлóпцям, як Грúць — гáрним, співýчим бандурúстам, що люблять жартувáти?

2. Мú живемó над óзером Мічіґáн. Пéрші дéсять рóків, кóли мú сюдú приї́хали, я́ кóжної зимú хворíла. Мáйже щомíсяця і гóрло болíло, і головá, і температýра булá висóка. Тáк мені цé набрúдло!.. Лíкар казáв, щоб мú переї́хали кудúсь у Флорíду абó Каліфóрнію, алé ж áні я́, áні чоловíк не моглú залишúти** своéї прáці. Та óсь минýло дéсять рóків, і тепéр я́ вжé більше не хворíю — за остáнніх трú рóки áні рáзу не захворíла. Я́ дýже рáда. Багáто приємнíше бýти здорóвою, ніж лежáти в лíжку з висóкою температýрою.

XIV. Answer the following questions to the reading passages.

(1)
1. Хтó вчóра прийшóв і чомý?
2. Чомý не прийшóв Мéльник?
3. Щó робúв Грúць цілий вéчір?
4. Щó вú знáєте про сестéр Тарновéцьких?
5. Щó Грúць кáже всім дівчáтам?
6. Чи мóжна вíрити Грúцеві?

(2)
1. Дé ця́ жінка живé?
2. Колú вонú тудú приї́хали?
3. Щó ї́й набрúдло?
4. Щó казáв лíкар?
5. Чомý вонú йогó не послýхалися?
6. Я́к вонá себé тепéр почуває?
7. Щó багáто приємнíше?

---

* особлúво — especially

** залишúти — to leave

XV. Answer the following questions to the dialogues.

"Макси́м захворі́в"

1. Що́ в Макси́ма боли́ть?
2. Яка́ в нього температу́ра?
3. Що́ хо́че зроби́ти Оле́на?
4. Які́ наро́дні лі́ки зна́є Макси́м?
5. Чому́ він не хо́че прийня́ти аспіри́ну?
6. Що́ Оле́на хо́че сказа́ти Палія́м?
7. Що́ ка́же Макси́м?
8. Що́ ду́має Оле́на?

"Ната́лка на діє́ті"

1. Чи Сла́вко голо́дний?
2. Що́ він ка́же про молоди́х дівча́т?
3. Чому́ Ната́лка і Га́ля ма́ло їдя́ть?
4. Скі́льки вони́ ва́жать?
5. Скі́льки вони́ хо́чуть ва́жити?
6. Що́ Сла́вко ї́м бажа́є?

"Загра́й на банду́рі"

1. Що́ ціка́во гостя́м?
2. Що́ вони́ чу́ли?
3. Що́ Оле́на про́сить Макси́ма?
4. Що́ Макси́м про́сить перекла́сти?
5. Що́ він співа́є?
6. Чи гостя́м сподо́балася пі́сня?

ДВАДЦЯТА ЛЕКЦІЯ

55 Психологічний роман A psychological novel

Дорога́ Наді́є Семе́нівно! 20-го лю́того

Ви́ проха́ли якнайскорі́ше написа́ти Ва́м мої́ думки́ про Ва́ш рома́н. Прочита́вши ті́льки пе́ршу части́ну, то́бто бі́ля двохсо́т сторіно́к, я́ мо́жу лише́ зроби́ти де́які заува́ження і да́ти Ва́м кі́лька пора́д. По-пе́рше, не ра́джу почина́ти зі сме́рти геро́я. Якби́ Ви́ писа́ли детекти́вний рома́н, тоді́ була́ б і́нша рі́ч, але́ Ви́, я́к я́ розумі́ю, пи́шете рома́н психологі́чний. Крі́м то́го, у Ва́с на са́мому поча́тку ги́не не ті́льки геро́й, але́ й дво́є його́ товариші́в — аж три́ вби́вства на пе́рших двохста́х сторінка́х. Чи це́ не забага́то? Якщо́ Ви́ ду́мали, що вби́вши геро́я і не вказа́вши на його́ вби́вцю, Ви́ ти́м заціка́вите читача́, то тре́ба було́ посла́ти товариші́в шука́ти того́ вби́вцю, а не дава́ти і ї́м відра́зу заги́нути. І що́ Ви́ тепе́р роби́тимете на насту́пних трьохста́х сторінка́х? Му́шу прочита́ти ре́шту рома́ну і тоді́ поба́чу.

Щодо сти́лю, то він у Ва́с непога́ний, особли́во в діяло́гах, але́, опи́суючи приро́ду, Ви́ ча́сом стаєте́ сентимента́льною. О́бсяг рома́ну до́брий — тро́хи ме́нше п'ятисо́т сторі́нок.

Оце́, ма́буть, і всі мої́ заува́ження. Пра́вду ка́жучи, я́ не ду́мав, що Ва́ш пе́рший рома́н ви́йде таки́й вда́лий. Якщо́ й дру́га його́ части́на така́, як і пе́рша, то Ви́ мо́жете, не вага́ючи́сь, посила́ти його́ до дру́ку. Я́ пе́вний, що він бу́де ма́ти у́спіх.

Щи́ро віта́ю, Ва́ш В. Гончаре́нко

P.S. Сподіва́юся поба́читися з Ва́ми в тра́вні.

Dear Nadja Semenivna! February 20

You have asked me to give you my opinion about your novel as soon as possible. Having read only part one, i.e. about two hundred pages, I can only make a few comments and give you some advice. First of all I would advise you not to start with the death of the hero. If you were writing a detective novel that would be a different matter, but as far as I can see you are writing a psychological novel. Moreover, right from the start you do away not only with your hero but also with his two companions — three murders on the first two hundred pages. Don't you think it's a bit too many? If by killing the hero and by not revealing the identity of the murderer you aimed at piquing the reader's curiosity, then you should have sent his companions in pursuit of the killer rather then letting them also be killed right away. What are you going to do on the next three hundred pages? I will have to read the rest of the novel and see.

And now about the style. It's not bad, especially in the dialogues, but when you describe nature you sometimes become sentimental. The size of the novel is good, somewhat under five hundred pages.

I guess these are all my comments. To tell you the truth, I did not think that your first novel would turn out so well. If the second part is like the first you may send it to the printers without any hesitation. I am sure it will be a success.

Sincere greetings, Your V. Hončarenko

P.S. Hope to see you in May.

56 Ми проїхали півдороги
We've gone half the way

Dialogue Paticipants:
Лари́са - Л, Оле́кса - О; Larysa - L, Oleksa - O

1. Л- Скі́льки ми́ль ми́ вже́ проі́хали?
2. О- Бі́ля трьохсо́т. Це́ прибли́зно полови́на доро́ги.
3. Л- Полови́на? Хіба́ туди́ шістсо́т ми́ль?
4. О- Тро́хи ме́нше шестисо́т. П'ятсо́т вісімдеся́т.
5. Л- А я́ чому́сь ду́мала, що бі́ля п'ятисо́т. Та́к, прина́ймні, виглядáло на ма́пі.
6. О- Твоя́ ма́па взагалі ні до чо́го. О́сь візьми́ мою́.
7. Л- Ні́, дя́кую. Я́ волі́ю свою́. Твоя́ така́ брудна́, що її́ неприє́мно бра́ти в ру́ки.
8. О- До́бре. Обіця́ю тобі́ її́ ви́прати, коли́ пове́рнемося додо́му.

1. L- How many miles have we made?
2. O- Around three hundred. It's approximately one half of the way.
3. L- One half? Is it six hundred miles to that place?
4. O- A little less than six. Five hundred eighty.
5. L- For some reason I thought it was about five hundred. At least that's the way it looked on the map.
6. O- Your map is no good anyway. Here, take mine.
7. L- No, thanks. I prefer mine, yours is so dirty that I hate to touch it.
8. O- O.K. I promise you I'll wash it when we get home.

57 Щасливої дороги!
Have a nice trip

Dialogue Paticipants:
Євге́н Гуме́цький - Є, Гуме́цька - Г
Jevhen Humec'kyj - J, Humec'ka - H

1. Є- Чи вже́ всі́ зібра́лись?
2. Г- Ні́, ще́ не всі́. Браку́є кілько́х хло́пців.
3. Є- Кого́ са́ме?
4. Г- Обо́х Ме́льників і Андрі́я Палі́я. Ме́льники побі́гли додо́му взя́ти све́три і за́раз ве́рнуться, а Палі́й дзвони́в, що тро́хи спі́зниться.
5. Є- Як звича́йно. Але́ ци́м ра́зом ми́ не бу́демо на ньо́го чека́ти. Неха́й навчи́ться, що "Се́меро одного́ не ждуть".
6. Г- Але́ ві́н каза́в, що ма́є якісь важли́ві спра́ви в науко́вім інститу́ті.
7. Є- А́, в тако́му ра́зі ми́ проба́чимо на́шому молодо́му науко́вцеві. О́тже, скі́льки на́с іде́?
8. Г- Во́сьмеро: двоє Ме́льників, че́тверо Тарнове́цьких, Палі́й і ти́.
9. Є- До́бре. А́! О́сь і Ме́льники з Андрі́єм іду́ть. Ну́, дівча́та, хло́пці, збира́йтесь, ході́мо!
10. Г- Щасли́вої доро́ги!
11. Усі- Дя́куємо. До поба́чення!

1.	J-	Is everybody here?
2.	H-	No, not yet. Several boys are missing.
3.	J-	Who are they?
4.	H-	Both Mel'nyks and Andrij Palij. The Mel'nyks ran home to get sweaters and will be right back, and Palij called that he will be a little late.
5.	J-	As usual. Well, this time we're not going to wait for him. Let him learn that "Seven do not wait for one".
6.	H-	But he said that he has some important business at the Science Institute.
7.	J-	Oh, in that case we will forgive our young scienstist. Well then, how many of us are going?
8.	H-	Eight. The two Mel'nyks, four Tarnovec'kyjs, Palij and yourself.
9.	J-	Fine. Hey, there come the Mel'nyks together with Andrij. Well, girls and boys, let's get going.
10.	H-	Have a nice trip!
11.	All-	Thank you. Good-bye!

СЛОВНИК

бракува́ти, браку́є I	to lack
забра́кнути, забра́кне P	to miss
(3rd. sg. only; + D + G)	
(за)вага́тися	to hesitate
важли́вий	important
вда́лий	successful
(по)верта́тися, -ються I	to return
(по)верну́тися, (по)ве́рнуться P	
відра́зу (= зра́зу)	right away (immediately)
віта́ти, -ють I	to greet
привіта́ти, -уть P (+ A)	
вка́зувати, -зують I,	to point (out), to indicate
вказа́ти, -жуть P	
воліти, -ють I (+ A)	to prefer
(no perf.)	
во́сьмеро	eight
геро́й (m)	hero
ги́нути, -уть I	to perish, to die
заги́нути, -уть P	
дво́є	two
де́який	some, certain
детекти́вний	detective
діяло́г, -у (m)	dialogue
доро́га (f)	way, road, trip
дру́к, -у (m)	print
заува́ження (n)	remark

збира́тися, -ються I	to gather; to intend
зібра́тися, зберу́ться P	to get ready
кі́лька	several
ми́ля (f)	mile
науко́вець, -вця (m)	scientist
науко́вий	scientific
неприє́мно	unpleasant
оби́два (m, n); оби́дві (f)	both
о́бсяг (m)	size, volume
півдоро́ги	half the way
по-дру́ге	secondly
по-пе́рше	firstly
полови́на (f)	half
пора́да (f)	advice
посила́ти, -ють I	to send (+A/G+D)
посла́ти, пошлю́ть P	
пра́ти, перу́ть I	to launder
ви́прати, ви́перуть P	
приблі́зно	approximately
принайм́ні	at least
приро́да (f)	nature
пробача́ти, -ють I	to forgive, to excuse
проба́чити, -ать P (+ D)	
проїжджа́ти, -ють I	to go through, to pass,
прої́хати, -дуть P	to cover (a distance)
проха́ти, -ють I	to ask (a favor)
попроха́ти, -ють I	
психологі́чний	psychological
ра́дити, -жу, -дять I	to advise (+D)
пора́дити, -жу, -дять P	
ре́шта (f)	the remainder
рома́н, -у (m)	novel; love affair
са́ме	just, precisely, namely
а саме́	namely
све́тр, -тра (m)	sweater
се́меро	seven
сентимента́льний	sentimental
сподіва́тися, -ються I	to hope (no perf.)
спра́ва (f)	business, affair
сти́ль, -ю (m)	style
сторі́нка, сторінки́, сторіно́к (f)	page
то́бто	that is (i.e.)
убива́ти, -ють I	to kill
уби́ти/уб'ю́ть P	
уби́вство (n)	murder
уби́вця (m)	murderer

уживáти, -ють I	to use
ужи́ти, уживу́ть P	
цікáвити, -лять I	to interest
зацікáвити, -лять P	(pfv. 'to begin to interest')
части́на (f)	part
чéтверо	four
читáч, -á, читáчу!; í (m)	reader
щи́ро	sincerely
щи́рий	sincere
щодо (+ G)	as for
я́к	as
якнайскоріше	as soon as possible

NAMES

Лари́са; Надія Семéнівна

IDIOMS

в такóму рáзі	in that case
інша річ	a different matter
ні до чóго	useless, no good
прáвду кáжучи	to tell the truth
ци́м рáзом	this time
Щасли́вої дорóги!	Bon voyage!

SUPPLEMENT

надія (f)	hope
надіятися, -ються (на + A)	to hope
понадіятися, -ються P	
наукóвий працівни́к (m)	research assistant
рóзмір (m)	size, dimensions

EXPLANATORY NOTES

1. The noun ромáн has two meanings, 'novel' and 'love affair'.

2. The verb (за)ги́нути means 'to perish', 'to be lost', 'ruined' as in

Хліб на полях ги́не. — Grain is perishing in the fields.

or 'to die', usually a violent death in some kind of major disaster, war, etc.

Він загúнув на війні.	He died in the war.
Люди гúнули з хóлоду й гóлоду.	People were dying from cold and hunger.

3. Note that the noun **вбúвця** 'killer' is masculine but follows the feminine a-declension:

Чи вжé знайшлú тогó вбúвцю?	Have they found the killer?

4. **Наукóвець** designates a research assistant, i.e. it is an equivalent to **наукóвий робітнúк** (**працівнúк**), either **стáрший** ('senior') or **молóдший** ('junior', see Lesson 16 p. 289). A scholar or scientist of some reputation is called **вчéний**.

5. The adjective **вдáлий** 'successful', 'apt', 'felicitous', 'good' is used in reference to events, actions, but not people. E.g.:

Цé бýв дýже вдáлий вéчір (концéрт)	It was a very successful evening (concert).
Перéклад вдáлий.	The translation is good (apt).

Мáти ýспіх means 'to have success', 'to be popular', e.g.:

Ромáн бýв вдáлий і мáв ýспіх у читачів.
The novel was good and had success with the readers.

Бандурúст мáв великúй ýспіх.
The bandurist was a great success (enjoyed great popularity).

Він мáє ýспіх у дівчáт.
He is popular with the girls.

There is no equivalent in Ukrainian to the English 'He is a successful man/lawyer/doctor, etc.', and the idea of 'being successful' is replaced by references to business going well, things turning out successfully, etc. E.g.:

У ньóго264 спрáви йшлú дýже дóбре.	He was doing very well.
Йогó спрáви йшлú дýже дóбре.	Things (business) went very well with him.
Він зробúв ýспішну кар'єру адвокáта	He pursued a successful career as a lawyer

Note: Unlike English, the term кар'єра 'career' usually carries a negative connotation in Ukrainian, and there is no equivalent for a 'successful career man/woman' so that кар'єрúст(-ка) denotes a 'go-getter' or a 'selfish opportunist', as dictionaries put it.

6. The words **щúрий, щúро** means 'sincere', 'true' as in the following examples:

Він говорúв щúро.	He spoke sincerely (truthfully).
Між нúми булá щúра любóв.	There was true love between them.
Він щúрий украї́нець.	He is a true Ukrainian (= a patriot).

7. The verb **сподіва́тися** has an equivalent **надіятися** (на + А). Both verbs are used in the sense of 'hoping', 'expecting', 'trusting', cf.:

Я́ наді́юся (сподіваюся) та́м бу́ти. I hope to be (expect to be) there.

The corresponding nouns are **сподіва́ння** and **наді́я** (the first is used mostly in pl. with the meaning 'expectations').

8. The verb **збира́тися (зібра́тися)** has two major meanings, 'to gather' and 'to be about to go s. thing', 'intend to do s. thing', cf.:

Ми́ ча́сто збира́лися у ни́х.
We used to get together at their place often.

Ми́ збира́ємося переїзди́ти у нове́ поме́шкання.
We intend to move to a new apartment.

Вона́ якра́з зібра́лася йти́, коли́ подзвони́в телефо́н.
She was just about to leave when the phone rang.

9. Research assistants in Ukraine's Academy of Sciences and similar institutions can be senior 'ста́рший науко́вий робітни́к' or junior 'моло́дший науко́вий робітни́к'. The masculine gender term is used for both males and females.

10. The word **о́бсяг** refers to size or dimensions in a non-physical sense as opposed to **ро́змір**: cf. **о́бсяг програ́ми** 'size of the program' and **ро́змір су́кні** 'dress size'.

NOTES ON GRAMMAR

I. GERUNDS (VERBAL ADVERBS)

Gerunds are an uninflected part of speech derived from verbs via suffixation. They function as verbal modifiers and designate a secondary or subordinate action, which either precedes the main action in time or is concomitant with it. Compare the examples from this lesson:

Опи́суючи приро́ду, ви́ ча́сом стаєте́ сентимента́льною.
Describing nature you sometimes become sentimental. (= simultaneity)

Прочита́вши пе́ршу части́ну, я́ мо́жу зроби́ти де́які заува́ження.
Having read the first part I can make certain comments. (= sequence)

1. Gerunds with the suffix **-чи** are formed from the 3rd person plural of the present tense imperfective verbs, both transitive and intransitive. The ending **-ть** is dropped and is replaced by the suffix **-чи**. The particle **-ся** in the -ся- verbs is modified to **-сь**. E.g.:

-Чи *suffixed gerunds*

3rd pl.	
співáю-ть	співáю-чи
пи́шу-ть	пи́шу-чи
вертáю-ть-ся	вертáю-чи-сь

2. The stress in the **-чи** gerunds is on the stem if the 3rd person plural of the verb has a stem stress. If the verb has end stress, the gerund carries the stress on the suffix **-чи**. Cf.:

Stem-stressed **-чи** *gerunds*	*Suffix-stressed* **-чи** *gerunds*
посилáють — посилáючи	беру́ть — беручи́
збирáються — збирáючись	живу́ть — живу́чи

Note 1: The gerund from the verb **хотíти, хóчуть** is **хотячи́** (it is actually formed from the form **хотя́ть** which is considered substandard in modern Ukrainian).

Note 2: In the three gerunds **лéжачи, си́дячи** and **стóячи** the regular final stress is usually shifted to the stem in conversational Ukrainian (see the discussion on the adverbialization of gerunds, p. 357).

Note 3: In the spoken language all **-чи** gerunds tend to be pronounced as if they were spelled with **-учи/-ючи**, e.g. /b'ižučy/ instead of /b'ižačy/ (from **біжáть**). However, the spelling rules require that they be spelled with an **-а-/-я-: боя́ться — боячи́сь, спішáть — спішачи́, біжáть — біжачи́**.

3. All the **-чи** gerunds express simultaneity:

Вони́ йду́ть, сміючи́сь і гóлосно співáючи.
They walk laughing and singing loudly.

Си́дячи за столóм, він читáв яки́йсь ромáн.
Sitting at the table he was reading a novel.

Вертáючись додóму, не забу́дь купи́ти хлíба.
On your way home don't forget to buy some bread.

Notice, that the gerund itself lacks time characteristics and can accompany an action which took place in the past, is taking place now or will take place in the future.

4. Gerunds with the suffix **-ши** are formed from the masculine past tense forms of verbs of either aspect by adding the suffix **-ши**. The stress remains the same as in the verb. The particle **-ся** is reduced to **-сь**.
-ши- *suffixed gerunds*

ішóв — ішóвши	диви́вся — диви́вшись
пішóв — пішóвши	подиви́вся — подиви́вшись
нíс — нíсши	
принíс — принíсши	

5. **-ши** gerunds formed from the verbs of the imperfective aspect indicate simultaneity, those formed from perfective verbs indicate sequence. cf.:

Simultaneity	Sequence
(**-ши** gerunds from imperfectives)	(**-ши** gerunds from perfectives)
Ішóвши вýлицею, він зустрів Надію. Walking down the street he met Nadija.	Прийшóвши додóму, він ліг спáти. He came home and went to bed.

Note: Of the two semantically identical forms in **-чи** and in **-ши** (imperfective aspect), both of which indicate simultaneity, the second is less common and usually accompanies a past tense verb.*

II. USE OF THE GERUNDS

1. Besides the aspectual features gerunds preserve another characteristic of the verb, i.e. the ability to govern objects. For example:

Дúвлячись прогрáму, він заснýв.	He fell asleep while watching a program.
Сказáвши цé, він вúйшов.	Having said that he left.

Syntactically, gerunds are verbal modifiers, but semantically they normally relate to the same subject which performs the main action.

2. In many instances the process of adverbialization of gerunds can be observed where they lose their ability to govern an object. In the case of the gerunds **лежачи, сидячи** and **стоячи** this is reflected in the difference of stress, where, the gerunds-turned-adverbs have the stem stress as opposed to 'true' gerunds with the stress on the suffix **-чи**:

Gerunds	*Adverbs*
Він пúв, лéдве стоячú на ногáх. He drank, hardly being able to stand on his feet.	Він пúв стóячи. He drank standing up.
Він читáв, лежачú в ліжку. Lying in bed he was reading.	Не читáй лéжачи! Don't read while lying down.
Він ї́в, сидячú за столóм. Sitting at the table he ate.	Зручніше ї́сти сúдячи. It's more comfortable to eat while sitting down.

3. Gerunds are used in many set phrases such as **прáвду кáжучи** 'to tell the truth, **починáючи з** 'beginning with', **кінчáючи** 'in conclusion', **поклáвши рýку на сéрце** 'to be honest', 'in all honesty', etc.

---

* A popular joke among Ukrainians is a take off on a saying "Не кажú 'гоп', пóки не перескóчиш " ("Don't say 'hop' before jumping"): 'Перескóчивши і сказáвши 'гоп', подивúсь, кудú тú скочив' (Having jumped across and having said 'hop', look where you jumped.)

4. Adverbial phrases with gerunds and isolated gerunds are separated from the rest of the sentence by commas, e.g.:

Говóрячи з ни́ми, він увéсь чáс диви́вся на годи́нник.
While speaking with them he kept looking at his watch.

Відпочи́вши, він знóв почáв працювáти.
Having rested he began working again.

Gerunds with a purely adverbial function are not separated by commas, e.g.:

Він ішóв не поспішáючи.	He walked unhurriedly.

(Exercises, 1, 2, 3, 4).

III. DECLENSION OF NUMERAL 200 — 1,000.00

The numerals 200 through 900 are compounds with each part declining separately (the hundreds have the plural forms.) For example:

	Двісті 200	Три́ста 300	П'ятсóт 500
N.	двісті	три́ста	п'ятсóт
A.	= N or G	= N or G	= N or G
G.	дв(о́)хсóт	трь(о́)хсóт	п'ят(и́)сóт
L.	(на) дв(о́)хстáх	(на) трь(о́)хстáх	п'ят(и́)стáх
I.	дв(о́)мастáми	трьом(а́)стáми	п'ятьмастáми
D.	дв(о́)мстáм	трь(о́)мстáм	п'ятистáм

1. The variant forms for numbers 500 through 900 (given here in parentheses) are less frequent with the exception of the instrumental where both forms are equally frequent.

2. The words **ти́сяча** 'thousand', **мільóн** 'million', **мілья́рд** 'billion', as well as **нýль** 'zero' (masc.) are nouns and decline as such. Nouns and adjectives following these numbers are always in the genitive plural throughout the declension, e.g.:

A.	Я́ мáю ти́сячу (мільйóн) питáнь. I have a thousand (a millon) questions.
G.	Нáм бракýє ти́сячі (мільйóна) дóлярів. We are lacking one thousand (one millon) dollars.
L.	Скільки грáмів у одній ти́сячі (у одномý мільйóні) кілогрáмів? How many grams are there in one thousand (one million) kilograms?

(Exercises 5, 6)

IV. COLLECTIVE NUMERALS

There is a special group of numerals in Ukrainian which are called 'collective'. They range from 2 to 30 and their forms are as follows:

(a) for 2 and 3 — **двóє, трóє**

(b) for 4 through 8 — **чéтверо, п'я́теро, шéстеро, сéмеро, вóсьмеро**

(c) for 9 through 20 and for 30 add **-еро** to the regular numeral, e.g.: **дéв'ятеро, дéсятеро, двáдцятеро, три́дцятеро.**

1. Collective numerals have no gender distinction. Their oblique case forms are identical to those of regular numerals: двóє — **двóх, двóм, двомá; сéмеро — сімóх, сімóм, сімом,** etc.

2. The noun which is used with the collective numeral is always in the genitive plural when the numeral-noun phrase functions as the subject or the accusative object of a sentence.

У ни́х в роди́ні трóє хлóпців і двóє дівчáт.
There are three boys and two girls in their family.

Я́ мáю тíльки двóє очéй.
I have only two eyes.

3. Collective numerals are normally used with:

(a) masculine nouns which designate human beings:

Усí трóє її́ синíв пішли́ на війну́.	All her three sons went to war.

(b) masculine and neuter nouns designating animals:

По ву́лиці бíгло трóє порося́т.	Three little pigs were running down the street.
Оцí чéтверо конéй хвóрі.	These four horses are sick.

(c) pluralia tantum:

В кімнáті булó двóє дверéй.	There were two doors in the room.
Оцí трóє штанíв ужé старí.	Those three pair of pants are old.

(d) nouns whose plural stems are different from their singular stems:

дити́на — дíти	У нéї булó сéмеро дітéй. She had seven children.
дру́г — дру́зі	Оцé нáші трóє дру́зів. Here are our three friends. (cf. also: **двóє людéй, дівчáт, росíян**, etc.)

(e) personal pronouns:

Нác булó всьóго двóє.	There were only two of us.

The verb is normally in the 3rd singular (neuter in the past tense).

4. Collectives stress the totality of a number, i.e. 'so many and no more'. They either refer to the whole group or to a definite part which is viewed as 'only so many and no more out of the total number'. E.g.:

У селí лиши́лося дéсять чоловíків.	There were ten men left in the village.
Усí дéсятеро були́ старí і хвóрі.	All ten were old and sick.
У селí лиши́лося дéсять чоловíків.	There were ten men left in the village.
П'я́теро з ни́х були́ старí, а п'я́теро хвóрі.	Five of them were old, and five were sick.

Because collectives refer to groups rather than individuals, the distinction between animate and inanimate categories is not so important so that the nominative form can be used in the accusative case for both categories, c.f.:

Inanimate	Animate
Він купи́в двóє штанів.	He bought two pair of pants.
Він кýпив двóє поросят.	He bought two piglets.
Вонá мáла трóє імéн.	She had three names.
Вонá мáла трóє дітéй.	She had three children.

(Exercises 7, 8)

V. DECLENSION OF ОБИДВА (ОБИДВІ, ОБОЄ), 'Both'

1. The word for 'both' is peculiar in that it has three forms: **оби́два** when the nouns are either neuter or masculine, **оби́дві** when they refer to two feminine nouns, and the collective **обóє** which is used when one noun is masculine and another feminine, or with nouns of any gender, cf.:

Оби́два брáти були́ висóкі.	Both brothers were tall.
Оби́дві сестри́ були́ гáрні.	Both sisters were pretty.

І чоловíк і жíнка, обóє були́ рáді йогó бáчити.
The husband and the wife were both glad to see him.

2. All three forms **оби́два, оби́дві, обóє** are declined like **двá**:

N.	оби́два, обóє
A.	= N or G
G.	обóх
L.	(на) обóх
I.	обомá
D.	обóм

3. The nouns following these collectives have the same declension and stress pattern as with the numeral 'two', i.e. when the numeral-noun phrase is the subject or the accusative (inanimate) object of the sentence the noun has the nominative plural form and the genitive singular stress. E.g.:

Вона́ покла́ла оби́дві руки́ на стіл.	She put both hands on the table.
Оби́два діди́ втоми́лися.	Both old men were tired.

3. Note that 'two of them' is **двоє з них** but 'both of them (like 'all of them') is **оби́два вони́, (усі вони)**.

(Exercises 9, 10)

VI. ПОЛОВИНА AND ПІВ

The noun **полови́на** has the same meaning as **пів**, cf.:

Ми́ пройшли́ полови́ну доро́ги.	We have walked half the way.
Ми́ пройшли́ пів доро́ги.	

1. **Полови́на** is declined like any feminine **a**-declension noun. The noun which follows it is always in the genitive (sg. or pl.)

Я́ познайо́мився з полови́ною студе́нтів.	I met half the students.
Я́ тепе́р чита́ю дру́гу полови́ну рома́ну.	I am now reading the second half of the novel.

2. **Пів** may combine with nouns to form a compound, e.g. **південь, північ, піврі́ччя** 'half a year', **півмі́сяць** 'half a moon', etc. In such instances it receives a secondary stress. As a separate noun **пів** is not declined.

Note: Remember that with hours ('half past') Ukrainian uses **пів** (**пів на** + A) and **полови́на** (+ G).

VII. MORE EXPRESSIONS OF APPROXIMATION

1. The preposition **біля** 'near', 'about', 'around' and **бли́зько** in its function of preposition 'near', 'about' are often used in expressions of approximation, e.g.:

Я́ прийду́ біля третьо́ї.	I will come around three.
Було́ бли́зько третьо́ї ра́нку.	It was nearly three in the morning.:

2. The adverb **прибли́зно** 'approximately' has more uses than **біля** and **бли́зько** since it can appear with various prepositions in phrases such as 'in about', 'for about', etc. E.g.:

Я́ та́м бу́ду прибли́зно через годи́ну.	I will be there in about an hour.
Він прибли́зно на рік ста́рший від не́ї.	He is about a year older than she.

(Exercise 11)

ВПРАВИ

I. Change the sentences to include gerunds in **-чи.**

Model: Він це́ **говори́в** і диви́вся на не́ї.
Гово́рячи це́, він диви́вся на не́ї.

1. Тому́ що вона́ **ма́є до́бре се́рце**, вона́ тобі́ ви́бачить.
2. Він **не зна́в украї́нської мо́ви** і тому́ не міг з ни́ми говори́ти.
3. Ти́ це сказа́в і **не ду́мав**, що́ з цьо́го ви́йде.
4. Вони́ працюва́ли до ве́чора і **не відпочива́ли.**
5. Вона́ не відповіда́ла, бо **не розумі́ла пита́ння.**
6. Ми́ **ду́мали**, що вже́ пізно, і тому́ не дзвони́ли ва́м.
7. Він роби́в усе́ са́м і **ніко́го не пита́в.**
8. Ви́ помили́лися, хоча́ **не хоті́ли цього́.**
9. Чи ви́ співа́єте, **коли́ купа́єтеся**?
10. **Коли́ помира́в**, він сказа́в усю́ пра́вду.

II. Change the sentences to include gerunds in **-чи** or -ши.

Model: Він **сказа́в це́** і подиви́вся на не́ї.
Сказа́вши це́, він подиви́вся на не́ї.
Після обі́ду він засну́в.
Пообі́давши, він засну́в.

1. Він **зрозумі́в**, що все́ ні до чо́го, і пішо́в додо́му.
2. Він за́вжди ї́в хліб, **коли́ вече́ряв.**
3. Вона́ зна́чно кра́ще себе́ почува́є **після відпочи́нку.**
4. **Я́ сподіва́лася** від ни́х листа́ і тому́ не дзвони́ла.
5. Вони́ це́ зрозумі́ли **після розмо́ви з науко́вцями.**
6. Вони́ це́ розумі́ли, **коли́ говори́ли з на́ми.**
7. Не вживайте таки́х слів, **коли́ відповіда́тимете на пита́ння.**
8. **Після відповіді** на це́ пита́ння ми́ вже́ нічо́го не боя́лися.
9. Вони́ **подарува́ли** си́нові банду́ру і надіялися, що він навчи́ться гра́ти.
10. **Під ча́с чита́ння** усім хоті́лося спа́ти.

III. Change the sentences so that they contain gerunds in -ши.

1. Коли́ він скінчи́в робо́ту, він пішо́в до ни́х у го́сті.
2. Після то́го як він поверну́вся, він до́вго до на́с не прихо́див.
3. Коли́ прочита́єш рома́н, віднеси́ його́ до бібліоте́ки.
4. Вони́ покра́яли хліб і шви́дко його́ з'ї́ли.
5. Ми́ налили́ собі́ ча́ю і почали́ пово́лі пи́ти.
6. Він сів за стіл і написа́в листа́.
7. Вони́ прийшли́ додо́му і почали́ пра́ти.

8. Я́ поміряв температу́ру і поба́чив, що вона́ висо́ка.
9. Лікар огля́нув хво́рого і да́в йому́ нові ліки.
10. Спочатку перевірте, а тоді дава́йте до дру́ку.

IV. Change the imperfective **-чи** gerunds to perfective **-ши** gerunds.

Model: Гово́рячи це́, він диви́вся на не́ї.
Сказа́вши це́, він подиви́вся на не́ї.

1. Пи́шучи це́, він смія́вся.
2. Поверта́ючись додо́му, вона́ співа́ла яку́сь весе́лу пісню.
3. Збира́ючись ї́хати, він купи́в собі валізку.
4. Віта́ючи госте́й, вона́ пита́ла, коли́ вони́ прилетіли.
5. Перучи́ його́ соро́чку, вона́ пла́кала.
6. Посила́ючи све́тр, напиши́ ї́й листа́.
7. Ціка́влячись да́вньою літерату́рою, він чита́в вірші Сковороди́.
8. Ра́дячи йому́ ї́хати, він не ду́мав про його́ здоро́в'я.
9. Проїжджа́ючи че́рез село́, вони́ поба́чили стару́ це́ркву.
10. Убива́ючи коня́, коза́к пла́кав.

V. Put the bracketed words in the correct case.

1. Ту́т браку́є (двісті ліжок, три́ста книжо́к, чоти́риста сторіно́к).
2. Ці робо́ти (п'ятсо́т студе́нтів, шістсо́т студе́нток, сімсо́т науко́вців).
3. Вони́ ціка́вляться (вісімсо́т до́ларів, дев'ятсо́т гри́вень, двісті копі́йок).
4. Пошліть це́ (три́ста шкіл, чоти́риста науко́вих інститу́тів, п'ятсо́т університе́тів).
5. Тоді заги́нуло біля (вісімсо́т украї́нців, дев'ятсо́т поляків, ти́сяча німців).
6. Вони́ керу́ють (двісті гру́п, сто́ хо́рів, сімсо́т людей́).
7. У ци́х (чоти́риста кімна́т, п'ятсо́т поме́шкань, двісті буди́нків) ме́шкають студе́нти.
8. Ту́т бу́де від (шістсо́т) до (сімсо́т) ми́ль.
Ту́т бу́де від (двісті) до (три́ста) ми́ль.
Ту́т бу́де від (чоти́риста) до (п'ятсо́т) ми́ль.
9. Це́ було́ напи́сане на (п'ятсо́т дощо́к, три́ста сторіно́к, ти́сяча квитків).
10. Це́й рома́н прочита́ло більше (шістсо́т читачів, мільйо́н читачів, сто́ читачів).

VI. Write out the numerals.

1. На́м браку́є ще́ приблизно 200 дол.
2. Що́ ти́ роби́тимеш з 1.000 гр.?
3. У цьо́му детекти́вному рома́ні біля 400 стор.
4. Тобі не ви́стачить і 1.000.000 дол.
5. Хто́ ме́шкає в ци́х 300 кварти́рах?
6. Вони́ продали́ ме́блі 500 людям.
7. О́сь ма́пи 600 міст.
8. На конфере́нції було́ бли́зько 700 учителів.
9. Лю́ди сиділи на всіх 900 місця́х.
10. Ця́ доро́га до́вша ніж та́ на 800 ми́ль.

VII. Replace the numerals by the corresponding collectives.

1. Прийшло́ сім хло́пців.
2. Дві дівчини щи́ро віта́ли госте́й.
3. Ту́т спи́ть два́дцять діте́й.
4. Та́м стоя́ло чоти́ри ко́ні.
5. Туди́ посла́ли вісім люде́й.
6. Заги́нуло три́дцять геро́їв.
7. Усі шість її синів уже́ одру́жені.
8. Поверну́лося додо́му тільки п'ять чоловіків.
9. Ту́т працю́є де́сять науко́вців.
10. Їде по доро́зі три́ козаки́.

VIII. Replace the numbers by any suitable collectives, and make corresponding changes in the nouns which follow.

1. Та́м одні две́рі.
2. У нього лише́ одні штани́, а ре́шту він пози́чив бра́тові.
3. Скільки у не́ї синів, оди́н?
4. Вона́ купи́ла одне́ порося́, а він прода́в одного́ коня́.
5. Ту́т живе́ оди́н росія́нин, а та́м — оди́н німець.
6. Лише́ оди́н мій до́брий дру́г це́ зауважив.
7. Хо́ч би одна́ люди́на прийшла́!
8. У ни́х тоді була́ вже́ одна́ дити́на.
9. Одна́ жінка купи́ла психологі́чний рома́н.
10. У не́ї одна́ сестра́ і оди́н бра́т.

IX. Change the sentences according to the model:

І він, і вона́ були́ сентимента́льні.
Обо́є вони́ були́ сентимента́льні.

1. І ї́й, і йому́ хотілося спа́ти.
2. Лари́су і її сестру́ всі ту́т до́бре зна́ють.
3. І йому́, і його́ жінці бракува́ло на це́ часу́.
4. Браку́є Мико́ли і його́ бра́та.
5. Вона́ щи́ро привіта́ла мене́ і мою това́ришку.
6. Проба́чте Оле́ксі і Лари́сі, що вони́ спізни́лися.
7. Я́ да́м пора́ду тобі і твої́й знайо́мій.
8. Це́, ма́буть, зацікавить ва́с і ва́шого знайо́мого науко́вця.
9. Я́ цікавлюся сти́лем і цього́, і того́ рома́ну.
10. Ми́ вже́ ї́здили бага́то разів і по ці́й, і по ті́й доро́зі.

X. Put the words in parentheses in the correct case.

1. Візьми́ це́ (оби́дві ру́ки) . . . . .
2. Ми́ зацікавлені (оби́два науко́вці) . . . . .
3. Ми́ проха́ли (оби́дві вони́) . . . . . приї́хати до на́с.
4. (Оби́два читачі) . . . . . сподо́бався рома́н.

5. На (оби́дві ді́вчини) . . . . . були́ га́рні све́три.
6. Про (оби́два ці геро́ї) . . . . . співа́ють пісні́.
7. Ми́ пе́вні, що зна́йдемо (оби́два вби́вці) . . . . .
8. Якнайскорі́ше подзвоні́ть (оби́два лі́карі) . . . . .
9. Я́ користу́юся (оби́два словники́) . . . . .
10. Ві́н гра́в у (оби́дві части́ни) . . . . . конце́рту.

XI. Change the sentences to expressions of approximation (use both 'approximately' and 'about').

1. У його́ рома́ні дві́сті п'ядеся́т сторіно́к.
2. Ми́ прої́хали сто́ два́дцять ми́ль.
3. Мені́ потрі́бно два́ ти́жні.
4. На́м браку́є шестисо́т карбова́нців.
5. Вона́ ва́жить вісімдеся́т кілогра́мів.
6. Сього́дні сімдеся́т три́ гра́дуси.
7. У нього́ висо́ка температу́ра, тридця́ть дев'я́ть гра́дусів.
8. Ві́н чека́в дві́ годи́ни.
9. Це́ було́ три́ста ро́ків тому́.
10. Ї́й вісімдеся́т ро́ків.

XII. Translate into Ukrainian.

1. Both of them are sentimental like all the novels of that time.
2. This is a novel about the heroes of the civil war.
3. I will wait till you come back.
4. To tell the truth, I don't like to read about murders and murderers.
5. These pants are dirty and must be washed.
6. We have walked at least ten miles in one day.
7. I sincerely wish you the greatest success.
8. She prefers detective novels.
9. First of all, they didn't know who the killer was.
10. This is approximately one hundred and fifty miles from here.

XIII. Read and translate.

1. Чому́сь у всі́х рома́нах, які́ я́ прочита́ла за оста́нні два́-три́ ро́ки, бу́в щасли́вий кіне́ць — як коли́сь у рома́нах вісімна́дцятого столі́ття. Тепе́р таки́х рома́нів ма́йже не пи́шуть, бо ма́ло лиши́лося люде́й, які́ ві́рять у щи́ру любо́в, щасли́ві роди́ни і до́брих люде́й. Та це й зрозумі́ло*, бо в на́ші часи́ сті́льки во́єн та вби́вств. Сього́днішній чита́ч шука́є у рома́нах того́, що́ ві́н ба́чить у житті́, то́бто у то́му житті́, яке́ пока́зує телеві́зор і про яке́ пи́шуть в газе́тах та журна́лах. Але́ це́ ті́льки части́на життя́, полови́на пра́вди. Ко́жний ба́чить те́, що́ хо́че ба́чити і знахо́дить те́, за чи́м шука́є. Хто́ ма́є здоро́вий по́гляд на життя́, знахо́дить ре́чі, які́ ва́рті любо́ви, які́ прино́сять ра́дість, а то́й, хто́ ніко́му і нічо́му не ві́рить, ба́чить скрі́зь ті́льки ци́ніків або́ ти́х, що́ кра́дуть і вбива́ють.

---

* зрозумі́ло — understandable

2. Ось і кінéць нáшої книжки. Хóчеться вірити, щó цé "щаслúвий кінéць", що вú багáто навчúлися. Вú тепéр знáєте багáто слів і вмíєте їх вживáти (принáймні знáєте, як і колú їх вживáти). Звичáйно, двадцятú лéкцій не дóсить, щоб дóбре вúвчити мóву. Цé тíльки почáток, алé якщó вáм сподóбалася українська мóва і вú захóчете дáлі її вивчáти, то за рік-двá вú дóбре говорúтимете і розумíтимете по-українському. Тоді вú змóжете познайóмитися з українською літератýрою, українською історією, а, можлúво, нáвіть поїдете в Україну, щоб на влáсні óчі побáчити, як живýть українці. Тоді — щаслúвої вáм дорóги!

XIV. Answer the following questions to the above passages

(1)
1. Щó булó в ромáнах 18-го столíття?
2. Когó тепéр мáло лишúлося?
3. Чомý цé зрозумíло?
4. Чогó шукáє сьогóднішній читáч?
5. Дé він цé знахóдить?
6. Щó знахóдить оптимíст?
7. Щó знахóдить песимíст?

(2)
1. Щó вú тепéр знáєте?
2. Чóго не дóсить/чомý?
3. Щó бýде за рік-двá?
4. Щó вú тоді змóжете зробúти?

REVIEW

XV. Change all singulars to plurals

1. Колúсь на цій горі жилú індіянці.
2. По сúньому мóрі плúв чóвен.
3. У чиїй голові народúлася такá дýмка?
4. На нáшому мíсці сидúть якúйсь чоловíк.
5. У тóму роцí грóші стáли нічóго не вáртими.
6. По ширóкій вýлиці їхало áвто.
7. На її дитúні булá червóна сорóчка.
8. Він жúв у дорогóму готéлі.
9. Дівчина сиділа у м'якóму кріслі.
10. Життя бýде крáще на новій землі.

XVI. Write out all the numerals and abbreviations

1. Мú тýт живемó вжé від 1948 р.
2. Цій цéркві вжé блúзько 1500 р.
3. З 200 крб. дóвго не проживéш.
4. Для цьóго мені трéба щонаймéнше 1/2 р. (рік).

5. У на́шому університе́ті вчи́ться біля 30.000 студе́нтів.
6. На конфере́нцію приї́хало 400 нау́ковців.
7. До 1861 р. люде́й мо́жна було́ купува́ти, я́к ме́блі.
8. 640 доце́нтам дали́ нове́ завда́ння.
9. Пі́сля 1919 р Украї́на ста́ла назива́тися "радя́нською".
10. Ки́ївська Ру́сь була́ ду́же сильна́ у XII ст.

XVII. Change the sentences according to the model

Я́ зна́ю ци́х дівча́т. — Я́ знайо́мий з ци́ми дівча́тами.

(поля́ків, люде́й, жіно́к, хло́пців, сесте́р, геро́їв, діте́й, ні́мців, росія́н, доце́нтів).

XVIII. Answer the questions according to the model:

Чи це́ не зана́дто шви́дко? — Ні́, ї́дьте якнайшви́дше.

1. Чи це́ не зама́ло? Ні́, кладіть . . . . .
2. Чи це́ не зана́дто бага́то? Ні́, да́йте. . . . .
3. Чи це́ не зана́дто ши́роко? Ні́, відчиня́йте . . . . .
4. Чи це́ не зана́дто ви́соко? Ні́, ста́вте . . . . .
5. Чи це́ не зана́дто те́пло? Ні́, вдяга́йтеся . . . . .
6. Чи це́ не зана́дто де́шево? Ні́, продава́йте . . . . .
8. Чи це́ не захо́лодно? Ні́, неха́й бу́де . . . . .
9. Чи це́ не забли́зько? Ні́, сіда́йте . . . . .
10. Чи це́ не задале́ко? Ні́, йді́ть . . . . .

XIX. Give the required form of participles (past passive)

1. З чо́го . . . . . це́ крі́сло?
   (зроби́ти)
2. Я́ ба́чив ли́ст, ... руко́ю Шевче́нка.
   (написа́ти)
3. Не бери́ хлі́б . . . . . рука́ми!
   (не ми́ти)
4. Що́ зроби́ти з . . . . . газе́ти?
   (прочита́ти)
5. З'ї́ж ці два́ . . . . . яйця́.
   (вари́ти)
6. Ти́ не бра́в . . . . . хлі́ба?
   (покра́яти)
7. Воні́ були́ у . . . . . сорочка́х.
   (вишива́ти)
8. Чи це́. . . . . поли́ця чи . . . . . ва́шими вла́сними рука́ми?
   (купува́ти) (зроби́ти)

9. Це́й рома́н ще́ не . . . . .
(надрукува́ти)
10. Усі гро́ші вже́ . . . . .
(порахува́ти)

XX. Change all singulars to plurals.

1. Подзвоні́ть цьо́му лі́кареві.
2. Пора́дьте це́ ва́шому у́чневі.
3. Подару́йте це́ на́шій америка́нці.
4. Да́йте це́ ва́шому си́нові.
5. Пошлі́ть це́ ї́хньому вчи́телеві.
6. Віта́йте від ме́не ва́шу сестру́.
7. Покажі́ть це́ ті́й ста́рій люди́ні.
8. Опиші́ть це́ ва́шій ма́тері.
9. Поясні́ть це́ своє́му това́ришеві.
10. Переда́йте це́ свої́й това́ришці.

XXI. Write out the numbers and open the brackets.

1. Що́ я́ ма́ю роби́ти з 15 (копі́йка) . . . . .
2. Я́ вже́ бу́в на 7 (по́льський фі́льм) . . . . .
3. Ми́ прої́хали 32 (ву́лиця) . . . . .
4. Мені́ браку́є 43 (ка́рта) . . . . .
5. Це́ ко́штує щонайме́нше 90 (карбо́ванець) . . . . .
6. У ме́не нема́є 100 (до́ляр) . . . . .
7. Йому́ бли́зько 80 (рі́к) . . . . .
8. Крі́м ци́х 6 (кни́жка) ві́н написа́в ще́ 2 (кни́жка) ві́ршів . . . . .
9. Чи ва́м ви́стачить ци́х 50 (кілогра́м) . . . . . ?
10. Вони́ пої́хали 10 (а́вто) . . . . .

XXII. Rewrite the sentences replacing the underlined verbs by corresponding gerunds.

1. Вони́ <u>гра́ли</u> в ка́рти і смія́лися.
2. Вона́ <u>ви́пила</u> ча́й і пішла́ на робо́ту.
3. Ві́н <u>писа́в</u> і вве́сь ча́с диви́вся на годи́нник.
4. Вони́ <u>переї́хали</u> у нове́ поме́шкання і купи́ли собі́ нові́ ме́блі.
5. Вона́ <u>сиді́ла</u> за столо́м і писа́ла листи́.
6. Ві́н <u>переві́рив</u> а́вто і пої́хав.
7. Ві́н <u>лежа́в</u> на бо́ці і спа́в.
8. Вона́ <u>купи́ла</u> ви́шень і звари́ла варе́ники.
9. Вони́ <u>пра́ли</u> сорочки́ і співа́ли.
10. Вони́ <u>влашто́вували</u> ве́чір і попроси́ли мене́ допомогти́.
11. Вони́ <u>смія́лися</u> й пили́ горі́лку.

XXIII. Open the brackets.

1. Він узя́в до́шку (оби́дві руки́).
2. У (оби́дві дівчи́ни) були́ си́ні о́чі.
3. На (оби́два хло́пці) були́ чо́рні штани́.
4. За (вони́ обо́є) говори́в голова́.
5. Від (вони́ обо́є) прийшли́ листи́.
6. За (вони́ обо́є) післа́ли а́вто.
7. Він стої́ть на землі́ (оби́дві ноги́).
8. Ци́м (оби́два студе́нти) браку́є папе́ру.
9. Ци́х (оби́дві студе́нтки) не було́ на ле́кції.
10. Він люби́в (оби́дві сестри́) і забу́в, як співа́ють "О́х! Та не люби́ дво́х!"

XXIV. Answer the following questions to the dialogues.

"Психологі́чний рома́н"

1. Чому́ Гончаре́нко поспіша́є написа́ти свої́ вра́ження?
2. Скі́льки він уже́ прочита́в?
3. Яка́ його́ пе́рша пора́да?
4. Чому́ він та́к ра́дить?
4. Що́, на його́ ду́мку, тре́ба було́ зроби́ти?
6. Що́ він ка́же про сти́ль?
7. Скі́льки в рома́ні сторіно́к?
8. Чого́ пе́вний Гончаре́нко?

"Ми́ проі́хали півдоро́ги"

1. Я́к дале́ко до то́го мі́сця, куди́ вони́ ї́дуть?
2. Скі́льки вони́ вже́ проі́хали?
3. Чому́ Лари́са ду́мала, що лиши́лося ті́льки п'ятсо́т ми́ль?
4. Що́ Оле́кса ї́й ра́дить?
5. Чому́ вона́ не хо́че його́ послу́хатися?
6. Що́ він ї́й обіця́є?

"Щасли́вої доро́ги"

1. Кого́ ще́ браку́є?
2. Чому́ ї́х ще́ нема́є?
3. Що́ Євге́н хо́че зроби́ти?
4. Що́ поя́снює Гуме́цька?
5. Що́ вирі́шує Євге́н?
6. Чого́ бажа́є ї́м у́сім Гуме́цька?

APPENDIX 1

THE ALPHABET

The Ukrainian alphabet is an adaptation of the old Slavonic alphabet called Cyrillic.

Tradition attributed its invention to St. Cyril (known also as Constantine the Philosopher), who with his brother St. Methodius made the first translations of parts of the Gospels into Slavonic in the 860's. As a matter of fact the alphabet elaborated by these "Slavic Apostles" was a totally different one, called glagolitic, but the Cyrillic letters were in use by the early tenth century and it was in this form that the Slavonic writings were imported by the Kyivans. Cyrillic is essentially the Greek alphabet, with additional letters for specifically Slavic sounds. The shapes of the letters were modified under Peter I (1708) in imitation of the style of Roman letters used in the West. Various adaptations of this "civil" Cyrillic (as opposed to the older "ecclesiastical" letters) are used by the Serbs, Macedonians, Bulgarians, Belarusians and Russians, and in recent decades alphabets based on these letters have been devised for the use of a large number of non-Slavic languages in the Soviet Union.

APPENDIX 2

TRANSLITERATION

Throughout this text we have used two systems by which Ukrainian words were represented aside from their cyrillic spelling. One was transcription and the other transliteration. The first reflected the actual pronunciation, while the second was a mere replacement of the Cyrillic by their Latin "equivalents". For example:

Ukrainian (Cyrillic)	Transcription	Transliteration
украї́нський	(ukrajín's'kyj)	ukrajíns'kyj
óтже	(ódže)	ótže
ди́вишся	(dývys͡'s'a)	dývyšsja

The transcription system was explained and illustrated in the Introduction ("Sound System"). Here we give the transliteration which is used by most Slavicists and adopted by the Harvard Ukrainian Research Institute. In addition the student will find the transliteration used by the Library of Congress (marked LofC).

Ukrainian	Transliteration	LofC
А	a	a
Б	b	b
В	v	v
Г	h	h

Ґ	g	g
Д	d	d
Е	e	e
Є	je	ie
Ж	ž	zh
З	z	z
И	y	y
І	i	i
Ї	ji	ï
Й	j	i
К	k	k
Л	l	l
М	m	m
Н	n	n
О	o	o
П	p	p
Р	r	r
С	s	s
Т	t	t
У	u	u
Ф	f	f
Х	x	kh
Ц	c	ts
Ч	č	ch
Ш	š	sh
Щ	šč	shch
Ю	ju	iu
Я	ja	ia
Ь	’	’
’	”	”

APPENDIX 3

SOUND SEQUENCING AND SPELLING

1. Assimilation takes place in sequences of hushing and hissing consonants:

hushing: /š/ /ž/ /č/ /ʒ/
hissing: /s/ /z/ /c/ /ʒ/ /s’/ /z’/ /c’/ /ʒ’/

The first consonant assimilates to the second, achieving the result **hiss + hiss** or **hush + hush** (and including the factor of palatalization).

The most important instance is in the second person singular of the reflexive verbs, when the ending -ш followed by the particle **-ся** is pronounced /-s's'a/, e.g. **поди́вишся** /podyvys's'a/. Here are other examples:

/s/ + /š/ = /šš/	нісши	/n'iššy/	'carrying'
/z/ + /š/ = /žš/	привізши	/pryv'ižšy/	'bringing'
	зши́ти	/žšyty/	'to sew'
/z/ + /ž/ = /žž/	безжа́лісний	/bežžál'isnyj/	'merciless'
/z/ + /č/ = /žč/	безче́стя	/bežčést'a/	'dishonor'
/z/ + /č/ = /šč/ (in initial position)	з чоловíком	/ščolov'íkom/	'with the husband'
/z/ + /ǯ/ = /ž ǯ/	з джерела́	/žǯerelá/	'from the source'
/š/ + /s'/ = /s's'/	жу́ришся	/žúrys's'a/	'you worry'
/ž/ + /s'/ = /z's'/	зва́жся	/zváz's'a/	'weigh yourself'
/č/ + /c'/ = /c's'/	не моро́чся	/nemoróc's'a/	'don't bother'
/š/ + /s'/ = /s'c'/	до́шці	/dós'c'i/	'to the board'
/ž/ + /c'/ = /z'c'/	у кни́жці	/uknýz'c'i/	'in the book'
/č/ + /c'/ = /c'c'/	дочці́	/doc'c'í/	'to the daughter'

At the word boundary this assimilation does not occur or is very weak.

2. As a part of the same series of assimilation, a /t'/ adapts to a following /s'/ by becoming /c'/. Therefore, in the third person forms, singular and plural, of reflexive verbs the ending **-ться** is pronounced /-c'c'a/ (but also /-t's'a/).

For example:

поди́виться	/podývyc'c'a/
поди́вляться	/podývl'ac'c'a/
купа́ється	/kup ájec'c'a/
купа́ються	/kup ájuc'c'a/

3. The spelling дз and дж usually indicates the units /ʒ/ and ǯ/ respectively. However, they may represent a sequence of separate sounds /d/ + /z/ or /d/ + /ž/ when a prefix ending in a /d/ such as **від**, **над**, **перед** joins a root which begins with /z/ or /ž/. For example:

під + жа́ти	= піджа́ти	/p'idžáty/	'to turn under'
від + звук	= ві́дзвук	/v'ídzvuk/	'echo'

4. Normally in Ukrainian a voiceless consonant (/p/, /t/, /s/, /š/, /c/, /k/, /x/, /f/) changes to voiced when followed by another voiced consonant (/b/, /d/, /z/, /z/, /h/), especially within a word or between closely related words, e.g.:

боротьба́	/borod'bá/	вокза́л	/vogzál/
о́тже	/óǯe/	о́сь де	/óz'de/
як же	/jágže/	якби́	/jagbý/

The opposite assimilation of a voiced to a voiceless consonant in a sequence voiced-voiceless is restriceted to a few instances such as **нігті** /n'íxt'i/ 'finger nails', **кігті** /k'íxt'i/ 'claws', **легко** /léxko/ 'light', **вогкий** /vóxkij/ 'damp' and to prefixes and prepositions ending in /z/. In the latter case, the spelling rules require that the prefix be written as **с** before consonants к, п, т, х, **ф**. Both the prefix and the preposition are pronounced /s/ (or /s'/ or /š/, depending on other assimilation rules). The prefix **з-** in this position assimilates most regularly, while prefixes **без-** and **роз-** may be pronounced with /s/ before voiceless consonants, but this is much less frequent. E.g.:

зсу́нути	/ssúnuty/	'to move'
зціпи́ти	/sc'ipýty/	'to link'
зши́ток	/ššýtok/	'notebook'
з ха́ти	/sxáty/	'from the house'
безпере́чно	/besperéčno/	'undoubtedly'
ро́зкіш	/rósk'iš/	'luxury'

Otherwise, Ukrainian, like English, tolerates groups with **voiced + voiceless** consonant, e.g. **шви́дко** /švydko/ **відповіда́йте** /v'idpov'idajte/. Russian and Polish, however, require assimilation to produce only **voiceless + voiced** or **voiced + voiced** groups; some Ukrainian speakers apply this principle to Ukrainian as well, but such pronunciation is to be avoided. Further, Ukrainian, like English, has voiced consonants at the end of words; Russian and Polish require devoicing. Thus, e.g., Ukrainian /raz/, but Russian and Polish /ras/.

5. Ukrainian has a feature called 'doubling' of consonants which refers to certain consonants being lengthened in pronunciation as the result of assimilation or coincidence. Coincidence occurs between suffixes or prefixes and the root or stem of a word, e.g.:

від + да́ти = відда́ти	/v'iddáty/	'to give away'
роз + збро́їти = роззбро́їти	/rozzbrójity/	'to disarm'
осін-ній	/os'ín'n'ij/	'autumn' (adj.)
хвили́н-ний	/xvylýnnyj/	'momentary'

It can also occur in reflexive verbs whose stems end in /s/, e.g. (понісся) /pon'is's'a/ 'dashed'.

Doubling of palatalized consonants /d'/, /t'/, /z'/, /c'/, /s'/, /l'/, /n'/, /ž'/, /č'/, /š'/ occurs as a result of assimilation in an intervocalic position, cf.:

життя́	/žyt't'á/	'life'
у житті́	/užyt't'í/	'in life'
суддю́	/sud'd'ú/	'the judge' (A.)
ні́ччю	/níč'č'u/	'in the night'

In addition, it appears in two verbs **лля́ти** 'to pour' and **сса́ти** 'to suck', cf.: **ллю́, лле́ш, ссе́, сса́ли**.

APPENDIX 4

(A) DECLENSION OF NOUNS
-a DECLENSION
(Fem. & Masc.)

Singular

N.	вода́	земля́	наді́я	ка́ша
A.	во́ду	зе́млю	наді́ю	ка́шу
G.	води́	землі́	наді́ї	ка́ші
L.	(у) воді́	(у) землі́	(у) наді́ї	(у) ка́ші
D.	воді́	землі́	наді́ї	ка́ші
I.	водо́ю	земле́ю	наді́єю	ка́шею
V.	во́до!	зе́мле!	наді́є!	ка́ше!

Plural

N.	во́ди	зе́млі	наді́ї	ка́ші
A.	во́ди	зе́млі	наді́ї	ка́ші
G.	во́д	земе́ль	наді́й	каш
L.	(у) во́дах	(у) зе́млях	(у) наді́ях	(у) ка́шах
D.	во́дам	зе́млям	наді́ям	ка́шам
I.	во́дами	зе́млями	наді́ями	ка́шами

-c DECLENSION
(Feminine)

	Singular			Plural		
N.	ніч	сла́бість	о́сінь	но́чі	сла́бості	о́сені
A.	ніч	сла́бість	о́сінь	но́чі	сла́бості	о́сені
G.	но́чі	сла́бости	о́сени	ноче́й	сла́бостей	о́сеней
L.	(у) но́чі	сла́бості	(в) о́сені	(у) ноча́х	(у) сла́бостях	(в) о́сенях
D.	но́чі	сла́бості	о́сені	ноча́м	сла́бостям	о́сеням
I.	ні́ччю	сла́бістю	о́сінню	ноча́ми	сла́бостями	о́сенями

MASCULINE — NEUTER DECLENSION

Masculines

Singular

N.	ді́д	сті́л	кі́нь	де́нь
A.	ді́да	сті́л	коня́	де́нь
G.	ді́да	стола́	коня́	дня́
L.	(на) ді́дові	(на) столі́	(на) коні́	(у) дні́
D.	ді́дові	столу́	коне́ві, -ю	дню́
I.	ді́дом	столо́м	коне́м	дне́м
V.	ді́ду!		ко́ню!	

Plural

N.	діди́	столи́	ко́ні	дні́
A.	діді́в	столи́	ко́ней	дні́
G.	діді́в	столі́в	ко́ней	дне́й
L.	(на) діда́х	(на) стола́х	(на) ко́нях	(у) дня́х
D.	діда́м	стола́м	ко́ням	дня́м
I.	діда́ми	стола́ми	кі́ньми (ко́нями)	дня́ми

Singular

N.	геро́й	ча́й	хло́пець	ра́нок
A.	геро́я	ча́й	хло́пця	ра́нок
G.	геро́я	ча́ю	хло́пця	ра́нку
L.	(на) геро́єві	(у) чаї́	(на) хло́пцеві	(у) ра́нку
D.	геро́єві	ча́ю	хло́пцеві	ра́нку
I.	геро́єм	ча́єм	хло́пцем	ра́нком
V.	геро́ю!		хло́пче!	

Plural

N.	геро́ї	чаї́	хло́пці	ра́нки
A.	геро́їв	чаї́	хло́пців	ра́нки
G.	геро́їв	чаї́в	хло́пців	ра́нків
L.	(на) геро́ях	(у) чая́х	(на) хло́пцях	ра́нках
D.	геро́ям	чая́м	хло́пцям	ра́нкам
I.	геро́ями	чая́ми	хло́пцями	ра́нками

Singular

N.	чита́ч	ні́ж	росія́нин
A.	читача́	ні́ж	росія́нина
G.	читача́	ножа́	росія́нина
L.	(на) читаче́ві	(на) ножі́	росія́нинові
D.	читаче́ві	ножу́	росія́нинові
I.	читаче́м	ноже́м	росія́нином
V.	чита́чу!		росія́нине!

Plural

N.	читачі́	ножі́	росія́ни
A.	читачі́в	ножі́	росія́н
G.	читачі́в	ножі́в	росія́н
L.	(на) читача́х	(на) ножа́х	росія́нах
D.	читача́м	ножа́м	росія́нам
I.	читача́ми	ножа́ми	росія́нами

Singular

N.	лі́кар	до́ктор
A.	лі́каря	до́ктора
G.	лі́каря	до́ктора
L.	(на) лі́кареві	(на) до́ктору
D.	лі́кареві	до́кторові
I.	лі́карем	до́ктором
V.	лі́карю!	до́кторе!

Plural

N.	лікарі́	доктори́
A.	лікарі́в	докторі́в
G.	лікарі́в	докторі́в
L.	(на) лікаря́х	(на) доктора́х
D.	лікаря́м	доктора́м
I.	лікаря́ми	доктора́ми

Neuters

Singular

N.	село́	мо́ре	прі́звище	пита́ння
A.	село́	мо́ре	прі́звище	пита́ння
G.	села́	мо́ря	прі́звища	пита́ння
L.	(у) селі́	(у) мо́рі	(у) прі́звищі	(у) пита́нні
D.	селу́	мо́рю	прі́звищу	пита́нню
I.	село́м	мо́рем	прі́звищем	пита́нням

Plural

N.	се́ла	моря́	прі́звища	пита́ння
A.	се́ла	моря́	прі́звища	пита́ння
G.	сіл	морі́в	прі́звищ	пита́нь
L.	(у) се́лах	(у) моря́х	(у) прі́звищах	пита́ннях
D.	се́лам	моря́м	прі́звищам	пита́нням
I.	се́лами	моря́ми	прі́звищами	пита́ннями

	Singular		Plural	
N.	дівчá	ім'я́	дівчáта	іменá
A.	дівчá	ім'я́	дівчáта	іменá
G.	дівчáти	íмени	дівчáт	імéн
L.	(на) дівчáті	(в) íмені	(на) дівчáтах	(у) іменáх
D.	дівчáті	íмені	дівчáтам	іменáм
I.	дівчáм	íменем	дівчáтами	іменáми

Pluralia tantum

N.	двéрі	лю́ди	штани́
A.	двéрі	людéй	штани́
G.	дверéй	людéй	штанíв
L.	(у) двéрях	(на) лю́дях	(у) штанáх (штáнях)
D.	двéрям	лю́дям	штанáм (штáням)
I.	дверми́, двери́ма	людьми́	штаньми́ (штанáми, штáнями)

(B) DECLENSION OF PRONOUNS

Personal

N.	я́	ти́	вíн	вонó	вонá
A.	менé (на мéне)	тебé (на тéбе)	йогó (на ньóго)	йогó (на ньóго)	її́ (на нéї)
G.	менé (у мéне)	тебé (у тéбе)	йогó (у ньóго)	йогó (у ньóго)	її́ (у нéї)
L.	на менí	на тобí	на ньóму	на ньóму	на нíй
D.	менí	тобí	йомý	йомý	і́й
I.	мнóю	тобóю	ни́м	ни́м	нéю

N.	ми́	ви́	вони́
A.	нáс	вáс	і́х (ни́х)
G.	нáс	вáс	і́х (у ни́х)
L.	на нáс	нá вас	на ни́х
D.	нáм	вáм	і́м
I.	нáми	вáми	ни́ми

Reflexive

N.	—
A.	себé (на сéбе)
G.	себé (у сéбе)
L.	на собí
D.	собí
I.	собóю

Interrogative pronouns*

N.	хтó	щó	скíльки	
A.	когó (на кóго)	щó	скíльки	
G.	когó (у кóго)	чогó (у чóго)	скількóх	
L.	на кóму	на чóму	на скількóх	
D.	комý	чомý	скількóм	
I.	ки́м	чи́м	скількомá	
N.	яки́й	якé	якá	якí
A.	яки́й, якóго	якé	якý	якí, яки́х
G.	якóго	якóго	якóї	яки́х
L.	на якóму (на якíм)	на якóму (на якíм)	на якíй	на яки́х
D.	якóму	якóму	якíй	яки́м
I.	яки́м	яки́м	якóю	яки́ми
N.	чи́й	чиé	чия́	чиї́
A.	чи́й, чийóго	чиé	чию́	чиї́, чиї́х
G.	чийóго	чийóго	чиéї	чиї́х
L.	на чийóму (чиéму, чиї́м)	на чийóму (чиéму, чиї́м)	на чиї́й	на чиї́х
D.	чийóму	чийóму	чиї́й	чиї́м
I.	чиї́м	чиї́м	чиéю	чиї́ми
N.	котри́й	котрé	котрá	котрí
A.	котри́й котрóго	котрé	котрý	котрí котри́х
G.	котрóго	котрóго	котрóї	котри́х
L.	на котрóму (котрíм)	на котрóму (котрíм)	на котрíй	на котри́х
D.	котрóму	котрóму	котрíй	котри́м
I.	котри́м	котри́м	котрóю	котри́ми

Demonstrative pronouns**

N.	цéй	цé	ця́	цí
A.	цéй, цьогó (на цьóго)	цé	цю́	цí, ци́х
G.	цьогó (у цьóго)	цьогó (у цьóго)	цiéї	ци́х
L.	на цьóму (цíм)	на цьóму (цíм)	на цíй	на ци́х
D.	цьомý	цьомý	цíй	ци́м
I.	ци́м	ци́м	цiéю	ци́ми

* The same pronouns may appear as conjunctions, in which case they are called "relative pronouns".

** The demonstrative pronouns **таки́й** and **стíльки** decline like the interrogative pronouns **яки́й** and **скíльки** respectively.

N.	тóй	тé	тá	тí
A.	тóй, тогó (на тóго)	тé	тý	тí, тúх
G.	тогó (у тóго)	тогó (у тóго)	тіéї (тóї)	тúх
L.	на тóму (на тíм)	на тóму (на тíм)	на тíй	на тúх
D.	томý	томý	тíй	тúм
I.	тúм	тúм	тіéю (тóю)	тúми

Possessive pronouns*

N.	мíй	моя́	моé	мої́
A.	мíй, могó	мою́	моé	мої́, мої́х
G.	могó	моéї	могó	мої́х
L.	на моéму (мої́м)	на мої́й	на моéму (мої́м)	на мої́х
D.	моéму	мої́й	моéму	мої́м
I.	мої́м	моéю	мої́м	мої́ми
N.	вáш	вáше	вáша	вáші
A.	вáш, вáшого	вáше	вáшу	вáші, вáших
G.	вáшого	вáшого	вáшої	вáших
L.	на вáшому (вáшім)	на вáшому (вáшім)	на вáшій	на вáших
D.	вáшому	вáшому	вáшій	вáшим
I.	вáшим	вáшим	вáшою	вáшими

Other**

N.	увéсь (ввéсь, вéсь)	усé (всé)	уся́ (вся́)	усí (всí)
A.	ввéсь, всьогó (на всьóго)	всé	всю́	всí, всíх
G.	всьогó (до всьóго)	всьогó	всіéї	всíх
L.	на всьóму (всíм)	на всьóму (всíм)	на всíй	на всíх
D.	всьóму	всьóму	всíй	всíм
I.	всíм	всíм	всіéю	всімá
N.	ніхтó	нíщó		
A.	нікóго (ні на кóго)	нічóго (ні на щó)		
G.	нікóго (ні в кóго)	нічóго (ні до чóго)		
L.	ні на кóму (кíм)	ні на чóму (чíм)		
D.	нікóму	нічóму		
I.	нікúм (ні з кúм)	нічúм (ні з чúм)		

* **Possessives твíй** and **свíй** decline like **мíй**, and **вáш** declines like **нáш**

** Indefinite pronouns such as **якúйсь, якúй-нéбудь, хтóсь, дéхто** decline like the corresponding definite pronouns. The pronouns **сáм, сáмий, íнший, цíлий** decline like hard stem adjectives.

(C) DECLENSION OF ADJECTIVES*

Hard stem

N.	до́брий	до́бре	до́бра	до́брі
A.	до́брий, до́брого	до́бре	до́бру	до́брі, до́брих
G.	до́брого	до́брого	до́брої	до́брих
L.	на до́брому (до́брім)	на до́брому (до́брім)	на до́брій	на до́брих
D.	до́брому	до́брому	до́брій	до́брим
I.	до́брим	до́брим	до́брою	до́брими

Soft stem

N.	си́ній	си́нє	си́ня	си́ні
A.	си́ній, си́нього	си́нє	си́ню	си́ні, си́ніх
G.	си́нього	си́нього	си́ньої	си́ніх
L.	на си́ньому (си́нім)	на си́ньому (си́нім)	на си́ній	на си́ніх
D.	си́ньому	си́ньому	си́ній	си́нім
I.	си́нім	си́нім	си́ньою	си́німи

(D) COMPARATIVE ADJECTIVES AND ADVERBS

Adjectives	Adverbs
бага́тий — бага́тший	бага́то — бага́тше
бли́зький — бли́жчий	бли́зько — бли́жче
важки́й — ва́жчий	ва́жко — ва́жче
вели́кий — бі́льший	бага́то — бі́льше
висо́кий — ви́щий	ви́соко — ви́ще
га́рний — кра́щий, лі́пший	га́рно — кра́ще, лі́пше
дале́кий — да́льший	дале́ко — да́лі, да́льше
деше́вий — деше́вший	де́шево — деше́вше
до́брий — кра́щий, лі́пший, добрі́ший	до́бре — кра́ще, лі́пше
до́вгий — до́вший	до́вго — до́вше
дороги́й — доро́жчий	до́рого — доро́жче
легки́й — ле́гший	ле́гко — ле́гше
мали́й — ме́нший	ма́ло — ме́нше
молоди́й — моло́дший	мо́лодо — моло́дше
пога́ний — гі́рший	пога́но — гі́рше
тяжки́й — тя́жчий	тя́жко — тя́жче
швидки́й — шви́дший	шви́дко — шви́дше
широ́кий — ши́рший	ши́роко — ши́рше

* The numeral **третій** 'third' declines like the soft adjectives. All other ordinals and possessive adjectives such as **батьків** decline like hard stem adjectives.

(E) DECLENSION OF PROPER NAMES (PEOPLE AND PLACES)

	Places		*Surnames*	
N.	Ки́їв	Льві́в	Ле́сів	Ле́севи
A.	Ки́їв	Льві́в	Ле́сева (-іва)	Ле́севих
G.	Ки́єва	Льво́ва	Ле́сева (-іва)	Ле́севих
L.	у Ки́єві	у Льво́ві	на Ле́севі	на Ле́севих
D.	Ки́єву	Льво́ву	Ле́севу (-іву)	Ле́севим
I.	Ки́євом	Льво́вом	Ле́севим (-івим)	Ле́севими
N.	Нью-Йо́рк	Монреа́ль	Івани́шин	Івани́шини
A.	Нью-Йо́рк	Монреа́ль	Івани́шина	Івани́шиних
G.	Нью-Йо́рка (-у)	Монреа́ля (-ю)	Івани́шина	Івани́шиних
L.	у Нью-Йо́рку	у Монреа́лі	на Івани́шинові (Івани́шині)	Івани́шиних
D.	Нью-Йо́рку	Монреа́лю	Івани́шину	Івани́шиним
I.	Нью-Йо́рком	Монреа́лем	Іванréши́ним	Івани́шиними

(F) DECLENSION OF NUMERALS*

N.	два́, дві́	три́	чоти́ри
A.	два́, двóх; дві́	три́, трьóх	чоти́ри, чотирьóх
L.	на двóх	на трьóх	на чотирьóх
D.	двóм	трьóм	чотирьóм
I.	двома́	трьома́	чотирма́

N.	п'я́ть	ші́сть	сі́м	ві́сім
A.	п'я́ть, п'ятьóх	ші́сть, шістьóх	сі́м, сімóх	ві́сім, вісьмóх
G.	п'ятьóх (п'яти́)	шістьóх (шести́)	сімóх (семи́)	вісьмóх (восьми́)
L.	на п'ятьóх (п'яти́)	на шістьóх (шести́)	сімóх (семи́)	на вісьмóх (восьми́)
D.	п'ятьóм (п'яти́)	шістьóм (шести́)	сімóм (семи́)	вісьмóм (восьми́)
I.	п'ятьма́ (п'ятьома́)	шістьма́ (шістьома́)	сіма́ (сімома́)	вісьма́ (вісьмома́)

N.	п'ятдеся́т	сóрок	стó
A.	п'ятдеся́т, п'ятдесятьóх	сóрок	стó
G.	п'ятдесятьóх (-десяти́)	сорока́	ста́
L.	на п'ятдесятьóх (-десяти́)	на сорока́	на ста́
D.	п'ятдесятьóм (-десяти́)	сорока́	ста́
I.	п'ятдесять(о)ма́	сорок(о)ма́	стома́

* Number 'one' **один** declines like pronoun **той**. Numbers 9 through 20, and number 30, decline like 5. Numbers 60, 70, 80 decline like 50, while 90 declines like 100. Numbers 600, 700, 800, 900 decline like 500.

N.	двíсті	трúста	чотúриста	п’ятсóт
A.	двíсті	трúста	чотúриста	п’ятсóт
G.	двóхсóт	трьóхсóт	чотирьóхсóт	п’ятúсóт (п’ятьóхсóт)
L.	на двóхстáх	на трьóхстáх	на чотирьóхстáх	на п’ятúстáх (п’ятьóхстáх)
D.	двóмстáм	трьóмстáм	чотирьóмстáм	п’ятúстáм (п’ятьóмстáм)
I.	двомáстáми	трьомáстáми	чотирмáстáми	п’ятьомастáми (п’ятьмáстáми)

APPENDIX 5

VERB GOVERNMENT

Verb	Object: Animate	Object: Inanimate	Examples
бажáти	D	G	Бажáю вáм ýспіху.
бáчити	A	A	Ми́ бáчили Марíю. Ми́ бáчили цéй фíльм.
бáчитися (по-)	з + I		Ми́ з ни́м чáсто бáчимося.
болíти (за-)	у + G D G	N	У мéне боли́ть головá. Менí боли́ть головá. Щó тебé боли́ть?
боя́ться	G	G	Когó ти́ боїшся? Усí боя́ться війни́.
бракувáти (забрáкнути)	D/G	D/G,N	Менí бракýє дóляра. (... тебе) Щó тобí бракýє? Цíй хáті нíчóго не бракýє.
брáти (взя́ти)	A	A,G	Я́ берý з собóю Петрá. Я́ візьмý цю́ кни́жку.
бýти	I, N		Він бýв учи́телем. Йогó жінка бýлá українка.
вари́ти (звари́ти)	A A	A A,G	Я́ варю́ бóрщ. (... ри́бу). Звари́ варéники (варéників).
вдягáти (вдягнýти)	A	A,G	Вонá вдягнýла дити́ну. Вдягни́ сорóчку. Він вдягнýв плащá.
вдягáтися (вдягнýтися)		у + A	Вдягати́ся у щóсь крáще.
вести́ (по-) води́ти	A	A	Вонá повелá дочкý до шкóли. Ми́ вели́ цікáві розмóви.
взя́ти — (див. 'брáти')			
викóнувати (ви́конати)		A	Вонá дóбре викóнує свою́ робóту.
відвикáти (відви́кнути)	від + G	від + G	Вонá від ньóго відви́кла. Він відви́к від важкóї робóти.
відноси́ти (віднести́)	D	A,D	Я́ віднесý йомý ви́шень. Віднеси́ кни́жку тíтці.
відповідáти (відповíсти)	D	на + A	Трéба їй відповíсти на її запитáння.
відчиня́ти (відчини́ти)		A	Відчини́ вікнó!

Verb	Object: Animate	Object: Inanimate	Examples
ві́рити (по-)	D, у+A	у+A, D	Він не ві́рить у Бо́га. Ми́ не повірили своі́м оча́м.
вибача́ти (ви́бачити)	D	за + A	Ви́бачте мені́ за те́, що я́ не писа́в.
вивча́ти (ви́вчити)		A	Ви́вчіть це́й ві́рш напа́м'ять.
вигляда́ти	I	I	Вона́ вигляда́є ще́ молодо́ю.
вистача́ти (ви́стачити)	D	G	Мені́ ви́стачить одного́ до́ляра.
вишива́ти (ви́шити)	D	A	Ма́ти ви́шила йому́ соро́чку.
води́ти (див. 'вести́')			
вози́ти	A	A	Вона́ вози́ла дити́ну до па́рку.
везти́ (по-)		A,G	Я́ везу́ з собо́ю словни́к. Повезі́ть йому́ я́блук!
говори́ти (по-)	з+I D до+G про	про+A I	Я́ хо́чу з ва́ми про це́ (про ва́с) поговори́ти. Чи ти́ і́й про це́ говори́ла? Я́ до те́бе говорю́! Він говóрить украі́нською мо́вою.
дава́ти (да́ти)	D	A,G	Да́й йому́ борщу́ і шмато́к хлі́ба.
дзвони́ти (по-)	до+G D	до+G на+A	Я́ до ва́с подзвоню́. Тобі́ хто́сь дзвони́в. Він подзвони́в на робо́ту (до інститу́ту).
диви́тися (по-)	на+A	в,на+A	Він на не́ї подиви́вся. Він диви́вся в ії́ си́ні о́чі.
жартува́ти (по-)	з+I/+G над+I	з+G над+I	Він з усіма́ жарту́є. Чи ти́ з ме́не жарту́єш? Вони́ над ни́м пожартува́ли.
жда́ти (підо-)	на+A;A	на+A G	Ми́ жда́ли Марі́ю. Підождіть на ме́не. Усі́ жда́ли кінця́ війни́.
жури́тися (за-)	за+I;I	за+I про+A	Вона́ жури́лася за си́ном. Чи́м ви́ зажури́лися? За чи́м жу́ришся? Про що́ зажури́вся?

Verb	Object		Examples
	Animate	Inanimate	
забува́ти (забу́ти)	за, про +A;A	за, про +A;A	Вона́ забу́ла (за, про) Ма́рка. Вона́ забу́ла (за, про) завда́ння
заважа́ти	D		Не заважа́й мені́!
займа́тися (зайня́тися)	I	I	Він зайня́вся свої́м го́стем. Він займа́вся пере́кладами.
закі́нчувати (закінчи́ти) кінча́ти (-ити)		A	Ми́ кінча́ємо (закі́нчуємо) тре́тю ле́кцію.
заува́жувати (заува́жити)	D	A	Вона́ заува́жила одну́ ціка́ву річ. Учи́тель заува́жив у́чневі, що то́й непра́вильно пи́ше.
зберіга́ти (зберегти́)		A	Ми́ зберіга́ємо статті́ про нього.
збира́ти (зібра́ти)	A	A	Тре́ба зібра́ти всі́х у́чнів. Він збира́є старі́ книжки́.
зверта́тися (зверну́тися)	до+G		До ва́с зверта́ється поет Гри́ць Весе́лий.
звика́ти (зви́кнути)	до+G		Я́ не зви́кла до тако́ї робо́ти.
знайо́мити (по-)	A; з+I	з+I	Я́ ва́с познайо́млю з мое́ю сестро́ю. Провідни́к знайо́мив на́с з істо́рією мі́ста.
знайо́митися (по-)	з+I	з+I	Познайо́мтеся з мої́м бра́том. Ми́ познайо́милися з ві́ршами.
знахо́дити (знайти́)	A	A	Вона́ знайшла́ това́ришку. Ви́ за́вжди знахо́дите такі́ ціка́ві ре́чі.
зна́ти	A	A	Хто́ зна́є цю́ студе́нтку? Хто́ зна́є доро́гу?
зустріча́ти (зустрі́нути)	A	A	Він зустрі́в свого́ старо́го дру́га. Учо́ра ми́ всі́ зустріча́ли Нови́й Рі́к.
зустріча́тися (зустрі́тися)	з+I	з+I	Ми́ з ва́ми зустріча́лися на конфере́нціях. Ми́ зустрі́лися з ціка́вим фа́ктом.
ї́сти (по-, з'-)	A	A G,A	Він ї́сть ка́шу. (... ри́бу) Він пої́в ка́ші.
каза́ти (с-)	D	A	Я́ тобі́ це́ кажу́. Хто́ тобі́ каза́в таку́ дурни́цю?
кла́сти (по-)	A, D	A A,G	Вона́ покла́ла дити́ну спа́ти. Він покла́в собі́ ка́ші. Поклади́ папі́р на сті́л.

Verb	Object Animate	Object Inanimate	Examples
кли́кати (по-)	A	I	Покли́ч О́лю. Його́ кли́кали "козако́м".
користува́тися		I	Я́ користу́юся словнико́м.
коштува́ти		A	Оліве́ць ко́штує одну́ копі́йку.
кра́сти (в-)	A	A	Диплома́та вкра́ли. Це́й диплома́т вкра́в які́сь папе́ри.
кра́яти (по-)		A A,G	Вона́ кра́є хлі́б. Вона́ покра́яла хлі́ба.
купа́ти (с-)	A		Коза́к купа́в коня́.
купува́ти (купи́ти)	A	A A,G	Ві́н купи́в коня́. Вона́ купува́ла собі́ су́кню. Купи́ ви́шень.
куштува́ти (по-)		G, A	Покушту́й цю́ горі́лку (цього́ вина)
люби́ти (по-)	A	A	Ві́н люби́в свою́ дружи́ну. Я́ люблю́ літерату́ру.
ма́ти	A	A	Ві́н ма́в сестру́. Хто́ ма́є ча́с на такі́ дурни́ці?
ми́ти (по-)		A	Поми́й го́лову.
мі́ряти (по-)		A	Помі́ряй цю́ соро́чку.
набрида́ти (набри́днути)	D/N	N	Ві́н мені́ набри́д. Це́ мені́ набри́дло.
навча́ти (-ити)	A	G	Я́ тебе́ навчу́ціє́ї пі́сні.
наді́ятися (по-)	на+A	на+A	Я́ наді́юся на те́бе. Я́ наді́юся на у́спіх.
назива́ти (-зва́ти)	A	I	Ві́н назва́в ї́ї своє́ю ми́лою.
носи́ти	A	A	Вона́ носи́ла дити́ну на рука́х.
нести́ (по-)			У руці́ ві́н ні́с валі́зку.
обіця́ти (по-)	D	A	Пообіця́й це́ мені́. Вони́ обіця́ли на́м золоті́ го́ри.
огляда́ти (огля́нути)	A A	A A	Лі́кар огля́нув хво́рого. Ми́ огляда́ли мі́сто.
одру́жуватися (одружи́тися)	з+I		Ві́н з не́ю одружи́вся.
ознайо́мити	A	з+I	Я́ ва́с ознайо́млю з на́шою пра́цею
опи́сувати (описа́ти)	A	A	Ви́ до́бре описа́ли цього́ профе́сора. Ві́н опи́сував своє́ життя́.
очі́кувати	A	G	Ми́ очі́куємо Ві́ктора в се́реду. Чого́ ви́ очі́кували?

Verb	Object: Animate	Object: Inanimate	Examples
пам'ята́ти (за-)	A	A	Я́ пам'ята́ю цю́ жі́нку. Я́ пам'ята́ю це́й ві́рш.
перевіря́ти (переві́рити)		A	Профе́сор переві́рив його́ пра́цю.
переклада́ти		A	Перекладі́ть це́ ре́чення з украї́нської мо́ви на́ англі́йську.
(перекла́сти)	з+G	на+A	
писа́ти (на-)	D до+G	A	Я́ написа́в йому́ листа́. Ві́н пи́ше рома́н. Напиші́ть до нього́.
пита́ти (с-)	A у+G	A про+A	Я́ хо́чу ва́с спита́ти одну́ рі́ч. Ві́н пита́в про Ки́ївську Ру́сь. (. . . про О́лю)
	G про+A	G	Я́ пита́ю ва́шої ду́мки. Спита́й (у) Мико́ли.
пи́ти (ви-)		A A,G	Вона́ пила́ ча́й. Ві́н ви́пив ча́ю.
підво́зити (підвезти́)	A	A	Я́ ва́с підвезу́. Тре́ба підвезти́ до́шки бли́жче до ха́ти.
підкре́слювати (підкре́слити)		A	Підкреслі́ть це́ сло́во.
пла́кати	за+I	за+I	"За тобо́ю, Морозе́нку, вся́ Вкраї́на пла́че." За чи́м ти́ пла́чеш?
поверта́ти (поверну́ти)	A D	A	Лі́кар поверта́в його́ на обі́два боки́. Поверни́ йому́ його́ кни́жку
повто́рювати (повтори́ти)		A	Повторі́ть ва́ше прі́звище, бу́дь ла́ска.
позича́ти (пози́чити)	D у+G	A G	Пози́ч мені́ твою́ ру́чку. Пози́чте мені́ папе́ру. Я́ в не́ї пози́чила гро́ші.
пока́зувати (показа́ти)	A,D	A	Ві́н пока́зував усі́м свого́ мало́го си́на. Покажі́ть мені́ ва́шу ру́ку.
поміча́ти (помі́тити)	A	A	Я́ ва́с відра́зу помі́тив. Я́ помі́тив одне́ непра́вильне ре́чення.

Verb	Object Animate	Object Inanimate	Examples
посила́ти (посла́ти)	A,D до+G	A,G до+G	Його́ посла́ли до Ки́єва. (. . . до лікаря). Вона́ посила́ла йому́ листи́.
потре́бувати	A	A,G	Чи ви́ мене́ ще́ потребу́єте? Я́ потребу́ю ва́шої пора́ди. Я́ потребу́ю ти́сячу до́лярів.
почина́ти (поча́ти)		A	Ми́ почина́ємо нову́ ле́кцію.
поя́снювати (поясни́ти)	D	A	Поясні́ть мені́ одну́ рі́ч.
прийма́ти (прийня́ти)	A	A	Його́ прийняли́ на слу́жбу. Прийми́ аспіри́ну.
присила́ти (присла́ти)	A,D до+G	A,G до+G	До на́с присла́ли ново́го вчи́теля. Пришлі́ть на́м ви́шень.
причепля́ти (причепи́ти)	D	A,D на+A до+G	Ві́н причепи́в собі́ на соро́чку яки́йсь значо́к. Що́ це́ ти́ причепи́в до свого а́вта?
про́бувати (по-)		A A,G	Попро́буй во́ду, чи не холо́дна. Попро́буйте ви́шень.
продава́ти (прода́ти)	A	A A,G	Прода́й мені́ твого́ коня́. Ці́ селя́ни продаю́ть капу́сту. Прода́йте мені́ я́блук.
пролива́ти (проли́ти)		A	Вони́ пролива́ли свою́ кро́в за Украї́ну.
проси́ти (по-)	A у+G G	G A	Я́ ва́с ду́же про це́ прошу́. Проси́ (у) ма́тері/матір. Ві́н про́сить одну́ копі́йку/ва́шої пора́ди.
прохо́дити пройти́	A	A	Ми́ пройшли́ оди́н кіломе́тр.
радити (по-)	D	A	Що́ йому́ пора́дити?
раху́вати (по-)	A	A	Учи́тель порахува́в усі́х діте́й. Ві́н раху́є гро́ші.
роби́ти (з-)		A	Ми́ ро́бимо дома́шнє завда́ння.
розповіда́ти (розповісти)	D про+A	A про+A	Ві́н на́м розпові́в про се́бе всю́ пра́вду. Розкажі́ть на́м про Украї́ну.
розумі́ти (з-)	A	A	Я́ ва́с до́бре розумі́ю. Чи ви́ розумі́єте це́ ре́чення?
слуха́ти (по-)	A	A,G	Я́ ва́с слу́хаю. Ми́ слу́хали украї́нських пісе́нь. Ми́ послу́хали цю́ пі́сню.

Verb	Object		Examples
	Animate	Inanimate	
слуха́тися (по-)	G		Слу́хайся ста́рших!
смія́тися (по-)	з+G	з+G	З нього всі сміються. Усі смія́лися з його́ соро́чки.
співати (за-)		A,G	Хо́р заспіва́в нову́ пі́сню. Ми́ співа́ли на́ших улю́блених пісе́нь.
спізнюватися (спізни́тися)		на+A до+G у+A	Він спізни́вся на робо́ту. Ми́ спізнимося в кіно́ (до кіна́).
става́ти (ста́ти)	I		Вона́ ста́ла лі́карем.
ужива́ти (ужи́ти)	A	A,G	Я́ рі́дко вжива́ю такі́ слова́. Я́ ужива́ю аспіри́ни.
улашто́вувати (улаштува́ти)	A	A	Тре́ба влаштува́ти його́ на робо́ту. Студе́нти влаштува́ли конце́рт.
учи́тися (навчи́тися)		G	Вона́ навчи́лася украї́нської мо́ви.
хворі́ти (за-)		на+A	Він хворі́в на яку́сь хворо́бу.
хоті́ти (с-, за-)		A,G	Я́ хо́чу цю́ кни́жку. Я́ хо́чу ча́ю.
хоті́тися (с-, за-)	D	G	Мені́ захоті́лося води́.
ціка́витися (за-)	I	I	Він ціка́виться О́лею. Чи ти́ ціка́вишся істо́рією?
цілува́ти (по-)	A		Він її́ поцілува́в.
чека́ти (по-)	A, на+A	на+A	На ко́го ви́ чека́єте? Кого́ (чого́) ви́ чека́єте?
чита́ти (про-)		A	Вона́ чита́є газе́ту.
чу́ти (по-)	A про+A	A, про+A	Я́ ва́с до́бре чу́ю. Я́ про ва́с бага́то чу́в. Чи ти́ чу́єш яку́сь пі́сню?
шкодува́ти (по-)		G	Ми́ його́ шкоду́ємо. Він шкоду́є мені́ гро́шей.
шука́ти	G,A	G,A	Кого́ ти́ шука́єш? Я́ шука́ю О́лю. Чого́ ви шука́єте? Ми́ шука́ємо до́брого папе́ру. Вона́ шука́ла вчи́тельки.

UKRAINIAN-ENGLISH VOCABULARY

The following notations are used:

Lessons are indicated by Roman numerals. Letters 'g', 'n', 's','r' after the Roman numerals mean: 'g' — Grammar notes, 'n' — Explanatory notes, 's' — Supplement, 'r' — Reading.

Perfective verbs are given together with the imperfective aspect and separately. Where the perfective differs from the imperfective by prefix only, the prefix alone is given, otherwise the verb notation is given as in Lesson 6.

No lesson numbers are given for the plurals of nouns. Plurals are separeted from the singulars by a semicolon. Stresses are provided over bisyllabic prepositions which are unstressed in speech. Proper names are given at the end of this list.

див. (= диви́сь) means "see"

А

а Introduction, I and
аби́ IX as ling as; in order to
або́ II or; either
  або́. . .або́ II either. . . or
а́вто́ (n) XI car; ї́здити а́вто́м XI to drive (ride in) a car; кермува́ти а́вто́м XI to drive a car;
а́вто́бус (m) XI bus
авто́бусна зупи́нка XIs bus stop
ага́! II aha! VII oh!
адвока́т, -а; -и XXn lawyer
адре́са (f) V address
аж X so that; even
але́ II but
америка́нець, -нця (m) III American (male)
америка́нка (f) III American (fem.)
америка́нський V American (adj.)
англі́йський V English (adj.)
ані V n not a; **ані...ані** IVs neither...nor
аніж XVIg than
аспіри́на (f) XIX aspirin; прийми́ аспіри́ну! XIX take aspirin!
аспіра́нт Xn graduate student
А́х! XII Ah! Oh!

Б

б (би) VII conditional particle
ба́ба; -и́ (f) XVg, XVIn grandmother; woman (peasant)
бабу́ня (f) XVI granny
бабу́ся (f) XVIn granny
ба́бця (f) XVIn granny (dial.)
бага́тий XVIg rich
бага́тший XVIg richer
бага́то X, XVIIIg much; many
бажа́-ти, -ють I (по-, P) intro (n) XIX to wish
база́р, -у (m) XV market
байду́же, ба́йдуже XIII no matter
  мені́ байду́же XIII I don't care
байду́жий XVIg indifferent
ба́л (ь) (m) VIIIn ball
банду́ра (f) XIX bandura (a musical instrument)
бандури́ст (m) XIX bandura player
ба́с, -у; -и́ (m) XIII basso
ба́тько; -и́ (m) V father; по ба́тькові I patronymic; Я́к ва́с по ба́тькові? I What's your patronymic?
батьки́ (pl.) X parents
ба́тьків XVIg father's
ба́ч-ити, -ать I (по-, P) II to see
ба́ч-итися. -аться I (по-, P) X to see each other

без (+G) V without
безкра́їй Vg endless
бе́резень, зня (m) XVI March
бібліоте́ка (f) V library
бібліоте́кар, -я (m) V librarian (male)
бібліоте́карка Vs librarian (f)
Біг (variant of Бо́г), XIIn God; бігме́ XVIn by God
біга-ти, -ють (I) XI to run (multi -d.)
бі-гти, -жа́ть I (по-, P) XI to run (uni-d.)
біг, -ла past imfv.
бій, бо́ю, у бою́; -ї́ (m) VIIg battle
бік, бо́ку; боки́ (m) XV side; з дру́гого бо́ку XV on the other hand/side; XIII з його́ боку on his part
білий XVII white
біля (+G) VII near, next to; XIX approximately, around
більйо́н — див. мільярд
більш XVIg more
більше XVIg more
більший XVIg larger
блаки́тний XIII light blue
бли́жче XV closer, nearer
бли́жчій XVg closer, nearer (adj)
близе́нько XV very close (adv.)
бли́зько XV close, near
близьки́й XVIg close, near
бо III because
Бо́г; боги́ VIII God; IVg; сла́ва Бо́гу! VIII thank God!
богослу́жба XIIIn church service
богослу́ження XIIIn church service
Бо́жий XIII God's, divine
болі́ти, боли́ть, боля́ть I (за-, P) XIX to; ache, to hurt (3rd sg.&pl. only); у ме́не боли́ть голова́ XIX I have a headache; у ме́не боли́ть горло XIX I have a sore throat
бо́рщ, -у́; -і (m) IX borsht
бо-я́тися, -я́ться (I) (no perfective) II to be afraid
бракува́ти, бракує I (забра́кнути, забра́кне P) XX to lack, to miss (3rd sg. only)
бра́т; -и́ (m) III brother.
бра́ти, беру́ть I (взя́ти, ві́зьмуть P) VI to take
бра́тів XIVg brother's
бру́д, -у (m) XVII dirt
брудни́й XVII dirty
буди́нок, -нку; -нки (m) III building, house
бу́дьколи XIV ever
бу́дьяки́й XIII whichever, any
бу́дь ла́ска Intro., I please
бу́ква (f) IIs letter (of the alphabet)
бу́-ти, бу́дуть IV to be (conj. has the future meaning) бу́в, -ла́ past t.; б. на "ти" (на "ви") to be on familiar (formal) terms VIIn

В

в = у
вага́тися, -ються I (за-, P) XX to hesitate
ва́ж-ити, -ать I (no perf.) XIX to weigh (= to have a certain weight)
важки́й XII hard, difficult, heavy
ва́жко II hard, difficult (adv.)
ва́жче XVIg more difficult (adv.)
ва́жчий XVIg more difficult (adj.)
важли́вий XX important
вазелі́на (f) XIXn vaseline
вака́ції (pl. only) XVIII vacation
валі́зка (f) XII suitcase
варе́ник (m) XII dumpling
вар-и́ти, ва́рять I (з-, P) XVII to cook
ва́рт(ий) XVIg worthy
ва́рто XV worthwhile
ва́ш, -а, -е I your (yours)
вбіга́-ти, -ють I (вбі-гти, -жа́ть P) Xvg to run into
вбіг, -ла past pfv.
вбі́гти P — див. вбіга́ти
вве́сь = уве́сь
вве́чері = уве́чері
вда́лий XX successful
вдо́ма = удо́ма
вдяга́-ти, -ють I (вдягну́ти, вдя́гнуть P) XIII to put on, to dress (одяга́ти/одягну́ти)
вдяга́-тися, -ються I (вдягну́тися, вдя́гнуться P) XIII to get dressed (одяга́тися/одягну́тися)
вдя́гнений (= одя́гнений) XIII (XIIIn) dressed
вдягну́ти P — див. вдяга́ти
вдягну́тися P — див. вдяга́тися
вез-ти́, -у́ть I (по-, P) XII to carry (= transport), to take (= to drive) (/uni-d.); віз, везла́ past pfv.

Вели́кдень, Великóдня (m) XIV Easter
вели́кий III large, big, tall; great
вельмишанóвний XIVs most honorable
вéресень, -сня (m) XVI September
верну́тися — див. вертáтися
вертá-тися, -ються I (верну́тися, вéрнуться P) XX to return
вéрх, -у; -и́ XIV top
вéрхи XVIn horseback
весéлий XVIg merry, happy
веселíше XVI happier, merrier
вéсело XVI happy, merrily
весíлля Xs wedding
веснá, вéсно!; вéсни, вéсен XI spring
веснóю XIg in the spring
ве-сти́, -ду́ть I (по-, P) XIV to lead, to take (uni-d), вів, велá imfv.
вéсь = увéсь
вечéря (f) IX supper
на вечéрю IX for supper
вечéря-ти, -ють I (по-, P) XVII to eat supper
вéчір, -чора; вечори́ (m) Introd. evening
Дóбрий вéчір! Introd. Good evening!
вечíрка VIIIn party
вжé = ужé
взагалí XIII in general
взи́мку = узи́мку
взя́ти (узя́ти) P — див. брáти
ви́ Introd., I you
вибачá-ти, -ють I (ви́бач-ити, -ать P) VIg to excuse Вибачте! Introd., I Excuse me!
вибачá-тися, -ються I (ви́бач-итися, -аться P) XIII to excuse oneself
ви́бачити P — див. вибачáти
ви́бачитися P — див. вибачáтися
вибирá-ти, -ють I (ви́брати, ви́беруть P) VII to choose, to elect
ви́брати P — див. вибирáти
вивчá-ти, -ють I (ви́вч-ити, -ать P) VII to study, to master
ви́вчити P — див. вивчáти
виглядá-ти, -ють I (no perf.) XVI to look like
ви́дно XIV one can see; XVIr it seems
ви́дужати P — див. виду́жувати
виду́жу-вати, -ють I (ви́дужа-ти, -ють P) XIX to get well
ви́йти P — див. вихóдити
ви́йшло XV it turned out
викладáти XIIn to teach
викóнувати, -ють I (ви́кона-ти, -ють P) VIIg, to perform, to execute
ви́нести P — див. винóсити
винó-сити, -шу, сять I (ви́нес-ти, -уть P) to carry (take) out; ви́ніс, ви́несла past pfv.
ви́нен (**ви́нний**) XIVg guilty; he owes
ви́пити P — див. пи́ти
ви́прати P — див. пpáти
вирішá-ти, -ють I IX to decide
вирішá-тися, -ються I (-аться P) XIIIg to be decided
вирíшу-вати, -ють I (ви́ріш-ити, -ать P) IX to decide
висíти, -ся́ть I, VIIs to hang
вирíшу-ватися, -ються I (ви́ріш-итися P) IX to be decided
висóкий XVI high, tall
ви́соко XVIg high(ly)
вихóд-ити, -жу, -ять I (ви́й-ти, -дуть P) XV to go out; to turn out;
ви́йшов, ви́йшла past. pfv.
вишивá-ти, -ють I (ви́ши-ти, -ють P) XVIII to embroider
ви́шитий XVIII embroidered
вишнéвий XV cherry (adj.)
ви́шня; ви́шень (f) XV cherry (fruit and tree)
ви́ще XVIg higher, taller
ви́щий XVIg higher, taller (adj.)
вівтóрок, -рка; -рки (m) IVs Tuesday
від (+G) V from
від'їжджá-ти, -ють I (від'ї́хати, від'ї́дуть P) XVg to drive away (від'їзди́ти, -жу́, -я́ть I)
від'ї́хати P — див. від'їжджати
віднести́ P — див. віднóсити
віднó-сити, -шу, -сять I (віднес-ти́, -у́ть P) XVIII to carry (take) back
віднíс, віднеслá past pfv.
відповідáйте Introd. answer!
відповідá-ти, -ють I (відповíсти — irregular P) II, VI to answer; відповíв, відповíла past pfv.
вíдповідь (f) II answer
відповíсти P — див; відповідáти

відпочива́-ти, -ють I (відпочи́-ти, -нуть P) XVII to rest
відпочи́нок, -нку (m) XVIII rest
відпочи́ти P — див. відпочива́ти
відпу́стка (f) XVIIIn leave
відра́зу XX immediately
відцура́тися — див. цура́тися
відчини́ти P — див. відчиня́ти
відчини́тися P — див. відчиня́тися
відчиня́-ти, -ють I (відчини́ти, відчи́нять P) VIII to open
відчиня́-тися, -ються I (відчини́тися, відчи́няться P) XIIIg to open (by itself)
війна́; ві́йни, во́єн (f) XVII war
вікно́; ві́кна, ві́кон (n) I window
він I he; it
ві́р-ити, -ять I (по-, P) X to believe
вірш (m) IV poem (pl. poetry)
ві́сім XV eight
вісімдеся́т, -ий XVI eighty, -ieth
вісімна́дцять, -тий XVI eighteen, -th
вісімсо́т XVII eight hundred
віта́-ти, -ють XX to greet, to welcome
ві́шати, -ють I (пові́сити -ять P) VIIs
вка́зувати I, **вказа́ти** P XX to point out
включа́ючи XV including
вкра́сти P — див. кра́сти
вла́сний XVII own
влашто́вувати —- див. улашто́вувати
влашто́вуватися — див. улашто́вуватися
влаштува́ти P — див. улаштува́ти
влаштува́тися P — див. улаштува́тися
влі́тку = улі́тку
вода́, во́ду; во́ди, во́д (f) XVII water
вод-и́ти, -жу́, -ять (I) XIV to lead, to take; XIVs to drive
водíй XIVs driver
во-зи́ти, - жу́, -зять (I) XII to drive, to carry (transport)
волі́-ти, -ють (no perf.) XIII, XX to prefer
Володи́мирський — диб. собор
вона́ I she; it
воно́ I it
восени́ XIg in the fall
во́сьмеро XX eight
во́сьмий VIII eighth
восьмисо́тий XVIIg eight hunderedth
впра́ва (f) I exercise
вра́ження (n) XIV impression
вра́нці — див. ура́нці
всі́ = усі́
ву́лиця (f) VII street
ву́хо (n) XVIIIg ear
вхо́д-ити, -жу, -ять I (увій-ти́, -ду́ть P) XVg to enter; увійшо́в, увійшла́ past pfv.
вче́ний, -ого XXn scientist, scholar
вчо́ра = учо́ра
вчора́шній = **учора́шній**

Г

газе́та (f) V newspaper
га́рвардський VIIIg Harvard (adj.)
га́рний VI nice, fine, pretty
га́рно XVIg nicely
га́ряче XVI hot
гаря́чий IX hot (adj.)
геро́й (m) XVIr. XX hero
ге́тьман; гетьма́ни XVIIg Hetman
ги́н-ути, -уть I (за-, P) XX to perish, to die
гі́рше XVIg worse
гі́рший XVIg worse (adj.)
гі́сть, го́стя; го́сті (m) VIII guest; іти́ в го́сті до (+ G) VIII to visit; у на́с го́сті VII we have guests
говори́ти, говоря́ть I (по-, P) II, VI to speak, to talk
говорі́ть Introd. Speak!
говори́тися, гово́риться I (no perf.) XIIIg to be said
годи́на (f) XI hour, o'clock; Котра́ годи́на? XI What time is it?; До котрої годи́ни? XI Till what time?
годи́нник (m) XII watch, clock годи́нник іде́; XII the watch (clock) is running; годи́нник запі́знюється XIIs the watch is slow; годи́нник поспіша́є XIIs the watch is fast
голова́, го́лову; го́лови, голі́в (f) XIX head; Ig chairman; у голові́ XIX on one's mind
го́лод, -у XVIIg famine
голо́дний IX hungry
голосні́ше Introd. louder
го́лосно Introd. loud
голосни́й XVIg loud (adj.)

горá, гóру; гóри, гíр (f) XI mountain; на/у гóрах VIIg in the mountains; у гóри XI to the mountains
горíлка (f) XIX whiskey
гóрло (n) XIX throat
горóд, -у (m) XVIII vegetable garden
готéль, -лю (m) III hotel
готíвка (f) XIIg cash
готóв XVIg ready
готóвий XII ready
грáм (m) XIXs gram
грá-ти, -ють (за-, P) XIX to play грáти на (+Loc.) XIX to play an instrument; **грáти в** (+Acc.) XIX to play a game
грáдус, -а (m) XIXs degree (°)
гречáний IXg buckwheat (adj.)
гри́вня (f) XVIIIn hryvnia (a monetary unit)
гріш, грошá (m) XVn penny
громáда (f) XVIIs community
громадя́нин; громадя́ни, громадя́н (m) XVIIs citizen (male)
громадя́нка(f) XVIIs citizen (female)
громадя́нський XVII civil
грóші, грóшей XV money
грýдень, -ня (m), December
грýпа (f) XIV group
губá; гýби, гýб and губíв (f) XVg lip
губ-и́ти, -лять (за-, P) VIIs to lose
гул-я́ти, -ють (по-, P) XIs to walk (go for a stroll)
гуртóжиток, -тку (m) VI dormitory

Д

да-вáти, -ють I (дáти — irregular P) XII to give; to let; дáв, далá past pfv.
дáвній XI old
давнó IX for a long time; long ago
далéкий XVIg far, distant
далéко XI far; XVIII by far
дáлі Introd. further; go on, next; і так дáлі (і т.д.) VII and so forth (etc.)
дáльше XVIg further
дáльший XVIg further (adj.)
дару-вáти, -ють I (по-,P) XIII to give a present
дáта XVIr date (calendar)
дáти P — див. давáти
двá (m & n) XII two
двáдцять, -я́тий twenty, -ieth
дванáдцятий XII twelfth
дванáдцять XV twelve
двéрі, -éй (pl.) I door
дві́ (f) XII two
двíр -орá XIs yard; надвóрі XIs outside, outdoors
двíсті XVIIg two hundred
двохсóтий XVIIg two hundredth
двóє XX two
дé I where
дев'янóсто, -тий XVI ninety, -ieth
дев'ятдеся́т XVIg ninety
дев'я́тий IX ninth
дев'ятнáдцять, -тий XVI nineteen, -th
дев'ятсóт XVII nine hundred
дев'ятсóтий XVIIg nine hundredth
дéв'ять XV nine
дедáлі XVIIIg increasingly
дéкілька VI some, a few
деклямувáти I, продеклямувати P VIIIr to recite
денéбудь IXg anywhere
дéнь, дня́; дні (m) introd. day; Дóбрий дéнь! Introd. Good day! Hello!
десéрт, -у XVIIn dessert; на десéрт XVIIn for dessert
деся́тий X tenth
дéсять XV ten
дéсь VIIIg somewhere
детекти́вний XX detective
дешéвий XV cheap, inexpensive (adj.)
дéшево XV cheap, inexpensive
дешéвше XVIg, XVIII cheaper
дешéвший XVIg cheaper (adj.)
дéякий XX some, certain
дзвони́ти, дзвóнять I (по-P) IV, VI to phone
диви́тися, ди́вляться I (по-,P) II, III to look, to watch; Подиви́ся! III Take a look!
ди́вний XVIII strange
диплома́т (m) XVIII diplomat
диплóмна прáця Xn degree thesis
дисертáція (f) X dissertation
дити́на; дíти, дітéй, дíтям (f) XII child, baby
ди́ха-ти, -ють I XVII to breath

дівча́ (n) XIVg girl
дівча́та (pl. of дівчина) XIII girls
ді́вчина; дівча́та (f) III girl
ді́вчинка (f) XII little girl; baby girl
ді́д, ді́ду!; діди́ (m) XVI grandfather діди́ й пра́діди XIX ancestors
діє́та (f) XIX diet
дізна-ва́тися, -ю́ться I (дізна́-тися, -ються P) IX to find out
дізна́тися P — див. дізнава́тися
дійти́ — див. дохо́дити
діста-ва́ти, -ю́ть I (діста́-ти, -нуть P)III, VI to get, to obtain
діста́ти P — див. дістава́ти
діяло́г, -у XX dialogue
для (+G) V for
до (+G) Introd., V to, for; X before; I, X till; до Хр. (до Христа́) XVIIs B.C.; до н.е. (до на́шої е́ри) XVIIg B.C.; до поба́чення! Introd. Good-bye!; до то́го VII in addition
доба́ (f) Xn day and night, 24 hours
добра́ніч! Introd. Good night! На добра́ніч Introd. Good night!
до́бре Introd. good, well; IV all right; На всé до́бре! Introd. All the best!
добри́день! Introd. Hello!
до́брий Introd. good, kind; до́брий ве́чір! Introd. Good evening!; до́брий де́нь! Introd. Good day!; до́брого здоро́в'я! II Good day! Hello!; до́брого ра́нку! Introd. Good morning!
добрі́ший XVIg kinder
до́вгий X long
до́вго X for a long time
довести́ P — див. дово́дити
дово́д-ити, -жу, -ять I (дове-сти́, -ду́ть P); XVg to lead to, to take; дові́в, довела́ past pfv.
до́вше XVIg longer (time)
до́вший XVIg longer (adj.)
додо́му VI home (homeward)
до́ктор, -а; -и́ (m) XIX doctor
до́ляр, -а (m) XV dollar
дома́шній II home (adj.) II дома́шнє завда́ння home work
доплива́-ти, -ють I (доплив-ти́, -у́ть P) XVg to reach by swimming
допливти́ P — див. доплива́ти
допомага́-ти, -ють I (допомогти́, допомо́жуть P) VI to help допомі́г, допомогла́ past pfv.
допомогти́ P — див. допомага́ти
доро́га (f) XX way, road; trip, journey Щасли́вої доро́ги! XX Happy journey!
дороги́й XII dear, expensive (adj.)
до́рого XVIg dear, expensive
доро́жче XVIg more expensive
доро́жчий XVIg more expensive (adj.)
до́сить VI enough
дохо́д-ити, -жу, -ять I (дійти́, ді́йдуть P) XIX to reach, to walk to дійшо́в, дійшла́ past pfv.
доце́нт (m) X docent (an M.A. holder)
дочка́, до́чко!; до́чки, -чок (f) IX daughter
до́шка; -и́, дошо́к (f) I (black) board
до́щ, -у́; -і (m) VI rain іде́ до́щ VI it's raining
дру́г, дру́же!; дру́зі, -в (m) XI, XIVg friend
дру́гий II second те́ й дру́ге II both на дру́ге XVIIn as a second course
дружи́на (f) XII spouse
дру́к, -у (m) XX print
друку-ва́ти, -ють I (на-, P) II to type; to print, to publish
ду́же Introd. very
ду́жий XVI strong (adj.)
ду́жче XVIg stronger
ду́жчий XVIg stronger (adj.)
ду́ма (f) XVIr duma (a historical song)
ду́ма-ти, -ють I (по-, P) II, VI think; А я́к ви́ ду́маєте? IIIr And what do you think?
ду́мка; -и́ (f) X thought, idea, opinion бу́ти якої́сь ду́мки XIV to be of a certain opinion; на мою́ ду́мку X in my opinion; те́ж тіє́ї ду́мки XIV of the same opinion
дурни́ця (f) XVIII trifle, foolishness зроби́ти дурни́цю XVII to do a foolish thing
душа́; ду́ші (f) IX soul
дя́ку-вати, -ють I (по-, P) II, VI to thank; Дя́кую! Introd. Thank you! Дя́кую ду́же! Introd. Thank you very much!

Е Є

е́ра (f) XVIIg era до н.е. (на́шої е́ри) XVIIg. B.S. н.е. (на́шої е́ри) XVIIg A.D.
є IV there is/are; is/are there; у мене є V I have

Ж

ж IV but (emphatic particle)
жа́рт, -у (m) XVI joke
жарту-ва́ти, -у́ють (по-, P) XVI to joke
жд-а́ти, -у́ть I (підо-, P) XVI to wait
же = ж
жени́тися I (о-, P) Xn to marry
живу́чий XIX of great vitality, endurance
жи́-ти, -ву́ть imfv. II to live жи́в, жила́ past imfv.
життя́ (n) IV life
жі́нка; -и́ (f) IX woman; wife
жо́втень, -тня (m) XVI October
жо́втий XIII yellow
жо́вто-блаки́тний XIII yellow-and-blue
жо́дний Vg none
жури́тися, жу́ряться I (за-, P) XVIII to worry
журна́л, -у (m) II magazine

З

з (+G) V from; (+ Instr.) X with
за (+ Acc.) II for; (+ Instr.) Xg behind; (+ Acc.) X in. within (time)
заба́ва (f) VIIIn dancing party
забага́то XV too much, too many
заболі́ти P — див. болі́ти
забра́кнути P — див. бракува́ти
забува́-ти, -ють I (забу́-ти, -дуть P) VIII to forget
забува́-тися, -ється, -ються I (забу́-тися, -деться, -дуться P) XIIIg to be forgotten (3rd sg. and pl. only)
забу́ти P — див. забува́ти
забу́тися P — див. забува́тися
зава́дити P — див. заважа́ти
заважа́-ти, -ють I (зава́д-ити, -жу, -ять P) XV to bother, to interfere
зavва́жити — див. заува́жити
зavва́жува́ти — див. заува́жувати
завда́ння (n) II assignment
завели́кий XVIIIg too large
за́вжди, завжди́ XI always
заво́д, -у (m) VII plant, factory
за́втра IV tomorrow
заговори́ти, загово́рять P XVIIg to begin speaking/talking
зажури́тися — див. жури́тися
займа́-тися, -ються I (зайня́тися, займу́ся, за́йму́ться P) XVIII to engage in, to be occupied with
зайня́тися — див. займа́тися
закі́нчу-вати, -ють I VIIn to end, to finish
закінч-и́ти, -ать P VIIn to end, to finish
закі́нчу-ватися, -ються IXIIIn to end
закінч-чи́тися, -а́ться PXIIIn to end
залиша́-ти, -ють I (залиши́ти, зали́шать P) XIXr to leave
залиша́-тися, -ються (залиши́тися, -шу́ся P) Xn to stay
залиши́ти — див. залиша́ти
за́між (ви́йти з.) X to marry (of women)
замі́жня XVIIIs married (woman)
за́мість (+ G) XVIII instead of
зана́дто XVIII too, excessively
запам'ята́ти (P) VIIIs to memorize
запита́ння IIn question
запі́зно XVIIIg too late
запі́знюватися — див. спі́знюватися
запла́кати — див. пла́кати
заплати́ти — плати́ти
запоро́жець, -жця; -жці (m) Vg Zaporižžja Cossack
запро́шувати, -ують I (запроси́ти, -сять P) VIIIs to invite
за́раз III now, right away
засі́дання (n) X meeting
засла́бнути XVIn to get sick
засмія́тися — див. смія́тися
заспіва́ти — див. співа́ти
заува́ження (n) XX remark
заува́жити — див. заува́жувати
зауважу-вати, -ють I (зауваж-ити, -ать P) XIV to remark, to notice
захворі́ти — див. хворі́ти
захоті́ти — див. хоті́ти
захоті́тися — див. хоті́тися
заціка́вити — див. ціка́вити
заціка́витися — див. ціка́витися
зачини́ти — див. зачиня́ти

зачини́тися — див. зачиня́тися
зачиня́-ти, -ють I (зачини́ти, зачи́нять P) VIII to close, to shut
зачиня́-тися, -ються I (зачини́тися, зачи́няться P) XIIIg to be closed/shut; to close by itself
зберегти́ — див. зберіга́ти
зберіга́-ти, -ють I (збере-гти́, -жу́ть P) XVI to preserve; зберíг, зберегла́ past. pfv.
збира́-тися, -ються I (зібра́тися, зберу́ться P) VIIIn, XX to gather; to intend
звари́ти P — див. вари́ти
зв-а́ти, -у́ть I XIVn to call
зв-а́тися, -у́ться I XIVn to be called
зверта́-тися, -ються I (зверну́-тися, зве́рнуться P) (до + G) VII to address s.one or s.thing
звика́ти (-а́ють) I, VII to get used to (зви́кнути, -нуть) II
звича́йно II usually; certainly, of course
зві́дки IX where from
зві́дси XI from here
зві́дти XIg from there
згі́дний IX agree; Я́ згі́дна I agree
зго́ден, зго́дний XVIg willing, agreable
здає́ться VII it seems
здíбний X gifted, capable
здíбність, -ости; здíбності (f) X ability
здоро́в XVIg Hi!
здо́ро́вий XVI healthy
здоро́в'я (n) Introd., II health; До́брого здоро́в'я! Introd., II Good day!
зеле́ний XVIII green
земля́, зе́млю, зе́мле!; зе́млі, земе́ль (f) XIV land, earth
зима́, зи́му; зи́ми (f) XI winter зимо́ю XIg in the winter
зі (+ G) Xg from; (+ Instr.) Xg with
зібра́тися P — див. збира́тися
з'ї́сти — див. ї́сти
змогти́ — див. могти́
знайо́мий XIII familiar; an acquaintance
знайо́м-итися, -ляться I (по-, P) X to get acquainted, to meet
знайти́ P — див. знахо́дити
зна́к, знаку́; знаки́ (m) Introd. sing
зна́-ти, -ють I (no perf.) II to know
знахо́д-ити, -жу, -ять I (знайти́, зна́йдуть P) VII to find знайшо́в, знайшла́ past pfv.
зна́ч-ити, -ать I (no perf.) XIV to mean, to signify
зна́чно XVIII considerably
значо́к, значка́; значки́ (m) XIII pin, badge
знести́ P — див. зно́сити
зни́мка (f) IIIn snapshot
знíмок, -мку (m) IIIn snapshot
зно́в(у) II again
зно́-сити, -шу, -сять I (знес-ти́, -у́ть P) XVg to carry down; зні́с, знесла́ past pfv.
зо (+ G) Xg from; (+I) Xg with
зо́всім X completely, quite
золоти́й XIVg golden
зо́лото (n) XIVs gold
золотове́рхий (= з золоти́м ве́рхом) XIV gold-domed (with a golden top)
зо́шит (m) I notebook
зра́зу XX immediately
зроби́ти — див. роби́ти
зро́блений XVIII made, done
зрозумíло XXr understandable
зрозумíти — розумíти
зру́чно VIIs convenient, comfortable
зумíти — див. умíти
зупиня́тися I, зупини́тися P XIs to stop
зупи́нка XIs stop
зустрі́нутий — див. зустріча́ти
зустріча́-ти, -ють I (зустрі-ти, -нуть; зустрін-ути, -уть P) XII to meet

И І Ї Й

і I and; XI even; XII (n)either XVI emphatic particle i...i IV both... and...
із (+ G) Xg from; (+ I) Xg with
ім'я́, і́мени; імена́ (n) I, XIV name; given name Я́к ва́ше ім'я́? What's your name?
індiя́нець, -нця (m) III Indian (American)
інжене́р (m) VII, XI engineer
інститу́т, -у (m) IX institute
і́нший VII, VIII other, different; між і́ншим VII, XIV among other things; incidentally
і́спит, -у (m) VI exam; склада́ти VIs to take an exam; скла́сти і. VIs to pass an exam.
істори́чний VIIIg history (adj.)
істо́рія (f) II history; story
і-ти́, -ду́ть I (пі-ти́, -дуть P) V to go, to come, to walk (uni-d.) ішо́в (пішо́в), ішла́ (пішла́) past

ї-здити, -жджу, -здять I XI to drive, to ride, to go (multi-d.); **їздити áвтом** XI to drive a car; **їздити конéм** XVI to ride a horse
її I her(s)
їсти, їдя́ть (irregular) I (з'-.P) IX to eat
їхати, -дуть I (по-, P) XI to drive, to go (in a vehicle) (uni-d.)
їхній I their(s)
його́ I his; II him, it

K

кáва (f) IX coffee
казáти, кáжуть I (с-, P) II, VI to say, to tell
канáдець, -дця (m) III Canadian (male)
канáдка (f) III Canadian (female)
канáдський V Canadian (adj.)
кандидáт (m) Xn candidate
кандидáтська прáця Xn PhD thesis
кандидáтський мінімум Xn prelims
канíкули XVIIIn vacation
капýста (f) XII cabbage **ки́сла капýста** XIIn sauerkraut
карбóванець, -нця (m) XVIIIs karbovanec' (ruble)
кар'єра, -и (f) Xxn
кар'єрист, -а (m), **кар'єристка, -и** (f) Xxn opportunist, go-getter
кáрта (f) XIX card
карти́на VIIs picture, painting
картопли́на (f) XIIn one potato
картóпля (f) XII potatoes
кáша (f) IX cooked cereal (any kind)
кв. = **кварти́ра**
кварти́ра (f) VII apartment
квитóк, -ткá, -тки́ (m) XV ticket
квíтень, -тня (m) XVI April
керівни́к, -á; -и́ (m) X director, leader
керівни́цтво (n) X leadership, direction
кермувáти áвтом XIn to drive a car
керу-вáти, -ють I (+I) XI to drive, to direct
ки́ївський VIII Kyivan
кілó (n) XIX kilogram
кілогрáм, -у (m) XIX kilogram
кíлька XIXg, XX several
кімнáта (f) I room
кінець, -нця, -нці (m) XIII end
кінó, -á; кíна (n) XVII movie(s)
кінотеáтр, -а XVIIs movie theater
кінчá-ти, -ють I (скінчи́ти, скíнчать P) VII to finish
кінчá-тися, -ються I (скінчи́тися, скíнчаться P) XIII to end
кíнь, коня́, кóню!; кóні, кóней (m) XVg, XVI horse; **їздити конéм** XVI to ride a horse
кíсть, кóсти; кóсті, -тéй, кістьми́ (f) XVIIIg bone
клáс (m) VIIg class; grade
клá-сти, -дýть I (по-, P) VII to put (lay down)
кли́-кати, -чуть I (по-, P) XIV to call, to summon
кля́са (f) VII class
кни́га, у кни́зі (f) XVIr book
кни́жка; -и́, -жóк (f) I book
кня́зь; князí (m) XIVg prince
кóжен XVIg every, each
кóжний X every, each
козáк, -á, козáче!; -и́ (m) XVI Cossack
козáцький XVI Cossack (adj.) "Козáцькому рóду немá перевóду" XVI "The Cossak stock will never cease to be"
колгóсп (колекти́вне господáрство) IXn collective farm
колгóсп -ник/-ниця IXn collective farmer (m/f)
коли́ IV when
коли́шній XII former
кóлір, -льору (m) XVIII color
кóло Xvn near, around
колумбíйський VIIIg Columbia (adj.)
комплімéнт (m) X compliment
комунíст (m) VII communist
конферéнція (f) VII conference
концéрт, -у (m) VIII concert **на концéрт** VIII to a concert
копíйка; -и́, копíйок (f) XVIII copeck (=penny)
корабéль -бля́; -блí (m) XIVs ship
користá-тися, -ються I (с-, P) IX to use, to make use of
користувáтися, -ýються I (с-, P) IX to use, to make use of
корóткий Xs short
котлéта (f) XVII meat patty
котри́й XI which, what
кохáний IIIs beloved
кохáння (n) IIIs love (romantic)
кохáти I (по- P) IIIs to love (romantically)
кохáтися, -ються I, по кохáтися P Xn to be in love

ко́шту-вати, -ють, коштува́ти I (no perf.) XVIII to cost
кра́й; краї́ (m) VIIg edge; land
крамни́ця (f) XV store
кра́-сти, -ду́ть I (в-, P) XVIII to steal
кра́ще Introd. better
кра́щий XVIg better; prettier
кра́-яти, -ють I (по-, P) XVII to slice
крім XI beside **крім то́го** XI besides
крі́сло; крі́сла, крі́сел (n) VII armchair
кро́в, -и (f) XVII blood
куди́ VI where (where to); XVIIIg by far
куди-не́будь IXg anywhere
куди́сь VIII somewhere
купа́-ти, -ють I (с-, P) XIVn to give a bath
купа́-тися, -ються (с-, P) XIV to swim, to take a bath
купи́ти — див. купува́ти
купу-ва́-ти, -у́ють I (купи́ти, ку́плять P) IX to buy
ку́рс, -у (m) VIII course; year (college) бу́ти на ... ку́рсі VIII to be in... year (in college); слу́хати ку́рс VIII to take a course

Л

ла́ден (ла́дний) XVIg ready, capable
ласка́в (ий) XVIg kind
легки́й XVIg easy, light
ле́гко XVIg easily; lightly
ле́гше XVI easier, lighter
леж-а́ти, -ать VII to lie
лежа́чий XIXg liyng
лейтена́нт XVIg lieutenant
ле́кція (f) I lecture; lesson
ле-ті́ти, -чу́, -тя́ть I (по-, P) XIV to fly (uni-d.)
ли́пень, -пня (m) XVI July
ли́ст, -а́; -и́ (m) V letter
листопа́д, -у (m) XVI November
ли́-ти, ллю́, ллю́ть I (на- P) XVIIs to pour
ли́хо XIIg mistortune
лиша́-ти, -ють (лиши́ти, ли́шать P) XIII to leave
лиша́-тися, -ються I (лиши́тися, ли́шаться P) X to remain, to stay
лише́ XVII only, merely
лиши́ти — див. лиша́ти
лиши́тися — див. лиша́тися
лі́вий XVII left
лі́кар, -я; -і (m) VII doctor, physician
лі́карка (f) IXs doctor (female)
ліка́рня (f) IXs hospital
лі́ки (pl) XIX medicine, drugs
лі́жко; -жок (n) VII, XVg bed
лі́тній IIn elderly
лі́пший XVIg better
лі́с, -у; -и́ (m) VIIg forest
лі́та, лі́т XVIg years, **мно́гая (мно́гії) лі́та** XVI Many happy returns!
літа́к, -а́; -и́ (m) XIVs airplane
літа́-ти, -ють I XIVs to fly (multid.)
лі́тера (f) II letter (alphabet)
літерату́ра (f) VIII lietrature
літерату́рний IV literary
лі́то (n) XI summer
лі́том XIg in the summer
літургі́я (f) XIIIn liturgy
лу́г, -у; лу́зі, лу́же! -и́ (m) Vg meadow
лю́бий XIVdear, beloved
люби́ти, лю́блять I (по- P) II, VI to love (pfv — to fall in love); люби́ти одне́ о́дного III to love one another
люби́тися Xn to love one another
лю́блячий XIXg loving
любо́в, -и (f) II love
лю́ди (pl. of люди́на)XIV people
люди́на; лю́ди (f) Xi person, human being
людськи́й XVIIIg human
лю́тий, -ого XVI February
ляга́-ти, -ють I (ля-гти́, -жуть P) XIII to lie down; лі́г, лягла́ past pfv.
ля́мпа (f) VIIs lamp

М

ма́буть VI probably
магази́н (m) XVn store (Russism)
ма́йже XIV almost
мали́й IX small, little

ма́ло X little; few; not enough
малю́нок, -нка (m) III drawing
ма́ма; -и́ (f) V Mom
ма́па (f) III map
ма́-ти, -ють I (no perf.) II to have
ма́ти, ма́тері; матері́ (f) V mother
ма́тер — див. ма́ти
ма́терин XIVg mother's
ма́тір — див. ма́ти
ме́блі (pl. only) XIV furniture
медици́на (f) VII medicine (science)
ме́нш(е) XVIg less, smaller, fewer
ме́нший XVIg smaller (adj.)
ме́шкання (n) VIIg apartment
ме́шка-ти, -ють I (no pfv) VIIg to dwell, to reside
ми́ I we
ми́лий XVII dear
ми́ло (n) XVII soap
ми́ля (f) XX mile
мина́-ти, -ють I (мин-у́ти, -у́ть P) XVIg to pass
мину́лий VII past; last
мину́ти — див. мина́ти
ми́р, -у (m) XVIIs peace
ми́-ти, -ють I (по- P) XVII to wash
між (+I) XIV among, between
мілйо́н (m) XVIIg million
мільйо́нний XVIIg millionth
мілья́рд (= більйо́н) XVIIg billion
мі́й, моя́, моє́ I my, mine
мі́ря-ти, -ють I (по- P) XIX to measure
мі́стер (m) IIg Mister
мі́сто; -а́ (n) VIII city, town; за мі́стом XI beyond the city limits, out of town
мі́сце; -я́, мі́сць (n) I place, seat; на твоє́му мі́сці VIII if I were you (lit. 'in your place')
мі́сяць; -і (m) XVI month; moon
мо́ва (f) I hanguage
могти́, мо́жу, мо́жуть I (з-, P) VIII to be able, can; may (з)мі́г, (з)могла́ past tense
мо́да (f) XVg fashion
мо́же VII maybe, perhaps
мо́жна III may; IX one can, it is possible
молоди́й XI young
молодший XXn junior
мо́лодо XVIg young
моло́дший XVI younger
молоко́ (n) XV milk
мо́ре; -я́, -і́в (n) XI sea
моє́ — див. мі́й
моя́ — див. мі́й
музе́й (m) III museum
му́-сити, -шу, -сять I (no pfv) X must
м'яки́й Introd. soft
м'яки́й знак Introd. soft sign
м'я́к(і)ший XVIg softer
м'я́ко XVIg softly
м'я́со (n) XVII meat

Н

на (+ A) II on, to; (+L) VII on, at, in
на! IV Here! Take it!
набага́то XVIg by far
набрида́-ти, -ють I (набри́дн-ути, -уть P) XVII to bore; набри́д, -ла past pfv
навесні́ XIg in the spring
на́віть XIII even
наві́що XV what for
навча́льний XIIIn **н. рік** school year
навча́-ти, -ють I (навч-и́ти, -а́ть P) XII to teach
навча́-тися, -ються I (навч-и́тися, -а́ться P) VIII to study, to learn
навчи́ти — див. навча́ти і учи́ти
навчи́тися — див. навча́тися і учи́тися
над (+ I) X over, above
наді́я (f) XXs hope
наді́-ятися, -ються I (по-, P) XXs to hope (на + A 'for')
надруку́вати — див. друкува́ти
на́дто = зана́дто XVIIIg too
на жа́ль XIII unfortunately
наза́д XVIII back
на́зва (f) Is name, title
назва́ти — див. назива́ти
назва́тися — див. назива́тися
назива́-ти, -ють I (назв-а́ти, -у́ть P) to name, to call
назива́-тися, -ються I (назва́тися, -у́ться P) XIIIg XIV to be called
найбі́льш XVIg most

найбі́льший XVIg the largest, biggest
найкра́ще XVIg best
найкра́щий XI the best (adj.)
найме́нш XVIg least
найме́нший XVIg the smallest, the least
найстарі́ший XIV the oldest, the most ancient
найста́рший XVIg the oldest
налива́-ти, -ють I (нали́ти, наллю́ть P) XVIIs to pour (in)
нали́ти — див. ли́ти, налива́ти
напа́м'ять VIII by memory, by heart; учи́ти напа́м'ять VIII to learn by heart
написа́ти — див. писа́ти
на́рід, -о́ду; наро́ди (m) XVIn people (W.Ukr.)
наро́д, -у (m) XVI people, nation
наро́дний XIX national, folk
наро́дження (n) XVI birth
наро́джу-ватися, -ються I (народи́тися, наро́джуся, наро́дяться P) XVI to be born
насту́пний V next, following
на́те IVn Here! Take it!
нау́ка (f) VI science; lesson
науко́вець, -вця (m) XX scientist
науко́вий XVIg, XX scientific, science (adj.) н. робітни́к XVIg, XXs research worker
навча́-ти, -ють I (научи́ти, нау́чать P) XIIn to teach
навча́-тися, -ються I (научи́тися, нау́чаться P) VIII to learn
наш, -а, -е I our(s)
н.е. (на́шої е́ри) XVIIIg A.D.
не I not
невже́ IV really?; Та невже́? IV You don't say!
невиліко́вний XIX incurable
невмиру́щий XIXg undying
невсипу́щий XIXg vigilant
неда́вно X not long ago, recently
недале́ко V not far
неді́ля (f) IV Sunday
незале́жний VII independent
незру́чно VII inconvenient, awkward
нема́ (нема́є) IV is/are not there; V does not/do not have; Нема́ за́ що! V Don't mention it!
нелолоди́й IIn elderly
непога́но Introd. not bad
непра́вильно Introd. incorrect, wrong
неприє́мно XX unpleasant
нес-ти́, -у́ть I (по-, P) XII to carry (by hand) (по)ні́с, (по)несла́ past t.
неха́й VIII let, may
нече́мний XVI impolite
неща́сний XVIII unhappy, miserable
ни́жче, -ий XVIs lower; shorter (of height)
низьки́й XVIs low; short (of height)
ни́зько XVIs low
ни́тка; -и́, -то́к (f) XVIII thread; pl. threads, yarn
ні Introd. no; ні (+G) XVII not a; ні...ні IV neither ...nor; ні до чо́го XX good for nothing
ні́би XVII as if
ніде́ XIIg nowhere
ніж II than
ніко́ли XI never
ні́коли XIIIg no time
ніку́ди XIIIg nowhere
ні́мець, -ця (m) XVII German (male)
німе́цький XVIIs German (adj.)
ні́мка (німке́ня) (f) XVIIs German (fem.)
ніхто́ (m) IV nobody
ніч, но́чі; но́чі, -е́й (f) X night
нічо́го II nothing; Це́ нічо́го! V It's all right!
нíщо́ II nothing
ніяк XIII in no way
ніяки́й XIII none, no
нови́й II new Що́ ново́го? II What is new? Нічо́го ново́го. II Noting new.
нога́, но́гу; но́ги, ніг (f) XVII foot; leg бу́ти на но́гах XVII to be on one's feet
но́мер (#) IIs number
носи́ти, ношу́, но́сять I XII to carry; to wear (multi d.)
но́та (f) XVg note
ну́ III well (interj.)
ну́ль, -я́; -і́ XXg zero
нью-йо́ркський VIIIg New York (adj.)

О

о (+L) XII at (time)
оби́два (m & n), **оби́дві** (f) XX both
обі́д, -у (m) IX dinner, lunch; на обі́д IX for dinner (lunch)

обі́да-ти, -ють I (по-, P) XVII to dine; to eat lunch
обіця́-ти, -ють I (по-, P) XII to promise
обов'язко́во XVIII by all means, absolutely
обо́є XX both
о́бсяг (m) XX size
огляда́-ти, -ють I (огля́н-ути, -уть P) XIV to see (to go sight-seeing), to inspect, to look around
Ого́! XII Oho!
оде́ржати — див. оде́ржувати
оде́ржу-вати, -ють I (оде́рж-ати, -ать P) XII to receive
оди́н, одна́, одне́ II one; а ні о́дного/о́дної V not one; одне́ о́дного III one another; ще́ одне́ II one more thing
одина́дцятий XI eleventh
одина́дцять XV eleven
одна́ — див. оди́н
однако́вий XIVr same, identical
одне́ — див. оди́н
одру́жений XVIII married
одружи́тися — див. одру́жуватися
одру́жу-ватися, -ються I (одружи́тися, одру́жаться P) X to get married
о́дяг, -у (m) XIII clothes, garment
одяга́ти(ся), одягну́ти(ся), одя́гнений — див. вдяга́ти(ся), вдягну́ти(ся), вдя́гнений
ожени́тися (з+I) Xs to marry (of men)
о́зеро; озе́ра, озе́р (n) XVg, XVII lake на о́зері XVII at the lake
ознайо́млюватися I, **ознайо́митися** P Xs to familiarize oneself
О́й! XI Oh no!
о́ко, в о́ці; о́чі, -че́й (n) XII eye ба́чити на вла́сні о́чі XVII to see with one's own eyes
оліве́ць, -вця́; -вці (m) I pencil
о́н, о́н та́м I there, over there
описа́ти — див. опи́сувати
опи́су-вати, -ють I (описа́ти, опи́шуть P) XIV to describe
оптимі́ст (m) XIX optimist
оповіда́ння (n) IIn story
о́сінь, о́сени; о́сені (f) XIs autumn
особли́во XIXr, XX especially
оста́нній VII, XVII last
о́сь, о́сь ту́т I here, over here
о́т, ото́ XVI that is/those are; о́т яки́й! II What a...!
о́тже X so (then), consequently
отри́мати, -ють P (**отри́мувати, отри́мують I**) Vs to receive
Ох! II Ah!
охоло́джений XVII cooled
охоло́джене пові́тря XVII air-condition
оце́й, оця́, оце́ III this
оці́нка (f) VIs grade, mark
очі́ку-вати, -ють I (no perf.) XII to expect

П

пам'ята́-ти, -ють I IV to remember, to recall (за-, P) VI to put to memory
па́м'ять (f) IVs memory
па́н; пани́ and **пано́ве** II, XIV Sir, mister, gentlemen, IIn master, Lord
п. II Mr.
пані (f) II Madam, Mrs., lady
п. II Mrs., Miss Дорогі́ (Шано́вні, Вельмишано́вні) па́ні й пано́ве! XIVs Ladies and gentelemen!
па́нна; -и́ IIg Miss
папі́р, -пе́ру; папе́ри (m) IV paper
па́ра, -ри; пар (f) XIII pair, couple
па́рк, -у (m) XIV park
пароплА́в, -а (m) XIVs steamboat
патріоти́чно XIII patriotic
пе́вен XVIg sure, certain
пе́вний VI sure, certain
пе́кло (n) XVII hell
пе-кти́, -чу́ть I (с-, P) XVII to bake (с)пі́к, (с)пекла́ past
пеніцилі́на (f) XIXn penicillin
переві́рити — див. перевіря́ти
перевіря́-ти, -ють; переві́рю-вати, -ють I (переві́р-ити, -ять P) X to check
пе́ред (+I) X before пе́ред ти́м я́к X before
переда́ча (f) IIn (TV, radio) program
переду́ма-ти, -ють P (no imperf.) XVII to change one's mind
переї́жджа́-ти, -ють; переї-зди́ти, -жджу́ - здя́ть I (переї́-хати, -дуть P) XV to move (over)

перейти́ — див. перехо́дити
пере́клад, -у (m) V translation
переклада́-ти, -ють I (перекла́-сти, -ду́ть P) V, VI to translate
перепли́ва́-ти, -ють I (перепли́в-ти́, -у́ть P) XVg to swim across
перепливти́ — див. перепливáти
перехо́д-ити, -жу, -ять I (перейти́, пере́йдуть P) XVg to walk over, to cross перейшо́в, перейшла́ past pfv.
перо́; пе́ра, пе́р (n) XVg feather
пе́рш(е) XVIg firstly
пе́рший I first; на пе́рше XVIIn for the main course
п'є́са (f) IIg play
пирі́г, -рога́; пироги́ (m) XIIn pie (dumpling in W.Ukr.)
пиріжо́к, -жка́; -жки́ (m) XVII small pie
писа́ння (n) II writing
писа́ти, пи́шуть I (на-, P) II, VI to write
писа́тися, пи́шеться, пи́шу́ться I XIIIg to be written (3rd sg. & pl. only)
пита́ння (n) II question відповіда́ти на пита́ння II to answer a/the question ма́ти до ... пита́ння II to have a question to/for s. one
пита́-ти, -ють (с-, за- P) II, VI to ask
п-и́ти, п'ю́ть I (ви́п-ити, ви́п'ють P) IX to drink пи́в, пила́ Past imfv.
пів XII half; пі́вдоро́ги XX half the road, half the way; пів до XIIg half past; пів на XII half past
півгоди́ни XIIs half an hour
пі́вдень, -дня — див. полу́день XIIIn afternoon
під (+ A and I) X under
підвезти́ — див. підво́зити
підво́-зити, -жу, -зять I (підвез-ти́ -у́ть P) XI to bring to/to give a ride; підві́з, підвезла́ past pfv
підкре́слити — див. підкре́слювати
підкре́слю-вати, -ють I (підкре́сл-ити, -ять P) VIII to underline, to stress
підло́га, на підло́зі (f) VII floor
піднести́ — див. підно́сити
підно́-сити, -шу, -сять I (піднес-ти́, -у́ть P) XVg to lift, to carry to; підні́с, піднесла́ past pfv.
підождáти — див. ждáти
пі́зній XI late (adj.)
пі́зно XI late
пі́сля (+G) X after; пі́сля то́го X afterwards, пі́сля то́го я́к Xg after
пі́сня; -сні́, -се́нь (f) XV song
піти́ — див. іти́
пі́ч, пе́чі, в печі́; пе́чі, пече́й (f) XVII stove, oven
пі́шки XI on foot
пла́ва-ти, -ють I XIV to swim (multi-d.)
пла́-кати, -чуть I (за-, P) XVII to cry
плати́ти, плачу́, пла́тять I (за-, P) XIIs to pay
пле́м'я (n) IIg tribe
плече́, -á; пле́чі, -че́й, -чи́ма (n) XVg XVIIIg shoulder
пливти́ (плисти́), пливу́ть I (по-, P) XIV to swim (uni-d.) пли́в, -ла́ past impfv.
по (+L) XI along; (+D) XIX each; (+L) XIIg after
по Хр. (по Христі́) XVII A.D.
по-англі́йському Introd. (in) English
побажа́ти — див. бажа́ти
по ба́тькові I patronymic; Я́к вас по ба́тькові? I What's your patronymic?
поба́чення (n) Introd. date, appointment; seeing До поба́чення! Introd. Good-bye! (I'll see you!)
поба́чити — див. ба́чити
поба́читися — див. ба́читися
побі́гти — див. бі́гти
по-ва́шому XVIIIs in your opinion; your way
повезти́ — див. везти́
по́вен XVIg full
поверну́ти — див. поверта́ти
поверну́тися — див. поверта́тися
поверта́-ти, -ють I (поверну́ти, пове́рнуть P) XVIII to return, to give back
поверта́-тися, -ються I (поверну́тися, пове́рнуться P) XVIIIs to return, to come back
повести́ — див. вести́
повече́ряти — див. вече́ряти
пови́нен, пови́нна, -нне XVI must, obligated
пови́нний XVIg must, obligated
пові́льний XVIg slow (adj.)
пові́льно Introd. slowly
пові́рити — див. ві́рити
пові́тря (n) XVII air
по́вний XVIg full
повтори́ти — див. повто́рювати і повторя́ти

Повторі́ть! Introd. Repeat!
повто́рю-вати, -ють; повторя́-ти, -ють I (повтори́ти, повто́рять P) VI to repeat
по́гляд, -у (m) XVI view, glance
пога́но II not good, bad
поговори́ти — див. говори́ти
пого́да (f) XIs weather
подарува́ти — див. дарува́ти
подару́нок, -нка; -нки (m) XII gift, present
подзвони́ти — див. дзвони́ти
подиви́тися — див. диви́тися
по́друга (f) XI girlfriend; **по́друга життя́** XIn wife
подо́ба-тися, -ються I (c-)XIII to like
по-дру́ге XX secondly
поду́мати — див. ду́мати
поду́шка; -и́ (f) XVIII pillow
подя́кувати — див. дя́кувати
пое́т (m) IV, XIIg poet
пожартува́ти — див. жартува́ти
пожи́-ти, -ву́ть P VIg to live for a while
позича́-ти, -ють I (пози́ч-ити, -ать P) XVIII to borrow; to lend
пози́чений XVIII borrowed
познайо́митися — див. знайо́митися
по-її́ XVIIIs her way; in her opinion
пої́хати — див. ї́хати
по-ї́хньому XVIIIs their way; in their opinion
по-його́ XVIIIs his way; in his opinion
показа́ти — див. пока́зувати
пока́зу-вати, -ють I (показа́ти, пока́жуть P) XII to show
по́ки XI until, while; **по́ки що** XIX so far
покида́-ти, -ють I (поки́н-ути, -уть P) Vg to abandon, to leave
покла́сти — див. кла́сти
покли́кати — див. кли́кати
покра́яти — див. кра́яти
по́ле; -я́, пі́ль and **полі́в** lg, XVg field
полеті́ти — див. леті́ти
поли́ця (f) XV shelf
полови́на (f) XX half
полта́вка (f) XVII native of Poltava (fem.)
полта́вський XVIII Poltava (adj.)
полу́день, -дня; -дні (m) XIII noon **пі́сля по́лудня** XIII afternoon **попо́лудні** XIIIn afternoon
полюби́ти — див. люби́ти
поля́к (m) XVII Pole (male)
по́лька (f) XVIIs Polish woman
по́льський XVIIs Polish (adj.)
поме́рлий XIXg deceased
поме́рти — див. помира́ти
поме́шкання (n) VIIs apartment
помили́тися — див. помиля́тися
по́милка; -и́, -ло́к (f) XIIIs mistake
помиля́-тися, -ються I (помили́тися, поми́ляться P) II, XIII to make a mistake
помира́-ти, -ють I (поме́рти, помру́ть P) XVI to die; **поме́р, поме́рла** past pfv.
поми́ти — див. ми́ти
помі́ряти — див. мі́ряти
по-мо́єму XVIII in my opinion; my way
по-на́шому XVIIIs in our opinion; our way
понеді́лок, -лка; -лки (m) IVs Monday
понести́ — див. нести́
пообіця́ти — див. обіця́ти
по-пе́рше XX firstly
popла́ва-ти, -ють P XIV to swim, to sail for a while
попливти́ (поплисти́) — див. пливти́ (плисти́)
попроси́ти — див. проси́ти
попроха́ти — див. проха́ти
попсува́тися — див. псува́тися
пора́да (f) XX advice
пора́дити — див. ра́дити
порахува́ти — див. рахува́ти
порозмовля́ти — див. розмовля́ти
по-росі́йському V (in) Russian
порося́, порося́ти; порося́та (n) XI piglet
поря́док, -дку (m) XV order; **усе́ в поря́дку** XV everything is in order
поси́д-іти, -жу, -ять P XI to stay, to sit for a while
посила́-ти, -ють I (посла́ти, пошлю́ть P) XX to send
послу́хати — див. слу́хати
послу́хатися — див. слу́хатися
посні́дати — див. сні́дати
поспіша́-ти, -ють I (поспіш-и́ти, -а́ть P) VI to hurry; XIIs to be fast (a watch)
поста́вити — див. ста́вити
по-тво́єму XVIIIs in your opinion, your way

по́тім XIV then, next
потребу-ва́ти, -ють I (no perf.) V to need
потрі́бен (потрі́бний) XVIg needed, necessary
по-украї́нському In (in) Ukrainian; по-украї́нськи I in Ukrainian
похо́д-ити, -жу, -ять I (no perf) IX to come from
поцілува́ти — див. цілува́ти
поча́ти — див. почина́ти
поча́тися — див. почина́тися
поча́ток, -тку; -тки́ (m) XIII beginning
почина́-ти, -ють I (поча́ти, почну́ть P) IX to begin
почина́-тися, -ються I (поча́тися, почну́ться P) XIII to begin
почита́-ти, -ють P VII to read for a while
почува́-ти себе́, -ють себе́ I Introd., VIg to feel Я́к себе́ почува́єте?Introd. How do you feel?
почу́ти — див. чу́ти
поша́на (f) XVI respect
пошкодува́ти — див. шкоду́вати
поясни́ти — див. поя́снювати
поя́сню-вати, -ють I (поясн-и́ти, -я́ть P) XIV to explain, to clarify
пра́вда (f) VII true, truth; пра́вду ка́жучи XX to tell the truth
пра́вий XVII right
пра́вильно Introd. correct
пра́во; -а́ (n) XVIn right, law
пра́дід (m) XIX great-grandfather
пра́пор, -а; прапори́ XIII flag
пра́ти, перу́ть I (ви́-, P) XX to wash, to launder
працівни́к XIs worker; **науко́вий п.** XXs research assistant
працю-ва́ти, -ють I VII to work; працюва́ти над X to work on
пра́ця (f) VII, XV work, job; на пра́ці XV at work
працьови́тий X hardworking
прега́рний XVIIIg most beautiful
прекра́сно XVIII excellent, beautiful, splendid
приблй́зно XIXs approximately
привіта́ти — див. віта́ти
приво́-зити, -жу, -зять I (привез-ти́, -у́ть P) XVg to bring (transport); приві́з, привезла́ past pfv.
прие́мно XII pleasant; Ду́же прие́мно! Introd. Pleased to meet you; Прие́мно познайо́митися! Мені́ ду́же прие́мно з ва́ми познайо́митися! XIIs I'm very pleased to meet you.
приїжджа́-ти, -ють; приї-зди́ти, -жджу́, -здя́ть I (приї́хати, -дуть P) VII, XVg to arrive, to come
приї́хати — див. приїжджа́ти і приїзди́ти
прийня́ття (n) VIIIn reception, party
прийо́м (m) VIIIn reception,
прийти́ — див. прихо́дити
принаймні XX at least
при́нцип (m) XVIII principle; за при́нципами XVIII according to principles
прино́-сити, -шу, -сять I (принес-ти́, -у́ть P) XVg to bring (carry) along; прині́с, принесла́ past pfv.
присила́-ти, -ють I (присла́ти, пришлю́ть P) XIV to send
прихо́д-ити, -жу, -ять I (прийти́, при́йдуть P) IV, VI to arrive, to come; прийшо́в, прийшла́ past pfv.
Прихо́дь! IV Come!
причіпля́-ти, -ють I причепи́ти, приче́плять P XIII to attach, to pin, to fasten
прі́звище (n) I last name,, surname; Я́к ва́ше прі́звище? I What's your last name?
про (+A) II about
пробача́-ти, -ють I (проба́ч-ити, -ать P) XX to forgive, to excuse
проба́чити — див. пробача́ти
пробіга́-ти, -ють I (пробі́-гти, -жа́ть P) XVg to to run (through); пробі́г, пробі́гла past pfv
пробі́гти — див. пробіга́ти
про́бу-вати, -ють I (с-, P) XVIII to try, to attempt
провідни́к, -а́; -и́ (m) XIV guide
провідни́ця (f) XIVn guide (female)
програ́ма (f) II program
прода-ва́ти, -ю́ть I (прода́ти - irregular P) XV to sell
прода́ти — див. продава́ти
проїжджа́-ти, -ють; проі-зди́ти, -жджу́, -здя́ть I (прої́-хати, -дуть P) XVg to pass to cover a distance
пройти́ — див. прохо́дити
пролива́-ти, -ють I (прол-и́ти, -лю́ть P) XVII to spill; проли́в, пролила́ past pfv

пропáщий XIXg lost
прóповідь (f) XVIII sermon
просúти, -шý, прóсять I (по-, P) IV, VI to beg, to ask (favor)
прóстий III simple
прóти (+G) XVI against
профéсія (f) VII profession
профéсор; -ú (m) I professor
прохá-ти, -ють I (по-, P) XX to beg, to ask (favor)
прохóд-ити, -жу, -ять I (пройтú, прóйдуть P) XVII to pass; пройшóв, пройшлá past pfv
прочитáти — див. читáти
Прóшу! Introd. Please!; You are welcome!; Прóшу дýже! Introd. You are very welcome!
психологíчний XX psychological
псу-вáтися, -ю́ться I (зі-, по-, P) XV to spoil; to break down
п'ятдеся́т, -ий XV fifty, -ieth
п'я́теро XXg five
п'я́тий V fifth
п'ятнáдцятий XV fifteenth
п'ятнáдцять XV fifteen
п'я́тниця IVs Friday
п'ятсóт XVIIg five hundred
п'ятисóтий XVIIg five hundredth
п'ять XV five

Р

рáд XVIg glad, happy
рáдий IX glad, happy
рáдо XVIg gladly
рáд-ити, -жу, -ять I (по-, P) XX to advise, to give advice
раднíше XVIg more gladly раднíший XVIg happier рáдше XVIg more, gladly, rather
рáз I once, one time в ýсякому рáзі X in any case цúм рáзом XX this time щé раз I once more
рáзом Introd. together
ранíш(е) XVIg earlier
рáно XI early
рáнок, -нку (m) Introd. morning; Дóброго рáнку! Introd. Good morning!
раху-вáти, -ють I (по-, P) XV to count
рáція (f) VII reason, cause; мáти рáцію VII to be right
ресторáн, -у (m) XIV restaurant
рéчення (n) VI.I sentence
рéшта (f) XX rest. remainder
рíвний XVIn even, equal
рівнопрáвність (f) XVI equality
ріг, рóгу, на рóзі; рогú XVII corner
рід, рóду; родú (m) XVI family, clan, descent
рíдко XIs seldom
Різдвó (n) XVIs Christmas
рíзний XVIs various, different
різнúця (f) XVI difference
рік, рóку; рокú, рóків (m) VII year Скíльки тобí рóків? XVI How old are you?
річ, рéчі; рéчі, речéй (f) III, X thing íнша річ XX a different matter
рíчка; -ú. -чóк (f) XVII river, rivulet на рíчці XVII at the river
робúти, рóблять I (з-, P) II, VI to do, to make
робúтися, рóбляться I (з-, P) XIIIg to be done/made
робітнúк, -á; -ú; робітнúця XIs worker
робóта (f)XI work, job; на робóту XI to work
родúна (f) XVI family
рóзмір, -у(m) XXs size
розмóва (f) X conversation, talk
розмовля́-ти, -ють I (по-, P) Xs to talk, to converse
розповідá-ти, -ють I (розповíсти — irregular — P) XI to tell (a story); розповíв, розповілá past pfv
розумí-ти, -ють I (з-, P) II, VI to undertsand; Розумíєте? Introd. Do you understand?; розумíю Introd. I understand
ромáн, -у (m) XX novel; romance
ромáнс, -у(m) XXn lyrical song; romance (W. Ukr.)
росíйський V Russian (adj.)
росія́нин; росія́ни (m) XIV Russian (male) pl. — Russians
росія́нка (f) XIVs Russian (fem.)
рр. = рóків, рокáх etc. XVIIs yrs.
рукá, рýку; рýки (f) XVII hand, arm
рýський XIV Rus' (adj.)
рýх, у рýсі (m) VIIg motion
рýчка (f) I pen
рушнúк, -á; -ú (m) XVII towel

С

са́д, -у; -и́ (m) XII garden
садо́к, -дка́; -дки́ (m) XV small garden
са́м, сама́, саме́, самі́ (сами́) XI oneself; alone
сам-оди́н XV alone
са́мий XVI the very; **а са́ме** XX namely **що́ са́ме** XVIg exactly what **то́й са́мий** XVII the same
св. = **святи́й**
све́тр, -а (m) XX sweater
свиня́; сви́ні, -не́й (f) XIIs, XVg pig
свіжий XV fresh
сві́й, своя́, своє́, свої́ V one's own
сві́т, -у; -и́ (m) XVIs world
світли́на IIIn photo
сві́тло (n) Xis light
світови́й XVII world (adj)
сві́тський XVII worldly, lay
святи́й (св.) XIII holy; saint (St.)
свя́то (n) XIII holiday
себе́ XII oneself
село́; се́ла, сіл (n) IX village
селяни́н (m), **селя́нка** (f), **селя́ни** (pl) IXs farmer, villager
се́меро XX seven
семисо́тий — XVIIg seven hundredth
сентимента́льний XX sentimental
серде́нько (n) VI darling (lit. 'little heart')
середа́ (f) IVs Wednesday
серйо́зний XIX serious
се́рпень, -пня (m) XVI August
се́рце; серця́, серде́ць XI heart; **від усьо́го се́рця** XII from the bottom of my heart
сестра́; се́стри, сесте́р (f) III sister
сестри́н, -на́, -не́ XIVg sister's
сид-і́ти, -жу́, -ять I VIII to sit; to stay; **сиді́ти вдо́ма** VIII to stay at home; **сиді́ти на ко́мусь** XIII to fit (clothes)
си́льний XVI strong
симпати́чний XIV nice, likable
си́н; -и́ (m) VII son
си́ній XVIII dark blue
си́ньо-жо́втий XIIIn blue-and-yellow
си́р, -у; -и́ (m) XII cheese
сіда́-ти, -ють I (**сі́сти, ся́дуть** P) VIII to sit down **сів, сі́ла** past pfv.
сі́м XV seven
сімдеся́т, -ий XVI seventy, -ieth
сімна́дцять, -тий XVI seventeen, -th
сімсо́т XVIIg seven hundred
сім'я́; сі́м'ї, сіме́й (f) XVg family
сі́сти — див. **сіда́ти**
сі́чень, -чня (m) XVI January
Скажі́ть! Introd. Say!
сказа́ли Introd. said
сказа́ти — див. **каза́ти**
скі́льки XII how much, how many
скінчи́ти(ся) — див. **кінча́ти(ся)**
склада́-ти, -ють I (**скла́-сти, -ду́ть** P) **+ і́спит** VI to take (pfv. — pass) an exam
скла́сти — див. **склада́ти**
скле́п, -у; -и́ (m) XVn store (W. Ukr.)
скориста́тися — див. **користа́тися**
скористува́тися — див. **користува́тися**
скорі́ш(е) XVIg sooner
ско́ро XVI soon
скрі́зь XIV everywhere
скупа́ти — див. **купа́ти**
скупа́тися — див. **купа́тися**
слаби́й; слабки́й XVIs weak
сла́ва (f) VIII glory; fame; hail!
словни́к, -а́; -и́ (m) I dictionary, vocabulary
сло́во; -а́, слі́в I, X word
слов'я́нський Ig Slavic
слу́жба (f) XIII service; **слу́жба Бо́жа** XIII liturgy
слу́ха-ти, -ють I (по-, P) VIII to listen
слу́ха-тися, -ються I (по-, P) XVI to obey
сльоза́; сльо́зи, слі́з (f) XVII tear
сма́ж-ити, -ать (по-, P) XVII to fry
смачни́й XVII tasty
сме́рть, -ти (f) XVI death
сміли́в-ий, -іший XVIg courageous, more c.
смі-я́тися, -ю́ться I (за-, P) XVII to laugh
сні́г, -у; -и́ (m) VIIg snow
сніда́нок, -нку (m) IX breakfast; **на сніда́нок** IX for breakfast
сні́да-ти, -ють I (по-, P) XV to eat breakfast
собо́р, -у (m) XIV cathedral **Володи́мирський собо́р** XIV St. Volodymyr Cathedral **Софі́йський собо́р** St. Sophia Cathedral
сове́тський, собі́тський VIIg Soviet (Russism)

со́нце (n) XIs sun
со́рок; сороко́вий XVI forty, -ieth
соро́чка; -и́ (f) XIII shirt
со́рт, -у; -и́ (m) XIVg sort
со́тий XVI hundredth
спаси́бі Introd., XII thank you
сп-а́ти, -ля́ть VII to sleep; лягáти спáти XII to go to bed/to sleep
спе́ка (f) XVII heat
спитáти — див. питáти
співá-ти, -ють I (за-, P) XIII to sing (pfv. — to begin singing)
співу́чий XIX fond of singing
спізни́тися — див. спізня́тися
спізня́-тися, -ються/спі́зню-ватися, -ються/запі́зню-ватися, -ються I (спізни́тися, спі́зняться/запізни́тися, запі́зняться P) XI to be late; XII to be slow (a watch)
сподівá-тися, -ються I (no perf.) XX to hope for, to expect
сподо́батися — див. подо́батися
спочáтку IX at first
спрáва (f) XX matter, business
спрáвді XVII indeed
спрáвжній III real, genuine, true
спро́бувати — див. про́бувати
ст. = століття (сторі́ччя) XIg, XIVn century
ста-вáти, -ю́ть I (стá-ти, -нуть P) IX to become
ста-вáтися, -ю́ться I (стá-тися, -нуться P) XX to happen
стáв-ити, -лять I (по-, P) VII to put, to stand
старенький IIs old
стари́й II old
старі́ший XVIg older
стáрший XVI older, XXn senior
старосві́тський XVI old-fashioned
стáти — див. ставáти
стáтися — див. ставáтися
статтяя́; -тті́, -тте́й (f) XVg article
сте́п, -у; -и́ (m) VIIg steppe
сти́ль, -лю (m) XX style
сті́л, столá; столи́ (m) I table, desk
стіле́ць, -льця; -льці́ (m) I chair
сті́льки XII so much, so many
сто́ VII hundred
столі́ття (сторі́ччя) (n) XIV century
сторі́нка; -и́, -но́к (f) XX page
сто-я́ти, -я́ть VII to stand
страшни́й XVII terrible
студе́нт; -и (m) I student (male)
студе́нтка (m) I student (female)
субо́та (f) IV Saturday
су́кня; -ні, -конь (f) XIII dress XIIg
схоті́ти — див. хоті́ти
сюди́ XI here, this way
сього́дні II today
сього́днішній V today's
сьо́мий VII seventh

Т

тá I that (fem. — see той); III and; VII but
тáк Introd. yes; III so, in such a way; X so
таки́ XXn yet, still
таки́й III such, so Щó такé? Щó тáм такé? V What's that? What's going on? What's the matter?
таки́й-то, такá-то IVn so-and-so
талanови́т-ий, -іший XVIg talented, more t.
тáм I there óн тáм I over there
тáнці (pl. of тáнець) (m) VIIIn dancing XIII
тáтів, -това XIII dad's
тáто (m) VII dad
тві́й, твоя́, твоє́ I I your(s)
тво́рчість (f) IV creativity, creative work
те́ — див. то́й
теáтр, -у XVIIs theater
те́ж II also
телебáчення (n) II television
телевізі́йний IIs television (adj.)
телеві́зія (f) IIn television
телеві́зор (m) II television set
телефо́н, -у (m) V telephone
телефону-вáти, -ють (I) (по-, P) IVs to make a phone call
те́мно XIs dark
температу́ра (f) XIX temperature
тепе́р Introd. now
те́пло XIs warm
те́хнікум, -у (m) IXn school of technology
ти́ I you
ти́ждень, ти́жня; ти́жні (m) V week
ти́сяча; і (f) XVII thousand

ти́сячний XVIIg thousandth
ти́хо XIs quiet
тільки III only
тітка; -и́ (f) XVIII aunt
то́ I that (is), those (are)
то III then, in that case; то я́к? XIII How about it?
то́бто XX that is, i.e.
товари́ство (n) VIs company; society
това́риш; -і́ (m) VI friend, comrade (m)
това́ришка; -и́ (f) VI friend, comrade (f)
тоді́ VII then, at that time
то́й, та́, те́, ті́ I that, the те́ й дру́ге II both то́й, хто́ XVII he who не то́й XIV different; wrong; до то́го VII in addition
тому́ X ago; рік тому́ X a year ago
тому́ VI why, the reason; тому́ що VI because
то́чний XVIg exact
то́чно XIII exactly
тра́вень, -вня (m) XVI May
тради́ція (f) XVIII tradition; за тради́цією XVIII according to tradition
тре́ба VI it is necessary, one must
тре́тій III third на тре́тє XVIIn for dessert
три́ XII three
три́дцять, тридця́тий XVI thirty, -ieth
тризу́б, -а; -и XIII trident
трина́дцять, -тий XV, XIII thirteen, -th
три́ста XVIIg three hundred
тро́є XXg three
тро́хи IX (a) little, some, somewhat
трудя́щий XIXg toiling; worker
трьохсо́тий XVIIg three hundredth
туди́ XI there, that way
турбува́ти (по-) II, VI to trouble
ту́т I here о́сь ту́т I over here
тяжки́й XII heavy
тя́жко XVI heavily
тя́жче XVIg heavier
тя́жчий XVIg heavier (adj.)

У

у (+ A) III in, into; (+ L) VII at, in; (+G) V at; has/have у нього є́ — he has; у ньо́го at his place
убива́-ти, -ють I (уб-и́ти, -'ю́ть P) XX to kill, to murder
уби́вство (n) XX murder, killing
уби́вця (m) XX killer, murderer
уби́ти — див. убива́ти
уве́сь, уся́, усе́, усі́ I all
уве́чері II in the evening; сього́дні вве́чері II tonight
увійти́ — див. входи́ти
уде́нь X in the day-time
удо́ма IV at home
уже́ II already; ready, done
ужива́-ти, -ють I (ужи́-ти, -ву́ть P) XX to use ужи́в, ужила́ past pfv.
узи́мку XI in the winter
украї́нець, -нця (m) I Ukrainian (male)
украї́нка (f) I Ukrainian (female)
украї́нський I Ukrainian (adj.)
улашто́ву-вати, -ють I (улашту-ва́ти, -ють P) IV to arrange, to organize
улашто́ву-ватися, -ються I (улашту-ва́тися, -ються P) XIIIg to get settled
улі́тку XI in the summer
улю́блений XV favorite
умі́-ти, -ють I (з-, P) XI to know how, pfv. — to be able, to manage
університе́т, -у (m) V university
університе́тський VIIIg university (adj.)
уночі́ X in the night
ура́нці X in the morning
усе́ everything, all; XVIIIg increasingly; II all the time; усе́ ж таки X still, nevertheless
усі́ Introd. all, everyone
уся́ — див. уве́сь
усміха́-тися, -ються I (усміхн-у́тися, -у́ться P) XIX to smile
у́спіх, -у (m) XIX success
у́спішний XIXs successful
утоми́тися — див. уто́млюватися
уто́млю-ватися, -ються I (утоми́тися, уто́мляться P) XVII to get tired
у́хо; у́ші, -е́й, -и́ма XVIIIg ear
учени́ця XIIs pupil (f)
у́чень, у́чня; -чні (m) XII pupil
учителю-ва́ти, -ють I XIIn to teach school
учи́тель; -і́ (m) IX teacher (male)
учи́телька (f) IX teacher (fem.)

учи́ти, у́чать I (навч-и́ти, -а́ть P) XII to teach
учи́тися, у́чаться I (навч-и́тися, -а́ться P) VII to study, to learn
учо́ра IV yesterday
учора́шній V yesterday's

Ф

факульте́т, -у (m) VIII department
фа́рба (f) XVII paint
філологі́чний VIII philological
фі́льм (m) II film іде́ фі́льм V a film is playing
фоте́ль, -лю (m) VIIIg armchair
фо́то IIIg photo
фотогра́фія (f) III photograph, photography

Х

ха́й VIIIg let
ха́рківський IX Xarkiv (Kharkiv) (adj.)
ха́та; -и́ XV house (in a village)
хвили́на (f) XIs minute
хво́рий XIX sick; patient
хворі́-ти, -ютьI (за-, P) XIX to be sick, pfv. to get sick
хворо́ба (f) XIX sickness, disease
хіні́на (f) XIXn quinine
хи́трий XIX sly, smart
хіба́ XIII really? XIX perhaps
хлі́б; -и́ (m) IX bread
хлі́б, -а́ XIVg grain
хло́пець, -пця (m) III boy, young fellow
ход-и́ти, -жу́; хо́дять I VII to walk, to go, to come (multi-d.) ходи́ти до шко́ли VII to attend school
холоди́льник, -а (m) IX refrigerator
холо́дний XVIg cold (adj.)
хо́лодно XI cold
хо́р, -у (m) XIII choir; chorus
хо́рий, хорі́ти, хоро́ба = хво́рий, хворі́ти, хворо́ба
хоті́ти, хо́чу, хо́чуть I (за-, с-, P) II, VI to want
хоті́тися, хо́четься I (за-, P) XIII to feel like
хо́ч (хоча́) XIII even though; at least
Хри́ст (= Христо́с) XVIIg Christ до Хр. (до Христа́) XVIIg B.C. по Хр. (по Христі́) XVIIg A.D.
хто́ I who
хтоне́будь IXg anyone
хто́сь VIII someone

Ц

це́ Introd. this (is), these (are)
це́й, ця́, це́, ці́ I this
це́нт, -а (m) XV cent
це́рква; -и́, -ко́в (f) XIII church
цибули́на (f) XVIIn one onion
цибу́ля (f) XVII onion
ци́нік (m) XII cynic
ціка́вий II interesting (adj.)
ціка́в-ити, -лять I (за-, P) IX, XX to interest
ціка́в-итися, -ляться I (за-, P) IX to be interested in
ціка́во II, XVIg interesting
ці́лий IX entire, whole
цілко́м XIII fully
цілу-ва́ти, -ють I (по-, P) X to kiss
цура́-тися, -ються VIII to shun, to reject
ця́ — див. це́й

Ч

ча́й, ча́ю; чаї́ (m) IX tea
ча́с, часу́ (ча́су) (m) IV time; тре́ба часу́ на (+A) X it takes time to; під ча́с XVIII during; ти́м ча́сом XIX meantime
ча́сом XV at times
часо́пис, -у (m) Vn newspaper
части́на (f) XX part
ча́сто XI often
чве́рть (f) XII quarter чве́рть на XII quarter after за чве́рть XII quarter to
чека́-ти, -ють I XI to wait
че́мний XVIs polite
че́рвень, -вня (m) XVI June
черво́ний XVII red

че́рез (+ A) X after, in; XIX because of
четве́р, -га́; -ги́ (m) IVs Thursday
че́тверо XX four
четве́ртий IV fourth
чи I interrogatory particle; II whether, if чи...чи II whether...or
чиє́, чиї́ — див. чи́й
чи́й, чия́, чиє́, чиї́ I whose
чийне́будь IXg anyone's
чи́йсь VIIIg someone's
чимра́з XVIIIg increasingly
число́; чи́сла, чи́сел (n) IIs numer; XVI date (calendar)
чи́стий XVII clean
чи́-стити, -щу, -стять I (по-, P) VIg to clean
чита́ння (n) II reading
чита́-ти, -ють (про-, P) II, VI to read
чита́-тися, -ється, -ються I XIIIg to be read (3 rd sg. and pl. only)
чита́ч, -ча́, чита́чу!; -і́ (m) XX reader
чия́ — див. чи́й
чо́вен, -вна́; -вни́ (m) XIV boat, row boat
чого́ III why, what for
чогоне́будь IXg for any reason
чого́сь VIIIg somehow, for some reason
чолові́к; -и́ (m) X man, husband, person
чому́ III why
чому́сь VIIIg for some reason
чо́рний XVII black
чоти́ри XII four
чоти́риста XVIIg four hundred
чотирна́дцять, -тий XVI, XV fourteen, -th
чотирьохсо́тий XVIIg four hundredth
чудо́вий VI, XVIg wonderful (adj.)
чужи́й VIII strange, foreign
чу́-ти, -ють I (по-, P) X to hear; to smell

Ш

шано́вний XIVs honorable
швидки́й XVIg fast (adj.)
шви́дко Introd. fast
шви́дше XVIg faster
ше́стеро XXg six
шестидеся́тники XVIIg people of the 60's
шестисо́тий XVIIg six hundredth
широ́кий XIV wide (adj.)
ши́роко XVIg wide
ши́рше XVIg wider
шістдеся́т, -ий XVI sixty, -ieth
шістна́дцять -тий XVI sixteen, -th
шістсо́т XVIIg six hundred
ші́сть XV six
шкода́ VI too bad; sorry
шкоду-ва́ти, -ють I (по-, P) XV to regret
шко́ла (f) IV school; ходи́ти до шко́ли VII attend school
школя́р (m) In student (school)
школя́рка (f) In student (school)
шмато́к, -тка́; -тки́ (m) IX piece, slice
шни́цель, -я (m) XVIIn pork chop; meat patty (W. Ukr.)
шо́стий VI sixth
штани́ XIII pants, slacks
шука́-ти, -ють VII to seek, to look for

Щ

щасли́вий XVIg, XVIII happy Щасли́вої доро́ги! XX Happy journey! Bon voyage!
щасли́віший, щасливі́ший XVIg happier
ще́ Introd. more; IV else; VI still (+ comparative); ще ні VI not yet; ще́ раз Introd. once more
щи́рий XXn sincere
щи́ро Introd., XX sincerely
що́ Introd. what А що́? II Why (do you ask)? А що́ таке́? V Why (do you ask)?; що́ як XIX what if
що II that (conj.)
щоб VII that, so that, in order to
щодо XX as for
що́йно XIX just now, this minute
щонайме́нше XVIII at least
щоне́будь IX anything
щора́з XVIIg increasingly
що́сь VIIIg something
щоти́жня XVIII weekly

Я

я́ Introd. I (1st person pronoun)
я́блуко (n) XII apple
яє́шня (f) XV omelette
яйце́; я́йця, яє́ць (n) IX egg
я́к Introd. how; I what; III if; XVI than, XX як as, я́к зна́єш XIX it's your business
якби́ VII if якби́ не X if it weren't for
яки́й, яка́, яке́, які́ II what (kind), which Ót яки́й! III What a ...!
якийне́будь IXg any (kind)
яки́йсь III some sort of
якнайбі́льше XVIIIg as much as possible
якнайскорі́ше XVIIIg as soon as possible
якне́будь IXg carelessly
я́кось VIIg somehow
якра́з X just, exactly
якщо́ IV if
я́сно XIs clear; bright

PLACES

Аме́рика (f) III America
Дніпро́ (m) XIV the Dnipro river
Кана́да (f) III Canada
Карпа́ти, Карпа́т (го́ри Карпа́ти) (pl.) XI Carpathians, Carpathian mountains
Ки́їв, Ки́єва (m) VII Kyiv
Льві́в, Льво́ва (m) VII L'viv
Монреа́ль, -ю (я) (m) V Montreal
Німе́ччина (f) XVIIs Germany
Нью Йо́рк, -у (а) (m) V New York
Полта́ва (f) XVIIIs Poltava
По́льща (f) XVIIs Poland
Радя́нський Сою́з, -зу (m) VIIs the Soviet Union
Росі́я (f) V Russia
Ру́сь, -и (f) XIV Rus'
Украї́на (f) II Ukraine
Ха́рків, -кова (m) IX Kharkiv (Kharkov)

PROPER NAMES (MALE)*

FIRST NAME

Андрі́й II Andrew; **Андрі́йко** II Andy
Богда́н III
Бори́с XVI Boris
Васи́ль, -я I Basil
Ві́ктор II Victor
Володи́мир VIIIs Volodymyr
Григо́рій, Григі́р XV Gregory; **Гри́ць, Грицько́** Greg
Дмитро́ VII
Євге́н XI Eugene
Іва́н IV John; **Іва́сь** VII Johnny
Ігор, -я III
Макси́м XI
Марко́, Ма́рко I Mark
Марти́н XVI Martin
Мико́ла II Nicholas
Миха́йло II Michael; **Михаї́л** XIII Michael
Оле́кса XIII Alex; **Олексі́й** XIII Alex
Оре́ст XIII
Оста́п XVIII
Павло́ III Paul
Петро́ II Peter
Рома́н X Roman; **Ро́мко** X
Семе́н XIII Simon
Сергі́й V Serge
Сла́вко XII; **Ростисла́в** XII; **Святосла́в** XII; **Яросла́в** XII
Степа́н V Stephen
Тара́с IV
Ю́рій VIII, George; **Юрко́** VIII

LAST NAMES

Гончаре́нко I
Гуме́цький XI
Дмитро́вський XII
Івани́шин X

---

* **English equivalents are provided wherever possible.**

Костю́к XX
Ле́сів III
Ме́льник III
Поліщу́к III
Сковорода́ X
Тарнове́цький XIII
Франко́ IX
Шевче́нко IX

PATRONYMICS

Володи́мирович XIII
Григо́рович IXs
Іва́нович IX
Миха́йлович I
Семе́нович XII

PROPER NAMES (FEMALE)

FIRST

Ва́ля XVIII; Валенти́на XVIII
Ві́ра V Vera
Га́ля III; Гали́на III
Га́нна VIII Ann
Да́рка XIII; Ода́рка, Да́рія XIII
Зіна XVI; Зіна́їда XVI
Іри́на XV Irene; Яри́на XV
Катери́на X Catherine; Ка́тря X Cathy
Лари́са XX
Ле́ся III
Лі́да II Lydia; Лі́дія II
Лю́ба III Amy; Любо́в III; Любоми́ра III
Марі́я II Mary
Ма́рта III Martha
Миросла́ва XIII; Сла́ва XIII
На́дя XIII; Наді́я XIII
На́стя XVI Anastasia; Анаста́сія XVI
Ната́лка IX Natalie; Ната́ля IX
Окса́на II
Оле́на XI Helen
О́ля I Olga; О́льга I
Тетя́на II

LAST

Гончаре́нко(ва) IIIg
Гуме́цька IIIg, XX
Дмитро́вська IXg
Івани́шина IXg
Костю́к XV
Ле́сева IXg
Ме́льник (Мельничи́ха) III (IIIg)
Палі́й (Палі́єва) III (IIIg)
Поліщу́к III
Прокопо́вич III
Сковорода́ X
Тарнове́цька XV

PATRONYMICS

Бори́сівна XV (from Бори́с)
Макси́мівна XI (from Макси́м)
Миха́йлівна II (from Миха́йло)
Семе́нівна XX (from Семе́н)
Сергі́ївна XIII (from Сергі́й)

ENGLISH-UKRAINIAN VOCABULARY

This section is provided for general reference (for more detailed information consult the Ukrainian-English part). Notation is the same as for the Ukrainian-English part plus the following: (n) — noun, (v) — verb, (adj) — adjective, (u) — undirectional, (m) — multidirectional

A

abandon Vg покида́ти (поки́нути)
ability X здібність, -ости
able to be a. VIII могти́ (з-) XI уміти (з-)
about II про (+ A)
above X над (+ I)
absolutely XXII обов'язко́во
accept XIX прийма́ти (прийня́ти)
according — see in my opinion
ache (v) XIX боліти (за-) I have a headache XIX У ме́не боли́ть голова́
acquaint-ance (person) XII знайо́мий, -ма; -ed: to get a. X знайо́митися (по-)
A.D. XVIIg по Хр. (по Христі) XVIIg н.е. (на́шої е́ри)
addition in a. VII ще́ й (до то́го)
address (n) V адре́са (v) a. a letter VII адресува́ти (за-); a. someone VII зверта́тися; зверну́тися (до + G)
advice XX пора́да; to give a, XX ра́дити (по-)
afraid: to be a, II боя́тися
after X після (+ G), Xg після то́го як XIIIg по (+ D) Intro.g X через (+ A)
afternoon XIII полу́день, -дня in the afternoon XIII після по́лудня XIIIn попо́лудні
afterwards X після то́го
again II зно́в(у)
against XVI про́ти (+ G)
ago X тому́; long a. IX давно́; not long a. X неда́вно; a year a. X рік тому́
agreeable (willing) XVIg зго́ден, зго́дний; agree IX згідний; I agree Я́ згідна
Ah! II Ох! XII Ах!
aha II а́га
air (n) XVII повітря; airplane XIVs літа́к, -а́; -и́; a. condition XVII охоло́джене повітря
all I уве́сь, уся́, усе́, усі ; a. right IV до́бре; All the best! Introd. На все́ до́бре!
almost XIV ма́йже
alone XI са́м; XV сам-оди́н
along XI по (+ L)
already II уже́
also II те́ж
although XIII хо́ч(а)
always XI за́вжди (завжди́)
America III Аме́рика; -n (male) III; америка́нець -нця; (fem.) III; америка́нка; (adj.) V америка́нський
among XIV між (+ I)
ancestors XIX діди́ й пра́діди
and I а, і; III та
answer (n) II відповідь; to a. II, VI відповіда́ти (відпові́сти); to a. a question II відповіда́ти на пита́ння; Answer! Intro. Відповіда́йте!
any -(kind) IXg яки́йне́будь; -one IXg хтоне́будь; -one's XI чи́йне́будь;-thing IX щоне́будь; -where (loc) IXg десне́будь; -where (dir.) IXg куди́не́будь XX будья́кий
apartment VIIs поме́шкання, VII кварти́ра, VIIg ме́шкання
apple XII я́блуко
appointment Introd. поба́чення
approximately XIXs прибли́зно
April XVI квітень, -тня
apt. VII кв.; VIIn пом.
arm XVII рука́; ру́ки; a. chair VII крісло, XVIIIg фоте́ль
around (ca) XIX біля (+ G), XXg бли́зько (+G)
arrange IV улашто́вувати (улаштува́ти)
arrive (by walking) IV, VI прихо́дити (прийти́); (by driving) VII, XVg приїжджа́ти/приїзди́ти (приї́хати)
article (written) XVg статтю́

as XX я́к; a. for XX що́до (+ G); a. if XVII ні́би; a. long as IX аби́
ask (a question) II, VI пита́ти (с-, за-); (a favor) IV, VI проси́ти (по-) XX проха́ти (по-)
aspirin XIX аспіри́на; take a. XIX бра́ти/ужива́ти аспіри́ну
assignment II завда́ння
association VIs товари́ство
at II на (+L); VII у (+ L), у (+ G); XII о (+L, ref. to time)
attend school VII ходи́ти до шко́ли
August XVI се́рпень, -пня
aunt XVIII ті́тка; -и́
autumn XIs о́сінь, о́сени; in the a XI восени́
awkward VII незру́чно

B

baby XII дити́на (ді́ти pl.)
back (ward) XVIII наза́д
bad II пога́но; not b. Introd. непога́но; too b. VI шкода́
bake XVII пекти́ (с-)
ball VIIIn ба́л (ь)
bandura XIX банду́ра; b. player XIX бандури́ст
basso XIII ба́с; -и́
bath: to give a b. XIVn купа́ти (с-); to take a b. XIV купа́тися (с-)
battle (n) VIIg бі́й, бо́я; бої́
be IV бу́ти
beautiful XVIII прекра́сно; most b. XVIIIg прега́рний
because III бо; VI тому́ що; b. of X че́рез (+A)
become IX става́ти (ста́ти)
bed VII, XVg лі́жко; to go to b. XII ляга́ти спа́ти
beg — see ask
before X до, перед (+ G); X перед ти́м як; b. Christ (B.C.) XVIIg до Хр. (до Христа́)
begin IX почина́ти (поча́ти) XIII почина́тися (поча́тися); -ning XIII поча́ток, -тку
behind Xg за (+ I, + A)
believe X ві́рити (по-)
beloved XIV лю́бий; IIIs коха́ний
besides XI крім (+ G); -s XI крім то́го
best XVIg найкра́ще, -щий; All the b.! Introd. На всé до́бре!

better Introd. кра́ще; XVIg кра́щий; лі́пший
between XIV між (+ I)
big — see large
billion XVIIg мілья́рд, більйо́н
birth XVI наро́дження
black XVII чо́рний
blue (dark) XVIII си́ній; (light) b. XIII блаки́тний; dark b. and yellow XIIIn си́ньо-жовтий
blood XVII кро́в, -и
board (black) I до́шка; -и́, що́к
boat (row b.) XIV чо́вен, -вна; -и́
bold — see courageous
bone XVIIIg кість; ко́сті
book I кни́жка; -и́ XVIr кни́га
boring: to become boring XVIII набрида́ти (набри́днути)
born: to be b. XVI наро́джуватися (народи́тися)
borrow XVIII позича́ти (пози́чити); -ed XVIII пози́чений
borsht IX бо́рщ, -у́; -і́
both II те́ й дру́ге; XX оби́два, оби́дві; обо́є; b...and... IV і...і...
bother XV заважа́ти (зава́дити)
boy III хло́пець, -пця
bread IX хлі́б; -и́
break down (v) XV псува́тися (зі-, по-)
breakfast IX сніда́нок, -нку; for b. IX на сніда́нок; to eat b. XV сні́дати (по-)
breathe XVIIg ди́хати
bring (by hand) XVg прино́сити (принести́), (transp.) XVg приво́зити (привезти́)
brother III бра́т; -и́; brother's XIVg бра́тів, -това
buckwheat (adj.) IXg греча́ний
building III буди́нок, -нка
bus XI авто́бус
business XX спра́ва; it's your b. XIX я́к зна́єш
but II але́; IV ж(е); VII та
buy (v) IX купува́ти (купи́ти)

C

cabbage XII капу́ста
call (v) XIV кли́кати (по-); XII назива́ти (назва́ти); XIVn зва́ти (по-); to be c-ed XIVn зва́тися, XIIIg, XIV назива́тися

can (v) VIII могти́ (з-); one c. IX мо́жна
Canada III Кана́да; -ian (male) III кана́дець, -дця (fem) III кана́дка; (adj.) III кана́дський
candidate Xn кандида́т
capable X здібний; XVIg ла́ден
car XI а́вто́; to drive a c. XI керува́ти а́вто́м XIn води́ти а́вто́, керму́вати, ї́здити а́вто́м
card XIX ка́рта
care: I don't c. XIII мені́ ба́йдуже; -lessly IXg якне́будь
career XXn кар'є́ра, -и
careerist XXn кар'є́рист (-ка)
carry (transport) XII везти́ (по-) (u) вози́ти (m), (by hand) XII нести́ (по-) (u) носи́ти (m); -c. out (by hand) XVg вино́сити (ви́нести); -c. back (by hand) XVIII відно́сити (віднести́); c. down (by hand) XVg зно́сити (знести́)
case: in any c. X в уся́кому ви́падку; in that c. III то
cash XIIg готі́вка
cathedral XIV собо́р, -у; St. Volodymyr Cathedral XIV Володи́мирський собо́р; St. Sophia XIV Софі́йський собо́р
cause — see reason
cent XV це́нт, -а
century XIg, XIV столі́ття, сторі́ччя
cereal (cooked) IX ка́ша
certain (sure) VI пе́вний; XIVg пе́вен; -ly II звича́йно
chair I стіле́ць, -льця́; -льці́
chairman IIg голова́; го́лови
change: ch. one's mind XVII переду́мати
cheap XV деше́вий, де́шево; -er XVIg деше́вше, -ший
check (v) X перевіря́ти (переві́рити)
cheese XII си́р, -у; -и́
cherry (fruit & tree) XV ви́шня; (adj.) вишне́вий XV
child XII дити́на; -dren XII ді́ти
choir XIII хо́р, -у
choose VII вибира́ти (ви́брати)
chorus — see choir
Christ XVIIg Хри́ст(о́с); before Christ (B.C.) XVIIg до Хр. (до Христа́)
church XIII це́рква; -и́ ch. service — see service
citizen (male) XVIIs громадя́нин (fem) XVIIs громадя́нка; (pl.) XVIIs громадя́ни
city VII мі́сто; -а́
civil XVII громадя́нський
clarify — see explain
class VII кля́са; VIIg кла́с
clear XIs я́сно
clock — see watch
clothes XIIIs о́дяг, -у
clean (adj.) XVII чи́стий; to c. VIg чи́стити (по-)
close XV бли́зько XVg бли́зький; very c. V близе́нько; -er XV бли́жче XVg бли́жчий; (v) VIII зачиня́ти (зачини́ти) to be c-ed XIIIg зачиня́тися (зачини́тися)
coffee IX ка́ва
cold XI хо́лодно; XVIg холо́дний
collective farm IXn колго́сп; c. farmer IXn колго́спник (m) колго́спниця (f)
color XVIII ко́лір, -льору
Columbia (Univ.) VIIIg Колумбі́йський (ун-т)
come (walk) V іти́ (u), IV, VI прихо́дити (прийти́); Come! Прихо́дь! (transp.) XVg приїжджа́ти/приїзди́ти (приї́хати); to c. from IX похо́дити (no pfv)
communist VII комуні́ст
community XVIs грома́да
company VIs товари́ство
completely X зо́всім
compliment X компліме́нт, -у
comrade — see friend
concert VIII конце́рт, -у; to a c. VIII на конце́рт
conference VII конфере́нція
consequently X о́тже
considerably XVIII зна́чно
conversation X розмо́ва; to converse Xs розмовля́ти (по-)
cook (v) XVII вари́ти (з-)
cooled XVII охоло́джений
copeck (penny) VIII копі́йка, -и́
corner XVII рі́г, ро́гу; роги́; on the c. XVII на ро́зі
correct Introd. пра́вильно; (v) II виправля́ти (ви́правити)
Cossack XVI коза́к, -а́; -и́ (adj.) XVI коза́цький "The Cossack breed will never end" XVI "Коза́цькому ро́ду нема́ перево́ду"; Zaporižžja c. Vg запоро́жець, -жця

cost (v) XVIII ко́штувати (no pfv)
count (v) XV рахува́ти (по-)
courageous XVIg смілúвий; more c. XVIg смілúвіший
course (school) VIII ку́рс, -у; to take a c. VIII слу́хати ку́рс; (meal): for the main c. XVIIn на пе́рше, for the 2 nd c. на дру́ге; of course II звича́йно
creativity (creative work) IV тво́рчість, -чости
cross (v) — (by walking) XVg перехо́дити (перейтú)
cry (v) XVII пла́кати (за-)
cynic XII цúнік

D

dad VII та́то; -'s XIII та́тів, -това
dancing VIIIn заба́ва, та́нці
dark XIs те́мно
darling VI серде́нько
date (calendar) XVI числó XVIg да́та; (appointment) Introd. поба́чення
daughter IX дочка́; до́чки
day Intro. де́нь, дня́; Good day! Introd. До́брий де́нь! Добрúдень!; d. and night Xn доба́; in the d. (time) X уде́нь
dear XII дорогúй XVIg до́рого; (beloved), IIIs коха́ний XIV лю́бий XVII мúлий
death XVI сме́рть, -ти
deceased XIXg поме́рлий
December XVI гру́день, -дня
decide IX вирі́шувати (вúрішити); to be d-ed XIIIg вирі́шуватися (вúрішитися)
degree XIXs гра́дус (temperature); d. thesis Xn диплóмна пра́ця
department (college) VIII факульте́т, -у
descent (family) XVI рі́д, ро́ду; родú
describe XIV опúсувати (описа́ти)
dessert XVIIIn десе́рт; for d. XVIIIn на десе́рт; XVIn на трете́
desk I сті́л, стола́; столú
detective (adj.) XX детектúвний
dialogue XX діялóг, -у
dictionary I словнúк, -а́; -ú
die (v) XVI помира́ти (поме́рти)
diet (n) XIX діє́та
difference XVI різнúця; -ent VIII і́нший, XIV не то́й
difficult II ва́жко XVIg важкúй; more d. XIg, XVIg ва́жче, ва́жчий
dinner IX обі́д, -у; for d. IX на обі́д; to eat d. XVII обі́дати (по-)
diplomat XVIII диплома́т
direct (v) XI керува́ти; -or X керівнúк, -а́; -ú -ion (leadership) X керівнúцтво
dirt XVII бру́д, -у; -y X×II бруднúй
dissertation X дисерта́ція
divine XIII Бо́жий
do II, VII робúти (з-); to be done XIIIg робúтися (з-); done XVIII зро́блений, II вже́
docent — see M.A.
doctor II, VII лі́кар, -я; -і́; IXs лі́карка; XIX до́ктор; -ú
dollar XV до́ляр
door I две́рі (pl. only)
dormitory VI гурто́житок, -тку
drawing III малю́нок, -нка
dream (n) VIIs со́н, сну́; снú
dress (n) XIIg, XIII су́кня; -ed XIII вдя́гнений; to get d-ed XIII вдяга́тися, одяга́тися, вдягну́тися/ одягну́тися
drink (v) IX пúти (вú-)
drive (v) — (a vehicle) XI керува́ти XIn кермува́ти, ї́здити (m) ї́хати (по-) (u), водúти (m), вестú (по-) (u); (to transport) XII возúти (m) везтú (по-) (u): to drive away XVg від'їжджа́ти, від'ї́здúти (від'ї́хати)
driver XIVs водí́й
duma (hist. song) XVIr ду́ма
dumpling XII варе́ник XIIn пирі́г, -рога́; пирогú (W. UKr.)
during XVIII під ча́с
dwell — see live, reside

E

each X ко́жний; XVIg ко́жен; XIX по (+ D)
ear XVIIIg ву́хо, у́хо
early XI ра́но; -ier XVIg рані́ш(е)
earth XIV земля́; зе́млі
Easter XIV Велúкдень, Великóдня
easy XVIg легкúй; -ily XVIg ле́гко; -ier XVI ле́гше

eat IX ї́сти (з-)
edge VIIg кра́й, -ю; краї́
egg IX яйце́; я́йця
eight XV ві́сім; XX во́сьмеро; -th VIII во́сьмий; -teen(th) XVI вісімна́дцять, -тий; -ty (-ieth) XVI вісімдеся́т, -ий; e. hundred XVIIg вісімсо́т; e. hundredth XVIIg восьмисо́тий
either II або́; e...or II або́...або́
elderly IIn старе́нький, немолоди́й, лі́тній
elect — see choose
electrician XIg еле́ктрик
eleven XV одина́дцять; -th XI одина́дцятий
else IV іще́
embroider XVIII вишива́ти (ви́шити); -ed XVIII ви́шитий
end (n) XIII кіне́ць, -нця́; -нці (v) XIII кінча́ти (кінчи́ти), VII закі́нчувати (закінчи́ти), XIII кінча́тися (кінчи́тися), XIIIn закі́нчуватися (закінчи́тися); -less Vg безкраї́й
engage in XVIII займа́тися (зайня́тися)
engineer VII, XI інжене́р
English V англі́йський; in E. Introd. по-англі́йському
enough VI до́сить; not e. X ма́ло
enter XVg вхо́дити, увійти́)
entire — see whole
especially XIXr, XX особли́во
etc. VIII і т.д. (і та́к да́лі)
even XIII на́віть, хо́ч; X а́ж; XI і
even (smooth) XVIIn рі́вний
evening Introd. ве́чір; Good e.! Introd. До́брий ве́чір!; in the e. II уве́чері
ever XIV будьколи
every X ко́жний XVIg ко́жен; -one Introd. усі́; -thing I усе́; -where XIV скрі́зь
exact XVIg то́чний; -ly XIII то́чно, X якра́з; e. what? XVIIn що́ са́ме?
examination VI і́спит, -у; to take an e. VIs склада́ти і́спит; to pass an e. VIs скла́сти і́спит
excellent XVIII прекра́сно
excessively XVIII зана́дто, на́дто
excuse (v) VIg вибача́ти (ви́бачити) XX пробача́ти (проба́чити); e. oneself XIII вибача́тися (ви́бачитися); Excuse me! Introd. Ви́бачте! XX Проба́чте!
exercise I впра́ва
expect XII очі́кувати XX сподіва́тися; -ation XXn сподіва́ння
expensive — see dear
explain XIV поя́снювати (поясни́ти)
eye XIII о́ко; о́чі; to see with one's own eyes XVII ба́чити на вла́сні о́чі
equal XVIIn рі́вний; -ity XVI рівнопра́вність

F

fame VIII сла́ва
familiar XII знайо́мий
familiarize oneself (v) Xs ознайо́млюватися (ознайо́митися)
family XVI роди́на; XVg сім'я́; XVI рі́д, ро́ду; роди́
famine XVIIg го́лод, -у
far XI дале́ко XVIg дале́кий; by f. XVIII дале́ко; not f. V недале́ко; so f. XIX по́ки що
farmer IXs селяни́н (m), селя́нка (f), селя́ни (pl.)
fashion XVg мо́да
fast Introd. шви́дко XVIg шви́дкий; -er XVIg шви́дше
father V ба́тько; -и́; 's XIVg ба́тьків, -кова
favorite XV улю́блений
feather XVg перо́; пе́ра
February XVIg лю́тий
feel Introd., VIg почува́ти себе́; How do you f.? Introd. Я́к ви себе́ почува́єте? f. like XIII хоті́тися (за-)
few X ма́ло; a f. VI де́кілька; -er XVIg ме́нше
field Ig по́ле; поля́
film II фі́льм, -у; f. is playing V іде́ фі́льм
find (v) VII знахо́дити (знайти́); f. out IX дізнава́тися (дізна́тися)
fine — see nice, good
finish (v) VII кінча́ти (кінчи́ти)
first I пе́рший; XVIg пе́рш; at f. IX споча́тку; -ly XX по-пе́рше
fit (v) XIII сиді́ти на (of clothes)
five XV п'я́ть; XX п'я́теро; f. hundred XVIIg п'ятсо́т; f. hundredth XVIIg п'ятисо́тий; fifth V п'я́тий; fifteen(th) XV п'ятна́дцять -тий; fifty (-ieth) XVI п'ятдеся́т (-ий)
flag XIII пра́пор
floor VII підло́га

fly (v) XIV летíти (по-) (u) XIVs літáти (m)
folk XIX нарóдний
following V настýпний
foolish to do a f. thing XVII зроби́ти дурни́цю; -ness XVIII дурни́ця
foot XVII ногá; нóги; on f. XI пішки; to be on one's feet XVII бýти на ногáх
for V для (+ G); II до (+ G); II за (+A); what f. XV навíщо; as f. XX щодо
foreign VIIIr чужи́й
forest VIIg ліс, -у; -и́
forget VIII забувáти (забýти); to be forgotten XIIIg, забувáтися (забýтися)
forgive XX пробачáти (пробáчити)
former XII коли́шній
forth and so f. VIII і т.д. (і тáк дáлі)
forty XVI сóрок; -ieth XVI сорокóвий
four XII чоти́ри; XX чéтверо; -th IV четвéртий; -teen XV чотирнáдцять; -teenth XIV чотирнáдцятий; f. hundred XVIIg чоти́риста; f. hundredth XVIIg чотирьохсóтий
fresh XV свíжий
friend XI дрýг (pl.) XIVg дрýзі), (fem.) XI пóдруга; VI (male) товáриш; -í, VI (fem.) товáришка
Friday IVs п'ятниця
from V від, з (+ G), Xg зі, зо, із (+G); f. here XI звíдси; f. there XIg звíдти; where f.? IX звíдки
fry XVII смáжити (по-)
full XVIg пóвний, пóвен; -y XIII цілкóм
furniture XIV мéблі (pl.only)
further Introd. дáлі; XVIg дáльше, дáльший

G

garden XII сáд, -у; -и́; small g. XV садóк, -дкá; -и́; vegetable g. XVIII горóд, -у
garment XIIIs óдяг, -у
gather VIIIn, XX збирáтися (зібрáтися)
general: in g. XIII взагалí
gentleman II пáн, -men XIV пани́, панóве Ladies and gentlemen! XIVs Вельмишанóвні (Шанóвні, Дорогí) пáні й панóве!
genuine II спрáвжній
German XVII (male) нíмець, -мця XVIIs (fem.) нíмка, німкéня; XVIIs (adj.) німéцький; Germany XVIIs Німéччина

get III, VI діставáти (дістáти)
gift XII подарýнок, -нка; -ed X здíбний
girl III дíвчина XIVg дівчá (pl. XIII дівчáта); little g. XII дíвчинка; baby g. XII дíвчинка; -friend XI пóдруга
give XII давáти (дáти); g.a present XIII дарувáти (по-)
glad IX рáдий; -ly XVIg рáдо; more g-ly XVIg рáдше
glance XVI пóгляд, -у
glory VIII слáва
go V (walk) іти́ (походи́ти) (u), ї́здити (m); g. out (walk o.) XV вихóдити (ви́йти); What's going on? V Щó тáм такé?
God IVg VIII Бóг; XIIn Бíг; Thank God! VIII Слáва Бóгу!; By God! XVIn бігмé
gold XIVs зóлото; -en XIVs золоти́й; g. -domed XIV золотовéрхий
good Introd. дóбрий; g. day! Introd. Дóбрий дéнь! Добри́день! Дóброго здорóв'я! g. evening! Introd. Дóбрий вечíр! g. morning! Introd. Дóброго рáнку! g. night! Introd. На добрáніч! Добрáніч! Good-bye! Introd. До побáчення!
grade VIs оцінка; school g. VII кля́са (клáс)
grain XIVg хлíб; -á
grandfather XVI дíд; -и́
grandmother XVg, XVIn бáба; баби́
granny XVI, XVIn бабýня, бабýся, бáбця (dial.)
great II вели́кий; g. grandfather XIX прáдід
green XVIII зелéний
greet XX вітáти (при-); -ings! Introd. Дóброго здорóв'я!
group XIV грýпа
guest VIII гíсть, гóстя; гóсті; we have guests VIII у нáс гóсті
guide (n) XIV провідни́к, -á; -и́; XIVs провідни́ця
guilty — see owe

H

hail! VIII слáва!
half XX полови́на, XII пів; h. past XII пів на, XII пів до; h. the road XX півдорóги; h. an hour XIIs півгоди́ни

hang VIIs висíти
hand XVII рýка; рýки
happen XX ставáтися (стáтися)
happy XVIg, XVIII щаслúвий, XVI весéлий, вéсело; -ier XVIg веселíше, веселíший, щаслúвіший; H. journey! XX Щаслúвої дорóги!
hardworking X працьовúтий
Harvard university VIIg Гáрвардський університéт
have II мáти, V (у + G); do/ does not h. V у + G + немá
he I він; H. who XVII тóй, хтó
head XIX головá; гóлови h. ache: I have a h. ache XIX у мéне болúть головá XIXn менé болúть головá
health II здорóв'я; -y XVI здорóвий
hear X чýти (по-)
heart XI сéрце; -цÿ; by h. VIII напáм'ять; to learn by h. VIII учúти напáм'ять; from the bottom of my h. XII від усьóго сéрця
heat XVII спéка
heavy XII тяжкúй; -ier XVIg тÿжче, -чий; -ily XVI тÿжко
hell XVII пéкло
Hello! Introd. Добрúдень! Дóброго здорóв'я! XVIg Здорóв!
help (v) VI допомагáти (допомогтú)
her (s) I її
here (loc.) I тýт (dir.) XI тудú; over h. (loc.) I óсь тýт Here! (Take it!) IV На! IVn нáте
hero XVIr, XX герóй
hesitate XX (за)вагáтися
Hetman XVIIg гéтьман; гетьмáни
high XVIg вúсоко, XVI висóкий; -er XVIg вúще, -щий
him II йогó
his I йогó
history II істóрія, VIIIg історúчний (adj.)
Holiday XIII свято
holy XIII святий
home (direct.) VI додóму, (adj.) II домáшній; h. work II домáшнє завдáння; at h. IV удóма
hope (n) XXs надія XXn сподівáння; (v) XX сподівáтися, XXs надíятися
horse XVI кíнь, конÿ; кóні; -back XVIn вéрхи; to ride a h. XVI їздити конéм (їздити вéрхи)
hospital IXs лікáрня
hot XVII гáряче; XI гарÿчий
hotel III готéль, -ю
hour XI годúна
house III будúнок, -нку; (in a village) XV хáта; -ú
how Introd. ÿк; h. many, h. much XII скíльки; XIII how about it? то ÿк?
hryvnia (money) XVIII грúвня, XVIIIn грúвна
human XVIIIg людськúй; h. being XI людúна (pl. XIV люди)
hundred VII стó; -th XVI сóтий
hungry IX голóдний
hurry (v) VI поспішáти (поспішúти)
husband X чоловíк; чоловікú

I

identical XIVr однáковий
i.e. XX тóбто
if III ÿк, IV якщó VII якбú I чи; if it weren't for X якбú не; if I were you VIII на твоéму місці
immediately XX відрáзу, зрáзу
impolite XVI нечéмний
important XX важлúвий
impression XIV врáження, вражíння (W. Ukr.)
in III, VII у (+ G), VII на (+ L), X через (+ A); Xn за (+A) -to III у (+ A); (time) X за (+ A)
incidentally VII, XIV між íншим
including XV включáючи
inconvenient VII незрýчно
incorrect Introd. непрáвильно
increasingly XVIIIg дедáлі, щé, усé, чимрáз, щорáз
incurable XIX невилікóвний
indeed XVII спрáвді
independent VII незалéжний
Indian (Amer.) III (male) індіÿнець, -нця; (fem.) індіÿнка
indifferent XVIg байдýжий
instead XVIII зáмість (+ G)
institute IX інститýт, -у
intend VIII збирáтися (зібрáтися)

interest (v) IX, XX цікáвити (за-), -ing II цікáвий XVIg цікáво; -ed: to be i. IX цікáвитися (за-)
interrogative particle Introd. чи
invite VIIIs запрóшувати (запросúти)
it I вонó, він, вонá

J

January XVI сíчень, -чня
joke (n) XVI жáрт, -у (v) жартувáти (по-)
journey XX дорóга; Happy j.! XX Щаслúвої дорóги!
July XVIs лúпень, -пня
June XVIs чéрвень, -вня
junior XVIg, XXg молóдший
just (just right) X якрáз; j. now XIX щóйно; (only) — see тíльки, лишé

K

karbovanec (=ruble) XVIIIs карбóванець, -нця
kasha — see cereal
Kharkiv IX Хáрків, -ва; (adj.) IX хáрківський
kill (v) XX убивáти (убúти); -er XX убúвця; -ing XX убúвство
kind (good-natured) Introd. дóбрий, XVIg ласкáв, ласкáвий; -er XVIg добрíший
kilogram XIX кілогрáм, -у; кілó
kiss (v) X цілувáти (по-)
know II знáти (no pfv.); K. how XI умíти (з-)
Kyiv VII Кúїв, -єва; -an VIII кúївський

L

lady II, XIV пáні (indecl.); Ladies and Gentlemen! XIV Вельмишанóвні (Шанóвні, Дорóгі) пáні й панóве!
lake XVg XVII óзеро; озéра; at the l XVII на озéрі
lamp VII лям́па
land XIV землá, зéмлі, VIIg крáй, -ю; -ї́
language I мóва
large III велúкий; -er XVIg бíльший; too l., XVIIIg завелúкий
last (past) XVIII минýлий; (in a series) VII, XVII остáнній
late XI пíзно, пíзній; too l. XVIIIg запíзно; to be l. XI спізнятися/спíзнюватися/, XII запíзнюватися (спізнúтися/запізнúтися)
laugh (v) XVII сміятися (за-)
launder XX прáти (вú-)
lawyer XXn адвокáт
lead (v) XIV водúти (m), вестú (по-) (u); l. to XV довóдити (довестú); XI керувáти; -er XI керівнúк, а; -ú; -ership XI керівнúцтво
learn VII учúтися (нав-) VIII навчáтися (навчúтися), научáтися (научúтися)
least XVIg наймéнш; at l. XX принáймні, XVIII щонаймéнше XIII хóч
leave (n) XVIIIn відпýстка; (v) XIXg лишáти (лишúти) XIIIr залишáти (залишúти)
lecture I лéкція
left XVII лíвий
leg XVII ногá; нóги
lend XVIII позичáти (позúчити)
less XVIg мéнш(е)
lesson I лéкція; VI наýка
let VIII нехáй, VIIIg хáй; to l. XII давáти (дáти)
letter V лúст, -á; -ú; (alphabet) I, II лíтера IIs бýква
lie (position) VII лежáти; l. down XIII лягáти (лягтú); lying XIXg лежáчий
light (weight) XVIg легкúй; -er XVIg лéгше; -ly XVIg лéгко
librar-ian V бібліотéкар, -я; (m) Vs бібліотéкарка (f) -y V бібліотéка
like (v) XIII подобатися (с-); -able XIV симпатúчний
life XIV життя́
lift (v) XVg піднóсити (піднестú)
lip XVg губá; гýби
listen VIII слýхати (по-)
litera-ry IV літератýрний; -ture VIII літератýра
little (quantity) X мáло, IX трóхи; (size) IX малúй
liturgy XIIIn літургíя
live (v) II жúти; l. for a while VIg пожúти (to reside) VIIg мéшкати
long X дóвго, дóвгий; -er XVIg дóвше, -ший; l. ago IX давнó
look (n) XVI пóгляд, -у; take a l. III Подивúся! (v) II, III дивúтися (по-); l. for VII шукáти (по-); l. like XVI виглядáти (no pfv.)

lose (v) VIIs губи́ти (за-, P)
lost XIXg пропа́щий
loud Introd. го́лосно XVIg голосни́й; -er Introd. голосні́ше
love (n) II любо́в, -и; IIIs коха́ня (v) II, VI люби́ти (по-); IIIs коха́ти (по-) to l. one another III люби́ти одне́ о́дного; Xn люби́тися, коха́тися; -ing XIXg лю́блячий
low XVIs ни́зько, низьки́й; -er XVIs ни́жче, ни́жчий
lunch IX обі́д, -у; for l. IX на обі́д; to eat l. XVII обі́дати (по-)

M

madam — see Mrs.
magazine II журна́л, -у
make II, VI роби́ти (з-); made XVIII зро́блений
man X чолові́к
manage (be able) — see able
many X, XVIIIg бага́то; too m. XV забага́то; how m. XII скі́льки; so many XII сті́льки; as m. as possible XVIIIg якнайбі́льше
map III ма́па
March XVI бе́резень, -зня
market XV база́р, -у
marry X одру́жуватися (одружи́тися); Xn вихо́дити (ви́йти) за́між, жени́тися (о-); -ied XVIII одру́жений XVIIIs замі́жня
M.A. holder X доце́нт
master (lord) IIn пан; -и́
matter XX спра́ва; What's the m.? V що́ (та́м) таке́?: no matter XIII байдуже; it's a different m. XX і́нша річ
may III мо́жна VIII могти́ (з-); -be VII мо́же
May XVIs тра́вень, -вня
meadow Vg лу́г; -и́
mean (v) XIV зна́чити (no pfv.)
means: by all m. XVIII обов'язко́во
measure (v) XIX мі́ряти (по-)
meat XVII м'я́со; m. patty XVII котле́та,XVIIn шни́цель (W. Ukr.)
medicine (science) VII медици́на (drugs) XIX лі́ки
meet (encounter) XII зустріча́ти (зустрі́ти/ зустрі́нути); (be introduced) X знайо́митися (по-); -ing (conference)X засі́дання
memory XIVs па́м'ять; by m. VIII напа́м'ять
mention: Don't m. it! V Нема́ за́ що!
mile XX ми́ля
milk XV молоко́
million XVIIg мільйо́н; -th XVIIg мільйо́нний
mine (possess.) — see my
minute XIs хвили́на; this very m. (just a m. ago) XIX що́йно
miserable XVIII неща́сний
misfortune XIIg ли́хо
Miss IIg па́нна
miss (v) XX бракува́ти (забра́кнути)
mistake II поми́лка; -и́; to make a m. II, VI помиля́тися (помили́тися)
mister Mr. II, XIV па́н. п.; IIg мі́стер
Mom V ма́ма; -и́
Monday I Vs понеді́лок, -лка
money XV гро́ші (pl. only)
month XVI мі́сяць; -і
moon XVI мі́сяць
more XVIg бі́льш(е); Introd. ще́; once m. Introd. ще́ раз
morning Introd. ра́нок, -нку; Good m.! Introd. До́брого ра́нку! in the m. X ура́нці
most XVIg найбі́льш
mother V ма́ти, ма́тері; XIV (pl.) матері́; -'s XIVg ма́терин
motion VIIg ру́х, -у
mountain XI гора́; го́ри; in the m-s VIIg у, на го́рах; to the m-s XI у го́ри
move (v) (across, in a vehicle) XV переї́жджа́ти/ переїзди́ти (переї́хати)
movie (-s) XVII кіно́; кі́на; m. theater XVIIs кінотеа́тр
Mrs. II па́ні, п.
much X бага́то; too m. XV забага́то; how m. XII скі́льки; so m. сті́льки; as m. as possible XVIIIg якнайбі́льше
murder — see kill
museum III музе́й
must X му́сити (no pfv.), XVI пови́нен, XVIg пови́нний one m. (it is necessary) VI тре́ба
my I мі́й, моя́, моє́

N

name (first) I, XIV ім'я́, і́мени; імена́; What's your n.? Introd. Я́к ва́ше ім'я́? (last) I прі́звище; What's your last n.? I Я́к ва̀ше прі́звище?; -ly XX а са́ме; n. (title) Is на́зва

nation IX нарóд, XVIg нáрід; -al XIX нарóдний

near VII біля (+ G), XV бли́зько, кóло XVIg бли́зький; -er XV бли́жче, XVg бли́жчий; -ly XX прибли́зно, XVI мáйже

necessary XVIg потрíбний, потрíбен; it's n. VI трéба

need (v) V потребувáти (no pfv.); -ed XVIg потрíбний, потрíбен

neither; n. ... nor IV ні...ні IVs áні...áні XII і

never XI нікóли; -theless X усé ж таки

new II нови́й; What's new? II Щó новóго?; Nothing n. II Нічóго новóго

New York V Нью Йорк, -у; VIIIg (adj.) нью-йóркський

newspaper V газéта; Vn часóпис, -у

next V настýпний

nice VI гáрний XIV симпати́чний; -ly XVIg гáрно

night X ніч, нóчі; нóчі; Good n.! Introd. Добрáніч! На добрáніч! in the n. X уночí

nine XV дéв'ять; -th IX дев'я́тий; -teen (-th) XVI дев'ятнáдцять;(-тий); -ty (-tieth) XVI, XVIg дев'янóсто, дев'янóстий; дев'ятдеся́т(-ий); n. hundred XVII дев'ятсóт; n. hundredth XVIg дев'ятисóтий

no Introd. ні XIII нія́кий; -body IV ніхтó; -where XI IIg нідé (loc.); нікýди (dir.)

none XIIn жóдний XIII нія́кий

not I не; n. a XVIII ні (+ G)

note XVg нóта

notebook I зóшит

nothing II нічóго, ніщó; good for n. XX ні до чóго

novel (fiction) XX ромáн, -а (-у)

November XVI листóпад, -у

now III зáраз Introd. тепѐр

number IIs числó; чи́сла IIs нóмер (№)

O

obey XVI слýхатися (по-)

obligated XVI пови́нен, XVIg пови́нний

occupy; to be occupied with XVIII займáтися (зайня́тися)

o'clock XI годи́на; at... o'clock XII о... -ій годи́ні

October XVIs жóвтень, -тня

often XI чáсто

Oh! II Á!; Oho! XII агá!; огó!; Oh no! XI óй! Oh you ...! XII Áх ти́ ...!

old II стари́й; IIs старéнький; XI дáвній; -er XVIg стáр(í)ше; -est XIV найстаріший, XVIg найстáрший; -fashioned XVI старосвíтський

omelette XV яéшня

on II, VII на (+ A/+L)

once Introd. рáз; o. more Introd. щé раз

one II оди́н, однá, - нé; not o.V ні óдного/ óдної; o. another III одне óдного; -self XII себé, XI сáм

onion XVII цибýля; one o. XVIIn цибули́на

only III тíльки, XVII лишé

open (v) VIII відчиня́ти (відчини́ти); (by itself) XVIIIg відчиня́тися (відчини́тися)

opinion X дýмка; -и́; in my o. XVII на мою дýмку, XVIII по-мóєму; to be of an o. XIV бýти якóїсь дỳмки; of the same o. XIV тіє́ї ж дýмки

optimist XIX оптимíст

or II абó; either...or II абó...абó

order XV поря́док, -дку; everything is in o. XV усé в поря́дку; in order to IX аби́, VII щóб

organize — see arrange

originate похóдити IX (no pfv.)

other VII, VIII íнший

outside, outdoors XIs надвóрі

oven XVII піч, пéчі; пéчі

over X над (+I)

owe: he owes XVIg ви́нен, ви́нний

own (adj.) XVII влáсний; one's o. V свíй, своя́, своє́

P

page XX сторíнка; -и́

paint (n) XVII фáрба

paints XIII штани́

pair XIII пáра

paper IV папíр, -пéру; папéри

parents XVI батьки́ (no sg.)

park XIV пáрк, -у

part XX части́на; on his part XX з йогo бóку

party (festivity) VIIIn вечірка, прийняття
pass (v) XVIg минати (минути); (walking) XVII проходити (пройти); (riding) XVg проїжджати/проїздити (проїхати); p. an exam VIs скласти іспит
patient (hospital) XIX хворий, XIXn хорий
patronymic I по батькові; What's your p.? I Як вас по батькові?
pay (v) XIIs платити (за-)
peace XVIIs мир
pen I ручка
pencil I олівець, -вця
penicillin XIXn пеніцилина
penny XVIII копійка; -й, йок; XVn гріш гроша; гроші
people XIV люди; XVI народ, -у; XVIn нарід, народу
perform VIIg виконувати, (виконати)
perhaps VII може; XIX хіба
perish XX гинути (за-)
person XI людина; (in counting) X чоловік
PhD thesis Xn кандидатська праця
philological VIII філологічний
phone (n) телефон, -у; (v) IV, VI дзвонити (по-); IVs телефонувати (по-)
photo IIIg фото; -graph III фотографія; IIIg світлина
physician — see doctor
pie XIIn пиріг, -рога; пироги; small p. XVII пиріжок, -жка; -жки
piece IX шматок, -тка; -тки
pig XIIs, XVg свиня; свині; -let XI порося, поросяти; поросята
pillow XVIII подушка;-й
pin (badge) XIII значок, -чка; -чки; pin (v) XIII причіпляти, причепити
place I місце; місця
plant (industry) VII завод, -у
play (n) (theater) IIg п'єса; (v) XIX (to p. a game) грати в (+ A); (an instrument) грати (за-) на (4-L)
pleasant XII приємно
please Introd. Будь ласка! Прошу! Pleased to meet you! XIIs Приємно познайомитися!; Introd. Мені дуже приємно з вами познайомитися.
poem IV вірш
poet IV, XIIg поет
point (out) XX вказувати (вказати)
polite XVIs чемний
Polish XVIIs (adj.) польський; P. woman XVIIs полька, полячка;
Pole XVII поляк;
Poland XVIIs Польща
potato (one) XI In картоплина; -es XII картопля
pour XVIIs лити/наливати (налити)
pork chop XVI In шніцель
Poltava XVIIs Полтава; (adj.) XVIII полтавський; (native of P. fem) XVII полтавка
possible III можна
prefer XIII, XX воліти (no perf.)
prelims Xn кандидатський мінімум
present — see gift
preserve Xv зберігати (зберегти)
pretty — see nice
prince XIVg князь; -зі
principle XVIII принцип, -у; according to p-s. XVIII за принципами
print (n) XX друк, -у; (v), VI друкувати (на.)
probably VI мабуть
program II програма, I In передача (TV, radio)
profession VII професія
professor I професор; -й
promise (v) XII обіцювати (обіцяти)
psychological XX психологічний
publish — see print
pupil XII (male) учень, -чня XIIs (fem) учениця
put (stand) VII ставити (по-), (lay) VII класти (по-); p. on XIII вдягати (вдягнути), одягати (одягнути)

Q

quarter XII чверть; q. after XII чверть на (+ A); q. to XII за чверть (+ N)
question II питання IIn запитання; to ask a q. II, VI питати (с-) IIn запитувати (запитати); to answer a q. II відповідати на питання
quiet XIs тихо
quinine XIXn хиніна

R

rain VI дощ, -у; -і; -ing: its r. VI іде дощ
reach (walking) XIX доходити (дійти); (swimming) XVg допливати (допливти)

read II, VI чита́ти (про-); to read for a while VII почита́ти; -er XX чита́ч; -і́; -ing II чита́ння; to be r. XIIIg чита́тися
ready II вже́XII гото́вий, гото́во XVIg гото́в, ла́ден; to get r. XX збира́тися (зібра́тися)
real III спра́вжній; -ly? IV невже́
reason (n) тому́ VII ра́ція; for some r. VIIIg чому́сь, чого́сь; for any r. IXg чоголе́будь
receive Vn отри́мувати (отри́мати) XII оде́ржувати (оде́ржати)
reception VIIIn прийняття, прийо́м
recently X неда́вно
recite VIIIr деклямува́ти (про-)
red XVII черво́ний
regret (v) XV шкодува́ти (по-)
refrigerator IX холоди́льник
reject — see shun
remain X лиша́тися (лиши́тися) Xn залиша́тися (залиши́тися)
remark (n) XX заува́ження; (v) XIV заува́жувати (заува́жити)
remember IV пам'ята́ти VI запам'ятати (P)
research assistant XVIg, XXs науко́вий працівни́к (робітни́к)
reside VI Is ме́шкати
repeat VI повто́рювати (повтори́ти); Introd. Repeat! Повторі́ть!
respect XVI поша́на
rest (n) XVIII відпочи́нок, -нку; (v) XVII відпочива́ти (відпочи́нути)
rest (remainder) XX ре́шта
restaurant XIV рестора́н, -у
return (v) XX вертатися (верну́тися), XVIII поверта́ти (поверну́ти) XVIIIs поверта́тися (поверну́тися); Many happy returns! XVIg Мно́гая (мно́гії) лі́та!
rich XVIg бага́тий; -er XVIg бага́тший
ride (v) XI ї́хати (по-) (и), ї́здити (m); r. a horse XVI ї́хати коне́м; (n): to give a r. XI підво́зити (підвезти́)
right (side) XVII пра́вий; (n) XVIn пра́во; r. away III за́раз; all r. IV до́бре; to be r. VII мати ра́цію
river (small) XVII рі́чка; -и́; at the r. XVII на рі́чці
road XX доро́га
romance XX рома́н, -у (-а), XXII рома́нс, -у (W. Ukr.)
room I кімна́та
run(v) бі́гти (по-) (u), бі́гати (m); r. into XVg вбіга́ти (вбі́гти); r. through XVg пробіга́ти (пробі́гти)
Rus' XIVs Ру́сь, -си; (adj) XIV ру́ський
Russia V Росі́я; -n (male) XIV росія́нин, (pl) росія́ни XIVs (fem.) росія́нка; (adj) V росі́йський; in Russian V по-росі́йськи

S

sail (v) XV пла́вати (m); пливти́ (по-)/пли́сти (по-) (u); s. a while XIV попла́вати
saint XIII святи́й; st. XIII св.
same XVI то́й са́мий; (identical) XIVr однако́вий
Saturday IV субо́та
sauerkraut XI In ки́сла капу́ста
say II, VI каза́ти (с-); Say! Introd. Скажі́ть!; You don't s.! XIV Та невже́!;
said Introd. сказа́ли; to be s. XIIIg говори́тися
school IV шко́ла; to attend s. IV ходи́ти до шко́ли; s. of technology IXn те́хнікум; s. year XIIIn навча́льний рі́к
science VI нау́ка; -tific XVIg науко́вий; -tist XX науко́вець, -вця; XXn вче́ний, -ого
seat I мі́сце; місця́
second II дру́гий; as a s. course XVIIn на дру́ге; -ly XX по-дру́ге
see II ба́чити (по-); s. each other X ба́читися (по-); one can s. XIV ви́дно
seek VII шука́ти
seem: it seems VII зда́ється, XVIg ви́дно
sell XV продава́ти (прода́ти)
send XX посила́ти (посла́ти) XIV присила́ти (присла́ти)
senior XVIg, XXg ста́рший
sentence (phrase) VIII ре́чення
sentimental XX сентимента́льний
September XIVs ве́ресень, -сня
serious XIX серйо́зний
sermon XVIII про́повідь

service XIII слу́жба; church s. XIII слу́жба Бо́жа XIIIn богослу́жба, богослу́ження
settled: to get s. XIIIg улаштовува́тися (улаштува́тися)
seven XV сім XX се́меро; -th VII сьо́мий; -teen (-th) XVI сімна́дцять, -тий; -ty (-tieth) XVI сімдеся́т (-ий) s. hundred XVII сімсо́т; s. hundredth XVIIg семисо́тий
several XIXg, XX кілька
she I вона́
shelf XV поли́ця
ship XIVs корабе́ль, -бля́; -блі́
shirt XIII соро́чка; -и́
short (height) XVIs низьки́й, ни́зько; -er XVIs ни́жчий, ни́жче; (length) Xs коро́ткий
shoulder XVg, XVIIIg плече́; пле́чі
show (v) XII пока́зувати (показа́ти)
shun VIII цура́тися (від-)
shut VIII зачиня́ти (зачини́ти); s. itself XIIIg зачиня́тися (зачини́тися)
sick XIX хво́рий, XIXs хо́рий; to be s. XIX хворі́ти/хорі́ти (за-); XVIn засла́бнути; -ness XIX хворо́ба, хоро́ба
side XV бік, бо́ку; боки́
sight-seeing XIV огляда́ти (огля́нути)
sign Introd. зна́к, -у; soft s. (letter of Ukrainian alphabet) Introd. м'яки́й зна́к
sincere XXn щи́рий; -ly Intro., XX щи́ро
sing XIII співа́ти (за-); -ing: fond of s-ing XIX співу́чий
Sir II па́н; Sirs XIV пани́, пано́ве
sister III сестра́; се́стри; -s XVIg сестри́н, -а́, -е́
sit VIII сиді́ти; s. down VIII сіда́ти (сі́сти)
six XV шість, XX ше́стеро; -th VI шо́стий; -teen (-th) XVI шістна́дцять -тий; -ty (-tieth) XVI шістдеся́т (-ий); s. hundred XVIIg шістсо́т; s. hundredth XVIIg, шестисо́тий; sixties: people of the 60's XVIIg шестидеся́тники
size о́бсяг, -у; XXs ро́змір, -у
slacks XIII штани́
Slavic Ig слов'я́нський
sleep (v) VII спа́ти; to go to s. XIIляга́ти спа́ти; (n) VIIs со́н, сну́; сни́
slice (n) IX шмато́к, -тка; (v) XVII кра́яти (по-)
slow XVIg пові́льний; -ly Introd. пові́льно
sly XIX хи́трий
small IX мали́й; -er XVIg ме́нш(е), ме́нший; -est XVIg найме́нший
smell (v) X чу́ти (по-)
smile (v) XIX усміха́тися (усміхну́тися)
snapshot IIIn зни́мка, зні́мок
snow XVIIg сніг, -у; -и́
so X так X о́тже III таки́й
so-and-so IVn таки́й-то (m), така́-то (f)
soap XVII ми́ло
society XVIIs грома́да;VIs товари́ство
soft Introd. м'яки́й; -er XVIg м'якше; -ly XVIg м'я́ко
some (quantity) VI де́кілька IX тро́хи; (quality) XX де́який; -how XVIIIg я́кось, чого́сь; -kind of III яки́йсь; -one VIII хто́сь; -one's VIIIg чи́йсь; -thing VIIIg що́сь; -where VIIIg де́сь (loc.), куди́сь (dir.); -what IX тро́хи
son VII си́н;-и́
song XV пі́сня; -і, -се́нь
soon XVI ско́ро: -er XVIg скорі́ш(е); as s. as possible XVIIIg якнайскорі́ше
sorry XVIg шкода́
sort XIVg сорт, -у; -и́
soul IX душа́: ду́ші
Soviet XVIIg сове́тський, совíтський (Russisms)
speak II, VI говори́ти (по-); Speak! Introd. Говорі́ть! to begin s-ing. XVIIg заговори́ти
spill XVII пролива́ти (проли́ти)
splendid XVIII прекра́сно
spoil XV псува́тися (зі-)
spouse XII (male & female) дружи́на
spring (season) XI весна́; in the s. XIg навесні́, весно́ю
stand (be standing) VII стоя́ти; (put) VII ста́вити (по-)
stay X лиша́тися (лиши́тися) Xn залиша́тися (залиши́тися); s. at home VIII сиді́ти вдо́ма; s. a while XI поси́діти
steal XVIII кра́сти (у-)
steamboat XIVs пароплав
steppe VIIg сте́п, -у; -и́
still (continuity) IV ще́; XVIg усе́; (yet) X усе́ ж таки XX таки́

stop (n) зупи́нка, Xs bus s. авто́бусна зупи́нка; (v) Xs зупиня́тися (зупини́тися)
store (n) XV крамни́ця, XVn магази́н (Russism), скле́п, -у (W. Ukr.)
story II істо́рія; IIn оповіда́ння
stove XVII піч, пе́чі; пе́чі
strange VIII чужи́й (=foreign); XVIII ди́вний (= amazing)
street VII ву́лиця
strong XVI си́льний, XVIg ду́жий; -er XVIg ду́жче, -чий
student (male) I студе́нт, (fem.) I студе́нтка In школя́р (m), школя́рка (f); graduate s. Xn аспіра́нт
study (v) VII учи́тися (нав-), VII вивча́ти (ви́вчити) VIII навча́тися (навчи́тися)
style XX сти́ль, -лю
success XIX у́спіх, -у; -ful XX вда́лий, XIXs у́спішний
such III таки́й
suitcase XII валі́зка
summer XI лі́то; in the s. XI улі́тку, лі́том
sun XIs со́нце
Sunday IV неділя
supper IX вечо́ря; for s. IX на вече́рю; to eat s. XVIII вече́ряти (по-)
sure VI пе́вний, XVIg пе́вен
surname I прі́звище; What's your s.? I Як ва́ше прі́звище?
sweater XX све́тр
swim XIV пливти́/плисти́ (по-) (u), пла́вати (m); s. a while XIV попла́вати (m); s. across XVg переплива́ти (перепливти́/переплисти́); s. to (reach) доплива́ти (доплив́ти/доплисти́) take a swim XIV купа́тися (с-)

T

table I сті́л, стола́; столи́
take VI бра́ти (узя́ти); t. an exam VI склада́ти і́спит
talented XVIg талантови́тий; more t. XVIg талантови́тіший
talk (n) X розмо́ва; (v) Xs розмовля́ти (по-), II, VI говори́ти (по-)
tall — see high
tasty XVII смачни́й
tea IX ча́й; чаї
teach XII навча́ти (навчи́ти) XII учи́ти (навчи́ти), XIIn виклада́ти, учителюва́ти; -er (male) IX учи́тель; -лі́, (fem.) IXs учи́телька; -и́
tear (n) XVII сльоза́; сльо́зи
telephone — see phone
television II телеба́чення, IIn телеві́зія, IIs t. (adj.) телевізі́йний; t. set II телеві́зор
tell II, VI каза́ти(с-); t. a story XI розповіда́ти (розпові́сти)
temperature XIX температу́ра
ten XV де́сять; -th X деся́тий
terrible XVII страшни́й
than II ніж XVI я́к XVIg аніж
thank II, VI дя́кувати (по-); Thank you! Introd. Дя́кую! Спаси́бі! XII t. you very much! Introd. Дя́кую ду́же!
that (indic.) I то́й, та, те; that is/those are I то́, XVI ото́, о́т; What's that? V Що́ (та́м) таке́?; so t. X а́ж; (conj.) II, що VII, щоб
the I то́й
theater XVIIs теа́тр
their (s) I ї́хній
then (at that time) VII тоді́; (next) XIV по́тім; (in that case) III то
there (loc.) I та́м; over t. I о́н та́м; (dir.) XI туди́
these I ці́
thesis (PhD) Xn кандида́тська пра́ця
thing III рі́ч, ре́чі; ре́чі; a different t. XX інша рі́ч; among other things XIV між і́ншим; one more thing II
think II, VI ду́мати (по-); And what do you t.? IIIr А я́к ви́ ду́маєте?
third III трѐтій
thirteen XV трина́дцять; -th XIII трина́дцятий
thirty XVI три́дцять; -tieth XVI тридця́тий
this I це́й, ця́, цѐ III оце́й, оця́, оце́; this is/these are Introd. це́
those I ті́
thought X ду́мка; -и́
thousand XVIIg, XVII ти́сяча; -th XVII ти́сячний
thread XVIII ни́тка; -и́

three XII трú XXg трóє; t. hundred XVIIg трúста; t. hundredth XVIIg трьохсóтий
throat XIX гóрло; I have a sore t. XIX у мéне болúть гóрло
Thursday IVs четвéр, -гá; -гú
thus X óтже
ticket XV квитóк, -ткá
till I, X до (+ G)
time IV чáс, -у; what t. is it? XI Котрá годúна?; Till what time? XI До котрóї годúни?; all the t. II усé; at times XIX чáсом; for a long t. X дóвго; it takes time to X трéба чáсу на (+ A); long t. ago IX давнó; no t. XIIIg нікóли; one t. I рáз; this t. XX цúм рáзом
tired: to get t. XVII утóмлюватися (утомúтися)
title Is нáзва
to V до (+ G)
today V сьогóдні; -'s V сьогóднішній
together Introd. рáзом
toiling XIXg трудя́щий
tomorrow IV зáвтра
tonight II сьогóдні ввéчері
too XVIII занáдто, XVIIIg нáдто
top on t. of it VII щé й
towel XVIII рушнúк, -á; -ú
town VIII мíсто; -a; out of t. (location) XI за мíстом
tradition XVIII традúція; according to t. XVIII за традúцією
translate V, VI перекладáти (переклáсти) -tion V перéклад, -у
tribe IIg плéм'я
trident XIII тризýб
trifle XVIII дурнúця
trip XX дорóга
trouble (v) II, VI турбувáти (по-)
true VII прáвда: truth VII прáвда; to tell the t. XX прáвду кáжучи
try (v) XVII I прóбувати (с-)
Tuesday XIVs вівтóрок, -рка
turn out XV вихóдити (вúйти); it turned out XV вúйшло
twelve XV дванáдцять; twelfth XII дванáдцятий
twenty XVI двáдцять; -tieth XVI двадця́тий
two XII двá, дві, XX двóє; t. hundred XVIIg двíсті t. hundredth XVIIg двохсóтий
type (v) II друкувáти (на-)

U

Ukraine II Украї́на; -nian (male) I украї́нець, -нця (fem.) I украї́нка, (adj.) I украї́нський; in U. I по-украї́нському In по-украї́нськи
under X під (+ A/+ I)
underline VIII підкрéслювати (підкрéслити)
understand II, VI розýміти (з-); Do you u.? Introd. Вú розумíєте? Excuse me, I don't understand. Introd. Вúбачте, я́ не розумíю.
undying XIXg невмирýщий
unfortunately XIII на жáль
unhappy XVIII нещáсний
university V університéт, -у
unpleasant XX неприéмно
until XI пóки
us II, XIV, IX нáс; нáм; нáми
use (v) IX користувáтися (с-), користáтися (с-) XX уживáти (ужúти)
usually II звичáйно

V

vacation XVIII вакáції (pl. only), XVIIIn канíкули (Russism)
vaseline XIXn вазелíна
vegetable: v. garden — see garden
very Introd. дýже; the v. XVI сáмий
view (point) XVI пóгляд, -у
vigilant XIXg невсипýщий
village IX селó; сéла
visit (v) VIII ітú в гóсті
vitality of great v. XIX живýчий
vocabulary I словнúк, -á; -ú

W

wait XI чекáти (по-); XVI ждáти (підо-)
walk V ітú (п-) (и), VII ходúти (m); w. across/over XVg перехóдити (перейтú); w. for pleasure XIs гуля́ти (по-, P)
want (v) II, VI хотíти (за-)
war XVII війнá; вíйни, вóєн
warm XIs тéпло

wash (v) XVII ми́ти (по-); (launder) XX пра́ти (ви́-)
watch (n)XII годи́нник w is running XII годи́нник іде́; w. is slow XII годи́нник запі́знюється; w. is fast XI Is годи́нник поспіша́є; (v) II, III диви́тися (по-) (на +A)
water XVII вода́; во́ди
way XX доро́га; half the w. XX півдоро́ги; my way XVIII по-мо́єму; in no way XIII нія́к; this w. XI сюди́; that w. XI туди́
we I ми́
weak XVIIs слабки́й (слаби́й)
wear (v) XII носи́ти
weather XIs пого́да
week V ти́ждень. -жня; -жні; -ly XVIII щоти́жня
wedding Xs весі́лля
Wednesday IVs середа́; се́реди
weigh (have weight) XIX ва́жити
welcome: You are w.! Introd. Про́шу! You are very w.! Introd. Про́шу ду́же!
well (interj.) III ну́
well: to get w. XIX виду́жувати (ви́дужати)
what Introd. що́; what for XV наві́що, III чого́; what if XIX що́ як; Introd. я́к; What's your name (surname)? Introd. Я́к ва́ше ім'я́ (пр́ізвище)?; What's your patronymic? Я́к ва́с по ба́тькові? what a ...! III О́т яки́й...! XI котри́й; what time is it? Котра́ годи́на? Till what time? До котро́ї годи́ни?
when IV коли́
where (loc.) I де́; (dir.) VI куди́
whether I чи; w...or II чи...чи
which XI котри́й, II яки́й
while XI по́ки
whiskey XIX горі́лка
white XVII бі́лий
who I хто; whose I чи́й, чия́, чиє́
whole IX ці́лий, I уве́сь
why III чому́, чого́, II А що́?
wife IX жі́нка; -и́; XII дружи́на; XIn по́друга життя́
willing VIg згі́дний (зго́дний), зго́ден
window I вікно́; ві́кна
winter XI зима́; зи́ми; in the w. XI узи́мку зимо́ю
wish (v) XIX бажа́ти (по-)
with X з (+ I), Xg зі, зо, із (+ I); -in (time) X за (+ A); -out V без (+ G)
woman IX жі́нка; -и́, XVIn (peasant w.) ба́ба;-и́
wonderful VI чудо́во; VI, XVIg чудо́вий
word X сло́во; -а́
work (n) XI робо́та, XV пра́ця; at w. XI, XV на робо́ті, на пра́ці; (v) VII працюва́ти; w. on X працюва́ти над (+ I); -er XIs робітни́к (m) робітни́ця (f) XVs працівник XIXg трудя́щий
world XVIs сві́т, -у; -и́; (adj.) XVII світо́вий; -ly XVIn сві́тський
worry (v) XVIII жури́тися (за-)
worse XVIg гі́рш(е), гі́рший
worth w. while XV ва́рто; -y XVIg ва́рт(ий)
write II, VI писа́ти (на-); written VII напи́сано; to be written XIIIg писа́тися (на-)
writing II писа́ння (n)
wrong (incorrect) Introd. непра́вильно; (different) XIV не то́й

Y

yarn XVIII нитки́ (p. of ни́тка thread)
year VII, XVIg рі́к, ро́ку; роки́; college y. VIII ку́рс, -у; to be in ... year (college) VIII на... -ому ку́рсі; yrs. XVII pp.
yellow XIII жо́втий; y. and blue XIII жо́вто-блаки́тний
yes Introd. та́к
yesterday IV учо́ра; -s V учора́шній
yet (still) X усе́ ж таки; not y. VI ще́ ні
you Introd. ви́, I ти́
young XI молоди́й, XVIg мо́лодо; -er XVI моло́дший
your (s) I ва́ш. тві́й

Z

zero XXg ну́ль. -ля́; -лі́

INDEX*

Consult also Appendices for Conjugation and Declension tables

---

* SS stands for the Ukrainian Sound and Writing System; other notations are the same as in the general vocabularies